The Cambridge History of the English Language is the first multivolume work to provide a comprehensive and authoritative account of the history of English from its beginnings to its present-day world-wide use. Its coverage embraces not only areas of central linguistic interest such as syntax, but also more specialised topics such as personal and place names. Whereas the volumes concerned with the English language in England are organised on a chronological basis, the English of the rest of the world is treated geographically to emphasise the spread of English over the last three hundred years.

Volume II covers the Middle English period, approximately 1066–1476, and describes and analyses developments in the language from the Norman Conquest to the introduction of printing. This period witnessed important features like the assimilation of French and emergence of a standard variety of English. There are chapters on phonology and morphology, syntax, dialectology, lexis and semantics, literary language and onomastics. Each chapter concludes with a section on further reading; and the volume as a whole is supported by an extensive glossary of linguistic terms and a comprehensive bibliography. The chapters are written by specialists who are familiar both with the period of the volume and with modern approaches to the study of historical linguistics. The volume will be welcomed by specialists and non-specialists alike and it will remain the standard account of Middle English for many years to come.

THE CAMBRIDGE HISTORY
OF THE ENGLISH LANGUAGE

GENERAL EDITOR Richard M. Hogg

VOLUME II 1066–1476

THE CAMBRIDGE HISTORY OF THE ENGLISH LANGUAGE

VOLUME II *1066–1476*

EDITED BY

NORMAN BLAKE

Professor of English Language and Linguistics, University of Sheffield

CAMBRIDGE
UNIVERSITY PRESS

Published by the Press Syndicate of the University of Cambridge
The Pitt Building, Trumpington Street, Cambridge CB2 1RP
40 West 20th Street, New York, NY 10011-4211, USA
10 Stamford Road, Oakleigh, Victoria 3166, Australia

First published 1992

Printed in Great Britain at the University Press, Cambridge

A catalogue record for this book is available from the British Library

Library of Congress cataloguing in publication data

The Cambridge history of the English language
Vol. 2 edited by Norman Blake
Includes bibliographical references and indexes.
Contents: v. 1. The beginnings to 1066 – v. 2. 1066–1476.
1. English language – History. I. Hogg,
Richard M. II. Blake, N. F. (Norman Francis) 1934 –
PE1072.C36 1992 420'.9   91-13881
ISBN 0-521-26474-X (v. 1)
ISBN 0-521-26475-8 (v. 2)

ISBN 0 521 26475 8 hardback

CONTENTS

Contents

Contents

MAPS

CONTRIBUTORS

NORMAN BLAKE *Professor of English Language and Linguistics, University of Sheffield*

DAVID BURNLEY *Reader in English Language and Linguistics, University of Sheffield*

CECILY CLARK

OLGA FISCHER *Senior Lecturer in English Language, Universiteit van Amsterdam*

ROGER LASS *Professor of Linguistics, University of Cape Town*

JAMES MILROY *Professor Emeritus of Linguistics, University of Sheffield*

It was with great regret that the General Editor, the Editor and the contributors to the first two volumes of the Cambridge History of the English Language learned of Cecily Clark's death on 26 March 1992. Although she was able to see the proofs of her chapters, she was unable to see the finished books. We hope that the chapters she has written for the first two volumes of the Cambridge History may stand as a memorial to her life and work.

GENERAL EDITOR'S PREFACE

Although it is a topic of continuing debate, there can be little doubt that English is the most widely spoken language in the world, with significant numbers of native speakers in almost every major region – only South America falling largely outside the net. In such a situation an understanding of the nature of English can be claimed unambiguously to be of world-wide importance.

Growing consciousness of such a role for English is one of the motivations behind this History. There are other motivations too. Specialist students have many major and detailed works of scholarship to which they can refer, for example Bruce Mitchell's *Old English Syntax*, or, from an earlier age, Karl Luick's *Historische Grammatik der englischen Sprache*. Similarly, those who come new to the subject have both one-volume histories such as Barbara Strang's *History of English* and introductory textbooks to a single period, for example Bruce Mitchell and Fred Robinson's *A Guide to Old English*. But what is lacking is the intermediate work which can provide a solid discussion of the full range of the history of English both to the anglicist who does not specialise in the particular area to hand and to the general linguist who has no specialised knowledge of the history of English. This work attempts to remedy that lack. We hope that it will be of use to others too, whether they are interested in the history of English for its own sake, or for some specific purpose such as local history or the effects of colonisation. Under the influence of the Swiss linguist, Ferdinand de Saussure, there has been, during this century, a persistent tendency to view the study of language as having two discrete parts: (i) synchronic, where a language is studied from the point of view of one moment in time; (ii) diachronic, where a language is studied from a historical perspective. It might therefore be supposed that this present work is purely diachronic. But this is not so. One crucial principle which guides The Cambridge History of the English Language is that synchrony and diachrony are intertwined, and that a satisfactory understanding of English (or any other language) cannot be achieved on the basis of one of these alone.

Consider, for example, the (synchronic) fact that English, when compared with other languages, has some rather infrequent or unusual characteristics. Thus, in the area of vocabulary, English has an exceptionally high number of words borrowed from other languages (French, the Scandinavian languages, American Indian languages, Italian, the languages of northern India and so on); in syntax a common construction is the use of *do* in forming questions (e.g. *Do you like cheese?*), a type of construction not often found in other languages; in morphology English has relatively few inflexions, at least compared with the majority of other European languages; in phonology the number of diphthongs as against the number of vowels in English English is notably high. In other words, synchronically, English can be seen to be in some respects rather unusual. But in order to understand such facts we need to look at the history of the language; it is often only there that an explanation can be found. And that is what this work attempts to do.

This raises another issue. A quasi-Darwinian approach to English might attempt to account for its widespread use by claiming that somehow English is more suited, better adapted, to use as an international language than others. But that is nonsense. English is no more fit than, say, Spanish or Chinese. The reasons for the spread of English are political, cultural and economic rather than linguistic. So too are the reasons for such linguistic elements within English as the high number of borrowed words. This history, therefore, is based as much upon political, cultural and economic factors as linguistic ones, and it will be noted that the major historical divisions between volumes are based upon the former type of events (the Norman Conquest, the spread of printing, the declaration of independence by the USA) rather than the latter type.

As a rough generalisation, one can say that up to about the seventeenth century the development of English tended to be centrifugal, whereas since then the development has tended to be centripetal. The settlement by the Anglo-Saxons resulted in a spread of dialect variation over the country, but by the tenth century a variety of forces were combining to promote the emergence of a standard form of the language. Such an evolution was disrupted by the Norman

Conquest, but with the development of printing together with other more centralising tendencies, the emergence of a standard form became once more, from the fifteenth century on, a major characteristic of the language. But processes of emigration and colonisation then gave rise to new regional varieties overseas, many of which have now achieved a high degree of linguistic independence, and some of which, especially American English, may even have a dominating influence on British English. The structure of this work is designed to reflect these different types of development. Whilst the first four volumes offer a reasonably straightforward chronological account, the later volumes are geographically based. This arrangement, we hope, allows scope for the proper treatment of diverse types of evolution and development. Even within the chronologically oriented volumes there are variations of structure, which are designed to reflect the changing relative importance of various linguistic features. Although all the chronological volumes have substantial chapters devoted to the central topics of semantics and vocabulary, syntax, and phonology and morphology, for other topics the space allotted in a particular volume is one which is appropriate to the importance of that topic during the relevant period, rather than some predefined calculation of relative importance. And within the geographically based volumes all these topics are potentially included within each geographical section, even if sometimes in a less formal way. Such a flexible and changing structure seems essential for any full treatment of the history of English.

One question that came up as this project began was the extent to which it might be possible or desirable to work within a single theoretical linguistic framework. It could well be argued that only a consensus within the linguistic community about preferred linguistic theories would enable a work such as this to be written. Certainly, it was immediately obvious when work for this History began, that it would be impossible to lay down a 'party line' on linguistic theory, and indeed, that such an approach would be undesirably restrictive. The solution reached was, I believe, more fruitful. Contributors have been chosen purely on the grounds of expertise and knowledge, and have been encouraged to write their contributions in the way they see most fitting, whilst at the same time taking full account of developments in linguistic theory. This has, of course, led to problems, notably with contrasting views of the same topic (and also because of the need to distinguish the ephemeral flight of theoretical fancy from genuine new insights into linguistic theory), but even in a work which is concerned to provide a unified approach (so that, for example, in most cases every contributor to a volume has read all the other contributions to that volume), such contrasts, and even contradictions, are stimulating and fruitful. Whilst this work aims to be authoritative, it is not prescriptive, and the final goal must be to stimulate interest in a subject in which much work remains to be done, both theoretically and empirically.

The task of editing this History has been, and still remains, a long and complex one. As General Editor I owe a great debt to many friends and colleagues who have devoted much time and thought to how best this work might be approached and completed. Firstly I should thank my fellow-editors: John Algeo, Norman Blake, Bob Burchfield, Roger Lass and Suzanne Romaine. They have been concerned as much with the History as a whole as with their individual volumes. Secondly, there are those fellow linguists, some contributors, some not, who have so generously given of their time and made many valuable suggestions: John Anderson, Cecily Clark, Frans van Coetsem, Fran Colman, David Denison, Ed Finegan, Olga Fischer, Jacek Fisiak, Malcolm Godden, Angus McIntosh, Lesley Milroy, Donka Minkova, Matti Rissanen, Michael Samuels, Bob Stockwell, Tom Toon, Elizabeth Traugott, Peter Trudgill, Nigel Vincent, Anthony Warner, Simone Wyss. One occasion stands out especially: the organisers of the Fourth International Conference on English Historical Linguistics, held at Amsterdam in 1985, kindly allowed us to hold a seminar on the project as it was just beginning. For their generosity, which allowed us to hear a great many views and exchange opinions with colleagues one rarely meets face-to-face, I must thank Roger Eaton, Olga Fischer, Willem Koopman and Frederike van der Leek.

With a work so complex as this, an editor is faced with a wide variety of problems and difficulties. It has been, therefore, a continual comfort and solace to know that Penny Carter of Cambridge University Press has always been there to provide advice and solutions on every occasion. Without her knowledge and experience, encouragement and good humour, this work would have been both poorer and later. After work for Volume I was virtually complete, Marion Smith took over as publishing editor, and I am grateful to her too, not merely for ensuring such a smooth change-over, but for her bravery when faced with the mountain of paper from which this series has emerged.

Richard M. Hogg

ACKNOWLEDGEMENTS

This volume has been a long time in the making. Inevitably, some chapters were finished before others, but they have all been revised for final submission in 1990. All chapters have been read by other contributors to the other volumes, and by the general editor. We are grateful to all these people for their comments. I hope it will not appear invidious if I particularly thank Richard Hogg, John Algeo and Robert Burchfield among the other editors for their helpful comments on individual chapters. We would particularly like to record our thanks to: John Anderson, Fran Colman, Catherine Coutts, David Denison, Heines Eichner, Gillian Fellows-Jensen, John Field, Margaret Gelling, Manfred Görlach, Suzanne Kemmer, Willem Koopman, Chris McCully, Hans Meier, Lesley Milroy, Oliver Padel, Matti Rissanen, Don Scragg, Ann Hurleman Stewart, Patrick Stiles, Mary Syner, Linda Thornburg, Elisabeth Traugott, Wim van der Wurff, Nigel Vincent, Tony Warner and Nancy Wiegand. There are many others who have helped us as we have struggled to complete our chapters, and I hope they will not feel slighted if they are included in such a general acknowledgement.

We acknowledge permission from Professor G. Kristensson and the editors of Lund Studies in English to reproduce the map '*a/o* forms in Lancashire, West Riding and Lincolnshire' on page 183.

ABBREVIATIONS

abstr.	abstract
acc.	accusative
adj.	adjective
AN	Anglo-Norman
AScand.	Anglo-Scandinavian
Bo	*Boethius* (Benson 1987)
BD	*Book of the Duchess*
CA	*Confessio amantis* (Macaulay 1900)
CF	central French
cl.	class
Co	coda
CSR	Compound Stress Rule
CT	*Canterbury Tales*
CWGmc	Continental West Germanic
dat.	dative
DB	Domesday Book
demonstr.	demonstrative
DEPN	*Dictionary of English Place Names* (Ekwall 1960)
Du.	Dutch
EME	Early Middle English
EPNS	English Place Name Society
F	French
fem.	feminine
G	German
gen.	genitive

Gk	Greek
Gmc	Germanic
Go.	Gothic
GSR	Germanic Stress Rule
HF	*House of Fame*
IE	Indo-European
imp.	imperative
ind.	indicative
inf.	infinitive
inst.	instrumental
Kt.	Kentish
LALME	*Linguistic Atlas of Late Medieval English* (McIntosh, Samuels & Benskin 1986)
Lat.	Latin
LGW	*Legend of Good Women*
LOE	Late Old English
Mars	*The Complaint of Mars* (Benson 1987)
masc.	masculine
MDu.	Middle Dutch
ME	Middle English
MED	*Middle English Dictionary* (Kurath, Kuhn & Lewis 1954–)
Med. Lat.	Medieval Latin
MLG	Middle Low German
Mod. F	Modern French
N	northern; nucleus
n.	noun
Nbr.	Northumbrian
neut.	neuter
NF	Norman French
nom.	nominative
NP	noun phrase
NSR	Nuclear Stress Rule
num.	number
O	onset; object
obl.	oblique

OE	Old English
OED	*Oxford English Dictionary*
OF	Old French
OHG	Old High German
ON	Old Norse
ONF	Old Norman French
ONGmc	Old North Germanic
OSc.	Old Scots
OScand.	Old Scandinavian
OSL	Open Syllable Lengthening
OSw.	Old Swedish
past pple	past participle
PC	*Peterborough Chronicle*
PDE	Present-Day English
perf.	perfect
pers.	person
PF	*The Parliament of Fowls*
POE	Proto Old English
PPl.	*Piers Plowman*
pres.	present
R	rhyme
Rose	*Romaunt of the Rose*
RP	Received Pronunciation
RSR	Romance Stress Rule
S	southern; strong
Sc.	Scots
Scand.	Scandinavian
SE	southeastern
sg.	singular
Skt	Sanskrit
subj.	subjunctive; subject
SW	southwestern
Troilus	*Troilus and Criseyde*
V; vb	verb
VLat.	Vulgar Latin
W	weak
WGmc	West Germanic
WS	West Saxon

*, **   a single asterisk precedes forms which are reconstructed or inferred; double asterisks precede forms which are (claimed to be) ungrammatical

þ, ð, etc.   a description of these Old English characters can be found on p. 35

A note on references

Since there are several different lineations available for *The Canterbury Tales* we have decided to provide two references for each quotation from this poem: one is to fragment number and line, e.g. III.845, which refers to lineation in Benson 1987; and the other is to section and line, e.g. 2: 819, which refers to the lineation in Blake 1980. The quotation is taken from the text with the first reference; the second is placed in square brackets immediately afterwards.

I INTRODUCTION

Norman Blake

1.1 Beginnings of the study of Middle English

Traditionally, the start of Middle English is dated in 1066 with the Norman Conquest and its finish in 1485 with the accession of Henry VII, the first Tudor monarch. Both dates are political and historical, and the events they represent may have an impact on the development of the English language in the longer term but they are hardly appropriate as guides to the dating of periods in it. In any case language does not change as abruptly as such stark dates would suggest and the whole matter of when Middle English began and ended depends on the features which are regarded as significant in marking a change in the language. The period is called 'Middle' English because it falls between Old and Modern English. To most people today Middle English has seemed closer to Modern than to Old English for a variety of reasons. Perhaps the most important of these has been the influence of Geoffrey Chaucer. His reputation as the 'Father of English Poetry' has meant that many people have some familiarity with Middle English through his writings. More importantly, his work has been almost constantly available since Caxton issued the *editio princeps* of *The Canterbury Tales* in 1476. Each subsequent century has seen its great editor of Chaucer (Ruggiers 1984) and these editors have kept Chaucer and Middle English very much in the public eye. The only other author who comes anywhere near Chaucer in this respect is Malory, whose *Le Morte Darthur* was published several times in the sixteenth and nineteenth centuries.

Both Chaucer and Malory are literary authors and the interest in the Middle English period which they have generated has been more connected with literary culture than with language. Interest in other

Middle English writings developed only in the nineteenth century, partly as a result of the Romantic revolution. Ballads, romances and prose texts all started to appear at this time. Thomas Ritson and Bishop Percy were among the first to popularise this type of literature through their editions, though the work of Sir Walter Scott should not be underestimated. More academic editions were produced by scholars such as Sir Frederic Madden, whose 1847 edition of the *Brut* is still valuable. However, it has to be said that the Middle English period did not have the same appeal as the Old English one, partly because of its nature as a transition period and partly because it does not have the attraction of the inter-relationship of pagan and Christian cultures. A period which is in transition does not have a point of focus unless that is provided by a great author such as Chaucer. But Chaucer was seen more as the initiator of a new age rather than as a typical product of the Middle English period.

The same attitude prevailed in the study of language. From the nineteenth century onwards there was great interest in the historical study of the language which expressed itself through the study of dialects, the development of phonology and the investigation of individual texts. Much of this work was done through the study of the phonology of individual literary texts, and was to that extent fragmented. A nineteenth-century edition of a Middle English work of literature is likely to contain an exhaustive account of the phonological features of that text together with some indication of what area of the country those features point to. It is unlikely to contain any description of the syntax or any formal analysis of the lexis, though individual words may well be commented on separately in the commentary. Sometimes this work was flawed because it did not pay sufficient attention to the various copies a text could go through or, in the case of rhyme, what the limits of acceptability were for rhyme in the period. A difficulty which presented itself to scholars was the greater profusion of available material as compared with Old English which allowed for the division of the country into a larger number of dialect and subdialect areas. Inevitably a great deal of information was assembled which could not always be fitted into a manageable pattern. The culmination of this work was the drawing of isoglosses to isolate various Middle English dialects in Moore, Meech & Whitehall's *Middle English Dialect Characteristics and Dialect Boundaries* (1935). This study is based on the examination of 266 texts from the twelfth to the fifteenth centuries and it proposed the establishment of characteristic features in Middle

English phonology whose limits could be represented as isoglosses. When plotted on a map, they divided the country into ten regions: northern, northeast midland, central-east midland, southeast midland, Kentish, southern, southwest midland, south central-west midland, north central-west midland and northwest midland. This study remained the basic framework for all phonological investigations until fairly recently. However, very little was achieved in the areas of morphology, lexis or syntax either generally or in relation to the charting of dialects.

1.2 The study of Middle English since the Second World War

Since the Second World War the study of Middle English language has made enormous strides, for which there are two major reasons: the first is the growth of modern linguistics, which has introduced a completely new approach to many areas of historical study; and the second is the establishment of comprehensive national surveys to study the modern language and earlier stages of English. In the latter the development of recording techniques and of computers has been of enormous influence. Shortly after the war a research programme to map out present dialect characteristics was launched by Dieth and Orton. This survey (Orton *et al.* 1962–71) isolated various rural localities and sought out older speakers who had lived in the area all their lives so that a network of dialect features could be plotted for the various sites investigated. The survey focused particularly on phonology and lexis. From the investigations dialect maps could be drawn, and usually they were portrayed historically through the advance or decline of features nationally. Inevitably, the most important point of comparison was the state of dialects in the Middle English period, because so little was known of dialects in the Early Modern period as a result of the spread of a standardised written language. The maps of Modern English dialect features provided a useful point of comparison for those studying Middle English. The Middle English period is much richer in its documentation than the Old English one, and the needs of the centralised monarchy meant that various national surveys were conducted and their results have often survived today. The earliest of these is the Domesday Book itself, but others, such as the Lay Subsidy Rolls, are equally important. Although such surveys and tax-rolls are in essence Latin documents, they contain personal names and place names in forms which are lightly enough Latinised to permit the underlying

English name to be recovered. A survey of dialect characteristics of Middle English using the Lay Subsidy Rolls is being undertaken by Professor Kristensson. Some of the results have been published already, and eventually the whole of England will be analysed (Kristensson 1967, 1987).

A different method of recording dialect features was initiated by Professor McIntosh at Edinburgh University in a project which had as co-members Professor Samuels of Glasgow University, Michael Benskin and others. This survey worked on the principle of establishing scribal profiles through the various letter forms and spellings which individual scribes employed. In this way it was possible to identify local or even at times individual characteristics so that the copying of individual manuscripts could be more specifically localised. This was achieved by working from the features of those texts which could be precisely localised through external information and by establishing a national grid on to which other texts could be plotted. The Edinburgh survey aimed at examining a very large corpus of material from the period, and this corpus continues to grow. It is now possible through the published atlas (McIntosh *et al.* 1986) to show more clearly how the language was changing at least at the written level and also to show how individual texts changed as they were recopied in different parts of the country. Articles by Professor Samuels and others have managed to exploit this material (Smith 1989). Perhaps particularly important has been the work done to show the various layers of language in the London area and their inter-relationship. The development of standards in this area before the acceptance of a single standard is now much better understood. An edition by John Fisher and others of texts written in the so-called Chancery standard has promoted understanding of this change (Fisher, Richardson & Fisher 1984).

In one respect the onset of modern linguistics has not had the impact on Middle English linguistic studies one might have expected. So much of modern linguistics has been concerned with the structure of language, particularly in the form of syntax, that one might have expected that this would encourage the wider study of historical syntax as well. Unfortunately, syntax still remains the Cinderella of Middle English linguistic studies. Professor Mustanoja completed only the first part of his *Middle English Syntax* (Mustanoja 1960), and so the Middle English period still has nothing to compare with Dr Mitchell's comprehensive account of Old English syntax (Mitchell 1985). Individual studies of special points continue to appear, but they cannot be fitted into a full historical, let alone a localised, dialect pattern. However, modern linguistics has altered most scholars' attitudes to the period profoundly. No longer is the language seen as no more than a series of marks on paper which have to be grouped into formal patterns. The language is accepted as a living and developing organism, and the certainties of the past have been abandoned to provide for a picture of language in use. No longer do scholars think in terms of a finite disappearance of one form or of one word to be replaced by another; they increasingly think in terms of competition between forms both geographically and chronologically. Choices were available to speakers of the language then as they are today, and reasons have to be offered for the preference of one over another. This in turn has led to the concentration on stylistics and features such as register. An understanding of the possibilities inherent in the language has in its turn bred a greater respect for the users of the language. The mindless scribe has given way to a copyist faced with a number of choices who tries to find his way through them in a way which was partly conscious and partly subconscious. The greater number of copies of Middle English texts and the wider range of material have made this approach more meaningful than it could possibly be for the Old English period.

1.3   English, French and Latin

It has already been suggested that the sources available for the study of Middle English are far greater than those for Old English, though it is appropriate to add a word of caution at this point. In this period three languages were used in England: French, Latin and English. French at both the spoken and written level existed at first in England in that variety known today as Anglo-Norman. It was used in literary works, official documents and religious writings. Anglo-Norman, the aristocratic vernacular used in England, gave way during the early thirteenth century to Anglo-French, which was essentially an administrative language which had to be acquired as a foreign language by the English. It was never a serious competitor to English. Latin remained the language of religion and administration through the whole of the Middle English period, and English was used only for specific religious purposes, as we shall see. English continued to be used at the spoken level, except in court circles, and consequently in status it was less well regarded than either Latin or French. It occurs in written texts sporadically at first, and then increasingly supplants first French and then Latin. It may be helpful to look at these sources in a preliminary way here.

In the late Old English period the flowering of literary studies is more associated with monastic establishments in the south and west of the country, where the Benedictine revival had its greatest impact. The standardised Late West Saxon written language was based on Winchester and its daughter houses (Gneuss 1972). The north of England had suffered most from the Scandinavian invasions and had taken time to reconstruct its cultural life, though there were naturally important religious centres in the north. The early eleventh century does not appear to be a rich period of writing, though this may be the result of manuscript loss. For after the Norman Conquest many Old English manuscripts continued to be copied and this suggests the survival of a tradition in the late Old English period. Some Old English texts survive only in post-Conquest copies, as is true of much of the material collected in Cockayne's *Leechdoms* (Cockayne 1864–6). The Late Old English period is associated with a vigorous prose tradition centred on the works of Ælfric and Wulfstan and their imitators. This prose tradition had developed to counter the decay of learning, particularly Latin learning, brought about by the Scandinavian invasions. The introduction of Anglo-Norman and, in particular, the greater use of Latin which was encouraged by the Norman conquerors and promoted through the twelfth-century Renaissance of Latin learning led to the gradual breakdown of this prose tradition. *The Anglo-Saxon Chronicle* is a good example of this situation. Several of the various recensions were recopied during the late Old English period and continuations were added. The latest text is the so-called *Peterborough Chronicle*, which was copied at that abbey ca 1121 from an original of indeterminate origin and then provided with sporadic continuations until ca 1155 (Clark 1970). From then on historical writing in England essentially uses Latin until the fifteenth century. Old English alliterative verse peters out towards the middle of the eleventh century, though some have argued for an eleventh-century date for *Beowulf*. *The Battle of Maldon* may have been composed in the eleventh century, but there are few significant poems from that century and certainly nothing that could be described as a vigorous poetic tradition. There are some modest attempts at alliterative poetry shortly after the Conquest, mostly associated with the west of the country, but these soon die out. In the early thirteenth century there is Laȝamon's *Brut* in alliterative long lines, although it is a translation of Wace's versified French version of Geoffrey of

Monmouth's *Historia regum Britanniae* (Brook & Leslie 1963–78). This text is from the southwest midlands. In the following century there is a revival of alliterative poetry in the west midlands associated particularly with *Piers Plowman* (Kane 1960; Kane & Donaldson 1975) and *Sir Gawain and the Green Knight*. Although the greatest impetus for these poems comes from the French and Latin traditions, their style has many links with the Old English alliterative tradition and it has proved difficult to determine how that tradition survived through a period when little poetry was written. Although a great deal of alliterative poetry may have been lost, it has also been suggested either that it survived at an oral level or that alliteration remained alive as a stylistic technique through prose.

Some prose writing in English occurred through most of our period, and it is especially associated with the homiletic tradition. At first there were writings in both the east and the west of the country, though by the end of the twelfth century it is particularly in the west that homiletic writing flourished. The writings of the so-called *Katherine* group and the *Ancrene Wisse* are linked with the dialect of the Old English *Vespasian Psalter*, and in Middle English these writings are mostly found in the west midland counties of Worcestershire and Herefordshire. Many of these works may have been written for women religious or for women who adopted a form of life which embraced some religious discipline, if not that of an established order. During the fourteenth century other writings in prose became more frequent, usually as translations from French or Latin. In part, these were intended to provide instruction for those unable to read Latin or French, though gradually they are written in English because the status of that language improved. By the fifteenth century prose in English was becoming the norm so that letters and records, such as those of London gilds, are found in English. The fifteenth century saw an enormous expansion of what was written in prose, and increasingly this is produced in London and its immediate surroundings. The growth of the civil service in London and the rise in patronage from the court made London a centre for English. London was now the largest city in the country and its merchants were powerful and wealthy. Inevitably, this generated a lot of writing, which was increasingly in English. The culmination of this development is the introduction of the printing press by William Caxton in 1476, for he set up his press in Westminster. The bulk of his output was in English and was clearly intended to appeal to the middle and upper classes who wanted reading material in their own language (Blake 1969a). The dominance of London in the production of written material in English was confirmed.

Apart from poetry in the alliterative style, Middle English poetry assimilated French metre and rhyme as its basic constituents. Once again one finds only sporadic examples appearing during the first two centuries following the Conquest. One of the best of these is *The Owl and the Nightingale*, probably written at the beginning of the thirteenth century in the south-east of the country (Stanley 1960). This poem shows already a clear assimilation of French language and poetic techniques, even if the number of French words it contains is relatively small. During the same century French romance begins to make an impact on English, and most of those which are found in Middle English have French sources or parallels. At the same time lyrics, perhaps prompted by the teaching requirements of the friars, begin to make their appearance so that by the end of the century the use of English for poetic purposes is widely accepted again. It is only in the fourteenth century that this trend turns into a flood, though again, apart from the alliterative poetry, much of this poetic activity is connected with London and the south-east. It culminates in the work of Geoffrey Chaucer, John Gower and John Lydgate. From this time onwards poetic composition not written in English will appear aberrant, though it needs to be remembered that Gower himself did compose poems in French and Latin as well as in English.

At a more official level administrative documents and letters were written at first in Latin or French, and throughout the period Latin remained the official language of the Church. Taxation and other surveys were written at first in Latin and sometimes from the mid-thirteenth century in French, and the same applies to judicial records. Although written in Latin or French, these documents contain such material as English names in a Latinised form which can be exploited for onomastic studies and more general linguistic surveys. The material can be important as it is often possible to localise the place where such documents originated, although extant copies are often from Westminster. In addition to the well-known English charter issued by Henry II in 1155, there is a small corpus of administrative documents in English dated before 1189, though it is not until the end of the fourteenth century that documents in English become common. The same applies to letter collections. Letters in French or Latin are found throughout the medieval period, but examples in Middle English are common only from the beginning of the fifteenth century. The earliest

English letter in the Paston collection is dated to 1425 (Davis 1971–6). It should be said, however, that insufficient attention has been paid by scholars to non-literary material in their work on the history and development of Middle English, often because many of these records have not been made available in modern editions (see Chambers & Daunt 1931; Fisher, Richardson & Fisher 1984). All the material which survives from the Middle English period is relatively formal, no matter whether it is literary or not, and so it is difficult to have much feel for informal varieties of the language. This restriction needs to be kept very firmly in mind in the chapters that follow, because the beginnings of the literary representation of low-class speech, as in Chaucer's *fabliaux*, might suggest to the modern reader that we do have access to these varieties.

1.4   Spelling and standardisation

As indicated in a previous section, people today find Middle English much easier to recognise as English than is true of Old English, which appears to be more like a foreign language. If we compare the same passage in both Old and Middle English, the differences are obvious. The following is Matthew 2.13 in an Old English (West Saxon) version and the longer Wycliffite version:

1   Þa hi þa ferdon, þa ætwyde Drihtnes engel Iosepe on swefnum, and þus cwæð, Aris and nim þæt cild and his modor, and fleoh on Egypta land, and beo þær oð þæt ic ðe secge; toweard ys þæt Herodes secð þæt cild to forspillenne.

('When they had left, then the angel of God appeared to Joseph in a dream and spoke in this way: "Arise, and take the child and his mother and flee to the land of the Egyptians and remain there until I tell you. The time is at hand that Herod will seek out the child to destroy him."')

2   And whanne thei weren goon, lo! the aungel of the Lord apperide to Joseph in sleep, and seide, Rise vp, and take the child and his modir, and fle in to Egipt, and be thou there, til that I seie to thee; for it is to come, that Eroude seke the child to destrie hym.

There are many contrasts between the two passages, but those which strike one immediately are changes in the spelling and letter forms, for it is these which create the air of unfamiliarity about Old English to modern speakers of English. Although immediately noticeable, changes in spelling may indicate only changes in the conventions of writing rather than any profound change in the structure or sound of the language.

Following the Norman Conquest many monastic institutions, which were the intellectual centres and scriptoria of their day, had an influx of monks trained in France accustomed to the spellings found in French even if these did not as yet constitute a French spelling system. When they copied texts in English they gradually transferred some of these spelling habits to English and so altered profoundly the look of English. Though these changes do not necessarily indicate any alteration in pronunciation, the attempt by French people to speak English and at a later stage bilingualism would inevitably promote changes at the spoken level as well. Old English contained the letters *æ*, *þ* and *ð*, of which in Middle English the first and the last were abandoned fairly promptly and the middle one was not much used except in special circumstances by the end of the fourteenth century. Some letters which were seldom or never used in Old English were gradually introduced in Middle English such as *k*, *q*, *x* and *ȝ*. What had been *cyning* in Old English is now *king*; and in the Old English passage above *cwæð* gave way to Middle English *quath*. This last example shows that different letter combinations were used in Middle English, for OE *cw* gives way to ME *qu*. The same applies to *c* (as in *cild*) becoming *ch* (PDE *child*), *sc* becoming *sh/sch* (OE *sceadu*, PDE *shadow*), and *cȝ* becoming *gg/dg* (OE *ecȝ*, PDE *edge*).

What in fact was happening was that the West Saxon standard was collapsing in the face of these new pressures. It should be remembered that this standard was the written language of an educated elite and was now somewhat archaic and had never represented the spoken language of most Anglo-Saxons. Naturally, this did not happen at once, for the standard was maintained in certain monastic institutions into the twelfth century. Gradually, as less writing in English was done under the impact of the use of Latin arising from the twelfth-century Renaissance and of French, the old spelling system was abandoned. No central unified system was put in its place to start with, so that early Middle English gives the impression of being far more fragmented than Late Old English. In practice, the introduction of new spelling habits allowed the scribes to make their written system reflect more closely the speech forms that they heard daily because they were no longer confined to the straitjacket of an imposed spelling system.

The freedom from the old spelling standard allowed the written language to take account of the different sounds introduced by the Viking and Norman settlers. It is an interesting feature of Late Old English that it contains little influence of Old Norse in either spelling or vocabulary. The pull of the standard was so strong that this new influence could not find full expression. It is also true that the areas of greatest Scandinavian settlement, the north and east, produced less written material in the late Old English period, in part at least because so many monasteries were destroyed or seriously weakened by the Vikings. The languages spoken by the Viking invaders were branches of the North Germanic variety of Indo-European and were not only mutually intelligible but were also largely comprehensible to speakers of Old English, a West Germanic language. Old Norse and Old English diverged in pronunciation in certain specific points, some of which are still traceable in the modern language. PDE *give* has as its ancestor OE *ȝiefan*, though that form would normally give something like PDE **yive*. In Middle English the reflex of OE *ȝiefan* was indeed *yive* or a variant of that spelling. In Old Norse the equivalent verb was *gefa*, and Middle English shows forms which exhibit features of this verb particularly initial <g> instead of <y>. These forms occur mainly in northern dialects, but gradually this <g> percolates south, where it merges with the southern form to produce *give* rather than *geve*. The same development accounts for forms like PDE *get* and *guest*, which in Old English were *ȝiet/ȝet* and *ȝiest/ȝest* as compared with ON *geta* and *gestr*.

The development of the Germanic sounds differed in the North Germanic dialects from the West Germanic ones so that many of the words introduced by the Viking invaders had phonological forms which were distinguished from those used by the Anglo-Saxons. In many cases these forms were adopted into northern dialects and surface in the Middle English varieties of those dialects. In some instances they were further adopted by the standard language as a result of the southward drift of northern dialect features. This results in further examples of that unexpected phenomenon that Modern English does not reflect the sound pattern of Old English, even though the modern standard is based on a Middle English London and east midland variety. For example, PDE *though* reflects an Old Norse form **þoh* which must be an intermediate stage between ONGmc **þauh* and standard ON *þó*.

The Old English form *þeah* reflects the development of Gmc *au* to OE *ēa*. In Middle English northern dialects have forms like *þogh* and *þough* for this word, whereas southern and midland ones are more likely to have forms like *þagh*, *þaugh* and *þeigh*. In such cases it may be difficult to decide why the standard language has finally chosen the reflex of the northern variety; but for our purposes it is important to recognise that the appearance of these forms in writing was occasioned by the breakdown of the old West Saxon standard. Forms of this type make their appearance from the earliest northern texts found in Middle English such as the *Ormulum* (White 1878). It is only later that such forms begin to extend southwards.

The breakdown of the Old English scribal tradition based on the West Saxon standard allowed for that diversity which we regard as typical of Middle English writing systems as compared with those in the Old English period. The diversity should not be interpreted as a free-for-all in which any spelling was possible, though that is perhaps the immediate impression a modern reader of Middle English has in comparison with Old English or Modern English. Standards or incipient standards developed in particular localities. Often these were based around a monastic foundation and may even have been regulated by a single teacher. The most famous example is the so-called AB language associated with certain manuscripts from the southwest midlands in the early thirteenth century and provisionally localised by Dobson at Wigmore Abbey, Herefordshire (Dobson 1976). The Corpus Christi College Cambridge manuscript of the *Ancrene Wisse*, a name sometimes given to this text to distinguish it from the *Ancren Riwle* version found in different manuscripts, is written in a consistent dialect which is also found in the Bodley manuscript of the *Katherine* group. The way in which the AB dialect could be copied is studied in some detail by Dobson in his edition of the Cleopatra manuscript of *Ancren Riwle* (Dobson 1972). The two most important scribes of that manuscript maintain many of the features of the main AB language but also diverge from it to some extent because of their geographical origins or incomplete training in the conventions of the AB language. Dobson's study, which supplements Tolkien's earlier one (Tolkien 1929), is important in showing how a set of conventions is generated and gradually breaks down with the passage of time.

The most important area for the development of writing standards is that of London and its immediate environs. Early scholars such as Mackenzie portrayed the London dialect in broad terms as one which turned from being an essentially southern dialect to one which became an east midland one (Mackenzie 1928). Ekwall in his study of personal names provided some social and economic reasons as to why this might have happened (Ekwall 1956). But more recent work by Samuels and by Fisher has revealed that it is possible to be much more specific about various standards within the London area itself. These may be associated with different types of work so that in the Chancery scribes developed their own standard which was by no means constant since it changed with time (Fisher 1977), whereas other standards developed in association with particular scribes who wrote literary and other works (Samuels 1963). The copying of manuscripts often produced mixed dialects or *Mischsprachen* as one scribe superimposed his own conventions on those of the manuscript he was copying, but this is something which is more particularly associated with literary and didactic texts since these are the texts which are copied most frequently. They are also the texts read most frequently today. It might be said that each local standard draws its conventions from a pool which consists of traditional, national and local features, with the local and traditional features being more important at first and the national gaining in importance as the fifteenth century progresses. In London itself it is perhaps surprising that so much standardisation is found, for although one might expect such standardisation in religious houses with their traditions, London is characterised by secular copying. As far as we can tell, secular scribes worked individually on a piece-work basis, though they might occasionally have teamed up to form a loose co-operative. However, many individual scribes may, like Hoccleve, have worked for a major organisation such as the Chancery during the day and done private copying at other times. Hence even in secular private copying the process of standardisation would gradually manifest itself.

The Chancery hand developed in Italian chancelleries in the thirteenth century and spread to France in the early fourteenth century. Later in that century it spread to London, and the standardisation of the handwriting went hand in hand with the standardisation of the spelling. Fisher, Richardson & Fisher have produced an important anthology of Chancery documents, and they note how the spelling adopted by the scribes became standardised.

> The Chancery clerks fairly consistently preferred the spellings which have since become standard. The documents in this anthology show the clerks trying to eliminate the kind of orthographic eccentricity found in the Privy Seal minutes, the petitions passed on to them for

entering in the rolls, and most of the documents printed by Chambers and Daunt. At the very least, we can say that they were trying to limit choices among spellings, and that by the 1440's and 1450's they had achieved a comparative regularization.

(Fisher, Richardson & Fisher 1984: 27).

Among examples of this regularisation process they note that *such* is the preferred Chancery form which had ousted *sich*, *sych*, *seche* and *swiche*. *Which* was replacing *wich*. The auxiliary verbs appear more regularly in their modern forms: *can*, *could*, *shall*, *should* and *would*. Furthermore it is difficult to detect spellings used by the Chancery scribes that can be described as phonetic. In other words a standardised spelling was developing which was divorced from the immediate phonetic environment so that sound and spelling were becoming two separate, if parallel, systems. As an example of this spelling system we may quote from a text printed in the Fisher anthology:

> The kyng by þadvise and assent of the lordes sp*irit*uell and temporell beyng in this *present* parlement woll and grantith þat þe said Sir Iohn Talbot haue and occupie the saide office of Chaunceller of Irelond by hym self or by his sufficient depute there after the fourme of the kynges *lett*res patentes to hym made þ*er*of. the which *lett*res patentes ben thought gode and effe*ct*uell and to be approved after the tenure of the same Also þat þe grete seal of þe saide lond belongyng to þe saide office. which þe said Thomas hath geton vn to hym be delyu*er*ed to þe said Sir Iohn Talbot or his sufficiante depute hauyng power of hym to resceiue hit.

(Fisher, Richardson & Fisher 1984: 265–6)

There are still features in the spelling of this text which appear old-fashioned to a modern reader: plurals in *-es*; double *l* at the end of words; variation between *i* and *y*; the retention of þ; the use of *-ie* for *-y* finally; the occurrence of final *-e* where we no longer keep it; the old arrangement of *u* and *v* according to position in the word rather than phonological function; and others. But most of these features will remain in standard English during the sixteenth century and even beyond. There is little in the above quotation that would cause difficulty to the modern reader, at least as far as the spelling is concerned.

In Middle English studies most attention has been devoted to attempts to localise sounds and spellings over space and time. Almost nothing has been done in this respect with regard to syntax. Although the origin of particular syntactic structures has been traced, no attempt has been made to see whether particular structures are more characteristic of one dialect in comparison with others. In so far as any attention has been paid to syntax it is more usually concerned with the question of how far a particular structure, such as the use of *gan*, is stylistic. The same may be said to apply in large part to the study of vocabulary. The history of the lexicon has been charted in the sense that the introduction of new words from other languages and the demise of words associated with traditional heroic vocabulary are noted. Some attention has been paid to the competition between various words to discover whether there are any general principles to determine which word might survive. Otherwise most attention has been paid to the register of the vocabulary of Middle English, for which the elucidation of the connotations of words in a literary context has been the driving force. Inevitably a lot of attention has been paid to Chaucerian writings. The greater variety of writing in English from the fourteenth century and the existence of a major author like Chaucer make this approach to vocabulary more rewarding than for any previous period. Full appreciation of some of the effects Chaucer aimed at can be achieved only through understanding how he exploited the connotative meaning and register of some of his words (Burnley 1979). The growth of romance and the development of mystical writings in English provide us with two genres with sufficient material to be able to plot more fully the vocabulary associated with each (e.g. Riehle 1981). Naturally, there has been some attempt to distinguish the vocabulary of alliterative poetry from that of rhyming poetry, but this has been geographically oriented only incidentally since the main motivation has been to distinguish between genres rather than to isolate geographical peculiarities.

1.5   Social and literary developments

As already suggested, the Norman Conquest of 1066 produced significant changes in Anglo-Saxon society and it is time now to consider some of these in greater depth. Despite the ravages of the Viking invasions, Anglo-Saxon England was a rich and sophisticated country, which is indeed one reason why it was attractive to foreign invaders like William. It was also a relatively centralised country, though the administration was still personal and peripatetic. Latin was the language of the Church, though it may not have been so extensively studied as it had been in the age of Bede. The teaching of the large mass of the people was done in English, though many monasteries still had extensive libraries with Latin manuscripts. A tradition of Old English prose writing was firmly established. The Norman invasion led to a reorganisation of the Church and the introduction of monks and clerics from France. At first these filled many of the higher positions in the Church, particularly in the east and south of the country. French became the language of the upper classes, both secular and religious. Latin was still the language of the Church and was available for religious writings and also for administration. The role of English was reduced in educational and religious matters, though it must be remembered that a greater proportion of the people living in the country still spoke English as their mother tongue. Some areas removed from the great metropolitan centres like London continued to copy manuscripts in Old English and to write new texts in a form of early Middle English during the eleventh and twelfth centuries. In particular, the west midlands in the area around Worcester maintained a strong link with the Anglo-Saxon past through the copying of manuscripts and the production of new texts such as *The Debate of the Soul and the Body*. Yet, throughout England individual texts could be copied or written, and it is difficult often to explain why they should have appeared at a particular place at that time, for so many of them exist in isolation, though part of the explanation may lie in the loss of material which has occurred since then. Usually these texts are religious or hortatory. The effect is of a relatively unified tradition producing a body of religious material in a standardised language fragmenting into a number of disparate and unrelated bits with the result that odd texts appear in more localised dialects. It is the fragmentation which allows us to see the changes which had taken place in the language and which are here given expression because of the loosening of the traditional scribal system.

The Norman Conquest brought England into close contact with France through the immigration of French-speaking people and through the ownership of lands on either side of the Channel. The kings of England were at first vassals of the kings of France for their possessions in France and in the end they came to claim the throne of France itself. The whole of the Middle English period witnessed a constant struggle between England and France for the control of all parts of France. English eyes were focused in this period on France, which remained at the centre of English foreign policy, and France was the spur of English cultural and literary ambitions. Gradually, French metre and stanza forms were introduced; French literary genres were imitated; and French vocabulary and syntax influenced English. At first the influence appears to be sporadic and fragmented, as is true of the appearance of *The Owl and the Nightingale* – a poem which has no immediate precursors or successors in English. Yet in its use of French-inspired metre and vocabulary it is extremely sophisticated. From the fragmentary evidence we have it is easy to assume that English was repressed and had largely gone underground, but the evidence of this poem would indicate that this is far from being the case. Because so much of what survives in Early Middle English is more practical than literary, the influence of French on English vocabulary appears to be more pragmatic. Many of the words borrowed at this stage have become so much part of the language that many modern speakers find it difficult to think of them as loan words. There are words of rank or status such as *duke* or *abbot*; words of religion such as *grace*, *mercy* and *miracle*; common words such as *mount* and *fruit*; as well as words of military meaning such as *war* itself. Many of these words are of one or two syllables only and have long become acclimatised in English.

The contact with France meant that England absorbed the new religious and cultural influences from the Continent quickly. In the religious sphere the rise of new orders and the movement towards teaching the laity were significant. From the twelfth century onwards new religious orders were established in England, often with the intention of re-establishing the fundamentals of Christian or monastic life. Some of these orders, like the Cistercians, were associated with new movements in spirituality and brought with them a heightened sensitivity. Others, such as the friars, were committed to teaching and preaching, and wanted to spread the word of God among those who may have been neglected by earlier orders, such as the urban poor. The Fourth Lateran Council of 1215 insisted on a certain minimum of instruction for all Christians and so encouraged the development of instruction in the vernacular. All of these influences worked towards the promotion of literature in English which would appeal to a wide cross-section of the population. Sermons and lyrics began to be produced in increasing numbers. The development of new orders also meant that many new houses were established, and as most of these had their own scriptoria the output of written material increased. More importantly, as these scriptoria were dotted around the country there was a marked increase in literary and religious texts from different areas of England. It was not until the fourteenth century that London started to be an important centre of literary output, and even then it was hardly the most important one. Monastic houses and bishops, and even possibly the local nobility, could act as patrons of literature and encourage writers in their own localities. The increasing importance attached to the role of women in religious life, whether in a formal order or in a looser attachment to the Church, meant that works in English were needed for their instruction. The *Ancrene Wisse* is a rule for anchoresses, and some of the mystical writings by people like Rolle were specifically intended for female disciples. It is hardly surprising that the amount of writing in English increased dramatically with each century in the Middle English period.

Academic life was fostered by the establishment of two universities in England. While these promoted the use of Latin more than of English, they also injected new ideas and concepts into the intellectual life of the country which in turn found their way into writings in the vernacular. In particular, there was an enormous growth in the amount of translation, from both Latin and French. In the fourteenth and fifteenth centuries it is through this translating activity that many loan words make their first appearance in English, for a translator often wishes his own version to be as stylistically elegant and ornate as the original. Many translators keep very closely to their original and in this way introduce both the words and the syntactic structures of their originals into English. How far these words and syntactic structures were adopted into ordinary speech is difficult to determine unless they are found in the works of later writers. One of the problems we continue to face in studying Middle English is that our sources are all written and it is impossible to determine what the nature of colloquial speech was like and what words and constructions it may have used.

The thirteenth and fourteenth centuries saw the growth of medieval English towns partly as a result of the growth of cross-Channel trade. Landowners increasingly took to rearing sheep, because the wool produced in England was in great demand on the Continent, particularly in the textile industries of the Low Countries. Parts of the country which had been relatively poor before now grew in importance and prosperity. The towns themselves also grew so that places like London, York and Norwich increased dramatically in population. This growth had important consequences for the language. Many country people were attracted to the urban centres, particularly London, so that the language heard in the town could become mixed or even undergo a significant change. Ekwall (1956) has suggested that it is immigration into London which caused its language to change from a southern dialect to a more north midland dialect. As the towns grew, there developed a new class – the merchant class. This class was wealthy and intermarried with the nobility. As it grew in wealth it could take an interest in culture and promote translations and other literary activities. It is from this class that our first printer, William Caxton, came, and it was probably to this class that he directed much of his published output (Blake 1969a). This class meddled in both trade and politics, for the preservation of its trade routes and friendly relations with its trading partners were essential to it. In the fifteenth century much of the focus of this trade was on the Low Countries, which had then passed under the control of the duchy of Burgundy. Flanders was one of the most important centres of manuscript production and the merchants brought manuscripts and other cultural artefacts with them on their return journeys. They also brought medieval Dutch words and expressions, but these seem not to have penetrated the English language very deeply.

Although the royal administration was at first peripatetic, later it came to be increasingly centred on London and Westminster. As it did so, a civil service developed which was responsible for copying the various charters, statutes and other government documents. Many of the scribes may at first have been clerics, though later they were probably little more than clerks in the modern sense. As the offices of government became established in London they developed their own scribal styles and orthographic preferences, as has been suggested above. Many of these documents were sent throughout the country and would have contributed to the standardisation of linguistic forms, though this was naturally a gradual process. But the choices made by the scribes probably had little to do with their actual speech forms, and may have been determined by chance among a series of available options. The influence of this Chancery language was not felt immediately on the writing of literary texts, where other traditions continued to prevail for some time. Fifteenth-century London saw a variety of writing traditions which gradually became reduced in number as the century progressed.

In respect of religion and politics two further points may be made. The first is that England in this period was relatively free of heresy in religion. It is only Wyclif and the Lollards who disturb this picture of conformity with the Church. While Wyclif wrote in Latin he was left in peace by the ecclesiastical and political authorities, but as soon as he started to appeal in English to a different audience the opposition to him became more determined and repressive. What is important about Lollardism from the language point of view is that so much literature of a potentially popular nature could be disseminated in English over different parts of the country (Hudson 1988). This production suggests that there were more centres of writing available than we might have assumed and that there were more readers who could read and assimilate the material which was produced. To take account of Lollard writings suggests that literacy was more widespread than we might otherwise have imagined. More importantly, much of what was produced appeared in a language which, while not standardised, shows signs of regularity to a surprising degree.

The second point is that although English foreign policy was focused on France, the kings of England had to contend with outlying districts of the British Isles. The Celtic-speaking areas – Scotland, Wales and Ireland – could always attack the English rear and these problem areas had to be dealt with. Generally, the English set about conquering and colonising these regions. The result was a decrease in the use of Celtic and the advance of English. The Celtic languages remained relatively unknown to most English people and they carried with them little cultural prestige. Hence the influence of Celtic on English remained insignificant; there are few words or syntactic structures which were borrowed into Middle English from Welsh or Gaelic, though the dialects and naming patterns of the Welsh Marches show more.

1.6   Concluding remarks

At the beginning of this Introduction I suggested that the major problem with Middle English was precisely that it is described as *Middle* English. With anything which comes in the middle, it is difficult to know when it begins and when it ends; how many of us know when middle age begins and ends? Consequently, much of the scholarship has focused on what constitutes the differences between Old and Middle English and what led to the development of Modern English. But a concentration on the beginning and end of the period would be limiting and distorting. Consequently in this volume the contributors have tried to present the whole history of Middle English without worrying overmuch about the boundaries of its beginning and end. It has been more convenient to deal with some aspects of the period in the previous or the following volume. What is more important is to present the general development of the language in the period from approximately 1100 to 1500 in a coherent and self-contained way.

FURTHER READING

Useful tools for the study of Middle English include the bibliographies, Arthur G. Kennedy (ed.), *A Bibliography of Writings on the English Language* (Cambridge, MA: Harvard University Press, 1927); J. Burke Severs & Albert E. Hartung (eds.), *A Manual of the Writings of Middle English 1050–1500*, 8 vols. to date (New Haven, CT: Connecticut Academy of Arts and Sciences, 1967–); George Watson, (ed.) *The New Cambridge Bibliography of English Literature*, volume 1: *600–1600* (Cambridge: Cambridge University Press, 1974); Jacek Fisiak, (ed.) *A Bibliography of Writings for the History of the English Language*, 2nd edn (1987); and Matsuji Tajima, *Old and Middle English Language Studies: A Classified Bibliography 1923–1985* (1988). Also to be noted are C. Brown & R. H. Robbins (eds.), *The Index of Middle English Verse* (New York: Columbia University Press, 1943; with supplement 1965), and R. E. Lewis, N. F. Blake & A. S. G. Edwards (eds.), *Index of Printed Middle English Prose* (New York: Garland, 1985). *The Middle English Dictionary* and the *Linguistic Atlas for Late Mediaeval English* (McIntosh *et al.* 1986) are indispensable. An earlier survey of Middle English sound changes is Moore, Meech & Whitehall 1935; a modern survey on different principles is Kristensson 1967, 1987, forthcoming. The exploitation of the Edinburgh survey of Middle English may be found in the essays collected in Laing 1989 and Smith 1989.

Collections of texts which can be used for historical linguistic study include for the early period Hall 1920, Dickins & Wilson 1951 and Bennett & Smithers 1966. For the fourteenth century there is Sisam 1921, and for the later period D. Gray (ed.), *The Oxford Book of Late Medieval Verse and Prose* (Oxford: Clarendon, 1985). For collections of non-literary material, mainly from the fourteenth and fifteenth centuries, there are Chambers & Daunt 1931 and Fisher, Richardson & Fisher 1984. A new collection of historical texts is now available in J. D. Burnley *The History of the English Language: a Source Book* (London: Longman, 1992).

Books dealing with the general history of the English language and with special features of Middle English are listed after later chapters and will not be repeated here. For the development of spelling see Scragg 1974. The collected papers of the conferences on English Historical Linguistics and on Historical Linguistics (various editors) often contain articles relevant to this period. There is no one journal which caters for Middle English seen from a language point of view, but important articles may often be found in the *Transactions of the Philological Society*, *Journal of English and Germanic Philology*, *Folia Linguistica Historica* and *Studia Anglica Posnaniensia*.

For the relation between literature and history which often provides important information about the background of the period, there are R. F. Green, *Poets and Princepleasers* (Toronto: Toronto University Press, 1980); V. J. Scattergood & J. W. Sherborne (eds.), *English Court Culture in the Later*

Middle Ages (London: Duckworth, 1983); Janet Coleman, *English Literature in History 1350–1400* (London: Hutchinson, 1981); V. J. Scattergood, *Politics and Poetry in the Fifteenth Century* (London: Blandford, 1971), and Anne Hudson, *Lollards and their Books* (1988). The historical background may be traced in the volumes of the Oxford History of England: A. L. Poole, *From Domesday Book to Magna Carta 1087–1216* (2nd edn, Oxford: Clarendon, 1955), F. M. Powicke, *The Thirteenth Century 1216–1307* (2nd edn, Oxford: Clarendon, 1962), M. McKisack, *The Fourteenth Century 1307–1399* (Oxford: Clarendon, 1959), and E. F. Jacob, *The Fifteenth Century 1399–1485* (Oxford: Clarendon, 1961). Important for the general background are David Knowles, *The Monastic Order in England* (2nd edn, Cambridge: Cambridge University Press, 1963) and *The Religious Orders in England* (Cambridge: Cambridge University Press, 1948–59).

Further reading for the relationship between French and English is dealt with at the end of chapter 5. The development of the London dialect is considered in Mackenzie 1928 and some background to immigration into London is provided in Ekwall 1956. Aspects of the development of London standards are considered in various articles by Samuels, now available in Smith 1989. The development of Chancery English is considered in Fisher 1977 and J. H. Fisher, 'Chancery standard and modern written English', *Journal of the Society of Archivists* 6 (1979), 136–44. This work is developed in M. Richardson, 'Henry V, the English Chancery, and Chancery English,' *Speculum* 55 (1980), 726–50; and T. Cable, 'The rise of written standard English,' in Aldo Scaglione (ed.), *The Emergence of National Languages* (Ravenna: Longo, 1984), 75–94.

2 PHONOLOGY AND MORPHOLOGY

Roger Lass

2.1 Introduction

2.1.1 *Middle English*

The period covered by this volume, conventionally Middle English, is of special importance for the history of the language – for precisely the reasons suggested by the adjective 'middle'. It marks the transition between English as a typologically 'Old Germanic' language and English of the type now familiar to us. These four centuries are particularly rich in radical and system-transforming changes in both phonology and morphology; they also provide a much richer corpus of evidence than Old English, both in numbers of texts and regional spread.

During this time as well, linguistic (along with political) dominance shifted from Wessex in the south-west to the south-east and particularly the southeast midlands, and the roots of today's standard dialects were laid down. The wider regional variety of texts allows us to examine more specimens of more dialect types than we could earlier; this is made even more helpful by another general characteristic of the period: the profound isolation of regional writing traditions. There was not, until quite late, much in the way of strong influence from any regionally localised standard or *Schriftsprache*.

In later Old English times, even regions far from the political centre in Wessex often showed West Saxon influence; after the Conquest anyone who wrote in English normally wrote in his own regional dialect, according to more or less well-defined local conventions, some of them of great phonological informativeness. This lack of standardisation also encouraged orthographic experimentation; and we have some very useful 'eccentric' texts like the *Ormulum* (see 2.1.3), whose authors have to one degree or another 'invented' their spelling systems, and in the process told us a great deal about aspects of linguistic structure that tend to be invisible in less fluid traditions.

The immediately following centuries (sixteenth to seventeenth) saw the rise of the first native descriptive phonetic tradition (see vol. III, ch. 1); from the mid-sixteenth century we have explicit and often quite reliable phonetic descriptions. Dating from less than a century after the end of our period, these give us for the first time relatively hard phonetic evidence, independent of our interpretation of spellings, and close enough to our major data so that backward projection becomes feasible, with rather less speculation than we need for earlier times.

2.1.2   When did Middle English begin?

In a paper with this title Kemp Malone (1930) argued that many features normally defined as 'Middle English' had already appeared in 'Old English'. Divisions between linguistic periods are of course no sharper than those between regional dialects: on either side of a chosen divide we find clearly characterisable or 'core' varieties; in the 'transition zones' we find varieties whose characterisation as one or the other may be a matter of taste. For instance, a 'southern' dialect of Modern British English may be defined as one with /ʌ/ in *but, come* (ME /u/), and /ɑ:/ or some other long vowel in *path, grass* (ME /a/ before voiceless fricatives) – as opposed to a northern or midland dialect that will have /ʊ/, /a/ respectively. But there are areas in the transition zone with /ʊ/ in *but* /ɑ:/ and in *grass* (see Wakelin 1984: map 5.1). Period boundaries in language history show the same kind of 'mixed lects'.

Periodisation, then, is partly conventional; if we take the Norman Conquest as a symbolic division between Old and Middle English we must use it with tact. There are texts after 1066 barely different from those before, and earlier ones with quite 'advanced' features. But even if we interpret the period divisions as broad zones rather than sharp lines, we can still talk rationally about 'different stages' of the language.

In Germanic linguistics Old vs Middle is in essence a typological distinction. A typical Old Germanic language (Gothic, Old English) will have: (a) a rich inflectional morphology, especially nominal case-marking and person/number/mood inflection on the verb; (b) a relatively full system of unstressed vowels, with little or no merger of distinctive qualities; and (c) relative freedom in the distribution of vowel length. From this perspective, a Middle Germanic language has begun (a') to lose its highly differentiated morphology; (b') to reduce its unstressed vowel system, often with neutralisation to one or two qualities; and (c') to reorganise vowel length, making it increasingly sensitive to syllable structure and phonetic context. (Points (a') and (b') are two sides of the same coin: see 2.5.3, 2.9.1.1 below.) These criteria are of course relative, and often obscured in the modern languages by subsequent changes.

Two extracts from texts dating from the relatively early and late ends of our period will illustrate the range involved:

I *Peterborough Chronicle* (1137; composed ca 1155)
Þa þe uureccemen ne hadden nan more to gyuen, þa ræueden hi and brendon alle the tunes, ðat wel þu mihtes faren al a dæies fare sculdest thu neure finden man in tune sittende, ne land tiled. Þa was corn dære and flesc and cæse and butere, for nan wæs o þe land. Wreccemen sturuen of hungær; sume ieden on ælmes þe waren sumwile ricemen, sume flugæn ut of land. Wes næure gæt mare wreccehed in land, ne næure hethen men werse ne diden þan hi diden, for ouer sithon ne forbaren hi nouther circe ne cyrceiærd, oc namen al þe god ðat þarinne was, and brenden sythen þe cyrce and altegædere.

('When the wretched men had no more to give, they robbed them and burned all the farms, so that you might well travel a whole day's journey and not be able to find anyone remaining on a farm, or tilled land. Then corn was dear, and meat and cheese and butter, for there was none in the land. Wretched men died of hunger; some who were once rich lived on alms, some fled from the land. There was never before more wretchedness in the land, nor did heathen men ever do worse than they did, for contrary to custom they spared neither church nor churchyard, but took all the goods inside, and then burned the church and everything together.')

II Geoffrey Chaucer, *The Tale of Melibee* (ca 1380)
Upon a day bifel that he for his desport is went into the feeldes hym to pleye. His wif and eek his doghter hath he laft inwith his hous, of which the dores weren faste yshette. Thre of his olde foos han it espied, and setten laddres to the walles of his hous, and by wyndowes ben entred, and betten his wyf, and wounded his doghter with fyve mortal woundes in fyve sondry places – this is to seyn, in hir feet, in hir handes, in hir erys, in hir nose, and in hir mouth, – and leften hir for deed, and wenten awey.

('One day it befell that for his pleasure he went into the fields to amuse himself. His wife and his daughter also he left inside his house, whose doors were shut fast. Three of his old enemies saw this, and set ladders to the walls of the house, and entered by the windows, and beat his wife, and wounded his daughter with five mortal wounds in five different places – that is to say, in her feet, in her hands, in her ears, in her nose, and in her mouth – and left her for dead, and went away.')

The language of these texts is strikingly different. Chaucer is recognisable without too much trouble as an older form of 'our' English, while the Chronicle passage is by and large in a 'foreign language'. Yet both possess many non-modern features: e.g. words with modern /aʊ/ like *tune* (I) 'farm' (cf. *town*), *hous*, *mouth* (II) would have had /u:/; words with modern /aɪ/ like *-wile* 'while', *finden* 'find' (I), *wif*, *espied* (II) had /i:/; *myhtes* 'might (2 sg.)' (I) and *doghter* (II) had a medial velar fricative /x/; words with modern short vowels in some cases had long ones (*flesc* 'flesh' (I), *deed* 'dead' (II) with /ɛ:/); some words with modern long vowels or diphthongs had short vowels (*myhtes* with /i/, *faste* (II) with /a/).

On the other hand, double-consonant graphs, as in *sittende* 'sitting', *alle* 'all' in the twelfth century represented distinctively long consonants; by the fourteenth (*setten*, *walles*) the long/short contrast had vanished or was on the way out (see 2.4.1.1). Similarly, many final <e> which in the twelfth century represented syllables (*sum-e* 'some', *cyric-e* 'church' < OE *sume*, *cyrice*) had by Chaucer's time been deleted, or were pronounced only optionally, mainly in verse (see 2.5.3), e.g. *pley-e*, *fast-e*, *nos-e* < OE *plegan*, *fæste*, *nosu*. Some categories of twelfth-century short vowels were by Chaucer's time lengthened and sometimes lowered in certain contexts, so that the class (modern /əʊ/) represented by *ouer* 'over' in I and *nose* in II had twelfth-century /o/ and fourteenth-century /ɔ:/ (OE *ofer*, *nosu*: see 2.3.2). The dative singular inflection (*in tun-e* 'on a farm', I) was generally lost by Chaucer's time (*inwith his hous*, where earlier we would have had *hūs-e*: OE *tūn-e*, *hūs-e*).

Change during the Old English period (though of course it took place) was much less radical; no two texts from say 830 and 1030 would have looked this different. Middle English, however, was a period of flux and transition. The major phonological and morphological changes defining Old English as a distinct Germanic dialect were over before the bulk of the texts were written; Middle English, on the other hand, shows a sequence of far-reaching changes within the sequence of texts. Hence its evolution can be studied at closer to first hand than that of earlier stages of the language.

2.1.3   Evidence and reconstruction

Our knowledge of the phonology of older languages is not a set of neat independent 'facts'; each fact (better, well-grounded belief) grows out of interlocking assumptions and arguments with varying degrees of support, confronting textual and other data, and fitting into intricate webs of inference. Sometimes everything dovetails so nicely with hard evidence that we feel sure of the basis for our beliefs; other cases are more controversial, and some problems are insoluble. All of our knowledge, though, of whatever degree of certainty, is built on arguments involving the following kinds of evidence.

1 *Comparative*. There are well-tried techniques of historical reconstruction, based on comparison of forms with known or presumed common ancestors. These may allow us to extrapolate earlier forms lying behind attested ones, or help us interpret the forms in our texts. This procedure is the foundation of historical phonology, and is perhaps the most reliable technique in the historian's armoury. Comparative evidence includes earlier languages (e.g. Latin, Sanskrit, Greek bearing on Gothic, Gothic bearing on Old English); closely related contemporary languages (e.g. Old Saxon for Old English); modern languages, both related and descendant (say German and Dutch as evidence for earlier stages of English, or modern dialects of English as evidence for the state of earlier ones).

2 *Written: texts*. Our data for earlier English are written texts, of all kinds (literary and non-literary, formal and informal). With what we know of earlier spelling conventions, assumptions about alphabetic representations within a given tradition, etc., we can often form a good idea of what a particular spelling ought to mean, which we support with other evidence.

3 *Written: direct description*. For most of the history of English we have no explicit phonetic descriptions; in the Middle Ages there is only the thirteenth-century Icelandic *First Grammatical Treatise*, which has some bearing (though mainly comparative) on our views about Old and Middle English. From the sixteenth century on we have a rich and often highly sophisticated indigenous phonetic tradition, which we can use for extrapolating back to earlier stages.

4 *Metrics and rhyme.* If we have reason to believe that a poet follows a strict metrical scheme, his verse may be evidence for things like syllable count and stress placement. If he rhymes strictly, we can get evidence for the merger of historically distinct categories (if he rhymes two vowel classes that we have good grounds for believing were once distinct); as well as splits (if he consistently fails to rhyme categories that on historical grounds he ought to).

5 *General linguistic theory.* The most important constraint on historical conjecture in any field is the general (non-historical) theory of the domain. Linguistic theory controls our reconstruction of the past in the same way that general biological theory constrains palaeontology, or physics controls cosmology. No system, sound type or process that our knowledge of present-day languages tells us is impossible may be reconstructed (the 'uniformitarian' principle: see Lass 1980: ch. 2, Appendix). Further, our knowledge of phonetics and phonology gives us reason to believe that certain process types are particularly likely in certain environments, and we can project this knowledge back as a constraint on the changes we reconstruct, and even use it to 'produce' history: if the evidence allows two courses of historical development and favours neither, the most probable one happened. Similarly, what we know about change in progress, on the basis of sociolinguistic research, can guide us in deciding whether some change is likely in a particular form within a given time-span.

Now an illustration of how some of these varied sources converge on a particular belief. In Middle English texts, words that in Modern English are spelled with < gh > (*night, bought, rough*) typically appear with < h > in early texts, later < gh >, < ch >, < ʒ > 'yogh'. 'Night' for instance has forms like *niht, nyʒt, nyght, nicht*. The usual view is that < ʒ > etc. represent a voiceless velar fricative /x/, as in G *Nacht*. The argument goes as follows:

1   We believe that the ancestor of the Middle English forms, OE *niht*, had /x/, and there is no reason to assume a change in Middle English. The arguments for original /x/ come first, then those for persistence.

2   Other closely related dialects show /x/ in equivalent positions: G *Nacht* /naxt/, similar forms in Dutch, Afrikaans, Frisian, Yiddish. This must represent an older state of affairs than

English /naɪt/, with nothing between the vowel and /t/, because:

3   Our knowledge of typical sound change says that insertion of fully articulated (i.e. non-glottal) segments in non-assimilating environments is extremely unlikely (for a rare exception that 'proves the rule' see Norman (1988: 140, 193) on Chinese [ʁ]-, [ŋ]-insertion). Methodologically, since more Germanic languages than not have /x/ here, English loss is likelier than many independent gains. More importantly,

4   This /x/ regularly corresponds to /k/ in other Indo-European languages: Lat. *nox*, gen. sg. *noct-is* (stem /nokt-/), Lithuanian *naktìs*, Skt *nakt-*, vs G *Nacht*, Lat. *octō*, Gk *oktō* 'eight' vs OE *eahta*, G *acht*, and so on. Therefore Gmc */x/ looks like a 'survival', in weakened form, of an original IE */k/.

5   But how late in the history of English can we assume /x/ in 'night'? Descriptions of the standard as late as the seventeenth century show a consonant here which is often identified with orthographic <h>, which is clearly described as [h]. On theoretical grounds we expect consonants to weaken rather than strengthen over time (in general); and [x] naturally weakens to [h], which just as naturally becomes zero (see Lass 1976: ch. 6). Thus the sequence [-Vkt-] > [-Vxt-] > [-Vht-] > [-Vt-] is just what we would expect; [h] supports an earlier [x], and virtually predicts modern zero.

6   In addition, many forms ending in OE /x/ have come down with /f/: e.g. *tough*, *rough*, *enough* (OE *tūh*, *rūh*, *genōh*); in the seventeenth century many forms that now have zero had variants with /f/ (*sought*, *brought* in Cooper 1687). Since /f/-forms are attested as early as ca 1300 (*thurf* 'through' < OE *þurh*), it is unlikely that /x/ had lost its oral articulation any earlier; [h] normally remains or is deleted, but does not turn into anything else. In addition, changes of velars to labials are well known (cf. Rumanian *lemn* 'wood', *opt* 'eight' < Lat. *lignum*, *octō*). Further, some modern dialects as late as the end of the nineteenth century show developments such as /k/, /g/ from our hypothesised /x/: /ɛkθ/ 'height' < OE *hēahþu* in the west midlands and Essex, /ɛkfə/ 'heifer' < OE *hēahfore* in East Anglia, /flɪəg/ 'flea' < OE *flēah* in Yorkshire (Wright 1905: § 360). These all presuppose a fully articulated consonant in this position.

7   In more conservative varieties of Modern Scots, a velar fricative occurs in the appropriate places: [nɛxt] 'night', [bɔxt] 'bought' < OE *niht*, *bōhte*. Some dialects in both England and Scotland must have gone through the whole modern period without even reaching the stage [h], at least in some items.

8   Throughout Middle English, forms in <gh> or <ȝ> where we posit /x/ generally rhyme only with forms of the same class, and not (until late: see 2.4.1.2) with the same vowel but no posited /x/. Chaucer rhymes *wight* with *knyght* (OE *wiht*, *cniht*), but does not rhyme *whit(e)* or *delit* (OE *hwīt*, OF *deliter*) with any member of the class, even though now *delight* (spelled with unetymological <gh>) and *white* rhyme with *wight* and *knight*.

9   Some modern dialects in west Yorkshire and neighbouring areas have a distinct development of forms with OE <h>, ME <ȝ>, where they do not belong to the same rhyme class as forms without: thus /iː/ in *night*, *right* (OE *riht*) vs /aɪ/ in *white*.

So a number of arguments, from different starting points, converge on an interpretation. This is a relatively straightforward (!) example; the arguments in the technical literature are often more elaborately based, if rarely spelled out in such tedious detail. The edifice of English historical phonology is largely based on inferential networks of this sort of complexity and sophistication.

A word is in order about what spelling itself can tell us, supported by other evidence. Obviously, no spelling in isolation tells us anything: Bernard Shaw's famous remark about *ghoti* being a good spelling for 'fish' (<gh> as in *rough*, <o> as in *women*, <ti> as in *nation*) should convince us (and see further Wrenn 1943). None the less, aside from such gross eccentricities, most spelling systems tend to be reasonably coherent, and we have bases for making assumptions about the likely ranges of phonetic values for particular letters. To begin with, we know a fair amount about the pronunciation of Latin, not only through comparative evidence but also through direct testimony (see Allen 1965). And Latin orthography – largely via Roman-trained missionaries – was the source of all Germanic writing systems except Gothic. Hence we have, at least as a working hypothesis, a set of limits on the possible values of symbols which can be checked against other evidence. We assume that <e> in accented syllables is something in the [e–ɛ] range, <o> in the [o–ɔ] range, <b> is [b] or some other labial

consonant, etc. These assumptions are boundary conditions on interpretation: it would take a lot of evidence to convince me that a <b>
in an older text represented [t], but much less to convince me that it
represented [v].

Periodically, we find texts by self-appointed spelling reformers; if
their systems are based on transparent and intelligent linguistic analysis,
we can often extract a good deal of information not available from more
conventional spellings. A case in point is Orm, author of the *Ormulum*,
a poem of some 20,000 unrhymed fourteen-syllable lines composed in
Lincolnshire around 1180. Even to one used to the vagaries of Middle
English spelling, the opening lines are rather striking:

> Nu broþerr wallterr, broþerr min
> affterr þe flæshess kinde,
> & broþerr min i Crisstenndom
> þurrh fulluhht annd þurrh trowwþe,
> & broþerr min i Godess hus...

> (Now brother Walter, my brother/ after the manner of the flesh/ and
> my brother in Christendom/ through baptism and through faith/ and
> my brother in God's house...)

Why so many double consonant graphs, and why in these particular
places? Why *broþerr* (*OE brōþor*) with two final <r>s, but *min*
(OE *mīn*) with one <n>, etc? It would be tempting to disregard this,
except for two things. First, Orm specifically calls the attention of
future copyists (who, alas, seem never to have materialised) to these
double letters; whoever copies this manuscript, he says, let him

> ...loke wel þatt he
> an boc staff wríte twiȝȝess,
> Eȝȝwhær þær itt upp o þiss boc
> iss wrĭtenn o þatt wise.
> Loke he wel þatt hĕt write swa,
> forr he ne maȝȝ nohht elles
> Onn Ennglissh wrítenn rihht te word,
> þatt wite he wel to soþe

> (...look well that he/ write a letter twice/ everywhere that it in this
> book/ is written in that way./ Let him look well that he write it so/
> for he may not otherwise/ write the word correctly in English/ let
> him know that for the truth)

Second, and more interestingly, his spellings are usually etymologically consistent. He writes <VC> (or alternatively <V́>) where

we have reason to suppose a historical long vowel, and <VCC> or
<V̆> where we expect a short one: *broþerr* < *brōþor*, *min* < *mīn*, but
onn < OE *on*, *rihht* < *riht*, etc. Or *wrĭtenn* vs. *wríte* (OE *writen*, *wrīte*, cf.
PDE *written*, *write*). He thus becomes a very important source of
evidence for vowel length in early Middle English – especially since, if
we take his etymologically supported spellings seriously, we can also
find in unexpected ones signs of historical changes taking place in his
time. For instance, *lufe* 'love' < OE *lufu*, *þolenn* 'endure' < OE *þolian*
where we would expect ***luffe, ***þollenn suggest the beginnings of a
process of open-syllable lengthening (see 2.3.2, 2.5.2).

2.1.4   Old and Middle English dialects and the London bias

This chapter and its equivalent in volume III are biased toward the
evolution of what we might loosely call the 'modern standard', or to use
a term of John Wells (1982), 'general English'. Geographically, this
means a bias toward the southeast midlands, in particular the educated
speech of London and the Home Counties. Not because of a social
prejudice, but a general matter of fact: 'English' in the normal sense
means one or more of the standard varieties spoken by educated native
speakers (e.g. as it appears in a title like *The Structure of Modern English*).
The sociohistorical development of the language has been such that the
most widely spoken and familiar varieties derive from the prestige
dialects of the capital and their near relations. For instance, the
upwardly mobile speaker of a broad local dialect in any part of Britain,
in attempting to become more 'standard', willy-nilly becomes more
'southern' as well. A northerner who learns to distinguish *cud* and *could*
(both natively /kʊd/) as /kʌd/ vs /kʊd/ is – whatever *his* view of the
procedure might be – from a dialectological point of view moving
south across a major isogloss. In addition, all the extraterritorial
varieties of English (American, Australasian, South African) are
broadly southern in type (see Lass 1987: §5.8.1); and the traditional
literary language of England and the (former) colonies (though not of
Scotland) is lexically, morphologically and syntactically of London/
Home Counties origin.

These considerations, as well as the weight of tradition, make it
natural for histories of English to be tilted southeastwards. In any case,
given the variety of dialects, it is impossible to write a coherent history
of them all simultaneously. Much of the regional history will be taken
up in the dialectology chapters of this and the next volume; here the

emphasis will be on the regions roughly in the line of descent to the modern standards. I will, however, refer to others here where their histories shed light on general trends in the evolution of English, and where they contribute to the clarification of southern (more accurately southeastern and southeast midland) developments: either by retaining older features or by being more innovative, or where features now standard originated outside the southeast midlands.

The shift of the political centre from Wessex to London during the post-Conquest period creates problems for the historian. Because of the geographical distribution of surviving Old English texts, there is no well-attested corpus directly ancestral to the modern southern standard – which in any case did not begin to emerge until the fourteenth century. The bulk of the 'classical' Old English texts are in dialects (loosely) ancestral to those of the modern south-west and southwest midlands (Dorset, Devon, Hampshire, Wiltshire, Gloucestershire, etc.); the rather small number of texts from the south-east are in the line of succession to the modern local dialects of Kent and Sussex.

The main contributors to the modern standard, the southeast midlands dialects, are mainly Anglian, not West Saxon. This part of the country (e.g. Essex, Middlesex, Surrey) is not well represented until Middle English times. The English of Chaucer or of the fourteenth–fifteenth-century Chancery, which are roughly precursors of 'our' English, do not have a detailed Old English ancestry.

Even the dialect of London itself is a hybrid, an emergent Late Middle English type combining south-west (Westminster) and south-east (Essex, City of London) sources. Sitting as it does on the Thames, a crossroads where East Anglia, Kent, the West Country and the midlands meet, London might be expected to present a regionally complex picture; and this is further complicated by the immigration typical of a capital city. The -(e)s marker on present third-person singular verbs, for instance, is probably northern (brought in via East Anglia), as are lexical items like *hale* (the northern form of *whole*: see 2.3.2); while the initial /v/ in *vat*, *vixen*, *vial* are southernisms (see 2.4.1.1), and the /ɛ/ in *merry*, *fledge*, *bury* is Kentish – though the <u> spelling of *bury*, like the /ʌ/ pronunciation of *cudgel*, *shut*, is southwestern (3.4).

The Middle English continuum is conventionally divided into five major dialect areas, roughly as shown (for refinements see ch. 3 of this volume). In terms of Old English, northern = Northumbrian, east midland and the northern two-thirds of the west midlands = Mercian,

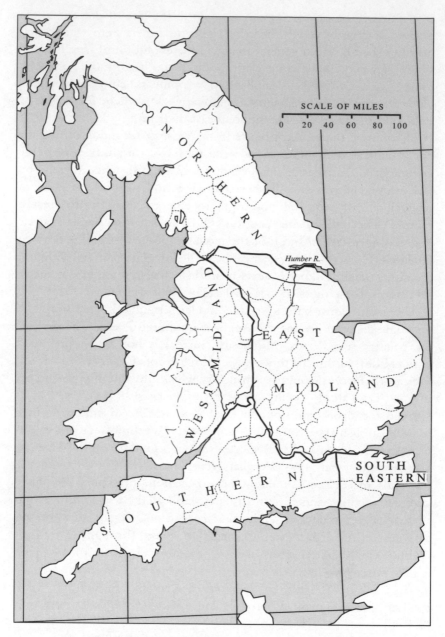

2.1   The dialects of Middle English

southwestern and the southern third of the west midlands = West
Saxon, and southeastern = Kentish.

Because of the dialectological complexities, and the fact that the bulk
of surviving Old English lexis is West Saxon, I will normally cite the
usual dictionary forms for Old English lexemes. Throughout this
chapter the term 'Old English' – unless further specified – will be used
more or less the way we use 'English' now: to denote a 'common core'
of features characterising the bulk of the dialects.

2.1.5   Middle English orthography

Old English (see vol. I, ch. 3) was written in a modified Latin alphabet;
the letters <k>, <q> and <z> were used rarely, and <j> and
<v> not at all. On the other hand, the alphabet was augmented by the
digraph <æ>, the crossed <d> or 'eth' <ð>, and two symbols of
runic origin, <þ> 'thorn' and <p> 'wynn'. Both <þ, ð> were
used for /θ/, and <p>, or in early texts <u> and <uu>, for /w/.
Other points worth noting are the following:

1   The same symbols were used for both palatal and velar
    consonants: ȝieldan 'yield' vs ȝyldan 'gild', cynn 'kin' vs cinn
    'chin'; i.e. /j g/ were spelled <ȝ>, and /tʃ k/ were spelled
    <c> (as the modern pronunciations suggest). The insular
    form of the letter <g>, which I represent here as <ȝ>, is
    usually changed to <g> in modern editions of Old English
    texts; for this section I retain <ȝ>, as its later shape played a
    special role in Middle English orthography distinct from that of
    <g> (see 5, below).

2   The cluster <cg> represented the palato-alveolar affricate
    /dʒ(ː)/ as in brycg 'bridge'; this was also written <ge> after
    nasals, as in sengean 'singe' (cf. singan 'sing').

3   <h> was used for [h], [x], and [ç], which were allophones of
    one phoneme (see 2.2.2, 2.4.1.2), e.g. hēah 'high' [hæax] =
    /xæax/.

4   Vowel length was rarely marked: manuscript ȝod could be
    either god 'god' or gōd 'good'. But consonant length was
    normally indicated (ofer /ofer/ 'over' vs offrian /ofːrian/
    'offer': see 2.4.1.1, 2.5.4 for later repercussions).

5   <y> was used only as a vowel letter, for front rounded /y(ː)/;
    the modern use for /j/ developed during the eleventh century.

The establishment of Middle English orthographic norms involves both endogenous changes to the earlier system and the introduction of French usages. The most important developments are as follows:

1   Old English had no voice contrast in its fricatives: [v z ð] were allophones of /f θ s/ (see 2.2.2, 2.4.1.1). Therefore it used <f> for [f v], <s> for [s z], and <þ/ð> for [θ ð]. With the rise of a phonemic voice opposition, French <z> was introduced (cf. *zeal* < OF *zele* vs *seal* < OE *segel*), and <u/v> (see 2, below) began to be used for [v] in both loans and native words (French *vice, virgin* vs. native *over, wolves,* formerly *ofer, wulfas*).

2   Many modern editions normalise the original conventions for the use of <u> and <v>. The standard medieval distribution is <v> initially for both /u/ and /v/ (*vp, virgin*) and <u> medially (*haue* 'have', *but*); though some texts use <v> initially only for /v/, and <u> initially for /u(:)/ and medially for /u(:)/ and /v/ (e.g. *Ancrene Wisse* has *van* 'foes' but *luue* 'love', *ure* 'our').

3   At the very beginning of the period, <þ> alternates in some texts with <u/uu> for /w/; beginning in the thirteenth century this is replaced by northern French <w>, which is standard by the fourteenth century.

4   The /θ/:/ð/ opposition has never been discriminated in English spelling (cf. *thigh, thy* still). <ð> began to yield to <þ> in the thirteenth century, though it remains sporadically through the fourteenth. In general, <þ> is the spelling for /θ ð/, though <th> appears in the twelfth century, and begins to take over towards the end of the period. A modified version of <þ>, virtually indistinguishable from <y>, remains in use well into the Early Modern period in abbreviations like y^e = *þ^e*: hence, by later misunderstanding, *Ye Olde Tea Shoppe*.

5   In around the twelfth century, Franco-Latin (Caroline) <g> is introduced, mainly for /g/ but also for /dʒ/, in place of insular <ʒ>. The latter, or some modification, then takes over the representation of /j/ (*ʒow* 'you') and /x/ (*nyʒt*). Later on <ʒ> for /j/ began to yield to <y>, following French practice. Early texts sometimes have <i> for /j/, as in the *Peterborough Chronicle*'s *iafen* 'gave' < OE *ʒēafon* beside conservative *gære* 'year (dat. sg.)' OE *ʒeare*. The letter <ʒ> continued in use well

into the fifteenth century. Early printers, especially in Scotland, often substituted <z> for it, producing 'false' spellings of Scots names and other items. Thus *Dalziel, Menzies, capercailzie*, where old <nz/lz> = palatalised /nʲ lʲ/. This led to spelling-pronunciations, so that now non-Scots tend to say /ménziːz/ for native /míŋıs/ (OSc. /nʲ/ > /ŋ/), and have no idea what to make of *Dalziel*, which is /dɪjél/.

6   In Old English /dʒ/ appeared only postvocalically; in Middle English it occurs in French loans initially as well (*joy, jewel*), spelled <i> or <j>. These two graphs are more or less equivalent, but <j> is rarer; in some texts it occurs for /i/ in certain positions, e.g. *jn* 'in', and commonly in Roman numerals like *iij*, etc.

7   OE /x/ is represented in earliest texts by <h>; later <ʒ> and <gh> become common in non-initial positions, and <ch> is used in the north (as still in Sc. *bocht, nicht*). By the end of the period <gh> is the norm except for the foot-initial allophone [h], which is still spelled <h>.

8   Velars and palatals become distinct in spelling, with <ch>, <cch>, for /tʃ/ and F <dg(e)> replacing both <cg> and <gg> in words like *bridge*.

9   <k>, rare in Old English, becomes common for /k/, substituting for older <c> before <i e l n> and post-vocalically, with <ck> typical after short vowels (*kiss, corn, back*); <c> also appears before front vowels for /s/ in French loans, e.g. *condicioun* /kondisiuːn/.

10   OE <sc> for /ʃ/ is gradually replaced by <sh>, <sch>, though some dialects use <s>, <ss>. In some Late East Anglian texts /ʃ/ in certain contexts, e.g. initially in modal auxiliaries, is spelled <x>: the *Book of Margery Kempe* (ca 1438) has *xal ~ schal, xulde ~ schulde*.

11   The digraph <æ> is lost in the thirteenth century, replaced by <a> or <e> if short (depending on dialect), and <ee>, <ea> and <e...e> if long (see 16 below and 2.5.4). The latest use of <æ> appears to be in a proclamation of Henry III of 1258.

12   After the unrounding of OE /y(ː)/, leading to merger with /i(ː)/ in non-western dialects (see 2.3.4), the graph <y> becomes equivalent to <i>; hence ME /i(ː)/ can be spelled <i> or <y>. As early as the *Peterborough Chronicle* 1137 we

find both spellings in the same word, e.g. *drihten* ~ *dryhten* 'God' < OE *dryhten*. In those dialects that retain distinct /y(:)/, it comes to be spelled after the French fashion with <u> (*Ancrene Wisse* has *buggen* 'buy' < OE *bycgan*).

13   Because of various later developments, OE <eo> spellings are retained in some dialects to represent mid front rounded /ø(:)/. This vowel is also spelled <oe/ue>, and in some texts <o> or <u> (see 2.3.4).

14   In later medieval hands, the letters <i u m n> were typically written as sequences of unligatured verticals or 'minims': *ͻ*, *11*, *111*, etc. This would make something like <l1111e> ambiguous: it could be read as *luue* or *lime*. The convention arose of writing <o> for <u> in these nasal environments: hence *come(n)* < *cuman*, *loue* < *lufu*, *sonne* 'sun' < *sunne*, etc.

15   Under French influence, <ou/ow> were increasingly used to represent /u:/, with <u> being reserved for short /u/ and (in those dialects where it remained) /y(:)/; thus *hows(e)* ~ *hous(e)* < OE *hūs*, *nou* ~ *now* < OE *nū*.

16   As Middle English progressed, vowel length tended to be more consistently indicated, especially for the mid vowels /eː ɛː oː ɔː/, in the form of doubling: *see* /seː/ 'see' < OE *sēon* or /sɛː/ 'sea' < OE *sǣ*; *boon* /boːn/ 'boon' < OScand. *bón*, or /bɔːn/ 'bone' < OE *bān*. Starting in the fifteenth century, the higher and lower mid vowels were often (though not uniformly) distinguished with <a> as a diacritic for the lower of each pair: <ee> /eː/ vs <ea> /ɛː/, <oo> /oː/ vs <oa> /ɔː/; F <ie> also appears for /eː/. (Thus modern *beet*/*beat*, *boot*/*boat* represent historical contrasts, merged in the first pair but not the second; for <ie> we have *pierce*, *thief* and the like.)

In later Middle English, due to the loss of final unstressed vowels and vowel lengthening in open syllables (see 2.5.3.4), the discontinuous representation <VCe> became available for long vowels, with <e> a 'dummy' graph or diacritic. The original use in words with lengthened vowels like *nose* /nɔːz(ə)/ < OE *nosu* is then extended to words that never had a final <e>, as in Chaucer's spelling *brode* for /brɔːd/ 'broad' < OE *brād*. Consonant length is indicated by doubling (e.g. *bitter* vs *biten* 'bitten'); after its loss CC spellings can be diacritics for the shortness of a preceding vowel (as already in Orm: see 2.1.3), just as a succeeding <e> can be a diacritic for length (see 2.5.4).

2.2 Phonology, origins: the Old English input systems

2.2.1 *Vowels*

This section and the following will repeat material already presented in vol. I, ch. 3 (if with some differing interpretation); this is necessary for an understanding of the major Middle English developments, and more convenient than requiring constant reference to another book. I will start a little further back than may seem strictly necessary, for the sake of historical perspective. For Old English of the eighth–ninth centuries, we can assume for all dialects this minimal or 'core' vowel system (on the representation of diphthongs, see below):

(1)

	Short		Long	
	Monophthongs	Diphthongs	Monophthongs	Diphthongs
	i y u		iː yː uː	
	e ø o	eŏ	eː øː oː	eo
	æ ɑ	æ̆ɑ	æː ɑː	æɑ

These are highly symmetrical systems, with a number of features worth noting: (a) phonetic as well as phonological symmetry throughout the long and short systems: matchings like [u]/[uː], [i]/[iː] instead of the modern types [ʊ]/[uː], [ɪ]/[iː] – a feature that was to persist well into the Early Modern period; (b) only three contrastive heights, as opposed to the four that were to develop in the thirteenth century (2.3.2); and (c) diphthongs only of the 'height-harmonic' type, i.e. with both elements of the same height, as opposed to the earlier and later closing types like /ai au/, and the much later centring types like /ɪə/ (*idea*).

The long/short diphthong contrast is conventionally indicated by marking the 'long' ones: *bēam* 'tree' vs *eahta* 'eight', *bēo* 'bee' vs *heofon* 'heaven' (and see the transcription /eːo/ vs /eo/ in vol. I). I have deliberately reversed the procedure here, using notations like /eo/ vs /eŏ/, to make a theoretical point, which helps explain why the two sets behaved as they did. This is that there is nothing 'extra' about the 'long' diphthongs; they functioned, as diphthongs typically do in languages with a long/short vowel contrast, as members of the long subsystem. It is the 'short' diphthongs that are the 'abnormal' or 'marked' category, since they pattern with the short vowels. We can see this clearly in the late Old English/Early Middle English mergers to be discussed in 2.3.1: 'long' /eo/ in *bēo* falls in with /eː/ in *grēne* 'green', while 'short' /eŏ/ in *heofon* falls in with short /e/ in *settan* 'set' (compare the vowels in the modern forms, /iː/ vs /ɛ/). I will return to this in more detail in 2.3.1.

In later periods, the most important change was the unrounding of /ø(ː)/, leading to merger with /e(ː)/; by the stage of Old English that can reasonably be seen as input to Middle English, we can assume for all dialects except Kentish a general vowel system of the type:

(2) i y u   iː yː uː
      e   o eŏ   eː   oː eo
      æ   ɑ æ̆ɑ   æː   ɑː æɑ

(/y(ː)/, /æ(ː)/ did not occur in later Kentish, having merged with /e(ː)/: Kt *hēdan* 'hide', *clēne* 'clean' vs WS *hȳdan*, *clǣne*.)

Since reference forms in dictionaries and grammars are often based on West Saxon literary language, although many of the target dialects of Middle English have a different provenance, there is a potentially misleading etymological relation as in the two historical classes of words commonly said to 'have OE *ǣ*'. In West Saxon, two etymological categories have /æː/, conventionally $\bar{æ}_1$ and $\bar{æ}_2$. In the usual terminology, $\bar{æ}_1$ represents WGmc */ɑː/ as in WS *sǣd* 'seed', *hǣr* 'hair' (cf. G. *Saad, Haar*); $\bar{æ}_2$ is the *i*-umlaut of WGmc */ai/, as in *hǣlu* 'health', *lǣdan* 'lead (vb)' (cf. G *Heil, leiten*). The $\bar{æ}_1/\bar{æ}_2$ contrast is important, because some Old English dialects have /eː/ rather than /æː/ for one or both of these categories, and OE /æː/ and /eː/ have different Middle English reflexes (/ɛː/ vs /eː/: see 2.3.1). It is only in West Saxon that both have /æː/; in Anglian $\bar{æ}_1$ is /eː/ (*sēd*) vs $\bar{æ}_2$ with /æː/ (*lǣdan*); in Kentish both have /eː/, and older /yː/ has become /eː/ as well. In terms of inputs into Middle English:

(3)

		West Saxon	Anglian	Kentish
$\bar{æ}_2$	'lead (vb)'	æː	æː	eː
$\bar{æ}_1$	'seed'	æː	eː	eː
$\bar{e}$	'green'	eː	eː	eː
$\bar{y}$	'hide'	yː	yː	eː

By these criteria, a London poet who rhymed *lead* and *seed* would show himself to be of southwestern or Kentish origin, or would at least be perpetrating a non-Anglian rhyme.

2.2.2 Consonants

The late Old English consonant system was:

(4) p t tʃ k   p: t: tʃ: k:
     b d dʒ g   b: d: dʒ: g:
     f θ s   ʃ x f: θ: s: x:
     m n   m: n:
        r l   r: l:
     w   j

Again quite symmetrical, with a length contrast for all consonants except /ʃ j w/. While the /C/ vs /C:/ contrast in final position may have been moribund in Old English (see vol. I, ch. 3), the medial contrast remained until late, and its loss triggered a major restructuring of the obstruent system (see 2.4.1.1). A few points with historical relevance:

1   While stops and affricates were paired for voice, the fricatives were not; /f θ s/ were in most dialects voiceless except medially in the foot (see 2.1.5). Thus [v z ð] appeared in native words only preceded by a stressed vowel (followed by an optional liquid or nasal) and followed by an unstressed vowel; they were always voiceless initially, finally and in clusters (see 2.4.1.1).

2   Old English had neither an /h/:/x/ contrast nor a phonemic velar nasal; [h] was the foot-initial allophone of /x/, and [ŋ] an allophone of /n/ before velars. Both features, unlike 1, remained stable throughout Middle English.

3   OE /g/ had the fricative allophone [ɣ] between back vowels as in dagas 'day (nom./acc. pl.)' /dagas/, [daɣas]; intervocalically if preceded by a front vowel it had the allophone [j], as in dæge 'day (dat. sg.)' /dæge/ [dæje]. (It is not clear whether unstressed -e was a front vowel or a central [ə]; this is problematic throughout the period; see 2.5.3.) Postvocalic [ɣ j], along with postvocalic [w], played an important part in the formation of the new Middle English diphthongs (2.3.3).

4   OE /l/ was 'dark' (velarised or uvularised) in syllable codas (e.g. eall 'all' [æaɫ:]); there is no way of telling whether it had 'clear' allophones prevocalically as in many present-day dialects. Dark /l/ in codas persisted into Early Modern English in most dialects, even those where it is now clear, as in Northumberland and parts of Durham. OE /r/ is a matter of

controversy; in codas it was clearly back, or had some back co-articulation, and this persisted through Middle English.

2.3 The formation of the Middle English vowel system

2.3.1 The short low vowels and the diphthongs

By the eleventh century a number of changes had begun which were to lead to the restructuring of Old English vowel phonology. The earliest involve the low vowels /æ ɑ/ and the diphthongs; they are hard to date accurately, because of the persistence of conservative spellings (see below), but the outlines are fairly clear.

These developments are hard to understand without an account of the relation between long vowels and 'long' diphthongs, and some idea of what the 'short' diphthongs were probably like. Let us assume that a long vowel and a diphthong in the ordinary case are equivalent structures, i.e. bimoric: so if /eo/ is a vowel cluster consisting of a short [e] plus a short [o], then /e:/ is a cluster of short [e] + short [e], giving a parallelism /eo/ = /ee/. A syllable peak, that is, has temporal 'slots' of short vowel length, and may have one or two of these. A short diphthong, in this framework, is also complex, but only occupies one mora or slot; it is made of two 'half-morae' of different quality, compressed into the normal temporal span of one. Thus any process of monophthongisation affecting say /eo/ and /eŏ/ would be the same in both cases – the only difference is the time-span over which the process occurs.

The monophthongisations of the Old English diphthongs involved two different types of assimilation between morae. In the /æɑ/ diphthongs the second mora assimilated completely to the first, so that /æɑ/ > /ææ/ (i.e. /æ:/), and /æ̆ɑ̆/ > /æ̆æ̆/ (i.e. /æ/). With the /eo/ diphthongs, the assimilation was bidirectional: the rounding of the second mora spread back to the first, and the frontness of the first forward to the second, producing a 'compromise' quality [ø] for both: short /eo/ as in *heofon* 'heaven' came out with /ø/, and long /eo/ as in *bēo* with /øø/ = /ø:/:

(5)   Type 1   Type 2

Systematically, the (a) changes result in loss of a phonetic category and merger with an already existing one, i.e. loss of an opposition; the (b) changes result in the loss of one phonetic type and the gain of another, with no change in oppositional structure.

At this stage two older lexical classes have fallen together with others by (a): *eahta* 'eight', *rætt* 'rat' now have /æ/, *bēam* 'tree', *glǣm* 'gleam' now have /æː/; while *heofon*, *bēo* 'bee' are still distinct from anything else, though in a different way phonetically. (At some time prior to the change to /øː/, some instances of long /eo/ seem to have undergone a change, often called 'accent shift'; this is a presumed shift of syllabicity to the /o/ mora, which then becomes long /oː/ and participates in the later history of OE /oː/. Thus *choose*, *lose* < OE *cēosan*, *lēosan* should have come down as PDE ***cheese*, ***leese* with /iː/, like *freeze* < *frēosan*; instead they have the reflex of OE /oː/ like *moon* < *mōna*, etc. In our model here there is no need for syllabicity transfer or other complex interpretations; what we have is simply a different version of the /eo/ > /øø/ change: instead of bidirectional assimilation, the first mora regressively assimilates to the second (a mirror-image of the /æa/ development), i.e. /eo/ > /oo/. This version in fact competes with the other; Chaucer's *chese*, *lese* for *choose*, *lose* show /eː/ < /øː/, i.e. the same development as in *freeze* (For details see Lass 1988.)

The changes in (5) restore (if briefly in most dialects) the original system type 2, with two front rounded vowels – though with no diphthongs, or with diphthongs of the new Middle English type (see 2.3.3) just beginning to appear. The total inventory of the non-Kentish dialects of the early to mid-eleventh century:

(6)   i y u   iː yː uː

        e ø o   eː øː oː

        æ   a   æː   aː

The new /ø(ː)/ were quickly merged with /e(ː)/ (another repetition of an earlier merger) in all except the southwestern and southwest midland dialects (see 2.3.4).

These mergers and phonetic changes resulted in a bewildering profusion of spellings. Thus the *Peterborough Chronicle* for 1127 shows <ea> for OE /eo/ (*heald* 'held' < *hēold*), and for /e/ (*Heanri* ~ *Henri*); as well as for /æa/ (*heaued* 'head' ~ *hæued* < *hēafod*); and <eo> and <e> for /ĕŏ/ (*eorl* 'earl' ~ *erl* < *eorl*). The twelfth century is still 'transitional'; the orthographic norms for these categories have not been stabilised (and see below on OE /æ/ and /a/).

Following, or perhaps partly overlapping with, this another set of mergers occurred; /æ/ (now consisting of original /æ/ plus mono-phthongised /æ̆a/) fell together with /ɑ/. In most of the country except parts of the west midlands and south-east this merger resulted in a vowel spelled <a>. There is a long-standing debate about this: what did graphic <a> represent at the Old/Middle English transition, and later in the period? The obvious facts are (a) that the original categories represented by <æ> in *rætt* and <a> in *catte* 'cat' merged in Late Old English, and have been indistinguishable ever since; (b) that comparative and historical evidence suggests a low front value for the merger in later Middle English (Lass 1976: ch. 4); and (c) that <æ> and <a> in Old English represented respectively front and back low vowels.

A merger of /æ/ and /ɑ/ could occur in principle in one of two ways: lowering of /æ/ to [a] and fronting of /ɑ/ to the same value; or, as some scholars have suggested (especially those who, like Jespersen (1909–49), believed that ME <a> was also a back vowel), retraction of /æ/ to [ɑ], and fronting of the merged result at some later stage (perhaps just before the seventeenth-century change to [æ]). In outline:

(7)

The second alternative is obviously less economical, since it involves two backness shifts in opposite directions; the first is simply a convergence on a new value, perceptually perhaps somewhat 'intermediate' between the two. Taking this option, the developments of the short low vowels and /æɑ/ are (see Lass 1977b):

(8)

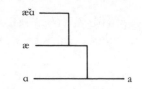

These mergers lead to extensive spelling variation in early texts. When formerly distinct categories merge phonetically, but traditional spellings are still remembered, scribes will often use the old spellings in a near-random way, since the actual pronunciations do not give a clear indication of how given items should be spelled. Thus in the aftermath of the /æ̆a/–/æ/ and /æ/–/ɑ/ mergers, the *Peterborough Chronicle* for

1127 and 1131 shows <æ> ~ <ea> ~ <a> variation for many
OE /æ/ words: *hæfde* ~ *hafde* ~ *heafde* for *hæfde* 'he had' and the like.

The changes in (8) radically altered the shape of the short-vowel
system; it now had only one low vowel, instead of the earlier front/back
symmetry. It also had more vowels at the front than the back, which
remained the case until well into the Early Modern period. After the
mergers, we are left with the following:

(9) i y   u   i: y: u:
     e (ø) o   e: (ø:) o:
     a   æ: ɑ:

In the eleventh or twelfth century, probably after the monophthongisations and mergers discussed above, /æ:/ raised to /ɛ:/. At
around 1100, then, we would have the following systems (/ø(:)/
omitted):

(10) i y   u   i: y: u:
      e   o   e: o:
      a   ɛ: ɑ:

Even though we have only three long unrounded front vowels at this
stage, they are distributed differently in the vowel space; there is a
potential 'empty slot' at low front which would allow for a new /a:/,
just as there had always been one in back between /ɑ:/ and /o:/ which
could accommodate a new /ɔ:/. This is obscured by the representation
in (10), which can be redrawn with the empty slots boxed:

(11) i: y: u:
      e: o:
      ɛ: □
      □   ɑ:

We will see in the next section how these were filled, creating the more
even, less gapped systems typical of later Middle English.

There are empty slots in the short system too:

(12) i   u
      e   o
      □   □
      a   □

Two of these, front /ɛ/ and back /ɔ/, were indeed filled, but not until
about the sixteenth century (see vol. III, ch. 1); later /ɔ/ lowered to /ɒ/,

filling in the lower back corner and creating a system much like that of earlier Old English, with /æ ɒ/ (*cat, pot*) balancing each other, and the old /e o/ slots (more or less) filled by the new centralised half-close /ɪ ʊ/ < older /i u/. The short /ɔ/ slot remained empty except in Scotland, where /ɔ/ never lowered to /ɒ/ in native varieties.

2.3.2 Filling out the system: OE /ɑ:/ and related matters

One striking difference between modern northern and southern dialects ('southern' including historically not only Received Pronunciation and the southern regional dialects, but the extraterritorial ones as well) is the reflex of OE /ɑ:/ (e.g. *bone, stone, home* < OE *bān, stān, hām*). In non-northern modern dialects, this category has, in conservative varieties, a mid back vowel of the [o:] type; in more 'advanced' (and more widely distributed) ones, it has a diphthong, usually [oʊ], [əʊ] or [ɵ̈ʊ], derived historically from Early Modern /o:/. In the 'traditional dialects' (conservative rural vernaculars: Wells 1982) of the north, the vowel is front: Sc. /hem/, /sten/, Nbr. /hɪəm/, /stɪən/ for *home, stone*. To anticipate material to be treated in vol. III, the northern front vowels in this class presuppose a Middle English low front input /a:/, and the southern back vowels and diphthongs an earlier half-open back vowel /ɔ:/ – both qualities missing from the system in (11). It now remains to unravel the rather complex developments that produced these new vowel types.

As early as the twelfth century we begin, in non-northern texts, to get a scattering of <o>, <oa> spellings for OE /ɑ:/ words. The sermon *In diebus Dominicis* (MS Lambeth 487: Hall 1920: 76ff.), written on the southern/midland border in the twelfth century shows *gast* 'spirit', *lauerd* 'lord', *swa* 'so' < OE *gāst, hlāford, swā* as well as *on* 'one' < OE *ān*, and the variant *louerd*; the *Peterborough Chronicle* for 1134 has a few <o> forms, including *noht* 'nothing' < OE *nāht, mor* 'more' < *māra*; and the Worcester Fragments (late twelfth century) have mainly <o> as in *bon* 'bone/leg' < *bān, more* < *māra*, but still show some <a>, as in *wa* 'woe' < *wā, lac* 'offering' < *lāc*. These spellings reflect a major change in progress, in which OE /ɑ:/ rounded and raised to /ɔ:/. Since spelling normally lags behind changes in pronunciation, and changes are implemented by long-term variation weighted in particular directions (see 2.8.3 below), we can assume that the change /ɑ:/ > /ɔ:/ was well under way by the time we have any graphic evidence for it. Despite its variable implementation in different texts and different areas, we can date it as coming to fruition in the late twelfth to early thirteenth century, beginning in the south-east and spreading northwards – and constituting from that time on one of the major north/south isoglosses.

At about the same time, OE /ɑ:/ in the north was undergoing a different change, fronting to /a:/ (though here the evidence is not from spelling, but from modern developments and indirect sources like rhymes: e.g. the undoubtedly front /a:/ in French loans like *dame* rhymes with OE /ɑ:/ in items like *hame* 'home'). The result of these two changes is – for a time – two quite different long vowel systems:

(13) South   North
      i: u: i: u:
      e: o: e: o:
      ɛ: ɔ: ɛ:
                    a:

(I omit /y(:), ø(:)/, as they played, when present, no part in the basic developments treated here: see 2.3.4).

The south, that is, lacks a long low vowel, and the north lacks /ɔ:/. Of the empty slots, low back /ɑ:/ was not refilled in any dialect until the nineteenth century, in words of the *path, far* classes (vol. III, ch. 1); but southern /a:/ and northern /ɔ:/ began to develop in the thirteenth century. Before we consider their sources, however, it would be well to look at two early 'archetype' systems, southern and northern, with long and short vowels together in a spatial array. The geometry of the paired systems is important:

(14) Southern   Northern
      i: i   u u: i: i   u u:
      e: e   o o: e: e   o o:
      ɛ: ɔ: ɛ:
          a   a: a

In the thirteenth century, as a result of a complex, controversial and ill-understood change called Open-Syllable Lengthening (OSL), a set of new vowel qualities was created, producing considerably more symmetrical long and short systems. On the traditional account, which I follow here (for others see below), short vowels lengthened in first syllables of disyllabic words with only one medial consonant; and if they were non-low (i.e. except /a/) they lowered by one height as well. (Not all vowels were equally prone to lengthening in all areas; while the non-high ones lengthened generally, the high ones tended to lengthen later, and more in the south than the north: see Brunner (1963: §12) for a summary.)

The overall effects of OSL can be summed up by the following examples:

> OE /i/: *wicu* 'week' /wiku/ > /wikə/ > [we:kə]
> OE /u/: *wudu* 'wood' /wudu/ > /wudə/ > [wo:də]
> OE /e/: *beran* 'bear' /berɑn/ > /berə(n)/ > [bɛ:rə(n)]
> OE /o/: *nosu* 'nose' /nosu/ > /nosə/ > [nɔ:zə]
> OE /ɑ/ (LOE/EME /a/): *sama* 'same' /sama/ > /samə/ > [sa:mə]

(On the change of final vowels to /ə/ see 2.5.3.)

With the loss of final /ə/ (2.5.3) and the dropping of various endings like the infinitival *-en* (2.8.3), the new qualities became distinctive. The effect on the vowel-quality systems overall can be illustrated this way (southern vs northern inputs as in (14)):

(15)

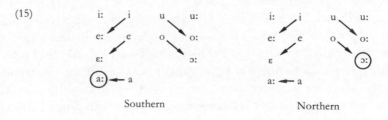

Southern   Northern

The circled qualities are new ones produced by OSL. Observe that after OSL and loss of /ə/ the vowel systems of the north and south were identical – even if the etymological sources of particular units, and hence the incidence of phonemes in particular lexical items, were different. Thus the south had /a:/ only from lengthened /a/, whereas the north had it also from OE /ɑ:/ (see 2.3.2); the south had /ɔ:/ both from OE /ɑ:/ and from lengthened /o/, whereas the north had it only from the latter. So southern /a:/ in *same*, as in the north, but northern /a:/ also in *home* (OE *hām*); northern /ɔ:/ in *nose*, as in the south, but southern /ɔ:/ also in *home*.

We now have in both major macrodialect areas long vowel systems with four distinctive heights at the front and three at the back, and short vowel systems with three heights at the front (a gap between /e/ and /a/) and two at the back. This basic configuration remained stable until the seventeenth century.

2.3.3   The new Middle English diphthongs

Recall that the Old English diphthongs were 'height-harmonic': one front and one back element of the same height. This was a relatively short-lived departure from the original Germanic input with /ai au ei eu/; these older types were revived in Late Old English or Early Middle English.

I have so far given the impression that during the whole set of 'gap-filling' operations on the early Middle English vowel system it remained in its Late Old English diphthong-free state. This is merely an artefact of the narrative. While the developments in 2.3.1–2 were taking place, a set of other changes, running to some extent in parallel, were creating a new diphthong system. Indeed, there is evidence for the combinative changes leading to the new diphthongs in Old English spellings as early as the eleventh century (Colman 1984), and a strong likelihood of Scandinavian loans with closing diphthongs of a non-Old-English type coming in quite early.

Diphthongal or 'perhaps-diphthongal' spellings are common in twelfth-century texts. In the *Peterborough Chronicle* we find < ei > for OE < eg > [ej], < æi > for OE < æg > [æj] (*ðeines* 'thane's', *dæi* 'day' 1127), suggesting /ei/, /ai/; we also find < uu > for postvocalic /w/ in *læuued* < *læwed* 'unlearned'. These are perhaps ambiguous, since < uu > could serve as a spelling for /w/ and < i > for /j/; but it seems quite likely that they did represent genuine diphthongs rather than /VC/ sequences. Early texts also show non-diphthongised forms like *nocht* 'nought' in the thirteenth-century *Kentish Sermons*, later typically *nouȝt*. Diphthongal spellings appear sporadically throughout the eleventh and twelfth centuries, increasing and stabilising in the thirteenth; it seems likely that the basic Middle English system was established in its final form by around 1250.

The new diphthongs from native sources (on borrowings see below) arise by two related processes, both involving original postvocalic consonants: (a) 'vocalisation' of [j] and [ɣ w] in syllable codas, yielding respectively [i] and [u]; and (b) what is best called 'Middle English breaking' (see vol. I, ch. 3 on breaking in Old English) – i.e. insertion of [ɪ] or [u] between a vowel and a following /x/. To illustrate:

(a)   *Vocalisation*
        OE [oɣ] > ME [ɔu]: *boga* 'bow' > *bowe*;
        OE [ej] > ME [ei]: *weg* 'way' > *wei*.

(b)   *Middle English Breaking*
        OE [ox] > ME [ɔux]: *dohtor* 'daughter' > *douȝter*;
        OE [eç] > ME [eiç]: *fehtan* 'fight' > *feiȝten*.

The principles are simple and natural: in (a) a voiced velar or palatal fricative or liquid after a vowel becomes a vowel with the same place of articulation (high front vowels are palatal and high back vowels velar); in (b) a high vowel with the same backness value as the following allophone of /x/ (which is in turn conditioned by the original preceding vowel) is inserted between the vowel and /x/.

Both these diphthongisations result in the neutralisation of vowel length: e.g. /ox/ as in *dohtor* and /o:x/ as in *sōhte* 'sought' both give ME /ɔu/. The Middle English length system did not allow for diphthongal length contrasts of the Old English type, e.g. **/ɔŭ/ vs /ɔu/, one behaving like a short vowel and the other like a long. Middle English allowed only monomoric (simple) and bimoric (two-piece complex) nuclei.

The main native sources of the new Middle English diphthongs are shown below; conventionally spelled Old English forms are given for identification. Note that, as above, both diphthongisation processes may give the same output:

(16)

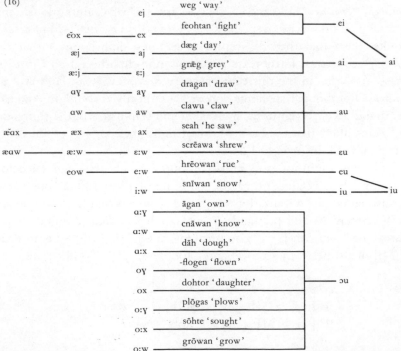

Note the later Middle English mergers of /ei ai/ in /ai/, and of /eu iu/ in /iu/.

These are all non-northern developments; diphthongisation was more restricted in the north, and did not occur before /x/, hence N *soçt, feçt* vs S *souȝt, feiȝt*, etc. Further, because of the different development of OE /ɑː/ in the north and south, a number of categories that fell together in southern /ɔu/ remained separate in the north: southern *grow, know* (OE *grōwan, cnāwan*) but northern *grow, knaw*. The southern development of OE [ɑːɣ], [ɑːw] is parallel to that of OE /ɑː/ to /ɔː/; it looks as if [ɑ] before a vowel or vowel-like segment in the south always became [ɔ]. Thus (given neutralisation of length as described above), the history of [ɑːw] (= [ɑɑw]) would be: [ɑɑw] > [ɑw] > [ɑu] > [ɔu], parallel to that of /ɑː/ (= [ɑɑ]), i.e. [ɑɑ] > [ɔɔ].

Diphthongs in borrowed words, and later native developments as well, increased the incidence of some of the new clusters. Thus F /au/ in *faut* 'fault', /eu/ in *peutre* 'pewter'; F / ieu/ and /yi/ gave /iu/ (*rule, fruit*), and palatal /ɲ/ and /ʎ/ formed diphthongs with preceding non-high front vowels: OF *plen* /pleɲ/ 'plain' > *plein/plain*, OF *bataille* /bataʎe/ > *bat(t)aile*. In addition, /v/ frequently vocalised to [u] before velars and syllable-final /l/, giving new /au/: so *hauk/hawk* from a late syncopated form of OE *hafoc* (e.g. pl. *hafces*), *crawl* < OScand. *krafla* [kravla], etc.

In line with these developments, the Old English high vowels in the relevant environments generally give Middle English long high vowels: [uɣ] > [uu] (*fugol* 'bird' > *fowl*: <ow> = /uː/, see 2.1.5), [yj] > [ii] (*ryge* 'rye' > *rīe* /riːə/). There were further developments in some cases: OE *bogas* 'boughs' and a number of others show [oɣ] > [ɔu] > [ou] (?) > [uu]: hence PDE /aʊ/ in *boughs*, rather than expected /əʊ/, the normal reflex of ME /ɔu/ (as in *bow* for shooting). Another case where monophthongised output was common was in the reflex of OE /eːx/, as in *hēh* 'high'. Whatever the diphthong was here (the usual Middle English spelling is <ei>), it was apparently distinct from /ai/, and monophthongised to /iː/ in Late Middle English: hence PDE /aɪ/ in *high* (the normal continuation of ME /iː/) rather than expected /eɪ/ < ME /ai/ as in *day*.

The phonological effects of these diphthong formations go beyond the addition of new nucleus types to the system. The segment [ɣ] vanishes completely, and /j w/ no longer occur in codas, but only syllable-initially.

The other major addition to the diphthong inventory comes from

French (though with some later additions from other sources). The Anglo-Norman dialect accounting for the bulk of French loans had two diphthongs of a distinctly non-Germanic type: /oi/ and /ui/, the former reflecting (among other things) Lat. /au/ (*joie* < *gaudium*, *cloistre* < *claustrum*), the latter largely Lat. /o:/ (*puison* < *pōtionem*) and special developments of short /u/ (*puint* < *punctum*). While there was some transfer of items between the /oi/ and /ui/ classes, and an increasing tendency in later Middle English to spell both with <oi/oy>, there is no doubt that they remained in principle distinct until the mid-seventeenth century (see vol. III, ch. 1). With this French contribution, then, we can assume for non-northern Middle English of around 1250 the diphthong system (18a) below, and around 1350 the reduced system (18b):

(18)   /Vi/   /Vu/
    (a) ei ai oi ui   iu eu ɛu au ɔu
    (b)   ai oi ui   iu   ɛu au ɔu

The borrowing of F /oi ui/ is of particular interest, as it violates a long-standing developmental principle in English. It is one of the rare cases (there are perhaps only two others of any consequence – see 2.4.1.1 and 2.6.2 below) where a foreign phonological element with no direct English parallel was borrowed and retained in its original form, rather than being assimilated to some already existing native category. A more characteristic treatment is that of Scand. /ey/, which falls in with the reflexes of OE /ej/ and /æj/ (*traisten* 'trust' < OScand. *treysta*). The borrowing from French is atypical behaviour: when dialects of English borrow without radical modification of the borrowed forms, the sources tend to be other dialects of English (see Lass & Wright 1986).

The peculiar type of borrowing involved in /oi ui/ and the fact that it has no native sources (all non-French examples are from other Germanic languages, like *loiter*, *toy* from Middle Low German and *buoy* from Dutch), are in a way reflected in both its later history and its modern status. It is the only Middle English diphthong that has undergone no major change since its first appearance. (I use 'it' to refer to the conflated category /oi ui/, since overall it has been historically unified.) The most that has happened, in some varieties, is lowering of the first mora along with the lowering of ME /o/, so that its basic range now is [ɔɪ ~ ɒɪ], with some dialects still having [oɪ]. Structurally, it participates in no productive (or even marginal) morphophonemic alternations of the kind entered into by the other long vowels and diphthongs, e.g. /aɪ/ ∼ /ɪ/ in *divine/divinity*, /eɪ/ ∼ /æ/ in *sane/sanity*, /iː/ ∼ /ɛ/ in *clean/cleanliness*, etc. (Unless pairs like *point/punctual, joint/juncture* could be claimed to be genuine alternations of this kind, which seems pretty far-fetched.) In other words, /oi/ has just sat there for its whole history as a kind of non-integrated 'excrescence' on the English vowel system.

2.3.4 Front rounded vowels, old and new

The southern English standard and its relatives are among the few modern Germanic dialects (aside from Yiddish) entirely lacking the front rounded vowel types [y ø œ] (as in G *kühne, Goethe, Götter*). The usual account is that at some stage /y(ː) ø(ː)/ 'were lost', and that 'English' has been without them ever since. This is indeed true by and large of the south-east and southeast midlands, but elsewhere such vowels are alive and well. Archaic rural Northumberland dialects have [ø œ] for ME /o/ (see Orton *et al.* 1962–71 at *fox* IV.5.11); in Scotland [y(ː)] is common in many varieties for ME /oː/ (*boot*) and /uː/ (*out*). And many varieties both in England and abroad (South Africa, New Zealand) have a mid front rounded (slightly centralised) [ö:] or [ö̈:] in *bird, hurt* and the like. The early loss – and continued absence – of such vowels is a southeastern mainland English phenomenon.

The loss of these vowels in the ancestor of the southern standard by 1300 (with one possible exception: see below) is part of a complex and interesting evolution, which needs looking at as a whole. We can begin by recapitulating the history up to the end of Old English (see 2.2.1 above):

1 Neither Proto-Indo-European nor Proto-Germanic had vowels of this type; they first appear in later West and North Germanic as the results of *i*-umlaut of back vowels: OE *mȳs* 'mice' < */muːsiz/, early *doehter* 'daughters' < */doxtri/.

2 Around the ninth–tenth centuries, /ø(ː)/ unrounded and merged with /e(ː)/, leaving only /y(ː)/.

3 During Old English times /y(ː)/ lowered and unrounded to /e(ː)/ in Kentish; thus the extreme southeastern dialects had by Late Old English reverted to the original state of having no front rounded vowels.

4 Beginning around the eleventh century, the diphthongs /ĕo eo/ (see 2.3.1) monophthongised to /ø(ː)/, thus (except in Kent) restoring the early Old English system with both /y(ː) ø(ː)/. We now see the beginnings of what might be called a 'southeastern distaste' for front round vowels.

We can assume, then, everywhere except in the south-east, an input to Middle English that had four vowel types in the high-to-mid front area:

(19) i: i y: y
      e: e ø: ø

Thus we seem to have recycled to the early 'full' front vowel system of the kind found in pre-Alfredian Old English.

By the early to mid-twelfth century, judging by the testimony of the *Peterborough Chronicle*, both /y(:)/ and /ø(:)/ had unrounded in the north and east, once again producing the old (pre-West Germanic) system type with only /i(:) e(:)/ in front. This is clear from the confusion of <e> and <eo> mentioned above (2.3.1), and the parallel treatment of <i> and <y>. For example, we get both graphs for OE /y/ (*circe* ~ *cyrce* 'church' < OE *cyrice*), and for OE /i:/ (*suyðe* 'very' < *swīðe*, *rice* 'powerful' < *rīce*).

In the south-west, west midlands and much of the central midlands, on the other hand, both front rounded categories remained unchanged into Middle English, and in one form or another persisted into the fifteenth century – as well as being added to by instances of the same vowels in French loans. Thus we have essentially three types of treatment of the Old English front rounded vowels, and three main patterns of distinctiveness and merger. We can illustrate this for the long vowels as follows:

(20) Old English	North, east midlands	South-west, south-west midlands	South-east
hȳdan 'hide'	hiden /i:/	hu(y)den /y:/	heden /e:/
bīdan 'wait'	biden /i:/	biden /i:/	biden /i:/
bēon 'be'	ben /e:/	bon /ø:/	ben /e:/
grēne 'green'	grene /e:/	grene /e:/	grene /e:/

Things in detail were unsurprisingly more complex than the neat trichotomy in (20) suggests; populations were mobile, and important places like London sat more or less on the borders of different areas. For instance, both the east midlands and south-east types of OE /y(:)/ reflex, at least in particular items, moved from one region to another; manuscript forms and place names show <e> spellings moving up as far north as south Lincolnshire, and the east midlands type <i> spreading westward into the south-west and west midlands (see Wyld 1927: 109).

This complex evolution and movement of forms has implications for

the emerging London standard; London being where it is, the total
speech community contained speakers of all three types, and southeastern (including Essex) and southwestern forms apparently remained
available for a long time. Early London is southwestern: the Proclamation of Henry III (1258), for instance, shows only <u> for OE /y/,
and <o>, <eo> spellings for /eŏ eo/ (*kuneriche* 'kingdom' < *cynerīc*,
beoþ 'be (3 pl.)' < *bēoþ*). Later texts show mainly <i/y>, with an
admixture of <u> and <e>. As late as the Mercers' Petition of 1386
we find, among general <i/y> like *kyng* < *cyning*, the westernism *lust*
'to wish' < *lystan*. The mid front rounded forms of 'be' and the like
vanished from London earlier; and indeed there is evidence in westerly
areas for early raising of /ø(:)/ to /y(:)/, and merger of both in the latter
value: the westerner John of Trevisa in 1385 has *buþ* 'they are' < *bēoþ*
and *burþ* 'birth' < (*ge-*)*byrd*.

In the late fourteenth century it seems as if the court/Chancery
language had available all three OE /y(:)/ reflexes (though only /e(:)/
for OE /eŏ eo/). Poets in particular whose basic dialects had /i(:)/ often
used 'Kenticisms' or 'Essexisms' with /e(:)/, especially in rhyme; and
there are some <u> spellings, whose interpretation is problematical.
For instance, a single text (*The Pardoner's Tale*) in the Ellesmere
manuscript of *The Canterbury Tales* has three spellings for 'merry' (OE
myrig): *myrie*, *murie* and *merie*, the last rhyming with *berie* 'berry' < OE
berie. It is not clear what the <u> in *murie* means; it could be /y/ (but
see below); or more likely /u/, which seems to be the usual outcome of
short /y/ that did not unround (PDE /ʌ/ in *cudgel, crush, rush* < OE
cycgel, crycc, rysc presupposes ME /u/, and this could only come from an
earlier western /y/: see Luick (1914–40: §375)).

Some scholars have suggested that the fourteenth-century London
standard did in fact have a front rounded /y:/, in French loans like
commune, fortune, nature, excuse, refuse. One problem here is that the vowel
spelled <u> in these forms falls in later with native /iu/, giving later
/(j)u:/ (cf. native *new* vs F *nude*). The argument is that since French was
actually a spoken language in educated circles, it was *a priori* likely that
at least upper-class speakers retained /y:/ in forms that had it in French.
The primary evidence is that, with one exception, Chaucer rhymes /y:/
only with itself (the exception is *Complaynte of Venus* 22–3, *aven-
ture:honoure*, which rhymes it with F /u:/ = ME /u:/). A check of
the first 3,000-odd lines of Gower's *Confessio amantis* (ca 1390) reveals
the same pattern: F /y:/ rhymes only with itself, and ME /iu/ only with
itself.

What are we to make of this? Absence of a rhyme is at best weak evidence for its non-existence: as William Wang once remarked (1969: 21) you can't prove that the platypus doesn't lay eggs with a photo of one not laying eggs. But it is at least curious. Part of the problem, however, may be that the sources of ME /iu/ (see 2.3.3) are such that it does not appear in the same environments as French /y:/, e.g. before /r/ and /n/; the number of possible rhymes is drastically limited in advance. A further difficulty is the bland assumption that in fact upper-class Englishmen spoke good French in the fourteenth century; John of Trevisa remarks that in 1385 the teaching of French was so bad that 'now childern of gramer-scole conneþ no more Frensch þan can hire lift hele' ('grammar-school children know no more French than their left heel'). The problem of /y:/ will surface again in the sixteenth century (vol. III, ch. 1); for the fourteenth I think the evidence for it is at best ambiguous, at worst absent (see Sandved 1985: 18ff.).

At least this is the case for London. Front rounded vowels, however, do appear once more – this time unambiguously – in a dialect from which they had apparently already been lost. This is in the north and outside my direct remit here, but it is important for two reasons: first, it helps to fill out the total evolutionary picture; and second, it has important repercussions for our understanding of the later history of the long vowels in all dialects (vol. III, ch. 1; and Lass 1976: ch. 2). Beginning in the late thirteenth or early fourteenth century, ME /o:/ from all sources fronted in the north, at first to /ø:/; later, but still in Middle English, it raised to /y:/, and then generally unrounded south of the Tweed. Thus modern northern dialects typically have a front reflex of ME /o:/ (*good*, *foot*); in England most often [ɪə] or [i:], in Scotland typically [y(:)].

This change is evidenced partly in <u> spellings for /o:/: Richard Rolle, from Yorkshire, has *gude* 'good' < *gōd*, *lufe* 'love' < *lufu* (with /y:/ < /o:/ < /u/ by OSL: see 2.3.2), which also rhymes with F /y:/, suggesting that in the north at least this French vowel may have been retained, not merged with /iu/. This can be seen as a 'co-operation' with the native development of /o:/: the quality [y] was not 'foreign' here, hence no pressure for alteration. Some of the more interesting rhymes in fact show no respelling: Rolle (see Jordan 1934: 54) has *fortune* rhyming with *sone* 'soon' < *sōna*.

The end result in the north is something like a 'reversion' to an earlier system type, rather like that of Late Old English:

(21)
```
i:  u:      i:  u:      i:  y:  u:
e:  o:   →  e:  ø:   →  e:
ɛ:  ɔ:      ɛ:  ɔ:      ɛ:      ɔ:
a:          a:          a:
```

2.3.5   Recapitulation: the standard Middle English vowel system ca 1350–1400

The changes discussed so far created, in effect, a quite new type of vowel system. By the fourteenth century, the incipient standard southeast midland dialects, as exemplified by those of Chancery and upper-class poets like Chaucer and Gower, would have had the following vowel inventory (I give it here with *modern* 'key words', to illustrate roughly which Middle English phonological classes are ancestral to which modern ones):

(22)   Short   Long
        i (*bit*)   u (*but*)   i: (*bite*)   u: (*out*)
        e (*bet*)   o (*pot*)   e: (*beet*)   o: (*boot*)
        a (*bat*)   ɛ: (*beat*)   ɔ: (*boat*)
                                 a: (*mate*)

            Diphthongal
        iu (*new*)   ɛu (*dew*)   au (*law*)   ɔu (*grow*)
        ai (*day*)   oi (*boy*)   ui (*poison*)

This is the input to the next major set of changes, which will be discussed in detail in volume III, chapter 1. For various quantitative changes that affected not primarily the vowels themselves but their distribution and the inventory of legal syllable types, see section 2.5 below.

2.4   Consonantal developments

2.4.1   The obstruent system

2.4.1.1   Degemination and the voice contrast
Major systemic changes, like those discussed above for the vowels, are not prominent in the history of English consonants. Indeed, the consonant system has as a whole remained relatively stable since Old English times. Except for the major restructuring discussed in this section, most of the consonant changes have been low level: adjustments

in allophonic distribution, loss in certain environments and the rise of a few isolated new contrasts.

Modern English contrasts voiced and voiceless fricatives freely in all positions. Taking the labials as an example, we have foot-initial *ferry*:*very*, foot-medial *loofah*:*louvre*, *selfish*:*selvedge*, and final *luff*:*love*. Old English had no such freedom (see 2.2.2). On the other hand, it did have a contrast of long vs short consonants that Modern English lacks. These differences are related.

The phonetic distribution of Old English fricatives (aside from /ʃ x/, which do not concern us here) was:

(23)

			Foot-initial	*Foot-medial*	*Final*
Labial	{	Short	f	–	f
			–	v	–
	{	Long	–	f:	f:
Dental	{	Short	θ	–	θ
			–	ð	–
	{	Long	–	θ:	θ:
Alveolar	{	Short	s	–	s
			–	z	–
	{	Long	–	s:	s:

To achieve the modern distribution there had to be four changes: (a) allowing [v ð z] to appear initially; (b) allowing [v ð z] to appear finally; (c) allowing [f θ s] to appear medially; and (d) disallowing the /C/ vs /C:/ opposition. As we will see, (c) and (d) are two sides of the same coin.

(a) After the Conquest, many French words with initial [v z] were borrowed, e.g. the ancestors of *veal*, *victory*, *zeal*, *zodiac*; this made possible contrastive English/French pairs like *feel*/*veal*, *seal*/*zeal*. Loans with initial [v] at least were in fact taken in during Old English times – but normally (unsurprisingly, considering the distribution in (23)) with /f/. Thus Lat. /v/ in *fann* 'fan' < *vannus*, *fers* 'verse' < *versus*, *Fergilius* 'Virgil' (see Campbell 1959: §539). Old English was not 'receptive' to initial [v]; something must have happened later to prompt the unmodified borrowing of voiced fricatives.

It is uncertain what this was; it may have been nothing more than the sheer numerical weight of loans in a contact situation, making initial [v z] more familiar. Degemination of medial /f: s:/ (see (d) below), if it was early enough, may have helped, by making a voiced/voiceless distinction in one environment available for the first time. A third factor, perhaps the most likely, was the existence in Middle English of varieties that had in Old English times undergone voicing of initial fricatives. Many southern dialects had voiced at least initial /f s/ – a development whose relics survive still in the rural West Country ('Zummerzet'). This parallels, and may well stem from, the same process in continental West Germanic: the <v> in G *Vater* 'father', now pronounced with /f/, and Du. initial <v> and <z> in *vader* and *ʒon* 'sun' (/f s/ in more innovating dialects, still /v z/ in conservative ones) reflect this. While the voicing in England was mainly southern, it did extend well up into the midlands in Early Middle English, and the standard still has a number of forms with voiced initials like *vat*, *vixen*, *vane* (OE *fæt*, *fyxen*, *fana*). Contact between speakers of these dialects and others without voicing may have facilitated borrowing of French /v z/, making them less 'outlandish'.

Be that as it may, by around 1250 /v/ and /z/ were separate phonemes in foot-initial position. The development of the /θ/:/ð/ contrast follows a different route, since no [ð] occurred in loan words. It is notable that modern forms with /ð/ are members of a very restricted class, all normally occurring under low sentence stress: deictics like *the*, *this*, *that*, *these*, *there*, *then*, *thou* and a few conjunctions like *though*. These items underwent initial voicing relatively late (around the fourteenth century); this is probably what Chaucer utilises in rhymes like *sothe*: *to the* 'sooth': 'to thee'), where *sothe* must be [so:ðə].

(b) The development of a final voice contrast is tied to the loss of final /ə/ (see 2.5.3 below), which probably began in the north and north midlands in the twelfth century, and spread southwards. The effect of this loss was to expose in final position voiced fricatives that were originally medial. For example, in OE *nosu* 'nose' we would have the following development: [nozu] > [nozə] > [nɔːzə] > [nɔːz]. The [z] here (and likewise the [v] in *love* < *lufu* [luvu]) was now free to contrast with voiceless fricatives in the same position.

(c, d) The medial voice contrast is contingent on the loss of the length opposition, as (23) should indicate. If long voiceless fricatives (the only voiceless ones in medial position) shorten, the original contrasts [sː]/[z], [fː]/[v], etc. will be replaced by [s]/[z], [f]/[v]. The double phonetic differentiation (length and voicing) is replaced by voicing alone. This shortening or degemination began in the north ca 1200, and extended southwards over the next two centuries, probably completing in London around 1400. The old medial voicing rule was no longer productive, so the new short [f θ s] in foot-medial position stayed voiceless; we now have a full voiced/voiceless opposition in fricatives, parallel to the ancient one in the stops.

These changes transformed the Old English obstruent system into a more symmetrical (and simpler) one, much more like today's. The systemic change can be represented like this:

(24)

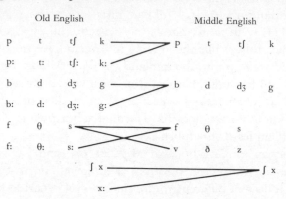

We have already seen that voicing of /θ/ to [ð] occurred initially in low-stressed words (*this*, *the*, etc.) In Late Middle English there was a parallel development which, though producing no new contrasts, increased the number of words with [v z] in places they did not occur before. This is a word-final voicing, e.g. in the noun plural ending -*es*, and low-stress words like *is*, *of*, *was*; it first shows up in fourteenth-century spellings like -*eʒ*, *oue* 'of' (see Jordan 1934 §159).

Even though the contexts for this voicing and that of *the* etc. are at opposite ends of the syllable, they are rhythmically parallel: i.e. in weak position in the foot, specifically in the margin of a weak syllable. Using S for strong or stressed and W for weak or unstressed, we can construct 'ideal' environments for both the voicings:

(25)   (a)   Initial voicing in *the* etc.

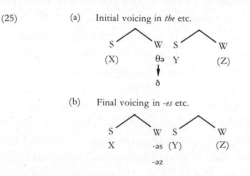

         (b)   Final voicing in -*es* etc.

The variables X, Y and Z stand for any other syllables, and parentheses around a variable mean that its occurrence is optional. The obligatory variables suggest that in (a) *the* and the like are typically followed by a strong syllable (e.g. the initial one of a noun), and in (b) typically preceded by one (e.g. the stressed syllable of a stem, subject of *is*, etc.) That is, these changes were probably syntactic in origin, first occurring in connected speech. The point is that both are essentially the same, even if the strong syllable is on the left in one case and the right in the other: the fricative in question is at the margin of a weak syllable, and there is a contiguous strong one.

These changes are in fact nothing new; they are 'recurrences' (see further 2.5.2) of a type of change that occurred at least once before. This is the Old English fricative voicing that was the original source of whatever [v ð z] there were before Middle English. Schematically, the rhythmic structure and changes in, say, *ofer* 'over', *ōþer* 'other', *rīsan* 'rise' are:

(26)

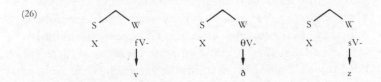

These processes illustrate the point that weak positions in the foot are prime sites for weakening: not only of consonants, but of vowels (i.e. this is where vowels reduce and delete: see 2.5.3).

2.4.1.2 [h]-dropping and the velar fricative

Old English /x/ appeared in all positions: initially probably as [h] (*heorte* 'heart'), medially as [x:] (*hlæhhan* 'laugh'), and preconsonantally and finally as [x] after back vowels (*bōhte* 'bought', *dāh* 'dough') and [ç] after front vowels (*niht* 'night', *hēh* 'high'). This distribution remained in principle throughout Middle English, though with considerable loss and articulatory change. Now [h] is a 'defective' or 'de-articulated' segment; i.e. it has no supraglottal stricture. Such segments tend to be weaker or more prone to loss than others. In all modern dialects /h/ deletes under low stress (*Give* (*h*)*im one*, *What's* (*h*)*e done?*); in most vernaculars in England (except Tyneside and parts of East Anglia) it is either completely lost or highly unstable. 'Dropping aitches' is a familiar stigmatised feature of most mainland vernaculars – though not in Scotland, Ireland or most extraterritorial dialects.

Standard opinion until recently has been that [h]-dropping is relatively new, on a large scale perhaps no earlier than the eighteenth century. Recent work, however (Milroy 1983; and see ch. 3 of this volume), suggests that it began in force as early as the eleventh century, and was common throughout Middle English. Erratic writing of <h> in early texts is well known – both omission where expected and insertion where etymologically unjustified. Milroy for instance gives examples from the thirteenth-century *Genesis and Exodus*:

(a)   *Missing* <h>
        forms of 'have', e.g. *adde, as, aue, aueð, algen* 'hallow', *ate* 'hate', *eld* 'held', *eui* 'heavy'.

(b)   *Excrescent* <h>
        halle 'all', *ham* 'am', *herðe* 'earth', *his* 'is', *hure* 'our'.

The question is how to interpret this. The conventional view is that it is not evidence of phonological change, but the work of 'Anglo-Norman scribes', the result of their imperfect command of English and lack of [h] in their own language. Milroy points out sensibly how unlikely it is that 'two centuries after the Conquest the majority of scribes were first-language Anglo-Norman speakers with a poor command of English' (1983: 45). Rather, the variation is precisely what we would expect if [h] were in process of variable deletion; assuming that written language may be rather like a 'transcription' of speech in communities without stable institutionalised spelling norms, spoken variation will have a written parallel (see Toon 1983 for a study of Old English spelling variation along these lines). On this interpretation the (a) spellings above show genuine loss, and the (b) spellings are hypercorrect.

There is also metrical evidence for [h]-loss. The *Ormulum*, for instance, has a metrical option allowing the deletion of final unstressed /e/ before vowel-initial words: thus line 101 *wiþþ all swillc ríme alls her iss sett* must be scanned ∪ – ∪ – ∪ – ∪ – to retain the rigid metrical pattern; so *ríme alls* must be a disyllabic foot, and the <e> on *ríme* is not pronounced. Environments before <h> pattern the same way: line 110 *þatt wite he wel to soþe* requires two syllables for *wite he* (see further Minkova 1984). So <h>-initial and vowel-initial environments pattern alike, as sites for deletion of final <e>, thus suggesting they are the same, i.e. that [h] is deleted.

Loss of [h] seems to have begun earliest in initial /xC-/ clusters, i.e. those spelled <hn hl hr> in Old English (*hnacod* 'naked', *hlūd* 'loud', *hrēowan* 'rue'); this starts in the eleventh century. Later, some dialects show loss before /w/ (*hwǣr* 'where', *hwīt* 'white', etc.); this became typical of the south, though [h] or something voiceless still remains in <wh>-words in Scotland, Ireland and many North American dialects. In the twelfth–thirteenth century prevocalic [h] began to be deleted; this spread in the fourteenth–sixteenth centuries to most dialects. It seems likely that the present '[h]-fulness' of the standard dialects is due at least partly to a late restoration, mainly via spelling and the influence of the schools, which was not firmly established until perhaps the eighteenth century (see vol. III, ch. 1). Certainly orthographic <h> was not uniformly pronounced as late as Elizabethan times, and it seems never to have been restored in some Romance loans (*honor*, *heir* and for older speakers of a certain class *hotel*); the now rather archaic use of *an* before words like *hotel* and *historian* must be a relic of earlier [h]-lessness.

While /x/ in the form of its allophone [h] was dropping in syllable onsets, things were happening at the other end, in codas. Two changes were starting in the fourteenth century: loss of final /x/, and a shift of [x] to [f] (*dough* < OE *dāh* vs *rough* < *rūh*). The written evidence for these changes is relatively sparse (they are still not noted in modern spelling); but <f> does appear as early as ca 1300 in the west midlands, e.g. *thurf* 'through' < *þurh*, *dwerf* 'dwarf' < *dwerh* (Jordan 1934: §196 Anm. 1). This change applies only to the velar allophone [x]; the palatal [ç] does not become [f]. (Forms showing apparent deletion of final [ç] as in *hi* 'high' beside *hiʒ* may not show deletion either; they may well descend from Old English inflected forms like nom./acc. pl. *hēa*, where intervocalic /x/ had been lost.)

In the fifteenth century we begin to find increasing evidence for both the change to [f] and loss: Jordan (1934: §294) gives examples of <f> spellings in *enough*, *plough*, *dough*, (and cf. the surviving doublet in (*plum-*)*duff*), *tough* and others. Loss in codas is attested earliest before /t/, e.g. *douter* 'daughter', *broute* 'brought'; some fifteenth-century texts also show final loss, as in *throu* ~ *throw* 'through', *thou* ~ *thow* 'though'. The palatal [ç] also begins to drop in the late fourteenth century: aside from spellings like *knit* 'knight', *brit* 'bright', there are rhymes in Lydgate and Gower like *bright*:*night*:*whit* (OE *-iht*: *-īt*). These developments are merely precursors of the major change (all instances of final or preconsonantal /x/ were either deleted or merged with /f/; this is later, and will be dealt with in vol. III).

2.4.1.3 Minor developments

The obstruent system (24) remains unchanged throughout the Middle English period, and indeed until the sixteenth or seventeenth century; but there are individual phonetic changes that redistribute phonemes, and produce the familiar shapes of words that had looked quite different in Old and Early Middle English. The most important of these concern the dental series, especially /θ ð d/.

1 *Presonorant strengthening.* As early as the twelfth century there is evidence of strengthening of [ð] to [d] before /r l n/ as in *spider* < *spīðra*, *fiddle* < *fiðl-* (inflected stem of *fiðele*), *burden* < *byrðn-* (inflected stem of *byrðen*). Strengthening before /l n/ can be considered an assimilation (since /n/ is a (nasal) stop and /l/ has some complete closure).

2 *Post-fricative strengthening.* This is a dissimilation: /θ/ > [t] after other fricatives, probably beginning in Late Old English. Familiar examples are *thefte* < *þēofþu*, *nostril* < *nosþyrl*, *height(e)* < *hēhþu*, *drought* < *drūhþu* (see Jordan 1934: §205). However early this change may have been, /t/ in many of these words did not become standard until much later (Milton still writes *heighth*), and some modern dialects still have /θ/ at least in *height* and *drought*.

3 *Fricative weakening before* /Vr/. Many words with OE intervocalic /d/ now have /ð/: e.g. *father*, *mother*, *gather*, *hither*, *whither*, *whether* (OE *fader*, *mōdor*, *gaderian*, etc.). Throughout Middle English the <d> spellings predominate, and the change is only attested on a large scale ca 1500 (Jordan 1934: §298); but it must have begun quite early, since geminate /d:/ does not undergo it (*bladder*, *adder*, *fodder* < *blæddre*, *næddre*, *fōddre*); the only explanation for the consistent failure of the process here is that /d/ > [ð] must have occurred while the /d/:/d:/ contrast was still stable.

The most likely reason for the lack of early written evidence is that the first stage of the weakening was an affricate [d̪ð], which had – as a new sound type – no institutionalised spelling, and in any case was predictable from a following /ər/. This is supported by the presence of [d̪ð] in precisely such forms in some modern northern dialects: e.g. *father* and *mother* have medial [d̪ð] in ten out of fourteen areas covered by the Survey of English Dialects in Cumberland and Westmoreland (Orton *et al.* 1962–71, s.v. *father*, *mother* VIII.1.1).

4 *Early palatalisation of* /sj/. There is some attestation in the fifteenth century of a change /sj/ > [ʃ], as in spellings like *confesschon, fessychen* 'physician', *fashon* and the like (Jordan 1934: §299); but this is sporadic until much later. In the sixteenth–seventeenth centuries there is a much more widespread palatalisation, affecting also the clusters /zj/ (*vision*), /tj/ (*Christian*), /dj/ (*soldier*).

2.4.2   The sonorant system

2.4.2.1   The nasals

After degemination (2.4.1.1), Middle English was left with a sonorant system consisting of the two nasals /m n/ (with [ŋ] an allophone of /n/ before velars), and the liquids /r l j w/. The major changes affecting the nasals were the following:

1 *Loss in weak final position.* Old English distinguished /m/ and /n/ in final unstressed syllables (infinitive *-an* vs dat. pl. *-um*, etc.). During Late Old English this contrast was already beginning to weaken, with neutralisation to /n/. Within the morpheme (as in *bottom, fathom*) this generally was blocked; it was also restricted in adverbial datives like *hwīlum* 'at times', which descends as *whilum/-om*. In the north there was already an Early Old English tendency to drop final /n/ (Northumbrian infinitives in *-a* vs other dialects in *-an*); from about the twelfth century this began to happen in the south as well in certain contexts: OE *gamen* > *game, mægden* > *maide*; in some dialects this occurs as well in words that elsewhere retained /n/, e.g. Kentish *ʒeue* 'seven'. Loss of /n/ was morphologically restricted: it is variable in past participles of strong verbs, and in weak noun plurals and verb plurals up to the late fourteenth century (see further 2.8.3 and 2.9.2.6 below).

2 *Nasal assimilation.* During the Middle English period we first get written evidence for assimilation of /m/ to [n] before dentals, as in *scant* < OScand. *skammt, ant(e)* 'ant' < *amte* < *æmete* (cf. the archaic doublet *emmet*), *Manchester* < *Mam(e)chestre*. Assimilation of /n/ to velars is much older, probably of Proto-Germanic date; runic Old English has a distinct [ŋ]-rune, and Gothic has special spellings for [ŋg], [ŋk] as in *siggwan* 'sing', *siqqan* 'sink' (OE *singan, sincan*).

3 *Stop epenthesis.* Beginning in the twelfth century, we find spellings suggesting insertion of a stop homorganic to a nasal preceding another

stop or liquid: *þundre* 'thunder' < *þunre*, *empty* < *æmtig* < *æmetig*; likewise *drempte*, *thimble*, *shambles*, *nimble* (the latter three from inflected stems, i.e. *thimble* not from nom. sg. *þȳmel* but obl. *þȳml-*). This appears to result from 'mistiming': raising the velum prematurely in transition from a nasal to a non-nasal segment, giving the oral equivalent of the nasal before the next consonant. The same process is normal in casual speech in many modern varieties, e.g. those where *prince* gets a [t] inserted before the [s], making it homophonous to *prints*.

2.4.2.2 The liquids
Under this heading I group the traditional liquids /r l/ and the 'semivowels' or 'glides' /j w/ (see Lass & Anderson 1975: Preliminaries). There are no major changes in this series, but a number of minor ones, one of which anticipates a very important later development.

1 /r/-*metathesis*. Since Old English times /r/ has shown a tendency to metathesis in the environments /VrC/ and /rVC/, where either configuration may yield the other. Familiar examples in the modern standard are *bright* < *be(o)rht*, *bird* < *bridd*. These metatheses were mainly northern in Old English, but tended to spread south. Examples of the two types: (a) /VrC/ > /rVC/: *briht* 'bright', *wrihte* 'wright', *þruh* 'through' (< *berht*, *wyrhta*, *þurh*); (b) /rVC/ > /VrC/: *bird*, *third*, *gers* 'grass' (< *bridd*, *þridda*, *græs*).

2 *Early loss of* /r/. In southeast England, postvocalic /r/ began to delete systematically in the seventeenth and eighteenth centuries, but there are earlier episodes of loss, more or less 'aborted' precursors. These losses are mainly before /n l ʃ/, and can be identified by spellings, and in some cases by their current forms – even if they are unattested in early texts. Typical early examples: *Dasset* 'Dorset' < *Deōrset*, *wosted* 'worsted', *passell* 'parcel', as well as inverted spellings like *marster* 'master', *farther* 'father' (Cely Papers: cited by Wyld 1936: 298). These become commoner in the sixteenth and seventeenth centuries, and will be treated in volume III.

Early /r/-loss can generally be distinguished from late loss in a simple way: in dialects that are now non-rhotic, the vowel in an original /-VrC/ sequence is long: e.g. PDE /ɑ:/ in *arse*, *cart*, *part*, /ɔ:/ in *fort*, *portion*, *coarse*, etc. This stems from seventeenth-century lengthening before /r/ followed by a consonant or pause. But if the loss was early, before the lengthening, the Present-Day English vowel is short: thus *ass* /æs/ for *arse* (USA, Somerset, Wiltshire, Norfolk, Essex, Herefordshire), rural British and US forms like *hoss*, *cuss*, etc. (Few of these except *ass* have survived in standard dialects; for more details see Jordan 1934: §166, Hill 1940.)

3 Like /r/, /l/ has some tendency to be deleted in syllable codas. The earliest cases are from the twelfth century: *Lambeth Homilies* already have *ech* 'each' < *ǣlc*; *such* < *swylc*, *hwich* 'which' < *hwylc* are also attested early. These sporadic losses may be precursors of later large scale loss of final /l/ in the south of England. In modern London and Home Counties vernaculars, for instance, dark [ł] in this position is often replaced by a back vowel reflecting its secondary articulation, giving realisations like [fɪo], [mɪok] for *fill*, *milk*. Presumably /l/ in codas was dark in Middle English and release of the dental/alveolar closure left behind a vowel-colour – which itself could be deleted. There was also some loss of /l/ in unstressed syllables, e.g. *wench(e)* < *wencel*, *much(e)* < *mycel*, and in low-stressed forms like *as* < *ealswā* (see Jordan 1934: §167).

4 From the twelfth century /w/ tends to be deleted before non-low back vowels (*suster* 'sister' < **swuster* < *sweostor*, *such* < *swuch* < *swylc*, *sote* 'sweet' < *swōte*, *þong* 'thong' < *þwong*). Parallel to this is deletion of /j/ before high front vowels, e.g. *icchen* 'itch' < *gyccan*, *if* < *gif*. These are obviously related: both involve loss of a close vowel-like segment before a vowel of similar articulation.

2.5   Length and quantity

2.5.1   Introduction: terminology and concepts

Our concern has been so far with individual segments (consonants and vowels), their relations to neighbouring ones, and the systems they make up. In this and the next section we shift to a higher level of organisation: syllable and foot structure. The terms 'length' and 'quantity' are often used interchangeably, which obscures an important distinction. Here 'length' denotes a durational property of individual segments (vowels or consonants can be long or short), and 'quantity' or 'weight' a structural property of syllables (syllables can be heavy or light). The intersection of these and related categories can be spelled out as follows:

1 A syllable (σ) is a hierarchical structure, with two main constituents: an onset (any material preceding the syllabic element) and a rhyme (the syllabic plus anything following: cf. the everyday use of the term). The rhyme in turn consists of the syllabic (normally a vowel or vowel cluster) and a coda (anything following the nucleus). Using the abbreviations O, R, N, Co, the structures of *a*, *at*, *cat* may be represented as:

(27)

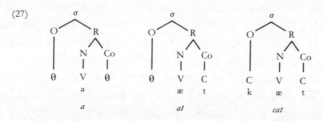

2 The weight of a syllable is defined by the structure of its rhyme. If neither the nucleus nor the coda is complex (made of more than one segment), the rhyme – hence the syllable – is light. If either the nucleus or coda (or both) is complex, the rhyme is heavy. If both are complex we have a special case of heavy rhyme, called superheavy or hypercharacterised. Thus a -V or -VC rhyme is light, a -VV or -VVC or -VCC rhyme is heavy, and -VVCC is superheavy.

To illustrate with forms occurring in the *Peterborough Chronicle* (1127), the basic rhyme types and weights are:

(28)

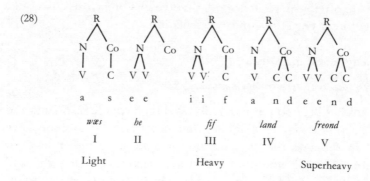

(Long vowels are interpreted as complex, e.g. /ee/ = /eː/: see 2.3.1.)

Weight, then, is a structural, not linear property. It is not the number of segments that makes a rhyme heavy (light -VC and heavy -VV both have two), but the way the complexity is distributed. A -VCCC rhyme is not superheavy, since only the coda is complex; superheaviness requires branching of both nucleus and coda.

3 *Syllable boundaries*. How does one decide where syllable divisions come in polysyllabic words, and which segments belong to which syllables? In *keeping* /kiːpɪŋ/, for instance, does the /p/ belong to the first syllable or the second? Decisions like this can largely be made on phonotactic grounds: in segmenting a string into syllables we try in the first instance to get only well-formed syllables, i.e. ones that could be monosyllabic words in the language – since in a monosyllable the boundaries are unambiguous. Take a simple case like *athlete* /æθliːt/. The syllabification is obvious: **/æ/ by itself is ill-formed, since in English the strong syllable of a foot may not terminate in a short vowel (see 2.5.2, 1 below); and **/æθl/ is illegal, as is **/θliːt/. Therefore we divide /æθ/–/liːt/.

In *keeping*, /kiː/ is well formed (*key*), as is /kiːp/ (*keep*) and so also is /pɪŋ/ (*ping*). Therefore the medial consonant or interlude belongs to both syllables; it is ambisyllabic. This is even clearer in a case like *kipping*, where **/kɪ/ is impossible for the same reason as **/æ/ above, and /pɪŋ/ is legal. Using numbered brackets to represent syllables, the divisions for *athlete*, *keeping*, *kipping* are:

(29) $[_1æθ]_1 [_2liːt]_2$ $[_1kiː [_2p]_1ɪŋ]_2$ $[_1k ɪ [_2p]_1 ɪŋ]_2$
        athlete   *keeping*   *kipping*

Clusters may also be ambisyllabic; a medial cluster that would be a well-formed coda for the first syllable and a well-formed onset for the second would be ambisyllabic, like the /st/ in *plastic*:

(30) $[_1plæ [_2st]_1 ɪk]_2$

We will see that the special properties of ambisyllabic consonants play an interesting part in the development of vowel length and syllable quantity.

4 At a higher level of organisation (the 'rhythmic'), syllables are grouped into feet. A foot (the prime unit of rhythm) consists of a strong (S) or stressed syllable plus any weak(er) (W) syllable(s) to its right. Foot boundaries do not have to coincide with word boundaries: e.g. *believer*

begins on the weak syllable of a preceding (notional) foot, whose strong syllable may be empty (a so-called 'silent stress': see Abercrombie 1964); while *rabbi*, with secondary stress on the second syllable, consists of two feet, one subordinated to the other, with the weak syllable of the second foot empty; *rabbit* consists of and coincides with a single disyllabic foot with both syllables filled; and *rat* is a monosyllabic foot with an empty or zero weak syllable:

(31)

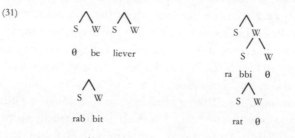

This somewhat breathless introduction to some basic concepts of suprasegmental phonology will, I hope, clarify the changes discussed below.

2.5.2   *The length and quantity conspiracies*

Segment length and syllable weight (at least in stressed syllables) were relatively unconstrained in Old English; long and short vowels contrasted freely nearly everywhere (though long consonants were restricted to syllable-final and foot-medial positions), and stressed syllables could be light, heavy or superheavy. From earliest Germanic times, however, there have been a considerable number of changes affecting both length and weight. These had overall two common effects: reducing the number of environments in which vowel length was contrastive; and tending to stabilise certain syllable shapes as 'preferred' or 'optimal'.

These developments can (metaphorically?) be interpreted as a kind of 'conspiracy'. In the sense in which I use the term here, a conspiracy is a set of rules or historical changes that are formally unrelated, but appear to act in concert to serve some particular 'goal'. At the very least the changes in question constitute a thematically related block, a distinct story within the larger history of English, because of their domains and effects; they are part of a long-term evolutionary pattern. The sequence spelled out below will make it clear how arbitrary the 'Old English'/'Middle English' division really is (see 2.1.2); the conspiracies are part of the history of English (even Germanic) as a whole, and make no sense if we consider only one 'period'.

I will therefore begin the story early, with some pre-Old English and Old English developments that are integral to the pattern that comes to fruition in Middle English times, and in which some changes look like 'revised versions' of earlier ones. I will give the changes in chronological order, with commentary; the names I give to them, with the exception of Open-Syllable Lengthening (5), are my own; there are no traditionally accepted designations.

1 *Foot-Final Lengthening.* In Common West Germanic (if not earlier, e.g. in Northwest Germanic), short stressed vowels lengthened in absolute final position (cf. Lat. *tŭ* vs OE *þū* 'thou'). In effect the strong syllable of a foot could not terminate with a short vowel (a condition that still holds for most Germanic languages). Thus even in earliest Old English vowel-length was neutralised in this position.

> *Length implications:* the /V/ vs /V:/ contrast is neutralised in favour of /V:/ in the zero-coda strong syllable of the foot.
> *Quantity Implications:* Only heavy syllables are allowed in the zero-coda strong syllable of the foot.

2 *Old English Quantity Adjustment*

(a) *Pre-Cluster Shortening I.* About the seventh century (Luick 1914–40: §204) long vowels shortened before /CC/ if another consonant followed, either in the coda or the onset of the next syllable, as in *brămblas* 'brambles' < */bræ:mblɑs/, *gŏdspel* 'gospel' < */go:dspel/. This removes one class of superheavy syllables.

(b) *Trisyllabic Shortening I.* At about the same time, long vowels also shortened before clusters of two consonants in stressed antepenultimate syllables: *ĕnleofan* 'eleven' < */æ:nd-/.

> *Length implications:* Length is neutralised in favour of /V/ before /CC/ if a third consonant follows, and before /CC/ in third from last syllables.
> *Quantity Implications:* Superheavy syllables are barred from environments before another consonant; a trisyllabic foot with a superheavy first syllable is disallowed.

3 *Pre-Cluster Lengthening.* Around the ninth century, short vowels generally lengthened before clusters of sonorant + obstruent at the same

place of articulation; this was especially clear if the obstruent was a voiced stop, but may also have occurred if it was a fricative (Luick 1914–40: §268). The most important environments are before /mb nd rd ld/: *cămb* 'comb' > *cāmb*, *fĭndan* 'find' > *fīndan*, *wŏrd* > *wōrd*, *cĭld* 'child' > *cīld*. Lengthening before final [ŋg], attested by spellings like *soong* 'sang' did occur, but was apparently undone later, and /nd/ and /mb/ seem never to have caused lengthening in the north (hence PDE [grʊn(d)] in the north of England, [grʌn(d)] in Scotland for *ground*, etc.).

Lengthening failed if another consonant followed the two relevant ones: *cīld* but pl. *cĭldru*. Thus the same environment that caused shortening in 2(a) inhibited lengthening as well: these are two sides of the same coin. Note also that in cases like 'child', lengthening and its failure produce a morphophonemic alternation /V:/ ~ /V/ (as still in *child/children*); we will see below that other changes in the sequence have contributed to the morphophonemic complexity of English.

> *Length implications:* The length opposition is neutralised to /V:/ in rhymes whose codas contain a sonorant + homorganic voiced stop.
> *Quantity implications:* A new class of superheavy syllables.

It is worth noting that these syllables and those with codas in /st/ are among the few left now where superheaviness can occur in a morphologically simple word: *priest*, *beast* and the like (see 4 below) are exceptional, as most superheavy rhymes containing obstruents are morphologically complex: e.g. pasts of verbs like *steeped* /sti:pt/, noun plurals like *lights* /laɪts/.

4 *Early Middle English Quantity Adjustment*: a generalisation to simpler (hence more inclusive) environments of the two changes in (2), beginning about the eleventh century (see Luick 1914–40: §§352ff.):

(a) *Pre-Cluster Shortening II.* Long vowels shortened before sequences of only two consonants – except, of course, those that caused Pre-Cluster Lengthening (3), and – variably – certain ones like /st/ that were typically ambisyllabic (see 2.5.1). So shortening in *kĕpte* 'kept' < *cēpte* (inf. *cēpan*), *mĕtte* 'met' < *mētte* (inf. *mētan*), *brĕst* 'breast' < *brēost*. Shortening failed in the same environment in *priest* < *prēost*; in words like this it may well be the reflex of an inflected form like *prēostas* (nom./acc. pl.) that has survived, i.e. one where the /st/ could be interpreted as onset of the second syllable; the same holds for *beast*, *feast* from French. This shortening accounts for the 'dissociation' between present and past vowels in a large class of weak verbs, like those mentioned earlier and *dream/dreamt, leave/left, lose/lost*, etc. (The modern forms are even more different from each other due to later changes in both long and short vowels that added qualitative dissociation to that in length: ME /keːpən/ ~ /keptə/, now /kiːp/ ~ /kɛpt/, etc.)

(b) *Trisyllabic Shortening II.* Long vowels shortened in antepenults before a single consonant, not just /CC/ as in 2(b): *sūþ* 'south' ~ *sŭþerne* 'southern', *divīn* 'divine' ~ *divĭnitie* 'divinity' and the like. The alternation pattern produced by this change, and as above enhanced by later changes, is now an important part of English morphophonology, especially of Romance loans: the above plus *sign/signify, serene/serenity, humane/humanity, profound/profundity, cone/conical.*

> *Length implications :* The length opposition is neutralised to /V/ before /CC/, and in virtually all antepenults.
>
> *Quantity implications :* The last major superheavy rhyme type (except those produced by 3 and before /st/) is removed; heavy syllables are barred from strong position in a trisyllabic foot.

5 *Open-Syllable Lengthening.* This change, described briefly in 2.3.2, is by no means as simple as it looks. Aside from the debate about its qualitative results, there is also controversy over whether the environment as traditionally conceived is the correct one. But the length and quantity implications are pretty much the same whatever position one takes.

The standard account is that about 1200 short vowels began to lengthen in stressed 'first open syllables' of disyllabic words. In purely linear terms the environment was /-V́CV-/. It made no difference if there was an initial consonant, though it seems that one closing the second syllable had an effect; at least lengthening was more likely to be inhibited if the last syllable was /-VC/ as in *gannet* < *gănot* without lengthening vs *same* < *săma* with lengthening. Lengthening also failed if the second syllable contained /i(ː)/ as in *body, many*; though this may simply be because such words had a secondary-stressed vowel in the second syllable, i.e. were composed of two feet – as in many modern dialects – and hence did not in fact meet the conditions for OSL.

More importantly, however, lengthening failed if there was a word-medial cluster (*sister, whisper*), or if the word had more than two syllables (*natural, bachelor*). Given the account of the conspiracy so far, this is precisely what we would expect; Pre-Cluster Shortening II had already ruled out most /-VVCC/ rhymes, and Trisyllabic Shortening I and II made sure that long vowels did not occur in antepenults (i.e. that they were as light as was consistent with the size of their codas). It looks as if some earlier changes got incorporated, more or less, as constraints or conditions on syllable structure in later times.

In the analysis here, the term 'Open Syllable' is really not appropriate. By Foot-Final Lengthening (1), /-V/ alone could not be a well-formed stressed rhyme even in Old English; any form with the configuration /-V́CV-/ would have the medial consonant ambisyllabic, as the strong syllable of the foot would have to be at least /-VC/. Therefore the environment for this change is more properly stated as 'short vowel in the strong syllable of a disyllabic foot, followed by an ambisyllabic consonant'. The 'open-syllable' analysis would, for instance, give for /nozə/ 'nose' < *nǒsu* the impossible syllabification **[nó] [zə] instead of [nó[z]ə]. This change might better be called 'Pre-Simple-Interlude Lengthening', but you can only go so far in bucking tradition, so I will stick with OSL (for the arguments see Minkova 1982; Lass 1985).

According to Minkova's argument, yet another revision is needed in the environment for OSL, which makes the name even less appropriate. It seems now that many of the final /ə/ that constituted the second peaks of the /-V́CV-/ sequence had already begun to be deleted earlier than the period when OSL was established. Orm, for instance (ca 1180), who shows only marginal OSL, has extensive (if variable) /ə/-deletion (see the discussion of the metrical sequence *ríme alls* with deleted *-e* in 2.4.1.2 above, and 2.5.3 below). It might well be that the prime environment for (so-called) OSL is really a monosyllabic foot with a light /-VC/ rhyme. If this is so, it makes very little difference; since the 'aim' of the change is to substitute heavy for light in the strong syllable of a foot, the only alteration would be visualising this in monosyllabic rather than disyllabic terms: the neutralisation of length would be the same, as would the overall quantitative effect (light > heavy). This requires more research, but there is no doubt that Minkova's solution, rather than the traditional one, is essentially right.

> *Length implications:* The length opposition is neutralised to /V:/ in strong syllables of disyllabic feet with a single medial (ambisyllabic) consonant.
>
> *Quantity implications:* Light rhymes are prohibited in the strong syllable of a disyllabic foot.

We have seen how OSL 'co-operates' with earlier changes in not occurring where new superheavy rhymes would be created. If we now look back at Foot-Final Lengthening (1), we see the other side of the conspiracy, and where OSL fits in. This is in ruling out 'overlight' syllables from strong position in the foot. OSL does just this, under either the monosyllabic or disyllabic interpretations. If pre-cluster shortenings get rid of superheavy strong syllables, foot-final lengthening and OSL get rid of superlight ones. The two tendencies converge in maximising simple heavy rhymes in strong positions.

These tendencies were in fact short-circuited in Late Middle English. With degemination (2.4.1.1) a host of new /-VCV-/ and /-VC/ sequences were created: e.g. *setten* 'set' /set:ən/ > /setən/, *katt* 'cat' /kat:/ > /kat/. Subsequent history shows that these consonants were not relengthened, and the vowels remained short. It looks as if Middle English was poised at one point to take what we might call the 'Scandinavian route': generalising heavy syllables to all strong positions in the foot, and doing away with superheavy syllables entirely (this is the case in all modern North Germanic languages except Danish). But for some reason the tendency was aborted, and English ended up later with a freer distribution of quantity.

If this conspiratorial picture makes sense, the one change that looks out of place is Pre-Cluster Lengthening (3). This is the only one that creates new superheavy syllables; it fits in with the neutralisation-of-length theme, but is quantitatively a misfit. It is odd in another way as well: it is the only change in the sequence that is sensitive to the phonetic quality of its environment, rather than more 'abstract' properties like syllable weight and syllable number. This is in its own way a precursor of later developments: in the seventeenth–nineteenth centuries this kind of 'concrete' or phonetically sensitive lengthening becomes the norm (e.g. before /r/), and virtually the only kind of length change that occurs.

Leaving this change out, then, we can trace developments to the time (late fourteenth century) when degemination interrupted the evolutionary sequence:

(32)   The quantity conspiracy

(a) *Weight increases*

1 Foot-Final Lengthening

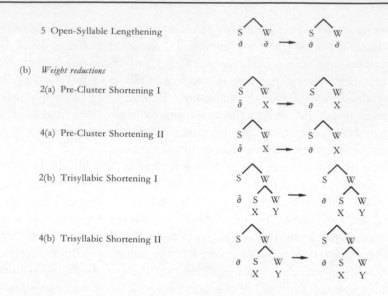

5 Open-Syllable Lengthening

(b) *Weight reductions*

2(a) Pre-Cluster Shortening I

4(a) Pre-Cluster Shortening II

2(b) Trisyllabic Shortening I

4(b) Trisyllabic Shortening II

($\bar{\bar{\sigma}}$ = superheavy syllable, $\bar{\sigma}$ = heavy, $\breve{\sigma}$ = light; X and Y indicate any syllable type, where weight is not at issue.) We will see in the next section that some rather different changes may also be related to this series.

2.5.3   More conspiracy: unstressed syllables and 'loss of -e'

In many Germanic (and other) languages, unstressed syllables tend to behave rather differently from stressed ones. Their vowels shorten, may be qualitatively unstable and neutralise, giving unstressed vowel inventories simpler than the stressed ones; the vowels are often less peripheral, so that the product of neutralisation may be a mid central [ə]-type; and the vowels, or even the whole syllables, tend to delete. These are only tendencies (if reasonably explicable ones), not universals. The view often expressed that 'strong initial stress' in English somehow 'caused' reduction or loss of unstressed syllables is untenable. Finnish, for instance, has as 'strong' an initial stress as English, yet maintains all quality and length distinctions in unstressed syllables. Cross-linguistically, there is a strong correlation between low prominence and reduction or loss – but not a causal relation.

Still, obscuration of contrast and loss in weak syllables are old Germanic tendencies, and the Middle English developments have a long pedigree. As with the quantity conspiracy, the antecedents go back to Germanic times; and some of the results tie in interestingly with later developments, and with those discussed in the last section. There are two separate but related evolutionary strands: (a) vowel reduction or obscuration in weak syllables; and (b) actual loss of such syllables.

(a) *Loss of contrast in weak syllables.* By the earliest historical Old English times, vowel length had generally been lost in weak syllables, so that all historically long inflectional vowels were shortened (compare Go. *a*-stem nom. pl. *-ōs* with OE *-as*, OHG *ō*-stem dat. pl. *-ōm* with OE *-um*). During Old English times, the phonetically distinct short vowels in these positions began to merge: by the mid-eighth century unstressed /æ/ and /i/ merged in /e/ (except for /i/ in certain suffixes like *-ing*); and later /u/, /o/ and /ɑ/ tended to merge in /ɑ/ (thus late dat. pl. *-an* for original *-um*, etc.).

By the eleventh century, it looks rather as if all original weak vowels except /i/ have merged in one value, usually spelled <e> – though early texts show complex vacillation. The mid-twelfth century situation can be summed up by spellings in the *Peterborough Chronicle*:

OE <e>: læred, gehaten; æfter ~ æftor; singað; hungær, forcursæd.

OE <u>: sun*u* ~ sun*e*; far*e*.

OE <o>: wær*o*n, seid*o*n, abb*o*d; wun*o*de ~ wun*e*de; heaf*o*d ~ hæu*e*d; broth*e*r, þol*e*den; cum*a*n.

OE <a>: dag*a*s, ath*a*s; abut*o*n, segg*o*n; blaw*e*n, tof*o*ren, cum*e*n.

(The use of <æ> stems from the merger of OE /æ/ and /ɑ/, as well as a local development of some /æ/ to /e/.)

The high vowel /i/ is distinct, but all other short vowels show both traditional and 'incorrect' spellings: original <e> is represented by <e, o, a, æ>, <u> by <u, e>, <o> by <o, e, a>, and <a> by <a, o, e>. This is as clear evidence as one needs for non-distinctness. (Some retained <i> spellings, as in the suffixes in *twenti*, *þrittig* 'thirty' < OE *-ig*, probably do not represent unstressed /i/, but secondary-stressed /iː/ < /ij/.)

By the end of the century, the characteristic spelling for all these categories is <e>: e.g. in the *Ormulum*, which shows quite consistent

<e> for OE /e/ (*erþe* 'earth', *kiþeþþ* 'shows'), /o/ (*wærenn* 'they were', *moderr* 'mother') and /ɑ/ (*þenkenn* 'think', *witenn* 'to know'). Other spellings appear in proper names (usually foreign): *Naȝaræþ*, *Beþþleæm*, etc.

The usual interpretation of these <e> spellings is not that the vowels in question merged in /e/, as the orthography suggests, but in some 'neutral' or 'colourless' vowel [ə], distinct from any stressed vowel in the system (at least phonetically: for the problems, see Minkova 1984). While it is not entirely clear what '[ə]' means (see Lass 1986), it represents a passable cover-symbol for generally non-peripheral mid vowels, and this is a reasonable interpretation. But the choice of <e> rather than <a, u, o> suggests that at least initially its quality was front enough for <e> to be an appropriate graph (unless it was simply that given an unrounded mid-vowel <e> was the only possible writing, since the other mid-vowel graph, <o>, indicated roundness). But there are later developments suggesting that this vowel was not always without 'colour', and also had a range of allophonic distinctions.

During later Middle English different regional traditions arose for spelling this 'colourless' vowel, whose implications are not entirely clear. From about the thirteenth century, it tends to be spelled (mainly in closed syllables) as <i/y> in the north and to some extent east midlands, and <u/o> in the west. Some authorities (e.g. Jordan 1934: §135) consider this a 'recolouring' of [ə], i.e. these spellings represent changes on the lines of [ə] > [i]/[ɪ], [ə] > [u]/[ʊ]. This is a minority opinion, and most scholars take the differences as 'merely ortho-graphic'; yet there is no reason in principle why these spellings could not represent something phonetic. After all, many modern dialects have quite different vowels for what is loosely written /ə/: e.g. a quite back [ä] on Tyneside, a much fronter and closer [ï] on Merseyside, etc.

In some forms <o> spellings were common in London and have remained (*abbot, bosom, weapon, iron, bottom*); <o> is most common in labial environments, as here, but also occurs for the reduced version of F -*oun* /uːn/ as in *nation* and *bacon*.

In some environments, especially before dentals and palatals, there was raising of this vowel; as early as the thirteenth century (*Havelok*) we find rhymes like *kitchin*:*in* < *cycene*:*in*; and in the next century Chaucer often rhymes -*is*/-*ys* (n. pl.) with the copula *is*. In the fourteenth-century London standard there was some distinction between the qualities [i] (or [ɪ]?) and [ə] in weak syllables: some [i] were apparently categorical norms, as in -*ing*, -*ish*, -*ic*, the prefixes *bi*-/*by*-, *i*-/*y*- < *ge*-; others were probably raised allophones of /ə/. Many modern dialects retain a similar distinction, e.g. RP weak /ɪ/:/ə/ in *taxies*:*taxes*.

(b) *Loss of final /ə/*. At some point in Late Middle English absolute final /ə/ as in *nose, same* /nɔːzə/ /saːmə/ were lost; it is not entirely clear when this loss was completed, but by Chaucer's time final /ə/ was an archaism, employable if necessary in verse, but not typical of the spoken language. Like many other processes we have been considering, this had a long pedigree; loss of weak vowels had begun as early as Late Proto-Germanic, and the Middle English developments are part of a long chain.

In trisyllabic forms, medial weak vowels were already lost in Proto-Germanic (Go. *duúhtar*, OE *dohtor* 'daughter' vs Skt *duhítar*, Gk *tʰugáter*: the accent had, of course, shifted to initial syllables in Germanic: see 2.6.2 below). A little later, final /i/ dropped in third syllables (OE pres. 3 sg./pl. *-eþ, -aþ* < */-iθi/, */-anθi/, cf. Skt *-e-ti, -a-nti*). Still later, probably in Northwest Germanic, medial /i/ dropped after heavy first syllables in trisyllabic words (OE *hȳr-de* 'he heard', *ner-e-de* 'he saved', cf. Go. *haus-i-da, nas-i-da*). Note that here syllable weight plays a part as well: a foot of the shape ōŏŏ is 'overheavy' and is reduced to ōŏ (this pattern should be familiar by now: see 2.5.2).

In Old English itself, a similar relation obtains between the weight of a stressed syllable and the loss of a following weak one. The clearest cases are nominative/accusative plural endings in *a*-stem neuter nouns (*scip-u* 'ships' vs *word* 'word(s)', with deletion after ō), and the nominative singular of many other noun classes (ō-stem *gief-u* 'gift' vs *bǣr* 'bier; *i*-stem *win-e* 'friend' vs *giest* 'guest'; *u*-stem *sun-u* 'son' vs *hand* 'hand'). Related to this there is syncope of medial vowels after heavy stem-syllables, but not after light: *wæter* 'water', gen. sg. *wæter-es* vs *tungol* 'star', gen. sg. *tungl-es*. In the first case ō-u, ō-i are overheavy and are reduced to ō, and the latter ōŏŏ is overheavy and is reduced to ōŏ. Thus what turns up in later Middle English as generalised post-stress /ə/-loss is very much in the tradition; if degemination had not yet fully taken place, the majority of final /ə/ in fact followed heavy syllables, since the vowels had been lengthened by OSL. It seems as well that syllable number has a kind of 'additive' effect in augmenting the weight of a foot (see Lass 1985 for a suggested explanation).

The first major Middle English deletion site is in hiatus (i.e. when another vowel follows directly); Old English already shows scattered examples like *sægdic* 'said I' < *sægde ic* (Luick 1914–40: §452), and there are some in Early Middle English texts like the *Peterborough Chronicle* (*maked hem* 'made them' < *macode heom*). Occurrences before ortho-graphic < h > are probably to be taken as instances of hiatus, or at least of an [h] so weak as barely to count as a consonant (see 2.4.1.2). By the late twelfth century deletion of /ə/ in hiatus is probably the norm, as it remains through most of the period – though it often does not show up in spelling. In the *Ormulum* for instance, vowels terminating the last weak syllable in a word usually drop before another vowel or < h >, especially in syntactically coherent groups like conjoined NPs or an Adverb + Verb cluster (in the examples below < ¢ > = non-pronounced but etymologically justified final orthographic < e >):

(33)

sun¢ and mone   son¢ on gann θ

'sun and moon'   'soon began'

< *sunne and mōna*   < *sōna ongann*

Deletion before word-boundary plus vowel or [h] was eventually extended to all word-final environments: though it was, except perhaps in the north, never categorical. In most dialects it was a variable process, increasing over time, with retention available as a rhythmic option. (The *Ormulum* also shows considerable variable /ə/-loss in non-hiatus position, e.g. in adjectives and the datives of nouns; it is not clear whether this is to be taken as an early extension of /ə/-deletion in its phonological sense, or as a morphological change – or both: see further 2.9.1 below.)

The late fourteenth-century state of affairs can be illustrated from Chaucer's metrical usage; in the examples below (*Troilus and Criseyde*, book I, after 1385), ¢ = unpronounced final < e >, and ë = pro-nounced final < e >:

1   For wel sit it, the sothë for to seynë (13)
2   Han felt that Lovë dorstë yow displesë (27)
3   O blyndë world, O blynd¢ entencioun (211)
4   And seydë Lord so ye lyv¢ al in lest (330)
5   In lovyng¢, how his aventures fellen (3)
6   Among this¢ other¢ folk was Criseyda (169)

Aside from retention of /ə/ at line ends, we see deletion in hiatus (3, 4, 5), and both retention (1, 2, 3, 4) and deletion before consonants (6). The clearest case is 3, with two forms of the same word in the same syntactic construction.

By the early fifteenth century all final /ə/ have probably dropped. The only persistent exceptions seem to be proper names (where the final unaccented vowel is often not spelled <e>, which may or may not be significant): examples from Chaucer and Gower which have kept /ə/ are *Attilla, Cane* 'Cana', *Cinthia, Cleopatre, Virginia, Pruce* 'Prussia' (Chaucer), *Athene, Caligula, Cassandra/-e, Medee/-a* 'Medea' (Gower). Most modern final /ə/ are in fact either in names or loan words – the above and *sauna, sonata*, etc. Or, in dialects that have lost postvocalic /r/, the remnant of earlier /ər/, as in *mother, victor, miller*.

The history of /ə/ in weak closed syllables is more complicated, subject to both phonological and morphological conditioning. The overriding phonological criterion is that /ə/ always remains if its deletion would cause an illegal cluster to arise: thus *weapon* keeps its /ə/ because it would otherwise end in **/pn/, and similarly *bottom, bosom*. With inflectional endings, deletion plus phonotactically derived constraints eventually give rise to variant allomorphs. Thus noun plurals and genitives in *-es* following a sibilant remain (*hors-es, hous-es*); otherwise /ə/ is lost (*catt-es* > *cat-s*), with assimilation of the remaining /z/ to /s/ after voiceless segments. After vowels /ə/ is lost on the general principle of hiatus avoidance (first seen in metrical practice much earlier): thus *law-es* > *law-s*. There is a similar pattern in weak past-tense and participial endings: retention after /t d/ (*want-ed, wound-ed*), loss elsewhere, with assimilation of /d/ to /t/ after voiceless segments (*kiss-ed*). Here, as in the genitive and plural, deletion is blocked if an illegal cluster would result: deletion in *wounded* would give **/dd/, just as in *houses* it would give **/zz/. The modern allomorphy of plural, genitive and weak past stems directly from constraints on /ə/-deletion in Late Middle English. These developments are only beginning in our period; the plural and genitive do not stabilise in their present forms until at least the sixteenth century, and the weak past much later.

Other morphological environments behave differently: strong past participles of vowel-final verbs tend to show deletion on the grounds of hiatus (*blown* < *blow-en*), or where a legal cluster remains after deletion (*born* < *bor-en*); otherwise /ə/ usually remains (*writt-en, chos-en, sunk-en*); this is of course a different matter from total loss of the ending (*drunk, sung*). In some cases, such as the superlative *-est*, /ə/ appears never to be deleted, even in hiatus (*free-est*).

2.5.4   *Hat, hate, hatter, hater*: sound change and diacritic spelling

The four words in the title illustrate a new set of spelling possibilities that arose in Late Middle English from the combined effects of a number of changes: specifically Pre-Cluster Shortening, degemination, OSL and loss of final /ə/. The principle involved – pervasive in Modern English orthography – is a switch from 'direct' representation to 'diacritic spelling': use of a letter not to indicate its own value, but as a cue to the values of other (not necessarily contiguous) letters.

Our concern here is with the spelling of syllable rhymes. Of the four key words, only *hat* has a directly spelled rhyme: orthographic <-VC> represents phonological /-VC/. In *hate*, <VCe> represents /VVC/ (/heɪt/), and <e> has no direct reference. In *hatter*, <VCC> represents /VC/, and the second <t> has no direct reference; in *hater*, the principle is related to that of *hate*, i.e. <VCe> represents /VVC/; only here the <e> has a direct value /ə/ as well.

The historical origins of these devices are transparent. The *hate* type derives from OSL and /ə/-deletion: since many final <e> in Middle English at one point represented pronounced vowels (as in *nose, same*), with loss of these vowels the sequence <VCe> could be used as an inverted spelling for any /VVC/ rhyme, whether or not there was a historical <e>. A case in point is *wrote* < OE *wrāt*, where <oCe> is simply a spelling for ME /ɔ:C/ (**wroat would be just as possible: cf. *throat* < *þrote* < *þrŏtu*, where the <e> has been dropped).

The *hatter* type, conversely, derives from Pre-Cluster Shortening and later degemination. The source is the subcase of shortening applying before geminates, which were typically written <CC> (a case in point would be *met* < *mĕtte*). If vowels are always short before <CC>, then <CC> can – conversely – be a device for indicating shortness: hence *written* < OE *writen* (this is the basic insight behind Orm's system: see 2.1.3). It has now become more or less the standard technique for handling cases where OSL has failed: *gannet, berry, hammer* < *ganot, berie, hamor*, etc. *Hat* and *hater* represent the original system: /-VC/ spelled <VC> and /-VVCV/ spelled <VCV>.

By the late fourteenth century, final <e> had become something of a scribal ornament, appearing both where it meant something and where it did not; it was not until much later that the above conventions were institutionalised, but the basic terms of reference were set by the time /ə/-deletion was well established. The dropping of /ə/ also left <e> free to be used for other purposes: e.g. after <u> to show that it meant /v/ rather than /u/ (*liue, loue, haue*); after <g> to indicate /dʒ/ rather than /g/ (*rage, bridge* vs *rag, brig*); after <c> to indicate /s/ rather than /k/ (*defence, mince*). It has also come to be used after a final <s> to show that a word is morphologically simple (i.e. that the <s> does not represent an inflection): *curse* vs *curs*, *tease* vs *teas*. Later conventions also established <e> to disambiguate what would otherwise have been homographs like *to/too/toe, do/doe*, etc.

2.6 Accentuation

2.6.1 *Preliminaries*

A stressed or accented syllable is 'prominent' compared to an unstressed one. The phonetic exponent of this prominence may be greater length or loudness or some salient pitch-difference – or any combination. Stress is thus not a strictly definable phonetic feature but a perceptual category that can be realised in different ways. In most Present-Day English dialects stressed syllables tend to be longer and louder than unstressed ones; but pitch relations vary from dialect to dialect (stressed syllables are higher in Received Pronunciation and most southern English dialects, lower in Northern Irish and much Scots and South African English). It is not clear what Old and Middle English stress were like phonetically, or indeed if they were any more homogeneous than now. For our purposes what counts is the phonological relation S(trong) vs W(eak).

In a typical stress-language, prominences or Ss are distributed over an utterance according to some kind of rhythmic principles, often interacting with syntax and morphology. Characteristically each linguistic unit (word, phrase, clause) has one main accent, i.e. syllable more prominent than any other(s) in the same unit. There may also be one or more subsidiary (weaker) prominences, traditionally called 'secondary stresses', within the unit – particularly the word-sized unit, which will be our concern here.

Given the S/W notation we have been using for stress, it seems natural to represent primary stress as S and unstress as W; secondary stress is then (according to conventions that have been fairly well accepted in one form or another for the last two decades) not an independent category, but simply a primary stress 'subordinated to' or 'weakened by' another primary stress. A modern example (relevant in principle to earlier periods) will perhaps clarify this.

The Present-Day English stress system operates at a number of levels.

First, individual words have their own stress contours, e.g. SW in *yellow*, *hammer*, WS in *believe*, *correct*. Second, higher-order units like compounds or phrases have their own independent contours: the compound *yellow-hammer* is overall SW (main stress on *yell*-), while the noun phrase *yellow hammer* is WS (main stress on *hamm*-). The syllables *-ow*, *-er* are weak in both. But it is also the case that relatively speaking, within the individual words themselves, the individual contours (here both SW) remain intact.

We can characterise this as follows: First, a rule for word stress (usually called the Main Stress Rule) assigns a contour at word level (the details are irrelevant here):

(35)

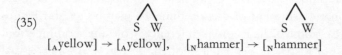

$[_A yellow] \rightarrow [_A yellow],$ $[_N hammer] \rightarrow [_N hammer]$

Then one of two higher-level rules, sensitive to morphosyntactic categories, assigns a secondary contour. The Compound Stress Rule (CSR) assigns SW to a string bracketed as a major lexical category (Noun, Verb, Adjective); the Nuclear Stress Rule (NSR) assigns WS to a string bracketed as a phrasal category (Noun Phrase, Verb Phrase, Sentence):

(36)   (a) Compound Stress Rule

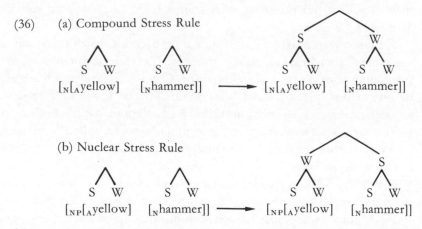

(b) Nuclear Stress Rule

In this notation a primary stress is then one that is S all the way up the tree; a secondary stress is one that has been weakened by subordination (indicated by a higher W); and an unstressed syllable is one that at the lowest level of the tree is W.

2.6.2 Left-handed to right-handed: Germanic to Romance stress

One of the most striking developments in the history of English stress is a shift from a system that assigns stress from the left-hand edge of the word and is insensitive to quantity and syllable structure, to one that starts from the right and is sensitive to these properties. English has undergone a change in prosodic 'handedness'.

In Indo-European and very early Proto-Germanic, accent was 'free': it could fall on any syllable of a polysyllabic root, or – under specific conditions – on a prefix or suffix. In a Greek paradigm like that of the verb 'leave', some forms are root-accented (pres. ind. 1 sg. active *leíp-ō*), some are prefix-accented (perf. ind. 1 sg. active *lé-loip-a*), and others suffix-accented (aorist ind. 1 sg. active *e-lip-ó-men*). Accent could also shift within a disyllabic root, as in *órni-s* 'bird' (nom. sg.), *orní-th-on* (gen. pl.).

One of the major Proto-Germanic innovations was an accent-shift that destroyed the older system. By the new Germanic Stress Rule (GSR), accent fell on the first syllable of the lexical root, and was withdrawn from all suffixes and most prefixes (see below). Like any stress rule, the GSR is essentially a 'foot-building' procedure: in principle, it simply begins at the left-hand edge of the word and assigns S to the first non-prefixal syllable – regardless of weight – and W to the one immediately to its right; the weight of this first root syllable is irrelevant:

(37)

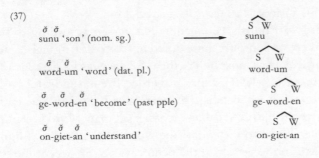

Like the other Germanic languages, Old English also had a number of stressable prefixes; these were prepositional or adverbial in origin, and often had unstressable ('normal') doublets. For example, corresponding to unstressed *on-* is stressed *and-* (*on-gíet-an* vs *ánd-gíet* 'understanding'), and so on. For historical reasons, stressed prefixes usually attach to nouns, as the examples here suggest.

These stressed prefixes were interpreted as full lexical items, rather than prefixes proper; a form like *and-giet* would be stressed on each of its elements, and the second stress subordinated to the first by the Old English equivalent of the modern Compound Stress Rule. Thus *and-giet* is like *hron-rād* 'whale-path' (= 'sea'); while a form with a true prefix like *on-gietan* would have its first root syllable only stressed by the GSR, and *on-* would be the W of a preceding foot:

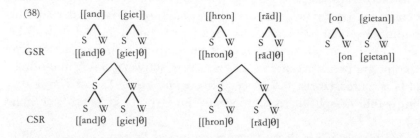

The main thing to note about the GSR is its simplicity: it is blind to weight and syllable count, and pays no attention to anything except the location of the first syllable of the root.

During the course of Old English, and much more extensively after the Conquest, the English lexicon was enriched by thousands of loans from other languages, notably Latin and its descendant Old French. These languages had a radically different kind of accentual system, which gradually came to replace the GSR – or, more accurately, to subsume the GSR in most instances as a special case.

Latin loans in Old English were generally stressed according to the GSR. This could create contours quite different from the originals, since the Latin Accent Rule was most unlike the GSR (as was its descendant, the Romance Stress Rule (RSR), which governed French and later Latin borrowings: see below for details). In very broad outline, the Latin accent was attracted to heavy syllables: it assigned main word accent to the heavy syllable closest to the end of the word. If the final was light, accent moved back to the penult; if the penult was light, accent moved back to the antepenult, regardless of weight – since there was an overall constraint forbidding accent to go further than three syllables from the end of the word (sometimes called 'the three-syllable rule' in classical grammars).

Old English restressing can be seen in *cándel* < L *candéla*, *ábbot* < *abbátem*, *mántel* < *mantéllum*. Any word with initial accent like *fébris* 'fever', *tábula* 'table' could of course be borrowed unchanged (OE *féfor, tæfel*). Aside from the modern developments of these and similar items, there is metrical evidence of restressing in words which now have Latinate accent: e.g. *Constantīnus, Holofernes* which alliterate on their initial consonants, thus presupposing initial stress; both are penult-accented in Latin, as now.

With the huge post-Conquest influx of both French and Latin loans, the overriding effect of the GSR weakened (cf. the similar constraint against initial [v] weakening at the same time: 2.4.1.1). French and Latin (and Greek) loans came to be accented according to the new Latin-based RSR, which is the foundation of the Middle English stress system (as a version of it still is today). This came about partly because the RSR was able to subsume most native words without altering their contours.

The RSR can be informally stated as follows (not the formally optimal statement, but one that shows clearly what its effects are):

(39)   *Romance Stress Rule*

(a)   (i) If the final σ is heavy, assign S:

arrḗst   θ   condiciōun   θ

(ii) If the final σ is light, go back to the penult.

(b)   (i) If the penult is heavy, assign S:

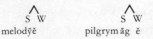

melodȳĕ   pilgrymāg ĕ

(ii) If the penult is light, go back to the antepenult.

(c)   Assign S to the antepenult regardless of weight:

clōistĕrĕr   băchĕlĕr

These are all words of three or more syllables; this will enable us to clarify how shorter words are stressed, and how the GSR is incorporated, virtually as a set of 'default' cases, within the RSR. The basic principle is that any subrule that says 'go back one syllable' obviously will not apply if there is no syllable to go back to. This can perhaps be seen most clearly in (39c) above, which stresses light antepenults by default, since any pre-antepenult syllables are invisible to the rule.

The same principle applies to (39a, i). The very existence of monosyllabic words ensures that they will be stressed, since option (39a, ii) is inapplicable. Hence automatic stress on heavy monosyllables like *clerk*, *cost*. Naturally all native monosyllables, both heavy (*see*, *word*) and light (*sit*, *fat*) would also be stressed this way.

Now (39a, i), of course, also assigns final stress to disyllables: *citéé*, *degréé*. That is, any word whose last two syllables show the profile ŏō will receive final stress (once ō is located, anything to the left is irrelevant). This applies then to perhaps the bulk of English monosyllables with unstressable prefixes (*y̆-séyn* 'seen', *bĕ-ráft* 'bereft'). This is a very clear case where the RSR and the GSR, starting from opposed first principles, do precisely the same work. The GSR is 'prefix-blind', so it reaches the final syllable in a string of the shape ŏ-ō by skipping the first; the RSR looks for the closest heavy syllable to the end, and thus accents the same one.

Now to (39b, i). This applies not only to French words like *nătŭrĕ*, *mĕlŏdy̆ĕ*, but to disyllables like *ágĕ*. It also applies, of course, by default to disyllables of the form ŏŏ, like *cătĕl*, *gálŏn*. Hence (39b, ii) covers all native words of the shape ōŏ (*bĕ-hóldĕn*, *kíssĕn*, *nósĕ*), as well as ŏŏ words where OSL did not apply (*bódĭ*, *gáthĕr*).

Finally, (39c). This accents the antepenult of any Romance word ending in -ŏŏ, whether -ōŏŏ like *clóĭstĕrĕr*, or -ŏŏŏ like *báchĕlĕr*. Since Trisyllabic Shortening (2.5.2) had more or less got rid of all native -ōŏŏ sequences, the remaining forms in -ŏŏŏ are covered by this subrule (*lŭvĕdĕ*, *wŭnĕdĕ* 'dwelt'). When, in Late Middle English, final /ə/ was lost (2.5.3), and various endings dropped, the reduced words came under other subcases of the RSR: thus *lŭvĕdĕ* is stressed by (39c), reduced *lŭvĕd* by the default case of (39b).

So the bulk of words originally stressed by the GSR would fall naturally under one or the other subrules of the RSR, which would produce the same stress contour. There is a historical coincidence which makes the fit even neater: since native Germanic roots were never more than three syllables long, and most, due to early unstressed vowel loss (2.5.3) were no more than disyllabic, there were virtually no native (non-compound) words longer than the RSR's three-syllable scope.

But the majority coincidence of the two rules did not mean that establishment of the RSR caused the *de facto* demise of the GSR. To begin with, there were two classes of native words that were still apparently subject to the GSR, since the RSR would produce the wrong contour. These were (a) prefixed light monosyllables like *ў-wĭs* 'certainly', *ă-fĕr* 'afar'; and (b) all forms with heavy (/-VCC/) suffixes, like present participles or gerunds in *-ing*, present second-person singular verbs in *-est*, and the like. The correct contours are *ŏŏ* for group (a) and *ŏ̄ō* for (b), as in *ă-fĕr*, *sĭng-ing*. In order for *a-fer* not to fall under the RSR subcase that produces *cătĕl*, the stress-assignment must skip the prefix: i.e. the GSR in its original morphologically sensitive form must apply. In the second case, the heavy final must not attract stress, so the same GSR principle – no stress on affixes, but only on roots – is still at work.

As usual, there are complications. The co-existence of the two stress rules, as well as the sensitivity of loan words to native processes like vowel reduction and loss, led to a great deal of variation, and numerous doublets. To begin with, many Romance loans apparently existed in two forms: an original type with a heavy final containing a long vowel, and an 'Anglicised' type with the vowel reduced. A typical case is the common Romance suffix *-oun* /-uːn/, which had the weak doublet *-on* /-on/ > /-ən/: *nacioūn* ~ *nacĭŏn*, *bacoūn* ~ *bacŏn*, etc. In these, the RSR alone could produce stress doublets like *băcoūn* ~ *băcŏn* (the first syllable heavy by OSL). In most instances, of course, the more 'native' version survived, as in PDE *bacon, nation*.

It was probably the existence of such doublets that helped to spread – at least in poetic usage – the domain of the RSR to some forms that clearly 'ought not' to be subject to it: in particular it led to the stressing of English suffixes. As early as the thirteenth century (*Floriz and Blauncheflur*) we find rhymes like *þíng*:*habbíng*, 'thing:having', *ríng*:*partíng*; or *tiþínge*:*sínge* 'tiding:sing' (*Owl and Nightingale*, ca 1220). There are even apparent RSR-like shifts of main word stress to the second elements of compounds, and to normally unstressed but not suffixal syllables: *Owl and Nightingale* has *tále*:*niȝtingále* 'debate: nightingale', *answáre*:*báre* 'reply:the open'. Conversely, the GSR could be extended to Romance words, producing initial stress on items with heavy final syllables. A classic case is Chaucer's use of both GSR and RSR versions of the same word in one line (Friar's Tale, *CT* 2:1460):

In *dívērs* art and in *dīvérse* figures.

This potential for doublet formation did not die out with the end of Middle English; as well integrated as the RSR seems to have been, the

GSR continued to exist, at least as a verse option, through the sixteenth and seventeenth centuries. Thus Shakespeare in *Romeo and Juliet*:

1	For *éxile* hath more terror in his look	(III.iii. 13)
2	And turns it to *exíle*, there art thou happy	(III.iii. 140).

GSR stressings of Romance words occur in Marlowe, Milton, Shelley and Byron as well – though of course the later the text, the more likely this is to be solely a poetic option, with no analogue in ordinary speech, rather like nineteenth-century uses of *thou* and *hath*.

2.7   When did Middle English end?

The official remit of this chapter covers developments until the mid-to-late fifteenth century (giving a sensible interpretation to the date 1476, which has iconographic rather than strictly language-historical significance – even more so than 1066). I have stuck, however, throughout the phonology section, mainly to developments up to about 1400. I justify this dereliction on the grounds that the main developments in fifteenth-century phonology are best seen, not as the 'end' of Middle English, but as the 'beginning' of Early Modern: e.g. changes in the vowel system as precursors of the Great Vowel Shift.

There are many changes, such as late vowel lengthenings and shortenings, diphthongisations and monophthongisations, which make little sense as codas to the larger movements I have been describing here, but 'look forward' to later developments. For this reason I will save them for the phonology chapter of volume III, which is a companion-piece to this.

The treatment of morphology, however, will be rather different: for the bulk of the fifteenth-century developments are of a piece with earlier ones, and English morphology by the 1480s is quite a lot more 'modern' looking than its phonology. This is not surprising: there is no reason why an active period in one component of a language's grammatical structure should be as active in others – except, of course, in particular cases where, for instance, phonological developments trigger morphological changes in a fairly direct way.

For this reason Middle English will 'end' rather earlier in the phonological sphere than it does in the morphological; the following volume, which is supposed to begin at 1476, will in fact start three quarters of a century or so earlier in phonology.

2.8   Morphology: general matters

2.8.1   Form and function

The term 'morphology' in these volumes is more or less equivalent to 'accidence' or *Formenlehre* in the handbooks: an account of word-shapes (hence 'morph-'): specifically inflection and related matters. This covers the system of word-level devices (affixes etc.) used by a language for signalling grammatical categories like tense, number, person, and the structure of certain closed paradigmatic sets like personal pronouns.

Inflectional morphology has two broad functions: (a) the actual marking of grammatical categories on words, and (b) establishing 'linkages' of various kinds between items in the sentence or discourse. An example of (a) would be number on nouns (*cat-s* = *cat-* 'plural'); of (b) agreement or concord (*I walk-0* vs *he walk-s*) and government (*I saw him*, not ****I saw he*), as well as anaphora within and beyond the sentence (relation of pronouns to their antecedents).

Morphology is thus something of a 'bridge' or interface between phonology and syntax. The examples above illustrate the syntactic connection (and see below); a simple phonological case would be the change of a morpheme's phonological shape in a particular grammatical environment (*knife* vs *knives* etc.). We will be concerned at a number of points with the interaction of phonological change and the structure of morphological systems (2.8.3, 2.9.1 below). Our main concern, however, will be with the forms themselves and their histories.

A general comment on the syntactic connection might be useful here, as a corrective to the image the handbooks often present of a language's morphology as a set of autonomous forms with no external connection. Morphology in any significant sense really exists only via a complex of dependencies and realisations involving not only syntax and phonology, but semantics as well; an understanding of this will clarify what is really meant by statements about morphological change.

For example, when we say that regular Present-Day English verbs 'have a present third-person singular in *-s*', we actually mean something quite complex and subtle. First, out of the inventory of possible grammatical categories to mark on the verb (tense, number, person, mood, aspect, etc.), English has chosen in this case three: tense, person (third vs all others) and number (singular only in conjunction with third person). As opposed, say, to German, which marks person and number symmetrically throughout the paradigm, or Swedish which marks neither.

Second, a statement like '*walk-s* is the present third-person singular of *walk*' is in the wider sense not about the paradigm of *walk* or any other regular weak verb, but about the language's choice of categories to represent, and the deployment of particular forms in the syntax. *Walk-s* in this perspective is the form the verb takes when the tense of the whole clause is present, the subject is third person and singular, there is no auxiliary (cf. *he can walk-*θ), and the verb is either in a main clause (*he walk-s*), or one of the subordinate clause types that allows tense marking on the verb (*I see (that) he walk-s* vs *I want him [to walk-*θ]).

As an illustration of the kind of context in which the following necessarily word-centred discussion should be seen, consider a simple transitive sentence showing all three relations mentioned so far: realisation of grammatical categories, concord and government:

(40)

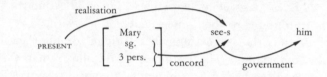

Both the higher sentential feature 'present' and the inherent features of *Mary* trigger -*s*, and the verb *see* triggers *him* rather than *he*. Any of these relations can be involved in historical change; number has ceased to be relevant in English except marginally for present concord on verbs, and government of nouns by verbs has vanished, since now only pronouns are case-marked; yet the situation was once very different (see further 2.9.1.3 below).

2.8.2   English as a morphological type

Languages may be classified by the type of morphology they have; this is relevant here, as the Middle English period saw a speeding up and virtual completion of a major typological change that had already begun in Old English. One traditional classification is based essentially on how much information is carried within the word, as opposed to being spread over or distributed among independent words.

At one extreme are 'isolating' or 'analytic' languages, which have (virtually) no inflectional morphology, but a basic one-category-per-word design, like Vietnamese:

(41) Khi tôi đền nhà bạn tôi, chúng tôi bắt dâu làm bài
     when I   come house friend I   PL   I   begin do   lesson

'When I came to my friend's house, we began to do lessons'

At the other pole are 'synthetic' languages, which incorporate several categories per word, like Kannaḍa:

(42) Saav-annu   taḍeyu-tt-a-de-yee
     death-ACC   stop-pres-3-NEUT-Question

'Does it prevent death?'

Some synthetic languages normally have only one category per morph, like Kannaḍa; these are called agglutinating. Others however pack more than one (often many more) into one morph, so that there are no definite boundaries between categories; these are called inflecting. A good example is Latin:

(43)

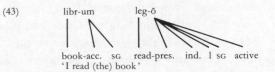

book-acc. SG read-pres. ind. 1 SG active
'I read (the) book'

While few if any languages are perfectly consistent examples of their type, most are predominantly one way or another. Indo-European languages (including Germanic) range from the nearly analytic (Present-Day English, Afrikaans) to the highly synthetic (Latin, Old English). When they are synthetic they are inflecting rather than agglutinating, often with a very complex distribution of categories among the elements of a word. Consider the present and past plural of an Old English strong verb: *rīd-aþ* 'they ride' vs *rid-on* 'they rode':

(44)

The discontinuous stem /r_d/ carries the lexical content of the verb, but both the stem vowel and the ending code tense: *-aþ* is 'present/plural' and *-on* is 'past/plural'. But the past is even more complex: number is marked on the stem vowel as well (cf. past 1, 3 sg. *rād*); and it is even worse for past second-person singular which has the vowel of the past plural plus its own ending:

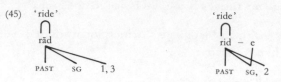

(45) 'ride'   'ride'

There are many ways to mark inflectional categories; the most important, which figure in the development of English to one degree or another, are the following:

1   *Affixation.* Marking grammatical categories by independent (bound) morphemes, attached at either end of the word or in the middle (prefixing, suffixing, infixing). Suffixation has always been the prime Germanic inflectional mode: OE *luf-o-d-on* 'we/they/you pl. loved' = *love* + conjugation marker + past + past/plural. Systematic prefixation is rare in Late Germanic, though in non-compound verbs Old English tended to mark past participles with a prefix *ge-* (along with a suffix: *ge-word-en*, past pple of *weorðan* 'become'). Infixing has never been productive, though there are scattered survivals of an earlier type, like the infixed /n/ in the present stems of certain verbs (OE *sta-n-d-an* 'to stand', past sg. *stōd*, where the stem is /st_d/).

2   *Word-internal change.* Categories signalled by phonological alternations, as in the strong verb (OE *rīdan/rād*, PDE *ride/rode*), or certain noun plurals (OE *mūs/mȳs*, PDE *mouse/mice*). etc. This may be combined with suffixation, as in the examples in (44)–(45).

3   *Suppletion.* Unrelated stems may code grammatical categories within a paradigm: OE *bēon* 'be' with an unrelated past stem (sg. *wæs*, pl. *wǣron*, PDE *be/was/were*, etc.). This may also be combined with suffixation, of course, as above.

Our starting-point, Old English, is a highly synthetic inflecting language. The Middle English evolution consists primarily in a shift towards a more analytic structure, eventually approaching that of today's language, which, except for the pronoun and some residues in the verb and noun, is close to isolating. Not only were distinctions like those between the past singular and plural root vowels of strong verbs lost (2.9.2.2); there was also degrammaticalisation of particular features, e.g. loss of gender, reduction of the three-way number opposition in the pronouns (singular vs dual vs plural) to singular vs plural, loss of case marking, the subjunctive and so on. The most marked characteristic of the evolution of English morphology from the Conquest to about 1500 is a reduction in morphological expressiveness: both the number of categories per word, and the number coded at all.

2.8.3 Modes of morphological change: autonomy and interfacing

Given the broad definition of morphology as anything to do with morpheme shape in inflectional contexts, there are a host of different processes that can affect it. These range from 'accidental' deformation due to purely phonological change, to changes involving both morphology and phonology, to purely morphological/syntactic ones, with no phonological involvement.

Since at one level of analysis morphemes are simply strings of phonemes, any synchronic phonological process or historical change can in principle have morphological implications. This may be quite adventitious: the neutralisation of unstressed vowels in /ə/ has as a spin-off the destruction of morphological distinctions, e.g. in certain noun classes nominative/accusative plural in -u and dative singular in -e collapse in -e (lim-u, lim-e 'limb' > lim-e), and so on.

In another common type of development, originally phonetic alternations may through phonological change take on a morphological function. Thus i-umlaut was originally a purely allophonic process: POE /u:/. for instance, had the allophones [y:] before following [i j], [u:] elsewhere: so *[mu:s] 'mouse', *[my:si] 'mice', phonemically /mu:s, mu:si/. When, however, the following /i/ dropped after heavy root syllables, [u:] and [y:] were no longer allophones of /u:/; the residue [mu:s] vs [my:s] is a minimal pair, and /u:/ and /y:/ are independent phonemes. But because of the original stem shape, the alternation /u:/ ~ /y:/ is now, in the absence of a suffix that could trigger umlaut, the sole plural marker for this noun class: the plural /y:/ in mȳs vs singular /u:/ in mūs is just a fact about 'mouse', as the unchanged vowel and -as ending in the plural are facts about 'house' (hūs, hūs-as). A phonological change has shifted an alternation to a new domain, and made it part of the morphology.

In Old English the umlaut class was already quite small, and has continued to decrease; but in German, when the point was reached where umlaut served as a sole morphological marker, it was extended to forms that could not have had it by regular development, e.g. 'tree', an *a*-stem (OHG *boum*, *boum-e*), now *Baum*, *Bäum-e*. This process, the extension of a morphophonemic alternation outside the class in which it is etymologically justified, comes under the general heading of 'analogy' (cf. the jocular *meese* as plural of *moose*).

There are two main types of morphological analogy, extension and levelling. Extension is the application of a process outside its original domain, like the spread of umlaut in German. To take an English example, the masculine *a*-stem inflection was extended in Late Old English and Early Middle English to many other noun classes: *hous-es*, *wolv-es* are regular descendants of OE *-as* plurals, but *son-s* (OE *sun-a*), *book-s* (OE *bēc*), *name-s* (OE *nama-n*), *hors-es* (OE *hors*) are analogical. By levelling we mean the ironing out of allomorphy within the paradigm; not only do consonant-stem nouns like *book* have a plural ending from another declension; the vocalism of the nominative/accusative/genitive has been extended to all forms, with one vowel for singular and one for plural, instead of the complex Old English system, where dative singular and nominative/accusative plural had one vowel and nominative/accusative singular and genitive/dative plural the other. With this kind of change we move from the phonological to the purely morphological domain: the arena for change is the paradigm itself, regardless of the phonological shapes of particular members.

But changes in paradigm structure, analogical levellings and extensions, are not the only kinds of non-phonological change in morphology. There are others, more closely linked to the syntactic deployment of morphological material, and these have been at least as important. Let us consider two major Middle English developments: (a) the loss of plural concord on the verb; and (b) the loss of the infinitive suffix *-(e)n*. If we think along the lines suggested in the previous section, taking into account the interdependence of morphology and syntax, then we are not really talking about 'loss of the plural marker' or 'loss of the infinitive suffix'. We are talking about changes in rules with a syntactic domain: e.g. the rule 'add *-en* to verbs with plural subjects', or 'add *-en* to verb stems in certain "infinitive" contexts'. The effect, to be sure, is morphological, but the context is syntactic – which explains, as we will see, why these changes were able to take place the way they did.

These two developments furnish a nice example of autonomous, purely morphosyntactic change, because the endings (a) represent

distinct grammatical categories, (b) are phonologically identical, and yet
(c) evolve independently. Their histories will illustrate the characteristic
mechanism by which morphological (and indeed nearly all other)
change occurs.

Through a series of developments that do not strictly concern us
here, it came about in Early Middle English that in the midlands, as far
south as London, the old opposition -*aþ* (pres.) vs -*on* (past) for verb
plurals was levelled under -*en* (or -*n* after vowel-final stems) for both
tenses. Thus *luv-en*, *luv-ed-en*, OE *luf-aþ*, *luf-od-on*. In the south, which
will be marginally relevant below, -*eþ* was the chosen ending for present
plural, and -*en* for past. The infinitive suffix -*an* also became -*en* by
neutralisation of unstressed vowels (2.5.3).

The history of these two categories from about 1250–1450 shows a
common tendency to loss; but they evolve independently, the infinitive
ending beginning to drop later but picking up speed until it outruns the
plural. The data here consists of a group of roughly 5,000-word samples
of relatively formal prose texts, one very early, to show the twelfth-
century state of play, the rest rather late, catching the changes in full
flight.

(46) *Peterborough Chronicle* (1127, 1131, 1137: Bennett & Smithers 1966)
      Verb plural: -Ø   -(V)n   Infinitive: -Ø   -(V)n
         N =   5   102   N =   0   48
         % = 4·7   95·3   % =   0   100

(47) Chaucer, *Treatise on the Astrolabe*, part I (1391–2; Robinson 1957)
      Verb plural: -Ø   -(V)n   -(V)þ   Infinitive: -Ø   -(V)n
         N = 10   49   4   N = 28   22
         % = 15·9 77·8   6·3   % = 56   44

The Chaucer text, coming from London, shows traces of southern -*eþ*
as well as midland -*en*; this pattern will continue in the rest of the texts,
which also have a London provenance.

(48) *Ordenances of the Grocers' Company* (1418: Chambers & Daunt 1931)
      Verb plural: -Ø   -(V)n   -(V)þ   Infinitive: -Ø   -(V)n
         N = 29   31   1   N = 33   11
         % = 47·5 50·8   1·7   % = 75   25

(49) Caxton, prologues and epilogues (1473/4–77)
      Verb plural: -Ø   -(V)n   -(V)þ   Infinitive: -Ø   -(V)n
         N = 49   18   1   N = 118   2
         % = 72   26·5   1·5   % = 98·3   1·7

Conflating the two marked plural types, the broad picture is (percentages rounded off):

(50) *Percentages of marked plurals and infinitives 1140–1480*

	Verb plural		Infinitive	
	Unmarked	Marked	Unmarked	Marked
ca 1140	5	95	0	100
ca 1390	16	84	56	44
ca 1420	48	52	75	25
ca 1480	72	28	98	2

Marked ~ unmarked variation in the infinitive has reached roughly 50:50 by the late fourteenth century; this ratio is not attained by the verb plural until well into the fifteenth. But by this time unmarked infinitives outnumber marked by 3:1. When the verb plural reaches this stage towards the end of the century, there is only a negligible remnant of infinitive marking. A closer examination of the actual texts, however, will display still other dimensions: of the eighteen marked infinitives in the Caxton sample, nearly 79 per cent are forms of the verb *be*; the other three consist of one instance each of a marked infinitive of *do, say, write*. So it is not only the numbers that are of interest; there is lexical involvement as well, in that the largest part of the marking residue is on one (frequent and common) verb, and none of the less common ones are marked at all. The same lexical dimension (and the same verb) is relevant to the plural: 88 per cent of the forms of *be* with plural subjects in the sample are marked, as against an overall marking frequency of 28 per cent. Morphological change, like phonological, proceeds through the lexicon by diffusion.

Speakers of modern 'codified' standard languages are unlikely to be familiar with this kind of grammatical variation; the 'normal' situation to us is that morphological rules either apply or not: there is no choice between *he walks* and *he walk*. This is simply a function of the fact that English happens not to be undergoing any change in this area at the moment: there was a time when standard speakers varied between *he walketh* and *he walks*, and the same was true of the verb plural and infinitive in Middle English. It might be of interest to look at a sample of variation *in situ*, rather than just at the numbers; a passage from the *Peterborough Chronicle* for 1137 will serve:

> Me *henged* bi the þumbes other bi the hefed, & *hengen* bryniges on her fet. Me *dide* cnotted strenges abuton hire hæued, and *uurythen* it ðat it gæde to þe hærnes.

('They/one *hung* (them) by the thumbs or by the head, and *hung* corselets on their feet. They/one *put* knotted strings about their head(s), and *twisted* it so that it penetrated to the brains.')

The indefinite pronoun *me* (< *man*) seems to be ambiguous as to number, though in fact singular in form. And it appears to 'attract' concord to singular, while the verbs further away take their endings from the sense of *me* as a collective. But other cases are not explicable this way:

Þa *namen* hi þa men þe hi *wenden* ðat ani god *hefden* ... and *diden* heom in prisun, and *pined* hem ...

('Then they *took* the men that they *thought had* any property ... and *put* them in prison, and *tortured* them ...')

Sumi hi *diden* in crucethus ... and *dide* scærpe stanes þerinne, & *þrengde* þe man þærinne, ðat him *bræcon* alle þe limes.

('Some they *put* in (the) torture-box ... and *put* sharp stones therein, and *thrust* the man inside, so that all his limbs *broke*.')

There seems to be a 'softening' of concord, particularly in situations where the first verb in a series carries plural marking; note that the plural marker returns when the subject changes. Certainly the categorical Old English concord rule is becoming variable.

About three centuries later the variation is much more striking, and begins – within any given portion of text – to look random (though historically it has been cumulative in a particular direction). A short extract from the *Grocers' Company Ordenances* (1418) illustrates variation in both our categories in a discourse context (plurals in *italics*, infinitives in small CAPITALS; <y, e> = /ə/):

And whan eny of the Brothyrhode *dyen* in London the Maystres that *ben* for the ʒer *shul* DON her Bedel to WARN hem in what clotyng they *schull* COMYN to the dirige ... And tho that *fayle paye* xijd.

(Chambers & Daunt 1931: 199)

The complex patterning will be clearer if we take just one construction type from this text as a whole: plural subject + 'shall' + infinitive. We find *schall comen* (two instances), *shall comyn*, *schullen comen*; *schull ben*, *schull be* (four instances), *schall haue*, *schull nought auentour*, *schull chesyn* ('choose'), *schall ofyr*, *shul don*, *schull constreyn*. Out of fifteen instances, only one marks both plural and infinitive; five have no marking at all. (Note also the variation in the plural vowel of *shall*, showing another ongoing restructuring: six with the old singular vowel extended to the plural (< OE *sceal*), the rest keeping /u/ (< OE *sculon*).)

2.8.4   *Middle English morphophonemics*

A morphophonemic alternation involves distinctive segments (or distinctive segments and zero) in a morphological context (see 2.8.3). At a given historical stage, some morphophonemic alternations will be synchronically productive (i.e. apply to (virtually) all forms of the appropriate shape, and to new ones); others will be non-productive residues of earlier productive types. So in Present-Day English the alternations in the shape of the plural suffix (/-s ~ -z ~ -ız/ in *cats*, *dogs*, *fishes*), while dating from Late Middle English (2.4.1.1, 2.5.3), are still fully productive: any new word takes the appropriate allomorph (cf. *sputnik-s*, *sauna-s*, *calabash-es*). Whereas the alternations based on the old Trisyllabic Shortening rule (2.5.2), like /aɪ/ ~ /ɪ/ in *divine/divinity*, *sign/signify* are residual: new formations of the apparently appropriate type usually fail to show them (the adjective *Bernsteinian* has stressed /aɪ/, not /ɪ/). Most of the morphophonemic alternations we have evidence for in Middle English are of this type, relics of old processes that were productive in Old or earliest Middle English.

Five major groups of morphophonemic alternations show up in Middle English inflectional morphology, only two of which are not of Old English date:

1 *Ablaut*. Old English had a complex (already residual, but in the relevant categories quite systematic) set of vowel alternations, stemming from formerly productive Indo-European processes that usually go under this name. The primary manifestation was in the shape of the tense/number forms in the strong verb classes, i.e. sets like class I /i: ~ ɑ: ~ i ~ i/ (*rīdan/rād/ridon/-riden*) or class IV /e ~ æ ~ æ: ~ o/ (*beran/bær/bǣron/-boren*), etc. This system began to deteriorate in Early Middle English, and while it remained in principle in the strong verb, it lost much of its regular structure. I will discuss this more fully in 2.9.2.2 below, in reference to the evolution of the strong verb.

2 *Umlaut*. The *i*-umlaut alternations were highly productive in Old English, more so perhaps in derivation than inflection (e.g. de-adjectival verbs were commonly formed by umlaut of the adjectival stem vowel:

trum 'strong', *trymman* 'strengthen', etc.). In inflection, certain umlaut-related alternations in the verb conjugation (*brūcan* 'use', pres. 3 sg. *brȳcþ*, and the like) were lost early; but umlaut survived in noun plurals and certain adjective comparisons. The class of umlaut plurals decreased during Middle English, but as late as Chaucer we still have *goos/gees*, *tooþ/teeþ* and the like, as well as *goot/geet* 'goat(s)', and *broþer/breþren*, *cow/keen* (the latter two with an extra weak plural). Other umlaut nouns like *book*, *nut* went over to the *a*-stem declension early. Umlaut also remains through most of Middle English in comparisons: Chaucer has *long/leng-er/leng-est*, *old/eld-er/eld-est* and a number of others.

3 *Fricative voicing.* The Old English allophonic alternations [f ~ v, θ ~ ð, s ~ z] (2.4.1.1) were phonologised in Middle English, and constituted part of a widely distributed morphophonemic system, major relics of which still survive. Taking examples from Chaucer, as representative of the later Middle English incipient standard, we find voicing alternations in the following main contexts:

(a) *Noun singular vs plural*: *elf/elves*, similarly *half*, *knyf*, *leef*, *lyf*, *staf*, *theef*, *wyf*; probably also in *hous*, *ooth* 'oath', but there is no orthographic evidence. There has also been some extension to new forms, as in *laxatyf*, pl. *laxatyves*. The adjective *leef/lief* 'dear' shows the same pattern in comparative and superlative: *levere*, *levest*, but this is not generally the case with other adjectives.

(b) *Present vs past in verbs*: In strong verbs with fricative-final stems, the environment for the voicing alternation appears: *delve(n)/dalf* 'dig', *sterve(n)/starf* 'die', *kerve(n)/karf* 'carve', *weve(n)/waf* 'weave', *heve(n)/haf* 'heave', *yeven/yaf* 'give'. The same thing occurs (with the voiceless form before a consonant) in some weak verbs as well, e.g. *leve(n)/left(e)*, *reve(n)/reft(e)* 'rob' (here with length alternation as well: see 4, below). In later times these alternations were ironed out in strong verbs that became weak (*starve/starved*, similarly *carve*, *delve*); or the consonantism of the present was levelled to the past (*give/gave*, *weave/wove*).

4 *Length alternations.* The complex of processes, grouped in 2.5.2 as the length and quantity conspiracies, left a considerable morphophonemic residue. The most important cases are:

(a) Originally short-stemmed adjectives showing long vowel allomorphs in OSL environments: e.g. *blăk*, *glăd*, *smăl* rhyming in Chaucer with *băk, adrăd, ăll* (Late OE /a/), but inflected *blāk-e, glād-e, smāl-e* rhyming with *māke, māde, tāle* with lengthened /aː/.

(b) Originally long-stemmed adjectives with gemination in the comparative and superlative showing Pre-Cluster Shortening: *greet* 'great'/*gretter*, similarly *reed* 'red', *whit* 'white', *hoot* 'hot', *late*. (The old short-vowel comparative of *late* has been lexicalised as a separate form, *latter*, with new analogical *later/latest*.)

(c) Pre-Cluster Shortening in the pasts of long-stemmed weak verbs: *feed/fĕdde, spēde(n)/spĕdde, mēte(n)/mĕtte*, etc.; likewise strong verbs that became weak (*slēpe(n)/slĕpte, wēpe(n)/wĕpte*). Some of these verbs were 'regularised' later: e.g. Chaucer has *grĕtte* as the past of *grete(n)*, as opposed to PDE *greeted*. (And cf. *lēve(n)/lĕfte* under 3(c) above.)

5 /ə/ ~ θ. These are of two main types:

(a) Alternations stemming from an Old English prohibition of sequences of two vowels back to back, where the first is strong and the second weak: already in Old English there were (variably) monosyllabic 'contract' verbs of the type *dōn* 'do' < */doː-an/, *slēan* 'slay' < */slæax-an* < slæx-an/, as opposed to the more usual disyllabic types like *ber-an, dēm-an*. The same alternation occurred with vowel-initial suffixes of other kinds: *bēoþ* vs *dēm-eþ*. This continued through Middle English, as we can tell by spelling and metrical practice: *been, doon* are metrical monosyllables, as opposed to *beer-en, deem-en*.

(b) Alternations stemming from /ə/-deletion in weak position in Middle English. In Present-Day English the two most striking cases are deletion of weak vowels in noun plurals (*cat-s, dog-s* as opposed to the earlier *catt-es, dogg-es*), and in weak-verb pasts (*walk-ed* /wɔːkt/). The vowel is of course retained where its deletion would produce an illegal cluster (see 2.5.3), as in *fish-es, wound-ed*. In the late fourteenth century these alternations had not been institutionalised, though deletion was an option; in the first 500-odd lines of the General Prologue to the *Canterbury Tales*, for instance, out of a total of 68 -(*e*)*s* plurals where /ə/ could have been deleted, the metre shows retention in 48 and deletion in 20, with deletion clearly favoured in polysyllabic nouns. Verbal pasts apparently remained variable much longer than plurals: well into the Early Modern period -*ed* could be pronounced (certainly in verse) in cases where it is now impossible (and there are scattered survivals of syllabic suffixes, sometimes with a semantic distinction, as in *learnèd* (adj) vs *learned* (past).

2.9   Morphology: the major syntactic classes

2.9.1   *The noun phrase*

2.9.1.1   Categories, paradigms and concord: the noun

The received wisdom is that Old English nouns 'were inflected for case, number and gender', or 'had three genders, four cases and two numbers'. This is globally true, but in detail just false enough to make the post-Old English developments explicable. This is not as para-doxical as it sounds: while the categories of gender, number and case were real enough, it was virtually impossible for any single noun form to be uniquely marked for all three (not so for determiners and pronouns: see 2.9.1.2–3). To illustrate this, and set the scene for the following discussion, it would be useful to review the inflection of the major Old English noun classes, so we can see what kind of system formed the input to Middle English. In the sections that follow I use the traditional stem-class names for the declensions (for details see vol. I, ch. 3 or any handbook). A name like '*a*-stem' means that in Proto-Germanic there was a thematic vowel */ɑ/ normally intercalated between the stem and the case/number ending: so the *a*-stem masculine *stān* 'stone' goes back to */stɑin-ɑ-z/ (nom. sg.), as opposed to the *u*-stem *sunu* 'son' < */sun-u-z/ or the *i*-stem masculine *cyre* 'choice' < */kur-i-z/. Most of these distinctions are already opaque in historical Old English, but they are useful cover terms for the declensions.

Here are the case/number endings of some of the most important noun types:

(51)

		a-stem (masc.)	*a*-stem (neut.)	*ō*-stem (fem.)	*u*-stem (masc.)
Singular	nom.	-θ	-θ	-u	-u
	gen.	-es	-es	-e	-a
	dat.	-e	-e	-e	-a
	acc.	-θ	-θ	-e	-u
Plural	nom.	-as	-u	-a/-e	-a
	gen.	-a	-a	-a/-ena	-a
	dat.	-um	-um	-um	-um
	acc.	-as	-u	-a/-e	-a

		i-stem (fem.)	n-stem (masc.)	Consonant-stem (masc.)
Singular	nom.	-∅	-a	-∅
	gen.	-e	-an	-es
	dat.	-e	-an	¨-∅
	acc.	-∅	-an	-∅
	nom.	-e/-a	-an	¨-∅
	gen.	-a	-ena	-a
	dat.	-um	-um	-um
	acc.	-e/-a	-an	¨-∅

Neuter a-stems were endingless in nominative/accusative plural if they had heavy stems; the same was true for nominative singular ō-stems, i-stems and u-stems (see 2.5.3 for details). The notation '¨-∅' = umlaut of stem vowel + zero.

It is clear from (51) that some Old English noun endings were uniquely recognisable as belonging to a particular case/number category: anything in -um is a dative plural, anything in -es is a genitive singular (and not feminine). But most of the endings were multiply ambiguous: -an marked all oblique n-stem forms except genitive/dative plural, -u could be nominative singular of feminine ō-stems, of light u-stems, nominative/accusative plural of light neuter a-stems. And -e is the worst: in the subset of paradigm-types shown here it marks no less than ten possible case/number/declension combinations. So while Old English indeed 'had a rich noun morphology' in the sense that there were a lot of endings, this morphology was relatively inexpressive and ambiguous. Certain endings were, however, more closely tied to particular categories (which has implications for later developments): e.g. -as could only be a plural, -es only a genitive singular; while -e, despite its many functions, was still the dative singular ending par excellence.

Such a situation was ripe for analogical remodelling; indeed, in Old English times there was already quite a lot going on. Some u-stems and i-stems had already taken masculine a-stem genitive singular in -es etc. (To get a good idea of the extent of variation, see the endings listed for nouns in a comprehensive Old English grammar like Campbell 1959.) Without going into more detail for the moment, it should be clear that the masculine a-stems play a crucial role in the subsequent history.

In principle, twenty-four Old English noun categories should be distinguishable (four cases × two numbers × three genders). But to make them there was only an inventory of nine devices: zero, umlaut, and the endings -*u*, -*a*, -*e*, -*an*, -*um*, -*as*, -*es*. Levelling of unstressed vowels had brought this about by classical Old English times. Even this restricted system was eroded by later phonological changes. Two in particular, collapse of weak vowels in -*e* /ə/ and merger of final /m/ and /n/ in weak syllables (2.5.3, 2.4.2.1) reduced the inventory still further in Early Middle English; and with loss of /ə/, it was even further reduced in Late Middle English. Schematically:

(52)   Old English   Early Middle English   Late Middle English

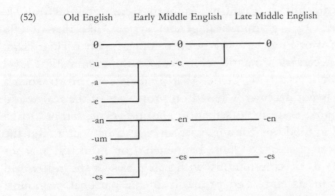

Phonological change 'forced' some restructuring of the morphology simply by eroding distinctions. The movement of English towards a more analytic type was supported by purely phonological developments, in principle unrelated to the morphology. The fact that Old English was a suffixing language simply put the bulk of its morphological markers in vulnerable positions.

But mere phonological erosion does not explain how case and gender as concordial categories disappeared. Even if the morphology of the noun itself was relatively inexpressive, there was much clearer case and gender marking elsewhere in the NP, e.g. on determiners and adjectives (see below and 2.9.1.2), and of course on anaphoric pronouns. There was in fact a deeper semantic/grammatical motivation of a rather complex kind.

To take gender first: even if it was in some sense inherent to nouns (*dæg*, *stān* simply 'are masculine', *giefu* 'gift' simply 'is feminine'), there is in most cases nothing in the form of the noun itself to indicate it. Gender may be a covert noun category; overtly it is realised only in concord and anaphora, i.e. the main signal of gender in Old English texts is the concordial relation between a noun and its modifiers and anaphors. (The same is true to a large extent of case, and even of number – e.g. in nouns with zero plurals, whose number is interpretable only from context, either semantic or grammatical.) Old English grammar is to a large degree built on this principle: the richest and most distinctive marking for nominal categories is on determiners, in the strong adjective declension (2.9.1.2) and in pronouns (2.9.1.3). This means that 'loss of gender' (or of case) is not coterminous with the erosion of noun endings; its domain is the whole NP, and to some extent even larger contexts like the sentence or text.

The historical shift in English has been from 'grammatical' to 'natural' gender. In a grammatical gender system, like that of Old English, German or French, every noun belongs to a particular class, which has no necessary semantic reference; on the grammatical level gender is simply a classifying device that predicts concord. In such a system gender is not necessarily based on properties of the real-world denotata of nouns: there is no semantic reason for *stān* 'stone' to be masculine, and a good one for *wīf* 'woman' *not* to be neuter. But the terms of the classificatory system happened (for historical reasons irrelevant here) to be coterminous with categories in the real-world referential system, as embodied primarily in the personal pronouns. Gender and sex (though one is grammatical and the other semantic) were expressed in the same vocabulary, so that conflicts could arise. To illustrate:

(53)   (a) Non-conflicting

	cyning 'king'	*cwēn* 'queen'	*scip* 'ship'
Gender	masculine	feminine	neuter
Sex	masculine	feminine	neuter

(b) Conflicting

	stān 'stone'	*duru* 'door'	*wīf* 'woman'	*wīfmann* 'woman'
Gender	masculine	feminine	neuter	masculine
Sex	neuter	neuter	feminine	feminine

Middle English saw a shift towards a system in which sex (or the lack of it) became the primary or sole determinant; objects that are male or female in the real world tend to attract masculine or feminine concords and pronouns; all other objects (concrete or abstract) are sexless or neuter (in the etymological sense of 'neither one nor the other'). There was a major change in the language's category space:

(54)

Old English

Middle English

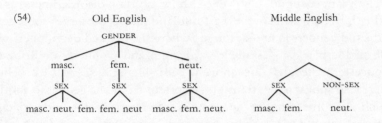

This did not come about through simple restructuring; it was rather the result of gradual relaxation of purely grammatical constraints. So, for instance, as Old English proceeded, there was a tendency for grammatical gender to weaken the further an anaphor was from its governing noun, e.g. if there was a gender conflict, a pronoun in a conjoined or subordinate clause would tend to agree with the natural gender of the noun, while agreement within the original NP would be in grammatical gender. So, for instance, in the Old English Gospel of Luke (1:59) the neuter *cild* 'child' (with male reference) appears in one clause with the neuter determiner *þæt*, and in a following conjunct is referred to by the masculine pronouns *hyne*, *his* (perhaps assisted by the topic of the discourse, circumcision):

> Þa on þam ehteoðan dæge hi comon *þæt cild* ymbsniðan, and nemdon *hyne his* fæder naman Zachariam.

> ('Then on the eighth day they came to circumcise the child, and called him by his father's name, Zacharias.')

Given this early conflict between two types of gender assignment, we can see the subsequent history as a cumulative weighting of 'decisions' in favour of natural gender – aided by decreasing distinctiveness of gender marking on those word classes that could carry the concordial information needed to sustain grammatical gender (articles and adjectives).

Like many major structural simplifications in English, gender loss began in the north; there are fluctuations as early as the tenth-century Lindisfarne Gospels, where, for instance, *endung* 'ending' appears as masculine (abstract nouns in -*Vng* are historically feminine), and *stān* 'stone' is both masculine and neuter. By around 1200 the old system is in considerable disrepair in most dialects, and except in Kent the shift to natural gender was pretty well complete by the end of the century.

The changeover does, however, show a certain disorderliness; as late as the thirteenth century the west midland dialect preserves some traces of the old genders in non-sex items where the marked determiners were still distinctive: e.g. 'assailede...*þen* toun and wonne *him*' (Robert of Gloucester, cited by Mustanoja (1960: 44), and see 2.9.1.2 below). There also appear to be 'transfers' of nouns from one gender to another, which to some scholars suggests a retention of the old principle, distorted by contact with French and Latin. Mustanoja (1960: 45ff.) argues that nouns denoting non-persons are often non-neuter, but have a gender corresponding to that of their French or Latin translation equivalents, not to Old English. So 'moon' (OE *mōna*, masc.) often takes *she*, *her* in pronominal reference, and 'sun' (OE *sunne*, fem.) often takes *he*, *him*; this he traces to Lat. *luna*, F *lune* (fem.), Lat. *sol*, F *soleil* (masc.). Again, 'ship' is often feminine (OE *scip*, neut. but F *nef*, fem.), and so on.

This is probably a mistaken interpretation; such cases do not represent grammatical gender in the usual sense any more than PDE *she* for ships does. They are not structurally 'linguistic' at all, but rather quite predictable personifications with clear extralinguistic models. To an educated medieval speaker with the usual knowledge of classical mythology, it would be natural to associate the moon with Diana and the sun with Phoebus; just as the feminine reference of 'church' (OE *cyrice*, fem.) is a natural association to the Church as Bride of Christ, or the Beloved in Canticles (which Mustanoja admits for this example, if not for the others). Such supposed gender survivals are the result of 'literary' decisions about appropriate personification, not relics of a grammatical system (see Mausch 1986).

The erosion of case marking on the noun goes hand in hand with restructuring of the declensional system, and the ultimate takeover by the masculine *a*-stems. No Old English nouns had more than six distinct forms for the eight case/number categories (nominative/genitive/dative/accusative × singular/plural); though the definite determiners made rather finer distinctions (in non-neuters the nominative/accusative opposition was maintained by *sě* vs *þone* (masc.), *sēo* vs *þā* (fem.)). But given the available noun endings and their natural developments (see (52)), it is clear that if any distinctions were to be maintained, the natural candidates would be the few likely to remain phonetically stable and perceptually salient, i.e. the *-as/-es* of the *a*-stems, and the *-an* of the *n*-stems. It was the former that won.

The *a*-stem declension had certain built-in advantages. Aside from the stability of the endings, it was the commonest noun type, and was already in Old English the target for analogical modification of other declensions. But the remodelling was not simply a migration of other nouns into the *a*-stem declension; there was a change in paradigm structure. By the end of the Middle English period, only two parameters were normally marked: singular vs plural, and non-genitive (often called 'common case') vs genitive. At first, there was a tendency to retain the *-e* of the dative singular, and extend the *-es* ending to all plurals, genitive and non-genitive, keeping the original genitive singular as well; later, with loss of /ə/, the dative singular vanished (it had in fact been variable from as early as the twelfth century). Taking 'stone' as an example, the sequence is:

(55)

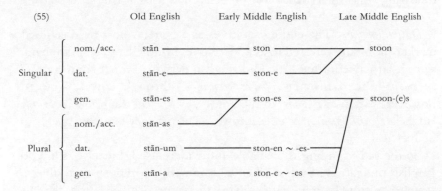

The *Ormulum* illustrates the Early Middle English state of play. This is a particularly useful text because its metrical rigidity allows us to determine whether any given final *-e* (not in hiatus: see 2.5.3) is pronounced, or is an orthographic decoration. The general state of the noun paradigm can be described as follows (based on the extracts in Dickins & Wilson 1956; Bennett & Smithers 1966, and in their discussion at xxiii ff.):

1 *Plurals.* Most nouns, of whatever historical class, have masculine *a*-stem *-es* for all cases: original *-as* plurals like *clut-ess* 'clouts' < *clūt-as*, *enggless* 'angels', as well as old zero-plural neuters like *word-ess* 'words', feminine *e*-plurals like *sinn-ess* 'sins'. There are also some weak plurals (*eʒh-ne* 'eyes') and umlaut plurals (*menn*). There is variability as well: the original types *word* and *sinn-e* also occur, showing that the new plural paradigm has not been fully established (as it still had not two centuries later – though the exceptions are fairly marginal).

There is virtually no case distinction in the plural: we find -ess in prepositional constructions that would take dative in Old English (*amang Goddspelless word-ess*) as well as genitives (*ʒer-ess, menn-ess*). Some genitive plurals, however, maintain relics of the old -*a* ending, especially feminines (*sawl-e* 'souls'' < *sāwl-a*), and some are variable (*neddre streon* ~ *neddr-ess* 'generation of vipers' < OE *nǣddr-a*).

2 *Genitive singular*. Virtually all in -*ess*, both original (*flæsh-ess* 'flesh's') and other types (e.g. feminines like *Marʒ-ess* 'Mary's', *bok-ess* 'book's'). Some feminines retain -*e*, particularly *sawl-e* (as in the plural). The old synthetic genitive, however, varies extensively with the new analytic *of-*genitive (*þe lannd off ʒerrsalæm* vs *Dauiþþ kingess chesstre*); the noun following *of* normally takes the 'prepositional' case form (see 3 below).

3 *Dative singular*. The ending -*e* serves as a general post-prepositional marker (normally referred to as a 'dative' in Middle English grammars, since it largely continues the Old English dative); *o lifft-e* 'in the air', *i an cribbe-e* 'in a manger', *þurrh trowwþ-e* 'through truth'. This is, however, variable: *i...hus* 'in the house', *on boc* 'on the book', *o þe lifft* 'in the air', *till þatt...tun* 'to that town'. The primary control appears to be metrical.

So the old -*e* ending is available and widely used, but not as in Old English obligatory: both marked and unmarked prepositional objects seem to be equally grammatical. Note that a metrical variation like this (especially where one of the variants is innovative) must be assumed to have its basis in speech: poetic 'deviations' from normal spoken usage are usually, at least in premodern times, conservative. Hence Orm is capitalising on available spoken variation, suggesting that /ə/-deletion is already active (if variable and morphologically controlled: plural -*e* does not delete except in hiatus) in the twelfth century (see 2.5.3). The fact that prepositional-case singular -*e* can delete freely but not plural -*e* suggests that number is already the most important parameter in the nominal inflection system, with (non-genitive) case reduced to an 'option'.

4 *Accusative singular*. There are still relics of the feminine accusative singular in -*e*, as in *icc hafe don þiss ded-e* 'I have done this deed' (OE nom. sg. *dǣd*, acc *dǣd-e*), *icc hafe wennd...Goddspelles hallʒhe lar-e* 'I have translated...(the) Gospel's holy lore' (OE *lār, lār-e*).

By the end of the twelfth century, generalising roughly over all dialects, we have a massive reduction of noun paradigm types. Aside from minor categories like umlaut nouns and zero plurals, there are two major declensions, which we can call (following Bennett & Smithers 1966: xxii) A and B. A is a modified continuation of the old masculine *a*-stems; B derives from the feminine *ō*-stems and certain weak *n*-stems. Examples would be *ston* and *tunge*:

(56)

		Type A		Type B	
Singular {	common	ston		all cases	tung-e
	genitive	ston-es			
Plural		all cases	ston-es	all cases	tung-en/tung-es

The type B plural derives either from *n*-stem *-un* or *a* stem *-as*; the singular comes from the collapse of *-e/-u* in *-e*. In the south there was a stronger tendency to retain the *-en* type, and even to extend it (see below); the modern standard retains only original weak *ox-en* (OE nom. sg. *oxa*, ME *oxe*) and the hybrid *childr-en*, but earlier London shows considerable southern influence, and Chaucer, as we will see, has quite a few other weak plurals.

Skipping over two centuries of development essentially along the lines just sketched out, we can take Chaucer's as an example of a typical Late Middle English noun system. Following the study in Sandved (1985), we can characterise his system as follows:

1 *Plurals.* The dominant form is *-(e)s* ($\sim$ *-is/-ys*), with *-e-/ə/* dropped after vowel-final stems (see 2.5.3, 2.8.4), and often in polysyllabic words: *book-es, soul-es, tree-s, herte-s, argument(e)s*. There appear to be no *-e* plurals (not surprising, since final /ə/ was only optionally retained, mainly in conservative styles). The weak plural class is larger than at present: *oxe-n* as expected, *eye-n/ye-n* 'eyes' < OE *ēag-an*. There are also shifts from other declensions like *doughtr-en*, as well as nouns varying between *-n* and *-s*: *foo-n/-s* 'foes', *bee-n/-s* 'bees', *shoo-n/-s* 'shoes'. This group includes both original *-n* plurals ('bee') and *-s* plurals ('foe', 'shoe'): the analogy could go in either direction.

The usual umlaut plurals are present (*teeth, feet*), as is the double umlaut + -*n keen* for *cow* (OE *cū/cӯ*). The zero plural is used not only for *deer, sheep, swine* and the like, but others that have since gone over to *-(e)s*: *hors, yeer, thyng, wynter* (all with *-s* doublets); zero also extends to some French loans, like *ca(a)s*, 'cases', *vers* 'verses'.

2 *Genitive singular*. Normally -(*e*)*s*, as in Present-Day English (*kyng-es*, *herte-s*); a few zero genitives occur, representing either historical -*e* (*his lady grace*) or zero (*my fader soule*); classical names in /s/ may also take zero, as they often still do (*Venus sone*).

3 *Dative/prepositional singular*. This has virtually disappeared; there are only a few post-prepositional -*e*, almost exclusively at line ends in verse: *in hond-e*, *to ship-e*; both marked and unmarked forms can be seen in the phrase *fro yer to yeer-e*.

So except for some marginal remnants of old zero genitives and dative -*e*, and a somewhat different distribution of certain lexical items among the noun classes, the late fourteenth-century system is essentially the same as today's.

2.9.1.2 Articles and adjectives

The Old English equivalent of the definite article was a fully inflected deictic ('demonstrative') adjective/pronoun, quite elaborately marked for case, number and gender:

(57)	Singular			Plural
	Masculine	Neuter	Feminine	(all genders)
Nominative	sĕ	þæt	sēo	þā
Genitive	þæ-s	þæ-s	þǣ-re	þā-ra
Dative	þǣ-m	þǣ-m	þǣ-re	þǣ-m
Accusative	þo-ne	þæt	þā	þā

Nowhere among the ten distinct forms, interestingly, is there a reasonable ancestor for the later Middle and Present-Day English definite article *the*. Old English had a relative particle *þe*, but this is (semantically and grammatically) an unlikely source. Perhaps the most plausible origin is analogical levelling of initial *þ*- throughout the paradigm (masc. nom. sg. *sĕ* and fem. nom. sg. *sēo* are the only forms in *s*-). Indeed *þe* for masculine nominative singular appears as early as the tenth century (~ *se* in the Mercian portion of the Rushworth Gospels, and about the same time in Northumbrian texts). The movement towards invariable *þe*, at least in the singular, can be seen in the *Peterborough Chronicle*. The earlier portion, written before 1132, has *se* ~ *þe*, but the final continuation (1132–55) has only *þe* for singular and *þa* for plural (all cases). As in the noun, number stabilizes early as the main inflectional category.

Loss of inflection is earliest in the east and north, the south and west generally remaining more conservative. As late as the thirteenth century we still find inflected article forms in southern and western texts, though there is virtually no trace in the east after 1150 of anything except number concord. So from the southwest midlands (*The Fox and the Wolf*, late thirteenth century) *He…þene vox i-herde* 'he heard the (masc. acc. sg.) fox', and Laȝamon's *Brut* (Cotton MS, ca 1250) has among others masculine genitive singular (*þes…kinges*), dative singular (*æfter þan flode*), and a distinct feminine dative (*þare æðelan Ælienor* 'to the noble Eleanor'). Forms like this also appear in London in the thirteenth century: the essentially southwestern Proclamation of Henry III (1258) has *þurȝ þan…rædesmen* 'through the counsellors', *ouer al þære kuneriche* 'over all the kingdom' (here, interestingly, fem. *þære* modifies an old neuter). And in highly conservative Kent, there are traces of masculine accusative singular as late as 1340 (the *Ayenbite of Inwit* has *nymþ þane viss* 'he takes the fish').

By the fourteenth century in general, however, invariable *þe/the* is normal for all singular gender/case categories, and plural *þo* is on the wane. Chaucer and Gower have only *þe/the*, (*þo(o)*, however, remaining as a plural demonstrative: see below).

The history of the deictic *this/these* vs *that/those* system is similar to that of the article (and the adjective). Even though the origins lie in an Old English system that was pronominal as much as it was adjective- or determiner-like, I treat them here because of the similarity in concord to the article, and the fact that the old neuter article *þæt* was incorporated into the new system.

The semantics of the Old English opposition between the proto-definite article *sē/sēo/þæt* and the 'emphatic' demonstrative *þes/þis/þēos* are not entirely clear; *se* could often translate well as 'this' and *þes* as 'the'. Generally, however, the sense of *þes* inclined more to the deictic than merely specifying, and this tendency became stronger in Middle English. Old English did not have a grammaticalised proximal/distal (speaker-centred vs non-speaker-centred) contrast, as with PDE *this* vs *that*. The original paradigm was:

(58)

		Singular		Plural
	Masculine	Neuter	Feminine	(all genders)
Nominative	þĕs	þis	þēos	þās
Genitive	þiss-es	þiss-es	þiss-e	þiss-a
Dative	þiss-um	þiss-um	þiss-e	þiss-um
Accusative	þiss-ne	þis	þās	þās

These inflections decayed more or less in tandem with those of the article; most case-marked forms are lost by the thirteenth century, though conservative texts that retain gender have fuller paradigms. *Ancrene Wisse* (southwest midlands, thirteenth century) has *þes king*, *þis scheld* 'shield', *þeos leafdi* 'lady', acc. *þisne swikedom* 'treachery'. A little later, *þis* (neut. nom./acc. sg.) is generalised in the north for singular, *þes* in the south, later replaced by *þis* as well. From these, a new plural type *þes-e/þis-e* (with *-e* presumably from the adjective plural: see below) was formed. In early texts *þos/þas* was used for plural; after the thirteenth century it was generally replaced by *þes-e*, and *þis-e* disappears during the fifteenth century.

After the twelfth century the old neuter nominative/accusative singular article *þat* begins to emerge with a clear distal sense (opposed to *þis*). Loss of gender facilitates its detachment from the article paradigm, so that it becomes free to take on its new function as one pole of a deictic opposition. (The picture is less clear than I imply: on the complex semantics of *that* in Middle English see Mustanoja 1960: 168ff.)

Early Middle English uses *þo* (N *þa*) as the plural of *þat* as well as of *þe*; during the thirteenth century the old plural is replaced in the north by *þas*. This looks like a relic of OE *þās*, but is more likely an analogical development of the plural article *þa* < OE *þā*, with added noun plural *-s*. The same development occurs in the south a good deal later, with the southern stem vowel, which makes Old English origin much less likely. Chaucer has only *that/tho(o)*, but Caxton has *those* as well, presumably to be analysed as *thoo-s*. This form then is a fifteenth-century development, and clearly analogical. The same principle can be seen in Modern non-standard (Irish, Scots, US, South African) *you-s* /juːz/ as plural of *you*. (Note that the early *þes-e* is formed with an adjectival plural ending; when this is no longer possible because of loss of final /ə/, the only remaining regular plural marker is used.)

The definite article and demonstrative are intimately connected, historically, with the adjective, since one of the main controls on adjective inflection in Old English was the definiteness of an NP. Old English had two distinct adjective declensions, normally called 'strong' and 'weak':

(59)

		Strong			Weak		
		Masculine	Neuter	Feminine	Masculine	Neuter	Feminine
Singular	nom.	-θ	-θ	-u/-θ	-a	-e	-e
	gen.	-es	-es	-re	-an	-an	-an
	dat.	-um	-um	-re	-an	-an	-an
	acc.	-ne	-θ	-e	-an	-e	-an

		Strong			Weak		
		Masculine	Neuter	Feminine	Masculine	Neuter	Feminine
Plural	nom./acc.	-e	-θ/u	-e/-a		-an	
	gen.		-ra			-ena/-ra	
	dat.		-um			-um	

(The '-θ' in masculine nominative singular and neuter nominative/ accusative singular stands for both true zero endings as in *gōd* 'good', and disyllabic or longer adjectives which have their own nominative singular endings, and never appear in zero form, e.g. *clǣne* 'clean', *grēne* 'green'. The -θ ~ -*u* alternation in neuter nominative/accusative plural depended on whether the stem was heavy or light.)

The concordial logic of this dual system is simple in principle, if enormously complex in detail. Since the two declensions differ in categorial 'informativeness', the richer strong declension tended to be used after uninflected determiners, quantifiers and other items poor in case/number/gender information, or when the adjective had no premodifiers. The weak form was used where categorial information was carried by the determiner.

This system underwent a two-stage restructuring in Middle English. In early texts there are recognisable relics of at least the most salient endings of the strong declension; e.g. Laȝamon's *æt...are chirechen* 'at a church' (*are* < OE *ān-re*, strong fem. dat. sg. of *ān* 'one'). But even some of these survivals show erosion of the original principles: from the same text *þes heȝes kinges* 'of the high king', which in Old English would have had the weak adjective following the inflected article, *þæs hēan cyninges*.

But as Middle English proceeded, the strong/weak opposition decayed, and with the loss of case and gender marking on the article, that on the adjective disappeared as well. The end result, typical of most of Middle English at least through the fourteenth century, was a simple opposition between forms with and without -*e*. As early as Orm we find variation in the same syntactic contexts (as with dative singular on the noun – see 9.9.1 – normally for metrical reasons): *annd habbenn aȝȝ* ['always'] *god wille, þat hafeþþ aȝȝ god wille* vs *þat hafeþþ god-e wille* (Bennett & Smithers 1966: xxvi).

By Chaucer's time the zero/-*e* distinction was sensitive to two parameters: 'definiteness' and number. The definite form in -*e* usually occurred after determiners (*the cold-e steele, this good-e wyf*), in vocatives (*O fals-e mordrour*) and in attributive plurals, whether prenominal (*the long-e nyghtes*) or postnominal (*shoures sot-e* 'sweet showers'). Endingless forms occurred in singular predicate adjectives (*it was old*), after indefinite determiners (*a good wyf*, *many a fals flatour*), and in other positions without determiner (*as hoot he was as...*).

In Late Middle English this pattern was mostly restricted to monosyllabic adjectives; longer ones were normally endingless everywhere (cf. /ə/-deletion in polysyllables, 2.9.1.1, and the general Germanic tendency towards vowel loss in longer items, 2.5.3). The adjectival *-e*, like others, was variable, and deletable in verse where metrically appropriate – suggesting once again that any distinction carried solely by a final /ə/ would have vanished by the end of the fourteenth century.

In fairly high-style literary texts, a rather short-lived new plural type appears in Late Middle English: an *-(e)s* which is found most often on postposed adjectives of Romance origin – since both the ending and the construction reflect a French pattern. Thus Chaucer has *places delitable-s*, *thynges espirituel-s* (cf. *espirituel freendes* with preposed adjective and no ending: Sandved 1985: 52f.). The N-*(e)s* + Adj-*(e)s* type was especially common in scientific and legal texts (*bestes crepandes*, *heirs males*), and persists into the fifteenth and sixteenth centuries. In a few instances the same *-(e)s* plural appears in preposed or predicate adjectives as well: Mustanoja (1960: 277) cites *sufficiauntȝ borwes* 'sufficient guarantees', and Chaucer's *romances that been roiales*.

Inflection for comparison remains throughout Middle English (and indeed today) in principle the same as in Old English, with minor simplifications. The main Middle English archaism is the retention until quite late of old umlauted comparatives and superlatives (Chaucer, for instance, still has *long/leng-er*, *-est*, *strong/streng-er*, *-est*, etc.). There are also some length alternations (see 2.8.4) as in *greet/grett-er* 'great', deriving from Pre-Cluster Shortening (2.5.2): OE *grēat/grēat-ra*, etc. The general modern rule that adjectives longer than two syllables take analytic comparison (*more beautiful*, **beautifuller*) was perhaps beginning to be established in Late Middle English, but the possibilities Adj-*er* ~ *more* Adj remain open through the seventeenth century (see vol. III, ch. 1).

2.9.1.3 Pronouns

The personal pronoun is the only word class that consistently, throughout the history of the language, maintains inflection not only for number and genitive/non-genitive, but also for other cases and gender as well. There was great simplification during Middle English, but the parameters of the old system remained intact at least in outline.

The first and second persons in Old English were inflected for three numbers (singular/dual/plural), and four cases, but not for gender; this was a category only of the third-person singular. Plural was the same for all genders. The basic Old English system was:

(60)

		First person			Second person		
		Singular	Dual	Plural	Singular	Dual	Plural
Nominative		ic	wit	wē	þū	git	gē
Genitive		mīn	uncer	ūre	þīn	incer	eōwer
Dative		mē	unc	ūs	þē	inc	eōw
Accusative		mē	unc	ūs	þē	inc	eōw

	Third person singular			Third person plural
	Masculine	Neuter	Feminine	(all genders)
Nominative	hē	hit	hēo	hī(e)
Genitive	his	his	hire	hira/heora
Dative	him	him	hire	him/heom
Accusative	hine	hit	hīe	hī(e)

Early Anglian and verse texts had a distinct first-/second person accusative (*þēc*, *mēc*, etc.); but the general trend was towards syncretism of dative/accusative under one form (see below).

By Late Middle English a number of major transformations had occurred: (a) the dual was lost; (b) dative and accusative had generally merged (usually to the dative form), so that there were at most three case distinctions – nominative vs genitive vs 'oblique' or 'objective'; (c) the old fem. nom. sg. *hēo* had been replaced in most areas by a new form in /ʃ-/, e.g. *scho*, *sche*; (d) new sandhi forms of the genitive singular and a new 'second genitive' had arisen; (e) the old third-person plural forms in *h-* had begun to yield to a new (Scandinavian) type in *þ-/th-*, the originals of *they/their/them*. We will look at these developments individually.

(a) The dual is an old Indo-European category; more archaic dialects like Greek and Gothic had it not only as a pronoun inflection but as a verb concord as well. Even earliest Old English, however, had lost it except in the pronoun, and this vanished by the thirteenth century. It is still systematically used in the twelfth by some writers, e.g. Orm, in passages in the dedication to the *Ormulum* concerning himself and his brother: *annd unnc birrþ baþe þannkenn Crist* 'and us-two (it) behoves to thank Christ', *witt shulenn tredenn unnderrfot* 'we-two must tread underfoot'. After 1200 number became a two-way opposition in all categories.

(b) Old English already showed a tendency towards dative/accusative syncretism, normally in favour of the dative form. In Middle English this trend continues in the masculine and feminine third-person singular. The collapse of *hine* and *him* in a general object-case *him* begins early, though *hine* remains as an alternative in southern texts into the fourteenth century (Dan Michel has *me hine anhongeþ* 'one hangs him' alongside *and him halt* 'and holds him'). This is a classic instance of the distortion of history produced by the standardisation of a language: from literary texts alone we would be justified in assuming that *hine* 'vanished' in the fourteenth century (and indeed this is true of the literary standard). But a reflex of *hine* (in the form /ən/, distinct from *him*) survives even now in the south-west of England, though it is not strictly differentiated as an accusative (see Wakelin 1972a: 113). Feminine acc. sg. *hi(e)* and related forms survive in the south until the late thirteenth century, but yield to *hir(e)/her(e)* afterwards. The dative/accusative distinction is, however, maintained for neuters during most of Middle English, and it is only later that *him* is dropped in the standard for neuter indirect objects (in many non-standard dialects, especially in the south-west, it still remains).

(c) The origin of *she* is one of the great unsolved puzzles of the history of English. One early view is that it descends from the feminine nominative singular article *sēo*, via syllabicity shift and palatalisation: i.e. [seǫ] > [sęo] > [sjo:] > [ʃo:]. This would give the N *scho* and similar forms, but not *s(c)he*: here the vowel would have to come from somewhere else, presumably an analogical transfer from *he*. One problem is that *sēo* appears to have died out rather earlier than one would like, which makes it too archaic to accord with the surfacing of *she*. A more likely account is what is sometimes called the 'Shetland Theory', since it assumes a development parallel to that of *Shetland* < OScand. *Hjaltland*, *Shapinsay* < *Hjalpandisey*, etc. The starting point is the morphologically and chronologically preferable *hēo*. Once again we have syllabicity shift and vowel reduction, giving [heǫ] > [hęo] > [hjo:]. Then [hj-] > [ç-], and [ç-] > [ʃ-], giving final [ʃo:]. The 'syllabicity shift' (or at least the development /eo/ > /o:/) is attested elsewhere (*ceōsan* > *choose*, not expected **cheese*: see 2.2.1); and [hj-] > [ç-] is also reasonable, as in many modern dialects that have [çu:-] in *hue*, *human*. Indeed Orm's fem. 3 sg. nom. *ʒho* may well represent either [hjo:] or [ço:]. There are, however, a few snags: first, chronological problems having to do with the /eo/ > /jo:/ development in Scandinavian, which is supposed to have influenced the

English development. Second, while [hj] > [ç] is reasonable, the further putative development to [ʃ] is only attested in a few (non-English) place names.

In addition, the simplest phonological solution, a normal development of the nucleus of *hēo* or *sēo* to /e:/, would make it impossible to get the right initial consonant; for [h] to give [ç > ʃ] requires a following [j], and this can only come from the aberrant development to /o:/, since it requires reduction of a desyllabified initial [e] in the diphthong. So any solution that gets [ʃ] from /eo/ also needs to 'correct' the resultant /o:/ (outside the north) to /e:/. This means an analogical transfer of (probably) the /e:/ of *he*. All this in just one word.

So none of the available stories is satisfactory. The only certainty is (a) that the northern *scho* type could have come easily from *sēo*, and less easily from *hēo*; (b) that all existing accounts, whatever the phonology, also require some morphological assistance to get the right vowel in *she*; and (c) that a form probably in the ancestral line of *she* occurs in the east midlands as early as the 1150s, i.e. the *Peterborough Chronicle*'s *scæ*. For most of the Middle English period *scho* is restricted to the north, and *sche* to the east midlands, while the south keeps the old *heo* or its descendants, e.g. *ho, hue, hi. Shoo* /ʃu:/, the natural descendant of *scho*, remains even today in rural dialects in a small part of West Yorkshire, and *hoo* /(h)u:/ < *hēo* in the northwest midlands, particularly parts of Lancashire, southwest Yorkshire, and scattered through Cheshire, Derbyshire and northwest Staffordshire (Duncan 1972: 188f.).

(d) During the course of Middle English the genitives of the personal pronouns were syntactically 'detached' from the pronoun paradigm, and came to function rather as adjectives than as true case forms. They could no longer occur as objects of verbs (as in OE *fanda mīn* 'try me'), or as partitives (*ān hīora* 'one of them') – the necessary translations illustrate what has happened (cf. **try my, **one their(s)).

Eventually the genitives became exclusively noun attributes, i.e. 'possessive adjectives'; this amounts to a retention of only one of their Old English functions – the type *mīn sunu* 'my son'. Morphologically these were much like other adjectives (as indeed they were in Old English in their adjectival function). pl. *mīn-e leov-e sustren* 'my dear sisters' and the like.

Beginning in the north and northwest midlands in the late twelfth to early thirteenth century, a new genitive type arose, with suffixed -(*e*)*s*, as in *your(e)s, her(e)s, our(e)s*, etc. These spread gradually southwards, appearing in the southeast midlands in the later fourteenth century. The new forms were used (as they still are) in constructions where the possessed noun did not directly follow the genitive of the possessor: e.g. Chaucer's *myn hous*...*or elles*...*your-es, al this good is our-es*.

In the south and parts of the midlands, the second genitive was apparently formed on the model of possessives like *min*, *þin*, with *-(e)n*: *ʒour-en, his-en* — a type that still survives in some dialects both in England and the USA. New forms of *min*, *þin* were also created by deletion of final *-n*, at first typically in sandhi before words beginning with a vowel or /h/ (cf. the modern distribution of *a, an*). This pattern is common but not obligatory; both the types *mi frend, min frend* occur.

(e) The entire third-person plural system has been replaced in the standard by a Scandinavian paradigm; but the different case forms were not uniformly replaced except in the north. The eventual merger pattern is the same as for the singular: dative and accusative fall together, and what remains is formally the historical dative (*them* < OScand. *þei-m*; cf. *hi-m*).

Northern Middle English dialects generally show a full Scandinavian paradigm from earliest times, with descendants of *þeir, þeirra, þeim* (nom., gen., obl.). The other dialects show a gradual southward movement of the *þ-* paradigm, the native *h-* type remaining longest in the conservative south. In the northeast midland *Ormulum*, the nominative is exclusively *þeʒʒ*; the genitive is mostly *þeʒʒre*, with a few *h-*forms; the oblique is *hemm*, with a few instances of *þeʒʒm*. This is the basic pattern: nominative *þ-*forms appear first, then the genitive, then the oblique. So *þei* appears in London in the fourteenth century, and Chaucer, typically for the period, has *þei/her(e)/hem*. London texts of the fifteenth century vary between *her(e)* and *their*, and towards the end of the century *their* begins to take over, and by Caxton's time is the only form in common use. *Them* is the last: Chaucer and the next-generation writers like Lydgate and Hoccleve use only *hem*, and Caxton has *hem* and *them*, with *hem* predominating. By the beginning of the sixteenth century the modern paradigm is fully established (Mustanoja 1960: 134f.; Wyld 1927: §§307, 312).

In summary, the late southeast midlands dialects show fairly stable first-, second- and third-person singular paradigms:

(61)

		1	2	3		
				Masculine	Feminine	Neuter
singular	nom.	I	þū	hē	shē	(h)it
	gen.	mī(n)	þī(n)	his	} her(e)	his
	obl.	mē	þē	him		(h)it

		1	2
	nom.	wē	ȝē
Plural	gen.	our(es)	ȝour(es)
	obl.	us	ȝou

The third-person plural, on the other hand, has a gradual three-phase development through the fifteenth century:

(62)

	I	II	III
Nominative	þei	þei	þei
Genitive	her(e)	her(e) ~þeir	þeir
Oblique	hem	hem	hem ~ þem

The only major changes in the pronoun system after this are the development of a new neuter genitive singular *its*, and a drastic remodelling of the second-person system (see vol. III, ch. 1).

2.9.1.4 Minor categories: interrogatives, indefinites, numerals

A number of categories show either pronoun- or adjective-like behaviour (or both), but lack full independent paradigms, and have simpler morphological histories than the true pronouns or adjectives. These include interrogatives, numerals and so-called 'indefinite pronouns' (a traditional catch-all including chiefly quantifiers like *all*, *any*, *each* and the like).

1 *Interrogatives*. Old English had two main interrogatives, one of which (*hwā/hwæt* 'who/what') was a true pronoun, while the other (*hwilc* 'which') was either pronoun or adjective, depending on syntax (see below). *Hwā* had two declensions, one primarily for reference to humans (hence conflating masculine and feminine), and one for non-humans (neuter). The paradigms and their Late Middle English descendants were:

(63)

	Old English		Middle English	
	Human	Non-Human	Human	Non-Human
Nominative	hwā	hwæt	who	what
Genitive	hwæs	—	whos(e)	—
Dative	hwǣm/hwām	—		
Accusative	hwone	hwæt	Oblique whom	what
Instrumental	—	hwȳ		

121

The old instrumental *hwȳ*, while pronominal in origin (= 'for what?'), is syntactically adverbial, and in Middle English is an indeclinable autonomous word. The others, with the expectable syncretism of dative/accusative under dative (cf. *hine/him* > *him*) form a coherent set parallel to the third-person singular masculine personal pronoun (*he/his/him*), and have a similar history. OE *hwilc* 'which' was declined like an adjective; in Early Middle English it retained the strong adjectival endings, especially in the south, but later, like other adjectives, developed a simple singular (θ) vs plural (*-e*) declension (see 2.9.1.2). Thus (Gower *CA* IV.1212f.) *which-e sorwes* vs *which...prosperite*. The same pattern holds for *whether* < OE *hwæþere* 'which (of two)'.

The interrogatives in later times were used as relative pronouns as well, and form the basis of the modern system; but this is more appropriately treated along with the syntactic evolution of the relative clause.

2 *Indefinite pronouns.* The Old English quantifiers (*e*)*all* 'all', *ān* 'one', *ænig* 'any', *mænig* 'many', *ælc* 'each', *ægþer* 'either', etc. survived into Middle English, and evolved much like adjectives, losing their inflections early in the more advanced northern dialects, and retaining fragmentary inflection further south. *All* keeps its endings longest, with dative plural still distinguished in Kent in the fourteenth century (*to all-en* 'to all'), and even Chaucer showing relics of a genitive plural (*at our all-er cost* 'at the cost of all of us' < OE *eal-ra*).

3 *Numerals.* While ordinals (*first, second*, etc.) are simply adjectives, and were generally treated in Old English as such, the cardinals (*one, two*, etc.) were somewhat ambiguous, and the morphology was not uniform for the whole series. Only 'one' to 'three' were regularly inflected (e.g. *twā* 'two' had forms like *twēgen* (masc. nom./acc.), *tweg(r)a* (gen.), *twǣm* (dat.), etc.) The higher ordinals were not usually inflected when prenominal (*syx wintra* 'six winters'), but could be when they stood alone (*fīf menn* 'five men' vs *ic sēo fīf-e* 'I see five': cf. Quirk & Wrenn 1957: 37). In Middle English the inflections began to vanish early, though in the south, especially in Kent, they remain to some extent into the fourteenth century (*Ayenbite of Inwit* has *to on-en* 'to one' < *ān-um* masc. dat. sg.). Except for these sporadic retentions in conservative areas, the numerals are treated as indeclinable words in Middle English; possibly because for any numeral higher than 'one' there is no possibility of a singular/plural or definite/indefinite opposition. Hence

the commonest loci for adjective inflection are absent, and the numerals fall away from the adjective paradigm faster than quantifiers or ordinary adjectives.

2.9.2   The verb

2.9.2.1   Introduction: Old English conjugation

The histories of the noun and adjective (2.9.1.1–4) suggest that English morphological evolution involves more than just simplification; there is a certain 'directedness', favouring particular categories at the expense of others. In the noun number expands or is retained at the expense of gender and case; in the adjective inflection is reduced to a singular/plural opposition, and then lost. The verb shows a similar (if longer-term) dominance pattern: of the potential inflectional categories in Old English (tense, mood, person, number), it is tense that becomes the single typifying inflection. Today there are only marginal exceptions: the present 3 sg. -(e)s on regular verbs, and a few recessive 'subjunctives', e.g. the was/were opposition (indicative if I was 'even though in fact I was' vs counterfactual if I were 'I am not, but if...'), or unmarked third-person singular verbs in complements like I insist that he leave (now mainly US).

The evolution in both noun phrase and verb shows a characteristic English (and to some extent Germanic – except for German and Icelandic) tendency: a move away from the multiparameter inflection typical of the older Indo-European languages to a restricted system with one exclusive or dominant parameter per part of speech.

Old English marked two tenses (past vs present), three moods (indicative vs imperative vs subjunctive), and three persons (first, second, third). All traces of both dual and passive inflection had already been lost in Northwest Germanic (only Gothic shows these). This suggests an 'ideal' maximum of twenty-six distinct forms for each verb: six each for present and past indicative and subjunctive (3 persons × 2 numbers), plus imperative singular and plural (only for second person). In fact, the system is not that symmetrical: person is marked only in the indicative singular. The inflectional categories for the Old English verb, overall, are as shown in (64).

(64)

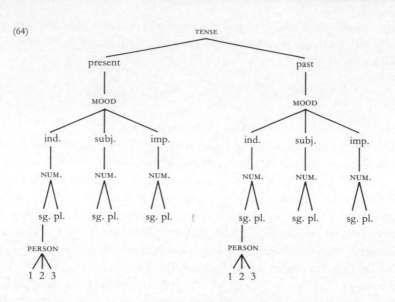

(I am counting only the finite forms as part of the verb paradigm proper; for the infinitive, participles and gerund see 2.9.2.6.)

This should give a total of sixteen forms for each verb; but the maximum is in fact only a little over 60 per cent of the expected yield: no more than eleven finite forms for any verb. This is due to the relative paucity of available inflectional material, which leads to massive homophony within the paradigm. To illustrate with one strong and one weak verb:

(65) Strong: Class I *drīfan* 'drive'
  drīf-e (pres. ind. 1 sg. pres. subj. 1–3 sg.); *drīf-st* (pres. ind. 2 sg.); *drīf-ð* (pres. ind. 3 sg.); *drīf-að* (pres. ind. 1–3 pl., imp. pl.); *drīf-en* (pres. subj. 1–3 pl.); *drīf* (imp. sg.); *drāf* (past ind. 1, 3 sg.); *drif-e* (past subj. 1–3 sg. past ind. 2 sg.); *drif-on* (past ind. 1–3 pl.); *drif-en* (past subj. 1–3 pl.)

  Weak: Class I *dēman* 'judge'
  dēm-e (pres. ind. 1 sg., pres. subj. 1–3 sg.); *dēm-est* (pres. ind. 2 sg.); *dēm-eð* (pres. ind. 3 sg.); *dēm-að* (pres. ind. 1–3 pl., imp. pl.); *dēm-en* (pres. subj. 1–3 pl.); *dēm* (imp. sg.); *dēm-d-e* (past ind. 1, 3 sg., past subj. 1–3 sg.); *dēm-d-est* (past ind. 2 sg.); *dēm-d-on* (past ind. 1–3 pl.); *dēm-d-en* (past subj. 1–3 pl.)

The inventory of inflectional material for the regular Old English verb then consists of: (a) the strong verb vowel alternations, which code tense/mood/number/person in an exceedingly complex way; (b) the weak tense suffix (here in the form -*d*-, but see the following section for allomorphy); and (c) zero termination plus the endings -*e*, -(*e*)*ð*, -(*e*)*st*, -*að*, -*on*, -*en*. This already shows a vast simplification of the original Germanic system: an archaic dialect like Gothic has twelve distinct person/number morphs just in the indicative and subjunctive singular and plural, compared to five in Old English.

So Old English is already reduced from a Germanic point of view; and it is clear that even this eroded system, like that of the noun, was bound to be further reduced. The -*en*/-*on*, -*eð*/-*að* oppositions would collapse in -*en*, -*eð* with the levelling of unstressed vowels; loss of final /ə/ would merge the present first-person singular with the imperative singular, and so on.

The story of the verb during Middle English is enormously involved, and nearly impossible to tell coherently. The noun was bad enough, with only case and number (and marginally gender) to worry about; here we have not only tense, person, number and mood, but a plethora of distinct strong and weak classes with partially independent histories, and numerous odd but important verbs like *be*, *do*, *can*, *must* (see 2.9.2.5). These complications make a neat category-by-category narrative nearly impossible. Still, we have to start somewhere; and since the 'victory of tense' is the main theme of the story, this is a good place to begin. For obvious reasons we will treat the weak and strong verbs separately; when we come to person and number we will consider both together.

2.9.2.2 The weak verb: tense marking and class membership

The strong verbs are largely an Indo-European inheritance in Germanic; their complex vowel alternations continue ancient Indo-European patterns. There have been far-reaching reorganisations: e.g. the distinct vowels in the past singular and plural reflect an Indo-European aspectual contrast, the singular vowel generally continuing an old perfect, and the plural vowel an aorist. But in principle they do not deviate as much from the Indo-European type as the weak verbs.

Semantically (and in a rather opaque way in some aspects of their morphology) the weak verbs are also Indo-European in type: that is, they can be related to certain classes of 'secondary' or 'derived' verbs in the other Indo-European dialects. Thus the -*ō*- in Gothic denominal weak class II verbs like *fisk-ō-n* 'to fish' is cognate to the -*ā*- in Latin first-conjugation denominals like *plant-ā-re* 'to plant', etc. But in terms of tense marking (see below) they are uniquely Germanic.

Most of the weak verbs, partly as a result of their historical background, differ from the strong verbs in being the outputs of productive word-formation processes. So, for instance, most class I weak verbs are either causatives (*settan* 'set' from umlaut of the past stem of class V *sittan* 'sit'), or 'factitives' (verbs indicating the coming into being of a state) formed from adjectives (*trymman* 'strengthen' < *trum* 'strong'). Since the morphology of the weak verbs was, compared to that of the strong, extremely simple, involving virtually nothing but suffixation, it was not only easy to make new ones, but also to borrow foreign roots and create still more weak verbs (e.g. OE *declīnian* 'decline' < Lat. *declīn-āre*).

In addition to this ease of formation – and to some extent because of it – weak verbs were the numerically preponderant type. They therefore were the natural analogical target for restructuring of the verb system, much as the *a*-stem masculines (2.9.1.1) were for the noun. Only with the verb the regularisation was much slower, and is still incomplete (about sixty-odd of the more than 300 Old English strong verbs still survive in one form or another). In general, though, if verbs changed conjugation type at any time after Old English, they went from strong to weak (*crēopan* 'creep', past sg. *crēap*, past pple *cropen* > creep/crep-t). The opposite change, as in *stick/stuck* (OE weak *stician/stic-o-de*) is much rarer, as is the borrowing of foreign verbs into the strong conjugation (*strive/strove/striven* < OF *estriver* is one of the few examples).

The conceptual basis of the weak conjugation is marking of the past by a suffix containing a 'dental' element, usually /t/ or /d/: OE weak *dēm-an* 'judge', past 1 sg. *dēm-d-e*, past pple -*dēm-e-d* vs *drīfan/drāf/-drifen*. Many weak verbs, owing to various sound changes, showed secondary vowel and consonant alternations as well: *sellan* 'sell', past *seal-d-e*, *sēcan* 'seek', past *sōh-t-e*, and so on. In Middle English there were also length changes that complicated the paradigms: OE *cēpan/cēp-te* 'keep', ME *kēpen/kĕp-te* and the like. But the suffix principle remains characteristic and defines the class; it can still be seen even in 'irregular' weak verbs, as in *keep/kep-t*, *seek/sough-t*, *bring/brough-t*.

For our purposes the most important of the Old English weak verb classes are the following:

Class I(a). Verbs with a historical */-jan/* suffix in the infinitive, and a heavy first syllable; either original (*dēman* <

*/doːm-jan/) or via West Germanic Gemination (*sellan* < */sal-jan/). The original thematic vowel /-i-/ connecting the stem and past suffix was lost in pre-Old English times after a heavy syllable (see 2.5.3): thus past 1 sg. *dēm-de* < */doːm-i-da/.

Class I(b). These have a light first syllable and no gemination, giving an infinitive in *-ian* and a retained thematic vowel *-e-* in the past: *herian* 'praise' < */xar-jan/, past 1 sg. *her-e-de* < */xar i da/.

In both groups the past participle was formed the same way: (*ge-*)*dem-ed*, (*ge-*)*her-ed* (on the fate of the prefix *ge-* see 2.9.2.6).

Class II. These had an original thematic */-oː-/ before the suffix, and could have had either light stems (*lufian* 'love' < */luf-oː-jan/) or heavy (*lōcian* 'look' < */loːk-oː-jan/). Though the *-ian* infinitives look like class I(b), the rest of the conjugation shows major differences; in particular the theme vowel, which is retained in the past and past participle of both light and heavy stems, is *-o-*, not *-e-*: *luf-o-de*/(*ge-*)*luf-od*, *lōc-o-de*/(*ge-*)*lōc-od*.

There was also a weak class III, including important verbs like *habban* 'have' (past 1, 3 sg. *hæf-de*); these tended to fall in with class I(a) in Middle English, except for *libban* 'live', which behaved more like I(b) or II.

Obviously one of the first things to go in the Old to Middle English transition was the *-o-d(e)*/*-e-d(e)* distinction, due to levelling in /ə/; the three types above collapse into two. We can call them new type I (athematic past) and type II (thematic past). Using examples cited above:

(66)		Infinitive	Past 1-singular	Past participle
Type I (athematic)		deem-en	deem-d-e	(y-)deem-d
		seek-en	souʒ-t-e	(y-)souʒ-t
Type II (thematic)		her(i)en	her-e-d(e)	(y-)her-e-d
		luv-(i)en	luv-e-d(e)	(y-)lov-e-d

The parenthesised (*-i-*) in type II is due to the retention of distinct endings for Old English classes I(b), II in some southern dialects; the thematic *-i-* did not level to *-e-*, and verbs like 'love' came down as *luv-ien*, later *luv-i*. This pattern was extended analogically to verbs of other classes as well. (These *-i-*forms never made it into the standard, but they did survive in some southwestern rural vernaculars at least into the late nineteenth century.)

At least in Early Middle English, type I generally contained the descendants of Old English heavy-stem weak verbs like *sette(n)*, *deeme(n)*, *wende(n)* 'turn', and most of class III, as well as perhaps the bulk of French loans with consonant-final stems (*joyne(n)*, *peinte(n)*, etc.). Type II was the model for most of weak class II (*love(n)*, *looke(n)*, *make(n)*) and I(b) (*were(n)* 'guard, wear', *styre(n)* 'stir'), as well as many French loans with vowel-final stems (*crye(n)*, *preye(n)*)) and some consonant-finals (*chaunge(n)*), though these often became type I as well.

The I/II distinction is not, however, quite as systematic as most handbooks imply. For one thing, there was already a certain amount of class confusion in Old English, with evidence of class I verbs going over fully or partly to class II and vice versa, as early as the ninth century (Mertens-Fonck 1984). The Mercian Vespasian Psalter, for instance, has some verbs with both class I and II conjugations: e.g. 'to build' with pres. 1 sg. *getimbru*, 3 sg. *timbreð*, pres. pple *timbrende* (class I), and pres. 1 sg. *timbriu*, 3 pl. *timbriað*, pres. pple *timbriende* (class II: *-i-* is the class marker). The two attested past forms happen to be unambiguously class II (*timbrade* (sg.), *timbradum* (pl.)); but the past participles, all of which show *-ed* rather than *-ad* < *-od*, are of a class I type. This suggests that the 'dictionary' class membership of a weak verb – normally based on its West Saxon morphology – may not be a good guide to its membership in Mercian; and Mercian is closer to the origins of the London standard than West Saxon. It is also quite possible for a verb to belong to more than one conjugation.

This simply exacerbates a further difficulty, having to do with spelling and the nature of /ə/-deletion. Given the instability of final /ə/, the type I/II contrast really boils down to whether the (potential) /ə/ comes before the past suffix (type II) or after (type I); or whether the past participle ending is syllabic (type II) or non-syllabic (type I). But the textual evidence is often ambiguous. There are certainly clear trisyllabic forms with the maximal type II pattern, e.g. in this line from the twelfth century *Poema morale* (Lambeth MS):

þa þe *luueden* unriht & ufel lif leden

'those who loved unrighteousness and led (an) evil life'

where the metre suggests that *luueden* be scanned όσσ. But other forms are ambiguous, especially those that are metrically disyllabic. This is bound to be so: assume that a trisyllabic past loses one syllable; if it is plural, there is no problem: *luueden* scanned όσ can only be /luv-dən/, since loss of the second syllable would give the impossible **/luv-ədn/. But a disyllabic *luuede* could in principle be /luv-də/ or /luv-əd/, and there is usually no sure way of telling. And if the verb in fact had an ancestry including both class I and II conjugations, either pronunciation would be available; and the tendency of scribes to write unetymological <e> all over the place obscures things further.

By the late fourteenth century increasing /ə/-deletion, both finally and in post-stress closed syllables, made it rare for any monosyllabic verb to have a past of more than two syllables; the modern monosyllabic type was commoner. Both do, however, still appear in Chaucer (examples from the General Prologue):

> Another nonne with hire *haddë* she (163)

> This ilke worthy knyght *haddẹ* been also (64)

This is Type I; for Type II we find both types as well:

> So hoote he *lovëd* that by nyghtertale (97)
> Wel *lovẹd* he by the morwe a sop in wyn (334)

While syllable count is generally unambiguous, this cannot be said for which vowel of two possibles is deleted, as in 166:

> An outrydere that *lovëdẹ* venerye

> An outrydere that *lovẹdë* venerye

The main evidence bearing on the ambiguous type II cases is that /ə/ in absolute finality is more likely to drop than when it is protected by a following consonant; this and the relative rarity of spellings like *lovde* as opposed to *loved* argues for some retention of the old distinction, if weakly. (Perhaps the most interesting evidence is Gower's apparent avoidance of pasts of type II verbs in his verse; it is nearly always the case that where such a past is likely to surface, he uses a present form instead, letting the tense of a past narration be carried by a strong or type I weak verb: thus 'Sche *loketh* and hire yhen *caste*' (*CA* II.1066) and many similar cases. See the discussion in Macaulay 1900: cxvi f.)

Unreduced type II pasts occur occasionally, including transfers from type I or strong verbs: thus Chaucer (*LGW* 1119):

> Ne ruby non, that *shynede* by nyghte

(where *shynede* ὅσσ is apparently a transfer to weak type II of the original strong verb *scīnan*; unless this is an error for or contamination by OE class II weak *scīmian* 'glisten, shine').

Later, the system was restructured; the only syllabic weak pasts now are in verbs with /t d/ finals (*seated, wounded, defeated, sounded*). And many of these have lost the vowel and separate ending, giving identical present and past (*fit, set*), or only a length/quality difference due to an original geminate (*lead/led < lēde(n)/lĕdde*). The main structural principle is now (and was beginning to become in Late Middle English) quite different: the old /-d/ vs /-əd/ distinction is still there, but the grounds for it are phonetic and non-historical: both types I and II are now monosyllabic (*had, loved*).

2.9.2.3 The Strong Verb: Root Vocalism and Tense/Number Marking

The strong-verb paradigm was organised around a set of vowel 'grades', typically represented as a set of 'principal parts', i.e. a set of qualities on the basis of which all members of the particular paradigm can be derived. The standard display includes present (= infinitive), past sg., past pl. and past participle. Some examples showing the most common vowel series in the seven major classes:

(67)	Class		Present	Past singular	Past plural	Past participle
	I	'ride'	rīdan	rād	ridon	-riden
	II	'creep'	crēōpan	crēap	crupon	-cropen
	IIIa	'find'	findan	fand	fundon	-funden
	IIIb	'help'	helpan	healp	hulpon	-holpen
	IV	'bear'	beran	bær	bæron	-boren
	V	'tread'	tredan	træd	trædon	-treden
	VI	'bake'	bacan	bōc	bōcon	-bacen
	VII	'blow'	blōwan	bleōw	bleōwon	-blōwen

(In addition, some verbs with present /e/ have /i/ in second- and third-person singular: e.g. *helpan/hilpst, hilpþ*.) The particular distribution of vowel grades in the various tense/number/mood forms is laid out in section 2.9.2.1; for our purposes here it is most important to note that a strong verb may have two (VI, VII), three (I, IIIa, V) or four (II, IIIb, IV) primary vowel grades, and that in all classes except VI–VII the past singular and plural have different root vowels.

There was a major distinction (except for classes VI–VII) between light-stemmed verbs, with a long vowel in past plural, and heavy-stemmed, with a short vowel (IV–V vs I–III). The long past plural is qualitatively the same as the short singular, except in a few odd verbs, like class IV *niman* 'take', past *nam/nōmon*; there is also an anomalous pattern in *cuman* 'come', past sg. *c(w)ōm*, pl. *c(w)ōmon*. This length regularity was one of the earliest Middle English casualties, for obvious reasons: (a) most of class IIIa (e.g. *find, bind, grind, climb*) end up with long vowels throughout the whole conjugation (Pre-Cluster Lengthening: 2.5.2); and (b) disyllabic forms with a -VC- first syllable were likely to end up with qualitatively altered long vowels (OSL: 2.5.2). So we might expect the series *findan/fand/-funden* to end up as *finden/fǫnd/ -funden* (ǫ = /ɔ:/ from earlier /a:/ by Pre-Cluster Lengthening); or *beran* to end up as *bēre(n)* with /ɛ:/ < /e/ (OSL and lowering). Since OSL of high vowels was less dependable than that of lower ones, we might expect the past plural and past participle of class I verbs like *wrītan* 'write' to end up either with /i/ or /e:/; indeed, Caxton at the end of the fifteenth century still has two participial forms, *writen* and *wreten*. So from the beginning the original vowel patterns were vulnerable to major phonological disruptions.

These changes did not themselves destroy the old structural principles; the real restructuring was at the morphological level. During the Middle English period (and indeed for another three centuries) the whole strong-verb system was in flux, with three major development patterns simultaneously (and variably) at work: (a) reduction in the number of vowel grades per verb; (b) 'hybridisation' or mixing of forms from more than one class in the conjugation of a given verb; and (c) movement of verbs wholly or partly into the weak conjugation. These produce a complex and apparently disorderly picture during our period; it is nearly impossible to set out 'standard' paradigms the way we can for Old English. We can, however, give some general illustrations of what was going on.

1 *Grade reduction*. The tendency was first to restrict the complexity of vowel alternations (e.g. by levelling the past singular under the vowel of the first- and third-person singular, thus stabilising a single singular/ plural opposition for the whole past); later, and more importantly, by eliminating the number opposition itself in the past, leaving concord to be marked (if at all) by endings, as in the weak verb. This is a good example of the problems in discussing tense and number separately for the strong verb: while the singular/plural collapse of course affects tense marking, it still belongs equally (perhaps more fundamentally) to

the history of number concord. It is probably no accident that the period in which the collapse is most noticeable (after ca 1450) also sees the speeding-up of loss of the -(*e*)*n* plural (see 2.8.3).

This simplification, like so many others, seems to have begun in the north (with a later wave, of a somewhat different character, in the west). Since both tendencies converge in the later London/east midlands dialects, and show up in the modern standard, they are worth isolating. Obviously the singular/plural distinction could be eliminated in three ways: levelling under the vowel of the singular, under that of the plural, or under that of the past participle. Only the first and last of these seem generally to have been taken up.

Levelling under the singular vowel grade (the 'Northern Preterite': Wyld 1927: 268) first appears in early northern texts, where the plural ending had already been lost: *Cursor mundi* (ca 1300) has past plurals with (historically) singular vowels like *rade* 'rode' (OE sg. *rād* rather than pl. *ridon*), *dranc* 'drank' (OE *dranc* rather than *druncon*). This spread south, and is well established for many verbs now (*rode, drank* as above, cl. III *sang, began*, cl. V *bade* /bæd/, *sat*). Not all collapses of this kind survived: Caxton, for instance, shows past sg./pl. *foond* < OE sg. *fand* for *fynde* 'find'.

The modern vowel in *found* stems from the other major collapse type, what Wyld calls the 'Western Preterite'. Here the past-plural grade (if distinct from that of the past participle, as in classes II, IIIb, IV) is eliminated by extending the participle grade to the whole finite past. This is now also a standard pattern, as in *found* < OE -*funden*, cl. I *slid*, *bit*, cl. III *bound*, cl. IV *bore*, *tore*. It is more sporadic in Late Middle English than the northern merger, showing up mainly in rather late texts; Margery Kempe, for instance, has one clear example in *breke* 'break', past sg. *broke*, pl. *brokyn* (with *broke* ~ older sg. *brakke* < *bræc*); there is also the ambiguous case of *syngyn* 'sing', past sg. *song*, pl. *songyn*, which is of the western type if <o> represents /u/ (OE -*sungen*), but northern if it represents /o/ (< OE /ɑN/: less likely in a text this far east). An additional pattern, extension of the past-plural vowel (where this is distinct from the participial one) to singular, also occurs, but is less common and generally has not survived. Chaucer, for instance, has *bere(n)* 'bear' with both the old past pattern *bar/bere(n)* < *bær/bæron*, and the innovative past sg. *beer* apparently with the vocalism of the Old English past plural (cl. V *sit* also has sg. *sat* ~ *seet*, the same pattern).

Any given writer of the period ca 1380–1450 is likely to show virtually all possible patterns of strong-verb vocalism, with the old singular/plural distinction predominant, and the northern the commonest merger. In Chaucer, for instance, classes I–III are largely intact, as in *creepe(n)* 'creep' /kre:pən/, past sg. *creep* /krɛːp/, past pl. *cropen* /krɔ:pən/ < *crēopan/crēap/-cropen*. The old pattern is retained for most strong verbs that have not gone weak (see below), though there are exceptions, such as 'sit' and 'bear', as cited above.

Roughly half a century later, Margery Kempe still shows the basic Old English pattern, e.g. cl. I *rydyn* 'ride', past sg. *rood*, past pl. *redyn* < *ridon*, cl. III *drynkyn* 'drink', past sg. *drank(e)*, pl. *dronkyn* (OE *dranc/druncon*). But she also has northern merger in *spekyn* 'speak', past sg./pl. *spak* < OE *spæc*, and the western types mentioned above ('break', 'sing'), though *spak* has a more conservative plural variant, *spokyn*.

At the end of the century, Caxton appears to show no singular/plural distinctions in past vocalism, and a mainly northern merger pattern: cl. I *wryte* has past sg./pl. *wrote*, cl. III *fynde* has past sg./pl. *fonde*, cl. IV *come* has past sg./pl. *cam*.

2 *'Hybridisation'*. Transfer of forms from one strong class to another had occurred sporadically even in Old English; it continues in Middle English but becomes prominent only rather late. The most striking Middle English examples perhaps are class V verbs taking on class IV participles: these become common in the fifteenth century. Margery Kempe, for instance, has *ʒouyn* 'given' and *spoken*, which reflect transfer from the class IV type of 'bear' (OE past pple *-boren*), with loss of the original type (OE *-giefen*, *-specen*), though in the first of these the old pattern has prevailed in the modern standard. These new participles tended later to engage in a western-type takeover in some verbs (as in PDE *spoke* as the past of *speak*).

3 *Transfer to weak*. This was common all through the period, but increased in the late fourteenth to early fifteenth centuries. Gower already shows cl. I *smot* ~ *smette* (OE *smāt*), cl. II *crepte* (OE *crēap*) – though this verb still has the strong participle *crope*; cl. I *chide* has the weak participle *chidd*. Chaucer has *smot* ~ *smette* as well, *shyned* ~ *shoon* (OE *scān*), cl. VII *wepte*, *slepte* (OE *wēop*, *slēp*); Margery Kempe has cl. II weak *fled*, *sowkyd* 'sucked' (OE *flēah*, *sēac*), cl. III *halpe* ~ *helpyd* (OE *healp*), cl. VI *schok* ~ *schakid* (OE *scōc*), cl. VII *beet* ~ *bett* 'beat' (OE *bēot*).

This small selection illustrates the variability characteristic of Late Middle English; in the next three centuries or so there was considerable tidying up, but by no means a complete regularisation. Even now there are verbs that are part weak and part strong, like *swell* (weak past *swelled*, strong participle *swollen*, similarly *show*, past *showed*, past pple *showed* ~ *shown*). There are also highly variable verbs like *shit*, which can serve as a model of what is likely to happen to a strong verb: cl. I *scītan* has had its plural or participial vowel transferred to the present (cf. northern and Sc. *shite*), and the past can be either a class V type (*shat*), or one of two weak types, *shit* or *shitted*. The original strong past, which would be **shote*, appears not to have survived at all, and the strong participle *shitten* is archaic.

2.9.2.4 The verb endings: person, number, mood

Aside from the rather unstable marking of number and to a lesser extent tense in the root vowels of strong verbs, most of the inflectional work in the verb paradigm was done by suffixes. The Old English system was, as we have seen, already considerably simplified (2.9.2.1), a generalised conjugation for the strong and weak verbs in non-northern Old English dialects (on the north see below) would look like this:

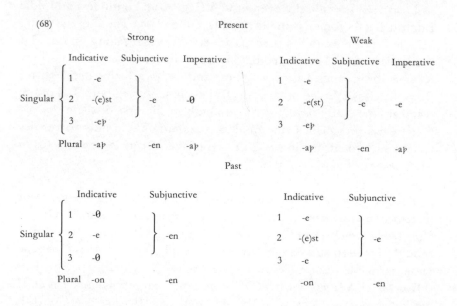

(68)

Present

		Strong				Weak		
		Indicative	Subjunctive	Imperative		Indicative	Subjunctive	Imperative
Singular	1	-e			1	-e		
	2	-(e)st	-e	-θ	2	-e(st)	-e	-e
	3	-eþ			3	-eþ		
	Plural	-aþ	-en	-aþ		-aþ	-en	-aþ

Past

		Indicative	Subjunctive		Indicative	Subjunctive
Singular	1	-θ			1	-e	
	2	-e	-en		2	-(e)st	-e
	3	-θ			3	-e	
	Plural	-on	-en		-on	-en

(The inflections for the weak past are those that follow the tense suffix: i.e. '-e' = -ed-e, etc.)

There were many variants: e.g. strong verbs tended to have syncopated present indicative second- and third-persons singular like *bir-st*, *bir-þ* < *beran* 'bear', and there were further phonological developments, especially in dental-stem verbs: *rīdan* 'ride' in West Saxon had pres. 3 sg. *rītt* < **rītþ* < **rīdeþ*, and so on. And weak class II had a theme vowel *-i-* in many parts of the conjugation, as well as other vowel differences (2.9.2.2). Still, (68) is 'basic', and underlies the main Middle English developments.

Given the tendencies at work elsewhere (e.g. in the noun and adjective), (68) suggests something of its own future. There is a relative paucity of inflectional material (see 2.9.1.1 on the noun): only seven endings for twenty-seven categories. But the original seven, -θ, -e, -(e)st, -eþ, -aþ, -en, -on would be bound to collapse to five with the Late Old English neutralisation of unstressed vowels: only -θ, -e, -(e)st, -eþ, -en could survive into Middle English. And with the loss of final /ə/, only four stable inflections would remain: -θ, -(e)st, -eþ, -en. So we can predict that certain distinctions will be non-sustainable: present first-person singular, imperative singular and the entire subjunctive singular will have to be reduced to the bare verb stem, present third-person singular seems likely to merge with present plural (but see below), and past indicative and subjunctive will collapse. The only potentially stable categories are present second- and third-persons singular in both strong and weak verbs, and the weak past second-person singular.

There are also obvious points for analogical remodelling. If, for instance, the verb were to follow the noun pattern, reducing the number of distinct inflectional classes, we might get a *rapprochement* of the strong and weak conjugations. Given the numerical superiority of the weak verbs, we could predict a reconstruction of the strong past on the weak model, with the addition of second- and third-person singular endings; on the other hand, given the simplicity of the strong past, the weak might follow it, and become endingless throughout. Except for a certain amount of analogical suffixation of the strong past second-person singular, however, it was generally the second option that was taken up.

Further predictions: (a) if anything remains stable, it will be the personal endings for present second- and third-person singular and plural; (b) the one thing that will remain is the present/past contrast. These are borne out in essence by the historical record, though it was not until the late sixteenth to early seventeenth century that the final remodelling was complete.

The modern verb paradigm shows that the essential outlines suggested above are right – though with differences in detail. The subjunctive is gone, and all we have is:

(69)   Present   Past
       1, 2 sg., pl   -θ   sg., pl. -θ
       3 sg.   -(e)s

The loss of contrasting present second-person singular is independent; it follows the loss of number in the pronoun (vol. III, ch. 1). The -(e)s rather than **-(e)th outcome for present third-person singular is another matter, which I take up below.

The verb inflections evolved rather differently in the various Middle English regional dialects; in order to understand these developments, some of which are relevant for the southwest midlands, we must go back briefly to Old English – but this time not to the more southerly dialects like West Saxon. In Old Northumbrian the present system was quite different from that in the other dialects. Aside from the expected forms, it had a highly innovative (probably Scandinavian-influenced) present, with frequent collapse of second- and third-person singular and of both with plural, and an ending in -s for all three collapsed categories. The variant forms in early Northumbrian texts (see Campbell 1959: §§735, 752) suggest these two basic paradigm types:

(70)   (a) Conservative   (b) Innovating
                 ┌ 1   -o, -e   -o, -e
       Singular ┤ 2   -s(t)   -as
                 └ 3   -eð, -að   -es, -as
                 Plural   -eð, -að   -es, -as

The innovating -s forms penetrated well into the more northerly reaches of the midlands during the Middle English period, and – as we can see from PDE -(e)s – eventually reached the south as well.

The paradigms in (68) and (69) give the basic material out of which the Middle English dialects formed their verb conjugations. By around 1300, the Old English system had been largely restructured everywhere; what with simplifications, and spread of parts of the northern system into other areas, the inherited material had been deployed as follows in the main regional dialects:

(71)

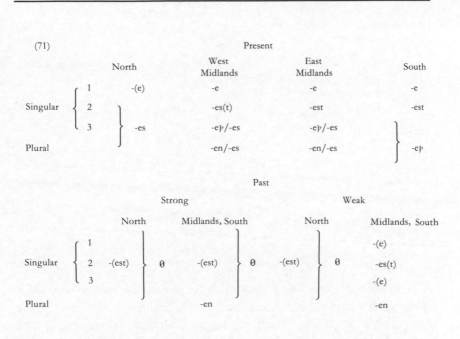

Present

		North	West Midlands	East Midlands	South
Singular	1	-(e)	-e	-e	-e
	2		-es(t)	-est	-est
	3	-es	-eþ/-es	-eþ/-es	
Plural			-en/-es	-en/-es	-eþ

Past

		Strong			Weak	
		North	Midlands, South		North	Midlands, South
Singular	1		θ			-(e)
	2	-(est)	-(est) θ	-(est)	θ	-es(t)
	3					-(e)
Plural			-en			-en

(This is for the indicative; the subjunctive was more or less as predicted, with variable -e in the singular, variable -e(n) in plural everywhere.)

Abstracting from this, the best regional indicators are the present third-person singular and the plural: 3 sg. -s is northern (though it occurs in the midlands as well), -en is a distinctively midland plural, and -eþ a distinctively southern one. This early clarity in dialectal forms will throw some light on what happened in London later. It is at least clear that the only trace of present-tense verb inflection in Present-Day English has a non-southern origin.

Early London texts show the typical southern pattern, with -eþ for third-person singular and all plurals; this remained until about the mid-fourteenth century, when the -eþ plural began to yield ground to the midland -en for both present and past. (Or, alternatively, the native southern past inflection began to invade the present; this is not strictly a factual question, but the location of London, as well as later developments, makes midland influence plausible.) The old -eþ survived as a minority variant in the indicative until well into the fifteenth century (see 2.8.3), and remained in the imperative plural.

By Chaucer's time the merging London standard had a generally stable verb conjugation of this kind:

(72)

		Present		
		Indicative	Subjunctive	Imperative
Singular	1	-(e)		
	2	-(e)st	-(e)	-e
	3	-eth		
Plural		-e(n)	-e(n)	-e(th)

		Past	
		Strong	Weak
Singular	1	-θ	-(e)
	2	-(est)	-(e)st
	3	-θ	-(e)
Plural		-e(n)	-e(n)

(*-eth* stands for both *-eþ* and *-eth*; at this late stage I use the more modern spelling to establish continuity with the later history. Since *-e* in the plural is also available, the ending might better be written *-(e(n))*. The past subjunctive is mostly non-distinct from the indicative, and is therefore not given separately.)

Given the instability of *-e* and its conservative/archaic status by the late fourteenth century, the 'real' (emergent) verb system in (72) was actually very like the modern one. Removing *-e*, the present and weak past are, by 1400, distinct from the modern system in only three particulars: marking of 2 sg., *-eth* rather than *-(e)s* for present 3 sg. and marking (variable and increasingly recessive) for plural.

The 3 sg. *-s* ending begins to appear in our period, under rather interesting circumstances. It is well known that for fourteenth-century London speakers it was a northern stereotype: in the Reeve's Tale Chaucer uses it as one of the markers of his northern clerks: they say *ga-s*, *fall-es*, *wagg-es far-es* while the narrator and the non-northern characters say *goo-th*, *mak-eth*, etc. But verbal *-s* is not merely for picturing comic northerners; while Chaucer uses it only for this purpose in the *Canterbury Tales*, it was known and available for other uses rather earlier. In *The Book of the Duchess* (ca 1370) and *The House of Fame* (ca 1375?) the *-s* ending is used in rhymes with noun plurals in *-s* and words like *elles* 'else':

That never was founde, as it *telles*,
Bord and man, ne nothing elles   (*BD* 73f.)

And I wol yive hym al that *falles*
To a chambre, and al hys halles   (*BD* 257f.)

Another case is *tydynges*: *brynges*, *HF* 1907f. This pattern of variation, with the -*s* ending available for rhyme, and apparently no sociolinguistic significance, was already attested at the beginning of the century, in areas further north; in the northeast midlands Robert of Brunne (1303) uses both endings in the same line: 'Þe holy man *telleþ* vs and *seys*' (Wyld 1927: 255).

The story of the spread of verbal -*s* in the southern standard belongs to the Early Modern period; but it was beginning to grow in the fifteenth century, and some writers use it quite frequently (e.g. Lydgate), others hardly at all, even rather late (Caxton). For this chapter it is a minority option, but one which we presume was in circulation in London at least as early as the 1370s, if not before.

Aside from later stabilisations and reductions, Late Middle English had clearly reached a point at which marking for person and number (and even mood) was becoming rather marginal; tense was the one obligatory category, with person second in importance, but only in the singular.

2.9.2.5   *Be, will, do, go* and the preterite-presents
There are a number of verbs of high text-frequency and great syntactic importance (most of them function as auxiliaries) that had problematic and 'irregular' morphology in earlier periods – and to some extent still do. I will look first at the very irregular group often called 'anomalous' in the handbooks, and then at the more coherent set (*can, may, shall* and the like) ancestral to the modern modal auxiliaries.

'ANOMALOUS' VERBS
1 *Be*. This is not really 'a verb' in Old English, but a collection of semantically related paradigms of various historical origins. There are three major stems (still visible): a synchronically messy but etymologically transparent group (*am, art, is*) cognate to Lat. *sum, es, est*; a *be-* group (cognate to Lat. *fīō* 'make', Skt *bhū-* 'dwell'); and a past stem (as in *was, were*) from a defective class V strong verb *wesan*, also with the historical sense 'dwell, remain' (Skt *vásati* 'he dwells'). The Old English paradigms can be represented (roughly: see the layout in Wyld 1927: 282, and Campbell 1959: §768) as follows:

(73)

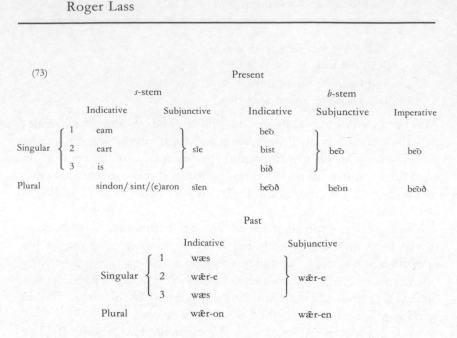

Present

		s-stem		b-stem		
		Indicative	Subjunctive	Indicative	Subjunctive	Imperative
Singular	1	eam		beō		
	2	eart	sīe	bist	beō	beō
	3	is		bið		
Plural		sindon/sint/(e)aron	sīen	beōð	beōn	beōð

Past

		Indicative	Subjunctive
Singular	1	wæs	
	2	wǣr-e	wǣr-e
	3	wæs	
Plural		wǣr-on	wǣr-en

The present plural (*e)aron* type was Anglian only; during Middle English it spread into the more southerly dialects, eventually becoming established as modern *are* (see below). The past stem *wes-* also formed an imperative *wes/wesað* (which still survives in *wassail* < *wes hāl* 'be healthy').

This collection of forms was dismembered in Early Middle English, and various portions spread over the dialects (see Mossé 1952: §84, for the major regional systems; and Lass 1987: §5.4, for modern non-standard survivals). In the dialects ancestral to today's standards, the *s*-stem type was generalised for present indicative, with *be(n)* ~ *are(n)* alternating for future until quite late. The *be-* paradigm remained, however, for present subjunctive. The *sīe-* forms were lost in Early Middle English, as was the *wes-* imperative; but this stem remained for the past, with the *-s-* for indicative, *-r-* for subjunctive contrast stable (as it still is in some dialects).

By the late fourteenth century the southeast midland dialects had stabilised a paradigm of this type:

(74)

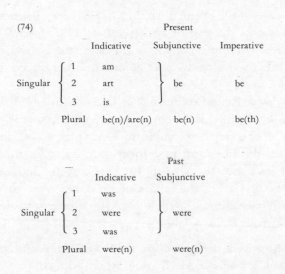

		Present		
		Indicative	Subjunctive	Imperative
Singular	1	am		
	2	art	be	be
	3	is		
Plural		be(n)/are(n)	be(n)	be(th)

		Past	
		Indicative	Subjunctive
Singular	1	was	
	2	were	were
	3	was	
Plural		were(n)	were(n)

The vowel-initial and /w/-initial forms also took negative clitics, giving *nam* 'am not' < *ne am*, and *nart, nis, nas, nere* (see below on *will*).

The *be(n)* plural is much commoner throughout the period than the northern *are(n)*. A sampling of letters written by Margaret Paston between 1441 and 1461 for instance shows a *be(n):are(n)* ratio of about 7:1; Caxton's prologues and epilogues from the 1470s–1480s show roughly the same. The controlling factors are difficult to unravel: a sentence like the following from book III, ch. 3 of Caxton's *The Game and Playe of the Chesse* (1474) is not atypical: 'I suppose that in alle cristendom *ar* not so many...men of the lawe as *ben* in englond.' Except for the triumph of *are* and the loss of the pres. 2 sg. *art*, the paradigm of *be* has remained virtually unchanged.

2 *Will*. The Old English ancestor had two tense stems: pres. *will*- vs past *wol*- (1 sg. *will-e, wol-d-e*). In the fourteenth century, the midland dialects began to show transfer of the past /o/ to the present, giving both *wil(l)-, wol(l)*- (though not transfer of present /i/ to the past). Present *wol*- is normal for Chaucer and Gower, and this stem has survived in *won't* < *wol not*. Other late Middle English writers, like the Pastons, have *wil-/wyl- ~ wol-*. One reason for this interchange of stem forms, as well as variant stems in other verbs like *shall* (see below), appears to be a weakening of the temporal meaning of the stems of some

modal verbs, as a first stage in the eventual split into (partially) distinct verbs: *would* is nowadays not 'the past of *will*' (see Lass 1987: §4.5.3). The old past forms can be used in distinctly non-past contexts (e.g. *I would like you to* ...), and this was already quite common in the fifteenth century.

So, for instance, Margaret Paston writes to her husband in 1443: 'I pray yow ... that ye *wollen* wochesaf ['vouchsafe'] to sende me worde', using a 'polite' present second-person plural form with a past vowel; in a letter of 1448 she uses the historical past form with its suffix in a present sense: 'for ... I *wolde* not for xl *li.* [£40] haue suyche anoþer trouble'. Two more passages from the letters of the same year, also including forms of *shall/should*, show the same weakening of past sense (and here the typical Norfolk <x> spelling):

> I sopose ye *xuld* haue seche thyngis of Sere Jon Fastolf if ʒe *wold* send to hym. And also I *wold* ʒe *xuld* gete ij. or iij. schort pelle-axis ...
> I pray ʒw that ʒe *wyl* vowchesave to don bye for me j *li.* of almandis and j *li.* of sugyre ... ʒe *xall* haue best chepe ['price'] and best choyse of Hayis wyf.
>
> (Davis 1971–6: I. 226–7)

In both verbs the past vowel and the /d/-suffix seem no longer associated with tense, but have become part of a new unitary lexical item.

It is also worth noting that in Old English *willan* did not take an *-eþ* suffix in present third-person singular; it is now the only verb outside the preterite presents (see below, pp. 143–4) that still shows this feature. *Will*, like *be*, also took a negative clitic in Old English, and this survived quite late: OE *nyllan* < *ne willan*, ME *nille*, etc. (cf. the modern remnant in *willy-nilly* < *will-he, nill-he*).

3 *Do*. In Old English this verb showed *i*-umlaut in present second- and third-person singular (1 sg. *dō*, WS *dēst, dēþ*), and an irregular (weak) past *dȳde*; the umlauted forms were lost early, but the weak past remained, with the expected regional variation of OE /y:/ (see 2.3.4 above): SW *dude*, SE *dede*, N, E Midlands *dyde/dide*. In general, London texts of the later period show <i/y> spellings, as expected; though standard writers like Malory with western origins often show <u> as a variant, and eastern texts like Margery Kempe and the Paston letters have <e>.

4 *Go*. This verb started out in Old English with a number of

complications: umlauted present second- and third-person singular like *dōn* (pres. 1 sg. *gā*, 2, 3 *gǣst*, *gǣþ*), and – more strikingly – a suppletive past, built on a different stem: *ēode*. As with *do*, the umlauted presents were lost early, but developments of *ēode* remained through the fifteenth century as *yede/yode*. In the north, however, a new suppletive past developed quite early: *wente*, originally the past of *wendan* 'turn'. This spread south in the thirteenth and fourteenth centuries, gradually replacing *yede/yode*. Chaucer has *wente* as his normal form, though *yede* still occurs occasionally, always in rhyme positions (e.g. *Troilus* 5.843 rhyming with *Diomede*). But *yede* occurs well into the next century along with *went(e)*.

PRETERITE-PRESENT VERBS

These have present systems which are historically strong pasts; the type is widely distributed throughout Indo-European (cf. Lat. *odī* 'I hate', where *-ī* is a perfect ending, as in *ama-v-ī* 'I have loved'). Since in Germanic these verbs took on most of the strong past conjugation to form a present, they are unique among Germanic present-tense forms in not having any inflection for present third-person singular and having different vowels in singular and plural (*will* – see above – shares the first of these properties but not the second). Thus OE *cann* 'I/he can', 2 sg. *cann-st*, pres. pl. *cunn-on*. Since the present is already a past, these verbs developed new (weak) pasts early on, producing a quite hybrid-looking conjugation. The most important Old English members were:

(75)		Present singular	Present plural	Past singular
'know'		wāt	wit-on	wis-te
'avail'		dēah	dug-on	dōh-te
'can'		cann	cunn-on	cū-ðe
'need'		þearf	þurf-on	þorf-te
'dare'		dearr	durr-on	dor-ste
'shall'		sceal	scul-on	scol-de
'must'		mōt	mōt-on	mōs-te
'may'		mæg	mag-on	mih-te
'owe'		āh	āg-on	āh-te

Most had infinitives as well, with still other vowel grades (e.g. *wītan*, *dūgan*, *cunnan*, etc.); these lost ground during Middle English though some (often with *to*) remained in use through the fifteenth century, and still survive in Scotland.

By and large the preterite presents developed phonologically on conventional lines; but the extreme formal differences between present and past led quite early to the kind of semantic dissociation between present and past that we saw above with *will* and *shall*. For example, the past of 'owe' (now the quite separate verb *ought*) was already being used as a present in the earliest Middle English texts: the twelfth-century *Poema morale* (Lambeth MS) has

> ich em nu alder þene ich wes awintre & a lare.
> Ich welde mare þene ich dede mi wit *ahte* bon mare
>
> (Hall 1920: I. 30)
>
> ('I am now older than I was in winters and in learning./ I possess more than I did – my wit *ought* to be greater')

(The Trinity MS of the same poem has *oh* instead of *ahte*, showing that both present and past could be used equivalently at this stage.)

The general strong/weak ambiguity of this verb class led to extremely complicated semantic developments, including splits into independent verbs (*owe* vs *ought*), loss of some forms (present *must* is an old past, and the verb has no formal present); and the class as a whole is still syntactically isolated. Certainly, the lack of a marked present third-person singular and early loss of the infinitive played a role in their eventual stabilisation as the unique class of modal auxiliaries, with idiosyncratic morphology and syntax.

2.9.2.6 Infinitive, gerund and participles

Modern English verbs are usually said to have four 'non-finite' forms (i.e. unmarked for tense and person/number): infinitive, past participle, present participle and gerund.[29] The last two are formally identical but functionally distinct:

(76) Infinitive (to) write
Past-participle writt-en
Present participle } writ-ing
Gerund

The infinitive and gerund are syntactically noun-like (*to write/writing is easy*); the participles are either adjectival (*written evidence/writing implements*), or complements to auxiliary verbs in aspectual constructions (*have written/be writing*). The four-way grammatical distinction is historically ancient, and was paralleled in Old English by a formal contrast:

(77) Infinitive wrīt-an
Past participle (ge-)writ-en
Present participle wrīt-ende
Verbal noun wrīt-ing

The term verbal noun rather than 'gerund' refers to the fact that the most characteristically gerundial uses, where the -*ing* form has both the subject and object (as in *John's writing the letter*), is a late development; for the distinction and history see Donner (1986). The Middle English developments include loss of the infinitive ending, so that the infinitive comes to be the same as the bare stem; merger of the original -*ende* present participle with the -*ing* noun; and loss of the *ge-* prefix. All of these are virtually complete by about 1500.

The story of the present participle and gerund is complex and somewhat murky; the two things we can be sure of are that, as in most major changes, there was a long period of complex variation, and that – surprisingly – the infinitive was involved as well. I begin with some odd infinitive developments, and bring the others in as relevant.

The Germanic infinitive is historically a neuter noun built on a verb stem; by earliest Germanic it had lost most of its nominal inflection, and consisted of a verbal stem + suffix: OE *ber-an* 'to bear' < */ber-an-a-m/ (cf. Skt *bhar-aṇ-a-m* 'the bearing'). The -*an* suffix was inflectable for dative in Old English, giving -*enne* (later ~ -*anne*); this occurred mainly after prepositions, e.g. *tō ber-anne*. The other two players, the present participle and the verbal noun, are respectively an old adjective and a derived noun. The present participle continues a verbal adjective in IE */-nt-/ (OE *ber-e-nd-e* = Lat. *fer-e-nt-* 'bearing'); the -*ing* noun continues a Germanic type called a 'feminine abstract', which in early times had the suffix */-inɣa ~ -unɣa/. By the end of Old English the -*ung* type had yielded to -*ing*, which was the only Middle English survival.

In early southern and southwestern Middle English, the inflected infinitive still occurs; but not only with reflex of -*enne*. Forms in -*ende* (identical with the present participle) also appear: Laȝamon B has *to flende* 'to flee', while the A text has *to fleonne* (see Mustanoja 1960: 512ff.). Beginning in the thirteenth century, southern and south midland texts show a further possibility, using either -*ende* or the southern variant -*inde* (identical again with the present participle), or -*inge* (which must owe something to the OE -*ing* noun, but has an -*e* from somewhere: either the present participle or, more likely, the dative singular of OE -*ing*). So Robert of Gloucester has *to doiinge* 'to do'; and well into the fourteenth century John of Trevisa and Wyclif maintain this as a variant. Mustanoja cites the following from Trevisa: 'they were ihote ['called'] Amazones, þat is *to menynge* "withoute brest"'.

We have seen present-participle-like forms for the verbal noun; the participle itself enters the story now. The most common Middle English endings are geographically distributed this way:

(78) North   Midlands   South
     -and   -ende   -inde

The northern form probably reflects Scand. *-andi*; the southern and midland ones continue OE *-ende* (S *-inde* may be significant, since it has the same vowel as *-inge*).

But even in very early texts like Laȝamon, there are some *-inge* endings for present participles; by around 1200 the variants *-inde* ~ *-inge* are available for this category in the south. By Chaucer's time the participle had stabilised in most dialects: e.g. Trevisa has *-ing(e)*, as does Chaucer, while Gower uses mainly *-ende* (with *-inge* mostly in rhyme), and the Kentish *Ayenbite* has only *-ind(e)*. By the fifteenth century *-ing(e)* was the dominant standard form.

The development for the London standard then must have been something like this:

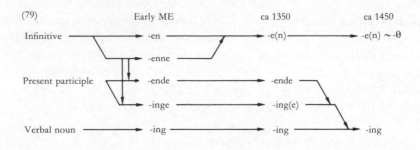

The past participle is historically an adjective formed off a verb stem; the suffix was IE */-no-/ for strong verbs (cf. Skt *va-vṛt-an-a-ḥ* 'having turned'), and */-to-/ for weak verbs (cf. Lat. *cap-tu-s* 'captured'). The weak participial suffix was retained throughout Middle English (as it still is); the strong was subject to variable nasal deletion, with variation of the type *-en* ~ *-e* ~ *-θ* common even in texts by the same writer. This variation did not stabilise into a set of categorical norms until modern times, except (largely, anyhow) in nasal-stem class III verbs like *sing*, *drink*, which tended to lose their endings earlier than others. The Late Middle English situation can be exemplified from Caxton's prologues and epilogues, which show a pattern very like Chaucer's nearly a century earlier. Some verbs always have *-n* (*goten, guyen, chosen,*

wreton/wryton), a few seem never to (*begonne, blowe*), while many others vary (*vnderstand(e)* ~ *vnderstanden, see* ~ *seen, found(e)* ~ *founden*).

The Old English past participle was commonly marked by a prefix *ge-*; this seems to derive from an old perfectivising/collectivising particle, and survives intact in all West Germanic languages except Present-Day English. It began to drop in Old English as early as the tenth century, especially in Northumbrian (possibly connected with the Scandinavian tendency to lose prefixes). By Middle English times it had vanished completely in the north and most of the midlands, and was stable only in the south and some south midland areas. In its normal reduced form *i-/y-*, it was for most of the period clearly a southernism; but it was available in London until quite late, and some writers like Chaucer used it extensively. It was particularly common in verse, probably because it enabled any participle with the prominence contour S(W) to be turned into WS(W), thus producing an iambic foot: *know(e)* S(W) > *y-know(e)* WS(W), etc. Use of the prefix seems to have been largely a personal matter; though it is typical of Chaucer, his contemporary, Gower, appears virtually never to use it (Macaulay 1900: cxx, cites one example, *y-bore* 'born' *CA* II. 499, where the metre demands an initial weak syllable).

By the late fifteenth century *i-/y-* had virtually died out; though it remained as a kind of 'Chaucerism' in archaistically inclined later writers like Spenser, and indeed occurs as late as Milton, who uses *yclept* 'called' (*L'allegro* 12).

FURTHER READING

General literature

Despite mountains of recent scholarship and revision of received wisdom (as this chapter is in part), the old standard handbooks are still the essential starting point, and my debt to them will be obvious. Any serious student will have to get to know them. The most thorough is Luick's gigantic *Historische Grammatik* (1914–40, reprinted 1964); this covers English historical phonology from Germanic to the present, and is a mine of original, powerful and occasionally mad ideas. Luick is available only in German; in English there is now a translation of the shorter but still classic Jordan (1934; rev. edn. Matthes 1968). Both Luick and Jordan deal only peripherally with morphology; there are, however, a number of excellent Middle English grammars covering both areas. In the old 'philological' tradition, Wright & Wright (1928) is thorough and useful, as is Brunner (1963). There is a shorter but more sophisticated outline grammar in Mossé (1952). In the structuralist tradition there is the excellent and too little known Fisiak (1968). There is no generative account of the same thoroughness as these earlier ones, though there are generative treatments of phonological and morphological topics in Jones (1972), which is a useful introduction to Middle English studies, and in Anderson & Jones (1977).

The more detailed general histories of the language also have useful overviews of the period; among the older ones Wyld (1927) is the most thorough and readable. If I were to recommend one modern history it would be Strang (1970), which though difficult and at times idiosyncratic is the most sophisticated and insightful one available. There are also brief and somewhat condensed treatments of historical phonology and morphology in Lass (1987), which might be useful introductions to the more detailed discussions here.

The references to this chapter are highly selective; the reader interested in pursuing given topics further should consult Fisiak's superb topical bibliography of English historical linguistics (1987). The current state of the field can be sampled through the papers from the International Conferences on English Historical Linguistics held since 1979 (Davenport, Hansen & Nielsen 1983; Blake & Jones 1984; Eaton *et al.* 1985; Adamson *et al.* 1990).

2.1.2 In addition to Malone's paper, there is a good discussion of the earliest 'transitional' changes in Moore (1928). See also Strang (1970: chs. IV–V).
2.1.3 On historical reconstruction and related matters see the notes to volume I of this history, chs. 1–3, and the discussion of reconstruction and written evidence in Bloomfield (1933: chs. 17f.) and Hockett (1958: chs. 42–62, *passim*). Hockett's views on the history of English are eccentric, but his argumentation and discussion of method are worth looking at. For a specific discussion of evidence and argument in relation to earlier English, see Lass (1987: §1.6).

On the evidential value (or not) of spelling see Wrenn (1943), and with special reference to Middle English McIntosh (1956), Samuels (1963).
2.1.4 On the development of the ancestor of the modern standard see Samuels (1963), Fisher (1977).
2.1.5 Middle English spelling is of course more variable and complex than is suggested here, and not all spellings have phonological relevance; on this see McIntosh (1956), and the studies of individual scribes in McIntosh (1974, 1975). For a structuralist study of the orthography of particular manuscripts and its phonological implications, see Francis (1962).
2.2.1 The account of the Old English inputs here is fairly traditional; for details of the controversies surrounding the vowel system in particular see volume I of this history, ch. 3. The traditional view that OE (and ME) /r/ was an alveolar trill [r] is untenable; for the history of this view and some criticism see Lass (1977a). The claim in Lass & Anderson (1975) that OE /r/ was uvular now seems misguided; the most likely value is an alveolar

approximant [ɹ], like Modern English /r/, but with velar and pharyngeal co-articulation. For detailed arguments for this controversial view see Lass (1983).

2.3.1 On the 'long' and 'short' diphthongs see Lass (1984a: 172–7). To give a somewhat simpler account, a normal (= 'long') diphthong, like a long vowel, can be seen as associated with two V-slots in the CV-skeleton of a form; a short vowel or 'short diphthong' is associated with only one. The CV-tier (see the diagram below) is where the weight or quantity of the syllable is determined (more details in 2.5.1). Using simple Old English examples:

Short vowel	*'Short' diphthong*	*Long vowel*	*'Long' diphthong*
C V C	C V C V	C V V	C V V
| | |	| ∧ |	| | |	| | |
r æ t	m eo d u	m e e	b e o
ræt 'rat'	*meodu* 'mead'	*mē* 'me'	*beō* 'bee'

The claim that the Middle English short low vowel was a front /a/ rather than a back /ɑ/ is based on arguments from modern dialect data and historical developments; for the full justification see Lass (1976: ch. 4). There is some recent discussion, with an attempt at explaining various changes in this vowel, in Adamska-Sałaciak (1984).

2.3.2 The assumption that Old and Middle English long and short vowels at a given height were the same in quality is controversial. The usual view (see e.g. Kökeritz 1961; Moore & Marckwardt 1964) is that the non-low long/short pairs had the 'modern' configuration:

i: u:

   ɪ ʊ

e: o:

   ε ɔ

There are, however, good (to my mind, convincing) arguments for a much more 'conservative' account, in which short /i e u o/ remained throughout Middle English, with /e o/ lowering to [ε ɔ] in the sixteenth century, and /i u/ not lowering and centralising to [ɪ ʊ] until after 1650 (see Lass 1981, and vol. III of this history, ch. 1). The arguments for putting the changes early can be seen in Luick (1914–40: §§ 378–80).

There is another – even more controversial – account of the Middle English long and short vowels, in which all the long vowels are assumed to be diphthongs; this was proposed by Stockwell (1961), and developed in a series of later papers (Stockwell 1978, 1985). The arguments are too complex to go into here, but the type of system proposed can be seen by juxtaposing my (actually quite traditional) view of the top three heights in the Middle English long front-vowel system with Stockwell's:

Lass Stockwell
i: iy (= [ij])
e: ɪə
ɛ: ɛə

I find Stockwell's account workable if one goes forward from presumed Old and Middle English values, but virtually impossible to square with the evidence from sixteenth- and seventeenth-century phoneticians. The argument, however, is by no means over, and my views should be compared with his, especially as set out in relation to Open Syllable Lengthening (Stockwell 1961, 1985).

Yet another view of the Middle English vowel system, recognising only three contrastive heights, is advocated by Chomsky & Halle (1968). They posit:

ī i u ū
ē e o ō
ǣ a ɔ̄ ā

where the distinction is not long vs short but 'tense' vs 'lax'. There is, however, no good evidence for either a three-height system (Lass 1976: ch. 4) or the feature 'tense' (Lass 1976: ch. 1, Appendix).

The account of OSL is oversimple and (given Stockwell's views) now controversial, if traditional. For detailed revisions of the traditional theory which I accept, see Minkova (1982) and the further discussion in Lass (1985); for Stockwell's views, with an interesting and detailed history of the relevant scholarship, Stockwell (1984).

One particular oversimplification merits some discussion. The historian constantly treads a difficult line between oversimplification and a somewhat more accurate complexity that can obscure the important outlines of a development. This is the case in my discussion of OSL. While the picture in (15) is overall a true one, and reflects the *ultimate* state of affairs in the ancestors of the modern standard, it fudges a number of details. First (though this is not strictly relevant to our concerns here), the merger of lengthened /e o/ with /ɛ: ɔ:/ never took place in parts of the midlands: these categories are still distinct in some modern rural dialects, e.g. in parts of Yorkshire, where we find [i:] in *wheat* (< /hwɛ:t(ə)/ < OE *hwǣte*) vs [ɪə] in *eat* < OSL of /e/ (OE *etan*: see discussion in Lass (1987: 227–9)).

Second, and more relevant, it appears that some London poets kept these categories apart in rhyme until quite close to the end of the fourteenth century. Gower (Macaulay 1900: xcviii ff.) apparently does not rhyme the outputs of OSL (e.g. *trede* 'tread' < OE *trĕdan*, *bore* 'born' < OE *-bŏren*) with original /ɛ:/ and /ɔ:/ (*dede* 'dead' OE *dēad*, *more* 'more' with /ɔ:/ <

OE *māra*). And both of these are kept apart from the closer /eː oː/. Gower thus appears to have three long mid vowel categories, all etymologically distinct. It is not clear what to make of this; Macaulay suggests 'imperfect lengthening', i.e. presumably the 'new' vowels from OSL were either shorter than 'true' long vowels (which seems dubious, since three-way length contrasts are not a Germanic type), or – more plausibly – variable, so that Gower would resist rhyming inconstantly long vowels with categorically long ones. Another possibility, consonant with their origins and with the modern north midland developments, is that they were phonetically different, perhaps slightly closer or more centralised (the most likely value, if they were still distinct, would be lowered and centralised, e.g. [ɪː] and [ʊː]: but this is problematical).

2.3.3 The account of the Middle English diphthongs is based generally on that in Lass & Anderson (1975: 194ff.). The term 'Middle English Breaking' is a coinage of Charles Jones (see Anderson & Jones 1977: §5.6). For another treatment of Middle English diphthongs, Phillips (1983).

On allophones of /x/: it is not clear (see Lass & Anderson 1975: 220) whether Old English palatalised /x/ to [ç] after front vowels. The German-based philological tradition posits an '*ich/ach* rule' for Old English, but the comparative evidence for this is weak: Dutch, Afrikaans and Yiddish, for instance, do not palatalise in this environment. The only evidence for an [x]/[ç] distinction that carries weight is the fact that only (supposed) [x] becomes [f] in Late Middle English (as in *rough* < OE *rūh*, etc. – see 2.4.1.2). The most conservative view would be that we have no information about the allophones of /x/ until well into Middle English, but that by the time the first <f> spellings appear for OE /x/ we must have [x] vs [ç].

2.3.4 On the front rounded vowels in the north, see Lass (1976: ch. 2); for an overall account of their loss, Reszkiewicz (1971).

2.4.1.1 The classic account of degemination and the rise of the voice contrast is Kurath (1956). On initial fricative voicing in OE and Middle English see Bennett (1955), Fisiak (1984b).

2.4.1.2 On weakening and the status of /h/ see Lass & Anderson (1975: ch. 5), Lass (1976: ch. 6; 1984b: §§8.3.1–3)

2.4.2.2 The account of /r/-metathesis is oversimplified; the process was apparently more widespread and less restricted than the handbook accounts (which I follow) suggest. For data and discussion see the intriguing study by Robinson (1985).

2.5.1 On quantity see the theoretical introduction in Lass (1984b: §§10.3.1–3). The characterisation of -VC rhymes as light is controversial, but seems valid for Germanic at least (Lass 1985: 261ff.). For length and quantity in Germanic see Árnason (1980); the metrical S/W model utilised here and in the treatment of stress in section 2.6 is outlined in Giegerich (1985), and in a detailed textbook introduction in Hogg & McCully (1987).

2.5.2 In my earlier (1974) paper I dealt with length, which I failed to distinguish from quantity; the introduction of quantity into the story is developed with more historical background in Lass (1985). The idea of conspiracy is derivative to a large extent from Sapir's 'drift' (1921: ch. VII). See also Lass (1977b). The Scandinavian languages also went through a quantity/length conspiracy, called by Árnason (1980) the 'Quantity Shift'; this is worth comparing to the English sequence.

2.5.3 On final /ə/-deletion: the idea that much Middle English verse was rigorously syllable-counted (at least, enough to provide evidence for the pronunciation of final unstressed vowels) is now nearly universally accepted by historians of English and Germanic. It stems originally from Tyrwhitt's remarks (1798) on Chaucer's versification, and was standard by the late nineteenth century (see Ten Brink's classic account, 1884). Recently, a contrary view has arisen, which denies that Chaucerian and much other Middle English verse was syllable-counted, and hence claims that both the pronunciation of -e and the evidential value of metrics are delusions. The controversy (notably restricted to literary circles) was started by South-worth (1954); an accessible, entertaining and intemperate further development can be seen in Robinson (1971). Whatever the literary issues at stake (the meat of Robinson's polemic), linguistically the Southworth school has nothing substantial to say, and can be dismissed as an eccentricity.

The most valuable recent work on /ə/-deletion is to be found in a series of papers by Donka Minkova (1982, 1983, 1984) and a classic book (1991); the view I take here on early loss of -e is based on her studies. For more on -e in metrical contexts see Iwasaki (1986a).

The story of the evolution of the plural morpheme, assuming deletion of /ə/ in certain contexts, is traditional; for a quite different account, claiming a rule of /ə/-insertion, see Keyser & O'Neil (1985).

2.5.4 On diacritics in English spelling see Fried (1969). For more on <e>, Jespersen (1909–49: §I, 6.28).

2.6.1–2 The characterisation of English stress (its nature, degree of rule-governedness, the appropriate rules and representation types for its description) has been a focal issue in phonological discussion for nearly thirty years. The early generative proposals in Chomsky & Halle (1968) have been much refined in the context of metrical phonology (see Hogg & McCully, 1987: ch. 3) and dependency phonology (Anderson & Jones, 1977: §§4.3, 4.8). For an introductory and informal metrical view of Present-Day English stress see Lass (1987: §§3.4–6). The treatment in the present chapter is really a sketch, and skirts many theoretical issues; for a detailed historical overview within the generative framework see Halle & Keyser (1971). For more on stress doublets, see Jespersen (1909–49: I, §§5.53ff.).

2.8.1 The best modern introduction to morphology is Matthews (1974). For some further introductory discussion of the morphology/syntax/semantics relation see Lass (1987: §4.1).

2.8.2 For a brief overview of morphological typology, Lass (1987: §4.2); for a thorough (though not elementary) introduction to typology, Comrie (1981).

2.8.3 On analogy, Bloomfield (1933: ch. 23) is still the best introduction; for more sophisticated accounts see Anttila (1972: ch. 4), Bynon (1977: ch. 1, §§ 5–6). Text sources: *Peterborough Chronicle* from Bennett & Smithers (1966), *Astrolabe* from Benson (1987), *Grocers' Ordenances* from Chambers & Daunt (1931).

2.9.1.1 The overviews of Middle English developments in the standard grammars and histories are a useful preliminary to the discussion here and in the rest of the chapter. Mossé (1952) and Fisiak (1968) are particularly useful, and Wyld (1927: ch. 9) has a good narrative history. There are useful discussions of morphological developments as they are implicated in syntax in the relevant chapters of Mustanoja (1960).

On early developments in the noun (and elsewhere) see Moore (1928); on grammatical gender Moore (1921), Clark (1957), Jones (1967), Mausch (1986). For Chaucer's morphology see Ten Brink (1884), Fisiak (1965), and the accessible but unhistorical Sandved (1985). For a generative account of Middle English noun morphology see Jones (1972: ch. 4).

2.9.1.2 On the article and adjective, Jones (1972: ch. 4). For the relation between syntax and adjective inflection, Mustanoja (1960: 275–89, *passim*). On demonstrative pronouns, Heltveit (1953).

2.9.1.3 On the personal pronouns, Mustanoja (1960: 122–51). *She* is a long-standing problem, which has generated a good deal of scholarship; for surveys and discussion Stevick (1964), Duncan (1972), who cite the relevant earlier work. Duncan is particularly worth reading, both for her general critical view of the literature, and her connection of the history with the modern rural dialect picture.

2.9.2.2 On the tense forms of the weak verb see any of the standard grammars; on class shifting and ambiguity in Old English, Mertens-Fonck (1984).

2.9.2.3 On the strong verb and its later history see Rettger (1934), Long (1944). There is a useful reclassification of Middle English strong verbs according to the number of stem allomorphs in Fisiak (1968: 106–10), and good class-by-class coverage in Mossé (1952) and Wyld (1927).

2.9.2.4 The present plural in *-en* is thoroughly discussed in Bryan (1921). The development of the *-es* present third-person singular is problematic; see vol. III, ch. 1, for discussion. On its early origins, Wyld (1927: 257) argues against the usual northern source, and derives it 'through the influence of, and by analogy with, the common Auxiliary *is*'. This is hard to maintain, especially in the light of early northeast midland occurrences, and other northernisms in the southern standard. Wyld is, however, surely right when he says (256) that -es is 'definitely colloquial in origin' – especially in the light of late retentions of -eth in elevated styles. On Chaucer's use of -es see also Burnley (1983: 127), and Shields (1980).

The southern present pattern, with its linking of third-person singular and all plural, has led Strang (1970: §119) to say that 'In this respect the morphology was abnormal and not illuminating, and … was ripe for change.' The first part of this claim is (self-evidently) true, the second a *non sequitur*. (Why has the linking of third-person singular and second-person plural in Dutch remained?) Closer to home, if identity of third-person singular and the plural is so 'abnormal', why was it allowed to develop in the first place, and why did it remain stable for nearly three centuries? Looking at 'abnormalities' as 'causes' of change is a dead end: it merely adds a specious drama or dynamism to the historical story, and produces an illusion of plausibility and understanding. We do not know why language changes; if we are lucky we can often see how. (On the fallaciousness of the argument from 'abnormality' see Lass (1980: chs. 2–3).)

2.9.2.5 The forms of the anomalous verbs are well laid out in the handbooks. On *be*, see the detailed study in Forström (1948). The preterite-present > modal story has been much discussed recently: see Goossens (1984), Plank (1984).

2.9.2.6 On the gerund and present participle see Rooth (1941–2), Dal (1952), Mossé (1957) and the discussion in Mustanoja (1960: 547). On the prefix *ge-* and its history, van Draat (1902–3), Pilch (1955).

TEXTUAL SOURCES

There are a number of easily accessible and well annotated collections of Middle English texts. I have, where possible, made use of these rather than standard full editions, so that the material I cite will be easily available to the reader who wants to check up or get an overview of what a particular text looks like. For Middle English overall the selection in Mossé (1952) is still to my mind the best; coupled with his outline grammar it forms an excellent introduction to the period. For Early Middle English there are three excellent collections: Hall (1920) has very clean texts with a minimum of editorial interference, which give a good idea of capitalisation and punctuation conventions, and are copiously annotated; Bennett & Smithers (1966) has a good linguistic introduction but somewhat modernised texts, and there is also a good selection in Dickins & Wilson (1956). For later Middle English Sisam (1955) has a good sample, but rather overmodernised. Chaucer citations are from Benson (1987), except for the *Canterbury Tales*, where the edition of Blake (1980) has now become standard; Gower from Macaulay (1900); Caxton from Crotch (1928) checked against Blake (1973); Paston Letters from Davis (1971–6); Margery Kempe from Meech & Allen (1940).

Some readers may note that my choice of texts is perhaps rather slanted toward the east, with much less mention than is usual of the great landmarks of the western prose and alliterative-verse traditions. This is deliberate, in keeping with the general view (the 'London bias', 2.1.4) that the further away from London and the southeast midlands a text comes from, the less is its direct relevance to 'the history of English' in the narrower sense.

3 MIDDLE ENGLISH DIALECTOLOGY

James Milroy

Dialectology is more central to the study of M[iddle] E[nglish] than to any other branch of English historical linguistics.

Strang (1970: 225)

3.1 Dialect method and the study of Middle English

3.1.1 Introduction

The most striking fact about Middle English is that it exhibits by far the greatest diversity in written language of any period before or since.[1] Before 1100 – in the Old English period – extant written sources for the study of variation are rather sparse, and much of the Late Old English literary output is in a relatively invariant West Saxon literary language. Similarly, close to the end of the Middle English period (in the fifteenth century), we witness the rise and subsequent spread of a relatively uniform written variety – the beginnings of 'standard English'. From that century onward, the vast bulk of printed documents is in this variety, regardless of the geographical provenance of the author: documents do not readily betray their region of origin, and the dialectal diversity that continued to exist in speech is suppressed in writing. For this reason, much of our knowledge of Early Modern English variation depends much more on indirect evidence, such as contemporary commentaries on pronunciation (on which see especially Dobson 1968), and much less on variable forms attested in the texts themselves. For written Middle English, on the other hand, our access to variation is direct, and it is this primary source that we use to reconstruct the diversity of spoken Middle English.

Variability in written Middle English is very wide-ranging at every linguistic level: spelling, morphology, syntax and lexicon. There are also several non-linguistic dimensions in which this variation can be observed. Of these, the geographical and chronological dimensions are most immediately obvious: texts from different areas are different, and later texts differ very markedly from earlier ones (for some examples see

Lass in this volume). For the dialect scholar, however, these dimensions intersect and overlap, as the date and place of origin of the relevant sources are not usually accurately known: thus, as the dialectologist's primary task is to describe aspects of variation as they exist *at a given time*, the need to take account of the chronology adds some complexity to the task of generalising correctly about Middle English dialect distribution. In addition to these, there is often quite considerable variability even within a single text: for example, the same recurrent word may be spelt in a variety of ways and different inflectional endings used on different occasions; frequently, different portions of a manuscript appear to be written in different dialects. This intratextual dimension of variation is in some ways analogous to what the present-day dialect investigator encounters as inherent variability in the speech of live informants, and it adds one further dimension to the task of analysis and interpretation. Much of the recent progress that has been made in Middle English dialectology, particularly in the work of Angus McIntosh and his colleagues, has depended on sophisticated analysis of this intratextual dimension.

Variation in written Middle English is so extensive that it is reasonable to ask in what sense we are dealing with a single state or stage of language. We can argue that the label 'Middle English' does not refer to a coherent entity, but to a complex series of divergent, rapidly changing and intertwining varieties retrospectively seen as transitional between 'Old English' and 'Modern English'. To research this variation, however, is essential if we are to explain how Modern English developed, and we approach the task in this chapter by asking the basic question: *why are the records of Middle English so variable?* We shall bear this in mind throughout, but we focus first on this general difference between Middle English and the preceding and succeeding stages: the relative variability of (written) Middle English, as contrasted with Old English and Modern English.

3.1.2   Variation and standardisation

Tolerance of variation in written Middle English can be ascribed to the absence of a fully institutionalised standard variety in Middle English; indeed, this is one of the most important sociolinguistic differences between Middle English and Modern English. Here we shall briefly notice two senses in which the notion of standardisation is relevant: the first is linguistic, and the second is sociopolitical. In the purely linguistic dimension, the main symptom of a standardised variety is *uniformity of usage* – a uniformity which for various reasons is most readily achieved in the *written*, rather than the spoken, channel. In this respect, Middle English (especially *Early* Middle English – approximately 1100–1300) is largely unstandardised, and there are rather few literary texts which have a high degree of uniformity of usage. The best-known example of a relatively uniform usage in Early Middle English is the so-called *AB language*. This is considered to be noteworthy because the same writing conventions are found in two substantial manuscripts in the hands of *different* scribes (they contain the *Ancrene Wisse* and a group of saints' lives), and it can be shown that these texts have a continuity with Old English writing conventions: their relative uniformity is the result of a continuous scribal tradition which was not disrupted by the Norman Conquest to the same extent that it was elsewhere (for a discussion, see Scragg 1974: 27–9, and for more detail Dobson 1962).[2] In the period 1100–1300 these relatively uniform varieties are the exception rather than the rule, and it may be thought remarkable that arguments for anything resembling a 'standard' in Early Middle English should depend here on as few as *two* manuscripts.

In the second sense (sociopolitical), a variety like the AB language is not precisely what a modern observer understands by a standard language, as its forms are localised and confined to two manuscripts; thus, they are very far from being universally accepted by all writers of English (contrast Present-Day English, in which thousands of documents appear daily in the standard variety). As time progresses, it becomes more common to find such relatively uniform (but localised) varieties used in different regions of the country – although personal documents, such as letters, can remain very variable up until the end of the period (and, indeed, thereafter). In the late fourteenth century the English nation still had not reached agreement on a single supralocal standard variety for use in literary texts, and the Scottish nation had its own written form of the language – Scots. These facts about Middle English variation are *prima facie* evidence that the attitude of writers to the language they were writing could not have been the same as that of present-day writers.

Indeed, as we are conditioned in the twentieth century to assume that there is a dominant 'correct' variety of written English, an understanding of attitudes to variation in Middle English requires from the modern observer a considerable leap of the imagination. For example, if we come across a document that uses localised and variable spelling conventions, we are not entitled for that reason alone to presume that the writer was careless or ignorant (uniform spelling in handwritten documents is largely a post-eighteenth-century phenomenon); therefore we are not necessarily entitled to 'correct' a text according to some notional 'standard' of Middle English spelling. One of the attitudinal differences between medieval and modern times is that in Middle English fluid and variable language states were accepted as appropriate vehicles for *written* use.

This attested variability is a matter of great good fortune for the dialectologist, whose natural interests are not in uniform states, but in variation. An analogy with the dialectology of present-day states may help to clarify this. When we interview a live informant, we are not normally interested in 'standard' or 'correct' forms, but in divergent forms, and we do not correct his/her usage; nor are we primarily interested in uniformity of usage: we want to know about variation. The point of studying variation, however, is not merely to describe the variation discovered, but also to draw from the study of variation conclusions about linguistic structure and in particular to locate patterns of linguistic change in progress; this is especially true of *social dialectology*, following Labov 1966, 1972b. These general points about the study of variation apply to Middle English just as much as they do to 'live' language states. A text that is variable within itself will often be of more interest than one which follows a uniform spelling tradition, for the obvious reason that conventional and standardised orthographies are likely to suppress change in progress in the spoken language. It is hardly an exaggeration to say that standardisation is the chief enemy of the dialectologist: the study of *variation* within and between texts gives us the best chance of coming close to knowing what variation in Middle English was actually like and hence to locate patterns of linguistic change. In Section 3.1.3, we review the aims and methods of dialectology, as these apply to Middle English.

3.1.3   *Dialectology*

Dialectology is the systematic study of variation in language – at any place or time – and in this chapter my brief is to focus on methods of systematic study and the kind of conclusions about language variation that can be drawn from such methods. This emphasis on methodology is essential, as our conclusions and interpretations are likely to be influenced by the methods we have used and the assumptions that lie behind these methods. As for the facts of variation in Middle English: this is so extensive that virtually every piece of research into Middle English language – whether it be textual commentary, a contribution to a dictionary (such as the *Oxford English Dictionary*), or a discussion of scribal practice – is, at least potentially, a contribution to Middle English dialectology. The difference in this respect between Middle English and other periods cannot be overstated: as virtually every commonly occurring lexical item is attested in a variety of *written* forms, the sources of our knowledge are extremely varied, and the task of making linguistically useful generalisations about the distribution of forms is an extremely challenging one.

The ultimate goal of investigating a historical state of language variation is the same as that of investigating a present-day state: to discover how language variants are distributed in some community – whether it be a small village or a whole country. Within this broad variationist aim, however, dialectologists have traditionally concentrated on the *geographical* dimension of variation, and in this respect, a large-scale Middle English project such as the *Linguistic Atlas of Late Mediaeval English* (McIntosh, Samuels & Benskin 1986; henceforth *LALME*) has the same goal as projects like the *Survey of English Dialects* (Orton *et al.* 1962–71) and the associated *Atlas* (Orton, Sanderson & Widdowson 1978): to make available detailed information on the geographical distribution of variants. Indeed, the geographical dimension has been so salient that it has sometimes been taken for granted that dialectology is by definition geographical in its aims and methods. In this chapter, I shall give considerable attention to geographical variation, but I shall also consider other aspects of variation.

While research on Middle English geographical variation is important for a number of purposes – some of them linguistic and others non-linguistic (literary and historical, for example) – dialectology has, for more than a century, had a much more ambitious aim than merely to describe variation in its geographical dimension. This is no less than to contribute to our understanding of the nature of linguistic change. The kind of questions considered in this perspective include the following: how and why are linguistic changes implemented at particular times and places? What patterns can be discerned in the diffusion of changes within and between communities? Why do some linguistic variants advance while others recede? These are theoretical questions, to which studies of present-day variation have made an enormous contribution and to which Middle English dialectology is also extremely relevant.

This theoretical aim is very much borne in mind in this chapter – for two major reasons. First, the background of theoretical interests at given times has always in some way influenced the methods of dialectology and the interpretations and explanations offered by investigators. Thus, in one respect, much nineteenth and twentieth-century regional dialectology can be seen as empirical testing of the Neogrammarian axiom that sound change proceeds blindly and without exceptions.[3] Second, recent developments in variation studies have suggested new perspectives and have brought to the forefront other theoretical issues to which satisfactory solutions might now be possible (see the review by Walters 1988). Here, the key perception is that variability in language may be shown to be *structured* and *functional* (Weinreich, Labov & Herzog 1968: 100–1) – *uniform states do not exist in reality: all states of language incorporate variation, and it is the dialectologist's task to reveal the orderliness in that variation.*

Within this broader theoretical perspective, however, Middle English dialectology has always had a more specific goal, which is to contribute directly to the historical description of the English language. In this respect Middle English dialectology links up with important work that has been carried out on the geographical dialectology of present-day states. The methods of the *Survey of English Dialects* (which concentrates on the language of rural people on the assumption that their speech is the most conservative) focus specifically on historical issues and select questionnaire items on the basis of their likely relationships to Middle English forms (Orton *et al.* 1962–71). The findings of the *Survey of English Dialects* can be and have been used to project backwards on to Middle English: for example, in an attempt to settle disputed questions about the pronunciation of Middle English (Lass 1976), or to demonstrate the present-day survival of Middle English variants in particular locations (Wakelin & Barry 1968). Of course, this process also works in the opposite direction: just as present-day findings can be, and have been, used to illuminate the past, so the findings of Middle English dialectology can be used to illuminate the present – or later stages of the language, such as Early Modern English.

3.1.4   *Middle English dialect method; written sources as evidence for spoken states*

The crucial difference between Middle English and Present-Day English research is that, whereas the Present-Day English dialectologist has direct access to speakers, the Middle English dialectologist is dependent on written records. Nevertheless, as Wyld (1927: 21) points out:

> we must never forget that while, from the nature of the case, the past history of a language must necessarily be traced by means of written records, these are to be regarded as affording us merely an indication of what was actually taking place in the spoken language itself... The drama of linguistic change is enacted, not in manuscripts nor inscriptions, but in the mouths and minds of men.

This has a number of consequences which greatly affect the methodology adopted and the kind of interpretation that scholars might wish to put upon the data. Our access to Middle English is plainly more indirect than our access to Present-Day English, and the practical difficulties of Middle English dialectology can be described as very largely a consequence of the differential *forms* and *functions* of writing and speech. There are consequences for the methodology, because the written nature of the evidence makes it necessary to adopt analytic methods that differ from those used in analysing spoken dialects. Here, however, we notice first that there is a very general consequence: this is that, because our evidence exists only in written form, there are limitations to what we can know for certain about variation in Middle English *speech*. We shall first notice some of the *formal* differences between the spoken and the written channels, and the limitations that these must place on the products of our research.

Alphabetic writing systems, even though they are ultimately based on phonology or phonemic structure, cannot (and do not attempt to) reflect all aspects of the spoken language. Suprasegmental features (pause, intonation, stress), for example, are either not shown or only very crudely indicated, as the writing system is based overwhelmingly on the segmental phonological structure. However, it is not a direct guide to the exact phonetic qualities of the sound segments. Thus, if we were ever to encounter a Middle English text with a perfect 'fit' between the orthography and the phonology, it would be like a 'broad' phonemic transcription and would thus reveal only (the scribe's interpretation of) the underlying phonemic (or systematic phonetic) contrasts in the dialect. (The *Ormulum* is the nearest we have to this ideal.) It would not indicate the exact phonetic qualities of different variants (allophones) of a phoneme and would also be a poor guide to the exact pronunciation of many of the phonemes.

It is because of these limitations on what we can know for certain that there can be so much dispute about early English pronunciation: for example, the qualities of the vowel sounds (for a discussion see Lass 1976). The use of a particular letter (or *grapheme*), such as <a> in a Middle English text normally gives no indication as to whether this represents a low or low-mid vowel, whether it was front, back or central, or indeed whether it might have been subject to lengthening, rounding or diphthongisation. (The *Ormulum* is the only text that can assist us in some of these respects.) The probabilities normally have to be assessed by the use of all manner of supporting evidence, none of which can ultimately tell us exactly how the vowel indicated by <a> was pronounced in a given area at a given date, or in a given word, or by a given person. Thus, Lass' conclusion that ME /a/ was probably a back vowel must be interpreted as applicable only in a broad sense, and does not rule out the possibility that at different times and places, and in varying phonetic environments, /a/ could have had other pronunciations. As for the consonant system, we can also ask whether ME /l/ was 'clear' or 'dark', or whether /t/ was aspirated in some contexts – in the knowledge that we would get little, if any, help in coming to a conclusion from the writing system alone. What we can know about Middle English pronunciation is thus limited by the fact that variation in Middle English speech is not directly accessible; therefore, our conclusions as to how things might have been are seldom authoritative: it is a matter of *reducing the margin of ignorance*, weighing up a set of probabilities and drawing conclusions of a rather generalised or idealised kind.

These difficulties are, of course, aggravated by the fact that Middle English writing systems are very far from being exact transcriptions. Apart from the additional problems caused by the fact that many literary texts were copied by scribes from different areas (on which see section 3.2), there are more general complications arising from the fundamental differences between speech and writing. A single letter (or 'grapheme') does not necessarily stand for a single sound (or sound segment) in Middle English any more than it does in Present-Day English or French (in *enough*, *thatch*, *chien*, for example). Thus, a sequence of letters may relate to a single segment, or to more than one segment, or to no segment at all; indeed, a discontinuous grapheme (such as *i...e* in PDE *site*) may refer to a single sound segment. Second, the same sound segment can be represented variably within the same text, or in the same region, by different graphemes. In a seminal article McIntosh (1956) sets out the general principles of the relation between writing and speech as they affect the methodology of Middle English dialect studies. He emphasises the independence of graphic and phonetic structures and the need to study graphic variation independently of supposed phonetic correspondences: there are many examples in Middle English of spelling variants that do not reflect phonetic/phonological differences. McIntosh calls attention to pairs like *erþe/erthe, noȝt/noght, up/vp*, which are graphic variants and are of interest in themselves for this reason (for example, such variants can be diagnostic for differentiating scribal practices), but they do not reflect phonetic differences. Thus, the whole situation is complicated by the fact that writing systems have their own dynamics, which are largely independent of spoken forms.

There are other complications involved in dealing with *written* dialects that are no longer spoken. Some of these are cultural or historical, rather than dialectological. In Middle English, one of the complicating factors is the demise of the West Saxon scribal tradition after the Norman Conquest. This tradition had achieved a high degree of uniform scribal practice, which implies also a high degree of uniformity in scribal training. It also implies the development of a relatively wide gulf between the standardised orthography and the norms of the spoken dialects of Late Old English, which must have been much more variable than the orthography – as spoken language always is. Beside Late Old English documents, Middle English documents from 1100 to 1300 appear at first sight to be quite chaotic scribally, and this arises – at least in part – from the mixing of different conventions in the work of scribes whose training was no longer in a single tradition (see Scragg 1974: 15–37). In varying mixtures, Early Middle English spelling incorporates aspects of Old English, Latin and Norman French spelling conventions, and the varying spellings in some cases indicate no more than graphic differences. Thus (for example), if one scribe uses <a> for OE *æ* where another uses <æ>, it does not necessarily follow that different pronunciations are indicated. Indeed, there are such tremendous difficulties in relating the extant written forms to what might have been the 'underlying' spoken forms that it is appropriate to consider the general nature of the problem here.

Emphasis on the different formal properties of spoken and written language is fundamental to the methodology of the *LALME* (McIntosh, Samuels & Benskin 1986), and is particularly prominent in the work of the founder of the project, Angus McIntosh. Effectively, the view adopted (McIntosh 1956, 1963, 1966) is that writing is a separate system of language that has its own structure and is not immediately derivative from speech (see also Vachek 1945–9; Haas 1970). Any 'fit' that we might discern between a writing system and its 'underlying' phonology is very complex. It seems that this view might further imply that it is very difficult (if not impossible) to show that there is a consistent fit between the writing system of some particular Middle English text and some underlying local phonology (or the phonological system of the writer himself). Although one very thorough attempt has been made (McLaughlin 1963) to specify the complex fit between orthography and phonology in the case of the *Gawain* manuscript, the conclusions that we are able to draw confidently are normally somewhat more generalised (indeed, idealised) than this. Thus, McIntosh *et al.* (1986) have preferred to treat the geographical distribution of forms in Middle English as specifically a distribution of written forms belonging to writing systems, with no claim that such forms necessarily reflect particular forms in speech (although, of course, they often might). The separation of writing from speech (as a methodological prime) is further justified by the functional differences between speech and writing, to which we now turn briefly.

The main functional difference between speech and writing is that, whereas speech is used mainly to communicate between interlocutors who are present at the time of utterance, writing is used to communicate with persons who are not present. To be effective the written channel has to be relatively unambiguous in its forms, as situational context cannot be used to clarify ambiguity or vagueness, and miscomprehensions cannot be repaired. Many important consequences follow from this. For the study of older stages of a language, the main consequence is that much of what remains is not necessarily very close in its forms to the conversational speech forms of the writer: written texts lean towards the more 'formal' registers and 'message-oriented' functions (Brown 1982) of language,[4] and they bear an indirect and idealised relation to speech. It is also partly because of this that the written channel tends to be more conservative: the writer follows conventions that are more generally agreed and prescribed by social groupings. For this reason, it becomes slightly dangerous for writers to introduce changes, as innovative forms may not be immediately understood outside a particular situational context. Thus, changes in progress are not easily admitted into writing systems: they do not normally appear in writing until some time after they have been adopted in speech. Sometimes, because of these functional differences, changes of certain kinds are *never* recorded in the writing system at all.[5] The

Middle English writing systems share these general characteristics with all others, except to the extent that in many Middle English sources writing conventions were less fixed and standardised than at other times. In these, therefore, we may have opportunities to come closer to what was happening in speech communities than is usually the case in the study of written sources, even though there are problems in interpreting them. So, despite all the difficulties, the Middle English dialectologist can be considered rather fortunate in this particular respect.

From what I have said above, it follows that writing is not a *social* activity in the same sense as speech, and this fact also places limitations on what we can know for certain about the roles and functions of speech varieties used in the Middle English period. Whereas present-day social dialectology has direct access to speakers in social and situational contexts that can be described by empirical observation, our knowledge of socially relevant detail in Middle English depends on indirect evidence – for example, on (rather rare) comments on the linguistic situation that have been accidentally preserved. The best known of these are Trevisa's comments (ca 1385) on the decline of French teaching in schools and the difficulty in understanding northern accents, and Caxton's famous complaint (ca 1490) about the variable and changing nature of the English language. Although comments of this kind are highly valued, we cannot of course know how representative they are of the attitudes of all speakers and users of Middle English; nor can we know *directly* what the precise role and function of other languages may have been in the Middle English speech community. For example, although we know that in general terms Anglo-Norman had a superordinate position in the early part of the period, we cannot have direct access by empirical methods to its detailed functions as they varied and changed at different times and places, and the sources available have been subject to varying interpretations by historians and language scholars.[6] However, these social matters are primarily relevant to more general questions regarding the social origins of linguistic changes across long periods in the history of English, rather than to analysing the language of the Middle English texts themselves. We shall therefore consider them only briefly in the concluding section of this chapter.

In this introductory section, I have attempted to sketch in some of the general considerations that affect Middle English dialectological method. In section 3.2, I focus on the kind of conclusions that have been drawn as to geographical distribution of variants in the Middle English period and the methods used to reach these conclusions. As we have noticed, this dimension is not the only dimension in which variation can be shown to exist; therefore, in section 3.3, I consider how far variability *within* texts can be shown to be linguistically systematic, and to what extent this dimension of variation can provide an additional perspective from which we can try to answer questions about change and variation in the history of English.

3.2 The study of geographical variation in Middle English

3.2.1 Introduction

The purpose of this section is to review a long tradition of work on the geographical distribution of Middle English dialects, focusing on the criteria that have been traditionally used to determine regional characteristics. This includes an assessment of the methods and aims of some of the surveys of Middle English dialects that have been carried out. The most extensive of these is that of McIntosh, Samuels & Benskin (1986) – and much attention is given to this. As the most immediate task of the Middle English dialectologist is to determine the *provenance* of surviving texts (McIntosh *et al.* 1986: I, 9), it is appropriate to start this section with a discussion of provenance.

3.2.2 Problems of provenance

Whereas the present-day fieldworker has direct access to speakers who live in particular locations and therefore knows the provenance of his/her data, the Middle English dialectologist is often reliant on texts of which the provenance is not divulged. For literary texts in particular we do not normally have direct indications of either geographical location or chronological date. Furthermore, literary manuscripts are nearly always copies, and the lost 'original' may not have been from the same part of the country as the surviving copy. For these reasons, the Middle English geographical dialectologist must find methods of determining provenance.

It is important to notice that in dealing with provenance, traditional aims have not always been purely linguistic; scholars have frequently been mainly interested in matters that are more properly described as literary or literary–historical. For example, they have sometimes been concerned with determining not only the date and place of the original version of a poem or prose-work, but also its authorship. As many Middle English texts survive in only *one* copy, which is at some distance from the original author, this is plainly a considerable undertaking, but we should note here that this type of aim is also divergent from what we have described in section 3.1 as the ultimate aims of dialectology in general: to contribute to a theory of linguistic change and to our knowledge of the history of the English language. For the textual commentator and literary historian, therefore, it may be of great importance to determine whether or not Nicholas of Guildford was the author of *The Owl and the Nightingale*; for the linguistic scholar, on the other hand, this is not of primary interest. None the less, the linguistic scholar must also be closely concerned with scribal and textual matters: I shall attempt to explain in later sections how important this is, and give a selective account of the contributions to our knowledge that have been made.

I shall focus first on traditional scholarship, and it is fair to say, I think, that much of the traditional interest in Middle English dialects arises from the needs of editors of literary texts. In this perspective, knowledge of regional variation has been seen largely as a contribution to studying textual transmission of particular documents, rather than as an immediate contribution to a theory of linguistic variation. As editors of texts are typically concerned with locating the provenance of the *original* version of the text in question, it is important for them to be able to strip away the layers of variation that might have been introduced by copyists from different dialect areas. The kind of assumptions on which these researches have been carried out are similar – in a broad sense – to those of geologists and archaeologists, and so the reference to 'layers' that are stripped away is a reasonably apt one. There are three problems for editors to solve: (a) Where does the attested version come from? (b) Where did the original come from? (c) What is the history of the transmission from the original to the surviving copy? The traditional method is best demonstrated by using simple examples.

In his edition of the *Bestiary*, Hall (1920: 590–1) concludes that the work was originally composed near the northern border of East Anglia, but that the extant copy was made near its southern boundary. This conclusion depends on certain linguistic forms in the copy, which we describe more fully in section 3.2.5. The northern forms identified include present-participle forms, certain rhymes depending on *a* (northern) rather than *o* (southern/midland) for OE [a:], such as *stedefast*: *gast* (lines 434–5: *gast*, but not -*fast* would have *o* as the vowel in more southerly texts), and, finally, a fairly high incidence of Scandinavian loan words. Other northern forms, such as -*es* for the third-person singular present tense of verbs, suggest to Hall transmission through a northern or north midland copy; however, he is sure that the final copyist was from the southern border of East Anglia. The reason for this is that the manuscript also contains some syncopated third-person singular present verb forms (such as *stant* 'stands', line 1) which can 'spoil the metre' because they reduce the words by one syllable: syncopated present forms are at this period characteristically southern (and recessive). The reasoning used in the argument depends on prior knowledge of the linguistic forms that are thought to be salient markers of particular regions. These are taken to be indicators of the probable provenance of the original version of a copied text and the history of its transmission.

The evidence of rhyming words, as in the above example, has often been found useful – especially in dealing with a period in which many extant literary texts are versified. Editors have assumed that when a copyist 'translates' from one dialect to another, he will be inclined to retain the rhyming pairs of the original, even when he has altered the original forms elsewhere. On this basis it can be argued that the original of *Havelok*, for example, had -*es* in the third-person singular present indicative. Although both -*es* and -*eth* are widely used in the text, the rhyming pairs are always in -*es*, except in one instance (lines 648–9). Therefore, it seems that the original favoured -*es* spellings and was probably composed in the northeast midlands. On the other hand, scribes may occasionally translate pairs which rhymed in the original but do not (apparently) rhyme in their own dialect. A familiar example is the pair *heonne* ('hence')/*kunne* ('kin') at lines 1673–4 of *The Owl and the Nightingale*. These are probably southwestern in this case; however, the only variety in which they could have rhymed is the southeastern dialect, where they would have been *henne*/*kenne*. We shall comment more fully on regional indicators in section 3.2.4, below.

It will be clear from these remarks that determining the provenance and textual history of literary texts is usually a difficult matter, and editorial conclusions in particular cases may be disputable. The reasoning used has depended on having reliable prior information about the regional distribution of linguistic forms. For this reason traditional scholars have set a high value on texts of which the provenance is accurately known. Other texts can then be located in terms of their similarities to and differences from these texts, much in the manner of solving a large jigsaw puzzle.

There are very few *literary* texts that give non-linguistic information as to provenance – for example, statements of the place and date of composing or copying the manuscript. The best-known exception is the fourteenth-century *Ayenbite of Inwit*, which is identified in the preface as being the autograph work of a monk of Canterbury – Dan Michel of Northgate. The 'anchor' texts, therefore, are mainly of other kinds – usually documentary records, such as legal texts, municipal records and the transactions of town guilds: the late-fourteenth-century *Norfolk Gilds*, for example, contain records from Norwich, King's Lynn and other towns. It is for this reason that much of the research carried out on Middle English dialectology has been based on texts that are not literary; indeed, Kristensson (1967: x) goes as far as to say that literary texts 'provide poor material'.

Apart from many detailed descriptions of individual literary texts (which cannot be listed here because of their number; but see McIntosh *et al.* 1986, vol. I, for references), many systematic studies of Middle English dialects (before *LALME*) have been based on material that can be precisely located. Not all of the studies have been comprehensive: often the scope has been limited either to relatively small areas or to the history and distribution of a particular sound segment or a small group of sounds. Such work includes that of Wyld (1913) and his associates (Serjeantson 1927; Mackenzie 1928), which is concerned largely with London, the south-east and the west midlands. Ekwall's onomastic work (on which see Clark in this volume), including, for example, his work on London street names, has also been of immense importance. In this tradition, there have been more recent studies which further explore the evidence of place name and by-name spellings (such as those by Sundby 1963 and Kristensson 1967, 1987). Kristensson's first volume surveys the 'the six northern counties and Lincolnshire' and his second the west midlands. The 1967 volume is based on the *Lay Subsidy Rolls* for five of the northern counties and documents of a similar type for the other two. We return below to a fuller discussion of the methodology and results of such surveys. Here, before we go on to look at the dialect areas in Middle English, I comment briefly on the question of *comprehensiveness* in dialect descriptions.

3.2.3 Comprehensiveness and selectivity

McIntosh *et al.* 1986 aim at exhaustiveness of coverage (of written English) in their new atlas, and lack of exhaustiveness in earlier work has come in for a good deal of criticism both from them and from Strang (1970). The first main attempts to generalise about the Middle English dialect areas were those of Oakden 1930 and Moore, Meech & Whitehall 1935. This is what Strang has to say about the work of Moore, Meech & Whitehall:

> it was clear that their findings were both impoverished and distorted by the small number of texts they analysed, the small number of criteria they employed, the discarding of much evidence, and, above all, the use of the written data simply as clues from which the phonemes and morphemes in the spoken language could be reconstructed ... the work covered such a large time-span that no accurate distinction was possible between strictly diatopic (place-to-place) variation, and diachronic (time-to-time) change.
>
> (Strang 1970: 225)

There are several criticisms here (all of which are well worth noting), but it is clear that selective use of the materials is one of them. This type of argument is in fact very common in dialect studies, and it can lead us into difficulties. *The Survey of English Dialects*, for example, can justifiably claim to be comprehensive, in that it covers the whole country; yet, it is at the same time selective in that it covers the speech of older rural informants, neglecting the young and the urban dialects. In social dialectology also, Labov's New York City study (1966) can be criticised for being selective in coverage, even though that study laid the basis for quantitative dialectology. Clearly, it is important to research materials in some dimension that will be as exhaustive as possible, and these materials then become a resource for other scholars who may wish to argue more selectively. At the same time there is room for more selective studies, which can be viewed as setting up *hypotheses* about dialect areas that can then be further tested and refined, and if necessary corrected. In fact, although they have been strongly criticised, the work of Moore, Meech and Whitehall was an advance in its day, and it has frequently been used as a kind of 'jumping-off' point by later investigators.

In work on present-day speech it has been very commonly observed that some differences in dialect are *salient* within and between communities in that speakers recognise them as social and geographical markers, whereas other differences are not so often noticed. This is so much of a truism that it makes sense to ask, as Trudgill (1986: 10–11) does, why speakers are so much more aware of some variables than they are of others. Therefore, it seems best to avoid arguments about *exhaustiveness* or *comprehensiveness* and advocate instead the principle of *accountability to the data*: whatever the scope and goals of the study may be, all the data relevant to these specific aims should be accounted for, and we should not ignore data that is inconvenient to our argument.[7] In this respect the programme of research leading to *LALME* is a model of accountability. Following these observations about method, we now pass on to a general description of the linguistic characteristics of the dialect areas of Middle English.

3.2.4   Middle English dialect areas

The general outlines of Middle English regional variation are quite well known, and texts can often be described in broad regional terms as 'southwest midland', 'southeast midland' and so on. The dialect areas traditionally recognised are quite closely based on those assumed for Old English. They can be described as: *southeastern* (corresponding to the distinctive Kentish dialect of Old English), *southwestern* (corresponding to West Saxon and ranging westward from west Surrey and Hampshire) – sometimes a middle south dialect is also distinguished – and *northern* (corresponding to Northumbrian and ranging from mid Yorkshire northward into Scotland). Northern texts are relatively few and are not attested in any quantity until late in the period. The *midland* dialects, stretching roughly north of a line from Gloucestershire to London, are divided into *east* and *west*, and these can be subdivided into southeast midland, northwest midland, and so on. Texts in these midland varieties are plentiful, and there are very marked differences between west and east. Finally, it is sometimes appropriate to distinguish also an *East Anglian* dialect area, as many East Anglian texts display features that distinguish them quite sharply from the east midlands.

As we have seen in our discussion of Hall (1920) above, arguments about regional provenance have traditionally tended to be based on selected data, rather than on fully exhaustive accounts, and editors of texts have normally relied on a restricted set of *indicators* of regional differences. This is in principle the same as Labov's (1966) socio-linguistic method, which was to select a small number of indicators of *social* differences in the New York City study. Essentially, these Middle

English dialect indicators are based on *variables*, and, where they are phonological, these variables are based on the phonology of Old English. For example, Old English long *a* is a variable, which can be represented in Middle English texts by the variants *a* and *o*. Thus, although Middle English scholars have not normally spoken of *variables*, *indicators* and the like, these are effectively what their studies make use of. In section 3.2.5, we proceed to a general account of linguistic differences amongst the regions.

3.2.5 *Phonological and morphological criteria for differentiating Middle English dialect areas*

In the following list of features that have been used as regional indicators, we bear in mind two important points that have been discussed in section 3.1. The first relates to the interpretation of written materials used as evidence for spoken states, and the second is the general principle that no language state is in reality uniform. We shall first briefly reconsider the interpretation of written materials.

Features in Middle English that are believed to relate to sound segments are *prima facie* orthographic features. The relation to phonology is not a simple one-to-one relationship, and it is a relationship that needs to be argued for rather than assumed beforehand. At the same time, we also bear in mind that, as Lass (this volume) points out, most spelling systems are reasonably coherent, 'and we have bases for making assumptions about the likely ranges of phonetic values for particular letters' (Lass, in this volume, p. 30). In other words, even when the relation of spelling to phonology happens to be complicated, there is still likely to be a relationship of some kind. We may not be able to project the detailed writing conventions of a particular text successfully on to the detailed phonology of the author of that text, but from comparisons of many texts, we may be able to draw broader conclusions about Middle English phonological variation.

The fact that no state of language is ever uniform is also relevant to projecting variation in writing on to the underlying forms of speech, partly because speech is always more variable than writing. Historical linguistics has been described as a 'search for invariance'; yet, it is through the study of variation that we hope to get access to this invariance. The paradox can be resolved only by viewing the different regional dialects of Middle English as idealisations: they could not have been uniform states in reality. They must also have been variable in dimensions other than the geographical one – a point that is not systematically taken into account in traditional studies of Middle English variation.

Systematically researched evidence of other dimensions of variation within particular regional 'dialects' at any given time was not easily available to investigators before the 1960s, and the consequences of research in social dialectology (following Labov 1966, 1972b) since then have not yet had much impact in Middle English studies. One relevant area here is the study of *contact varieties* (e.g. by Trudgill 1986), as we know that early English was in direct contact with Danish and Norman French. There have also been developments in historical linguistics which are relevant to interpreting Middle English sound changes and which greatly modify the traditional Neogrammarian framework that was traditionally assumed. I have in mind here especially *lexical diffusion* (Wang 1969; Toon 1978; Labov 1981), which holds that sound change can be lexically gradual and does not necessarily apply to all items in a phoneme class at the same time. From this perspective, the Middle English data consists of transitional language states that may exhibit changes spreading through the lexicon and also a range of alternations between conservative and innovative forms. These perceptions are most relevant to traditional arguments about textual histories (e.g. Hall 1920). Although many texts have a history of copying of the kind proposed for the *Bestiary*, it is also more likely than it seemed to early investigators that some of the textual variants are due to variability and change in progress in the speech community of the author or copyist himself. The work of McIntosh and his colleagues, which I shall review below, employs a very careful and comprehensive methodology, well informed by advances in linguistic theory and analysis, and in their work, matters of this kind are taken into account.

Bearing in mind these general points about the relation between writing and speech and the non-uniformity of language states, we now proceed to a selective account of variables that have been used as indicators of regional provenance.

> OE *a* (long) continues to appear as < a > in northern dialects (and often as *ai*), whereas from quite an early date in Middle English it begins to appear as < o > in texts from south Lincolnshire southward. Thus items like *home*, *stone* will be *ham*, *haim* in the north and *hom(e)* in the south and midlands. When, as sometimes happens, a text contains both types of

spelling, this has been traditionally taken to indicate a border area between north and south, or to be due to the activities of copyists from different areas; it can also indicate an early date.

OE *y* (long and short) appear as <u> in the south-west, middle south and southwest midlands, as <e> in the south-east and as <i> elsewhere. Thus OE *brycg* 'bridge', for example, appears in forms such as *brugge, bregge, brig(ge)*.

OE *æ*, as in *dæg* ('day'), usually appears as <a>, except that southeastern and west midland dialects often have <e>.

OE *a* before nasals, as in *hand*, appears as <o> in west midland texts, but gains a wider distribution later in the period; it is found, for example, in Chaucer (southeast midland; late fourteenth century).

In northern and many east midland dialects, digraph spellings for OE *eo, ea*, etc. are relatively rare (<e> and <a> being preferred), and such spellings can often point to southern or west midland provenance.

Southern dialects and some southwest midland ones often represent the OE voiceless fricatives [s, f] as <z>, <v> in initial positions (as in *zea, vox* 'sea', 'fox'). Western and southern texts may also show a good deal of graphic variation in the use of <u>, <v> and <w>, so that 'fox', for example, can appear as *wox*.

Northern dialects favour <g>, <k> where southern and midland sources have spellings that are thought to indicate affricate pronunciations, e.g. *ch*. Thus *rigg, kirk(e)* appear in northern texts for southern and midland *rigge, ridge, chirch(e)*; forms like *brig, kirk* survive in northern dialects until the present day.

OE *hw* (as in *hwæt* 'what') is represented as <wh>, <w>, <quh> and other <q>-type variants. Later in the period <qu->, <q-> spellings become distinctively Scots and East Anglian. Many early texts, however (often east midland and East Anglian), have <w> for OE *hw*, as in *wat* for 'what'.

There are also a number of lexical and morphological (or morpholexical) criteria that are regionally distinctive. The main ones are: (a) the forms of the present participle; (b) presence or absence of the past-participle prefix (OE *ge-*); (c) forms of the personal pronouns – especially third-person plural and third-person singular feminine; and (d) variant verb endings, especially the singular and plural of the present tense.

In the north, and to some extent, north midlands, the typical present-participle ending is *-and(e)*; in other dialects it is *-inde*, *-ende*, *-iende*. However, by 1350 or so, the forms in *-ing(e)*, *-yng(e)* have become common in southeast midland and East Anglian dialects (they are found in Chaucer), whereas in the north *-and(e)* forms persist into Late Middle Scots (sixteenth century). As for the Old English past-participle prefix, southern, south and west midland texts generally retain it in the form *i-* or *y-* (it occasionally occurs as late as Milton and in later archaising poetry), whereas it is lost early in the north, north midlands and East Anglia.

The third-person plural pronoun (*they*, *them*, *their*) is a Scandinavian borrowing into northern or north midland dialects, which later spreads southward. It first appears in writing in the *Ormulum* (north midland, ca 1200). By Chaucer's time the *th-* form has been adopted in London for the subject case only, whereas the oblique cases remain in their native form (*hem*, *here* < OE *heom*, *heora*). At the same period (and indeed before), Scots texts, such as Barbour's *Bruce*, have the *th-* form in all cases. The history of third-person singular feminine pronoun *she* is similar. Forms such as *sche*, *scho* spread from the north and midland and are so slow to penetrate some southern and western dialects that the *h-* form *ho* (and similar variants) is attested even in some present-day dialects. The origin of the *sh*, *sch* form has long been a matter of dispute. It has been suggested (Bourcier 1981: 146) that it arises from stress shift in the pronoun *hie*, which may have developed to [hje], followed by palatalisation of [hj] to [ç] and reinterpretation of [ç] as [ʃ] (see Lass, this volume). Our interest here, however, is not in the origin of forms, but in their regional distribution.

The history of the present-tense endings is of general interest. The *-s* ending for the third-person singular, which is now general, originated in the north, and it is regular in e.g. fourteenth-century Scots texts. Indeed, in these texts the *-s* ending is often added to plural forms as well as singular, just as many present-day dialects (see e.g. Milroy 1981) allow sequences like *Them fellows likes gambling*. Many southern texts, however, have the *-th*, *-þ* ending in both singular and plural forms, whereas midland texts have *-th* in the singular and *-en* in the plural. Later in the period the third-person singular *-s* ending spreads into London English, together with the other northern morphological forms that we have discussed. By Shakespeare's time alternation between *-s* and *-th* in standard literary English (as in *goes*, *goeth*) has plainly become marked for style, with *-th* (the recessive form) preferred in formal contexts.

Recalling my remarks (above, section 3.2.3) on comprehensiveness and selectivity in dialect research, it will be clear even in this brief account that variation in aspects of morphology and pronoun forms is very salient (and hence important diagnostically), and it may be thought remarkable that in these centuries there appears to have been so much variety in these forms. The language was undergoing a process of generalising certain of these forms at the expense of others, and this is (indirectly) relevant to another more general point about the history of English – the trend towards morphological simplification in Middle English that led to the reduced morphological apparatus of Present-Day English. This process is of great theoretical interest, as it is through simplification that the typological difference between Old English and Modern English comes about: the first is a *synthetic* (inflected) language, and the second *analytic* (largely uninflected). In the study of Middle English variation we may hope to find explanations of how and why this came about, as certain Early Middle English dialects were in advance of others in the process of simplification. In order to put some flesh on these general observations, we now briefly examine three short excerpts from Middle English texts.

3.2.6   *Some specimens of regional Middle English*

We now examine a set of excerpts from three selected texts and comment on their dialectal characteristics. For reasons of space, our discussion of these cannot be an exhaustive exercise, but even from these short extracts we may be able to get some idea of the diversity of Middle English. Fuller texts and commentaries can be found in certain histories of English, for example Strang 1970. The extracts printed here are early (from the twelfth and thirteenth centuries): 1 is from one of the earliest texts in Middle English, the *Peterborough Chronicle* annal for 1137 (probably composed after 1154): this is east midland; 2 is from Laȝamon's *Brut* (southwest midland: ca 1200): and 3 is an early northern fragment composed around 1272, which is housed in the York Cathedral Chapter Library.

> 1   Þa was corn dære, and flesc and cæse and butere, for nan ne wæs o
> þe land. Wrecce men sturuen of hungær. Sume ieden on ælmes þe
> waren sum wile rice men. Sume flugen ut of lande. Wes næure gæt
> mare wreccehed on land ne næure hethen men werse ne diden þan

hi diden; for ouer sithon ne forbaren hi nouther circe ne cyrceiærd, oc namen al þe god ðat þarinne was and brenden sythen þe cyrce and al tegædere. Ne hi ne forbaren biscopes land ne abbotes ne preostes, ac ræueden munekes and clerekes, and æuric man other þe ouermyhte. Gif twa men oþer iii coman ridend to an tun, al þe tunscipe flugæn for heom, wenden ðat hi wæron ræueres. Þe biscopes and lered men heom cursede æure, oc was heom naht þarof, for hi uueron al forcursæd and forsuoren and forloren. War sæ me tilede, þe erthe ne bar nan corn, for þe land was al fordon mid suilce dædes. And hi sæden openlice ðat Crist slep and his halechen. Suilc and mare þanne we cunnen sæin we þoleden xix wintre for ure sinnes.

(Adapted from Clark 1958/1970: 56)

('Then corn was dear, and meat and cheese and butter, for there was none in the land. Poor wretches perished from hunger. Some went begging who were formerly wealthy men. Some fled out of the land. There was never yet greater misery in the land, nor did heathen men ever do worse deeds than they did, for in defiance of custom they spared neither church nor churchyard, but took all the wealth that was therein and then burned the church and everything with it. Nor did they spare bishop's land, nor abbot's nor priest's, but robbed monks and clerics, and every man who had the power (robbed) the other. If two or three men came riding to a town, all the township fled before them – they thought that they were robbers. The bishops and learned men cursed them continually, but it was nothing to them – they were all accursed and perjured and damned. Wherever men tilled, the earth yielded no corn, for the land was completely ruined by such deeds. And they said openly that Christ slept, and his saints. Such things, and more than we can say, we suffered nineteen winters for our sins.')

2 'And ich wulle uaren to Aualun to uairest alre maidene,
　to Argante þere quene, aluen swiðe sceone,
　and heo scal mine wunden makien alle isunde,
　al hal me makien mid haleweiȝe drenchen.
　And seoðe ich cumen wulle to mine kineriche,
　and wunien mid Brutten mid muchelere wunne.'
　Æfne þan worden þer com of se wenden,
　þat wes an sceort bat liðen sccouen mid vðen,
　and twa wimmen þer-inne wunderliche idihte,
　and heo nomen Arður anan and aneouste hine uereden,
　and softe hine adun leiden and forð gunnen liðen.
　Þa wes hit iwurðen þat Merlin seide whilen,
　þat weore uni-mete care of Arðoures forð-fare.

Bruttes ileueð ȝete þat he bon on liue,
and wunnien in Aualun mid fairest alre aluen,
and lokieð euere Bruttes ȝete whan Arður cumen liðe.

(Adapted from Brook & Leslie 1963–78: 750)

('"And I will journey to Avalon to the fairest of all maidens – to the queen Argante, most beautiful of divine creatures [lit: 'elves']. And she will heal all my wounds and make me whole with health-giving draughts. And thereafter I will come to my kingdom and dwell among the British with great joyfulness". Upon those words there came moving in from the sea – it was a short boat gliding, driven through the waves, and in it two women wondrously dressed. And straightway they took Arthur and speedily carried him, and laid him down gently, and journeyed forth. Then it had come to pass as Merlin had prophesied of old – that there was excessive grief at Arthur's passing. The British still believe that he is alive and dwells in Avalon with the fairest of divine beings, and the British still await the time that Arthur will return.')

3 Wel, qwa sal thir hornes blau
   Haly Rod thi day?
   Nou is he dede and lies law
   Was wont to blaw thaim ay.

(Dickins & Wilson 1956: 118)

('Alas who shall blow these horns, Holy Cross, on thy day? Now he is dead and lies low, (who) was wont to blow them always.')

It is plain at first sight that these three extracts are linguistically highly divergent from one another. We shall examine them briefly by commenting on: (a) variability within texts, and (b) divergence between them in terms of: (i) spelling/phonology and (ii) grammar.

3.2.6.1 Variability within texts

Although these extracts are too short to display much internal variation, the *Peterborough Chronicle* (*PC*) extract shows variability in the preterite plural verb inflections (OE -*on*): *coman, flugæn, wæron* ('came', 'fled', 'were') and others retain the OE -*n* inflection, but spell the ending in three different ways; *cursede* ('cursed') drops the distinctive plural marking and becomes the same as the singular. Other cases of variation in this ending from the same source are pointed out by Lass in this volume. Divergence in spelling also is attested in *wæron* as against *uueron* ('were') (lines 10 and 12). There is in fact much more variability in this text than is apparent from this brief extract. As for the York fragment: despite its brevity, it has two different spellings for the word 'blow'.

However, divergence *between* the texts is easier to demonstrate from these short extracts than is internal divergence.

3.2.6.2   Divergence between texts
SPELLING/PHONOLOGY

Extracts 1 and 2 are too early to show much evidence of <o> and <a> in OE [a:] words, although <o> spellings do occur elsewhere in the *Peterborough Chronicle*. This feature progresses northward through the midlands as time goes on (see map 3.1 on p. 183 representing the situation in the early fourteenth century, which shows <o> spellings as far north as Lancashire). Extract 1 has *naht, nan* ('nought', 'none'), and *Brut* has *hal, ane* ('whole', 'one'). The York fragment retains *a* in *qwa, blau, Haly, law*, as is to be expected in a northern text. For OE short /a/, *Brut* shows a preference for <o> before nasals (as in *mon* for 'man') – this is originally a west midland characteristic. The most salient orthographic difference between the *Brut* extracts and the others is the appearance of <u>/<v> for OE [f] in *uaren, uairest* ('fare', 'fairest'). This points to voicing of initial voiceless fricatives – a southern and southwest midland characteristic which is well attested in present-day southwestern dialects (Wakelin & Barry 1968). Both 1 and 2 have *heom* for 'them': *hem* becomes usual in later east midland texts. *Brut* has <u> for OE [y] in *muchelere* (cf. *PC micel, mycel*), but <i> in *kineriche* (OE *cynerice*). Text 1 has <i> and <y>, but not <u>. The characteristic northern <q-> form for *wh-* appears in the York fragment as <qwa> ('who').

GRAMMAR

By far the most profound difference between these three texts is in the grammar. Extract 2 (although it is later than 1) is highly conservative in retaining much of the Old English inflectional morphology, and it is no exaggeration to state that the morphological differences between 2 and the others are as great as the difference between modern standard German and standard Dutch. After the Conquest, texts in Old English continued to be copied in the diocese of Worcester well into the Middle English period, and as we have noted in section 3.1.2, above, the west midland AB language shows a clear continuity with Old English in various respects. As for the *Brut*, it is possible that its grammatical conservatism is partly literary and that colloquial English in the area was more advanced in the loss of inflections, and it has recently been suggested that there is deliberate archaism here (Laing 1990; Smith forthcoming). However, inflectional loss (and the associated loss of grammatical gender, on which see Jones 1988) is the most important general linguistic development in Early Middle English; it is difficult to explain why this should happen by purely intralinguistic arguments, and it seems that sociopolitical developments may be implicated. It has been widely suggested that phonological and grammatical distinctions are most readily lost from speech when there is extensive language contact (Labov 1972b: 300) and when supralocal norms develop (Jakobson 1929). The reduction in inflectional morphology (which is clear enough in a comparison of these extracts) seems to have been most rapid in the east and north of England and in Scotland. It is tempting, therefore, to suggest that a history of relatively strong contacts with Danes and (to a lesser extent) Normans may be implicated here, and that traditional forms survived where these contacts were less strong.

Amongst the case inflections of nouns and adjectives which the *Brut* retains (according to the Old English pattern, but with some orthographic changes) are the following: *alre maidene* has the genitive plural adjectival ending in *alre* ('of all') and the genitive plural noun ending in *maidene*. In *þere quene* ('to the queen'), the dative singular feminine ending appears in *þere*. Grammatical gender is retained in this and also in *mid muchelere wunne*: *wunne* ('joy') is feminine, and *muchelere* ('much, great') is dative singular feminine. As early as the mid-twelfth century, the east midland *Peterborough Chronicle* has already lost overt grammatical gender marking, together with many of the Old English noun/adjective inflections; demonstratives and relatives are generally reduced to *the*, *that* (variously spelled). In both extracts 1 and 2, however, many verbal endings are retained, variably in the *Peterborough Chronicle*, but scrupulously in the *Brut*: for example, the infinitive ending in -*n* is usual in these, e.g. *makien*, *sæin*; but it has disappeared entirely in *blau*, *blaw* in the York fragment (for a much fuller discussion of morphological changes, see Lass in this volume and Jones 1988).

As for pronouns and the third-person singular present verb inflection, extract 3 has *thaim* ('them') for *heom* in 1 and 2. The *Peterborough Chronicle* and *Brut* retain initial *h*- forms in all cases including the nominative (*hi*, *heo*). The York text already has the third-person singular -*s* inflection in *lios*, whereas *Brut* has the -*eth* type in *habbeoð*. Although the present tense does not occur often in the extracts, the texts of the *Peterborough Chronicle* and the *Brut* do use the -*eth* type of ending consistently. Indeed, it is consistent also in Chaucer's London English two centuries later. The York fragment has the northern *sal* ('shall') and omits the nominative relative pronoun in the last line (also a northern tendency found, for example, in the Border Ballads). Another specifically northern feature of the York text is the occurrence of the plural demonstrative *thir*. This occurs in later Scots texts also (e.g. Barbour's *Bruce*) and in present-day Scots dialects. In most of its grammatical characteristics, however, it is the far-northern text which at this early date evidently looks most similar to Modern English.

This last point has some importance for historical descriptions of developments in English and for studying the causes of linguistic change in general, and I shall return to it in the concluding section of this chapter. Our primary task here, however, is to describe the methods by which scholars arrive at generalisations about variation in Middle English itself, rather than to discuss the causes of change. Accordingly, in the following sections, I pass on to consider survey methods in Middle English dialectology.

3.2.7 *Survey methods in Middle English dialectology*

Amongst the methodological and interpretative challenges that face the Middle English dialectologist, the question of *provenance* is crucial. For this reason, scholars have placed a very high value on texts that can be reliably located, and much research has been carried out on non-literary sources of known provenance. The seminal work here is that of Ekwall (1913, 1917, etc.), who advocated the study of place names as *Hilfsmittel* ('support, assistance') to Middle English dialect research (for greater detail on place-name and byname research, see further Clark in this volume). Ekwall's work has been built on by many, including other Scandinavian scholars such as Holm, Sundby and Kristensson. From amongst the more recent surveys, we focus here on Kristensson 1967 as an example.

Kristensson's argument for relying on texts of this type is explicitly based on the parallel with modern regional dialectology (such as the *Survey of English Dialects*). In such a method precise geographical location of sources is all-important, and the time-span should be as limited as possible (in this case 1290–1350). Kristensson's sources are the Lay Subsidy Rolls and other onomastic documents, and on this basis he constructs maps showing the diffusion of changes in Middle English, which define more precisely the geographical movements of these changes than previous scholars have been able to do. He refers frequently to Moore, Meech & Whitehall (1935) and to Ekwall (1947,

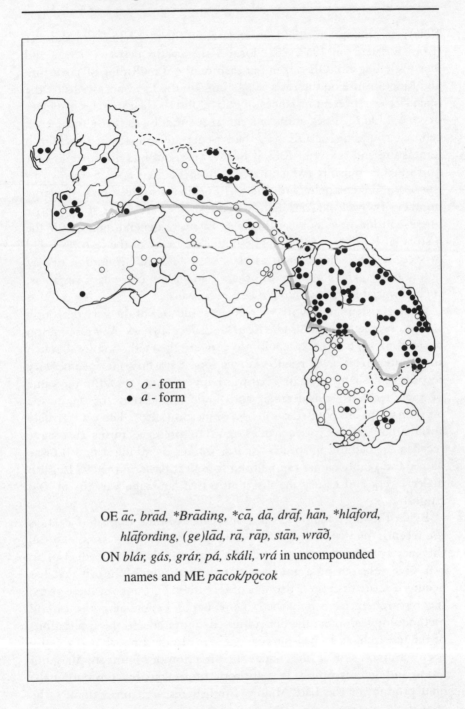

OE *āc, brād, *Brāding, *cā, dā, drāf, hān, *hlāford, hlāfording, (ge)lād, rā, rāp, stān, wrāð,* ON *blár, gás, grár, pá, skáli, vrá* in uncompounded names and ME *pācok/pǭcok*

3.1   *a/o* forms in Lancashire, West Riding and Lincolnshire

1956); he attempts to build on and refine their conclusions. Map 3.1 (from Kristensson 1967: 283) locates the *isogloss* between <o> and <a> spellings for OE /aː/ in Lancashire, the West Riding of Yorkshire and Lincolnshire on the basis of spellings in the Lay Subsidy Rolls: the open circles represent instances of <o> and the black circles instances of <a>. On the basis of this we can argue that by the early fourteenth century rounding of OE /aː/ had penetrated northward well into Lancashire and the West Riding in the west, but had not spread as far north in Lincolnshire (which has a high incidence of <a> forms). In this way, Kristensson records the spellings in his sources for a very large number of vowel and consonant variables which are either of diagnostic interest in locating regional forms or of more general interest for the history of English – or both. These include many of the features listed in section 3.2.5 above (such as the 'west midland' rounding of /a/ before nasals) and a number of others – including consonant variables, such as variable loss of initial *h* before vowels.

From Kristensson's work we can get some idea of the very thorough and careful methods of Middle English dialect surveys. Any reservation we might wish to express would not concern the methodology so much as the interpretation of results, i.e. we might ask how far documentary records can reliably indicate what was happening in *speech*. But the value of such work is considerable, and some applications of onomastic investigations are pointed out by Kristensson (1989). These are largely antiquarian, in that place names tend to preserve forms that have receded or died out in speech: hence, studies of Middle English place names and family names can be used to reflect back on the *Old* English dialect areas and clarify the distribution of language variants in Old English.

By far the most comprehensive survey of Middle English dialects is the recently published *Linguistic Atlas of Late Medieval English*. To call this merely a survey seems to belittle it, as it is the final product of an extensive research programme initiated by Angus McIntosh that has occupied more than three decades of research. Throughout these years, the researchers have published many papers, explaining the careful methodology adopted, the difficulties encountered and the applications of the research, and a new survey of *Early* Middle English has recently been set up on similar lines under the direction of McIntosh, Margaret Laing and Jeremy Smith. It is appropriate to start by considering the final product of the Late Middle English research programme – the atlas itself.

This is in four volumes and is equipped with full references to the sources on which it is based and accounts of the methodology adopted. There are hundreds of maps of different kinds, including 'dot maps', which show the distribution of linguistic items throughout the country, and 'item maps', which show in detail the occurrence of particular variants in smaller geographical sectors. It is important to understand the methodology of such a survey as a basis for assessing its results, as it raises many of the issues we have discussed in section 3.1: one that concerns the presentation of the atlas itself is the question of handling the two intersecting dimensions of chronology and geography.

One of the difficulties faced by so comprehensive a survey is that there are bound to be chronological differences amongst the surviving documents. Although the 'later' medieval period covered by the atlas is approximately 1350–1450, the investigators have not found it practicable to restrict themselves to so short a time-span. The reasons for this are in themselves of some interest. The first reason is that whereas texts from the south and south midlands are plentiful before 1350, there are relatively few extant northern and north midland texts before that date. The atlas therefore includes earlier (late-thirteenth- and early-fourteenth-century) texts from the southern part of the country. The second reason given by the editors for differentiating chronologically between north and south is that the influence of the official 'Chancery' standard language becomes noticeable in southern texts, especially in legal and administrative documents, from quite early in the fifteenth century. To that extent, therefore, southern texts become less valuable as evidence for strictly geographical variation from about 1425. Northern texts, however, which become plentiful in the fifteenth century, continue to provide evidence for distinctively northern dialects, and a few of the northern texts used are Scottish texts from as late as the early *sixteenth* century. Thus, whereas the present-day dialectologist may claim to present a still 'photograph' of variation at a restricted point in time, the medievalist is governed by the accidents of historical preservation and – especially in such a comprehensive survey – must find principled ways of dealing with it.

The new atlas is explicitly an atlas of written Middle English. The investigators have addressed themselves to coping in the first place with the vast amount of written variation that is extant from the period – in a multitude of sources listed in volume I, ranging from legal, municipal and official documents to literary texts. Thus, if a map shows the distribution of < wh- > forms (as in *what*, *where*), varying with < qu- >

spellings and others, the investigators are not claiming that they have determined whether these different spellings necessarily indicate different pronunciations, nor are they claiming to specify what the pronunciations might have been. It is up to others to base arguments about phonology on the written data, and many of the variants shown must be purely scribal.

As for provenance – the investigators are explicitly concerned with determining the provenance of texts that do not openly divulge it, i.e. chiefly literary texts. The value of documentary records is that they can often be precisely located; however, McIntosh *et al.* (1986: I, 9) note that their *linguistic* value is limited in certain ways. In particular, lexical coverage is limited in such sources. They are sparse on certain lexical items of special historical interest: for example, items such as *she, eye, world, fruit*; and (according to McIntosh *et al.* 1986) it is only in literary texts that adequate lexical coverage is found. There are indeed other limitations on the value of documentary material: certain syntactic forms, such as certain verb tense forms and embedded clauses, are also likely to be more restricted than in literary texts, and non-literary records of some kinds may be relatively conservative in language. The goal, therefore, is to devise a method for locating literary manuscripts (especially) very precisely – much more precisely than has been possible in the past.

The methodology depends first on the use of 'anchor' texts – those that can be located on non-linguistic grounds. The next step is to relate other texts to these by using a 'fit' technique: briefly, to the extent that other texts have linguistic features in common with the anchor texts, they are tentatively plotted on maps, and as more and more texts are taken into account, the plotting of their relative geographical positions becomes more and more refined. In general, although absolute positions of texts may not always be located, relative positions can reasonably be located. In some areas (e.g. the southwest midlands, where texts are plentiful), the authors believe that the locations are probably accurate to within 10 miles. This advance in precise localisation of the data is a result of the comprehensive and detailed nature of the research carried out.

There are of course difficulties in using the fit technique, as McIntosh *et al.* (1986) point out. For example, although it is true that dialect variation forms a continuum and that there are no absolute boundaries between dialects, modern dialectology has shown that isoglosses can 'bundle' at certain points and that something reasonably called a dialect boundary sometimes intervenes between one town and another only a few miles distant. However, as the aim of this research programme is to extend and refine our knowledge of detail, the boundaries themselves should now be definable with greater accuracy than in the past.

The results are presented in the form of maps. The dot maps consist mainly of core vocabulary items, inflectional and derivational morphemes and salient spelling conventions (such as variation in <wh->forms). The lexical items covered include both 'grammatical' words (such as forms of the verb *be* and pronouns) and 'lexical' words (nouns, adjectives, etc.). The first section of maps covers the whole country as far north as the Firth of Forth; the second section concentrates on the northern part of this and the final section on the southern.

So detailed is the material presented that it would be incautious to make too many generalisations about the atlas distributions of forms before other investigators have had an opportunity to explore the material more fully. However, a few general comments can be made. In many cases the maps confirm and refine traditionally recognised boundaries, especially (it seems) when Scandinavian invasions have affected the east and north. For example, initial <k-> spellings for *church*, *at* for infinitive *to*, and many other features coincide roughly with the boundaries of the Danelaw. In other cases, however, some of the traditional views may have to be modified or corrected. For example, the distribution of <u, e, i> for OE <y> proves to be much more fuzzy and overlapping than traditional accounts would lead us to believe (see section 3.2.5, above). Although <e> spellings are somewhat more favoured in the south-east and East Anglia, they are very well distributed in western areas also. Similarly <u> spellings, which were traditionally viewed as western, also have a distribution in the south-east.

These few remarks are intended to give some idea of the usefulness of the atlas for research that others might now wish to carry out, and the great advances here are in comprehensiveness and precision. However, successful dialectology depends crucially on adequate *methods* of research, and to understand the product, one also has to understand the methods used in arriving at it. In section 3.2.8, therefore, I shall attempt to describe some of the main principles of the research programme and the methods adopted.

3.2.8   The LALME research: some principles and methods

It is appropriate here to recall the parallel that has been mentioned before in this chapter – the parallel between the study of present-day spoken dialects and of medieval written dialects. If, at the present day, a person has lived for long periods in different parts of the country, his/her speech is normally affected by this experience: hence, we may be able to detect (for example) Scottish, northern English and southern English features in his/her speech. The traditional regional-dialect researcher, who is normally interested in examples of 'pure' regional speech, will not want such a person as an informant and will reject him/her in favour of true natives of the areas concerned. In traditional Middle English studies, the focus on precisely locatable written texts is exactly parallel to this. Texts that appear to show mixed dialects, or which seem to have been copied by different scribes, and which are difficult to localise for these and other reasons, have traditionally been undervalued and neglected as materials for dialect description. However, the Middle English scholar is in a very unhappy position here, because the vast majority of surviving documents are of this problematic kind. We cannot afford to be purists, and so we must devise methods for exploring the materials that have survived and account systematically for all the data. This, essentially, is what the *LALME* programme has tried to do, and it is easiest to clarify this by referring to some publications by the researchers themselves.

McIntosh has consistently emphasised the importance of this work for linguistic theory, and has pointed out the failures of the past in the respects I have mentioned. There is such a wealth of surviving material that 'linguists fall regrettably far short of exploiting anything like all there is or even of making optimum selective use' of what is available (McIntosh (1975) 1989: 32). The researchers have set out to correct this, and the task has involved not only an enormous commitment of time and energy, but also a wide range of sophisticated analytic skills. It is important to remember that many of the relevant documents have never been published: thus, an essential task has been to track down and analyse unpublished manuscripts in addition to those that have been published, and to prepare (amongst other things) what the researchers call *scribal profiles* for the documents (McIntosh 1975).

Most of the surviving literary texts are copies, and these are often at more than one remove from the original. Some copies are in the hand of a single scribe, but others are by two or more scribes. McIntosh and Wakelin (1982) discuss the case of Mirk's *Festial*, which is in the hands of five different scribes – but one of these scribes seems to have copied material in no less than fourteen different dialects. Although this may be an extreme case, the example does make it clear how important it is to explore the scribal and linguistic make-up of the texts, and McIntosh *et al.* have therefore suggested a classification of text types in terms of the history of copying and of the different patterns of textual mixing that may arise.

In some cases, a single scribe seems to have translated from an original into his own dialect, but he may have done this inconsistently to a greater or lesser extent. Sometimes, for example, the translation is 'progressive': the scribe starts by copying more or less faithfully from his exemplar, but as he begins to work more quickly, he resorts more and more to the forms of his own 'dialect' (or scribal practice). Other texts, however, are *composite*: two or more different copyists have been at work on the text that has come down to us, or a single scribe has faithfully copied an exemplar which is itself the work of two scribes. The Cotton MS of *The Owl and the Nightingale* is a well-known example of the latter, and in this case the place where one scribe finished and the other began can be accurately determined: the scribe of the final version seems to have made few changes. In extreme cases of mixed origin, we encounter *Mischsprachen*, in which (according to McIntosh *et al.* 1986) the variation encountered is random and unpredictable. However, it is a measure of the great progress that these scholars have made that Laing (1988) has been able to illuminate the textual histories of two manuscripts of Richard Rolle's *English Psalter*, which are effectively *Mischsprachen*. She demonstrates, using quantitative methods (amongst others), that even in these extreme cases, the layers of copying may be separable.

As many Middle English literary texts survive in only one copy, methods of 'internal reconstruction', in addition to comparative methods, are essential. What we can know about the original depends on interpretations of internal variation in the text, which lead to hypotheses about the provenance of the original, and to some extent these interpretations have traditionally depended on rather purist notions about relatively uniform dialects. McIntosh *et al.* (1986) have given attention to the possibility of personal and social variation affecting the language of the texts. They note the possibility that a writer of mixed upbringing may betray in his usage the influence of two or more different dialects, and that a text may be affected by mixing of what they call a sociolinguistic kind, especially through influence from the spread of standard English, which becomes noticeable in later Middle English. McIntosh *et al.* also note that it is possible to find, especially in the fifteenth century, an extremely wide range of spelling variation in the work of a single writer. Thus, we should be able to acknowledge that when a text contains variation, this may not all be due to the activities of copyists from different regions: the copyist of the extant version, or his speech community, may have tolerated a good deal of variability in usage. Indeed, one thing is obvious: the copyists evidently thought that the mixed and variable usage of their copies was *acceptable* in some way, and McIntosh, Samuels and their colleagues have given much more weight to this aspect of variation than have previous scholars.

3.2.9   Some applications

I pointed out in section 3.1 that the goal of a dialect survey is primarily linguistic and is specifically to describe and account for variation in language. But it is clear that such an extensive exploration of manuscript sources can have applications to other kinds of research. The most immediately obvious applications are literary, editorial and textual. The case of *Havelok the Dane* (MS Bodley Laud Misc. 108 (A) plus some other fragments) is important linguistically, but it is also of interest for literary history. To demonstrate the *LALME* method, I shall now briefly review some of McIntosh's arguments about the localisation of Laud Misc. 108.

McIntosh (1976) argues that this text may be from Norfolk, south-west of King's Lynn, a long distance south of the town that is pre-eminently associated with it – Grimsby, in north Lincolnshire. The -*es* verbal ending that we have noted above (p. 169) makes it quite possible that the original was composed in north Lincolnshire, but we do not know how many copies intervene between the putative original and the manuscript we have to hand. It has long been clear that *Havelok* has much mixing of forms that are not characteristically northeast midland (e.g. a fairly high incidence of <o> for OE /a:/, on which see map 3.1), and, despite the attribution to north Lincolnshire by Dickins & Wilson (1956: 34) and others, the surviving manuscript has never seemed to be from as far north as Grimsby. McIntosh uses the 'fit' technique to suggest a more precise location for the text than has been suggested before – an area in west Norfolk south-west of King's Lynn. Various comparisons are used here, but an important one is the comparison with the work of scribe D of BM Cotton Cleopatra C vi. McIntosh shows that this is probably from west Norfolk rather than Lincolnshire, and it displays many similarities to *Havelok*. The majority of the key forms in *Havelok* that McIntosh uses to refine the 'fit' turn out to have a distribution to the south of west Norfolk (e.g. in material located in Ely, near Cambridge) more often than to the north of it. Indeed, when some variants (e.g. *togidere* 'together') do have a distribution north of Norfolk, they are usually also found to the south. The incidence of these more southerly variants is greater in *Havelok* than in Cleopatra C vi; therefore, *Havelok* may be from somewhere to the south of Cleopatra C vi.

Another theme running through this research programme is the application of its findings to questions of importance in the history of English. In a very influential paper, Samuels (1963) has considered changes in the London dialect of the fifteenth century and the varieties that may be said to have been competing at that time for pre-eminence as the basis of modern literary standard English. These varieties are classified into four types, of which the Chancery standard is the ancestor of the modern literary standard. Samuels also argues that the main regional influence on London English and the early standard language is not the whole east midland area, or areas to the east of it, but the central midlands. Again, the relative precision here is made possible by work on the atlas project.

I have noted above that the *LALME* researchers have taken more account than previous scholars of sociolinguistic factors. Unlike traditional scholars, they have pointed out that some of the variation encountered may be inherent in the written language of one particular scribe, and they have mentioned the *acceptability* of variant forms to the copyists. It is appropriate, therefore, to go on to consider in section 3.3 another perspective on variation in Middle English documents, which is not primarily about geographical provenance and not primarily devoted to reconstructing textual histories, but which may be seen as complementary to these. This perspective is informed mainly by the results of variation studies on present-day dialects: it depends on the perception that variation may itself be structured and is not necessarily the result of errors or carelessness. Therefore, it can be studied in itself as a matter of linguistic interest and as a contribution to historical linguistic theory.

3.3   Variation theory and Middle English dialectology

3.3.1   Introduction

Present-day dialectology has developed an additional dimension of interest which focuses on variation in the speech of individual speakers and speech communities rather than on broader geographical patterns, and it is the purpose of this section to consider how far this perspective can contribute to the analysis and interpretation of variation in Middle English. The primary interest of *social dialectology* is in tracing the origins and diffusion of linguistic changes, and these patterns are typically discovered in language variation *within* communities in the different speech styles of individuals and of social groups. From an analysis of these patterns, changes in progress can be located, and their path through the community can be described. The most important principle is that languages (or dialects) are never 'pure' or uniform states of language, and further that variation in speech is itself structured and functional; e.g. it may be shown to serve social purposes. As Weinreich, Labov & Herzog (1968) have pointed out, structuredness should not be equated with uniformity; for a language state to be structured it does not have to be uniform. As Middle English language states are very far from being uniform, they should in principle be suited to this kind of analysis.

The claim that variation is structured in communities has been tested by numerous studies (Labov 1966; Trudgill 1974a; Milroy & Milroy 1978 – to name a few), which have demonstrated regular patterns of variation according to speech style, social context and social group, and the basic perception has been formalised in the idea of *variable rules* (Labov 1972a; Sankoff 1978, etc.). Rules of this kind specify the *constraints* on the variation that has been discovered by empirical observation. In a present-day community, these appear as constraints on variation in speech: in Middle English we must locate these constraints initially through the writing system.

The consequence of this is that, in general, variable texts can become more valuable for our researches than relatively uniform ones. Let me clarify this by comparing a modern case with a medieval case. Suppose we show that in a present-day vernacular, there is structured variation in verb forms of the type *he does/he do* (see Cheshire 1982 for a relevant study), with one form perhaps being preferred in formal styles and the other in casual styles; we may also – by comparing the speech of different social groups and age-groups – additionally show that one form is progressing at the expense of the other. As it happens, Middle English texts also frequently exhibit variation in verbal inflections. Suppose, for example, a text (such as the *Bestiary*, discussed in section 3.2.2) exhibits third-person singular verb-form variation in *-es*, *-eth* and syncopated forms (e.g. *stant* for *standes*, *standeth*): it may be possible in many cases to show that the text is composite and expose the 'layers' of copying (see Laing 1988). On the other hand, it may also be the case that all three forms (or perhaps two of them) were current in the underlying dialect of the scribe (or of the author), or – more properly – of the speech community to which he belonged. Indeed, as the writing system was not standardised, it is likely that structured variation of this kind would enter more readily into the texts than it would today.

Clearly, in this approach, the *exact* geographical provenance of texts is no longer the primary, or exclusive, interest (important as it is to establish this as far as possible). The method can be seen as complementary to geographical dialectology: the goal is to contribute to theories of change, and within this to our understanding of the history of English, which is of course a multidimensional history focusing on variation of all kinds. One possible result may be to show that variation attested in later periods of English can be traced back to these early sources.

3.3.2   The neglect of structured variation in Middle English studies

Variability in Middle English has sometimes been perceived as an obstacle rather than a resource, partly because of the broadly literary emphasis on which we have commented above. In editorial and descriptive commentary, it is very easy to find comments about chaotic or 'lawless' spelling (e.g. Sisam 1915: xxxvii) and even editorial judgements to the effect that a given scribe could not have been a native English speaker – so variable is his orthography. This last judgement (although it is commonly made) is speculative, of course, as the scribe is normally anonymous. However, judgements of this kind can effectively block further investigation of variable constraints in the texts in question: they can be dismissed as 'corrupt' or 'unreliable' specimens of language. One way in which variation of this kind is discounted is to claim that the scribe was Anglo-Norman, or that the spellings are Anglo-Norman and therefore not valid evidence for the history of English.

The Anglo-Norman argument goes back to Skeat (1897), who

specified particular features of spelling as Anglo-Norman. These are discussed by Milroy (1983), and it is noticeable that many of these features, such as < w > for *wh*, have reflexes in later English. As a result of Skeat's claims, the very fact of variable spelling in an Early Middle English document became in itself a reason for concluding that the scribe was Anglo-Norman and that his spelling could be corrected by editors and ignored by historical commentators. The work of scribes writing centuries after the Conquest has even been dismissed in this way, seemingly mainly because it is *variable*, and not because we can (usually) know whether the scribe was a first-language speaker of Anglo-Norman, or whether it would have been relevant if he had been.

Leaving aside this argument, we must also recognise that scholars have sometimes been more generally influenced by the notion that written language *should be* uniform, even in a period in which it plainly was *not* uniform, and they sometimes appear to chide the scribes for spelling variably. Scragg (1974: 26), for example, comments that 'The existence of regional orthographies, and their confusion in the copying of texts resulted in a very lax attitude to spelling in most scribes.' In the context, this 'very lax attitude' seems to be measured against circumstances (such as Late Old English or the present day) in which there is a uniform standard of spelling: thus, all this really means is that in Early Middle English there was no uniform standard. Scragg adds that these scribes had 'no conception of a spelling standard' and then – much more dubiously – that they used 'variant forms at will'. However, if the scribes really had used variants 'at will', we would actually be unable to read the texts, as there would be no system in the spelling; but there must always be *some* order in any spelling system that we can read, even if it is a variable system. Therefore, the scribes did not spell 'at will', but according to variable (and historically mixed) conventions. It is our task to attempt to specify the constraints on spelling under which they were working, always admitting that even after we have done this, there may well be residues of apparent randomness that we cannot explain.

3.3.3   *Orderly variation in spelling*

The existence of variable orthographies is an advantage to the Middle English dialectologist in exactly the same way that the existence of spoken variation is an advantage in present-day research. Although the scribes no doubt made 'errors', it should be possible to investigate variable texts *in extenso* to determine the extent to which the variation in spelling (or indeed in other linguistic dimensions) is in fact orderly, and whether this variation can help us to work out what might have been happening in spoken English at the time. As an example, let us briefly consider some aspects of spelling in *Havelok the Dane*.

The *Havelok* text is one of those sources that has been traditionally thought to be the work of an Anglo-Norman scribe (Sisam 1915) on the grounds that the spelling is highly variable in the respects specified by Skeat. However, although it doubtless contains some forms that are simply 'errors',[8] it also exhibits the kind of orderly variation that could be captured within a variable-rule framework, *but in spelling variation rather than phonology*. The scribe does not have a free hand with spelling variation: there are constraints on the variants he uses. OE postvocalic /ht xt/, for example, can be represented in the spelling of *Havelok* by <st>, <ht>, <th>, <cht>, <cth> (in words of the type *riht*, *niht*), but *not* by, e.g. <gt>, <ght> or by random and unpredictable forms such as *tc* or *m*. The variation is constrained in much the same way as present-day *phonological* variation in speech communities is observed to be constrained. Therefore, just as present-day phonological variation can be used as a clue to change in progress, so it may be possible here to use orthographic variation in the same way.

The spelling variants for OE (ht)[9] overlap with spelling variants for other forms (from different sources in Old English), just as phonological variants in present-day studies are found to overlap (see Milroy & Harris 1980; Milroy 1981). Thus, if we take the realisation *th*, we find that this can be used word-finally, not only for (ht), but also for (t) and (th). The result of this is that a spelling like *with* can realise three separate classes: OE *wiht* ('wight, person'), OE *wiþ* ('with') and OE *hwit* ('white'), and this of course applies to other items of these types. To formalise this – the following (Old English) classes can appear with final *th*:

1   Final (postvocalic) dental fricatives: /þ ð/ e.g. *with* (OE *wiþ*, PDE *with*).

2   Final (postvocalic) dental stop: /t/ e.g. *with* (OE *whit*, PDE *white*).

3   Final /ht xt/: e.g. *with* (OE *wiht*, PDE *wight*).

The *potential* realisations of these three classes are, however, different: (ht) items can also appear with <st>, <cht>, etc. (e.g. *wicht*): the other two classes cannot; (th) items can also appear with final <þ>,

<δ> (e.g. *wiþ*): the other two classes cannot; (t) items can appear with final single *t* (e.g. *wit*, *whit*): the other two classes cannot. Thus, 'with, wight' cannot appear as *wit*, whereas 'white' can. To this extent, therefore, the variation is constrained, and not random. Applying the principle that change in progress is manifested in variation, let us consider its possible implications for spoken variation in Middle English.

The study of (ht) in *Havelok* is of course relevant to the date at which the velar fricative [x] before [t] (in *right*, *might*, etc.) was lost in English. The *prima facie* conclusion to be drawn is that in the variable phonology of the 'underlying' (east midland/East Anglian) speech community, loss of the fricative and merger of *wight*, *white* or close approximation and overlap, had already taken place. It is also possible that in this variable phonology there was some tendency to merge final /þ/ with /t/. If developments of this kind were not in some sense in progress, then there would have been less likelihood of the scribe observing precisely *this* pattern of orderly spelling variation, because, given the variable state of the orthographic conventions known to him, he could have chosen to vary in other ways. Of course, it is quite another matter to go on to argue from this very limited piece of evidence that loss of the fricative in /xt/ was generally accepted as a completed sound change in the English language as a whole at this early date. Yet, if we take this together with the fact that many other forms characteristic of Modern English spread in these centuries from the east midlands and the north (see the discussion of morphological dialect indicators in section 3.2.5), we can advance the hypothesis that this change was in progress in the east midlands around 1300 and look for further evidence to support or refute this. If, however, we insist that many Middle English scribes were simply careless or poorly acquainted with English, we shall be inclined to reject the evidence and date this sound change much later – at a time when it was actually completed in 'standard' English. This, of course, will not bring us anywhere near the *origin* of the change.

Loss of the velar fricative is a change that was finally adopted in standard English and formal styles. Middle English sources, however, also contain variation that may be relevant to non-standard varieties and casual styles of speech; hence, there may be considerable time-depth to these variables also. In section 3.3.4, therefore we consider how far studies of variable spelling in Middle English are capable of throwing light on this.

3.3.4   The time-depth of non-standard variants

A number of present-day non-standard and casual speech forms appear
to be indicated by some features of variable Middle English spelling.
Some of these are recognised as regional and have been studied as such
(e.g. in Wakelin & Barry 1968 the study of the voicing of initial
fricatives in southwest England); others are more widespread in
English. One of these is 'final-stop deletion' (loss of /t, d/, and
sometimes other stops, in final clusters in words such as *mist, mend*). This
is today very common in many varieties of English (Guy 1980; Romaine
1984), but not common in careful styles of Received Pronunciation
(hence its exclusion from many accounts which claim to be accounts of
'English'). The *LALME* maps show a distribution of final-consonant
loss also in medieval *written* English, and I have noted a number of
examples in *Havelok* and other texts. Thus, the phenomenon may have
been part of variability in English for many centuries – more common,
perhaps, in some dialects than in others, receding at some periods and
progressing at others. Yet it plays little part in standard accounts of
the history of English before about 1600, and Middle English stop-
deleted forms (such as *bes, lan* 'best', 'land') are amongst the forms that
are typically corrected by editors as errors.

There are other features that may have much earlier origins than is
generally believed. These include: (a) the (casual style) *-in'* ending on
present participles; (b) certain widespread socially or regionally marked
alternations in Modern English, such as 'stopping' of dental fricatives
in, e.g. *thick, that*, and [h]-dropping. One of the most important points
arising is that studies of these variables contribute to the history of the
language as a multidimensional phenomenon. They accept as a principle
that, just as English is variable today, so it has constantly incorporated
variation through the centuries. Indeed, as some of this 'stable'
variation may have been very long-lasting, we may have to reconsider
what it means to say that some *categorical* change was completed at some
specific date in history. Bearing in mind also the points made above on
the structured nature of variation, I now consider as an example the case
of [h]-dropping in English, i.e. variable loss of [h] in stressed syllables
initially before vowels.

Although scholars have noticed instability in initial <h> spellings
in Middle English, the traditional view (e.g. Wyld 1936: 296) is that
there is little reliable evidence for '[h]-dropping' in English much
before the end of the eighteenth century, and earlier instability in

spelling is usually dismissed as unreliable in handbook accounts of the history of English sounds (e.g. Brunner 1963; Ekwall 1975). One reason given for the alleged lateness of the phenomenon is its apparent absence from colonial English (Wyld 1927: 220). From a variationist point of view, the reasoning here is not necessarily acceptable, as colonial forms of English may have changed; for example, there is evidence that, although Australian English is [h]-ful now, it *used to* have [h]-dropping (Trudgill 1986: 138–9). The evidence of variable spelling in Middle English seems to point to an early origin, and if the arguments for this can be sustained, they have a clear relevance to understanding patterns of variation in Middle English.

In modern times [h]-dropping – like *-in'* for (ing) – is extremely widespread and well established: it is not confined to a particular region (as voicing of initial fricatives is, for example). In fact, most people in England and Wales drop their [h]s to a greater or lesser extent. Therefore, if the origin of the phenomenon is as recent as the late eighteenth century, it is difficult to explain how it could have become so geographically widespread in so short a time. It was already highly salient and overtly stigmatised by the latter half of the nineteenth century (for evidence of this, see Milroy 1983: 40). It is reasonable to assume that if a linguistic variant is so widespread and strongly established, it probably has quite a long history in the language. The late-eighteenth-century evidence adduced by Wyld and others is therefore likely to indicate the date at which it had become stigmatised as a 'vulgarism', rather than its date of origin.

The most important reason for questioning the traditional view, however, is that variation in initial <h> usage is a very common pattern in Middle English texts. Whereas we have discussed orderly variation in spelling (above) by looking at distribution within a single text, the evidence for early [h]-loss depends on spelling variation across a number of texts. Many Middle English sources exhibit variable use of the letter <h> in syllable-initial positions (i.e. in words like *hate*, *hopper*). Sometimes it is omitted where it is historically expected to be present, and sometimes it is added where it is not expected.

This pattern of variation is widespread in Early Middle English, and the *LALME* maps also show a distribution at later periods. It has been very widely noted by careful editors such as Hall (1920), and (although the atlas map shows some west midland distribution) it seems in the early part of the period to be most common in texts originating in the east midlands, East Anglia and the south. It is quite common in southern texts of ca 1200, such as *Poema morale* (Lambeth and Trinity MSS) and *The Owl and the Nightingale*, in early east midland/East Anglian texts such as *Genesis and Exodus, King Horn, Havelok*. It is found in the Otho MS of Laȝamon's *Brut*, but not in the Caligula MS, which is certainly south*west* midland. It is not characteristic of early texts known to be west midland, such as those of the Katherine group. The geographical distribution of relevant texts from ca 1190–1320 is from Lincolnshire or Norfolk (in the north) to the southern counties, but the instability seems to be greatest in the east midlands. Certain later texts, mostly of a non-literary kind, display the same phenomenon. It is found in Kristensson's (1967) northern onomastic sources in the period 1290–1350, and Wyld (1927, 1936) documents a number of later examples, from sources that include the *Norfolk Gilds* (late fourteenth century), *The Paston Letters* (fifteenth century), and the mid-sixteenth-century *Diary of Henry Machyn* (for a fuller discussion, see Milroy 1983: 48–9). In my own investigations of many of these texts, I have noted additional examples. The following selective lists are from the thirteenth-century *Genesis and Exodus* (Morris 1873a), which is believed to originate in East Anglia. They include examples additional to those given by Wyld. List 1 documents omission of *h*, and list 2 addition of 'unhistorical' *h*:

1   *a, adde, adden, as, aue, auede, aued, auen, aue* (parts of the verb 'have': lines 239, 240, 1251, 1505, 1760, 2388, 2425, 2720, and very commonly – considerably more so than forms with *h*); *algen, aligen* ('hallow'): 258, 918; *ail* ('hail'): 3066, 3183; *ate* ('hate'): 373, 3638; *alt* (< infin 'hold'): 924; *atteð* ('is called' < OE *hatan*): 813; *e* ('he, they'): 2341, 2708, 4094; *egest* ('highest'): 143, 1224; *eld* ('held'): 2999; *elles* ('of hell'): 4157; *ere* ('of them' < OE *heora*): 2855, 3773; *eðen* ('hence'): 2188; *eui* ('heavy'): 2559; *is* ('his'): 482, etc; *opperes* ('hoppers' i.e. 'locusts'): 3096; *ostel* ('hostel' i.e. 'lodging'): 1056; *om* ('home'): 2270; *oten* ('called'): 1131.

2   *hagte* ('wealth'): 431; *hagt* ('grief'): 486, 2044, 2082; *halle* ('all'): 2340; *ham* ('am'): 926; *helde* (i.e. *elde* 'age'): 457, 1527; *her* ('before'): 801; *herf* (i.e. *erf* 'cattle'): 2991; *herðe* (i.e. *erde* 'land'): 806; *hic* ('I'): 34, 2783; *hinke* (i.e. *inke* 'dread'); *his* ('is'): 2935; *hore* (i.e. *or* 'before'): 958; *hunframe* (*unframe*): 554; *hunkinde* (*unkinde*): 534; *hunne* ('grant'): 2249; *hunwreste* ('wicked'): 537; *hure* ('our'): 322, 2206.

The most immediate 'explanation' for such substantial instability in the use of <h> is that syllable-initial [h] was not present, or only variably present, in the speech of the relevant regions. The letter was, however, present in the orthographic tradition (regardless of the mixed origins of the tradition in Old English, Anglo-Norman and Latin): thus, in the absence of strong orthographic standardisation, the scribes would omit it on some occasions and insert it 'hypercorrectly' on others.

As instability of <h> is extremely common, it is remarkable that careful scholars, such as Wyld, could have been so much aware of this type of evidence, but could nevertheless have rejected it. I have suggested above some of the reasons why this should be so and have elsewhere (Milroy 1983) reviewed some of the arguments that have been used to reject variable evidence; however, as it happens, instability of <h> is one of the putative 'Anglo-Norman' features distinguished by Skeat (1897).

Frequently, this orthographic evidence for variation in Middle English is rejected on the grounds, not that the scribe was literally an Anglo-Norman, but that uses such as variable <h> are originally scribal importations from French or Latin usage. However, the origin of scribal habits is not in itself valid proof that variable use of the conventions in written English do not *also* relate to variable usages in spoken English. This is because variable scribal usage is likely to be functional in some way, and the most immediately obvious function of an alphabetic writing system is to relate writing to speech forms (however complicated this relationship may be). Thus, especially in a time of unsettled orthography, it is extremely likely that current sound changes will be admitted into writing, whatever the historical origins of the writing conventions may be. Moreover, the *prima facie* evidence for [h]-dropping continues well into Early Modern English – long after there can be any suspicion of direct Anglo-Norman scribal interference. The evidence from spelling strongly suggests that (h) has been a *variable* in English for many centuries: [h]-loss may have gone to completion in some varieties at particular times and places, but in general speech communities have used the variation over these centuries as a stylistic and social marker. In other words, whatever the origin of the phenomenon may be (in phonotactic constraints, in rapid speech processes or in language contact, for example), it has probably had a social and stylistic function in the language for centuries.

Although a sociolinguistic perspective does suggest some possible interpretations of the social and stylistic functions of [h]-dropping and other kinds of variation at different times and places, we are not primarily concerned with these here and will refer to them briefly in section 3.4. The case of [h]-dropping is discussed here as an example of the possible contribution that a variationist perspective may make to a multidimensional account of linguistic variation in Middle English, and through that to a multidimensional history of the structure of the English language.

3.4 Concluding remarks

In this chapter I have concentrated on *methods* of ascertaining the distribution of linguistic variants in Middle English rather than attempting to give a full account of the details of variation. This latter task would involve reporting massive variation, which is best appreciated by direct study of the texts themselves and of the surveys and maps that have been discussed above. I have also been very much concerned with how the variation discovered is to be interpreted, as the aims of dialectology are more far-reaching than merely to record the distribution of variants. Ultimately they are concerned with explaining linguistic change, the seeds of which are manifested in variation.

Historical dialectology has always been modelled to some extent on the methods and principles of present-day researches, and investigators, such as Kristensson (1967), have normally emphasised this dependence. This chapter has focused on two branches of the subject – regional and social dialectology – and we have assessed what each of these can contribute to the study of variation in Middle English. Of these two, however, it is social dialectology that has been most explicitly concerned in recent times with the theoretical issue of how linguistic change is to be explained. In this concluding section, therefore, I should like to take up two points connected with social dialectology that are relevant to the exploration of past states. The first concerns the idea of uniformity in language as it applies to historical description and interpretation. The second concerns the social nature of language and, within this, how far the framework of social dialectology can help us to understand the social motivations of change and variation in the past.

Most branches of linguistic enquiry have been influenced by the doctrine that only uniform language states can be regular or structured. Therefore, when variation is encountered, it may well be discounted as 'irregular'. We have noticed above that this doctrine has in the past influenced the analysis of Middle English in the tendency to dismiss variant forms as errors or to explain them away as 'Anglo-Norman'. I have suggested in section 3.3 that, although there may often be errors in the texts, it is appropriate in the first place to determine the extent to which the variation displayed is actually structured, and I have attempted to demonstrate this by looking at constraints on variation in *Havelok*. The belief in uniformity has, of course, had a more general and diffuse effect on the historical description of English, chiefly in the form of emphasising the history of *standard* English, at the expense of 'vernaculars'. Although this is less relevant to Middle English than to later periods, it has resulted in some selectivity in reporting the data in handbooks of Middle English. Thus, the time-depth of such phenomena as final-stop deletion and [h]-dropping may well have been underestimated by many. The general effect of this is to understate the multidimensionality of language and its history.

As for the social motivations of change, it is clear that although linguistic changes are initiated and diffused by live *speakers*, they become apparent in changes in the language *system*. What we have to explain is how innovations initiated by speakers find their way into language systems, at which point, of course, they become linguistic changes. For this reason it is useful in social dialectology to bear in mind a distinction between speaker-based and system-based accounts (Milroy & Milroy 1985), and to look at how speakers are motivated to innovate and to accept innovations by others. Yet, whereas present-day dialectologists have access to speakers in social contexts and can therefore form hypotheses of a social kind on the basis of fieldwork and empirical explorations, Middle English dialectologists must attempt to get access to speaker motivations by very indirect means. One source is the general sociopolitical situation as studied by historians; within this branch of enquiry we also gain insights from, for example, comments by contemporary observers on the language situation and documentary evidence of population movements. Thus, from Ekwall's (1956) study, we can deduce that the change in London dialect from a southern/southeastern to a midland type is related to large-scale immigration into London from the east midlands and north. Another method we can use is to project the social argumentation of sociolinguistics on to the past.

One aspect of this argumentation concerns *evaluation* of linguistic variants by communities. This may be relevant to explaining the change in the character of London English noticed above, as population movement does not in itself explain why the dialect of the in-comers should prove to be dominant: why was their speech not simply assimilated into the pre-existing London dialect? It seems that certain features of the in-coming dialect were evaluated more highly, and sociolinguists might explain this kind of pattern in terms of *prestige* or – preferably – in terms of the changing identity functions of language. Present-day studies in the rise and development of urban vernaculars (Milroy 1981, and Harris 1985, on Belfast, for example) help to provide a framework additional to the findings of historical investigations, in which these historical phenomena can be further considered.

It has also been clearly established that in the course of time evaluation of particular variants can change or even be reversed. Therefore, it is most unlikely that present-day stigmatised forms have always been stigmatised, and I have suggested elsewhere (Milroy 1983) that in the Middle Ages [h]-dropping may have been a marker of more cultured speech. Although in a particular instance like this such an interpretation may be debatable, the belief that 'vulgarisms' have always been 'vulgarisms' is much more dangerous. Apart from specific cases, however, there are broader trends in the history of English for which sociolinguistics can provide an interpretative framework. One of these is the trend toward simplification that was mentioned in section 3.2: it seems fairly clear that such a sweeping change is at least to some extent associated with *language contact*.

Language-contact studies form an important background to present-day social dialectology in the work of Weinreich (1953), and the topic is further developed in Trudgill's *Dialects in Contact* (1986). In a suggestive study Anderson (1986) has examined simplification patterns in a wide variety of European dialects and proposed a distinction between *open* and *closed* communities – those that are open to outside influences as against those that are not. We (Milroy & Milroy 1985) have proposed that *speakers* are open to outside influences to the extent that their social links within close-tie communities are weakened and, further, that simplification is associated with weakening of links (Milroy 1992). Studies of this kind seem to be suggestive as projections on to the past: late medieval London, for example, seems to have been an open community in this respect, and changes in the London dialect may have depended on the development of weak personal ties resulting from population movements.

The most extreme cases of simplification are pidgin/creole languages, and these have been empirically studied very widely in recent years (e.g.

by Mühlhäusler 1986). Using pidgin/creole arguments, the most extreme solution to the Middle English simplification question is that of Bailey & Maroldt (1977), who argue that Middle English was a French-based creole – a view that few have accepted as it stands. Yet, it seems likely that language-contact phenomena may be implicated in a more general way: the advanced inflectional loss in twelfth- to thirteenth-century east midland dialects, for example, may be in some way associated with heavy Danish settlement in these areas – even if the language varieties that resulted from this were not creoles. In general, these observations on language contact, rooted as they are in empirical research, provide a well-motivated framework in which simplification – and variation in the speed of change at different periods – can be discussed and debated.

There are many other matters of interest to theories of change that I have not been able to discuss in this chapter. However, I hope that I have said enough to make the point that continuing study of Middle English dialects is of crucial importance to writing a realistic multi-dimensional history of English, and of considerable importance also to theories of linguistic change in general.

FURTHER READING

Elementary introductions to variation in Middle English are available in standard histories of the English language. These vary in the amount of attention given to dialect variation, and some are quite poor in this respect. Amongst those that give attention to variation, the appropriate chapters of the following are recommended: Baugh & Cable (1978), *A History of the English Language*, 3rd edn; Bourcier (1981), *An Introduction to the History of the English Language* (English adaptation by Cecily Clark); Strang (1970), *A History of English*. The collections of Middle English texts by Dickins & Wilson (1956) and by Bennett & Smithers (1966) have useful general introductions to Middle English dialect variation and useful commentaries on the individual texts. Martyn Wakelin's *English Dialects: an Introduction* (1972a) contains a good deal of historical material.

Amongst more recent writers on regional dialects of Middle English, the work of Kristensson and Sundby is recommended, together with the classic work of Ekwall, which underlies their work. However, the most important contributions to Middle English dialectology are those of McIntosh, Samuels and their colleagues. The introduction to the first volume of *LALME* is very important. The complexity of the work that has gone into Middle English dialectology can be further investigated in, for example, McIntosh's study of the provenance of *Havelok the Dane* and the McIntosh & Wakelin study of

John Mirk's *Festial*. The recent collection of essays edited by McIntosh, Samuels and Laing is recommended. Apart from the studies mentioned, this includes an important article by Samuels on the origins of early standard English and one by Laing on linguistically composite texts. The maps themselves will be very useful to investigators who have specific aims in mind (for example, compiling a history of /h/-dropping!).

There has been very little work on sociolinguistic variation in Middle English. Some of my comments in this chapter are discussed more fully in J. Milroy (1983) and treated in the context of variation studied in J. Milroy, *Linguistic Variation and Change* (1992). The classic essay on backward projection of variation studies is Labov, *On the Use of the Present to Explain the Past*, which is most accessible in the reprint by P. Baldi and R. Werth (eds), *Readings in Historical Phonology* (University Park: Pennsylvania State University Press, 1978).

NOTES

1 There is a tremendous bibliography relevant to the study of variation in Middle English that stretches back for well over a century. I have not attempted here to review this in detail, as good reviews are available in the best histories of English, such as Baugh & Cable (1978). The main focus of this chapter is on methodology and interpretation.

2 Another manuscript from ca 1200 that is very consistent in spelling is the *Ormulum* – from the east midlands. This, however, is experimental – a conscious attempt to devise a consistent orthographic system that represents the phonological system (especially vowel length) accurately.

3 Recent developments – in particular the idea of *lexical diffusion* (Wang 1969) have questioned the Neogrammarian axiom, which often lay behind earlier interpretations of sound change. For an assessment of the controversy, see Labov 1981 and Kiparsky 1988.

4 As systematic change in language (e.g. in phonology as against lexical borrowing of learned words) is initiated and diffused by speakers (and not writers) in casual and informal *conversational* contexts, the styles and modes of writing conspire to 'cut off' the origins of linguistic changes. They represent 'planned' rather than 'unplanned' discourse (Ochs 1983).

5 For example, most dialects of English have merger of words of the type *pair/pear/pare* and many other sets of items. However, the writing system, here as elsewhere, retains older spelling distinctions.

6 There are many studies of particular instances in historical records of the use of French in the medieval English speech community, and the place and function of Anglo-Norman has been widely debated. Some commentators have tended to emphasise its importance and its longevity as a mother tongue (see, e.g. Legge 1941). A different view is expressed, however, by

some others, for example, Rothwell (1966, 1968, 1975). He has shown that certain thirteenth-century scribes (who would be amongst the most educated persons of the time) did not have a native-like command of French, and were given to quite systematic errors in translation. Thus, the position was fluid and changing, ultimately resulting in the disappearance of Anglo-Norman from the speech community. It is discussed in many histories of English, such as Baugh & Cable 1978.

7 One way of achieving 'accountability to the data' is to *quantify* the relevant variation (as Labov 1966 does). There is considerable scope for doing this in Middle English studies, and it has been used in the *LALME* project: for example, by Laing (1988).

8 Here, I distinguish an 'error' from an 'orderly variant' by considering the latter to be reasonably frequently attested in a text, and not just once. Ultimately, there is bound to be some difficulty in making such a distinction in every instance – partly because what appear to be 'errors' may sometimes be the beginnings of linguistic changes.

9 The parentheses enclose variables. Thus (ht) is a variable which may be differentially realised.

4 SYNTAX

Olga Fischer

4.1 Introduction

In many ways 'Middle' is an appropriate term for the syntax of the period that will be the subject of discussion in this chapter.[1] As Roger Lass says in chapter 2 (section 2.2) of this volume, 'middle' indicates the transitional nature of the language in this period; 'transitional', of course, only with hindsight. Lass further refers to the typological use of the term 'middle' within the family of Germanic languages, representing among other things a language with a relatively 'poor' inflectional system. Translated into syntactic terms, a 'middle' language tends to have a fairly strict word order, and to make greater use of periphrastic constructions; i.e. it relies more heavily on auxiliary verbs, prepositional phrases, etc.

Compared with the Old English period, when the syntax of the language was relatively stable (see vol. I, section 4.1), the Middle English period is indeed one of change. Much has been written about the causes of the rapid loss of inflections, which started in the Late Old English period in the northern part of the country and which was more or less concluded in the fourteenth century with the exception of some enclaves in the extreme south. Without doubt the fact that Old English had initial stress played a role. It must have contributed to the neutralisation of vowel qualities in inflectional endings and their almost total subsequent demise. However, when we consider the fact that other Germanic (initial-stress) languages did not all lose their inflections, it cannot have been a decisive factor. More important may have been the influence of the Viking settlements in the Danelaw, which, according to some scholars, led to a process of pidginisation, with a concomitant loss of morphological structure and the development of a more analytic language (see O'Donnell & Todd 1980: 47–8; Poussa 1982; but also Hines forthcoming).

Since *change* is the term associated with the middle period, this chapter will be largely devoted to the *changes* in syntax that were taking place. Each discussion of a particular structure will start off with a brief description of the Old English situation (in many cases this will be no more than a reference to the corresponding sections in vol. I, chapter 4) followed by a discussion of the developments taking place in Middle English. Where possible, an explanation for these developments will be provided.

The emphasis, as stated, will be on the diachronic aspects of the syntax. Questions of a diatopic nature will be largely ignored, for several reasons. First of all, space does not permit a discussion of syntactic change as well as syntactic dialectal variation (some of this variation will be found in chapter 3 of this volume). Methodologically, it may seem a hazardous decision to ignore dialectal variants: change often originates in variation. However, as far as we know, the major syntactic changes in the Middle English period do not find their origin in dialectal variants, but are a result of the morphological developments discussed above. These are common to all Middle English dialects. It is true that individual dialects may have undergone these changes at different times, but the ultimate results do not essentially differ. Moreover, syntactic change seems more often caused by language-internal factors than is the case with changes on the other linguistic levels, with the exception perhaps of the morphological one. This makes dialectal variation less important for our purposes. A second reason for ignoring dialectal variants is the lack of dialectal evidence of such syntactic variants. The *Linguistic Atlas of Late Medieval English* (1986) provides an extensive survey of dialectal differences in the fields of phonology, morphology and lexis, but it has nothing on syntactic variants. In the introduction it is stated that 'it may well be that syntax will perforce remain the Cinderella of Middle English dialectology' (McIntosh *et al.* 1986: 32). This lack of a syntactic survey is understandable. Not only is it far more difficult to establish syntactic profiles on the basis of the often relatively short documents used for the survey, but it is also a major problem to decide to what extent two different syntactic constructions are in fact variants of one another. In this light it is not surprising that the only plan for a syntactic dialect survey that I know of involves a survey of *Present-Day* Dutch dialects, whereby informants can actually be consulted about the variants involved (see Gerritsen 1988). (For the lack of informants as one of the major problems facing a student of historical syntax, see also vol. I, section 4.1.[2])

As I have indicated, in syntax it is more difficult than in phonology, morphology and lexis to identify items to be compared. One needs a much larger corpus, and one needs to establish how far two surface structures actually represent the same construction. It will only rarely be the case that one can compare completely identical structures (for this problem — and ways of overcoming it — and the resultant 'lag' of the study of historical syntax, see Lightfoot 1979 and Warner 1982). Ideally, for a survey of syntactic developments in a particular period, one should only use texts that are similar in nature, representing the different stages of the period under discussion. That is, one should use only prose texts; texts that are not translated or at least not influenced by their source text; and texts that are similar in style and dialect. On the other hand, one would like to use texts that are widely available to the reader. And, even though prose texts may be our preference, it should be borne in mind that in the Middle English period, most prose texts were more formal in style than a lot of the poetry. For all these reasons I have not hesitated to select illustrative examples from a variety of texts. For instance, I have often used Chaucerian poetry (because of its familiarity to the reader) when I am convinced that the nature of the text has had no effect on the construction under discussion, because the construction in question occurs in all types of Middle English texts. Where a construction is more typical of either poetry or prose, this is made explicit. Information about textual sources is provided at the end of the chapter.

The structure of the chapter is similar to the chapter on Old English syntax in volume I. It begins with a discussion of the syntactic properties of the nominal phrase (section 4.2). Section 4.3 deals with the verb phrase: with the arguments dependent on the verb and the changes taking place in the mood and tense systems, leading to, among other things, the development and consolidation of a whole range of periphrastic constructions. Sections 4.4 and 4.5 are short treatments on the nature of interrogative and negative (mainly simple) clauses. Section 4.6 is very extensive; it deals with subclauses, finite as well as non-finite. The discussion of finite clauses is mainly an inventory of the type and range of clauses available in Middle English. An exception is the discussion of the relative clause, where a great deal of attention is given to the many differences in complementisers between the Old and Middle

English periods. What will be central in the discussion of the non-finite constructions is a description and, as far as possible, an explanation of the new constructions that have arisen since the Old English period. Section 4.7 deals with the types of agreement that exist between sentence elements, and centres on the differences between Middle and Present-Day English. Section 4.8 concerns word order. It is a crucial, but at the same time tentative, section. It is crucial because many of the changes discussed in the other sections are related to the changes discussed here. It is tentative because the opinions of linguists concerning the nature of the basic word order in Old and Middle English still differ considerably, if they accept at all the notion 'basic word order'. Section 4.9 deals with developments concerning passive and preposition stranding constructions, topics that in recent years have attracted the attention of more theoretically inclined linguists. They constitute important areas of English historical syntax in their own right and are not fully dealt with in the preceding sections.

4.2 The noun phrase

Noun phrases are phrasal units with a noun, an adjective or pronoun as head. The noun may be premodified by a quantifier, adjective (including pronominal adjectives such as demonstratives, interrogatives, etc.) or an adjective phrase, and postmodified by a prepositional phrase or an adjective (phrase). As in Present-Day English, noun phrases may be definite or indefinite (see section 4.2.2). In Old English noun modifiers agreed with their head in number, case and gender. With the loss of inflections in the Middle English period, this kind of agreement fairly quickly disappeared, for details see chapter 2 of this volume. Case inflections on the head of a noun phrase dependent on another noun phrase will be discussed in section 4.2.4. The first section will address the possible orders of modifiers within the noun phrase.

4.2.1 Word order

Although quite a number of detailed studies have appeared on sentential word order, very little has been written on the position of elements within the noun phrase. The reason for this neglect may be the diachronic rather than synchronic bias of many Middle English syntactic studies, set beside the absence of any notable changes in this area between Middle English and the modern period. Basically, the internal

Table 4.1. *Premodifiers in the Present-Day English noun group*

Predeterminer	Determiner	Postdeterminer	Modifier	Head
all	articles, demonstrative	other quantifiers,	adjectives,	
both	adjective, possessive	numerals	genitive	
half[a]	adjective, interrogative		phrases	
	adjective, quantifiers: *some*,			
	any, no, enough, each, every,			
	much, (n)either			

[a] Expressions like *twice a day* also occur in Middle English. However, *twice* is not considered a predeterminer here but a separate adverbial adjunct, which has its own adverbial – genitive – ending in *-es* (the spelling in Middle English is usually *ones*, *twies*, etc.).

order of the premodifiers follows the Present-Day English patterns, as represented in table 4.1. Table 4.1 does not represent all the Present-Day English possibilities. Moreover, only a small number of combinations are in fact permitted. Concerning the Middle English possibilities, only those features will be discussed in which the Middle English system differs markedly from that of Present-Day English.

The number of quantifiers that can appear before the determiner position is somewhat larger in Middle English. Thus we find:

(1) ... þurh out *vch a* toune ...

(*Horn* (Hrl) 218)

'Throughout each [a] town'

(2) And God forbede that *al a* compaignye / Sholde rewe o singuleer mannes folye.

(*CT* VIII.996–7)

Each a is also found in Old English; in Middle English it occurs only in the early period (see Rissanen 1967: 247–50). Other Middle English predeterminers that begin to occur in combination with *a* are: *many, such, which, what*. The earliest instances are found in thirteenth-century texts. The separation of the (pronominal) adjective from the following noun makes the whole phrase more emphatic (see Rissanen 1967: 252). In this connection it is interesting to compare the Caligula and Otho manuscripts of Laȝamon's *Brut*:

(3)a. Selkuð hit þuðte *moni* cnihte ...

(*Brut* (Clg) 3746)

'Strange it seemed to many knight'

   b. Sel-cuþ hit þohte *maniane* cnihte...

(Brut (Otho) 3746)

     'Strange it seemed to many a knight'

(4) Michel was *svich a* king to preyse...

(Havelok (Ld) 60)

(5) Lokes nu... *hwuch a* merke he leide up on hise icorene...

(Ancr. (Tit) 85.9–11)

     'Look now what sign he put on his chosen [ones]'

Which a is not very common, examples of *what a* seem to be later and are also not frequent. Other quantifiers can occur before *an*, but in that case *an* has the numerical/intensifying meaning of *one* (see Rissanen 1967: 258–60):

(6) ...I wot well *non oo* man a-lyve hathe callyd so oft vpon yow...

(Davis 1971–6: 386, 16–17)

Next to *all, both, half* some other quantifiers occur in combination with the definite article, such as *some* and *any*. Present-Day English would use an *of*-phrase here:

(7) some þe messagers

(Glo.Chron.A (Clg) 2718) (other manuscripts have some of)

(8) ony the other eyght

(Caxton's Preface, Vinaver 1967: cxii, 6)

(the other extant copy of the Caxton edition has *ony of*...)

In Middle English it was possible to combine the predeterminers *all* and *both* (see Lightfoot 1979: 174):

(9) alboth this thynges owyth euery good Iuge to haue.

(Yonge S.Secr. 207.37–8)

All both is also found in independent use in combination with a personal pronoun:

(10) & paye hem alle bo

(SLeg.Fran(2) (Bod) 256)

Note that this combination is still common in Dutch (e.g. *allebei*). Since *all* always precedes *both* it is likely that this *all* was, at least in origin, an intensifier rather than a quantifier (cf. the use of *al* in Middle English as a degree adverb).

Next, one finds examples of two determiners combined together;

especially common is that of an article or possessive adjective followed by a possessive noun phrase:

(11) for þare aller right

(*Cursor* (Vsp) 469)

   'for the right of them all'

(12) hare baðre luue

(*St.Kath.* (Tit) 1212–13)

   'the love of both of them'

(13) her eitheres werke

(*Palladius* (Tit) 808)

   'the work of both (each) of them'

When inflections were lost in the Late Old English/Early Middle English period, it was not always possible to recognise a genitive case in these constructions (quantifiers did not develop an analogical -(*e*)*s* genitive). Ambiguity, too, could easily arise since *both* was also used attributively after determiners (cf. the Middle English adjectival use of *al* 'complete' and *much* 'great') as in *his boþe armes* (*Gawain* 582) 'his two arms'. This probably accounts for the fact that these genitives were replaced by *of*-constructions in the course of the Middle English period.

In Old English it was also possible to combine the demonstrative and the possessive adjective. Some instances are still found in Early Middle English but they are rare:

(14) hyre þa leofstan hlaford &   sunu...
      her the dearest lord   and son

(*PC* (Ld) 1093: 26–7)

According to Mustanoja (1958: 14ff.), the possessive is placed before the demonstrative for emphasis. Rather similar is the construction *oon the best man*, which will be discussed below.

Middle English quantifiers also show more freedom when used independently in combination with personal pronouns. *All* and *both* occur both before and after the pronoun: *we alle/alle we*. *Alle we* is used all through the period but later disappears, presumably because of the rise of *all of us* constructions. The latter constructions were formed in the modern period on analogy with quantifiers such as *many* which allowed of a partitive construction, e.g. *many of us*.

The word *other* is not as positionally restricted in Middle English as it is in Present-Day English. In Middle English we still find traces of the Old English *oþer sum* construction:

(15)   And oþer-sum said...

(Cursor (Vsp) 6491)

'and some others said...'

and also *other all, other many, other more.*

The position of adjectival modifiers in Present-Day English is normally before the head; the exceptions are found mainly in poetry, in instances where they can be regarded as reduced relative clauses, and in certain idiomatic phrases like 'the Lords temporal'. The position was somewhat freer in Middle English (but there, too, more so in poetry than in prose) so that postmodification was not infrequent. Lightfoot (1979: 205ff.) suggests that in Middle English we see a tendency developing towards postmodification as a result of the word-order change from SOV (Subject–Object–Verb) towards SVO (for details on word order, see section 4.8); i.e. Middle English follows its typological course in that, with the change from SOV to SVO, it also changes from Adjective–Noun to Noun–Adjective order (according to the universals formulated by Greenberg 1966). However, Noun–Adjective order in Middle English tends to be restricted in two ways; these restrictions cannot be explained with reference to the above universal. First, under French influence so-called 'learned adjectives' borrowed from French (i.e. those adjectives that were also postnominal in Old French; see Harris 1978: 58–60) are often placed after the head word (note in (16) the use of the French-type plural inflection on the adjective):[3]

(16)   ...oure othere goodes temporels

(CT VII.998 [10:998])

(17)   Ful weel she soong the service dyvyne

(CT I.122 [1:122])

Second, when two adjectives are involved, it is possible for the first adjective to precede and the second to follow the head or for both adjectives to follow. (This was usual in Old English, i.e. when the language was presumably still SOV.) In the latter case, *and* was normally used as a connector (as in Old English), but from the thirteenth century onwards *and* also begins to be found when just one adjective follows, e.g. *a good man and (a) fair* (see Rissanen 1967: 293).

The only detailed study of the position of the adjective is that by Schmittbetz (1909) on *Sir Gawain and the Green Knight*. He finds, with a single adjective, Adjective–Noun order is the most common (in about 80 per cent of all cases), and that 66 per cent of instances of Noun–Adjective order can be explained on metrical grounds. With two adjectives, postposition is slightly more frequent: there are seventeen instances of *Noun–Adjective and Adjective/Adjective–Noun (and) Adjective* against sixteen instances of *Adjective–Adjective–Noun*.

As in Present-Day English heavy adjective phrases normally follow the head,

(18) ...and wise advocatz lerned in the lawe.

(CT VII.1007 [10:1007])

Occasionally, however, one also comes across examples where the adjective precedes the head while the prepositional phrase follows:

(19) ... þei þat scholden ben conuerted to crist...be oure gode ensamples
& be oure *acceptable lif to god*,

(Mandev. (Tit) 90: 2–4; see also 190: 6–8)

'...and by our [way of] life, acceptable to God'

Another adjectival construction that typically occurs after the head word is the one introduced by *al* or *so*, e.g. *of face so fere* 'of such a bold mien' *(Gawain* 103), *lyouns all white (Mandev.* (Tit) 193.24). These occur side by side with *so hardy a here* 'such a brave army' *(Gawain* 59) and the older construction *a so hardy here*. *So hardy a here* first occurs in the thirteenth century. Here again predeterminer position is selected for purposes of emphasis. The emphatic nature of the phrase is clear in this case from the use of degree adverbs before the adjective. Similar constructions with *too*, *how*, *full* and *thus* do not occur until the fourteenth century (see Rissanen 1967: 266):

(20) I sal þe ken ful gode a gin;

(Cursor (Vsp) 3644)

'I shall show you a very good trick'

Finally, in Middle English we find instances in which a simple adjective phrase precedes the determiner. These are undoubtedly a survival from Old English (see Mossé 1952: 123), and, like their Old English counterparts, are restricted to poetry (Mossé 1945: 168). They seem to be exceptionally frequent in the Cotton Caligula manuscript of Laȝamon's *Brut*, which also has a number of examples with the even rarer construction with the indefinite article (see Rissanen 1967: 265). In the less archaic Otho manuscript, we usually find the normal word order:

(21)a. mid godene heore worden
        with good   their words

    'with their good words'

  b. mid hire gode wordes

    'with their good words'

The Otho manuscript uses this construction only when the metre needs to be filled out, thus Clg 384, *mid richere strengðe* becomes Otho 384 *mid riche his strengþe*, to fill the gap left by the omission of the inflection.

In this section belongs perhaps the well-known Middle English phrase *oon the beste knyght* 'the very best knight'. This construction, rare in Old and Early Middle English, is regular in the Late Middle English period. The use of *oon* here may have been a development of what Mustanoja (1958: 293) has called the 'exclusive use' of the Old English numeral *an*, in which *an* denotes singleness, uniqueness (see also Rissanen 1967: 189ff.). *An* is put in an unusual position (usually initial but occasionally final position) to give it extra emphasis. It is most commonly found in combination with a superlative. Because it expresses uniqueness, it is often referred to as 'intensifying *one*'. The close connection of this use of *oon* with its original numeral function is brought out by the fact that plural constructions occur too, such as:

(22) Þre þe beste yles þese beþ & mest couþe

                                                  (Glo.Chron.A. (Clg) 34)

in combination with a superlative. Rissanen (1967: 200ff.) gives some examples of intensifying *oon* with a positive adjective, but they are much less frequent. Mustanoja argues convincingly that these were not partitive constructions, at least in origin. However, formally and also semantically, they were very close to partitives of the type *oon of the beste knyghtes*, and it is therefore not surprising that in Late Middle English we begin to come across hybrid constructions showing the partitive marker *of* combined with a singular rather than a plural noun:

(23) Oon of the beste entecched creature...

                                                  (Troilus V 832)

    'One of the most gifted/The most gifted creature(s)'

The rather exceptional form of these *oon* constructions and the existence of the semantically and syntactically close, but far less opaque, partitive constructions probably led to their disappearance in the course of the Modern English period.

The word order in the case of personal names accompanied by a noun denoting rank or title has undergone a notable change. In Old English the most common order was proper noun + rank, *Ælfred (se) cyning*, with or without a determiner. *Se cyning Ælfred* occurred, but mainly in writings influenced by Latin. In Middle English the latter became the normal order, very likely influenced by French.[4] Most of these nouns would be preceded by the definite article although it could be dropped at all times especially in Early Middle English and in poetry. Only with the titles *king* and *queen* (usually unique by themselves) was there a strong tendency to drop the article, especially when the noun was followed by an *of*-phrase (cf. the use of a zero article discussed in the following section):

(24) to King Petir of Spayn

(Capgr.Chron. (Cmb) 198.13)

but the amount of variation is striking in this period.

4.2.2 *Definite and indefinite noun phrases*

Whereas in Old English the use of a weak versus strong adjective helped to signal definite and indefinite noun phrases respectively, this distinction in adjectival inflections disappeared in Middle English. It remained longest in the case of monosyllabic words (for details see chapter 2, section 2.9.1.2). Chaucer's metre, for instance, shows that he still recognised weak and strong adjectives. The loss of this distinction led to a further systematisation in the use of the articles in Middle English.

The Old English deictic *se (seo, þæt)* fulfilled the functions of both definite article and demonstrative adjective. In Middle English a clear-cut distinction developed between these two functions with the invariant form *the* taking the role of the former and the Old English neuter form *þæt* > *that* (plural *tho*, northern *tha*, later *those*) beginning to function purely as a deictic.

In the earliest Middle English manuscipts one still finds inflected forms of the definite article (and also in later manuscripts in the more conservative south), especially the plural form *þa*, but in the course of the thirteenth century *the* had become the rule in most dialects. Compare, for instance, the replacement of inflected forms by invariant *the* in the Otho manuscript of Laȝamon's *Brut* (e.g. the accusative *þa Englisca boc* (Clg 16) becomes *þe Englisse boc* in Otho). By Chaucer's time, one would normally only come across inflected forms before words like *oon, other* (*that oon* > *the toon*; *that other* > *the tother*), and in set expressions like *atten ende* (< *at þæm ende*) (PDE 'at an end' goes back to this). In the phrase *for the nones* (< *for þan anes* < **for þæm anum*) the process of metanalysis or abduction has removed the original inflection (for more details see chapter 2, section 2.9.2.1).

The distal demonstrative adjective *that* is used in opposition to the proximal one *this/thes* in a deictic locative function (see further chapter 2, section 2.9.1.2). However, both adjectives are also used in a more metaphorical way, with *that* referring to what the speaker emotionally sees as removed from him or her, often carrying a tone of disapproval or dislike:

(25) Ar ich utheste uppon ow grede,/ Þat ower fihtlac leteþ beo,

(Owl&N (Clg) 1698–9)

'Before I raise the hue and cry on you, stop that fight of yours'

and *this* signifying a certain intimacy between the speaker (author) and the subject, or the speaker and the audience (as it still does in modern story-telling). The latter is frequently used by Chaucer before personal names and creates a chatty atmosphere (see Coghill 1966):

(26) Now, sire, and eft, sire, so bifel the cas/ That on a day *this hende Nicholas…*

(CT I.3271–2 [1: 3265–6])

The indefinite article developed out of the Old English numeral *an* (OE *sum* disappeared early on in the period, for its use see vol. I, section 4.2.1). In Middle English the indefinite article is usually unstressed *a(n)*, the stressed form *oon* being preserved for its function as a numeral. In Old English the rule had been to have no article with indefinite noun phrases unless they were referential (Givón 1981)/individualising (Mustanoja 1960), i.e. *an* was only used to introduce an entity that would be a topic later on in the discourse. In Middle English *a(n)* became a regular feature with indefinite noun phrases, used in more or less the same functions as in Present-Day English.

There are differences between Middle English and Present-Day English in the use of the (in)definite article, but usage varies even within

Middle English, which makes it difficult to give definite rules. As in Present-Day English, unique nouns usually have the definite article unless the object is unique in itself, in which case zero article is more common (see (27), (28)). In poetry, its presence or absence is often influenced by the requirements of metre (see (29), (30)):

(27) Þere is grete holownesse vnder erþe

(Trev.*Higd.* (St J-C) vol. 2, 23: 15)

(28) ...to destruye þe weres yn Tempse,

(Chambers & Daunt 1931: 151, 327)

'...to destroy the weirs in [the] Thames'

(29)a. In worshipe of Venus, goddesse of love,

(*CT* I.1904 [1: 1906])

b. Bitwixe Venus, the goddesse of love,

(*CT* I.2440 [1: 2442])

(30)a. Crul was his heer, and as the gold it shoon,

(*CT* I.3314 [1: 3308])

b. For his crispe heer, shynynge as gold so fyn,

(*CT* III.304 [2: 304])

Zero article is also more common when the noun (phrase) emphasises function rather than denoting a particular specimen:

(31) Brutus nom Ignogen, & *into scipe* lædde...heo wunden up *seiles*

(*Brut* (Clg) 551–3)

'Brutus took Ignogen, and led [her] into ship [= on board]...they hoisted [the] sails'

(32) ...freris han tauȝt in englond þe Paternoster *in engliȝsch tunge*

(Wycl. *Sel.Wks* 429: 30–1)

A zero article is especially common when the head noun is further specified by a following *of*-phrase or *þat*-clause, most regularly when it is an abstract noun preceded by a preposition,

(33) all þat sorwe & mischance schall turne to himself *þorgh vertue of þat ston*...

(*Mandev.* (Tit) 106: 10–11)

(34) & þei [diamonds] ben square & poynted of here owne kynde... *withouten worchinge of mannes hond*...

(*Mandev.* (Tit) 105: 17–19)

(35) This false knyght was slayn for his untrouthe/ *By juggement of Alla* hastifly;

(*CT* II.687–8 [3: 687–8])

and in expressions like *in hope þat* etc. It is very likely that the determiner is left out in these cases in Middle English because the *of*-phrase functions like a determiner just as the prenominal possessive phrase does. Note that some of these expressions still show variation in Present-Day English, such as *in (the) light of*.

Finally, Present-Day English must use the definite article before a substantival adjective when the reference is generic, i.e. to all members of a class. In Middle English this is less strictly necessary,

(36)   saynt germayn hit hedde al yeve to pouren.

(Ayenb. 190: 8)

‘Saint Germain had given it all to [the] poor’ (but cf. *þe poure* in 190: 9)

The indefinite article is regularly absent in Middle English when the noun phrase is used predicatively; this is especially so with non-concrete nouns, i.e. abstract or non-count nouns:

(37)   Þær wes feiht swiðe strong

(Brut (Clg) 856)

‘There was [a] very hard fight’

(38)   ...þat it is meruaylle...

(Mandev. (Tit) 104: 17)

‘that it is [a] miracle’

(39)   ...uram þet he wes child...

(Ayenb. 191: 8)

‘ever since he was [a] child’

On the other hand, it could occur before non-concrete nouns in order to individualise them, as in:

(40)   Agains him he tok a pride

(Cursor (Vsp) 448)

In that case the indefinite noun phrase is often referential, i.e. it is further specified in the discourse:

(41)   ...Shal falle a reyn, and that so wilde and wood/ That half so greet was nevere Noes flood.

(CT I.3517–18 [1: 3511–12])

‘There will be a [deluge of] rain, so violent and stupendous, that Noah’s flood will be nothing compared with it’

Givón (1981) gives an implicational hierarchical scale that is intended to show the possible historical development of the numeral *one* from a referential indefinite article to a non-referential indefinite article.

predicate nouns, object in future scope	>	generic subject	>	object in modal scope, object in negative scope, indefinite object[5]

It is clear that Present-Day English is positioned at the far end of the scale, while in Old English all indefinite articles can still be interpreted as referential (vol. I, section 4.2.1). But what is the position of Middle English in this scale? The indefinite article is not consistently used before predicate complements. Rissanen (1967: 278) shows some of the ratios in Early Middle English texts, but this does not take account of the referential/non-referential parameter. The evidence seems to show, though, that the indefinite article is decidedly more frequent in predicate complements than in generic subjects in Early Middle English. Rissanen gives examples of the type *An hors is strengur þan a mon* (*Owl&N* (Clg) 773), but says they are sporadic. On the other hand, indefinite articles seem to occur quite regularly before objects in modal or negative scope (42), although articleless objects are not infrequent (43):

(42)   For certes, every wight wolde holde me thanne *a fool*;
                                                    (*CT* VII.1055 [10: 1055])

(43)   ... but certes, of alle wommen, *good womman* foond I nevere.
                                                    (*CT* VII.1057 [10: 1057])

Clearly more research is necessary to establish the validity of this scale for Middle English.

Rissanen also writes (1967: 281) that the indefinite article seems to be more acceptable before objects of result as in,

(44)   þe hali gast lette writen *o bok* for to wearne men of hore fol sihðe.
                                                    (*Ancr.* (Tit) 5: 26–7)

   'the Holy Ghost let write a book to warn people of their foolish looking.'

but most of his examples seem to be referential indefinites. The use of the indefinite article is rare according to Rissanen (1967: 280) after verbs like *consider* and *regard*. This is not surprising because these objects could hardly be referential,

(45)   & halden hine for lauerd
                                                    (*Brut* (Clg) 2441)

   'and regarded him as lord'

4.2.3   Adjectives

As with other parts of speech, case and gender inflections for adjectives were lost in the Middle English period. Case and gender distinctions disappear very early on in the period, and even number distinctions (in contrast to nouns) are lost, apart from some occasional French plural markers (see (16)). This should not surprise us. Adjectival inflections carried no functional load because adjectives were normally supported by nouns. Problems only arose where these endings *were* functional, as was still the case to some extent in the weak/strong distinction, but especially when adjectives were used substantivally, without a head word (see section 4.2.3.1). The inflections of comparison constituted a separate system; these remained highly functional, and were therefore not lost. (For a discussion of these and other morphological details concerning adjectives, see chapter 2, section 2.9.1.2.)

4.2.3.1   Substantive use of adjectives and the development of the propword *one*

In order to preserve number distinctions when adjectives were used substantivally, nominal plural endings (-(*e*)*s*, and also -(*e*)*n* in the south, see (36)) were sometimes added in Early Middle English. This is to some extent still possible, but the group of such adjectives is highly restricted and includes mainly adjectives referring to humans (see the remark on the importance of gender distinctions below): *blacks, Christians, savages,* etc. Note too that the above adjectival nouns have undergone semantic narrowing; they have moved away from their 'companion' adjectives and have in fact become separate nouns. Thus, *blacks* does not normally refer to miners, chimney-sweeps, etc.

These singular and plural forms, when used, were not amenable to gender distinctions, i.e. they could not distinguish between human and non-human (for developments in the category of gender, see chapter 2, section 2.9.11). These deficiencies probably initiated the development of another system, which made use of propwords such as *man/men, thing(s)* and later also *one*, as in *Give me a good one*. This is basically the system that was adopted in Modern English. The only case in which a substantival adjective remains possible in Present-Day English is when the noun (phrase) is used generically, referring to the whole class, as in *the poor, the blind, the fabulous*, etc. We see it also in the superlative *the best, the worst*, but in a sense this is a generic reference as well: the superlative constitutes the whole class by itself. There are a few exceptions to this rule, but they are relics; they no longer form part of a productive system: *my beloved, the intended*. Such substantival adjectives were still quite common in Early Middle English, but towards the end of the period they began to be restricted to a smaller group of adjectives, or they became a stylistic device employed especially in alliterative poetry. Some examples:

(46) Þe   deade nis   namare of scheome þen of menske,
To-the dead not-is nomoreof shame   than of honour,
of *heard* þen of *nesche*, for he ne   feleð nowðer.
of hard than of soft,   for he not feels neither

(Ancr. (Corp-C) 180: 14–16)

'To someone dead there matters neither shame nor honour, hardship nor ease, for he feels neither.'

(47) Gauan gripped to his ax, and gederes hit on hyʒt.../ Let hit doun lyʒtly lyʒt on *þe naked*,/ Þat *þe scharp* of þe schalk schyndered þe bones.

(Gawain 421–4)

'Gawain took hold of his axe, and lifted it up high ... let it come down deftly on the naked [flesh] so that the sharp [axe] of the man cleaved the bones.'

The development of the propword *one* itself is still one of the more contentious areas of Middle English syntax. Like the indefinite article and intensifying *one*, the propword *one* can be traced back to the Old English numeral *an*. Rissanen (1967), following Mustanoja (1960), claims that the propword *one* developed out of pronominal and anaphoric uses. He rejects the notion that the propword is derived from the appositive use in Old English as in:

(48) Ic wat hea burh her *ane* neah lytle ceastre

(Gen. 2519)

'I know [a] high fort here, one near [a] small camp'

because this use is found almost exclusively in poetry, where the presence of *one* can be explained on metrical or rhythmical grounds. The earliest Middle English examples where *one* (ME *o(o)n*) follows an adjective date from the thirteenth century. Rissanen points to two interesting facts: (a) most of the early examples of adjective + *one* refer to persons not to inanimate objects; (b) examples of *so* + adjective + *one*, and superlative adjective + *one* are more common at first than non-degree adjectives. The first of these facts seems to suggest that the pronominal use of *one*, which developed in Early Middle English, see (49), made the development of these new constructions possible:

(49)   and þo heo weren alle i-sete,/ Þare cam *on* and seruede

(SLeg. (Ld) 227: 281–2)

'and when they were all seated, one came in and served'

This was also supported by the use of *æghwilc oon* and *such oon*, already occurring in Old English. An example is,

(50)   'Nai', quoð þe cuddest *an* of ham alle

(St.Kath. (Bod) 304–5)

The second fact seems to suggest that the intensifying use of *oon*, as in (51) (and see also section 4.2.1), must have been a factor too:

(51)   He was þe wisiste mon þad was in engelonde *on*.
       He was the wisest man that was in England   one

(Prov.Alf. (Trin) 72: 23–4)

'He was the very wisest man in England'

Meanwhile, anaphoric *one* develops out of pronominal *one* (see Rissanen 1967: 64–5). Anaphoric *one* replaces a noun (phrase) mentioned earlier in the sentence as in:

(52)   He haues a wunde in þe side.../ And he haues *on* þoru his arum...

(Havelok (Ld) 1981–3)

(53)   ...a moche felde,/ So grete *one* neuer he behelde.

(Mannyng *HS* (Hrl) 3267–8)

This probably led to an extension from persons to things in general and to the propword proper.

Another important development arising from the pronominal use of *one* was the rise of the indefinite pronoun *one* as in,

(54)   euery chambre was walled and closed rounde aboute, and yet
       myghte *one* goo from one [anaphoric!] to a nother.

(Caxton *Eneydos* 117: 17–19)

The earliest instances of this generalised *one* are from the fifteenth century (see Rissanen 1967: 65–8), but earlier fourteenth-century examples already show how indefinite *one* could develop out of pronominal *one*, referring not to an individual but to any one representative of the species under discussion,

(55)   Quat! hit clatered in þe clyff, as hit cleue schulde,/ As *one* vpon a
       gryndelston hade grounden a syþe;

(Gawain 2201–2)

'Hark, it re-echoed within the cliff, as though it would split it, as if someone were grinding a scythe on a grind-stone'

This development of *one* may have been assisted by the French indefinite pronoun *on*; but French influence is unlikely to have been the main cause since, as Mustanoja (1960: 223) points out, the earliest instances of indefinite *one* show it not in subject position but in oblique position. The rapid rise of *one* after the Middle English period is probably due to the fact that the Old English indefinite pronoun *man* (also *men*, *me* in Middle English) began to disappear. The reason for this disappearance is still the subject of some controversy, but contributing factors may have been the co-existence of the noun *man* 'man', the association of *man* with male gender, problems in agreement and anaphoric reference and the fact that there were already many other expressions in current use that could take the place of *man*, such as *you*, *they*, *we*, *people*, etc. (see Meier 1953: 235–8; Jud-Schmid 1956: 105–13).

4.2.4 *Case assignment within the noun phrase: the genitive case*

In this section we will primarily be concerned with the genitive case and its developments in Middle English, since the genitive constitutes the prime case assigned by a nominal phrase. Attention will also be paid to the genitive case assigned by the adjective phrase. In section 4.3.1 cases governed by the verb will be discussed. For developments in the use of a dative case after a noun or adjective, see section 4.8.4.1.

In Old English the genitive governed by a nominal phrase could express a variety of functions, which have been given terms, such as possessive, subjective, objective, partitive genitive, etc. The occurrence of the inflectional genitive becomes sharply reduced in the Middle English period in the general erosion of inflections. By the end of the period the inflectional genitive had become restricted to adnominal usage, with mainly a possessive or subjective function. Genitive case assigned by the verb or an adjective was lost very early in our period. In most instances the original genitive is replaced by a prepositional phrase, usually *of* + NP. Sometimes an uninflected form is used, especially where the Old English noun had zero-genitive inflection or *-e*, which was reduced to zero in Middle English:

(56) this lady name

(*Troilus* 1.99)

(57) thi brother wif

(*Troilus* I.678)

Inflectionless forms are also often preserved in compound nouns, as can still be seen in PDE *ladybird*, *mother tongue*. It is often difficult to tell, however, whether the compound contains a reduced or zero-genitive form or is simply a combination of two nouns (see Mustanoja 1960: 72).

The use of the *of*-phrase to replace the genitive is a native development (cf. similar developments in the Romance languages from Latin *de*, and in Dutch and German: *van* and *von* respectively), but it may have been helped along by the parallel French construction with *de*. There is some evidence that the frequency of the *of*-construction was higher in some works written under strong French influence. Mustanoja (1960: 75) presents tables that show roughly how the periphrastic genitive spread from just 1 per cent of all genitive constructions in Late Old English to roughly 85 per cent in Late Middle English. These tables also show that the inflectional genitive held out longest with personal nouns as heads, with singular heads rather than plural ones, and in verse. It is difficult to establish whether there was also dialectal variation in this case.

It is not hard to see why the inflectional genitive lingered on in verse; poetic language often shows archaic features, and besides, it gave the poet the opportunity to vary rhythm and stress patterns. That the *of*-phrase was more regular at first in the plural has mainly a phonological cause. The Old English genitive-plural endings in *-a*, *-ra*, *-ena* were weak and among the first inflections to disappear, while in the singular the masculine and neuter strong *-(e)s* had early on replaced the pho-nologically weaker singular endings of the feminine nouns and the *-n* declension nouns. It was some time before the singular *-(e)s* form also came to be generally accepted in the plural. This happened first in the north, at the end of the period also in the south, where older inflections (in this case *-ene*) were usually kept longest.

There is not much discussion in the handbooks about why virtually only the possessive and subjective genitives remained in the language and why most of the other functions dropped out of the system, leaving only some idiomatic residues behind. I think it is possible to establish a number of factors that go some way towards explaining this.

In Old English the genitive had a fairly free position; it could occur both before and after its head word (for more details, see Mitchell 1985: §§ 1304ff.). Mustanoja (1960: 76) and others have noted, however, that front position prevailed with proper names and personal (human) nouns in Old English, that is those nouns that still occur most frequently in genitive forms today. Most of the Old English genitives involving personal nouns have a possessive function. For that reason it is not surprising that this genitive appears before the head word in Old English since it reflects the Old English sentential order in which the subject appears normally before the object; i.e. a phrase like *Alfred's book* reflects the clausal structure 'Alfred a book has'; in both the two nouns function as subject and object respectively. Subject followed by object was still the sentential order in Middle English ('Alfred has a book'), so this type of genitive could easily survive. Likewise the subjective genitive survived into Middle English because it too reflected the Middle English sentential word order. The chances of survival for the Old English objective genitive, however, were considerably smaller. In all instances the head word is not a concrete noun like *book* but an abstract noun often related to a verb. Since in Old English the underlying (basic) order was presumably still SOV (see section 4.8 for more details), a phrase like *his feonda* (gen.) *slege* 'the killing of his enemies' (*ÆLS*(Oswald)14) presented no problem because the genitive *feonda* stood in object relation to the (verbal) noun *slege*. This type of construction became opaque in the course of the Middle English period when the language developed towards a SVO type. Thus, in Middle English the first noun *feonda* would tend to be interpreted as the subject rather than the object of *slege*. Therefore, this genitive was early on replaced by the *of*-phrase *following* the head word. (Note that the objective genitive is still in use when there is no ambiguity, i.e. when *only* the object interpretation is plausible as in phrases like *the king's assassination* or *his death*.) In theory, the problem could also have been solved by placing *feonda* after the head word. This, however, would have clashed with the general rule in Middle English that noun modifiers precede their heads (see section 4.2.1). It is interesting to see, then, that the objective genitive in the more archaic manuscript of the *Brut*, *for mines Drihtenes lufe* (*Brut* (Clg) 9844) is replaced by *for loue of mine Drihte* in the Otho manuscript.

The above also applies to genitives dependent on adjectives. In most instances, the genitive bore an object relation to the adjective; most of these adjectives occurred after a copula verb, the subject of which stands in subject relation to the adjective. Thus we find that already in Early Middle English the genitive is replaced by a prepositional phrase *following* the adjective. In the earliest texts we still find examples of the inflectional genitive and also of the periphrastic genitive preceding the adjective:

(58) ðu art deaðes   sceldi(h)
      you are of-death guilty

(Vices&V(1) (Stw) p. 51: 23–4

'you are guilty of death'

(59) teres wet
      of-tears wet

(*Gen.&Ex.* 2288)

'wet with tears'

(60)a. he wes ʒeua   custi

(*Brut* (Clg) 2033)

   b. he was ʒeftes custi
       he was of[-]gifts generous

(*Brut* (Otho) 2033)

'he was generous with gifts'

In the case of verbs, genitives were often replaced by the oblique form (as well as by prepositional phrases). This does not happen, however, with genitives assigned by adjectives. The reason is that this would create opacity; a phrase like *wet tears* would more naturally be interpreted as a noun phrase in which *wet* modifies *tears*. Moreover – and this is not the case with verbs, where oblique use was already the rule – such a phrase would have constituted a completely new type in the language.

In Old English the partitive genitive most commonly appeared after numerals and after quantitative nouns like *fela* 'many' and *unrym* 'a great amount'. Already in Old English the genitive inflection could be absent here, and many numerals were declined like adjectives. This is also the development in Middle English. The genitive was lost in phrases like *twa hundret sicles* 'two hundred shekels' (*Ancr.* (Corp-C) 203: 7) because the numeral now functioned as a modifier to the noun. The *of*-periphrasis, however, is also found,

(61) fif & sixti hundred of heðene monnen

(*Brut* (Clg) 9110)

'sixty-five hundred [of] pagan men'

Where the case-assigning noun could not function as a modifier the *of*-phrase became the rule: in Old English we have *husa selest* 'of houses the best' ('the best of houses'), in Middle English we find *best of alle* (*Ancr.* (Corp-C) 178: 3–4). Likewise, measure words like *busshel*, *pece* 'piece', *pound*, etc. now also require an *of*-phrase. Old English constructions like *þara fiftig* 'of-them fifty' ('fifty of them') also appear with an *of*-phrase, because in these cases the numeral could not become adjectival, since a pronoun does not normally take modifiers.

In a similar way, many locative and temporal nouns usually found in the genitive in Old English (the so-called genitive of measure) became inflectionless in Middle English because standing before the head word they could function as adjectival modifiers. Compare OE *fotes* (gen.) *trym* 'of-foot space' ('space of a foot') (*Mald* 244) with ME *foure myle weye* 'four mile way' ('a distance of four miles') (*KAlex.* (Ld) 4096). However, the genitive can also still be found here (next to the *of*-phrase) especially if the phrase would be ambiguous without this, e.g. *a day's journey* is clear in reference, whereas *a day journey* might also mean 'a journey taken during the day'. Presumably this type of genitive could go on existing because it was restricted to a small and well-defined set of nouns; it did not in any way upset the system.

A new development in Middle English was the so-called 'group genitive'; that is, a genitive inflection could come to be attached to a *group* of noun phrases as in *The Wife of Bath's Tale*, where, before, only a single noun phrase could be inflected (*The Wyves Tale of Bathe, CT* III.1264/5 [2: 1238/9]). When the genitive noun in Old English was followed by another noun in apposition, this appositive noun usually followed the head word and also carried a genitive inflection; when the genitive noun was followed by a prepositional phrase, this usually also followed the head word and had its own case: *neah Rines* (gen) *ofre þære ie* (gen.) 'near of-Rhine shore of-the river' ('near the shore of the river Rhine') (*Or.* 1 1.14: 28), *Malcolmes cynges* (gen.) *dohter of Scotlande* (dat.) 'the daughter of King Malcolm of Scotland' (*Chron.*E (Plummer) 1100: 47). In Middle English this order is also the usual one but the noun in apposition is put in the common case:

(62) þuruh   Iulianes (gen.) heste   ðe amperur
     through Julian's   command the emperor

(Ancr. (Nero) 109: 11)

  'by the command of Julian the emperor'

In the case of the appositive noun, the group genitive appears early in Middle English,

(63) Þe Laferrd Cristess karrte

(Orm. 56)

  'The Lord Christ's chariot'

and is found all through the period, although less frequently than the split construction (62). It became the rule first in the case of a title or rank followed by a proper name, which was looked upon as a unit. In a looser kind of apposition the split construction remained possible especially in formal or poetic styles, cf. *Hamlet* V.i.175 (Arden edn), 'This same skull, sir, was Yorick's skull, the King's jester.'

The split construction remained the norm with prepositional phrases all through the Middle English period. The earliest examples of the group genitive here seem to be the phrases *God of Loves (servantz)* (*Troilus* I.15) and *god of slepes (heyr)* (*BD* 168) both in Chaucer's poetry. Notice that in both these examples the *of*-phrase is descriptive and functions like a 'restrictive' phrase, i.e. it further identifies the type of god. Not surprisingly therefore the group genitive first occurs here and not in phrases like *the Wyves Tale of Bathe* (Chaucer, *CT* III.1264/5 [2: 1238/9]) where *of Bathe* is non-restrictive (it gives additional information about the *Wyf*, as is clear from *CT* I.445) and locative rather than descriptive.

A construction that also becomes current in Middle English is the type *The Man of Lawe his tale* (*CT* II.133/4 [3: 133/4]), in which the genitive inflectional *-(e)s* is replaced by a possessive pronoun; a construction common colloquially in other Germanic languages like German and Dutch. This occurs rarely in the north and not very frequently in the south. It becomes more widespread only after the Middle English period. Janda (1980) believes that this type of construction shows that English lost the morphological genitive inflection, i.e. that genitive *-(e)s* was reanalysed as a syntactic clitic element *his*. His main support for this argument is that genitive case according to Greenberg's universals (Greenberg 1966) is a marked case, and it would be highly exceptional for a marked case to be preserved where less marked cases (such as dative and accusative) have disappeared; and secondly that there are no other languages that have only genitive case. It also explains, it is claimed, the disappearance of the Old English postnominal possessives such as *cyrce Romes* '(the) church of Rome' because one cannot have *his* positioned after the noun phrase.

There are a number of problems, however, with this theory. First of all Mustanoja (1960: 162) shows that these 'genitive-equivalent' constructions (as he calls them) already occur in Old English, when the nominal inflectional system was still intact. They are found in Old English especially when a genitive inflection was problematic, for instance in the case of a foreign name or a compound head. Secondly, this theory cannot explain why German developed a similar construction in spite of the fact that it is still a fully inflected language. Thirdly, there is insufficient evidence that there was a general reanalysis of *-(e)s* to *his* although one or two examples are found where *his* is used with a feminine noun.[6] What *is* remarkable is that the genitive-equivalent is rarely found with inanimate nouns. This shows that *his* and later also *her* were used primarily to indicate gender, which in Middle English was tied up with animacy. We should recall here that the Middle English genitive case (*-(e)s*), unlike in Old English, could no longer mark gender distinctions. The occurrence of some feminine *his* constructions does show, as Mustanoja (1960: 162) has remarked, that the phonetic similarity between *-(e)s* and *his* actually strengthened the use of the genitive-equivalent construction. The overall conclusion, therefore, is that the genitive case in Middle English was still a morphological case – a case that could go on existing, although highly marked, because it had become very restricted in its use. The loss of the Old English postnominal possessive is explained by the fact that the Old English genitive functions which survived into Middle English most commonly occurred in prenominal position.

The well-known Present-Day English construction in which a genitive is used without a head word ('Marks and Spencer's', 'St Paul's'), often called the 'absolute genitive' (see van der Gaaf 1932) is first found in Middle English in the latter part of the thirteenth century. The earliest examples involve the omission of the word *church*:

(64) he was at seint poules

(SLeg. (Ld) 109.91)

From *church* it spread to the abode of the friars (from 1300 onwards) and hence (mid fifteenth century) to any house where one could lodge (this, by the way, gives an interesting insight into the social role the friars played in the late medieval period):

(65) ...þat þis nyght at soper I was with my maistresse your wyff *at my Maistresse Cleres*,

(Davis 1971–6: 445, 2–3)

After our period it becomes common usage in reference to colleges, shops, etc. In Middle English the absolute genitive is still strictly locative, i.e. it occurs only after such prepositions as *on, to, at*. The use of this genitive as subject or object is found from the sixteenth century onwards. The only exception seems to be *St Paul's* which already in Chaucer was used adjectivally:

(66) With Poules wyndow corven on his shoos

(CT I.3318 [1: 3312])

The loss of the locative nature is, however, already clear from 'contaminated' expressions such as:

(67) the Nonnes of the hows of seynt Eleynes of London

(EEWills, an.1395, Hampshire, 7.1–2)

in which the name of the building has been inserted before the absolute genitive to emphasise the locality.

Finally, the Middle English period saw the rise of a construction that some have termed 'the double genitive', i.e. the type *a friend of mine*. It is very likely (see Mustanoja 1960: 165ff. and Schibsbye 1974–7: 71ff.) that this filled the gap that had been left by the disappearance of Old English constructions in which determiners and possessive pronouns could still co-occur as in *to ðysum urum gebeorscipe* 'to this our party' (cf. vol. I, section 4.2.1). There seems to be general agreement that the new construction developed out of an original partitive, or more precisely an 'ablating' type, i.e. something taken *out of* a larger set (see van der Gaaf 1927), which in Late Old English began to be constructed with *of*:

(68)   sumne of ðam witeȝum

(Mk.(WSCp) 8.28)

'one of the prophets'

The first examples in Middle English in which the head word in the partitive construction is left out, thus resembling the type *a friend of mine*, are from the early thirteenth century:

(69)   Gif ðu him lanst ani þing *of ðinen*

(*Vices&V*(1) (Stw) 77: 21)

'if you lend him anything of your [things, property]'

In all the early examples the partitive nature is still obvious; the head word presumably could be left out in these cases because the reference is clear, usually it refers to part of someone's property or household. This theory of its origin also explains the fact that it could occur in Middle English after the definite article, which is no longer possible in Present-Day English, **the friend of mine*:[7]

(70)   ... shuld set or cause my lord to do thynges oþerwise þan accordith to *the pleasir of my lordes*.

(Davis 1971–6: 908, 8–9)

and it explains its relatively frequent occurrence in the legal language of wills etc. (It is not restricted to colloquial language as stated by van der Gaaf 1927.) When the idea of 'part of the property' was lost and the construction came to be used in expressions like *that car of yours* (where no reference is intended to one car out of many or to the car as just one of one's possessions), the type with the definite article was lost. There was no longer a need for it since *the car of yours* was already adequately represented by *your car* (but see note 7). The construction was quite possibly also helped along by the existence (by then) of other *of*-constructions without partitive sense such as *all of them*.

4.3 The verb phrase

4.3.1 *Verb valency*

One of the most important developments that has taken place in the constitution of the verb phrase is the levelling of the case system. Whereas in Old English verbs could take arguments in the genitive, dative or accusative (leaving the nominative or subject out of consideration for the moment since they are not *direct* arguments of the verb), this is reduced to just one case, usually termed oblique case, in the course of the Middle English period. This case is only overtly visible with some of the pronouns (especially personal pronouns), but is indistinguishable from the nominative case with nouns, certainly by the end of the Middle English period. This levelling again (see section 4.2) takes place much earlier in the north. In southern dialects (especially Kentish) different case forms are distinguished as late as the fourteenth century.

One of the important effects of this change is that, whereas in Old English there was still a more or less direct relation between case form and semantic function (see Anderson 1986; Fischer & van der Leek 1987), this is no longer so for the two remaining case forms in Middle English, nominative (or 'common' case) and oblique. They have acquired purely syntactic functions and can bear a large number of semantic roles. (For the general development concerning the grammaticalisation of verb arguments in the Germanic languages from Primitive Germanic onwards, see Seefranz-Montag 1983, ch. 1.) This does not mean that Middle English was less well equipped than Old English for expressing the semantic functions of verbal arguments. Other ways of expressing these became current in this period. For instance, instead of case inflections prepositions came to be used much more frequently. Thus in Old English the verbs *wundrian* 'to wonder' and *bereafan* 'to rob' are construed with a genitive. In Middle English we find:

(71)   Lest they *berafte* .../ Folk *of* her catel or of her thing.

(Rose 6669–70)

(72)   Þar*of* ich *vvndri*,

(Owl&N (Clg) 228)

There is a lot of fluctuation. Many verbs occur with an oblique case as well as a prepositional phrase. It is striking that in the early texts the preposition replacing, for instance, the genitive is usually *of*; other prepositions begin to appear later. Thus, 'wonder of', 'forget of' become 'wonder about', 'forget about'. In short, what we see developing is a system that at first shows a more or less one-to-one correspondence between the new prepositions and the old case forms; more prepositions enter into it at a later stage which could then be used to signal finer semantic role distinctions.

Word order, too, became more and more fixed so that subject and object functions could be distinguished by their positions, as a rule immediately before and after the verb respectively. The indirect object and direct object, which both show oblique case in Middle English, are also kept apart in this way. For a discussion of the position of the indirect object in Middle English, see section 4.8.4.

Another means of preserving semantic role distinctions was to replace one of a pair of constructions by a construction containing a different lexical verb (which was often borrowed from French or Latin). In Old English there were a large number of verbs that could express semantic differences by means of case (see Plank 1983), e.g.:

(73)a. hie   getreowlice Gode [dat.] hyrdon swa heora hlafordum [dat.]
　　　　they loyally   God   'heard' as   their lords

(LS 32 (Peter & Paul) 259)

　　　　'they loyally obeyed God as well as their lords'

b. Þa   se   cyng þæt [acc.] hierde
　　when the king that   heard

(*Chron.*A (Plummer) 894.38)

In Middle English the differences would be expressed by using two different verbs, 'obey' and 'hear'.

4.3.1.1 Predicates with zero-arguments

As in Old English there are predicates with zero arguments, notably the so-called 'weather verbs', a subdivision of the impersonal verbs discussed in the next section. Whereas in Old English these verbs would still occasionally occur without a syntactic subject altogether (see Wahlén 1925; Ogura 1986), in Middle English the subject position is practically always filled by a so-called dummy (*h*)*it*, as in Present-Day English:

(74) Now it shyneth, now it reyneth faste,

(*CT* I.1535 [1 : 1537])

4.3.1.2   One- and multi-argument predicates without a subject
When (an)other argument(s) is/are present, the syntactic subject can still be left out, in contrast to Present-Day English, where dummy *it* or *there* is a necessity. This is the case with the impersonal verbs and with the existential verb *be*:

(75)   ... And *happed* so, they coomen in a toun ...
(*CT* VII.2987 [10: 2959])

(76)   For sikerly, *nere* clynkyng of youre belles/ ... I sholde er this han fallen doun for sleep,
(*CT* VII.2794–7 [10: 2766–9])

However, the use of dummy (*h*)*it*/*there* becomes more and more frequent towards the end of the period. The reason a subject becomes more or less obligatory in Middle English is linked to the fact that the word order became fixed as SVO (see section 4.8). In this order the subject took up first position. When the subject was a clause, an infinitive or a heavy NP – these would normally be placed at the end of a clause, cf. Old English – the initial position was filled with a preliminary or dummy subject. Likewise, in completely subjectless constructions (i.e. in impersonal constructions that remained 'impersonal') this (*h*)*it* became the rule as well, so that all constructions (with only a few clearly defined exceptions such as questions etc.) conformed to the fixed order.

A lot has been written on the causes of the demise of the impersonal construction. One of the main problems in accounting for its loss has been the analysis of the Old English data. Jespersen's (1909–49, III) hypothetical example,

(77)   þam   cynge (dat.) licodon (pl.) peran (nom.)
       to the king   'liked'   pears

changing into Middle English,

the king (subj.) liked (sg.) pears (obj.)

has been very influential and was used by, among others, Lightfoot (1979) as the basis of subsequent analysis. Jespersen essentially sees an impersonal construction as one in which the animate experiencer ('the king') is not the subject (as it usually is in English), and not as a construction *without* a subject. It is clear that this hypothetical example in fact has a subject, *peran*. According to Jespersen, the change therefore involves a swopping around of the original nominative (which becomes object) and accusative/dative (which becomes subject). The explanation he gives for this change is basically psychological: it 'was brought about by...the greater interest taken in persons than in things, which caused the name of the person to be placed before the verb' (II, 2). His explanation is related to changes in word order in that it implies that the *pre*verbal element (i.e. the experiencer) came to be interpreted as a subject when SVO word order became the regular order in Middle English. Jespersen also refers to the loss of the case system, as do most linguists (i.e. van der Gaaf 1904; Visser 1963–73), since this made it possible for the original dative/accusative to be reinterpreted as subject (but see McCawley 1976).

Word order and loss of case are also the basic ingredients in the explanation given by Lightfoot (1979/1981a and b). Lightfoot does not question Jespersen's data, and he also accepts the meaning change that impersonal verbs undergo when the original functions are swopped around (see above). Elmer (1981) and Fischer & van der Leek (1983) have shown that Jespersen's example is only part of the story and that different construction types exist. Fischer & van der Leek (1983) recognise three basic types and hypothesise that each lexical verb can appear in all three types except in cases where the semantic nature of the impersonal verb does not lend itself to its usage in all three constructions. Elmer's subdivisions into types is much finer (see also Anderson 1986), but his work is basically descriptive, whereas we more rigidly formalise the data in order to be able to provide a theoretical account for the changes taking place. In doing this we have somewhat idealised the data. It is possible that, instead of treating all the impersonal verbs in the same way, it is better to recognise different subclasses occurring in slightly different argument structures (see Anderson 1986; Denison 1990a). On the other hand, it can also be said that syntactically they form a class because they differ from 'personal' verbs in one respect: they do not require any *direct* arguments (i.e. structural cases assigned at surface level); or, to put it differently, they are the only verbs that can be generated with arguments that do not depend for their case on the verb but which provide their own case and corresponding semantic role (see also below). The differences in argument structures among the impersonal verbs themselves could be explained on semantic rather than syntactic grounds, according to Fischer and van der Leek (1987).

The basic difference between our account and Jespersen's and others' is the suggestion that impersonal verbs have one basic meaning which is modified according to the different constructions in which they occur. We reject the postulated semantic change in a verb like *lician* from Old English causative 'to please' to Middle English receptive 'to like'.

Instead, we suggest that the verb *lician* simply indicates the 'existence of pleasure'. This core meaning is present in all constructions in which *lician* appears; it is made more specific by the alternative argument structures in which the verb can appear. In general, each Old English impersonal verb can appear in three different argument structures (one without a syntactic subject – the 'true' impersonal construction – one with the experiencer as subject, one with the cause/source as subject), which give it a neutral, a receptive or a causative meaning respectively.

In our view, therefore, the change concerning the impersonal verb in Middle English does not involve a change of meaning, but a loss of one or usually two constructions with their concomitant meanings. This theory has several advantages: it takes better account of the diversity of the data; it does not have to postulate a meaning change that is theoretically dubious and not supported by the data (see Fischer and van der Leek 1983: 342ff.; 352ff.); and it also fits the slow implementation of the change (Lightfoot's radical reanalysis links it too rigidly to the change in word order from SOV to SVO (see Fischer and van der Leek 1983: 342)), i.e. it allows for impersonal constructions as late as the sixteenth century.

In Early Middle English the impersonal construction was still thriving. There clearly was a need for the semantic possibilities it could express, i.e. a verbal process without any direct participants. Van der Gaaf (1904: 12ff.) notes that verbs of Old French and Old Norse origin joined the system (e.g. from ON *dremen, geynen, happen* and from OF *greven, plesen*) and he also shows (pp. 143ff.) that some existing personal verbs developed impersonal variants, e.g. the modals *must* and *ought*:

(78)a. Ded *he* aght to thole for-þi,

> *(Cursor* (Vsp) 9636)

     'Death he ought to suffer therefore'

b. dethe *hym* owith to thole for-þy...

> *(Cursor* (Frf) 9636)

     'death "him" ought to suffer therefore' (death he must suffer therefore)

A very interesting development is the occurrence of impersonal constructions with originally reflexive verbs. Van der Gaaf (pp. 148ff.) gives examples with such verbs as *repenten, remembren*, both borrowed from Old French. This origin cannot be a coincidence. Old English was not very familiar with pure reflexive verbs (except verbs of motion

which could take a dative reflexive pronoun; see vol. I, section 4.4.3.2).
Most Old English reflexive constructions are of the following type:

(79) And þa Pyhtas heom   abædon wif   æt   Scottum
      And the Picts   for-them asked   wives from Scots

*(Chron.*E (Plummer) 15)

'And the Picts asked for wives for themselves from the Scots'

The difference between this construction and those with the Old French
verbs is that in the Old English one, (79), the reflexive pronoun has its
own semantic role; the reflexive has no separate semantic function in the
Middle English example as given under (80a). It must have been difficult
to fit the Old French pure reflexives into the grammar of Middle
English, witnessing the variety of constructions we encounter with
these French verbs:

(80)a. First a man shal remembre hym of his synnes;

(*CT* X.133 [12: 133])

b. Why ne haddest thow remembred in thy mynde/ To taken hire,

(*LGW* 2717–18)

c. …that me remembreth of the day of doom…

(*CT* X.159 [12: 159])

The examples show that there was felt to be a relation between
impersonal constructions and these French reflexive constructions. A
similar relation can be shown to exist in Dutch, where original
impersonal constructions have in some cases changed into reflexive ones
(see van der Leek 1989: 40–1, note 13).

Yet, in spite of its semantic possibilities, the impersonal construction
was lost in English. The reason for this was purely syntactic. In Fischer
and van der Leek (1987) we explain this loss as follows. In Old English,
cases could be syntactically determined, e.g. nominative and accusative
case could be direct arguments of the verb, whose semantic roles were
also assigned by the verb. As direct arguments, they represent direct
participants in the process expressed by the verb. However, the cases,
especially genitive and dative, could also still be semantically autonomous (see section 4.3.1); we could call these 'concrete cases'. These
are independent of the verb and provide their own semantic role. They
do not directly participate in the process expressed by the verb.
Normally in Old English all verbs would require at least one direct
argument (nominative), but the impersonal verbs are semantically
anomalous in that they do not require a direct argument (see McCawley's

(1976) characterisation of impersonals as a class of verbs that allow of a human experiencer 'unvolitionally' involved in a situation).

Syntactically, this situation changed drastically in Late Middle English because the concrete cases disappeared due to the collapse of the inflectional case system, with the result that bare NPs could only represent direct arguments or direct participants. At the same time the presence of a subject became more and more obligatory, due among other things to the loss of distinct verbal endings. As a consequence of this the impersonal proper, which showed no direct arguments, had to disappear. In principle the concrete cases could have been replaced by prepositional phrases, but the position of the experiencer before the verb (the normal subject position in Middle English) and the growing need for a syntactic subject (due to, among other things, the loss of inflections on the verb) decided the direction of the development. The semantic notion formerly expressed by the impersonal proper now found its expression in different surface forms. In some cases this was done by adopting new lexical items such as *please* and *seem* to stand beside *like* and *think*, and by using passive or adjectival constructions such as *I am ashamed, he was sorry* for the older constructions *me sceamaþ* and *me hreoweþ*. In the latter case the verb *be* is used, which does not assign a thematic role to its subject, thus approaching most closely the impersonal proper which had no subject at all (see Fischer and van der Leek 1987: 111ff.).

4.3.1.3 Reflexive intransitive verbs
Some verbs which are usually intransitive in Middle English are also found with a reflexive pronoun, which was either originally a dative pronoun in Old English (especially with verbs of motion) or an accusative. There is clearly a tendency in Middle English to drop the reflexive pronoun wherever possible (see the previous section and Mustanoja 1960: 431). Thus we find both,

(81)   And to the launde he rideth hym ful right,

(*CT* I.1691 [1: 1693])

(82)   This knave gooth hym up ful sturdily,

(*CT* I.3434 [1: 3428])

and

(83)   No neer Atthenes wolde he go ne ride,

(*CT* I.968 [1: 970])

The use of the reflexive pronoun seems to be more common in poetry and may therefore have become to some extent a metrical device.

However, the frequent use of expressions like 'riden forth *his wey*' etc. in Middle English, where the intransitive verb of motion is accompanied by some sort of object, seems to suggest that there was a tendency to use these verbs with some kind of pseudo-object, whether reflexive or otherwise. (For more information on the types of reflexive constructions in Early Middle English and for developments taking place between Old and Middle English, see Ogura 1989.)

4.3.2 The finite verb

4.3.2.1 Tense

As in Present-Day English there are, morphologically, two tense categories in Middle English: past and non-past. These are the main indicators of temporal relations, in combination with lexical devices such as adverbs and conjunctions of time. Periphrastic constructions (perfect, pluperfect, future) also play a role in the tense (and aspect) system of Middle English, but in most cases they are still interchangeable with the above two tense categories with or without other temporal indicators. The periphrastic forms will be discussed separately below (section 4.3.3).

NON-PAST

As in Old English (and Present-Day English) the non-past may be neutral as regards time; it is therefore used to express general truths and habitual or repeated actions:

(84) Eft me seið & soð hit is, þet a muche wind *alið* wið alute rein, ant te sunne þrefter *schineð* þe schenre.

   (Ancr. (Corp-C) 126: 14–16

   'Often people say, and true it is, that a strong wind subsides with a little rain, and the sun shines the more brightly afterwards.'

(85) Fro Ethiope men *gon* into ynde be manye dyuerse contreyes…

   (Mandev. (Tit) 104: 24–5)

The other primary function of the non-past is that it indicates that an action is going on or that a state exists at the moment of speaking. Here it covers the function of the progressive (or expanded) as well as the simple form of Present-Day English:

(86) Thow *walkest* now in Thebes at thy large,/ And of my wo thow yevest litel charge.

   (CT I.1283–4 [1: 1285–6])

(87) 'What! Alison! Herestow nat Absolon,/ That *chaunteth* thus under oure boures wal?'

   (CT I.3366–7 [1: 3360–1])

In Middle English the non-past is still regularly used to refer to the future, although periphrastic constructions are more numerous, even in the Early Middle English texts. Quite often a periphrastic (future) form (or some other lexical marker of future time) is used elsewhere in the preceding discourse, as in (89). (We have a similar case in (93), where the non-past is used for the perfect, i.e. another periphrastic perfect precedes the non-past.)

(88) And wel I woot, as ye goon by the weyc,/ Ye *shapen* yow to talen and to pleye;

(CT I.771–2 [1:773–4])

(89) And whase wilenn shall þiss boc efft oþerr siþe writenn,/ Himm bidde icc þatt het *write* rihht, swa summ þiss boc himm tæcheþþ.

(Orm. 48–9)

'And whoever shall wish to copy this book at some other time, him I ask that he copies it correctly, just as this book shows him.'

As in Present-Day English the non-past is common in adverbial clauses (e.g. temporal, conditional clauses) which themselves have future reference. For the same reason it is usual in object clauses after verbs like *hope*, *expect*, etc. because their sentential arguments are necessarily part of the speaker's future:

(90) ʒif ðu ðus *dost*, ðanne berest þu þin rode.

(Vices&V(1) (Stw) 33: 30–1)

'If you act like that, then you [will] bear your own cross'

(91) For after this I hope ther *cometh* moore

(CT I.3725 [1: 3718])

Mustanoja (1960: 582) and Visser (1963–73: §726) give examples from Early Middle English that show that forms of the verb *be* still regularly express futurity as they did in Old English (in contrast to *wesan*; see vol. I, section 4.3.1.2):

(92) ... vor ase softe ase he is her, ase herd he *bið* ðer, and ase milde ase he is nu her, ase sturne he *bið* þer.

(Ancr. (Nero) 137: 25–6)

'... for as soft as He is here, as hard He will be there, and as mild as He is now here, as stern He will be there.'

Occasionally (see for Old English, vol. I, section 4.3.1.2), the non-past was still used to indicate that an action which had its origin in the past was still relevant in the present. Normally the perfect form (as in Present-Day English) would be used here.

(93) Considered this, that ye thise monthes tweyne/ Han taried, ther ye
seyden, soth to seyne,/ But dayes ten ye nolde in oost sojourne –/
But in two monthes yet ye nat *retourne*.

(Troilus V.1348–51)

'When one considers this, that you have tarried for [the past] two months, whereas you said, truly, that you would only stay ten days with the host, but yet in these two months you return not [you have not returned].'

THE HISTORICAL PRESENT

The use of the non-past in a past-time narrative context is a new phenomenon that is first encountered in Late Middle English. It does not occur in Early Middle English texts (see Zimmermann 1968), whether poetry or prose, irrespective of the area of provenance. Some examples are found in the romances of *King Horn* and *Havelok* (for references see Fridén 1948), but the usage becomes regular only in Chaucer, Gower, the later romances and the Middle English alliterative poems. There is a considerable amount of controversy concerning both the origin of this construction and the function it performed. Some linguists (notably Mätzner, Sweet, Einenkel, Mossé) believed that it was due to foreign (Latin or French) influence (see Fridén 1948: 15ff.). If Latin is responsible for its use, some explanation must be given for why the historical present is never found in Old English: the Latin historical present, when it occurs, is consistently rendered by a past-tense form. The possible influence of Old French is difficult to prove or disprove (see Visser 1963–73: §762). On the one hand, we have the translation of *Havelok*, where the Old French historical present is usually rendered by a preterite in Middle English (see Steadman 1917: 23), and there are also Middle English texts with a high frequency of historical presents which have no French origin. On the other hand, the occurrence of the historical present in Middle English poetry roughly coincides with French literary influence on Middle English verse (see Trnka 1930). Jespersen (1935: 258), followed by Fridén (1948: 14ff.), believed the historical present was popular in origin; this would link up with the fact that it is found in other Germanic languages. Its absence in Old English they explain stylistically: the extant Old English texts were not colloquial enough to show the use of the historical present. No hard proof can be given for this, but it must be noted that the historical present in Middle English is especially common in popular poetry (for criticism of Jespersen, see Steadman 1917: 24ff.).

Visser (1963–73: §§764ff.) notes that the historical present is used exclusively in poetry (the instances in the Wycliffite Bible he refers to Greek influence). This in itself is true, but one should not rely too heavily on this fact since it is possible that the more literary style used in the prose texts (such as Chaucer's *Boece* and *The Tale of Melibee*, and *Mandeville's Travels*) accounts for its absence. Starting from the premise that the historical present is exclusive to poetry, Visser suggests that it is to be accounted for solely by the exigencies of rhyme and/or metre. For this reason he prefers to call the historical present the 'substitutive present'. Some of his examples are quite convincing:

(94) For in the lond ther was no crafty man/ That geometrie or ars-
metrike *kan*,

(*CT* I.1897–8 [1: 1899–1900])

(95) Now he *strykes* for þe nonys/ Made þe Sarazenes hedebones/
Hoppe...

(*Perceval* (Thrn) 1189–91).

In (94) the present *kan* is used to rhyme with *man* (although it seems to me that *kan* could also be interpreted as a 'neutral' present); in (95) the preterite *strook* would have been metrically too short. In the following instances, however, the past tense would theoretically have fitted the rhyme or metre pattern:

(96) Wo was this knyght, and sorwefully he *siketh*;/ But what! He may
nat do al as hym *liketh*./ And at the laste he chees hym for to
wende...

(*CT* III.913–15 [2: 887–9])

(97) She *gropeth* alwey forther with hir hond,/ And foond the bed, and
thoghte noght but good,

(*CT* I.4222–3 [1: 4214–15]).

In (96) both *siketh* and *liketh* could have been preterite forms (*siked*, *liked*) without any harm done to either rhyme or metre, similarly *groped* in (97) would have fitted the metre as well as *gropeth*. Visser's theory does explain why the historical present did not appear in Old English verse (which had neither rhyme nor fixed syllabic metre) (see Visser 1963–73: §774), but it does not explain why the historical present does occur in Middle English alliterative verse such as *Patience*, *Purity* and the alliterative *Morte Arthure*. Visser (1963–73: §771) provides additional evidence of a morphological nature, which may partly explain the use of the historical present and especially the rapid alternation of past and non-past forms. In certain dialects the endings -*eth* and -*ed* were variants, as is shown by the occurrence of -*eth* endings in past participles. This may have become – as a handy device – part of the common poetic language, just as certain Kentish or strictly northern forms were used outside their own area, and may have spread from weak to strong verbs.

Visser's hypothesis entails that a purely technical function is attached to the use of the historical present. This seems a rather doubtful assumption. In language, differentiations express some meaning difference, however slight, and if they do not at first, they often develop one later. It is also doubtful when we consider the fact that we frequently encounter fairly long passages with a quite consistent use of the historical present e.g. in a by now famous passage from Chaucer's *Knight's Tale* (*CT* I.2600–14 [1: 2602–16]) and in other descriptions of battle scenes, such as this one from *The Legend of Good Women*:

> Up goth the trompe, and for to shoute and shete, 635
> And peynen hem to sette on with the sunne.
> With grysely soun out goth the grete gonne,
> And heterly they hurtelen al atones,
> And from the top doun come the grete stones.
> In goth the grapenel, so ful of crokes; 640
> Among the ropes renne the sherynge-hokes.
> In with the polax preseth he and he;
> Byhynde the mast begynnyth he to fle,
> And out ageyn, and dryveth hym overbord;
> He styngeth hym upon his speres ord; 645
> He rent the seyl with hokes lyke a sithe;
> He bryngeth the cuppe and biddeth hem be blythe;...
> Tyl at the laste, as every thyng hath ende, 651
> Antony is schent and put hym to the flyghte,
> And al his folk to-go that best go myghte.

Note that past tenses in lines 644 and 647 would have fitted better metrically but that still the non-past is used (*dryveth*, *bryngeth*[8]) in spite of Visser's hypothesis. Instances like the above seem a confirmation of the idea, put forward among others by Benson (1961), that the historical present suggests continuing or repeated action, while the past (in the above example the perfect (line 652)) denotes the climax or the rounding off of the activity. It is noteworthy that many of the verbs that are found in the historical present are inherently imperfective, while the past is used for punctual or perfective verbs. It is possible that the historical present may have filled a grammatical gap that was later filled by the progressive. The progressive form was used in Middle English but had not become grammaticalised yet. It seems likely, however, that at the same time poets were able to use the historical present to some extent whenever it suited their purposes.

Steadman's (1917) account of the rise of the historical present is also closely linked to its aspectual function, but he approaches it from a different direction. According to him the historical present could not be generally used as long as there was a clear morphological distinction between perfective and imperfective verbs, as there was to some extent still in Old English. He shows that in Old English future time was still as a rule expressed by the present tense of perfective verbs, while the present of imperfective verbs denoted only present time. The present of perfective verbs, therefore, could not be used to describe activities in the past. With the loss of morpholexical aspect in Late Old English/Early Middle English a periphrastic future evolved. This was necessary because the combination of morpholexical aspect and tense no longer could fulfil that role. As the tense system became separated from the aspectual characteristics of individual verbs, a new way of expressing the future became necessary, with the result that the present tense was now free to refer to actions taking place in the past. The theory is of interest because it nicely accounts for the various stages in the development of periphrastic future and historical present. Whether the aspectual functions of the Old English verbs were as important as Steadman believes is a question that still needs looking into (see Strang 1970: 190, 280). So far it has not received the serious consideration it deserves.

PAST

The past-tense forms express an action completed in the past. They are especially used in a narrative context, often accompanied by past-time adverbials:

(98) And ʒee schull vndirstonde…þat at myn hom comynge I cam to Rome & schewed my lif to oure holy fadir the Pope & was assoylled of all þat lay in my conscience…

(*Mandev.* (Tit) 209: 31–4)

This past tense is also found where Present-Day English would prefer the past progressive; the latter is rare in Middle English. Zimmermann

(1968: 173) found only five instances in his corpus of Early Middle English texts; in later Middle English it is somewhat more frequent.

When an action starts in the past but continues into the present, a perfect is usual in Present-Day English. In Middle English past-tense and perfect forms are found side by side. An example of the past tense is:

(99)   here is wayth fayrest/ Þat I *seʒ* þis seuen ʒere in sesoun of wynter.

   (Gawain 1381–2)

   'this is the finest kill that I saw [have seen] these seven years in the winter season.'

With the temporal adverbs *ever/never* the past tense is almost the rule (see Fridén 1948: 31),

(100)   For thys ys the moste shamefullyste message that *ever* y *herde* speke off. I have aspyed thy kynge *never* yette mette with worshipfull man.

   (Malory *Wks* (Add.59678) 55: 6–8)

For the difference in usage between past tense and perfect see section 4.3.3.2.

To refer to the past within the past both preterite and pluperfect are found, as in Old English, seemingly without any distinction in meaning (see Fridén 1948: 34; Zimmerman 1968: 166):

(101)   Moyses was bliðe.../ And ches ðo men god made wis.

   (Gen.&Ex. 3671–2)

   'Moses was glad...and chose those men God [had] made wise.'

For the so-called modal preterite see section 4.3.2.2.

4.3.2.2   Mood

As in Old English, there are three terms within the mood system: the indicative, the subjunctive and the imperative. The indicative is the unmarked term, the subjunctive and the imperative are modally marked. The function of the imperative is fairly clear, but those of indicative and subjunctive often overlap. In general, the indicative is used to indicate the factuality of a report or statement, while the subjunctive expresses contingency and supposition. However, there are exceptions to this rule especially in dependent clauses (for details see section 4.6.2).

The three moods are still formally differentiated in Middle English but this becomes less and less so in the course of the period. One can question how far one should go on using terms like imperative and subjunctive when the form(s) has/have become identical to the indicative form(s) (see Visser 1963–73: §§ 834–7). There is a tendency to preserve the term imperative, presumably because a formal difference is still visible (i.e. the subject pronoun is normally absent) and its function has remained clear-cut. This is not the case with the subjunctive. It serves more functions, and in some cases, e.g. in certain dependent clauses, subjunctive and indicative alternated.

Formally, the imperative singular and the subjunctive present singular could, effectively, no longer be differentiated. In the plural the distinction was usually preserved in all dialects (for details see chapter 2, section 2.9.2.4), except when the subject pronoun immediately followed the imperative; in that case the ending (as in Old English) was normally -*e* and therefore indistinguishable from the subjunctive. The inflectional differences between indicative and subjunctive were considerably reduced. In the present tense only the second- and the third-person singular were distinctive (except in the south, where the plural forms were still distinct: -*eþ* in the indicative, -*en* in the subjunctive). In the past tense of strong verbs only the first and third person were distinctive, and of the weak verbs only the second-person singular. Under these circumstances it is not surprising that the periphrastic construction (which was already used in Old English) gained ground rapidly. Mustanoja (1960: 453) writes that by the fifteenth century the ratio between the periphrastic and inflectional subjunctive was nine to one in non-dependent clauses.

Another development is the use of the past-tense indicative as a modal marker, the so-called modal preterite (see Visser 1963–73: §§ 812ff.) This is in fact a continuation of the Old English past subjunctive, which had become virtually indistinguishable from the past indicative in Middle English. When in Middle English this past form comes to be used in present-tense contexts, its function as a modal marker becomes clear-cut. In Late Middle English this development, called 'tense-shift', is also found in past-time contexts, where, in contrast, a pluperfect comes to be used to give the clause modal colouring:

(102) And she hym thonked with ful humble chere,/ And ofter wolde, and it *hadde ben* his wille,

(Troilus I.124–5)

(103) Haddestow as greet a leeve as thou hast myght/ To parfourne al thy lust in engendrure,/ Thou *haddest bigeten* ful many a creature.

(CT VII.1946–8 [10: 1946–8])

The use of the modal preterite is most common when other elements in the clause are indicators of modality, such as conjunctions (*if*, *as if*, etc.), adverbs (*perhaps*), or when the clause is preceded by a class of verbs that semantically expresses non-fact (*desire*, *hope*, etc.). The periphrastic subjunctive will be discussed separately in section 4.3.3.3. Here we will only discuss the use of the subjunctive in independent clauses; for its use in dependent clauses see sections 4.6.2 and 4.6.3.

SUBJUNCTIVE

The subjunctive was distinguished for tense (non-past, past) on the plane of modality but not of temporality. The present subjunctive expresses a realisable wish (104) or an exhortation (105):

(104)   God *shilde* that he deyde sodeynly!

(CT I.3427 [1 : 3421])

(105)   Þatt mann þatt wile follȝhenn me/ & winnenn eche blisse,/ He *take* hiss rode, & *bere* itt rihht,

(Orm. 5606–8)

'That man who wants to follow me and attain eternal bliss, let him take up his cross and bear it well.'

The hortatory subjunctive is in Middle English usually expressed by a periphrastic construction with *let*. Unlike the Old English construction with *uton* (see vol. I, section 4.3.1.3), which still occurs in Middle English (*ute(n)*) until the late thirteenth century, *let* is not restricted to the first-person plural. *Let* and the subjunctive can occur side by side:

(106)   Now *lat us stynte* of Custance but a throwe,/ And *speke we* of the Romayn Emperour,...

(CT II.953–4 [3: 953–4])

Let was the accepted construction in Late Middle English except in biblical contexts (see the examples given by Visser (1963–73: §846)) and in rules, regulations, prescriptions and recipes.

The past subjunctive expresses an unrealisable wish (107) or a hypothetical situation (108):

(107)   Allas, for wo! Why *nere* I deed?

(Troilus II 409)

(108)   For though I *write* or *tolde* yow everemo/ Of his knyghthod, it myghte nat suffise.

(CT VII.2653–4 [10: 2653–4])

IMPERATIVE

In Middle English the forms of the imperative singular and the subjunctive present singular coalesced, as noted above. In function, the hortatory subjunctive and the imperative were practically similar already in Old English, where one finds them used side by side (see vol. I, section 4.3.1.3). In the plural there was still a morphological distinction, as we have seen, when the subject pronoun did not immediately follow the verb. This situation was not to last, as the hortatory subjunctive was on its way out. The imperative has a tendency to become invariant in form (this happened also in other Germanic languages), because it functions like a self-contained, exclamatory expression. Mustanoja (1960: 473) compares its function to that of (invariable) interjections. In an example like,

(109)   Help! Water! Water! Help, for Goddes herte!

(*CT* I.3815 [1:3807])

help is as much an interjection as an imperative. In Chaucer and Gower one often finds instances of singular and plural forms used in one and the same sentence:

(110)   *Telle* forth youre tale, *spareth* for no man,/ And *teche* us yonge men of youre praktike.

(*CT* III.186–7 [2: 186–7])

By the middle of the fifteenth century the plural imperative ending disappears.

As in Old English, the subject pronoun, although not common, could be present. When added, it usually points out the person addressed more distinctly. It does not occur more often in negative than in positive clauses, as was the case in Old English (see vol. I, section 4.3.1.3). Normally, the pronoun follows the verb (111), but preposing of the pronoun is also found (112):

(111)   Be as be may, *be ye* no thyng amased;

(*CT*. VIII.935)

(112)   Thesiphone, *thow help* me for t'endite/ Thise woful vers, that wepen as I write.

(*Troilus* I 6–7)

The perfect imperative is rare in Middle English, being restricted to the expression *have done*, which may be considered a special idiom (see Visser 1963–73: §2017).

4.3.2.3 Voice

As in Old English, there are two terms in the system of voice, the active and the passive. The passive is formed by means of the auxiliary *ben* (for the occurrence of the Middle English inflectional passive *hiht* (< OE *haten*: *heht*) see vol. I, section 4.3.2.4). *Weorþan*, which was employed along with *beon* in the Old English passive construction, is still found in Early Middle English texts, but its frequency is greatly reduced and practically zero at the end of our period (see Zimmermann 1968: 51ff.). The agent, when present, is usually expressed by *of* + NP, later also *by* + NP although other prepositions are also found (*from*, *through*, *at*). As in Old English the subject of the passive construction corresponds as a rule to the direct object of the active construction, but in the course of the Middle English period two new passive constructions appear: the so-called indirect object passive and the prepositional object passive. For these developments see section 4.9.

4.3.3 Periphrastic expressions

In Old English we see a beginning of the development of periphrastic constructions in the systems of tense, aspect and modality, but it is difficult to decide how far verbs like *habban*, *beon*, *willan*, *sculan*, etc. already enjoyed auxiliary status (see vol. I, section 4.3.2). In Middle English we see a very rapid increase in the use of periphrastic constructions especially of the so-called perfect and future 'tense', and in the use of modals where Old English had the subjunctive. The progressive form becomes more frequent towards the end of the period. Middle English also marks the beginning of the development of the auxiliary *do*, although its greatest growth will take place outside our period. A new construction not found in Old English (to any extent) is the periphrasis with the aspectual verb *ginnen*.

How far these different constructions contain true auxiliaries is a matter of debate. According to Lightfoot (1979) – whose main concern is modal auxiliaries – English only acquired the category Aux(iliary) in the sixteenth century. Others (e.g. Plank 1984) see a more gradual development. We will address the question of auxiliary status for each verb in the relevant sections.

4.3.3.1 The progressive or 'expanded' form

Although we lack clear evidence such as tag questions and reduced forms to decide whether the verb *be(n)* is a true auxiliary, its frequent co-occurrence with temporal adverbs and the word order (the progressive form is not often separated by other sentence elements, except in cases of subject–verb inversion) indicate that *be(n)* has auxiliary status in Middle English. On the other hand, the stages of development of the progressive for Old English (see Mitchell 1985 §§ 685, 698–9) can still be seen in constructions where it is not clear whether the -*ing*-form is an adjective (113), an appositive participle (114) or already part of the progressive:

(113)   What ladyes fairest been or best daunsynge,

(CT I.2201 [1: 2203])

(114)   Heere is the queene of Fayerye,/ With harpe and pipe and symphonye,/ Dwellynge in this place.

(CT VII.814–16 [10: 814–16])

The reasons for the increase in the use of progressive forms are not clear. In the Early Middle English period their frequency is very low; on the whole, their number is no higher than in comparable works in Old English, and in some cases it is even remarkably lower. For instance, Nehls (1974: 139) gives as the frequency rate for the translation of the Old English *Orosius*, 518 (rate per 100,000 words), while the comparable Middle English *Polychronicon* (also a chronicle translated from Latin) has a frequency of only six. The use of the progressive in didactic and homiletic prose is comparable, although slightly lower in Middle English; the frequency in poetry is also low, as in Old English. At the end of the Middle English period the frequency almost doubles, and from the beginning of the Modern English period onwards the use of the construction rises astronomically (see Strang 1982). One of the interesting observations one can make for this period is that overall the use of the progressive is much higher in northern texts than in midland or southern texts.

Various explanations have been given for the increase in the use of the progressive. A clear picture has not yet emerged, but most of the following factors probably contributed to its development.

1 Nickel (1966) has remarked in his study of the Old English *Orosius* that verbs that are inherently punctual or perfective – this concerns especially prefixed verbs (*a-*, *be-*, *ge-*, etc.) – occur almost without exception in the simple form, while durative verbs (in many cases the same verbs without the prefix) often appear in the expanded form. In Middle English this morphological means of showing aspectual

differences was lost with the disappearance of the prefixal system, and this may have created a need for other means of showing aspect (see Strang 1970: 190–1; 280; Samuels 1972: 161ff.).

Visser (1963–73: §1857) is not convinced that the 'Aktionsart' of verbs played a role. He points out that in many Late Old English works this distinction is not preserved, especially in the *Lindisfarne Gospels*. However, it is very likely that already in Late Old English the prefixal system was in decay, especially in the north. Samuels (1949) has shown that *ge-* in the *Lindisfarne Gospels* had become meaningless. The glossator even seems to manipulate *ge-* to match the length of the Latin word he is glossing. In that context it should not be surprising to find *ge-* verbs in the progressive form.

2 In the Late Old English/Early Middle English period the inflectional endings of the present participle, (inflectional) infinitive and verbal noun began to be confused (see Visser 1963–73: §§1018–34, and chapter 2, section 2.9.2.6 of this volume). At the same time, or perhaps even because of this, there was syntactic confusion in that the verbal noun (in Old English ending in *-ung*) began to develop verbal properties, i.e. it acquired the ability to take a noun phrase as its direct object (in Old English the genitive case was the norm); and it could be modified by adverbs that normally only modify verbs etc. (see Visser 1963–73: §1035). Curme (1912) places these developments as early as the ninth century, mainly on the basis of adverbial modifiers accompanying the gerund or verbal noun. He does not notice, however, that these adverbials (mainly instrumental) can also accompany nouns other than gerunds. Tajima (1985) dates the occurrence of gerunds followed by adverbial adjuncts from Early Middle English. The evidence given by Visser shows that unambiguous examples of the gerund showing verbal properties all belong to the early part of the fourteenth century, with the exception of cases like *þe sonne rysyng*, where the original Old English genitive has become subject. These already occur in the early thirteenth century (see Visser 1963–73: §1099). Some of these 'subject gerunds' could be explained away as present participles, and this may account for their earlier occurrence. It seems likely, therefore, that the syntactic confusion noted above was more a result of the phonological developments than that it occurred independently of it. An immediate consequence of all this was an enormous expansion of the functional load of the form in *-ing*. This may well have assisted in the breakthrough of the progressive form. An example of this is the gradual replacement of the Old English construction *he com ridan* by the *he com*

ridyng/ridand construction (see Mustanoja 1960: 557; Nehls 1974: 122–3). (For the dialectal distribution of the *-yng/-and* form, see chapter 2, section 2.9.2.6.)

More specifically, it is suggested in connection with these phonological changes that two separate Old English constructions, i.e. *he wæs huntende* and *he wæs on huntunge* (and see similar pairs discussed in vol. I, section 4.3.2.1) became very similar in Middle English *he was huntyng(e)* and *he was on/an/in/a huntyng(e)*, and that they ultimately coalesced, thus sharply increasing the frequency of the progressive form proper. The hypothesis is that the preposition *on* weakened first to *an* and *a* and then disappeared altogether. However, it is difficult to ascertain such a chronological development in the actual examples. Although instances with *a/an* occur quite early, but infrequently – Visser's first example dates from 1205 (1963–73: §1866) – examples with *on/in* (and even *upon*) occur all through the period and beyond as well. Visser (1963–73: §1859) also gives examples where *a* has been elided. It should be noted, however, that in none of his examples does this *a* function as a preposition; on the contrary, *a* is still going strong even in Present-Day English (e.g. *asleep, alive*; see Nehls 1974: 166ff.). This theory also runs counter to the observation made above that the progressive form was much more frequent in the north – where the present participle (*-ande*) and the verbal noun (*-yng*) remained strictly separate – than in other areas. Jespersen (1909–49, part IV: 168–9), who supported this theory, gave as evidence for the stage *a* > θ the appearance of constructions like *he was writing of a letter* (where *writing* is clearly a noun, as shown by *of*). He does not discuss the form *he was awriting a letter*, which also appears. According to Nehls (1974: 168) the latter type clearly does not fit the pattern of *a*-disappearance. His suggestion is, therefore, that both types are to be explained by false analogy. For this reason, Nehls rejects the above theory and suggests the following scenario: the two types (i.e. nominal and verbal *-ing*) were functionally almost equivalent; as a result mixed forms (like the above) appeared; the progressive finally replaced the *on huntyng* type, which became dialectal and/or non-standard. Evidence for this he sees in a sharpening of the function of the progressive once it had replaced the *on huntyng* type, and in the fact that this did not take place in Scotland, where the progressive and the gerund were still kept apart.

3 Foreign influence. Although it seems likely that Latin played some role in the origin of the construction (see vol. I, section 4.3.2.1), there is far less evidence for the influence of French or – even less – Celtic on

the development of the construction in Middle English. Although Old French has a similar construction in *estre* + *V-ant* (which, by the way, is less frequent in Old French than the type *aller* + gerund; see Gougenheim 1929), the *-ant* form in Middle English is very infrequent and, when found, more commonly has strong adjectival force (see Visser 1963–73: § 1860):

(115) Hir diete was accordant to hir cote.

(*CT* VII.2836 [10: 2808])

'Her food was in keeping with her cottage.'

Moreover, as we have seen, the progressive is most frequent in northern texts, which were least influenced by French.

A separate question in connection with the expanded form is the matter of 'continuation'. Is there a steady development from the Old English period into Middle English and beyond, or is there a break between the usage of the form in the two periods? Clearly there is room for disagreement here. It all depends on how one defines the various functions of the progressive in the respective periods. Two things are quite clear: (a) the Middle English (and Old English) constructions are not exactly equivalent to the Present-Day English ones; (b) the use of the progressive in Old and Middle English is optional; only in the Modern English period (according to Strang 1982 by about 1700) did it become obligatory. Thus it was only in the modern period that the progressive form became grammaticalised and formed part of the aspectual system of English. Before that it must be mainly seen as a stylistic device, one that was to a certain extent limited in usage. With hindsight one can see the development of the progressive form towards its employment as an aspectual marker. As in Old English, the progressive in Middle English is largely restricted to activity verbs,

(116) Polidamas.../ Broght hym [the horse] full bainly to þe bold
Troiell,/ Þat *was fightand* on fote in þe felle stoure.

(*Destr. Troy* (Htrn) 8336–9)

'Polidamas...brought it very quickly to the bold Troilus, who was fighting on foot in the fierce battle.'

It seems to be especially frequent in so-called frame situations; i.e. it is used to express the activity that is limited or framed by some other activity. Thus it is particularly frequent in temporal subclauses (Strang 1982 notes this also for the later periods):

(117) ...As Canacee *was pleyyng* in hir walk,/ Ther sat a faucon over hire
heed ful hye,

(*CT* V.410–11 [4: 402–3])

On the other hand, the progressive is also found with activity verbs where Present-Day English would not use it because the context shows the action to be habitual or to be essentially timeless:

(118)   Ther takth Asie ferst seisine [= possession]/ Toward the West, and over this/ Of Canahim wher the flod *is*/ Into the grete See *rennende*, ...

                                        (*CA* (Frf) VII.564–7)

(119)   Arestotill sais þat þe bees *are feghtande* agaynes hym þat will drawe þaire hony fra thaym

                                        (Allen 1931: 55.19–20)

Other ways in which the use of the progressive differs from standard usage today are its occurrence in imperative constructions:

(120)   John, *be thou* here *abydand*, ...

                                        (*Towneley Pl.* (Hnt) 19, 197.83)

and its occurrence with essentially stative verbs:

(121)   The tour, ... *Was joynynge* in the wal to a foreyne;/ And it *was longynge* to the doughtren tweyne/ Of Mynos,

                                        (*LGW* 1960–4)

'The wall of the tower adjoined the outer privy, and it belonged to the two daughters of Minos'

It is remarkable that in both Old and Middle English the progressive is frequent with certain kinds of verbs that are inherently imperfective or continuative: *flowen*, *irnen/rinnen*, and verbs meaning 'to live, dwell'. This seems to point to a certain stylistic preference for the progressive with these verbs.

When looking at the absence of the progressive, Nehls (1974) noted a clear continuity all through the history of English in that he has not found any instances of the progressive in so-called performative utterances, or in demonstration or running comment. The absence of the progressive in the latter two text types, however, may well be due to their scarcity in written English. The progressive *is* recorded in certain types of reportage as is clear from Crystal & Davy's (1969) chapter on 'The language of unscripted commentary'.

The process of grammaticalisation of the progressive can also be seen in the development of a much fuller range of patterns. In Old English the progressive appeared only in the past and the non-past and after modals. In Middle English the progressive perfect and pluperfect are first recorded from the mid/late fourteenth century (see (122)); but they remain sporadic. Likewise future (past and non-past) progressives enter the language in the fourteenth century, first in the north (123).

> (122) Heere in this temple of the goddesse Clemence/ We *han ben waitynge* al this fourtenyght.
>
> *(CT* I.928–9 [1: 930–1])
>
> (123) ... and *lyfand shall* I *be* ...
>
> *(Towneley Pl.* (Hnt) 20, 218.459).

The only missing forms in our period are the future perfect (*will have been -ing*) and all the passive forms. Occasionally we find the *on huntyng* type used where Present-Day English would have a passive progressive (see Visser 1963–73: §§ 1884–6). The forms with *in* are the earliest (early fourteenth century):

> (124) and he ordeynede þat everiche man schulde stonde while þe gospel is in redynge...
>
> (Trev. *Higd.* (St J-C) vol. 5, 213.5–6)

Visser (1963–73: §§ 1876–7) also notes the use of *be + ing* in this case, but many early examples can be otherwise explained; either the *-ing* form may represent the *-in* ending of the past participle or the verb could be both transitive and intransitive. Some examples, however, are less ambiguous:

> (125) þai crist till hething driue/ Sli men quen þai þam coms to scriue,/ þat þere *er* dedis *doand* neu,/ þat þai agh sare wit resun reu.
>
> *(Cursor* (Vsp) 26810–13)
>
> 'they drive Christ to scorn, people such, that when they come to be shriven, deeds are being done again, which with reason they ought to rue deeply.'

Only in the sixteenth century does this construction become truly frequent.

4.3.3.2 The perfect and the pluperfect

In Old English the verb *habban* could already be used as an auxiliary in the periphrastic (plu)perfect (see vol. I, section 4.3.2.2). In Middle English the frequent alternation between the perfect and the preterite in different manuscript versions of the same text (see Visser 1963–73: § 805) and the haphazard use of the inflected past participle (the plural *-e* ending is frequently used with singular correlates; see Zimmermann 1968: 36) show that this development is complete. In word order, the Middle English construction reflects its origin in that the construction with the object before the past participle remains very common until the sixteenth century (Zimmermann 1968: ch. 3). (This word order is still found in many non-standard dialects, e.g. in Hiberno-English, where its usage resembles the original Old English construction with *have* as a full lexical verb denoting possession and the participle as a complement of the object NP (see Harris 1984).) This is presumably due to the persistance of the so-called Verb-Second rule, which in Old English placed the finite verb immediately after the subject – so *before* the object – in main clauses (for the rule of Verb Second see also section 4.8). This makes it difficult to distinguish the perfect from the construction in which the past participle following the *main* verb *have* is used attributively. Only the context offers a clue. In Present-Day English the two constructions are distinguished by differences in word order: *I have cut out the pattern* versus *I have the pattern cut out* (in British English there is usually also a lexical distinction: *have* is commonly replaced by *have got*). An example of a perfect construction is:

(126) ... þe feader hwen he haueð inoh ibeaten his child ant *haueð hit ituht* wel, warpeþ the gerde i þe fur.

(Ancr. (Corp-C) 96.13–14)

'... the father when he has beaten his child enough and has brought him up wel, throws the rod into the fire.'

and of an attributive construction,

(127) Ant hu schulen þeose chirch ancres þe tilieð oðer *habbeð rentes isette*, don to poure nehburs dearnliche hare ealmesse?

(Ancr. (Corp-C) 212.25–7)

'And how can those church-anchoresses who cultivate some ground or have fixed incomes give unobtrusive alms to poor neighbours?'

The frequency of the (plu)perfect increases enormously in the Middle English period, although its use in comparison with the preterite is still limited. It is unlikely that either Latin or French played any significant role (see Zimmermann 1968: 17–26). Mustanoja (1960: 504) offers a psychological reason for the increase of the perfect: '[the] compound tense form is longer and therefore more emphatic than the simple preterite ... A more emphatic verb form is desirable for indicating the completion of an action which continues up to the moment of speaking than for expressing an action which clearly belongs to the past.' This may be correct, but it does not explain why this desire would have become stronger in the Middle English period. The infrequent use of the perfect in Old English may also be partly a matter of the style and subject matter of the extant manuscripts. Zimmermann has noted that the Middle English (plu)perfect occurs more often in colloquial style; it is rare in purely narrative contexts and frequent in instructional texts. Thus, in the Early Middle English texts he has examined (*Ancrene Wisse*, the 'Katherine Group', Laȝamon's *Brut* and *The Owl and the Nightingale*), the perfect occurs almost exclusively in direct speech. This also explains why the perfect occurs mostly in the first and second person, while the preterite and pluperfect are rare in these cases. He also shows (pp. 155–8) that in the Old English *Orosius*, where the perfect is seldom used, it is found in places where the sentence structure is looser, especially in conclusions of chapters and in connecting passages. Thus it is possible that the greater frequency of the (plu)perfect in Middle English not only reflects a change in actual usage but is also related to the nature of the extant texts. However, another cause might be the general change in the English language from a morphological tense/mood (aspect) system to a grammaticalised auxiliary system. As such it shares a trend found in other Germanic languages.

The (plu)perfect is not fully grammaticalised in Middle English: it freely alternates in almost all its functions with the preterite. The type of constructions, however, in which the (plu)perfect occurs already anticipates its later usage in present-day standard English.

The primary function of the perfect is to indicate that an activity has started at a certain moment in the past but that it is still relevant/continuing at the moment of speaking:

(128) And alle þo þat seyn for me a Pater noster…I make hem parteneres
       & graunte hem part of all [þe] gode pilgrymages & of all the gode
       dedes þat I *haue don*, ȝif ony ben to his plesance.

                                                    (*Mandev.* (Tit) 210.36–211.4)

The preterite is also commonly found in these constructions. When the relevance of the activity is related not so much to the moment of speaking but to the future or the generic present (which includes the future), the perfect is clearly favoured over the preterite. Zimmermann (1968: 110–12) has found no examples of the preterite here:

(129) Ase ofte as ȝe *habbeð ired* eawiht her on, greteð þe leafdi wið an aue;
       for him þet swonc her abuten.

                                                    (*Ancr.* (Corp-C) 222.12–14)

       'As often as you have read anything in this [book], greet the Lady
       with an *Ave* for him who took pains over it.'

(130) þe hen hwen ha *haueð ileid*, ne con bute cakelin.

(*Ancr.* (Corp-C) 36.18)

'the hen when she has laid, knows no better than to cackle.'

As in Present-Day English certain temporal adverbs favour a particular construction. Thus, *now*, *here*, *today*, etc. are usually found with the perfect, whereas *(n)ever*, *þa*, etc. are commonly combined with the preterite. But it is not unusual in Middle English (especially in poetry, so metrical considerations could play a role here) to find a perfect with a past-time adverbial:

(131) I am youre doghter Custance.../ That whilom ye *han sent* unto Surrye.

(*CT* II.1107–8 [3: 1107–8])

Just like the non-past, the perfect is found in narrative past-time contexts often in conjunction with the preterite. It is not clear how far the perfect has a special function, and how far the exigencies of rhyme and metre are responsible, since this phenomenon occurs mainly in poetry (see Mustanoja 1960: 506–7; Visser 1963–73: §§ 766, 772):

(132) His brother, which that knew of his penaunce,/ Up *caughte* hym and to bedde he *hath hym broght*.

(*CT* V.1082–3 [6: 374–5])

The pluperfect occurs exclusively in narrative passages and always refers to a completed action. In most cases it is used, as in Present-Day English, to indicate a past within the past. It is often accompanied by clarifying temporal adverbials such as *(þer)biuoren*, *ear* 'ere', etc. and occurs especially in temporal subclauses. In Middle English, however, a preterite can also be used.[9] The first example shows a pluperfect, the second a preterite:

(133) ...I schewed hym this tretys þat I *had made* after informacioun of men þat knewen of thinges þat I had not seen my self,

(*Mandev.* (Tit) 210: 1–3)

(134) Moyses was bliðe.../ And ches ðo men god *made* wis.

(*Gen.&Ex.*3671–2)

'Moses was glad... and chose those men that God had made wise.'

The description of the knight in Chaucer's 'General Prologue' (*CT* I.47–63) shows that preterite and pluperfect forms could easily be interchanged.

The pluperfect was used in hypothetical contexts to indicate what could or should have happened but did not ('counterfactuals'). This use is equivalent to that of the modal preterite, except the pluperfect refers to a past in the past. Like the modal preterite, the modal pluperfect was originally a subjunctive, but the loss of inflections caused the indicative and the subjunctive past forms of *habben* to become alike, with the exception of the second-person singular. This subjunctive form, however, was soon levelled out in favour of the indicative:

(135) '...*Haddestow* be hende', quod I, 'þow woldest haue asked leeue.'

(PPl.B (Trin-C) xx, 188)

(For the use of the inverted word order in this clause, see section 4.6.3.3.) The modal pluperfect is also found in main clauses where nowadays we prefer a modal verb:

(136) And ʒif here fader had not ben dronken he *hadde not yleye* with hem.

(Mandev. (Tit) 68: 10–11)

In addition to the (plu)perfect formed with the auxiliary *habben/hauen*, there was a form with *ben*. As in Old English, this was mainly restricted to the so-called mutative verbs (i.e. intransitive verbs involving a change of place or state). However, the distinction in Middle English becomes less clear-cut. *Habben* encroached upon the *ben*-domain, while *ben* is found with some intransitive, non-mutative verbs. A number of verbs occur with both auxiliaries. Attempts to describe the difference between the two constructions have not been completely successful so far in that they always admit of exceptions. Some linguists have described the *habben* construction as denoting an action and the *ben* construction as denoting a state (see Bøgholm 1944; Fridén 1957; Visser 1963–73: §1898). It is unlikely that such a clear dichotomy exists in view of the facts that the two constructions often seem to be interchangeable and that in the later development *have* ousts the *be* forms. Such a dichotomy would also mean that a structure like *he is come* always referred to state, never to completed action. Fridén (1948) formulated the rule that mutative verbs take *have* when they are used transitively as in *he has gone half a mile*. Visser (1963–73: §1898) objects to this because, he says, there are many exceptions. However, a large number of these exceptions can be explained if one widens Fridén's rule (see also Zimmermann 1973) so that with mutative verbs *be* is normally used when location (in time or place) or direction is emphasised, while *have* is used to refer more purely to the activity conveyed by the verb, as the following examples show:

(137)a. Be wel avysed on that ilke nyght/ That we *ben entred* into shippes bord,'/ That noon of us ne speke nat a word,

(CT I.3584–6 [1 : 3578–80])

b. For ye *han entred* into myn hous by violence,

(CT VII.1812 [10 : 1812])

(138)a. The nexte houre of Mars folwynge this,/ Arcite unto the temple *walked is*/ Of fierse Mars to doon his sacrifise, ...

(CT I.2367–9 [1 : 2369–71])

b. 'Saw ye,' quod she, 'as ye *han walked* wyde,/ Any of my sustren walke yow besyde ...'

(LGW 978–9)

For this reason it is not surprising to find adverbials of manner or degree, which highlight the activity of the verb, more often collocated with mutative verbs in *have* constructions, and adverbials of time and place with the same verbs in *be* constructions (as in the above examples). It also explains why the *have* construction prevails in hypothetical statements: there the emphasis is always on the *activity*, on what should have *happened*:

(139)a. She wende nevere *han come* in swich a trappe.

(CT V.1341 [6 : 633])

b. He wende *have cropen* by his felawe John,/ And by the millere in he creep anon,

(CT I.4259–60 [1 : 4251–2])

Fridén (1948 : 43–57) gives a list of contexts in which *have* is preferred to *be*. They all agree with the above observation except for one category: '*Have* is used if the sentence contains an adverb or adverbial phrase denoting the *place* of action' (p. 48; italics mine). However, in all the examples he quotes this adverbial can be interpreted as one of degree: 'and when you have gone *as far as you can*', 'thy slander has gone *through and through her heart*'.

Finally, it remains to consider the reason(s) why *have* ousted *be* in the formation of the perfect. Various factors are at work (see Zimmermann 1973): (a) the greater functional load of *be* (used as an auxiliary of the passive, progressive and perfect) compared to *have* (at this stage only perfect) and the ambiguity that could arise because of this (i.e. *be* + past participle of a transitive verb could be perfect as well as passive; the progressive in *-ing* is sometimes found written as *-en*, the same ending as the past participle of strong verbs) made *have* a more suitable candidate for the perfect; (b) *be* had become the auxiliary *par excellence* of the passive voice. One might have expected *wurthen* to play a larger role here as it did in other West Germanic languages like German and Dutch. But from earliest Old English, *weorþan* had been far less frequent in the passive, and it became very infrequent in Early Middle English, when the auxiliary system was undergoing great change. Why *wurthen* disappeared is still unclear; reasons for this development have been sought in the nature of the verb itself, while it has also been ascribed to foreign influence (for a discussion of the possible factors, see Mustanoja 1960: 616–19).

When the (plu)perfect became frequent in Middle English, it was necessary to streamline the various constructions; and *have*, which already acted as the auxiliary of the perfect with most types of verbs and even occurred with mutatives in special constructions, slowly took over the functions of *be*. This development was possibly also facilitated by the fact that in co-ordinate constructions the auxiliary was usually not repeated so that *have* was often used where *be* was expected. Another factor that is frequently adduced is the influence of the use of the reduced form *'s* (especially in spoken language), but evidence for *has* reduced to *'s* (from spelling and metre) is mainly post-Middle English.

4.3.3.3 Modal auxiliaries

In section 4.3.2.2, we have seen that by the end of the Middle English period periphrastic constructions far outweighed subjunctive forms. This development started in Late Old English when periphrastic constructions became increasingly common. What probably happened is this: on the one hand, the gradual erosion of verbal inflections made it necessary to replace the subjunctive by something more transparent; on the other, the use of periphrastic constructions at a fairly early stage was itself responsible for the disappearance of the subjunctive. The early use of the periphrastic construction may be due to a desire to be more emphatic and possibly to be more specific than was possible with the subjunctive form. Interesting in this respect is the use in Old English of periphrastic auxiliaries which are themselves in the subjunctive form.

Together with the loss of the subjunctive came a grammaticalisation of the modal verbs, which in Old English in many ways still had the status of full verbs (but see Warner 1990). A full list of changes that the modal verbs underwent can be found in Plank (1984). This list shows that the development was gradual and not of a radical nature, as suggested in Lightfoot (1979). Some of the more important changes taking place in Middle English but not completed in that period (and continuing for a long time after in certain dialects) are: (a) the modals lost the possibility of appearing in non-finite forms and of taking objects; in general they move towards an invariable form. This is related to the loss of the notional meaning of the modals. (b) Tense differences in modals no longer serve a temporal purpose. (c) The close relation between a modal and its infinitive is emphasised by the fact that the *to*-infinitive never replaces the bare infinitive as happened after most other full verbs, and also by the increasing unwillingness of modals to appear without an infinitive of another verb in series. In Middle English we still find the modal verbs used in some of their 'non-auxiliary' functions (for Old English see vol. I, section 4.3.2.3); (140) shows them as full verbs, (141) in non-finite forms.[10]

(140)a. She *koude* muchel of wandrynge by the weye.

(CT I.467 [1: 469])

      'She knew a lot about travelling.'

   b. And by that feith I *shal* Priam of Troie.

(Troilus III.791)

      'And by the faith I owe Priamus of Troy.'

   c. And seyde he *moste* unto Itayle,...

(HF 187)

      'And said he had [to go] to Italy'

(141)a. Þatt mannkinn *shollde muȝhenn* wel/ Upp cumenn inntill heoffne

(Orm. 3944–5)

      'that mankind should be able to go up to heaven'

   b. But Pandarus, if goodly hadde he *myght*,/He wolde han hyed hire to bedde fayn,...

(Troilus III.654–5)

Next to the so-called 'core' modals (*shal*, *wil*, *may*, *mot*, *can*) periphrastic constructions also expressed modality. Some of these occur in Old English (e.g. 'to be to', 'to have to'). These, together with the Middle English innovation borrowed from Old French 'to be able to', remain sporadic until they come to fill a systemic gap left by the grammaticalisation of the core modals, which, as we have seen, lost all but their non-finite forms (and to a great extent they even lost their finite past forms). For other examples of periphrastic constructions conveying modality, see Plank (1984: 321–2).

A rather special development is the use of the modals, especially *shal* and *wil* (but in some cases also *mot*), as markers of the future. Since, however, these constructions remain modally marked for the greater part of the period (see Mustanoja 1960: 490–1), they are discussed here and not under *tense*. Already in Old English **sculan/willan* are used with predictive meaning, but in these cases **sculan* usually expresses obligation or necessity as well, and *willan* volition. (Traugott (in vol. I, section 4.3.2.3) states that there are no examples in Old English where **sculan* or *willan* has pure future reference. Warner (1990), however, shows that these verbs must be mere futurity markers when they occur in impersonal constructions in Old English (see also Mitchell 1985: §§ 1023ff).) This situation continues in Middle English:

(142) And rightful folk shul gon, after they dye,/ To hevene;

(PF 55–6)

In the above example *shul* expresses future as well as 'ordained event'. Thus, *shal* is more frequent in prophesies, in contexts in which a sense of obligation is present, in commands and instructions. Because of this modal function, *shal* is particularly common in the third person. *Wil*, on the other hand, occurs far more often in the first person, since modally it is connected to the desire of the speaker/subject:

(143) we wulleð folhi þe, we wulleð don alswa, leauen al as þu dudest

(Ancr. (Corp-C) 87.6–7)

> 'we will follow you, we will do likewise, [we will] leave everything [behind] as you did'

Wil occurs especially in promises, wishes and resolutions.

Because *shal* is not related to the will of the subject, it develops into a pure future marker earlier than *wil* (see Mustanoja 1960: 490). The more frequent use of predictive *shal* in Early Middle English may, however, also be due to other factors. It could be partly a matter of style. In biblical writings *shal* is preferred to *wil* (*wil* is reserved for the translation of Latin *velle*). *Wil* seems to be a product of a more popular style. The pure future use of *wil* may have developed out of its use in generic and habitual contexts,

(144) He is a fool that wol foryete hymselve

(Troilus V.98)

Examples that indicate that *wil* is used without any modal colouring are those that have inanimate subjects (although note the personified nature of the subject in this particular instance):

(145) And I, book, wole be brent but Iesus rise to lyue...

(PPl.B (Trin-C) xviii, 255)

Other verbs employed in periphrastic future expressions were *wurthen* (see Mustanoja 1960: 495), in Late Middle English *to be about to* (Mustanoja 1960: 354) and right at the end of the period *to be going to* (Mustanoja 1960: 592). The expanded form *be + ing* was not used for future reference in Middle English (except with the verb *to come* which is inherently futural) even though it was fairly frequent in Old English particularly as a translation of Latin *esse + -urus* (see Visser 1963–73: §1830).

4.3.3.4 The periphrasis with *gan*

The verb *ginnen* is used in Middle English, just like *beginnen*, to refer to the beginning of an action:

(146) Seþþen þat ich here regni *gan*/ Y no fond neuer so fole-hardi man

(Orfeo (Auch) 425–6)

'From the time I began to rule here I have never found anyone so foolhardy.'

However, there are many contexts in which such an inchoative meaning does not fit:

(147) þus þe bataile *gan* leste long/ Til þe time of euesong, ...

(Bevis (Auch) 797–8)

'thus the battle went on a long time, till evensong'

(148) A knaue he *gan* imete.

(Horn (Cmb) 940)

'He met a lad'

In (147) the inchoative function of *gan* is incompatible with the adverbial adjunct *long*, which expresses duration. In (148) the inherently punctual (non-durative) verb *mete* cannot be combined with ingressive *gan*, which only collocates with durative verbs. It is clear that in these examples *gan* has a different function. The very beginnings of this new function of *gan* are found in Old English with the related verb *onginnan*, as shown by Funke (1922: 8–9).

As to what this new function of *gan* entails, there seem to be two schools of thought. One maintains that *gan* is a mere stopgap and is exclusively used as a metrical device (Visser 1963–73: §§1477ff.; Smyser 1967; Terasawa 1974; Tajima 1975). The other believes that *gan* has a particular descriptive function, that it is used as a stylistic device, which later also becomes, or could become, a mere line-filler (Funke 1922; Homann 1954; Mustanoja 1960, 1983; Kerkhof 1982; Brinton 1983; cf.

Brinton 1988: § 3.8). The evidence available strongly supports the 'mere stopgap' theory: the *gan*-periphrasis occurs almost exclusively in poetry. In Chaucer, for instance, nearly 700 instances have been found in his poetry, and only three in his prose (all in *Melibee*) of which two are probably a direct translation of OF *commença*. Likewise, in his study of the Gawain-poet, Tajima notes that *con/can* (the northern form of *gan*) appears only very sporadically in the unrhymed alliterative lines, but is frequent in rhymed lines. Ninety-five per cent of the examples put the infinitive in rhyme position. In Chaucer the equivalent figure is 73 per cent, according to Smyser. Another interesting feature is that the construction occurs only in the past tense (with the exception of *Pearl*, where some present-tense forms are found). Smyser (1967: 74) explains this as follows: the preterite, especially of weak verbs, is very difficult to rhyme; for that reason, the infinitive is preferred in rhyming position. His evidence supports this: verbs that have the same form in preterite and infinitive (*hente, sette, sterte, stente*) only occur twice in Chaucer in the *gan*-periphrasis (compared to eighty-two times in the simple form). This should be contrasted with e.g. *cried/gan crye*: *cried* occurs six times in rhyme, *gan crye* twenty-one times.

The evidence provided by the second school of thought for their hypothesis is based on the presumption that a great poet like Chaucer, who uses the construction frequently, would not have stooped to the use of stopgaps (Homann 1954; Brinton 1983). Funke (1922) suggests that there must have been an intermediate stage between inchoative function and pleonastic use. He suggests that *gan* was used as a signal to introduce a new event, that it has a descriptive, intensive function. Although such an intermediate stage is likely before *gan* was semantically reduced to zero, we are quite in the dark as to the meaning of *gan* at that stage. This is clearly shown by the many different interpretations that have been offered for this descriptive function. It is also difficult to prove conclusively whether this descriptive function continued to exist side by side with stopgap *gan* at a later stage.

That different linguists give widely different interpretations of the meaning of the descriptive function of *gan* is a serious weakness of this theory. Homann believes that Chaucer 'utilized "gan" to add vitality to dramatic scenes, intensity to emotional situations, and an inner meaning and depth to his characters' (1954: 398). Brinton (1983: 244) very tentatively suggests that *gan* may convey a notion of contingency. The problem with all these suggestions, especially Homann's, is that they can be read into the context, the danger of 'hineininterpretieren' looms large. On the other hand one can see that if *gan* was used as a stopgap, it could be easily turned to stylistic use. In the following example from Chaucer, for instance:

> (149)   For with that oon encresede ay my fere/ And with that other gan
>   myn herte bolde;/ That oon me hette, that other dide me colde;
>
> (*PF* 143–5)

it is likely that Chaucer used *gan* not just to put *bolde* in rhyming position, but also to put it in a symmetrical position to *fere* with which it forms a contrast. Notice also the completely symmetrical ordering of all the other clause structures in these lines.

Just as it is virtually impossible to decide whether *gan* has a descriptive function along with its line-filler function, and, if so, which of the two it is in each individual case, it is also almost impossible to distinguish between the ingressive function of *gan* and its other uses. Brinton (1983) gives criteria to do just that (criteria that have been used by Smyser before). She discusses the collocation possibilities between aspectual *ginnen* and the main verb (*be*)*ginnen*. What needs to be realised, however, (and this clearly diminishes the overall usefulness of these criteria) is that, if the collocation indeed allows of an ingressive interpretation, that does not necessarily mean that *gan* could not in that very example also be a stopgap. Once *gan* has developed that function one can expect to find it everywhere.

4.3.3.5   The verb *do*

The Middle English period is a time of rapid expansion in periphrastic constructions involving the rise of an auxiliary system, including perfect *have/be*, progressive *be* and the modals. The development of a periphrastic verb *do* in this period is of considerable importance on account of the later establishment of this *do* as an empty syntactic marker in constructions in which the simple verb no longer suffices (e.g. in negative and interrogative clauses). As we will see, *do* begins to fill a gap that results from the development of the auxiliary system described above.

Before we look at Middle English developments, we will consider the way the verb *do* was employed in Old English. OE *don* was used (a) as a full lexical verb ('notional' or Visser's 'factitive *do*'):

> (150)   Uton... don hyne on þone ealdan pytt
>
> (*Gen.* 37.19)
>
> 'Let us do [= put] him in this old well'

(b) Two other usages develop from (a), the use of *do* in a vaguer, more general sense, i.e. 'anticipative' *do* (151) and 'vicarious' *do* (152) (together often referred to as the propverb *do* or substitute *do*):

(151)   utan   don swa us mycel þearf is, habban   æfre rihtne geleafan...
        let us do   as   us great   need is, have (inf.) ever   right   belief

(WHom. 7a 42)

'let us do what is necessary for us, (i.e.) to have the true faith...'

(152)   ...he miccle ma on his deaðe acwealde, ðonne he ær cucu dyde

(Judg. 16.27)

'...he killed many more in death than he did before [when he was] alive'

In both cases *do* replaces a lexical verb used elsewhere in the clause, thus avoiding repetition. The difference is that in (151) *do* precedes and in (152) *do* follows the lexical verb. Notice that this *do* is parallel to the lexical verb, i.e. it appears in the same person, tense, mood, etc. as the lexical verb it replaces.

(c) *Do* could be used as a causative verb in Old English. It is usually followed in that sense by a *þæt*-clause construction. Infinitival constructions (which are of greater interest in the light of the syntactic structure in which periphrastic *do* will later appear) are rare in Old English, especially those without an object (Visser's cdi-type; 1963–73: § 1213), and are usually considered to have been influenced by Latin (but see Visser, § 1212):

(153)   And treowa he deð færlice blowan and eft raðe asearian

(HomU 34 (Nap 42) 109)

'And trees he does [= causes] to bloom suddenly and again to wither quickly'

These three uses continue into the Middle English period, in which they are joined by the new type: periphrastic *do*. So far I have ignored so-called 'emphatic *do*', as in PDE *Do have another drink!* According to some linguists (discussed by Ellegård 1953: 23ff., 121ff.) emphatic *do* is an auxiliary that developed from vicarious *do* and which provided the basis for later periphrastic *do* when it became unstressed in colloquial speech. This theory of the origin of periphrastic *do* is now generally rejected. First of all it is unprovable because there is no way of telling what is colloquial and what is not. Secondly, most of the early examples of periphrastic *do*, which appear mainly in verse, occupy unstressed position.

Since most linguists agree that periphrastic *do* developed out of (one of) the earlier uses of *do*, it is worthwhile to look at further developments in Middle English, concerning notional, substitute and causative *do*. The idea that periphrastic *do* was a borrowing from Celtic is now no longer generally upheld (see Ellegård 1953: 119–20; Visser 1963–73: §1415; but cf. Poussa 1990), likewise French influence is usually ruled out (Ellegård 1953: 92; Visser 1963–73: §1416), although Ellegård believes that the French construction *faire* + infinitive may have influenced the English development indirectly (see also below).

Notional *do* is an unlikely candidate for the origin of periphrastic *do* for the simple reason that it is not normally followed by an infinitive. However, due to the loss of inflections there are quite a few nouns in Middle English that could be interpreted as verbal elements. Consider the following examples:

(154) To *doon* yow *ese*, and it shal coste noght.

(*CT* I.768 [1: 770])

Cf. To *esen* hem and doon hem al honour

(*CT* I.2194 [1: 2196])

(155) …at every tyme that a man eteth or drynketh moore than suffiseth to the sustenaunce of his body, in certein he *dooth synne*.

(*CT* X.372 [12: 372])

It is unlikely that this would have happened before periphrastic *do* had developed because, as Ellegård (1953: 144) points out, the nominal interpretation would be elicited by examples where an element like *synne* would be clearly nominal because it is in the plural or preceded by an article, adjective, etc. Also the fact that the noun was often far removed from *do* would preclude a periphrastic interpretation. Ellegård (p. 146) also adds that if this ambiguity did indeed lead to the development of periphrastic *do*, one would have expected it to happen first in the north where the endings were lost earliest. But the northern areas are the last to acquire periphrastic *do*. So at most this development could have been a contributory factor.

In connection with notional *do*, I wish to touch upon a development noted for a number of (Germanic) languages in present-day colloquial speech.[11] In some dialects of modern spoken Dutch (similar examples are found in German; see Hausmann 1974 and Stein 1990), we often come across constructions such as the following,

(156) En dan doen we eerst even afwassen (inf.)

'And then do we first wash up'

where the Dutch noun *afwas* has been replaced by the verbal infinitive *afwassen* as a kind of afterthought. Presumably the verb *doen* 'do' has been forgotten by the time the speaker comes to the noun (due to the non-specific meaning of *doen* (and *do*)), and he replaces the noun by a verb that expresses specifically the activity that *doen/do* does not. In other words, it is possible that the verb *doen/do* has inherent propensities to develop into a semantically empty verb. We can hypothesise that in the grammar of a language this will only be used when there are other syntactic needs for an empty *do*, as was presumably the case in English (Denison 1985b shows that periphrastic *do* filled a slot in the highly structured and formally patterned auxiliary verb subsystem – see below), and not in Dutch.

Substitute *do*, and especially anticipative *do*, is considered a candidate for periphrastic *do* by a number of linguists, notably Visser. A problem with this idea is that anticipative *do* is not usually followed by an infinitive. It is only in late Middle English that we come across examples where the following lexical verb is unambiguously an infinitive, as in,

(157)   so ded sir Galahad delyver all the maydyns oute of the woofull castell.

(Malory Wks (Add.59678) 892.13–14)

Denison (1985b) (and see also Mitchell 1985: §666) has shown convincingly that all the earlier examples attested by Visser are suspect in a number of ways. The majority of Visser's Old English examples are of the form shown in (151), where the infinitive (*habban*) depends on *uton* and not on *don*. Other instances show verbal forms that are ambiguous. Ambiguity is of two kinds: (a) the verbal form following *do* can be interpreted as an infinitive as well as a finite form due to the confusion of their endings (infinitival *-an*, finite *-on*, *-en* all became [ən] in Late Old English, joined in Middle English by the replacement of finite *-eþ*: *-en* in many dialects); (b) the verbal form can be interpreted as directly dependent on *do* or as dependent on some other element present in the clause. Concerning the latter Denison points out that in all the early examples *do* has a complement in its own clause, usually *swa*, *swa* + clause, or *ægðer*. This suggests that the following lexical verb does not depend on *do* but is a further explication of the object of *do* (see also Ellegård 1953: 133). Examples (158) and (159) represent two of those given by Visser (1963–73: §1413) for Old and Middle English respectively:

(158)   And we lærað þæt preostas swa dælan folces ælmessan þæt hig ægðer don ge God gegladian ge folc to ælmessan gewænian.

(WCan.1.1.1 (Fowler) 55)

'And we teach that the priests so divide up the people's alms that they do both [that is] please God and…'

(159) *So* he deð alse ofte   ase he ne mei mid openlich vuel, *kuðen*
So he does as   often as he not can by   open   evil, show
*his strenc*ðe.
his strength

(Ancr. (Nero) 99.16–17)

'This he does whenever he cannot show his strength by means that are clearly evil.'

Anticipative *do* is unlikely to have generated periphrastic *do* because examples of periphrastic *do* appear about two hundred years before unambiguous examples with anticipative *do* are found. Furthermore, development from anticipative *do* is unlikely because usually a clause or phrase intervenes between *do* and the infinitive. Although Visser argues here that deletion of this clause would yield periphrastic *do*, this is not convincing since there is no reason why such a deletion process should take place (see Denison (1985b: 49), who comments in some detail on the confusion present in Visser's account).

Causative *do* has been put forward most frequently as the originator of periphrastic *do*. The postulated development is roughly as follows. Ellegård distinguishes two main types of constructions which he calls *do ac* (160) and *do x* (161) (in Visser *cdsi* and *cdi* respectively). *Do ac* contains an oblique noun phrase that functions as object of *do* and as subject of the infinitive; this makes *do ac* usually unambiguously causative. *Do x* has no such noun phrase and can therefore in principle also be interpreted as a non-causative:

(160) Þe king dede þe mayden arise,…

(Havelok (Ld) 205)

'The king did [= made] the maiden rise'

(161) He dude writes sende…
he did   letters send

(Horn (Cmb) 1001)

'He sent letters' or 'He had letters sent'

(162) A noble churche heo dude a-rere
A noble church she did   raise

(SLeg. (Ld) 4.118)

'She built a noble church' or 'She had a noble church built'

Ellegård claims that the change from causative *do* to periphrastic *do* occurred in *do x* constructions in a process which he calls 'permutation' (1953: 29). He illustrates that with the following example:

(163) Henry... þe walles did doun felle, þe tours bette he doun

(Mannyng *Chron.Pt.2* (Petyt) 97.22)

The equivalence of *did felle* and *bette* implies that there is a causative element in both expressions. Now if a verb like *bete* can mean both 'beat' and 'cause to beat', this would also be true for *felle*. In that case *did* can be interpreted as a non-causative, and is semantically empty. Visser (§ 1417) does not find Ellegård's semantic change convincing because he does not believe that a verb like *fell* could be both causative and non-causative at the same time. Marchand (1939:123) even considers the semantic change a mental impossibility. Denison (1985b: 48), however, shows that language does tolerate this kind of 'equivocation' with examples from Present-Day English involving *get* and *have*. In addition, examples like *Nixon bombed Cambodia* and *The pilot had bombed Dresden* show that the same verb can be both causative and non-causative depending on context. Thus, two surface structures were in existence which could express the same thing. This then, according to Ellegård, could lead to constructions where *do* is used without any causative implication as in:

(164) His sclauyn he dude dun legge,

(*Horn* (Cmb) 1057)

'He laid down his pilgrim's cloak'

Ellegård believes that this development took place earliest in areas where causative *do* was weak, and where what he calls equivocal *do* (as in (161)) occurs frequently. Such a situation is found in thirteenth-century southwestern poetic texts.

Denison (1985b) notes two problems in connection with Ellegård's proposal. First, Ellegård offers no motivation for the semantic change except that it provided poets with a handy device that could be used at any time to salvage their rhyme or metre. The second concerns the chronology. Ellegård posits a development from causative *do x* > equivocal *do x* > periphrastic *do x*, but there are few examples of causative *do x*, while equivocal and periphrastic *do x* occur at about the same time rather than consecutively. These two objections, presented as separate, are in fact interconnected. Denison (p. 48) believes that Ellegård sees the semantic change as motivated by rhyming verse because the latter does not offer any linguistic factors to explain the change. These linguistic factors (see below), however, are linked to the appearance of the construction causative *do x* in the first place. Ellegård acknowledges that the causative *do x* construction – a prerequisite to the semantic change – is in fact not at all frequent. (Thus, when he wants to show whether in a certain dialect causative *do* is weak or not, he mostly relies on occurrences of *do ac* which are unambiguously causative.) This infrequency of course upsets his putative development, as mentioned above, which starts off from causative *do x*. Ellegård holds on to this 'putative development' and does not see the implications of the fact that causative, equivocal and periphrastic *do x* occur at the same time (as Denison makes abundantly clear). That this should be so is in itself not surprising because it is difficult to imagine examples of unambiguous causative *do x* (they do indeed hardly occur). Thus, as soon as the *do x* construction appears, equivocal *do x* is bound to appear as well together with periphrastic *do x*, unless the causative notion of *do* is clearly present in (usually) unambiguous *do ac* constructions. This would presumably prevent the last stage of the development to periphrastic *do x* as it has done for texts written in the eastern dialect.

So the important question is not the occurrence of the semantic change, but the occurrence of causative *do x* which (almost automatically) triggers it. Ellegård (1953: 62ff., 118ff.) does in fact give a linguistic motivation for its appearance, i.e. the translation of the French construction *faire x*, which occurs in French texts that have been translated into Middle English verse. He argues why in this case the translator usually opted for *do x*, rather than *make, cause* or *let x* (pp. 90–108). It is Denison's achievement that he focuses on the true motivation for the whole change, the appearance of the *do x* construction alongside clearly causative *do ac*. As linguistic factors for this appearance he gives, next to the influence of French *faire*, the analogical effect of the occurrence of subjectless constructions with similar causative verbs like *haten* and *leten*.[12]

The advantage of Denison's approach is that, by focusing on the appearance of the *do x* construction, he finds that there is no need to split up this construction into causative, equivocal and periphrastic *do x*. The context will make clear 'whether or not an intermediary actually performed the action' (1985b: 52), and he goes on to argue – in order to explain how these semantic subtypes could all function in one construction – that the performer of the action is of no importance: 'the construction is used to focus not on who did it but on what happened' (p. 53). Looking for an interpretation that might cover all three subtypes, he suggests that the *do x* construction might have developed a perfective or completive aspect. There are good reasons for accepting this possibility. He mentions (a) that a development from *do* to a perfective marker is widely paralleled cross-linguistically, and (b) that the disarray in aspect marking occurring after the obsolescence of the Old English prefixal system explains a groping around for other ways to mark aspect, as is clearly the case in the Middle English period, where we see all kinds of new aspectual structures appear and disappear. Something else that may support the suggestion of a relation between causation and perfective aspect is the frequent appearance in Middle English of constructions such as:

(165)a.   ...wiþ michel honoure, þat he hade *done made* in remembrance of þe Britons...

(*Brut*-1333 (RwlB.171) 64.31–65.1)

(other mss. have *done make* (D), *do made* (O))

b.   '...but God of his mercy/ And youre benyngne fader tendrely/ *Hath doon* yow kept.'

(*CT* IV.1096–8 [8: 1096–8])

c.   Item, I haue *do spoke* for yowr worstede,...

(Davis 1971–6: 192.126)

These constructions have been explained in a variety of ways. Ellegård (1953: 141ff.) believes that what is normally the infinitive donned the morphological appearance of *do* (i.e. both are past participle) by a process he calls 'attraction' or 'contamination'. For him the construction is a sign of the uneducated. This is strongly objected to by Mustanoja (1960: 605–6) and Davis (1972). Visser (1963–73: §1414a) interprets *do* here as anticipative *do*. This may be true in some cases, but Ellegård clearly shows that it does not account for all instances since the phenomenon occurs with other causative verbs. Royster (1918: 84) gives a hint to its true meaning. In his discussion of the causative nature of the Old English verb *hatan*, he writes, "the verb of causing predicates the accomplishment of an act that has been brought about by the exercise of an influence of some one or of some thing upon some person or some object. The causative verb affirms accomplished action; it is a perfective verb." He explains an Old English example where *hatan* is followed by a past participle rather than the expected infinitive (like the examples quoted above) as a mental process whereby the speaker has shifted his mind from the giving of the order (*hatan* + infinitive) to the accomplishment of it (*hatan* + past participle).

What makes the notion of a stage in which *do x* was perfective so attractive is the use Denison makes of it in connection with the regulation of periphrastic *do*. If *do* is perfective, it would co-occur with telic and punctual verbs. It would not be compatible with activity verbs and states. Denison checks this for the relevant examples and comes to the conclusion that it works for most of the *do x* constructions. If Denison's theory is correct, it would nicely explain the non-occurrence of *do* with the main verbs *be/have* and most of the auxiliaries (which are neither telic nor punctual), i.e. precisely those verbs that do not show *do*-support once *do* has become grammaticalised. Denison believes that this happened when *do x* became completely isolated due to the fact that both *do ac* was lost as well as the subjectless patterns of the other causative verbs. It was then that *do x* began to function (1985b: 55ff.) within the modal verb subsystem which it already resembled formally. As we have seen, Denison states that most of the *do x* constructions he has looked at can be interpreted aspectually as perfectives. He does not show the results of his investigation, but presumably examples like,

(166)a.　His menbres, þat he carf of: euer eft he dude misse, ...

(SLeg. (Ld) 45.380)

　　　b.　... and wulleth that if the seid Thomas paie or do paie to the seid Margaret yerly xviij li. ...

(Davis 1971–6: 229.39–40)

cannot be interpreted as having perfective aspect. Example (166a) is purely periphrastic (*misse* is not a telic verb), while (166b), to make sense, must be strictly causative. This would mean that Denison's putative development for *do x* from a loose causative to a (causative) perfective marker to a purely periphrastic verb (1985b: 55) may not be so clear-cut, because pure periphrastic *do* appears rather early and causative *do* is still found fairly late. There may after all be a case for Ellegård's subdivision of *do x* into three subtypes. The use of the pattern was strengthened by the presence of substitute *do*, which was in existence from earliest Old English and which also played a role in the modal subsystem, as can be seen from examples such as *I deny this and so does my employer, I can prove this and so can my employer*. Later on, then, the pattern could serve a new and useful function in interrogative and negative clauses, in which it would preserve (the new) SVO order (see section 4.8) whenever another auxiliary was not present to do so. To conclude, it is clear that there are still points to be settled and that further investigation is needed on the following: is there a stage at which *do* functions as a perfective marker; and, what account can be given for the loss of this perfective marker later on, for which Denison (1985b) does not offer an explanation?

A final remark should be made about the occurrence of *did do* (Ellegård 1953: 110–15) as in:

(167) Þe tresurer dyde do make a dich

(7 Sages (1) (Balliol) 1269)

(earlier manuscripts have single *do* or *let*)

This construction occurs very frequently in some late-fifteenth-century texts, notably in Caxton. Ellegård rejects the idea that the phrase is simply a double causative because the usefulness of such an expression must have been very restricted, and *did do* usually parallels simple *do* in other manuscripts of the same text. Also, the explanation that *did* is simply periphrastic with respect to *do*, which is causative, is not adequate because there are texts in which *did do* is frequent, but periphrastic *do* is almost non-occurrent. Ellegård finds that *did do* occurs mainly in eastern texts, where causative *do* is also used and periphrastic *do* is infrequent. For that reason he believes that writers like Caxton, who witnessed the rise of periphrastic *do* elsewhere, wished to emphasise the causative nature of *do*, when they used it, by doubling the verb. Once causative *do* was completely lost, the phrase had lost its usefulness, and not surprisingly it dies out very soon after its introduction. Ellegård's idea correlates with other phenomena found in Late Middle English texts (see Fischer forthcoming b) such as Malory's use of *make* or *let* in addition to *do* when *do* is used as a causative (a rare phenomenon in Malory):

(168) ..., and so thus he *ded lete* make and countirfete lettirs from the Pope, and *dede make* a straunge clarke to brynge tho lettyrs unto kynge Marke,...

(Malory *Wks* (Add.59678) 677: 27–9)

In Gower we find the order reversed, here *let* + *do* is used as a (single) causative,

(169) And so the vessel which for blod/ Was made, Silvestre.../ With clene water of the welle/ In allc haste he *let do* felle [= fill],/ And sette Constantin therinne/ Al naked up unto the chinne.

(*CA* ii.3445–50)

4.3.3.6 Sequencing of auxiliaries

Middle English can be characterised as the period in which the modern auxiliary system becomes established. Of special importance is the development of the perfect, realised by the auxiliaries *have* and *be* + past participle. Although this sequence occurred in Old English, *have* and *be* still behaved like full verbs in many ways. They could not be combined with other verbs such as 'progressive' *be*[13] and passive *be* that functioned partly as main verbs and partly as auxiliaries. It is surprising, however, that the auxiliary of the perfect did not combine with the modals in Old English, especially since passive and 'progressive' *be* are found with modals at that stage.[14] In Middle English perfect *have/be* develop into true auxiliaries functioning in the tense/(aspect) system and they freely combine with passive and 'progressive' *be* and with the modals. Thus, purely formally, the Modern English stage has almost been reached except that examples combining passive and 'progressive' *be* have not been attested so far in Middle English.

An interesting consequence of the grammaticalisation of the modals, which takes place all through the period (and beyond), is the new combination of two modals within the verb phrase. Visser's earliest examples (1963–73: §1685) are from the *Ormulum* (ca 1200):

(170) Þatt mannkinn shollde muȝhenn wel/ Upp cumenn inntill heoffne
(*Orm.* 3944–5)

'that mankind should well be able to go up to heaven'

Lightfoot (1979: 110) argues that this combination of modals was always possible and only became defunct in the mid-sixteenth century when the modals, as he claims, undergo the radical change from full verb to auxiliary (see also section 4.3.3.3). This presentation of events is most unlikely. All the instances in Visser (1963–73: §§1685, 2134) show that this combination occurs almost exclusively with the modal *shal*. Visser offers no explanation for this, but it is very likely that this is related to the fact that *shal* (much earlier than *wil*) became the auxiliary of future reference. As such it became grammaticalised and emptied of meaning (as part of the Middle English tense system) earlier than the other auxiliaries and could therefore more easily occur in combination with another modal verb.

The sequence in which the auxiliaries can occur within the verb phrase in Middle English is then more or less the same as the one we find in Present-Day English, except that passive and 'progressive' *be* cannot yet be combined. Further differences from Present-Day English are: (a) there may be more than one modal in the sequence and the modal can still occur as V, either by itself or in the form of a past or present participle (see the examples in (140) and (141)); (b) whereas in Present-

Day English only an adverb can be placed between the finite verb and the rest of the verb phrase, other sentence elements could still occur there in Middle English, especially pronouns (see also section 4.8):

(171)   lef me þ[et] ich mote þe treowliche luuien.

(St. Juliana (Roy) 25.244)

'allow me that I may thee truly love.'

Concerning the position of the infinitival verb with respect to the auxiliary, in Early Middle English (as in Old English) the infinitive was still often positioned before the auxiliary in subclauses, a feature typical of SOV languages. In the later periods it can still be preposed but only as a marked construction. Sanders (1915: 11ff.) shows that in Early Middle English texts (poetry and prose) the infinitive precedes the modal auxiliary in about 15 per cent of all occurrences in subclauses, against only about 2·5 per cent in main clauses. In later Middle English Aux–V becomes the norm everywhere in prose, in poetry we still find V–Aux, mainly for rhythmical or emphatic reasons. The same observations apply to the order of auxiliary and participle.

4.4   Questions

In this short section main as well as subordinate interrogative clauses will be discussed. Questions are of two types, they are either yes/no questions or wh-questions (see vol. I, section 4.5.9). Inversion of subject and finite verb is the rule in simple clauses of both types:

(172)a.   Woot ye nat where ther stant a litel toun...

(CT IX.1 [11: 1])

   b.   Hastow had fleen al nyght, or artow dronke?

(CT IX.17 [11: 17])

(173)   Why make ye youreself for to be lyk a fool?

(CT VII.980 [10: 980])

unless, as in Present-Day English, the wh-word is itself the subject. Although *do* is found (albeit rarely) in questions in Middle English, such constructions should probably not be interpreted as containing empty interrogative *do*; rather, they are the questioned counterpart of a clause already containing *do*. The first attested example is from Chaucer:

(174)   Fader, why do ye wepe?

(CT VII.2432 [10: 2728])

Only in the Early Modern English period is there a sharp rise in the occurrence of *do* in interrogative (and negative) sentences (for the introduction of *do*, see also section 4.3.3.5).

Rhetorical questions are often introduced by *what*:

(175)a. What nedeth it to sermone of it moore?

(*CT* VI.879 [9: 877])

b. What sholde I al day of his wo endite?

(*CT* I.1380 [1: 1382])

In Old English *hwæþer* could be used in simple interrogative clauses followed by normal word order in a rhetorical context (see vol. I, section 4.5.9). Examples of this seem to be extremely rare in Middle English; one instance is found in Chaucer's *Troilus and Criseyde* in a highly rhetorical passage. The verb is usually in the subjunctive because the construction as a rule is used as an expression of doubt:

(176) 'O Troilus, what dostow now?' she seyde./ 'Lord! wheyther thow yet thenke [subj.] upon Criseyde?'

(*Troilus* V.734–5)

Far more frequent is a construction with *whether* followed by inverted word order and the indicative mood in so-called alternative questions.

(177) Wheither seistow this in ernest or in pley?

(*CT* I.1125 [1: 1127])

Subordinate interrogative clauses occur in the same functions that complement clauses can occur in, i.e. as a complement to a noun phrase, as object of a verbal or adjectival predicate, as subject (but see section 4.6.2.1). Dependent interrogatives are found after nouns and predicates that are concerned with the truth value of the complementation, such as *ask*, *(not) know*, *(not) say*, *wonder*, *doubt*, etc. The usual subordinator in yes/no and alternative questions is *whe(the)r* (178) but *ʒif* is also found (179):

(178)a. I noot wher she be womman or goddesse,

(*CT* I.1101 [1: 1103])

b. ...of which he is in doute wheither he may parfourne it or noon.

(*CT* VII.1221 [10: 1221])

(179) She frayneth and she preyeth pitously.../ To telle hir if hir child wente oght forby.

(*CT* VII.600–2 [10: 600–2])

As a rule the subjunctive – or an appropriate auxiliary – is employed when there is an element of doubt or uncertainty.

Dependent wh-questions are introduced by the wh-element just as in simple clauses; this element can be an adverb (*where*, *how*, *why*, etc.) or an interrogative pronoun (independent or used attributively):

(180) But sikerly she nyste who was who,

(CT I.4300 [1 : 4292])

(181) Who coude wryte which a dedly cheere/ Hath Thisbe now, and how hire heer she rente,...

(LGW 869–70)

The mood in these clauses is as a rule the indicative.

4.5 Negation

Between the Old and the Middle English periods some important changes took place in the system of sentence negation. In Old English the negative adverb was *ne*, which was commonly placed before the finite verb (for more specific details see vol. I, section 4.5.10). Negation could also be expressed by indefinite pronouns such as *nan*, *naþing*, *næfre* 'none', 'nothing', 'never', but in that case the negative adverb *ne* was still usually present (this phenomenon is called multiple negation or negative concord). It was possible to use a more emphatic form of negation in Old English, 'by no means, not at all', by combining *ne* with *na* 'never' or *naht* (from *nawiht* 'nothing'). *Na* and *naht* could both precede and follow *ne* (see examples (249) and (255) in vol. I, ch. 4), although the latter is more frequent.

In Early Middle English the Old English emphatic negative *ne ... naht* (*na* disappears here quite quickly) begins to be used more and more frequently and can no longer be considered to be truly emphatic. Jack (1978b: 300) shows that in the earliest preserved text, the *Peterborough Chronicle*, the percentage of *ne ... naht* is still small (about 17 per cent) but that in the *Ancrene Wisse* the number has risen steeply to about 40 per cent. In Early Middle English *naht* has also acquired a fixed position; it now, practically without exception, follows *ne* and is placed after the finite verb. In the course of the Middle English period, *ne ... naht* (also ... *nat*, *nought*, *not*, etc.) becomes the regular negator. Because *ne* was now normally supported by *naht*, it could be dropped (cf. the similar dropping of *ne* in the combination *ne ... pas* in present-day colloquial French). This indeed was the situation in Late Middle English: *nat/not* has become the common negator, while *ne* (which still occurs – see below) and *ne ... not* have become infrequent (see Jack 1978a).

To some extent *ne...na(h)t* was still emphatic in the earliest texts, when its frequency compared to unsupported, unemphatic *ne* was quite low, but this changed rapidly. That it was originally emphatic can be deduced from the fact that *naht* is not normally found in combination with other emphatic negatives like *noon, never*; there, *ne* alone is the rule:

(182) ...ne beon ha   neauer se ancrefule ne se fulitohene,
            not are   they never so anxious nor so ill-disciplined,
       þe deouel of helle duteð ham swiðe
       the devil of hell fears them greatly

(Ancr. (Corp-C) 125.8–9)

'even if they are ever so anxious or ill-disciplined, the devil in hell fears them greatly.'

In fact, most of the positions in Middle English in which unsupported *ne* occurs can be explained with reference to this original distinction between *ne* and *ne...na(h)t*. Jack (1978b) shows that in Early Middle English *ne...na(h)t* predominates in declarative, optative and imperative clauses, while unsupported *ne* is the rule in interrogative clauses and clearly preferred with *but* 'only'. Some examples:

(183) Nis þis god foreward?

(Ancr. (Corp-C) 184.10)

'Is this not a good plan?

(184) cwench hit wið teares weater, & mid iesu cristes blod hwil hit nis [= ne + is] bute a sperke.

(Ancr (Corp-C) 153.6–8)

'quench it with the water of tears and with the blood of Jesus Christ while it is [still] only a spark.'

In Late Middle English *no(gh)t* has become the rule, but there are some texts of the southeastern region (notably Chaucer's prose and contemporary London documents (see Jack 1978a)) where *ne...not* and unsupported *ne* are still regularly used. At first sight it looks as if *ne* and *ne...not* were on the whole simply alternatives except that *ne...not* was more frequently found when *ne* could be cliticised to an auxiliary (see vol. I, section 4.5.10), especially *is*:[15]

(185) Ther nys nat oon kan war by other be.

(Troilus I.203)

while *not* alone was used after the conjunction *ne* 'nor', presumably in order to avoid the rather awkward *ne|ne*.

The distribution of *ne*, however, is significant and correlates with the use of *ne* in Early Middle English. Again *ne* is the rule with other negatives such as *non, never* (supported *ne*). Unsupported *ne* is found with the (negative) adverb *but* and in complement clauses following a negative or interrogative clause (compare the use of *ne* in interrogative main clauses in Early Middle English):

(186) For ther nys no creature so good that hym ne wanteth somewhat of the perfeccioun of God,...

(*CT* VII.1080 [10 : 1080])

The subclause in (186) in fact contains a positive statement (i.e. every creature, however good he is, *does* lack something in comparison to God's perfection). The presence of negative *ne* there should be seen as a case of negative concord due to the negative character of the main clause. An interrogative clause, too, very often carries negative implications. This is clear, for instance, from the fact that in Present-Day English the indefinite pronouns *any, anything, anywhere*, etc. are used in interrogative as well as negative clauses rather than *some, something, somewhere* in use in positive statements.

Other types of clause in which unsupported *ne* occurs are rather similar: it is found in inherently negative situations (i.e. contexts which are semantically negative and therefore may dispense with an explicit negator; for a list of these see Klima 1964) such as comparative clauses (see (187)), conditional clauses (188), after verbs like *douten, denyen, forsaken*, etc. (189), after *lest* (190).

(187)a. And thanne al the derknesse of his mysknowynge shall [schewen] more evydently to the sighte of his undirstondynge *then* the sonne *ne* semeth to the sighte withoute-forth.

(*Bo*.III m.11, 24–7)

Notice in this connection also the sporadic use of *na/nor* for *than* (still found in some Present-Day English dialects):

(187)b. And the lest party of thame twa/ Wes starkar fer na he and ma

(Barbour *Bruce* vi, 537–38)

'And the lesser party of the two was far stronger than him and more'

(188)a. *If* God *ne* kepe the citee, in ydel waketh he that it kepeth.

(*CT* VII.1304 [10 : 1304])

b. &, *nad it be* for drede of our lord the kyng, I wot wel eueri man sholde haue be in others top. [= attacking one another]

(Chambers & Daunt 1931 : 28.169–71)

(189)a. ...that no man *douteth* that he *ne* is strong in whom he seeth strengthe.

(*Bo*.II pr.6, 95–6)

b. *Denyestow*...that alle schrewes *ne ben* worthy to han torment?

(*Bo*.IV pr.4, 224–5)

(190)   ... ther bihoveth greet corage agains Accidie, *lest* that it *ne* swolwe
the soule by the synne of sorwe, or [!] destroye it by wanhope.

(*CT* X.731 [12: 731])

In all these instances, then, the presence of unsupported *ne* can be
explained as a case of negative concord, i.e. *ne* is induced by the
(implicit) negative already present.[16] The situation is thus similar to the
regular use of supported *ne* in Old English and (although already less so)
in Middle English in combination with another negative element in the
clause:

(191)   And therfore he, .../ Nolde *nevere* write in none of his sermons/ Of
swiche unkynde abhomynacions, ...

(*CT* II.86–8 [3: 86–8])

The following example shows that not only unsupported *ne* is employed
in these cases but also other negative adverbs or indefinite pronouns
(Present-Day English usually has their antonyms here):

(192)   For, be we *never* so vicious withinne,/ We wol been holden wise
and clene of synne.

(*CT* III.943–4 [2: 943–4])

'For, even if we are ever so vicious within, we want to be considered
wise and clear of sin.'

See also (182) above.

We have seen that in the course of the Middle English period *ne*
begins to disappear. Phonologically, it is a weak element. It can be
dropped because it is now normally supported by *not*. The disappearance
of *ne* in the combination *ne ... not* is soon followed by the disappearance
of unsupported *ne* in the instances discussed in (187), (189) and (190).
The situation is different in the conditionals (188) and the interrogatives.
Here, depending on the way the question or condition was phrased, the
clause became either overtly negative or positive. In the former case *ne*
was replaced by *not*; in the latter case, *ne* was left out. For example,
Baghdikian (1979: 678) gives an example of a conditional clause in the
Latin text of *Boethius*, which contains a negative in Chaucer's translation,
while it is positive in Queen Elizabeth's version. The explanation why
ne rather than (*ne ...*) *not* was employed in (187)–(190) is now also fairly
straightforward: emphatic *not* was from the very beginning not used in
cases where another negative was already present (whether overt or
implicit).

The disappearance of *ne* precipitates the corrosion of multiple
negation. Clauses like the one in (191) in Late Middle English vie with
clauses without *ne*. The next step in this process will not be taken until

the Modern English period, i.e. it is still normal in Middle English, when two or more indefinite pronouns or adverbs are present, for them all to be negative rather than for the negative element to be attached to the first indefinite in the clause (or expressed by *not* when present) as is the case in Present-Day English. Thus, Chaucer still writes,

> (193) But *nevere* gronte he at *no* strook but oon,...
>
> (CT VII.2709 [10: 2613])

where Present-Day English would prefer 'but he *never* groaned at *any* of the blows except one...'. In Middle English the use of *any* etc. is still confined to implicit negative contexts (as defined above), it does not as a rule occur in explicit negative clauses.[17] Therefore, where Present-Day English has *not ... anything, not ... ever*, etc., Middle English normally (and this usage persists into the seventeenth and eighteenth century) has *nothing, never*:

> (194) He was despeyred; no thyng dorste he seye,
>
> (CT V.943 [6: 235])

The distribution of negative elements in co-ordinate constructions follows more or less the same patterns. It also shows similar developments as far as negative concord is concerned. Thus, when the initial clause is affirmative and the second clause negative, the conjunction *ne/neither* rather than expected (from a Present-Day English point of view) *and/or* can be used. This is especially common in the so-called AB language[18] and in Chaucer's *Boece* (see Jack 1978a, c). What has happened is that the conjunction is attracted into the sphere of the second clause by negative concord. In the following instance, however, the conjunction is negative because, although the first clause looks positive, it is really implicitly negative:[19]

> (195) But securly þo þat lie in dedely synne, noþur amendes hem not by confession hastely, Crist woll not dwell with hem
>
> (ME Sermons 285.8–10)

When both clauses are negative the usual connector is *ne*:

> (196) Lifte not vp youre horne on hiȝe ne speke ȝe no wickenes aȝeyns God
>
> (ME Sermons 68.25–6)

but *and* (showing the absence of negative concord) is also found, especially towards the end of the period:

> (197) For of þat werke þat falliþ to only God dar I not take upon me to speke wiþ my blabryng fleschely tonge; &, schortly to say, al-þof I durst, I wolde not.
>
> (Cloud (Hrl 674) 62.19–21)

Notice, however, that here an infinitive construction and a subclause intervene between the two co-ordinate clauses.

Jack (1978c) draws attention to constructions like (198) and (199):

(198) wið eise & wið este ne buð me nawt blisse

(Ancr. (Corp-C) 220.15–16)

'through ease and pleasure one does not buy bliss'

(199) & makeð þe heorte schir & of briht sihðe, þt nan ne mei habben
wið monglunge of unþeawes, ne wið eorðlich luue of worltliche
þinges.

(Ancr. (Corp-C) 196.22–4)

'and make the heart shining and bright which no one may possess who is contaminated by vices or has earthly love of worldly objects.'

Example (198) looks like a counter-example to the general rule stated above. Notice, however, that in (198) & conjoins two NPs, i.e. *eise* and *este*, and not two clauses. For (199) to make sense it must be clear that *ne* does not conjoin the two noun phrases but rather two clauses, in the second of which the verb is deleted. So *ne* is the conjunction 'nor', which one would expect here since both clauses are negative.

Instances of negative raising (*I don't think it is true* instead of *I think that it is not true*) are not yet very frequent in Middle English but some examples can be found:

(200) He thenkith nought that evere he shall/ Into ony syknesse fall.

(Rose 5621–2)

The following instance looks like a case of negative concord rather than negative raising (see vol. I, section 4.5.10):

(201) … amonges thise thynges *I ne trowe nat* that the pris and the grace of the peple nys neyther worthi to ben remembred, ne cometh of wys jugement, …

(Bo.III pr.6, 27–31)

4.6   Composite sentences

Traditionally, a distinction is made between complex sentences and compound sentences, the former comprising a combination of a main clause and a (number of) subclause(s) (here discussed in the subsection on subordination), the latter consisting of main clauses only (discussed in the subsection on co-ordination). Purely formally, this distinction works fairly well for Middle English (as it does for Present-Day English) in contrast to Old English. In Old English it is not always clear whether a conjunctive element functions as an adverb or a conjunction in any given clause, and consequently whether that clause is used dependently or independently. In many cases, however, word order and/or the use of the subordinating particle þe help to decide the matter (see vol. I, section 4.5). In Early Middle English some of this Old English 'vagueness' is still present, e.g. in the use of correlative constructions like þa... þa, þonne... þonne, 'then... when' and swa... swa, 'so... so', but this is rapidly replaced by a more transparent system, in which conjunctions are distinct from adverbs. Word order no longer plays an important role in Middle English since the tendency was for all clauses (main and subclauses) to have the same word order (see section 4.8). Thus in early texts, we can still come across examples like the following:

(202) And *so* hi were in þo ssipe, *so* a-ros a great tempeste of winde

(Ken.Serm. (Ld) 32.14–15)

'and when they were in the boat, a big storm got up'

(203) & Đat oþer dei *þa* he lai an slep in scip, *þa* þestrede þe dæi ouer al landes...

(PC (Ld) an.1135; 54.2–3)

'and the next day, when he lay asleep in the boat, (then) it became dark everywhere in the country...'

(204) *Þanne* he com *þenne* he were bliþe,...

(Havelok (Ld) 778)

'when he came, [then] they were glad'

Notice that word order still plays a role, at least in the first two examples, which show inversion of subject and verb in the main clause but not in the subclause.

In later texts the correlative adverb is often dropped or one of the two conjunctives is replaced by another different in form. Thus for example in Chaucer, *tho* (< OE *þa*) no longer functions as a conjunction, only as an adverb; and the same is true for *þonne/þenne*. There is just one exception:[20]

(205) For which I seye, if that yow list to heere/ Moralitee and vertuous mateere,/ And *thanne* that ye wol yeve me audience/ I wol...

(CT X.37–40 [12:37–40])

but notice that here the conjunction *thanne* is accompanied by the subordinator *that* (the role of *that* will be discussed in the subsection on subordination). Normally, Chaucer uses *whan (that)* (< OE *hwænne*, an interrogative adverb) with or without a correlative in the main clause:

(206) Thanne rekke I noght, whan I have lost my lyf,...

(CT I.2257 [I: 2259])

Likewise *though/þeih/þah* can still function as adverbs as well as conjunctions in early texts:

(207) Ich wat þah to soðe þ[et] ich schal bituhen ham neomen deaðes
wunde.

(Ancr. (Corp-C) 199.11–12)

'Yet I know for certain that among them I shall receive death's wound.'

(208) þah ich ȝeue poure al þ[et] ich hefde, ȝef ich nefde luue þerwið, to
godd, ... al were i spillet,

(Ancr. (Corp-C) 196.13–15)

'although I give to the poor all that I have – if I do not do it out of love for God, ... all would be in vain'

but in Chaucer *though* has become almost exclusively a conjunction. An example of adverbial usage is:

(209) And thogh wherto? For trewely/ I holde that wyssh nat worth a
stree!

(BD 670–1)

An adverbial value for *though* does survive in Present-Day English, e.g. *It is clear though that ...*

In one other respect we can see a development towards more clarity and greater explicitness in the system of complex clauses. In Old English the conjunctions, or rather conjunctive phrases, were of a rather general nature usually consisting of a preposition followed by a demonstrative pronoun and the relative marker or subordinator *þe* (*for þæm þe* etc.; see the subsection on subordination, pp. 293–5, for the status of this *þe*). Consequently, the same phrase could be used in a range of semantic types of clauses, and each type of subclause could be represented by quite a number of phrases. This becomes more streamlined in Middle English when the conjunctive phrases become fossilised and their applicability is narrowed down.

As was said above, formally it is usually not difficult in Middle English to separate main clauses from subclauses (for asyndetic relative clauses, which can be interpreted as subjectless main clauses, see section 4.6.1.1). Quite often, however, a co-ordinate clause may well be subordinate semantically. Although this is true for Present-Day English as well, this remark is more relevant for the older stages of the language, for Old English even more than for Middle English. At that time the written language often presented ideas paratactically where written Present-Day English would use subordination (hypotaxis). In Old and

Middle English the written language was still closer to the spoken language, which has always made heavier use of parataxis than of hypotaxis (see Phillipps 1966a; Leith 1983: 112). It is only at the end of the Middle English period, with the development of a written standard, that the written language begins to make more extensive use of complex structures, under the influence of both French and Latin prose styles (see Fisher 1977). Here follow some instances of such paratactic structures:

(210) and ek wondit so,/ *And* in his syd ware brokyne Ribys two.

(Launc. 2729–30)

'and also so wounded *that* two ribs were broken in his side'

(211) Now, or I fynde a man thus trewe and stable,/ *And* wol for love his deth so frely take,/ I preye God let oure hedes nevere ake!

(LGW 702–4)

'now, before I find a man so true and loyal, *who* will...'

Similarly, we see that subordinators which are associated with certain types of syntactic subclauses sometimes occur with another type of clause, thus giving it an extra semantic colouring:

(212) Mercy me meuyþ by her praier.../ forr of that wrecche I haue pyte...

(Cursor (Ffr) 9738–40)

'Mercy moves me with her prayer because/that I have pity on that wretch'

Here *for* is used instead of *that* because the clause denotes reason in this context. It is also possible that the conjunction *for* is used because it resembles the preposition *for*, in which case purpose or result may have been intended.

Another consequence of the proximity of written and spoken language is the high frequency of so-called anacolutha, sentences which are 'illogically' constructed from a purely formal point of view:

(213) The reule of Seint Maure or of Seint Beneit –/ By cause that it was old and somdel streit/ This ilke Monk leet olde thynges pace,...

(CT I.173–5 [1: 173–5])

In this example the first line – the syntactic object of *leet pace* – has been left dangling since a new object *olde thynges* is introduced later. We have no difficulty in understanding what is said. These anacolutha may also be used for special stylistic effect (see Fischer 1985: 218), as is the case in the above example.

Likewise, we often come across constructions that contain elements which look pleonastic in modern written English.

(214) Thanne dame Prudence, whan that she saugh how that hir housbonde shoop hym for to wreken hym on his foes and to bigynne werre, *she* in ful humble wise, whan she saugh hir tyme, seyde...

(CT VII.1050 [10: 1050])

'Then lady Prudence, when she saw how her husband prepared himself to take revenge on his foes and to start a fight, [she] very humbly, when she saw an opportunity, said...'

or examples such as (215), where the subject pronoun of *casten* has been left out in spite of the fact that there is no syntactic antecedent. The context, of course, makes clear that the subject is the people of the *town* (of Troy), which has been mentioned before,

(215) Gret rumour gan, whan it was first aspied/ Thorugh al the town, and generaly was spoken,/ That Calkas traitour fled was and allied/ With hem of Grece, and casten to be wroken/ On hym...

(Troilus I.85–9)

In this section, we will only be concerned with relations of clauses *within* the sentence. It must be clear, however, that the expression of causal, adversative, consecutive, etc. relations does not take place on the level of the sentence only, but also for a large part on discourse level. Adverbial linkage (by means of adverbs like *so*, *therefore*, etc.) and clause-integrated linkage (*that's why*..., *the result was*...) will be left out of account.

CO-ORDINATE CLAUSES

Looking at co-ordination from a purely syntactic point of view, one may distinguish three types: syndetic, asyndetic and polysyndetic co-ordination. Syndetic co-ordination comprises clauses with overt conjunctions, the most usual type. In asyndetic clauses the conjunction has been omitted; this is mainly a question of style:

(216) No wonder is, he herde it al the day;

(CT I.641 [1: 643])

(217) Thow farst by love as oules doon by light:/ The day hem blent, ful wel they se by night.

(PF 599–600)

In the first example *for* could be added, in the second *for* as well as *but*. In asyndetic constructions it was also possible to leave out the personal pronoun in the second clause. This is especially frequent in the colloquial language of the mystery plays:

(218) Greatte mystis, sir, ther is both morn and noyn,/ [θ] byte vs full bytterly;

      (Towneley Pl. (Hnt) 73.286–7)

(219) I was bowne to by store,/ [θ] drofe my shepe me before,...

      (Towneley Pl. (Hnt) 104.130–1)

      'I was on my way to buy provisions, drove my sheep before me'

For (218) it could also be argued that it is the relative pronoun that is left out (see also section 4.6.1.1).

Polysyndetic clauses, in which all connections are overtly expressed, are more frequent in the spoken language than in the written (see Poutsma 1929: 550). This may be one of the reasons why they occur more frequently in Middle English than in Present-Day English texts:

(220) & for the grete lust þat he had to hire he wente in the nyght vnto hire tombe & opened it & went in & lay be hire and wente his wey.

      (Mandev. (Tit) 16.29–17.1)

Semantically, one can broadly distinguish three types of co-ordination. The first is copulative co-ordination, expressed in Middle English by *and*, occasionally *ac*, the negative *ne* (rarely *nor*) and the correlative conjunctions *both...and*; *ne...ne*, *neither...ne/nor/neither*. Below follow some examples with the more unusual conjunctions:

(221) he wes Arðures mæi, of aðelen his cunne/ ah cniht he wes wunder god.

      (Brut (Clg) 12713–14)

      'he was Arthur's kinsman, of his noble race, and he was an exceedingly good knight.'

(222) And also the Sarazines bryngen forth no pigges nor þei eten no swynes flessch,

      (Mandev. (Tit) 47.17–19)

The co-ordinate conjunctions link not only clauses but also parts of the clause such as noun phrases, adjective phrases, adverbial adjuncts, etc. The correlatives *both...and* usually link smaller constituents, only rarely do they combine two clauses. In (223), for instance, *both...and* does not combine two clauses but co-ordinates two nouns functioning as the antecedents of relative clauses:

(223) For *bothe* I hadde thyng which that I nolde,/ *And* ek I nadde that thyng that I wolde.

      (PF 90)

Second is adversative co-ordination, in Middle English expressed by *ac* (especially in older texts), *but*, *or/oþer* and the correlative conjunctions *either … o(þe)r*, *o(þe)r … o(þe)r*.

(224) For either mot I have yow in my cheyne/ Or with the deth ye mote depart us tweyne;

(Anel&Arc.284–5)

Finally, there is causal (also called illative) co-ordination, introduced by *for* and *forhwi*,

(225) And atte laste the feend, oure enemy,/ Putte in his thought that he sholde poyson beye,/ … *For-why* the feend foond hym in swich lyvynge/ That he hadde leve him to sorwe brynge.

(CT VI.844–8 [9: 842–6])

Forhwi can also still be used in Middle English as an adverb in the sense of 'therefore' (see *Troilus* II.12). *For* is also employed as a subordinating conjunction. Jespersen (1909–49: part V, 392) believed that subordinate *for* was earlier than co-ordinate *for*. However, the earliest examples containing *for* (it does not really occur before the twelfth century, but see Mitchell 1985: §3037) show that it could already have both functions:

(226) ac hit naht ne beheld, for se biscop of Særesbyrig wæs strang…

(PC (Ld) an.1123; 43.30–1)

'but it had no effect because the bishop of Salisbury was powerful'

(227) Alle he wæron forsworen & here treothes forloren, for æuric rice man his castles makede & agænes him heolden;

(PC (Ld) an.1127; 55.13–14)

'They were all forsworn and their oaths broken for every great man built himself castles and held [them] against him'

It is not always easy to distinguish between the two types of conjunction. In general, it can be said that subordinate *for* introduces clauses which give the cause or reason for an event mentioned in the main clause; as such it has a close connection with the main clause. Co-ordinate *for* introduces a clause which amplifies or explains the reason for a statement contained in the main clause. It is therefore much more loosely connected with the main clause, and must necessarily follow that clause. This also explains why co-ordinate *for* sometimes expresses purpose or result as well as cause as in:

(228) no man hire mete ne 3af ne drunch… for heo scholde to heore lawe hire þou3t tuyrne.

(SLeg. (Ld) 97.171–2)

'no one gave her either food or drink for/ so that she should turn her mind to their law.'

That *for* (which is presumably an elliptic form of OE *for þæm* (*þe*)) already had both functions in Middle English is not surprising since its ancestor in Old English also functioned in both ways (for examples and discussion see Mitchell 1985: §§ 3014ff.; vol. I, section 4.5.5).

Of these three types of co-ordinators, *and* is the most neutral one for linking clauses together. It has already been shown above that *and* can be used in Middle English where Present-Day English would normally employ a subordinating conjunction. Likewise, in co-ordinate use, *and* frequently occurs where Present-Day English would prefer a more explicit co-ordinator. In the following instance *and* has adversative meaning:

> (229) and thou, Virgine wemmelees,/ Baar of thy body – and dweltest mayden pure –/ The Creatour of every creature.
>
> (*CT* VIII.47–9 [7: 47–9])
>
> 'and you, spotless Virgin, gave birth – and [yet] remained a pure maiden – to the creator of every creature.

Normally, in Present-Day English as well as in Middle English, the subject of the co-ordinate clause is omitted if it is co-referential with the subject of the main clause. However, the omission of the subject was more extensive in Middle English (as it was in Old English). This may be a left-over from the time when the inflection on the verb made a pronominal subject less necessary; or, more likely, it may be a result of the greater looseness of syntax, which is characteristic of the Old and Middle English written language. In Middle English it was possible to leave out the subject when it was co-referential with a (noun phrase that is part of a) possessive phrase (231), with a prepositional phrase or with a noun phrase that functions as (in)direct object (230),

> (230) His modir him baþede in þe water of helle,/ And [θ] was honged by þe feet & þries deopped adown/ Body and blod, hed and croun,/ Bote þeo soles of his feet/ Þer his modir hondes seet.
>
> (*Siege Troy(1)* (LinI) 1345–9)
>
> (231) ... By cause that he was hire neighebour,/ And was a man of worshipe and honour,/ And [θ] hadde yknowen hym of tyme yoore,...
>
> (*CT* V.961–3 [6: 253–5])
>
> 'because he was her neighbour and [he] was an honourable man and [she] had known him for a long time,...'

The subject can even be understood from a *by*-phrase in a passive construction which is not expressed:

(232)   A Cloþ bi foren him was drawe/ And ȝaf him wyn...

(*Greg.Leg.* (Vern) 1162–4)

'A cloth was laid before him and [they] gave him wine'

SUBORDINATE CLAUSES

In this subsection we will address the status of the complementisers *þe* and *þat*, frequent in many types of subordinate clause. In the section following, the subordinate clauses themselves will be considered, finite as well as non-finite. Special attention will be given to the relative clause, which underwent a number of important changes in this period, notably the introduction of interrogative pronouns as relative pronouns. Further, there will be extensive discussion of non-finite complement types; especially the use of the bare versus the *to*-infinitive and the emergence of new complement types such as the *for NP to V* construction. A final section will deal with the various types of adverbial clauses, the conjunctions introducing them and the choice of mood in each type.

Þe and *þat*, originally both deictic markers, developed from the same Germanic root. They were used as complementisers in Old and Middle English, but in Middle English *þe* gradually gives way to *þat*. Any explanation of this development depends heavily on the syntactic status one assigns to *þe* in Old English (for the various theories see vol. I, section 4.5.3.1). Geoghegan (1975), for instance, argues that the Old English complementiser *þe* is not a relative particle but a marker of subordination, which introduces many types of subordinate clause. It has the same status therefore as OE *þæt*, which also introduces subordinate clauses. The explanation for the replacement of *þe* by *þat* in Middle English is then relatively simple: because *þe* in Middle English acquired too many functions (it was by then also used as a definite article), it became ambiguous and disappeared in favour of *þat*.

On the other hand, Kivimaa (1966) and Allen (1977) (and see also Mustanoja (1960) and most traditional accounts) believe that OE *þe* was basically a relative particle.[21] It does appear in other types of subordinate clause but these are almost all of the type introduced by *for þæm þe, mid þæm þe*, etc. According to Allen, these conjunctive phrases consist of a preposition followed by a demonstrative pronoun, which acts as the antecedent of relative *þe* introducing the clause. The demonstrative pronoun is usually in the dative case because most Old English prepositions govern the dative. Prepositions governing an accusative, such as *þurh* 'through' or *oð* 'until' are followed by the accusative demonstrative form, i.e. *þæt*, which in turn is followed by the relative pronoun. This is *þæt* rather than *þe*, because that is the more usual relative after demonstrative *þæt* (see McIntosh 1948). Thus we find *þurh þæt þæt*, *oþ þæt þæt* usually simplified to *þurh þæt*, *oþ þæt* (for examples see Allen 1977: 134). Thus, the argument runs that in Old English *þe* and *þæt* are kept apart: *þe* functions strictly as a relative particle; *þæt* is used as a subordinator in non-relative subclauses (especially clauses of purpose and result and content or complement clauses).

We saw that the demonstrative pronoun *þæt* can also be used as a relative pronoun. There are only sporadic uses of *þæt* as relative particle in Late Old English (see vol. I, section 4.5.2.1). There are some exceptions to this statement in that *þæt* is also found in some conjunctive phrases in which *þe* is normally used, notably in *to þon þæt*, *for þæm þæt*. Interestingly enough, these phrases all introduce consecutive clauses in which *þæt* alone is normally the complementiser (cf., in contrast, *for þæm þe*, which introduces almost exclusively *causal* clauses in Old English). The use of *þæt* here rather than expected *þe* can therefore be explained as a kind of analogy. (There are a few more minor exceptions, but most of these can be accounted for; see Kivimaa 1966: 160ff.; Allen 1977: 139ff.)

It is clear then that if *þe* is a relative particle rather than a general subordinator, the explanation for its displacement by *þat* given by Geoghegan does not work. The development must have been roughly as follows:

1   due to the loss of case forms and grammatical gender the relative pronoun most frequent in Late Old English and Early Middle English was the neuter form *that* (*þæt*);

2   *that* was the new relative particle developed from the demonstrative pronoun;

3   *that* and *þe* co-occurred as relative particles side by side for some time, with *þe* finally giving way to *that* presumably because (a) *þe* was phonologically rather weak; moreover, it was now primarily used as a definite article (from earlier *se* with *þ-* analogically extended from other forms in the paradigm); and (b) *that* already occurred as a subordinator in other types of subclauses and in conjunctive phrases (see above).

Kivimaa (1966: 248) shows that the earlier conjunctive phrases with *þe* generally lost *þe* in the twelfth century and began to be found with *that* only in the thirteenth century. The scenario therefore is not that *þe* was *replaced* by *that*; rather, *that*, by now the general subordinator, becomes added, as a kind of pleonastic element, to all kinds of conjunctions. Thus we find in Middle English, *now that*, *(g)if that*,[22] *when that*, and after prepositions (prepositions not encountered in Old English conjunctive phrases) *before that*, *save that*, *in that*, etc.

Another reason which makes the theory that the subordinator *þe* is replaced by the subordinator *that* in Middle English unlikely is the evidence provided by McIntosh (1948), Kivimaa (1966) and Jack (1975) in their articles on the use of *þe* versus *that* in some Middle English dialects. If it were true that *þe* is simply replaced by *that*, one would not expect neat patterns such as they encountered. They find that the relative particle *þe* is found mostly with animate antecedents, to distinguish it from *that*, which normally follows inanimate heads.[23] Connected with this is the preference of *þe* to *that* when it functions as the subject of the clause; this is most frequently animate. Further, *þe* is used with *in*animate plurals, where it is the reduced form of Old English plural *þa*. And finally, *that* is often used with animate antecedents precisely in those places where Old English tended to use the *se*, *seo*, *þæt* sequence, e.g. after personal names and indefinite pronouns like *al*, *an*, *lut* 'little'. This last point clearly shows that this Middle English *that* is a development of the Old English demonstrative relativiser and does not represent the Old English subordinator *þæt*. More details about the use of *that* will be given in the sections following.

4.6.1   Relative clauses

4.6.1.1   Finite relative clauses

For Present-Day English it is possible to set up a system for relative clauses to explain the choice of relative marker (*who*, *which*, *that*) in most instances (see Quirk 1957). Basically, two parameters are at work: the animacy parameter and the 'information' parameter. The first decides the choice of *who* (*whom*, *whose*[24]) against *that*, *which*[25]; the former being used strictly with a personal antecedent, the latter with inanimate antecedents (but see also below). The information parameter distinguishes between so-called restrictive and non-restrictive clauses. In the first, the information given in the relative clause particularises the antecedent, while in the second the information given is additional; it does not serve to delimit the potential referents of the antecedent. *That* is the prototypical relativiser in restrictive clauses, which can overrule the animacy parameter by replacing *who* after a personal antecedent. *That* is barred from non-restrictive clauses; here *who* and *which* are used in accordance with the animacy parameter.

Matters are less well defined in Middle English. In the corresponding chapter on Old English it was shown that there is a tendency for *þe* to appear in restrictive clauses and *se* (*þe*) etc. in non-restrictive ones. The reason for this may be that the antecedent of a restrictive clause typically contains a demonstrative pronoun so that the weakened deictic marker *þe* was enough to establish the link between the antecedent and the relative particle that is co-referential with it. The animacy parameter was less relevant for Old English, which had grammatical gender.

In Middle English the Old English system collapses, due to the gradual loss of *þe* and the replacement of the paradigm *se, seo, þæt* by indeclinable *that*. In some Early Middle English texts remnants of the *se, seo, þæt* system are still found, often with analogical *þ-* rather than *s-*, but these are regular only in rewritings of Old English texts (see Allen 1977: 197ff.). Kivimaa's detailed study of the distribution of *þe* and *þat* in Early Middle English (Kivimaa 1966) shows that *þe* is more frequent than *þat* in south and southeast midland texts in the twelfth century, while in northeast midland texts (e.g. in the *Ormulum*) *þat* is the usual form. From the north *þat* rapidly spreads to the other dialects, and in the thirteenth century *þat* (also *þet*) is the rule everywhere. The only exceptions are southwestern and especially west midland texts, where *þe* is found next to *þat* much longer, where the influence of the West Saxon 'Schriftsprache' was still strong in some of the scriptoria.

All this means that in the thirteenth century *that* stood practically alone as a relativiser. Consequently, it was used in restrictive as well as non-restrictive clauses, with animate as well as inanimate antecedents. *That* was also used in Old English and Early Middle English to refer to a clause (see Mustanoja 1960: 190; this usage can still be found in Early Modern English) but was gradually replaced in Early Middle English by *what* and in Late Middle English by *which*. This was presumably part of the development in which *that* became confined to restrictive clauses. The beginnings of this latter development can be seen in Middle English, but it took place mainly outside our period (see Mustanoja 1960: 196–7).

The use of wh-relatives (*whom, whose, what, (the) which (that)*) dates, it is true, from the beginning of the Middle English period, but they are very rare everywhere in the twelfth century, and rare enough in the thirteenth. *Which* is at first highly infrequent; *whom* and *whose* less so. They are more often found in non-restrictive clauses. *Whom* and *which* are generally preceded by a preposition (for this restriction in their use see also below). *Which* is found with both animate and inanimate antecedents, *whom* and *whose* mainly with animate ones.[26] *Which* begins to supplant *that* only in the fifteenth century. In the fourteenth century *that* remains the usual relative, especially in poetry; in the more formal prose *which* is somewhat more current. Chaucer, for instance, still uses *that* in 75 per cent of all cases; in Caxton the use of *that* has been reduced to 50 per cent (see Mustanoja 1960: 197ff.).

In Old English the wh-pronouns (*hwa, hwæt, hwylc*) were not used as relative pronouns. The use of *hwæt* after *eall* in Old English looks like an exception, but most examples can be explained interpreting the *hwæt*-clause as being in apposition to *eall* (see Karlberg 1954: 63; Mitchell 1985: §360):

(233) nu ic wot æall hwæt þu woldest

(Solil.2 57.9)

'now I know all, [I know] what you wanted'

The earliest instances of wh-pronouns preceded by an antecedent are from Early Middle English:

(234) Ac he hafde many wimmen hi-hafd to his bedde,/ Bi woche he hadde on liue twenti sones bliþe,

(Brut (Otho) 1343–4)

'But he had had many women as his bedfellow, by whom he had alive twenty blithe sons'

(235) Þatt Jesu Crist wass witerrli/ Þatt illke, off whamm profetess/ Haffdenn forr lannge cwiddedd ær,/ Þatt...

(Orm. 6994–7)

'That Jesus Christ was clearly the same [man] about whom prophets had for a long time said that...'

(236) All þatt ȝho sahh & herrde off Crist,/ Whas moderr ȝho wass wurrþenn.

(Orm. 3424–5)

'all that she saw and heard about Christ whose mother she had become'

The development of an interrogative pronoun into a relative pronoun is in itself not an unusual process; it is well attested in a number of other

Germanic and Romance languages. A point of contact is the use of interrogative pronouns in indirect questions such as *She asked who struck him*. Here the nature of *who* is still clearly interrogative because of the verb *ask*. But in *They knew who did it* or *They wanted to know who did it* the function of *who* comes very close to a so-called free relative, also called independent or headless relative ('the one who') or to a generalising relative ('whoever'). It is difficult to keep generalising and independent relatives apart. A generalising relative can often be interpreted as an independent relative and vice versa, but the following Present-Day English example shows that this is not always so. In *After what you have told me, you ought to see a doctor*, *what* can only be an independent relative.

In Old English the wh-pronoun (*hw*-pronoun would be more appropriate) is normally found in clear indirect questions, just as the wh-conjunction (*hwæþer*) is used for introducing interrogative sentential complements:

(237)   ... þa acsode he hwa ðær ferde.

(ÆCHom.I, 10 152.11)

'then he asked who went there.'

After verbs like *know*, *wonder*, *see*, etc. usage varies in Old English. In texts translated from Latin wh-pronouns are quite common, but wh-pronouns also occur when there is no (wh-pronoun in the) Latin source, as in (238). Otherwise, the common Old English independent (free) relative *se þe* is used – see (239) (see vol. I, section 4.5.2.3) or *þæt* by itself – see (240).

(238)a.   Ic wundrige swiðe ungemetlice hwæt þe sy?

(Bo. 5.12.24)

'I wonder very much what [the matter with] you is?'

  b.   and hi sceolon geseon æt ðam micclan dome hwæne hi gewundodon

(ÆCHom.II, 15 159.317)

'and they shall see at the Last Judgement whom they wounded'

(239)   ... waldon gesea ðaðe gie geseað

(Lk. (WSCp) 111)

'... wanted to see what you saw'

(240)   Eala, hu manful man.þu eart, ðu ðe wast þæt þu æfter axsast

(Ap.T 7.12)

'Alas, what a wicked man you are, you who know what you ask for'

The wh-form was also frequently used in constructions following *nabban/habban* (see Karlberg 1954: 48ff.), which show independence of Latin:

(241) for ðan ic leng næbbe   hwæt ic on his lacum aspende
      because I long not-have what I in his service could spend

(ÆLS (Lucy) 66)

'because for some time I have had nothing to spend in his service'

Here, *hwæt* stands somewhere between its use as an indefinite pronoun (another common use of wh-words in Old English – see below) and its use in indirect questions.

Wh-words are, of course, also common after verbs introducing indirect questions and verbs like *know* and *wonder*, when used adjectivally:

(242) Sage me hwilc word ærust forðeode of Godes muðe?

(Sol.I 2.1)

'Tell me which word first went forth from God's mouth?'

Another situation which may have influenced the development of wh-pronouns into relatives is that in which the interrogative pronoun stands in a position where it could be interpreted as relative, i.e. in so-called double-object constructions:

(243) Ne meahte hire Iudas, .../ sweotole gecyþan be ðam sigebeame,/ on
      hwylcne se hælend ahafen wære, ...

(El. 859)

'Nor could Judas tell her clearly about the victorious tree,[tell her] on which [tree] the Saviour was raised up'

But, as shown by means of the translation (for a more detailed discussion see Mitchell 1985: §359, Karlberg 1954: 55ff.), *hwylcne* still functions as an interrogative pronoun; it introduces a subclause which is parallel to a preceding object.

It must be clear that all these different uses of the wh-forms opened up the way for their development into relative pronouns. It is likely that Latin and French played a role here too. In most accounts, however, it is believed that this influence was only slight and that it strengthened rather than initiated a new trend (see Kivimaa 1966: 143–4, but see also Meier 1967: 280). A final, important influence was the use of Old English wh-words as generalising relatives (next to *se þe*, which was the common free and generalising relative in Old English) in the combination *swa hw ... swa* and in Late Old English also *loc(a) hw ...* In

Early Middle English the first *swa* tended to be lost, while the second was often reduced to *se* (*whose*) and later replaced by *þe*, *þat* or deleted. This development reinforced the trend to use wh-forms as free relatives rather than *se þe* etc., which were also still used in Early Middle English.

For the wh-word to develop from an independent or generalising relative into a strict relative requires the presence of an antecedent. The following example shows how this could have come about:

(244)   hwam mai he luue treweliche hwa ne luues his broðer.

(Wooing Lord (Tit) 238–40)

'whom can he love truly, who(ever) does not love his brother.'

Here *he* can be interpreted as the antecedent of *who*, since it precedes this generalising or free relative. Other instances where a preceding NP could be interpreted as an antecedent are the so-called double-object constructions discussed above (243). The status of the subclause in such cases is ambiguous. Once the function of the wh-form started to shift, it is not difficult to imagine that this clause could quite easily develop into a non-restrictive relative clause.

The first occurrences of wh-relatives date from the twelfth century (with the possible exception of *hwær* (see Kivimaa 1966: 35)). The wh-form does not become frequent, however, until the fourteenth century. The earliest ones are found as a rule in non-restrictive clauses (which may point to the important influence of ambiguities such as presented in (243) above), and preceded by a preposition. It seems clear that the inability of the relative particle *that* to take a preposition in front of it (just like its sister-particle *þe* in Old English) contributed to the rise of this new pronoun which did allow a preposition. (For the place of the preposition in these clauses, see section 4.9.) This may be one of the reasons why the non-prepositional, nominative form *who* lagged behind in its development into a strict relative pronoun. Another possible reason may be that the generalising relative was used far more often in subject position than in any other function, so that *who* was still too strongly generalising in sense to become a mere relativiser.

Romaine (1982), studying the Middle Scots relative system, notes two important factors in relation to the introduction of relative wh-forms and the lag of nominative *who*. First of all, the further one moves down the hierarchy of syntactic positions that are relativisable (she refers to Keenan and Comrie's accessibility hierarchy for relatives, with subject position as the most accessible, via direct and indirect object to genitive position as the least accessible) the more wh-dominated the system becomes. In other words the new wh-system enters the grammar by way of the back door, that is, first in the least salient positions (see Romaine 1982: 151ff.). Secondly, Romaine notes (213ff.) that the wh-system enters English by way of the most complex styles of writing. It is probable in this light that French and Latin influence prompted or strengthened the adoption of the wh-relatives. This would explain why the wh-relatives appear last in subject position since that represents according to the hierarchy the least complex syntactic position in which relatives occur.

The first example of relative *who* usually given in the literature (Karlberg 1954: 60; Mustanoja 1960: 199) is from 1297:

(245)   Vor he nadde bote an doȝter wo miȝte is eir be

(Glo.Chron.A (Clg) 1977)

'For he had an only daughter to be his heir.'

Meier (1967: 281) shows quite convincingly, however, that this *wo* is too early and too sporadic to function as a strict relative, and that the sentence must be interpreted roughly as follows 'as far as the heir (the question of heritage) was concerned, he had only a daughter (i.e. not a son)'. The first true examples of relative *who* date from the fifteenth century and involve stereotyped closing formulas found in letters (cf. also Rydén 1983). The earliest attested instance is:

(246)   I submitte me and alle þis matier to yowr good discrecion, and
        euere gremercy God and ye, who euere haue yow and me in his
        gracious gouernaunce.

(Davis 1971–6: 4.44–6)

It took almost another century before relative *who* became established outside these formulas. Rydén (1983) shows how Latin and French examples may have played a role in the choice of *who* in this very specific context (i.e. the antecedent is always the deity, the relative clause is barely subordinate and in each case contains an optative element). Seen from the point of view of the language system, the choice of *who* was not remarkable since the introduction of *who* filled a systemic gap: it filled out the paradigm already containing *whose* and *whom*, which were likewise used mainly with personal antecedents. It is interesting to note in this respect that Dutch, which also saw the development of wh-forms into relative pronouns, uses the *who* form (Du. *wie*) still only after prepositions and in the genitive, and as a generalising pronoun; nominative (and accusative) *wie* has never become part of the relative paradigm.

Next to the wh-forms discussed so far, there developed certain elaborations of these forms, i.e. *which*, *whose* and *whom* preceded by *the* or followed by *that* or occasionally even both.

Which that occurs all through the Middle English period and becomes rare by the end of the fifteenth century. *Whose that* remains a rare form throughout, while *whom that* is somewhat more frequent. *What* (...) *that* is also found, but usually has generalising force.

The wh-form is first followed by *that* in the so-called free relatives. It is a development from Old English *swa hw... swa* (see Bødtker 1908–10; Allen 1977), where the loss of the first *swa* led to the replacement of the second *swa* by *þe* and later in the thirteenth century by *that*, as described above:

(247)   ...hwo þet bere a deorewurðe licur...in a feble uetles...nolde heo gon ut of þrunge bute ȝif heo were fol:

(Ancr. (Nero) 72.35–73.2)

'whoever carries a precious liquid in a frail vessel should not go out in a crowd unless she were a fool'

This development is rather similar to the OE *se þe* development into a free relative, but is independent of it (see Allen 1977: 384).

The next stage is the appearance by the end of the thirteenth or beginning of the fourteenth century of *that* after wh-forms which function as strict relatives (so after an antecedent) or in indirect questions,

(248)   First, I.../ Am dwellynge with the god of thonder,/ *Which that* men callen Jupiter,

(HF 606–9)

(249)   Nat wot I wel *wher* [= whether] *that* I flete or synke.

(PF 7)

(250)   Þan askede he here, *why þat* hyt was/ Þat she suffred swyche peyne...

(Mannyng HS (Hrl) 3287–8)

It is noteworthy that the early examples of *that* in indirect questions tend to have generalising force – see (250). It is clear, too, that many of the later *which that* relatives retain this generalisation,

(251)   He which that hath no wyf, I holde hym shent;

(CT IV.1320 [5: 76])

(cf. CT I.3152 [1: 3148]: 'Who hath no wyf, he is no cokewold.')

which is particularly true for the combination *what that*, as noted above. The reason for this spread of *that* is clear. We have seen in section 4.6.2 that *that* became the general complementiser for many types of subordinate clauses. Thus it could spread from the free relative wh-form to other wh-forms introducing subclauses. Once *that* was established after *wh-* it became a handy metrical device. It should therefore not be surprising that this pleonastic *that* is in, for instance, Chaucer twice as common in verse as it is in prose (Kivimaa 1966: 10).

In contrast to *which that*, the use of *the which* (*the whom* and *the whose* occur only rarely) is much more frequent in prose, especially in the fifteenth century. It occurs first in the north in the early part of the fourteenth century (the earliest recorded instance is in *Cursor Mundi*) and slowly winds its way south in the course of that century. Its antecedent is more often inanimate than animate (in contrast to *which that*, where the antecedent is frequently animate, especially in verse) and often stands some way away from the relative, which usually introduces a non-restrictive clause.

The development of *the* before *which* has often been ascribed to French influence. It was said to have been formed on the analogy of forms like *liquels* etc. Curme (1912) and Reuter (1937) have shown, however, that French *liquels* cannot have initiated the form (it can at most have supported its continuing use in later texts) because the earliest instances are found in the north, where French influence was slight, and because a certain number of syntactic peculiarities of *the which* (such as the initial reluctance to use it after a preposition) cannot be explained with reference to the French form. Curme and Reuter believe that *the which* is the result of a contamination of the Old English generalising relatives *se þe* and *swa hwylc swa*, used independently. Curme (1912: 153) has found forms like *seðe suahuelc* and *ðone suæ huælc* in Late Old English northern glosses, which suggest that contamination has taken place. What may have happened then is that these forms developed into *þe* (< *se*) *hwich* (with loss of *swa* – see above) and came to be used as strict relatives just as the generalising *se þe* could function in Old English as both generalising and headed (strict) relative. What is important in this explanation is that *the* goes back to an Old English demonstrative. This may account for the fact that *the which* occurs in Middle English in places where there was need for a relative capable of recalling the antecedent more strongly, i.e. in non-restrictive clauses, particularly in clauses separated from their antecedents:

(252) þat ilk dai a propheci/ Said symeon of vr leuedi,/ Of hir and of hir sun iesu,/ þe quilk i sal sai yow nu.

(*Cursor* (Vesp) 11357–60)

'that same day Simeon uttered a prophesy about our Lady, about her and her son Jesus, which I shall tell you now.'

and is used especially after an antecedent that has itself no demonstrative before it. For this reason it is also found frequently in so-called continuative relative clauses,

> (253)   ȝyt þer ys anoþer sweryng/ where-þurgh comþ ofte grete
> cumbryng,'/ Þe whyche ys, an oþe oute of mesure…
>
> (Mannyng HS (Hrl) 2765–7)
>
> 'yet there is another oath through which often arises great trouble, which is an oath without measure…'

that is, in relative clauses that are only loosely connected to what goes before and often serve as a summing up of previous thoughts (see Reuter 1938). In view of the above it should not come as a surprise that *the which* occurs far more often in texts of a didactic nature, which make much more intensive use of non-restrictive and continuative clauses. This explains the much higher percentage of *the which* in prose as compared to verse.

So far we have looked at the major types of relativisers in Middle English. Two other types remain to be discussed, (a) adverbial relatives and (b) zero relatives. Following that, we will have a look at two other topics in connection with relative clauses: (c) the occurrence and the function of resumptive pronouns in certain types of relative clause, and (d) the type of mood used in relative clauses.

ADVERBIAL RELATIVES

As in Old English the adverbial relative *þær* > ME *ther(e)* was used after an antecedent with locative meaning:

> (254)   But I cam in þere & in othere places þere I wolde…
>
> (*Mandev.* (Tit) 53.28–9)

It could also be used as a free relative, i.e. without a head:

> (255)   Arður him lokede on, þer he lai on folden.
>
> (*Brut* (Clg) 14270)
>
> 'Arthur looked at him, where he lay on the earth.'

With the replacement of the demonstrative pronoun by the interrogative pronoun, *there* was gradually ousted by *where*. *There* is still the common form in Early Middle English; in Late Middle English both *there* and *where* are common. The last instances of *there* date from the sixteenth century.

Just as in the case of the relative pronoun, the relative adverb could be followed by pleonastic *that*, but even more frequently by *as*:

(256) To Engelond been they come the righte way,/ Wher as they lyve in joye and in quiete.

$\qquad$ (*CT* II.1130–1 [3: 1130–1])

(257) But bad his folk to gon wher that hem liste.

$\qquad$ (*Troilus* I.357)

Kivimaa (1966: 103) explains this use of *as* as follows. *Ther/wher* from Old English onwards could also express temporal meaning (there are many examples where *there* has both temporal and locative reference – see Dubislav 1916: 295; and, in general, time deixis is characteristically parasitic on space deixis). As such they belong to the same paradigm as *as*, which functions among other things as a temporal conjunction. Consequently *ther/wher* came to be used where one would expect *as*, and *as* could be used instead of *ther/where*.

(258) ...he heolde him et hom ine ierusalem, ase he wunede.

$\qquad$ (*Ancr.* (Nero) 75.37–76.1)

$\qquad$ 'he kept him at home in Jerusalem where he lived.'

(259) ...domesdai þer þe engles schulen cwakien.

$\qquad$ (*Ancr.* (Nero) 51.10)

$\qquad$ 'Doomsday when the angels shall tremble.'

Ther and *as* are virtually interchangeable, too, as introducers of main clauses expressing a wish (see e.g. *CT* III.201 [2: 201] and *Troilus* V.1787). We also find the occasional use of *as* in relative clauses, after *which* and by itself:

(260) Hir tretys, *which as* ye shal after heere, ...

$\qquad$ (*CT* IV.331 [8: 331])

(261) ...ne ther lakked nought,/ Neither his collect ne his expans yeeris,/ Ne his rootes, ne his othere geeris,/ *As* been his centris and his argumentz...

$\qquad$ (*CT* V.1274–7 [6: 566–9])

These can be explained as an extension of the regular Middle English relative construction with *swich...as* (cf. PDE *such...as*). But it is also quite likely that the use of relative *as* is connected with Scandinavian settlements (see Hines 1984). The latter would provide an explanation for the dialectal spread of *as* in the modern period, this being confined to originally non-West-Saxon areas (see Poussa 1988: 459).

Once *where* could occur by the side of *there* in relative clauses, it also became possible for *where* to be combined with prepositions, just as *there* was,

(262) Veire weies manion þer beþ in englonde/ ...ȝwar þorȝ me mai wende...

(Glo.Chron. A (Clg) 169–70)

'Many beautiful roads there are in England...along which people may go...'

ZERO RELATIVES

Absence of the relative marker is in Present-Day English commonly only found when the absent relative pronoun functions as object (including indirect and prepositional object) in the relative clause as in, *The secretary I wanted to see was not there*. In Middle English (as in Old English), zero relative is more common in subject position:

(263) Adam ben king and eue quuen/ Of alle ðe ðinge [θ] in werlde ben.

(Gen.&Ex. 296–7)

'Adam and Eve are king and queen of all the things [that] are in the world'

(264) Leir þe king wende forh, to is dohter [θ] wunede norð.

(Brut (Clg) 1719)

'King Lear went forth to his daughter [who] lived in the north.'

(265) ...I know no knyght in this contrey [θ] is able to macche hym.

(Malory Wks (Add.59678) 377.35–6)

However, it is certainly not true that any subject relative may be left out in Middle English; omission is heavily constrained. Most often the finite verb of the relative clause is a stative verb (cf. the frequency of verbs like *hatan* and *wesan* in such clauses in Old English, vol. I, section 4.5.2.1), usually the verb *to be* or a verb expressing existence in time or place, i.e. verbs that could easily be left out because they add little in the way of information (cf. the absence of a verb of movement in Old and Middle English after a modal auxiliary when an adverbial locative phrase is present, i.e. of the type *I must to my house*). Thus, in examples (263)–(265) the relevant information is contained in the locative phrases *in werlde* and *north* and in the subject complement *able to macche hym*; the relative pronoun (*and* the verb for that matter) can easily be omitted because the relation of the noun preceding the subclause (the antecedent) to the above-mentioned italicised phrases is always that of subject (stative verbs do not normally take other arguments). Example (265) is interesting from another point of view: it closely resembles the zero-subject relative constructions still acceptable in colloquial Present-Day English, a type that also occurs frequently in Middle English:

(266) No lim nas þat he smot, [θ] mid þe bodi beleued.

(*Glo.Chron.A* (Clg) 403)

'(there) was no limb that he struck (that) remained part of the body.'

(267) With hym ther was dwellynge a poure scoler,/ [θ] hadde lerned art,...

(*CT* I.3190–1 [1: 3184–5])

(268) Hyt is nothing [θ] will byten the;

(*HF* 1044)

The zero relative occurs here after existential *there is* and in cleft sentences introduced by *it is*. Erdmann (1980) has called these constructions 'focusing constructions', constructions in which a person/thing is identified for a course of action. Notice that example (265) identifies the antecedent in a similar way.

There is controversy whether these clauses are truly relative or whether they are paratactic with the subject pronoun left out (see Bødtker 1908–10; Phillipps 1965; Ohlander 1981). This depends very much on the type of clause used. A zero pronoun in a non-restrictive clause can be interpreted as both relative and personal:

(269) For he hadde founde a corn [θ] lay in the yerd.

(*CT* VII.4365 [10: 3147])

(270) An preost wes on leoden, Laʒamon wes ihoten.

(*Brut* (Clg) 1)

'[There] was a priest in the country, [who/he] was called Laweman'

Restrictive clauses, however, such as examples (263) and (265), can only be interpreted as subordinate, i.e. with ellipsis of the relative pronoun.

In addition to the zero-subject relative constructions we also find constructions in which the object relative pronoun has been left out. In most accounts one reads that this construction developed later than the one just discussed (see e.g. Mustanoja 1960: 205; Phillipps 1965: 329). Visser (1963–73: §§627ff.), however, disagrees, and gives a number of Old English examples showing object-pronoun deletion. However, all the instances, except the last two, are dubious in that they involve a demonstrative pronoun as antecedent placed immediately before the zero relative. This makes it likely that these examples should be interpreted as so-called 'attracted relatives' (see vol. I, section 4.5.2.1), even though they are not, as is usually the case, accompanied by the relative particle þe. The Middle English instances are interesting in that they are basically of two types. They either involve the verbs *clepen* 'call' or *callen* (cf. the use of *hatan/haten* in the zero-subject relative discussed above) or the idiom *by the faith I owe to God*:

(271) Sir, be þe faith [Ø] i haue to yow,...

(Cursor (Vesp) 5145)

(272) Of Northfolk was this Reve of which I telle,/ Beside a toun [Ø] men clepen Baldeswelle.

(CT I.619–20 [1: 621–2])

Other examples usually contain possessive *have* (and are thus similar to subject zero relatives with stative verbs) or verbs similar in meaning to possessive *have*.[27] It seems as if the earliest object constructions are an extension of the (older) subject constructions. It is only after the Middle English period that the object construction gains ground, when it begins to appear with all kinds of verbs in the subclause. Phillipps (1965) connects this with the change in word order (from Old English SOV to Middle English SVO) and the loss of inflections. This causes the pronoun before the finite verb of the subclause to be interpreted as subject rather than object, so that the zero relative came to be interpreted more easily as object rather than subject.

RESUMPTIVE PRONOUNS

In the discussion of relative clauses in volume I (section 4.5.2.2) reference is made to the appearance of so-called resumptive pronouns in certain types of relative clauses. These resumptive pronouns (i.e. pronouns that fill the gap left by the absent relativised NP) occur with the relative particle þe. If it is accepted that the relative particle is generated in position and not moved (see vol. I, section 4.5.2.2, for analysis), we have an explanation why resumptive pronouns should only occur with þe and not with demonstrative relatives in Old English, since the latter have moved from their original position. It is a principle of generative grammar that a moved element cannot be replaced by an element of the same category.[28] There are some examples in Old English of resumptive pronouns occurring with þæt, but the þæt-clauses appear to be of the consecutive type, discussed below and more fully in section 4.6.3.1.

The resumptive pronouns seem to have a clearly defined syntactic function in both Old and Middle English, i.e. they indicate the case of the relative particle (its function in the subclause), which is incapable of expressing case itself. This interpretation of the role of the resumptive pronoun is based on the following observations:

1 In Middle English, as in Old English,[29] they occur almost exclusively with the indeclinable relative particle: Early Middle English þe, later þat; and then only when the pronouns express oblique case. Þe and þat functioned most often as nominative and so they were nominative almost by default. Other functions sometimes needed to be expressed explicitly, this is especially true in the case of the genitive. The frequency of the resumptive pronouns is sharply reduced once the wh-pronouns, which have overt case,[30] have taken up position, i.e. in the fourteenth century. This may also explain why the wh-pronouns at first occur almost exclusively after prepositions and in the genitive (*whose*). There they filled a systemic gap. Nominative *who* was not needed syntactically and consequently developed more slowly. (Other/additional explanations for the late arrival of nominative *who* were discussed earlier in this section.) Some examples:

(273)   ... it was þat ilk cok,/ þat petre herd *him* crau,...

(Cursor (Vesp) 15995–6)

(another manuscript (Trn) has '... þat petur herde crowe')

(274)   Ther-ynne wonyþ a wyȝt, þat wrong is *his* name,...

(PPlC (Hnt 143) i, 59)

'There lives a creature whose name is wrong'

When only the relative particle *that* was available to form a relative clause (as is practically the case for a while in Middle English), the genitive created a real problem since relative *that* had no genitive form *that's*; it could not be preceded by a preposition, ******of that*, nor could the preposition be stranded because possessive *of* is never stranded (not even in PDE ******I want to question the man that the gun has been found of in the canal*). The extent of the problem is shown by the awkwardness of the constructions found to express the genitive:

(275)   And drof hem intil Engelond,/ Þat al was siþen in his hond,/ *His* þat Hauelok was þe name.

(Havelok (Ld) 726–8)

2 When the resumptive pronoun *is* found in the nominative – which, as I have just stated, is rare – usually the clause introduced by þat is not

a true relative clause, or the resumptive pronoun is necessary because another clause intervenes. Consider the following examples:

(276) Wot ic ðor non ðat he ne biueð...

(*Gen.&Ex.*2280)

'I don't know anyone there who would not tremble.../ I don't know of anyone such that he would not tremble...'

(277) Now turne we unto sir Trystrams, that uppon a day he toke a lytyll barget...

(Malory *Wks* (Add.59678) 441.27–8)

(278) ...the damesell of the castell, that whan Alysaundir le Orphelyne had forjusted the four knyghtes she called hym to her...

(Malory *Wks* (Add.59678) 640.1–3)

Clauses such as exemplified in (276) approximate consecutive clauses (for a discussion see section 4.6.3.1). Example (277) is a frequent type in Malory's *Morte Darthur*. Instances of it all occur in the same context, after the phrase 'now turne we' or 'lat us now spekyn of' etc. Clauses of this kind hover between object clauses (with a phrase like 'it happened that...' left out), consecutive clauses ('it so happened that...') and relative clauses. In (278) a subclause intervenes between the relative particle and the clause, which accounts for the repetition of the pronoun. In these cases a resumptive pronoun even occurs after *which* and *who* (see Visser 1963–73: §§75, 606). Example (278) could also be explained on other grounds. It is rather similar to cases like,

(279) þe scorpiunes cundel ðet heo bret in hire boseme, schek hit ut mid schrifte,

(*Ancr.* (Nero) 91.34–5)

'the scorpion's offspring that she breeds in her bosom, shake it off through confession'

which show topicalisation of the object but with a pronoun in the position vacated by the topicalised NP. That the resumptive pronoun in (279) has nothing to do with the relative clause is clear from the fact that a resumptive pronoun is also found in (280):

(280) Noght him allon bot al his kin,/ In thraldam has he broght *þaim* in,...

(*Cursor* (Göt) 9657–8)

(cf. also (Frf) '...he hath to thraldom brot ynne')

Example (278), then, may be a case of topicalisation of the subject.

MOOD

Normally, the verb in the relative clause is in the indicative. In Old English there were certain situations in which a subjunctive was preferred (e.g. after an imperative, or when the principal clause contained a negative or a subjunctive expressing a wish). Traces of this remain in Middle English. The subjunctive mood is also used when the relative clause is part of a hypothetical or potential situation:

(281)   Fele of yow fareþ as if I a forest hadde/ That were ful of faire trees,
                                                        (*PPl.B* (Trin-C) xv.333–4)

'many of you act as if I had a forest that was full of faire trees'

It is quite common in clauses introduced by free relatives when they contain an element of concessivity:

(282)   For hem semeth þat whosoeuere be meke & pacyent he is holy...
                                                        (*Mandev.* (Tit) 113.19–20)

'for to them it seems that whoever is meek and patient is holy'

4.6.1.2   Non-finite relative clauses

Instead of a relative clause, a participial construction can be used. The use of the past participle here is common, as it was in Old English:

(283)   swete iesu uor minne sunnen anhonged oþe rode
                                                        (*Ancr.* (Nero) 11.27–8)

'sweet Jesus, for my sins hung on the cross'

The use of the present participle developed under the influence of Latin and was also due to a widening of the function of the *-ing* form in Middle English (the result of the coalescence of the Old English verbal noun in *-ung* and the present participle in *-ende*; for more details, see section 4.3.1.1).

(284)   And thilke fooles sittynge hire aboute/ Wenden that...
                                                        (*Troilus* IV.715–16)

The disappearance of the zero-relative subject construction, discussed above, can also be partly a consequence of the rise of these participle constructions, which perform a similar function.

A construction new in Middle English is the infinitival relative clause,

(285)   She has no wight to whom to make hir mone.
                                                        (*CT* II.656 [3: 656])

It appears late in our period; no examples have been attested before the fourteenth century. In Old English a relative pronoun was not possible here: the *to*-infinitive by itself was used. This new construction presumably developed out of questioned infinitives, which also first appeared in Middle English but quite a bit earlier. Examples with bare infinitives are found in Early Middle English:

(286)   ant nuste hwet seggen.

(St.Kath.(1) (Bod) 563–4)

'and did not know what [to] say'

Examples with (*for*) *to*-infinitives are somewhat later,

(287)   heo nusten ȝwat forto do,...

(SLeg. (Ld) 153.1624)

'they did not know what to do'

Again we see how this particular construction with a relative wh-pronoun could develop out of a similar use of wh-forms in indirect questions (see section 4.6.1.1).

4.6.2   Complement clauses

Complement clauses are nominal or adjectival in nature and function as complements to a noun phrase, an adjective phrase or a verb phrase. They can be both finite and non-finite. In this section only nominal complements will be discussed. Adjectival complement clauses (= relative clauses) have been treated in section 4.6.1.1, which also deals with nominal relative clauses (i.e. clauses without an antecedent).

4.6.2.1   Finite complement clauses

Nominal complement clauses occur in the functions a NP can take in the higher clause, i.e. as object of a verbal or adjectival predicate, in apposition to another NP, and as a subject complement. In Present-Day English a clause can also replace a subject NP. There are constructions in Middle English that could be interpreted as subject clauses:

(288)   But bet is that a wyghtes tonge reste/ Than entermeten hym of such doinge,...

(PF 514–15)

(289)   Now is it resoun and tyme that I shewe yow...

(CT VII.1223 [10: 1223])

However, since the 'subject-clause' in Middle English only rarely occurs in initial position,[31] it is not clear whether such clauses are true subjects. It is perhaps preferable to interpret the above clauses as complements to the adjective (*bet*) and the noun (*resoun*, *tyme*) respectively (see also vol. I, section 4.5.3.1). As in Old English, these clauses occur especially with impersonal verbs, which often lack a subject (for a discussion of the status of these clauses when non-finite see section 4.6.2.3):

> (290)　Hym thynketh verraily that he may see/ Noees flood come
> 　　　　walwynge as the see...
>
> (CT I.3615–16 [1 : 3609–10])

Again, the *that*-clause here should presumably be interpreted as object of the verb *thynken* rather than subject.

The complement clause is normally introduced by *that* when it is a statement. For interrogative complement clauses see section 4.4.

THE CLAUSE AS OBJECT OF THE VERBAL PREDICATE

> (291)　ichulle þt　ȝe　speken selde,
> 　　　　I want that you speak　seldom
>
> (Ancr. (Nero) 31.19)
>
> 　　　　'I want you to speak seldom'

As in Present-Day English it is possible for *that* to be omitted, but this phenomenon seems to be more restricted in Middle English (but see Warner 1982: 169–70) than it was in Old English (see vol. I, section 4.5.3.1). It is mainly found after *seyn*, *thinken*, *witen* and verbs with similar meanings, and performative verbs like *sweren* etc., when the clause reports more or less directly the actual words spoken or thought. Warner (1982: 175ff.) shows that *that*-deletion is more likely when its function as clause-boundary marker is less needed because some other element, such as initial pronoun, can serve that function:

> (292)a.　...and on this book he swoor anoon/ She gilty was,...
> (CT II.667–8 [3: 667–8])
>
> 　　　b.　And þei seyn þei sinnen ȝif þei refusen ony man.
> (Mandev. (Tit) 118.29–30)

The omission of *that* also depends on style, and may be used for metrical purposes. It is found far more frequently, for instance, in poetry than in prose (see Eitle 1914: 9). Chaucer omits it regularly in so-called free indirect speech (see Guiraud 1971), which is more lively than ordinary reported speech:

(293) In al the court ne was ther wyf, ne mayde,/ Ne wydwe, that
       contraried that he sayde,/ But seyden he was worthy han his lyf.

(*CT* III.1043–5 [2: 1017–19])

That-clauses may also occur without a full main clause in what are sometimes termed independent desires:

(294) Mercy! And that ye nat discovere me, ...

(*CT* IV.1942 [5: 698])

and in exclamations,

(295) That I was born, allas! What shal I do?

(*LGW* 1308)

After verbs of 'fearing' and the like, negative *lest* is often found instead of *that*:

(296) Thow hast a ful gret care/ Lest that the cherl may falle out of the
       moone!

(*Troilus* I.1023–4)

For the use of negative sentential complements after verbs like *douten* etc., see section 4.5.

The subjunctive occurs regularly in object clauses. The subjunctive mood gives the activity expressed in the verb a certain modal colouring so that it conveys no longer a fact, but something that is possible, probable or desirable. Not surprisingly, therefore, the subjunctive occurs especially after (a) verbs expressing a wish, a command or exhortation, where the subclause denotes a prospective event (cf. the use of the subjunctive in clauses of purpose and result, section 4.6.3.1) as in (291) above; and (b) verbs expressing some mental activity:

(297) Hi weneþ þat þu segge soþ.

(*Owl&N* (Clg) 844)

       'They think that you speak the truth.'

or after a negated verb, denoting the uncertainty of the action conveyed in the complement clause. For the same reason the subjunctive is fairly frequent in indirect questions. This contrasts with Old English, where the subjunctive occurs regularly in reported speech without any implication of uncertainty on the part of the speaker (in Old English the subjunctive could still be used in its original function of syntactic marker of subordination).

Instead of the subjunctive, which in Middle English is only distinctive for some forms (for details see chapter 2 and section 4.3.2.2), we often find auxiliaries used, especially after the verbs mentioned in (a) above. *Should* is the most common auxiliary, from about 1300 onwards also found after present-tense matrix verbs; in Early Middle English we also come across *mote* 'may', while in later Middle English *would* occurs too. An example with *should* is:

(298)   And manie gon nakede; and bidde þæt sum man heom scholde
        biweue,...

(SLeg. (Ld) 420.7)

'and many go naked and ask that some one would clothe them,...'

THE CLAUSE AS OBJECT OF AN ADJECTIVAL PREDICATE

These are not common in Middle English except in so-called semi-impersonal expressions like (*it*) *is bet* etc., where the clause might also be a subject clause. More instances are found in prose than in poetry. An example of the construction with the adjective *certeyn* is:

(299)   I am certein by many resouns that schrewes been unsely.

(Bo. IV, pr.4, 227–8)

'for many reasons I am certain that wicked people are unhappy.'

Much more common is the expression *I woot certain that*..., where the clause depends on the verb *woot*, or expressions where the complement depends on the noun *certain, I am in certein that*...

APPOSITIVE COMPLEMENT

The clause occurs in apposition to another noun:

(300)   And aske hym counseill how thou may/ Do ony thyng that may hir
        plese;

(Rose 2868–9)

The nouns are always abstract nouns. They correlate with the verbs found before object clauses or are nouns that convey an experience or the content of a statement, fact, etc. The use of the subjunctive after these nouns is also the same as in object clauses.

THE CLAUSE AS SUBJECT COMPLEMENT

(301) In Cipre is the manere of lordes & all oþere men all to eten on the erthe, for þei make dyches in the erthe...And the skyll [reason] is *for þei may be the more fressch* for þat lond is meche more hottere þan it is here.

(Mandev. (Tit) 17.29–35)

The subordinator is usually *that* as in the other cases, but the quoted example shows that it may also be *for* when the complement expresses the ground for a statement. See also the use of *for* in (212).

4.6.2.2 Non-finite complement clauses

The most frequent type of non-finite complement is the infinitival construction. There are many differences in form within this group. First, there is the difference in infinitive marker: it can be zero (bare infinitive), *to* or *for to*. The Middle English infinitive also shows a distinction in voice (active vs passive infinitive) and tense/(aspect) (present vs perfective infinitive). Finally the infinitive construction can have an explicit subject (lexical subject) or an implicit one (PRO subject). In the latter case, no lexical NP is present, the subject is 'controlled' (i.e. has as its antecedent) either by a NP argument in the matrix clause, as in (302) (i.e. PRO is co-indexed or, in other words, the empty subject finds its referent in another NP in the clause) or by some entity outside the clause, as in (303) (i.e. PRO is arbitrary: there is no referent for the empty subject within the clause):

(302)a. I_i thenke [PRO_i] make/ A bok for Engelondes sake,...

(CA (Frf) Prol.23–4)

  b. sche bad me$_i$ [PRO_i] telle and seie hir trowthe.

(CA (Frf) i, 181)

In (302a) the empty subject (PRO) is co-indexed with the subject of the matrix verb, *I*. In generative grammar terms this is called 'subject control'. In (302b) the empty subject is co-indexed with the object of the matrix verb, *me*, which is called 'object control'.

(303) ...as whan thou comandest [PRO_{arb}] to sleen a man.

(CT X.570 [12: 570])

Below, we will discuss the various types of infinitive constructions one by one.

4.6.2.3 Bare versus (*for*) *to* infinitive

In Old English the bare infinitive was by far the most frequent of the infinitives (see vol. I, section 4.5.3.2). This situation is completely reversed in Middle English, where the *to*-infinitive becomes the most common form and the bare infinitive gets restricted to an increasingly smaller number of verbs. One of the causes for this development is the progressive weakening of the infinitive marker *to*. *To*, in origin a directional adverb/preposition, started off as an indicator (mainly) of purpose, but by Late Old English/Early Middle English it had lost that function so that it began to occur where previously only the bare infinitive was found. It is very likely that *to* increased its territory because it became a useful sign of the infinitive form, to distinguish it from other forms of the verb. Due to the reduction and loss of inflections, the infinitival endings (-(*i*)*an* and -*enne* for the bare and inflected infinitive respectively) could no longer serve that purpose. Also the introduction of the *for to* marker in the Early Middle English period (a few examples with *for to* were already found in Late Old English), which, likewise, serves at first as an indicator of purpose, makes it clear that *to* by itself no longer satisfactorily fulfilled that role. Soon, however, *for to* follows its predecessor and degenerates into a mere infinitive marker. In the late thirteenth and fourteenth century it alternates freely with *to* (and even in some cases with the bare infinitive), especially in poetry, where it was a useful metrical device. (See, for instance, the list of verbs given in Kenyon (1909: 90ff.), which shows that in Chaucer some verbs such as (*bi*)*ginnen*, *desiren*, *hopen*, *lernen*, etc. allowed all three infinitival constructions as complements.)

However, it is not true that the use of these infinitive markers was entirely haphazard and free in the Middle English period, certainly not as far as the selection of zero versus (*for*) *to* was concerned. The statistical studies by Kaartinen & Mustanoja (1958) for Late Middle English prose and Quirk & Svartvik (1970) for Chaucer show that at least two parameters are of importance: (a) what they and others (e.g. Sanders 1915; Ohlander 1941) have called the 'intimacy' of the relationship between the matrix verb and the infinitive; (b) the physical distance between the matrix verb and the infinitive.

Concerning (a), it seems clear that the more grammaticalised the matrix verb is, or, in other words, the emptier it is of referential meaning, the more likely it is that the bare infinitive is found.[32] Thus, already in Old English the core modals – *shall*, *will*, *can*, *may*, *must* – are normally followed by the bare infinitive and this trend continues in Middle English.[33] Likewise, verbs such as *haten*, *bidden*, *let*, *gar*, *do* and *maken* are almost always found with the bare infinitive when used as causatives. True causative verbs have little semantic content because the emphasis is not on *who did* it but on whether something *gets done* (see Royster 1918: 84: '[it] affirms accomplished action'), which is expressed by the infinitive following the causative verb. The verb *do* behaves a little awkwardly with respect to the form of the infinitive. At the end of the Middle English period causative *do* tends to prefer the *to*-infinitive, but it has to be remembered that this behaviour of causative *do* represents, as it were, its last convulsions (see section 4.3.3.5): *to* was reintroduced to distinguish causative *do* from the increasingly popular, but even more semantically empty, periphrastic *do*. This trend also explains why *(bi)ginnen*, once it has developed into a kind of aspectual auxiliary or a purely periphrastic verb (especially in the past tense), normally appears with a bare infinitive.[34] That the tendency for *to* to disappear is still active in Modern English is shown in the form of 'conjunction contraction' in verbs that have developed modal or aspectual characteristics: *wanna*, *gonna*, *bounta*, *gotta* (from *want to* etc.) (see Plank 1984: 339).

It follows from this theory that we do not expect a bare infinitive to appear where such grammaticalisation is out of the question. And indeed the above-mentioned studies show that only the (*for*) *to*-infinitive is found after nouns and adjectives (this was already so in Old English – see vol. I, section 4.5.3.2):

(304) That no manere man ne child,...be so hardy to wrestell, or make ony wrestlyng within the seintuary ne the boundes of Poules,...
(Chambers & Daunt 1931: 93.1–3)

(305) ...John White,...was holde in prison in london tille he had founde surete to paie it hym.
(Chambers & Daunt 1931: 226.33–5)

and also when used adverbially (i.e. when it is not part of the VP),

(306) ...he presentit hym self a surgeon & a visicion to disseiue the peopl...
(Chambers & Daunt 1931: 124.79–80)

For the same reason one would expect the (*for*) *to*-infinitive to be selected rather than the bare infinitive when it is used as a subject.

However, we find a good many examples in Middle English where the subject-infinitive is the bare infinitive.

(307)   And if yow liketh knowen of the fare/ Of me, ...
(Troilus V.1366–7)

Interestingly enough, though, almost all these examples have as a matrix predicate an impersonal construction (containing either an impersonal verb or *to be* + adjective/noun used as a semi-impersonal *it is good, me is loth*, etc.). One of the characteristics of impersonal verbs is precisely that they lack a subject. The use of the bare infinitive, therefore, in these cases may provide corroborative evidence that this infinitive was still looked upon as an object (see the discussion in section 4.6.2.1). The infinitive also usually *follows* the matrix verb. That the *object* infinitive of impersonal verbs could take *to* or not is not surprising considering the proximity of impersonal verbs to modal verbs. In Middle English quite a number of instances are found where modal verbs behave like impersonals e.g. *must, dare, ought* (see Mustanoja 1960: 436),

(308)   Us moste putte oure good in aventure.
(CT VIII.946)

Consider also the case of *need*, an impersonal verb that developed into a modal (see note 33).

When the infinitive functions as a subject complement after *to be*, (*for*) *to* is again the rule. This predicative infinitive (as it is called) is a comparatively recent development. It does not occur in Old English, and is rare in Early Middle English (see Sanders 1915: 45). The exclusion of the bare infinitive here is not surprising when one considers that *to be* is used as a full verb (in the sense of 'exist', 'consist in'), while the infinitive functions as a kind of adjunct (usually expressing purpose):

(309)   ... al my walkynge out by nyghte/ Was for t'espye wenches that he dighte.
(CT III.397–8 [2:397–8])

The idea that the matrix verb needs to be grammaticalised to a certain extent to allow the bare infinitive also explains the occasional occurrence of *to*-infinitives after modals. These usually concern cases in which the modal verb is still used as a full verb and not as an auxiliary:

(310)   Telle me which thow *wilt* of everychone,/ *To han* for thyn, and lat me thanne allone.
(Troilus III.412–13)

   'Tell me which one of all these you desire to have for yourself and then leave me alone.'

or where the infinitive is placed in front position:

(311) And certes yow to haten shal I nevere;[35]

(Troilus V.1079)

In that case the infinitive approximates to the function of an object NP; preposed, it is no longer felt to be part of the VP (see also Ohlander 1941: 66). Warner (1982: 133) offers the interesting suggestion that the fronting of some element within the infinitival construction may involve increased infinitive marking for perceptual reasons.

There is at least one group of verbs that seems to form an exception to the rule stated above: the verbs of perception – *see*, *feel*, *hear*, etc. These clearly retain their full semantic content but nevertheless normally take the bare infinitive:

(312) For sorwe of which she felt hire herte blede,...

(Troilus V.17)

(313) This sely wydwe and eek hir doghtres two/ Herden thise hennes crie and maken wo,...

(CT VII.3375–6 [10: 3347–8])

This is even the case with perception verbs borrowed from French:

(314) ... what maner man can aspie any maner persoune make, medle or consent in any wyse...

(Chambers & Daunt 1931: 98.24–6)

We can perhaps interpret the rather vague notion of 'intimacy' here in another way. What distinguishes the infinitival complements of perception verbs from those of other verbs is that the perception verb almost always shares the tense domain of the infinitive. In other words, the bare infinitive is used to indicate as it were the 'intimacy' of tense, i.e. the simultaneity of the actions expressed by matrix verb and infinitive (simultaneity in the case of perception verbs implies also direct perception). When simultaneity (see (315a)) or direct perception (see (315b)) is absent, a finite complement is used instead:

(315)a. Up to the tree he caste his eyen two,/ And saugh *that Damyan his wyf had dressed*/ In swich manere it may nat been expressed,...

(CT IV.2360–2 [5: 1116–18])

   b. The sothe is this, the cut fil to the Knyght,/ ... And telle he moste his tale, as was resoun,/ ... And whan this goode man saugh *that it was so*...

(CT I.845–50 [1: 847–52])

This identity of tense domain may have wider implications for the choice between bare and (*for*) *to*-infinitive. While in Present-Day

English, usage has become more or less fixed for each verb, many verbs in Middle English waver between bare and marked infinitives. This choice may be lexically determined and therefore grammatically arbitrary, but it is quite possible that a structural factor is also at work. It seems to me that the identity of tense domains plays an important role in deciding which infinitive was used. Compare the following examples:

(316)a. God leue hem in his blisse spilen...

*(Gen.&Ex.*2532)

'may God let them dwell in his bliss'

b. Ure louerd ihesu crist leue us swo ure synnen to beten, and swich elmesse to wurchen...

*(Trin.Hom.*59.6–7)

'May our lord Jesus Christ permit us so to atone for our sins and to do such alms...'

(317)a. Ic wende habben strengþe of me seluen...

(Vices&V.(1) (Stw) 83.23–4)

b. ...ah þeo þe wenden to fordon him

(St.Marg.(1) (Bod) 8.29–30)

'but those who thought to destroy him'

(318)a. O brother deere,/ If thow a soth of this desirest knowe,...

(Troilus V.1458)

b. wel wostow that I/ Desire to ben a mayden al my lyf,...

(CT I.2304–5 [1: 2306–7])

(319)a. but softely/ By nyghte into the town she thenketh ride.

(Troilus V.1153–4)

b. for sith that day that I was bore,/ I nas, ne nevere mo to ben I thynke,/ Ayeins a thing that myghte the forthynke.

(Troilus II.1412–14)

In general the (*for*) *to*-infinitive is used when in some way the activity is seen as taking place in the future. The distinction is subtle but future reference may be indicated by a temporal phrase referring to or including the future (*al my lyf* (318a), *nevere mo* (319b)) or it may be implicit in the activity expressed by the verb (*fordon* (317b), *beten...wurchen* (316a)). Simultaneity, on the other hand, may be indicated by an adverbial phrase of manner (*softely* (319a), *in his blisse* (316a)) or by the 'stativeness' of the verb (*habben strengþe* (317a), *knowe* (318a)). In many cases only the context can make clear what is meant. Sanders' remark (1915: 73) about the verb phrase *leue gifen* 'to give leave' is interesting in this respect. He states that this verb only occurs with the *to*-infinitive, in contrast to the verb *leuen* 'to allow, let'. Now it must be obvious that 'leave' can only be given for something that has still to take place; for this reason, the verb necessarily selects a *to*-infinitive. Moreover, *leuen* followed by the bare infinitive is partly grammaticalised; it is closer to a causative 'auxiliary' than that it is a verb of full referential meaning.

Since in Present-Day English the use of *to* has become lexically determined for almost every verb, this kind of variation no longer plays a role within the individual verb, but it may be noted that the function of the bare infinitive seems to have been taken over to a large extent by the *-ing* form, so that variation is still possible albeit with different forms. Although further research is needed to establish more firmly the accuracy of the above remarks, I hesitate to concur with Kaartinen & Mustanoja and others who have stated that in poetry 'the form of the infinitive is largely dictated by metrical conditions' (1958: 179). If that were so, one would expect variation with a large number of verbs. Only a fairly small number, however, allow two or three forms of the infinitive, a fact that needs to be explained. I do agree, however, that the use of *to* versus *for to* may be more a matter of rhythm and metre.

Concerning the second parameter, the distance between the matrix verb and the infinitive, Middle English usage shows that increased infinitive marking sometimes occurs when the infinitive becomes separated from the verb that governs it – this applies particularly to infinitives in co-ordination. This is especially noteworthy in the case of modals, which, although normally selecting a bare infinitive, may take a *to*-infinitive in this case. Some typical examples:

(320)   leue me vnderstonde/ þi dol & herteli to felen sum hwat/ of þe
         sorhe þ[et] tu þa hefdes...

                                                        (*Wooing Lord* (Tit) 561–3)

         'let me understand your grief and [to] feel something of the sorrow
         that you had then in my heart...'

(321)   Cheos nouþe ȝwaþer þov bi-leue wolt: oþur heonnes for-to gon,...
                                                        (*SLeg.* (Ld) 199.46)

         'choose now whether you want [to] stay or to go from here,...'

(322)   And sende his sonde þen to say þat þay samne schulde,/ And in
         comly quoyntis to com to his feste...

                                                        (*Cleanness* 53–4)

         'and sent his messenger then to say that they should gather and [to]
         come to his feast in seemly, fine clothes'

The explanation usually given is that a preposition is inserted to mark off the infinitive as infinitive in order to emphasise the close relation between matrix verb and infinitive, which has become obscured by the intervening elements (see Sanders 1915: 31). It has also been noticed that this special use of *to* may be occasioned by the exigencies of metre (see Ohlander 1941: 66).

Although the above factors may be relevant, it is worthwhile observing that there are some facts of Middle English that cannot be easily reconciled with the above. First of all Kenyon (1909: 159–62) and Quirk & Svartvik (1970: 402ff.) have shown that in the case of co-ordinated infinitives the second element is usually identical with the first when this concerns the bare infinitive, while in the case of the *to* or *for to* infinitive, the infinitive marker is usually left out before the second infinitive; a repetition of the first form is here less common. This seems to indicate that there was no real need for an extra marking of the second infinitive. In this connection Warner (1982: 127ff.) has found that it is not so much separation as such that may be responsible for increased infinitive marking, but separation of a very specific kind. What seems to be important is the presence of preposed material between the conjunction (*and*, *or*, etc.) and the second infinitive. Warner explains this as follows: increased infinitive marking (especially *to* instead of zero) may be necessary for perceptual reasons in order to avoid mis-interpretation on the part of the hearer/reader, who could interpret the conjunction as relating (some element in) the previous clause with the preposed material – especially when this material can be sentence-initial – rather than the infinitive itself.

Secondly, as the use of a *to*-infinitive as an extra marker of a second infinitive is not all that common, the question arises why this device was not used more often if the aim was to indicate more clearly the nature of the second infinitive. For these reasons I am inclined to believe that the function of the second *to* is not simply limited to that of increased infinitive marking, but that it may add something extra to the meaning of the sentence. The second *to*-infinitive often conveys the aim or result of the action expressed by the first infinitive, or indicates the next stage in the proceedings. In other words, *to* has a function similar to the one discussed above: it indicates a difference in tense domain:[36]

(323) Graithli taght he [Satan] him [the adder] þe gin,/ How he suld at þe wyf be-gin,/ And thorw þe wijf to wyn þe man;

(Cursor (Vesp) 741–3)

'promptly he taught him the scheme, how he should begin with the woman, and through the woman [to] win over the husband'

(324)   ... þat he shulde go on fote fro the Tour þrouȝ þe toun of London
        vnto Tyburne, and þere to be hangyd, ...

        (*Brut*-1419 (CmbKk) 362.6–8)

(325)   He þowȝte that he wolde go/ For hys penance the pope to,/ And
        heuen for to wynne.

        (*Emare* 955–7)

A note of authority and pre-ordainedness is often conveyed by *to*. All
the above examples are given as straightforward instances of increased
infinitive marking by Ohlander. He does mention, however, that there
are instances in which the second infinitive may be 'associated with the
final or absolute use of the infinitive' (1941: 60). This is clear, for
instance, in

(326)   And trust wel that a coveitous man ne kan noght deme ne thynke,
        but oonly to fulfille the ende of his coveitise;

        (*CT* VII.1130 [10: 1130])

A final remark should be made about the distinction between *to* and
for to. So far we have mainly set off the bare infinitive against the *to* and
for to infinitive together. I think this is correct. All the evidence shows
that there is much less difference, especially in Late Middle English,
between *to* and *for to* than between zero and (*for*) *to*. Quirk & Svartvik
(1970), for instance, show that in Chaucer *for to* can occur wherever *to*
occurs with only one exception – as a complement of a copula – but
this must be due (as they themselves admit) to the paucity of the data,
since Kenyon (1909: 133ff.) gives many examples with *for to* in this case.
Warner too has noted a similar distributional parallel between *to* and *for
to* in the Wycliffite sermons (1982: 116). Other evidence in Kenyon (pp.
9ff.; 90ff; 102ff.) suggests that the difference between *to* and *for to* is
mainly a question of lexical preference or style (metre), while that
between bare and (*for*) *to* infinitive seems to indicate a grammatical
function, as I have shown above. Quirk & Svartvik (1970: 399) and
Warner (1982: 123ff.) mention a few areas where the choice of *for to* over
to is more structurally conditioned, the main one being the preference
for *for to* in adjuncts.

4.6.2.4   The perfect infinitive

Although Mustanoja (1960: 517) gives an example of the perfect
infinitive in Old English from Alfred's translation of *Boethius*, the
construction is extremely rare then and remains so in Early Middle
English (see Sanders 1915: 4; Miyabe 1956). Only from the fourteenth
century onwards do we come across it with any frequency (see

Mustanoja 1960: 518). By nature, the perfect infinitive refers to an action that has taken place before the moment of speaking or before some other point of reference given in the clause.

(327) The worste kynde of infortune is this,/ A man to han ben in
       prosperitee,/ And it remembren whan it passed is.

(Troilus III.1626–8)

(328) ich... schulde mid rihte beon more scheomeful uorte habben i
       speken, ase ich spec,

(Ancr. (Nero) 143.18–20)

'I should rightly be more ashamed to have spoken as I spoke'

However, must of the early examples do not concern an action in the past; most often the perfect infinitive expresses the non-realisation of an action (the Latin 'irrealis'). This is because the perfect infinitive is usually found in combination with modal verbs which express contingencies rather than facts (e.g. the only Old English examples Visser gives (1963–73 §§ 2044; 2154) are of a modal + perfect infinitive):

(329) Than if I nadde spoken.../ Ye wolde han slayn youreself anon?

(Troilus IV.1233–4)

In Middle English the expression of the irrealis rather than tense becomes the main function of the perfect infinitive, for examples like (328) are rare. Although (327) may look like a straightforward 'tense' example, it resembles the 'irrealis' perfect in that *A man* clearly is only an example, he does not exist; i.e. the situation is not 'real'. Most of the Middle English examples in Visser (1963–73) which do not take a modal, represent unreality of one kind or another:

(330) And she no husbonde had I-had/ hir to haue gouerned & lad...

(Cursor (Trin) 10803–4)

This association of unreality and the perfect infinitive led to what Mustanoja (1960: 517) has called the 'peculiar' Middle English use of the perfect infinitive in cases where the action expressed in the infinitive is simultaneous with that of the matrix verb, where Present-Day English would employ a present infinitive:

(331) And on hir bare knees adoun they falle/ And wolde have kist his
       feet...

(CT I.1758–9 [1: 1760–1]).

'they fell down on their bare knees and wanted to kiss his feet'

As such it also comes to be used in adverbial adjuncts (even of purpose):

(332) he smot mid more maine,/ To abbe icloue him al þat heued...

(Glo.Chron.A. (Clg) 1134–5)

'he struck with more power in order to split his head right open...'

As Visser shows (1963–73: §2050), these occur not only in Middle English but in the modern period as well.

4.6.2.5 The passive infinitive

In Old English the passive infinitive (*wesan/beon/weorðan* + past participle) is rare and has generally been ascribed to Latin influence (see Callaway 1913: 271–2; Scheler 1961: 101). There is some confusion as to what constitutes the passive infinitive. The problem is that in Old and Middle English an active infinitive is often used where Present-Day English would employ a passive one, as in:

(333)a. and yf ye thynk it be to doo...

(Davis 1971–6: 184.70)

'and if you think it can be done...'

b. þai ordent him to hange on rode.

(Cursor (Frf) 14879)

'they commanded him to be hung on the cross.'

For this reason Quirk & Wrenn (1957: §131) include the above infinitives under the passive infinitive, but one expressed with the active form. Other linguists (Callaway 1913: 29ff.; van der Gaaf 1928a, b) more guardedly speak of the infinitive used in a passive sense. Bock (1931: 200ff.) and Fischer (1991), on the other hand, believe that there are good reasons to interpret the infinitives in (333) as truly active within the grammatical system in which they function. Mitchell (1985: §923) sees the whole thing as a pseudo-problem; according to him the 'argument is largely terminological'.

Mitchell's 'solution' may be acceptable when one looks only at Old English. It is not sufficient, however, when one also wishes to explain the changes that take place in Middle English. Why is it that in the course of the Middle English period this formally active but semantically passive infinitive becomes passive also in *form*? (Mitchell calls the latter the periphrastic passive infinitive.) Van der Gaaf's explanation (1928a: 110; and see also 1928b: 133) is of a psychological nature, based on analogy:

the circumstance that the passive sense of what was originally the inflected infinitive…, was not expressed by any distinctive form, while otherwise passivity was reflected in the language, must have been felt to be an anomaly. If this psychological factor had not asserted itself, no innovation would probably have been introduced.

However, it does not solve the problem, it merely shifts it. Why otherwise would this tendency to have congruity between function and form suddenly show itself in Middle English and not in Old English, where other passive forms were also current? (See also languages like Dutch, which still employs infinitives such as (333) in spite of possessing other passive forms (finite and non-finite) as well.)

Bock (1931: 204ff.) looks for the solution in the spread of the *to*-infinitive marker. In Old English the periphrastic passive infinitive is only found as a bare infinitive (see vol. I, section 4.5.3.2) and it could therefore only occur as a complement to a verb. Once it had acquired *to*, the passive form could spread to other functions. This is an interesting, but not quite satisfactory, solution because it does not explain why the periphrastic passive does not occur in constructions like *Scipia het ealle burg towearpan* (*Or*.4 13.212.19) 'Scipio commanded the town [to be] destroy[ed]', which has a bare but active infinitive, and where Present-Day English would use a passive infinitive.

It is noteworthy, though, that in Old English the periphrastic passive is indeed found only as a complement to the verb, which is always a modal verb (see van der Gaaf 1928a: 108–9). It is true that some occasional periphrastic passives occur in other functions, but these are all faithful translations of Latin passive infinitives. There is good reason to believe therefore that the (bare) periphrastic passive in Old English was a native phenomenon after modal verbs but a borrowing from Latin in other functions (i.e. when used predicatively, postadjectivally, and after verbs of perception, causation etc.; see Fischer 1991).

The answer to the question why the periphrastic passive spread in Middle English must start out from the Old English situation. In other words, why did Old English modal verb complements require a passive form, while in other functions the active form sufficed? In Fischer (1991) I have suggested that it is related to a change in basic word order that English underwent in this period. More research is needed here, but the basic idea is as follows. In Old English, a SOV language (for a brief discussion of basic word-order typology, see vol. I, section 4.6.1), *ealle burg*, in the *Orosius* example above, would be interpreted as the object of

the infinitive, and therefore an active infinitive – in form as well as sense
– is appropriate; in Middle English, a SVO language, the same phrase
would be interpreted as subject of the infinitival complement and so a
passive infinitive is to be expected (for more details, see also section
4.6.2.10).[37] Notice that in constructions where the passive infinitive
occurs after a modal, an active form cannot be used because that would
change the meaning of the utterance:

(334)   ne ðearf he beon eft gefullod

(ÆCHom.II, 3 25.224)

'he may not be baptised again'

An active infinitive is clearly impossible because that would result in the
reading 'he may not baptise again'. The *Orosius* example and (334) differ
as well in that *he* can only be the subject of the clause, while *ealle burg* is
an object.

Thus, the active infinitive with so-called passive sense was replaced
by a periphrastic passive in the course of the Middle English period in
the functions mentioned above. Apart from those positions, it started to
appear postnominally and as an adjunct of purpose in Middle English:

(335)   ...he till hiss Faderr wass/ Offredd forr uss o rode,/ All alls he
        wære an lamb to ben/ Offredd...

(Orm. 12644–7)

'he was offered to his Father for us on the cross as if he were a lamb
to be offered'

(336)   & puplicaness comenn þær,/ Att himm to wurrþenn fullhtnedd,

(Orm. 9295–6)

'and publicans came there to be baptised by him'

Again, in Old English, it was possible in some cases for an active
infinitive to appear in these positions, although finite clauses were more
usual. An example of a postnominal active infinitive is given in (337)
and of an active adjunct of purpose in (338):

(337)   næs   þær... wæteres drync to brucanne
        not-was there of-water drink to use

(And. 23)

'there was no drink of water to be (that could be) used'

(338)   hine... of   þære byrig gelæddon to stænenne
        him   from the city led   to stone

(ÆCHom.I, 3 46.32)

'[they] led him out of the city to be stoned'

A passive infinitive came to be preferred in Middle English because in a SVO language the relation between subject and verb is primary, hence the empty NP position of the infinitive (PRO) can syntactically only be a subject. This can be achieved by interpreting *drinc* in (337) as subject (a passive infinitive becomes necessary) or by inserting an explicit (lexical) subject, such as '*for us* to use'. The same applies to (338). The empty subject of the infinitive is either co-referential with the matrix subject, in which case we get 'they$_i$ led him out of the city PRO$_i$ to stone him', or with the matrix object, which will give 'they led him$_i$ out of the city PRO$_i$ to be stoned' (for the use of the term *PRO*, see section 4.6.2.2). In the latter case a passive infinitive becomes again necessary. In Old English, which is still SOV, the relation between object and verb is primary (see Strang 1970: 345ff.) and the subject is often left unexpressed. For these reasons the infinitive in (337) and (338) is not syntactically related to a subject but to an object (*drinc* and *hine* respectively) and the infinitive remains active.

4.6.2.6   The 'split' infinitive

Considering the relatively recent attacks levelled at this construction by language purists, one would think that it is a fairly new development. However, instances of the so-called split infinitive have been found, albeit sporadically, as early as the thirteenth century. In the earliest examples it is most frequently the negative adverb or the personal pronoun as (in)direct object that is placed between (*for*) *to* and the infinitive. Before Pecock (fifteenth century) adverbial phrases are not found there, with the exception of adverbs of manner and degree – which, by the way, are the adverbs that most favour preverbal position with finite verbs too. Pecock, indeed, is the most prolific splitter of infinitives of all times. Whereas nowadays longer phrases are usually only put in between *to* and the infinitive for jocular effects (see Visser 1963–73: §972, p. 1038), Pecock can insert whole sentences quite seriously. Some examples of the earlier type of split infinitive are:

(339)   and he cleopede him to, alle his wise cnihtes,/ for to *him* reade,...
　　　　　　　　　　　　　　　　　　　　　　　　　　(*Brut* (Otho) 5495–6)

'and he called to him all his wise knights (in order) to advise him'

(340)   ... þou3 þei not laboure forto *so* gete þe same contemplaciouns...
　　　　　　　　　　　　　　　　　　　　　　　　　　(Pecock *Rule* 475.23–4)

A typical Pecockian example is:

(341)   Also if þis man myȝte assigne þee, lord, *for to freely and in no weye of his owne dette or of eny oþer mannys dette to ȝeve* and paie eny reward to þe seid oþer man,...

(Pecock Rule 182.22–5)

Nowadays, the preplacing of the direct object is no longer current. The personal pronoun in this position is without doubt related to the old SOV word order, in which object pronouns were most commonly placed before the verb whether finite or non-finite. That the split infinitive does not occur yet in Old English must be due to the fact that *to* and the infinitive (usually marked by a dative inflection) were still considered too much a unity.

4.6.2.7   The *(for) NP to V* construction

The construction in *It is time for you to go*, which is frequent in Present-Day English, is new in the Middle English period. In the past and also more recently, a great deal of attention has been paid to the origin of the construction and to the changes in *for* from a preposition marking the benefactive function of the following NP to a complementiser introducing a non-finite complement (in the traditional literature the former is often called 'organic' *for*, the latter 'inorganic' *for*). Some linguists (Stoffel 1894; Lightfoot 1981a; but cf. Fischer 1988) have explained the rise of the complementiser *for* as being due to the spread of the so-called accusative and infinitive construction (for the latter, see section 4.6.2.10). It has also been related (Lightfoot 1979; but cf. Fischer & van der Leek 1981) to the disappearance of the *for to* infinitives.

The important thing to realise is that when the *for NP to V* construction first makes its appearance in Middle English, *for* is definitely a preposition; the development to complementiser is of later date (Lightfoot 1979, 1981a fails to make this distinction). In Middle English the construction takes the place of the Old English construction in which the benefactive function was expressed by the dative case. With the loss of inflections, this dative was slowly replaced in the course of the Middle English period by a prepositional phrase, in Early Middle English usually *to* + NP, later also *for* + NP. This benefactive dative is especially frequent after semi-impersonal constructions such as *it is good/bad/shameful* etc. Here follow some examples showing the various stages of development of the benefactive:

(342)a. Hit is swiðe earfoðe *ænigum* [dat.] to þeowienne twam hlafordum

(ÆAdmon.1 2.46)

'it is very difficult [for] anyone to serve two lords'

b. For it was not semely *to þe* to folowe swych a rowte,...

(Allen 1931: 23, 119–20)

'it was not fitting for you to follow such a company'

c. ...that it is bet *for me*/ To sleen myself than been defouled thus.

(CT V.1422–3 [6: 714–15])

However, as well as the prepositional phrase, the dative NP – or rather the oblique NP (in Middle English dative and accusative are virtually indistinguishable) – is also still found in Middle English:

(343) it es vncuth and vnwon,/ *þe fader* to be-cum þe sun,

(Cursor (Vsp) 10139–40)

'it is strange and unusual [for] the father to become the son'

The change from preposition into complementiser presupposes the following reanalysis:

1   for = preposition: NP V_{fin} for NP_i [$_s$ PRO_i to V]
2   for = complementiser: NP V_{fin} [for [$_s$ NP to V]]

In structure 1, the *for NP* is an argument of the matrix verb and the infinitive has an empty subject (PRO; for the use of this term, see section 4.6.2.2), which is co-indexed with the benefactive NP. In structure 2 the same NP is no longer an argument of the matrix verb but of the infinitive; the infinitive, in other words, has acquired a lexical subject. The earliest unambiguous examples of reanalysed *for NP to V* constructions after semi-impersonals date from the sixteenth century (Fischer 1988 disagrees here with Lightfoot 1979, 1981a, who dates them in the fourteenth century).

    The older construction without *for* was reanalysed in a similar way, and this happened earlier than in the corresponding *for NP to V* constructions. There are various criteria on the basis of which one can establish whether reanalysis has indeed taken place (for a complete list and discussion see Fischer 1988) such as front placement (344), placement after *as, than, but* (345), *NP to V* in predicative function (346) etc.:

(344) A kynges sone to ben in swich prysoun,/ And ben devoured,
        thoughte hem gret pite.

(LGW 1975–6)

(345) ...no thyng...is so muchel agayns nature as a man to encressen his
owene profit to the harm of another man.

(CT VII.1584–5 [10: 1584–5])

(346) The thridde grevance is a man to have harm in his body.

(CT X.665 [12: 665])

The questions to be answered are, firstly, why did this reanalysis take
place in Middle English and not in Old English,[38] and secondly, why
was it earlier in the *NP to V* construction than in the corresponding *for
NP to V* construction? Various factors played a role. With the loss of
inflections, dative and accusative cases were no longer distinguishable
so that the *NP to V* construction formally resembled the *NP to V*
construction found after perception verbs and causatives in Old English
and Middle English, where the infinitival construction, as in *I saw him go*,
is equivalent to an object clause *I saw that he*... The loss of verbal
inflections may have been influential too since in some cases it became
difficult to distinguish the subjunctive – which could be used in *finite*
semi-impersonal complements – from the (bare) infinitive, as in:

(347) 'Bet is', quod he, 'thyn habitacioun/ *Be* with a leon or a foul
dragoun,/ Than with a womman usynge for to chyde.'

(CT III.775–7 [2: 749–51])

This is a less likely factor, however, since after most finite verbs *to* was
present to indicate the nature of the verbal form. Moreover, ambiguity
could only arise in the present tense, not in the past. Zandvoort (1949)
suggested that the order of elements in the sentence plays a part in the
reanalysis. This is taken up by Fischer (1988), who believes that the
change in word order from SOV to SVO and the fixation of this order
in Middle English are important. In Old English the benefactive NP
would normally precede the matrix verb, and the object of the infinitive,
if it had one, would usually precede this. In other words in Old English
benefactive NP and infinitive were hardly ever adjacent. This situation
changes drastically in Middle English. The normal order there was for
the benefactive dative to follow the matrix verb and to stand
immediately before the infinitive. To analyse that NP as the subject of
the infinitive would be the next logical step in a SVO language (see also
the discussion in section 4.6.2.10).

A final influential factor may have been the existence of nominative
and infinitive constructions of the type illustrated in (348), which are
attested from Late Middle English onwards:

(348) he het   men   to ȝyve hem mede/ If þei
he commanded people to give them reward if they
coude hit   riȝtly   rede/ And *þei   to   ȝyve*
could it [a riddle] correctly guess and they to give
þe   same   aȝeyn ...
the   same   in return ...

(*Cursor* (Trin) 7121–3)

'he commanded people to give them a reward if they could guess it
correctly while they should give the same in return'

After semi-impersonal constructions nominative forms are also found
occasionally only in structure 2 (shown in the following example by
front placement):

(349) ..., and *thou to love* that lovyth nat the is but grete foly.

(Malory *Wks* (Add.59678) 322.3)

It is also possible, however, that the development that took place within
the *NP to V* construction after semi-impersonals was in fact responsible
for the use of the 'absolute' construction of (348). Many instances in
which it is used implicitly contain a semi-impersonal expression:

(350) ... and I to take þe lesse when I may have þe more, my ffrendes
wold þenke me not wyse ...

(*Stonor* an.1472, 123, p. 126.7–8)

Compare this to 'it is not wyse (for) me to ...'.

The reason why the reanalysis took place later in the *for NP to V*
construction is not hard to find. First of all, the *NP to V* was much older
than the *for NP to V* construction and therefore likely to be subject to
reanalysis earlier. Secondly, the introduction of *for* itself stood in the
way of reanalysis. It was introduced in order to emphasise the
benefactive function of the NP in question, so *for* re-established the link
between the NP and the matrix verb. A possible link with the infinitive
could only take place after *NP to V* had been reanalysed. This paved the
way for the reanalysis of the *for NP to V* construction, which in other
ways so closely resembled it.

THE FUNCTION OF INFINITIVAL COMPLEMENTS

The following sections deal with the use of the infinitive as a
complement of a verb (subject complement after copula verbs, object
complement), or of an adjective. Although not strictly a complement,
the use of the infinitive in subject position is also discussed. Infinitival

constructions following nouns have been dealt with in section 4.6.1.2. Infinitives used in an adverbial function are treated together with their finite counterparts in section 4.6.3, which ends with a discussion of the so-called 'absolute infinitive'.

4.6.2.8　The infinitive as subject

In Old English the infinitive as subject is rare (see vol. I, section 4.5.3.2). When it occurs with a copula it is usually a direct translation from Latin; when it occurs with an impersonal verb, it should presumably not be interpreted as subject but as a complement of the impersonal verb, as has been argued above (section 4.6.2.3). The subject infinitive becomes more frequent in the Middle English period because of a reanalysis that took place in the Old English period (a development that is supported by the need to translate the Latin subject infinitive), which is very lucidly described by Bock (1931). He shows (p. 129) that Old English infinitives, which linguists in the past had often interpreted as subjects, were in fact adnominal infinitives. As an example he gives:

> (351)　Nis　þæt uneaðe eallwealdan　gode (dat.) to gefremmanne
> 　　　　not-is that uneasy to-Almighty God　　　　to do
>
> <div align="right">(<i>And.</i> 205)</div>

which according to him means,

> 'that-to-do is not difficult for the Almighty God'

with the infinitive dependent on *þæt*, which functions as the subject of the clause. It does not mean 'to do that is not difficult', where the infinitive would be subject and *þæt* dependent (as object) on the infinitive. Bock convincingly shows that this is the only way to explain why it was the *to*-infinitive rather than the plain infinitive that first developed a subject function in the history of English. Still, many linguists are convinced – Bock (1931: 132, note 1) refers to Callaway (1913), Einenkel (1914, 1916) and others; Visser (1963–73: §§898–901) is the most recent – that it was the plain or bare infinitive that first developed a subject function. Presumably, this is because these linguists ascribe a nominal function (that of subject and object) to the bare infinitive, while the *to*-infinitive is preserved for prepositional objects (see Bock 1931: 132). Visser (1963–73: §901) even maintains that the *to*-infinitive occurs far less frequently in Old English and Middle English than the plain infinitive in this function in spite of many opinions to the contrary (e.g. Kenyon 1909: 112; Sanders 1915: 37; Mustanoja 1960:

522–4, all note that *to* is far more common). Visser writes (1963–73: §901, p. 952): 'When after about 1500 the construction with plain infinitive is on its way towards obsolescence, the construction with the *to*-infinitive begins to spread with the result that eventually the older idiom is completely ousted', thus completely inverting the actual state of affairs. This is made abundantly clear by the statistics provided by Bock. The plain infinitive only begins to occur as subject on analogy with the *to*-infinitive, and never acquired a very strong position there, except to a certain extent in poetry for metrical reasons.[39] The examples in Visser show that when a plain infinitive does occur it is often in apposition to another noun as in:

(352) For þet is aa hare song, þonki Godd ant herien þet...

(HMaid. (Bod) 11.4–5)

'for that is always her song to thank God and praise that...'

In this function the plain infinitive can still be used as 'subject' even in Present-Day English: cf. *that is something he could never do, speak frankly.* Notice that the relation between the infinitive and the noun is quite different here from the example in (351), where the infinitive stands in a kind of purpose relation to the noun – 'that in order to do (it)' – which explains why the *to*-infinitive is used here rather than the plain infinitive. From the very beginning there is strong competition between the infinitive and the verbal noun in *-ing* (< OE *-ung*) in subject position. In Middle English, the two could be used without much difference in meaning, to judge from the following example:

(353) Wepynge, and nat for to stynte to do synne. may nat avayle.

(CT X.90 [12: 90])

4.6.2.9 The infinitive as subject complement (predicative infinitive)
The infinitive has this function mainly after the verb *to be*. In the Middle English period, the following types, some of which begin to merge syntactically and semantically, can be distinguished.

1   THE INFINITIVE AFTER A COPULA

(354) As gret a craft is kepe wel as winne

(Troilus III.1634)

Sanders (1915: 45) and Mustanoja (1960: 526) write *contra* Visser (1963–73: §917) that this infinitive does not occur in Old English. Visser's examples are suspect, since all but two come from the *Old English Homilies*, which is an Early Middle English version of an Old

English text. Its use remains rare in Early Middle English (both with and without *to*) and only becomes slightly more frequent in Late Middle English. Besides the infinitive, the present participle (in *-ende, -yng*, north *-ande*) comes to be used in Middle English in this position seemingly without much difference in meaning (see Visser 1963–73: §916). For the difficulty in distinguishing between a subject function of the infinitive and a subject–complement function (as is relevant also to (354)), see Sanders (1915: 37–45).

2   THE TYPE *ME IS TO DONNE HIT*

This impersonal construction expresses obligation or necessity. It occurs frequently in Old and Middle English and is presumably of native origin. It changes into a 'personal' variant (following the development of other impersonal constructions – see section 4.3.1.2) in the Late Middle English period. The earliest instance is found in Wyclif:

(355)   for he wist what he was to do

(Wycl.Sel.Wks I.120.25)

Visser (1963–73: §369) quotes an earlier instance from *Cursor Mundi* (Edinburgh MS) but this example is suspect since it is more likely to be an instance of type 3 (see below).

3   THE TYPE *HE IS TO CUMENNE*

This construction differs from type 2 in that it has a personal subject. (When the personal variant of 2 developed, however, types 2 and 3 became identical on the surface.) It occurs in Old English only in translated prose; essentially it remains a construction foreign to the Old English grammatical system. The meaning of the phrase depends on its Latin original, since it was used to translate both the Latin periphrastic future (*-urus esse*) and the gerund after the preposition *ad*. Thus, it could express future, as it does in *he is to cumenne* (Latin *venturus est*), and also purpose, as in:

(356)   drihtnes mægen wæs hig to gehælenne
        (et virtus erat domini ad sanandum eos)

(Lk.(WSCp) 5.17)

'the Lord's power was [there] to heal them'

The construction becomes more common English idiom in the Middle English period, especially the one containing the infinitive *to cumen*. The reason for this is clear (see Klöpzig 1922: 382ff.). It became confused with a native Old English construction consisting of a form of the verb *to be* and the adjectival present participle *tocymende* (from the complex verb *tocuman*). In Late Old English/Early Middle English the inflected infinitive (*-enne*) and present participle endings (*-ende*) became confused, and the loss of the Old English prefixes caused *to* in *tocymende* to be reinterpreted as an infinitival marker. This made the infinitival *he is to cumen* more acceptable to the grammar. With other verbs the construction becomes only more frequent at the very end of the Middle English period.

4   THE TYPE *HE IS TO BLAME*

Superficially, this type resembles 3, but there are some important differences: first of all, it is only used with transitive verbs (unlike type 3); secondly, its meaning is neither purpose nor future but it expresses possibility or obligation depending on context; finally, it is very frequent in Old and Middle English, and although it is used to translate the Latin gerundial construction (*audiendus est* 'he can/must be heard'), it clearly is native since it occurs in most extant Old English texts and in other Germanic languages. The reason why only transitive verbs occur in this construction lies in the fact that the subject functions as object of the infinitive ('one can/must blame *him*'). The existence of this construction in Old English must be held responsible for the fact that type 3 did not spread in Old English, and that, when 3 was used, it occurred only in unambiguous situations in which the two could not be confused. Klöpzig (1922) shows that type 3 only occurs with intransitive verbs or with transitive verbs that have their own object (see (356)), so that the subject of the sentence cannot be interpreted as the object of the infinitive as is the case in type 4.

The question that should be asked now is why it is that type 3 becomes acceptable in English grammar from the Middle English period onwards, whereas type 4 starts to decline at about the same time and is ultimately replaced (except in a few idiomatic phrases like *he is to blame*, *the house is to let*) by a construction with a passive infinitive. The latter begins to occur from about 1300 onwards:

(357)   þey beþ to be blamed eft þarfore...

(Mannyng HS (Hrl) 1546)

Klöpzig (1922) suggests that the reason for the decline of type 4 is the increasing frequency of the passive infinitive; this made the older (active) construction superfluous and so it disappeared. This, however, only shifts the problem, because the question then is, why did the passive infinitive become the norm in this construction at all? Although Old English had a periphrastic passive after modals, it never occurs in type 4 constructions. It was suggested above (section 4.6.2.5), that the development of the passive infinitive is connected with the change in basic word order in English around this time. It is not unlikely that this plays a role in the rise and decline of types 3 and 4 respectively, too.

The use of the active infinitive is related to the 'interpretability' of the initial NP as object, since the active infinitive lingers longest where this NP is inanimate rather than animate, and therefore typically object rather than subject. In the Old English grammatical system it is unproblematic, even natural, to interpret preverbal arguments, even animate ones, as objects, due to SOV order. In Middle English, however, this becomes increasingly difficult. With SVO as basic order, any preverbal NP will tend to be given a subject interpretation. This interpretation is also in line with a general tendency for the subject of an auxiliary – and *to be to* clearly functions within the system of modal auxiliaries in Middle English – to control the empty subject (PRO; for this term, see section 4.6.2.2) of the infinitive (see Denison's (1985b: 54) remarks concerning the development of full verb *do* into auxiliary *do*). This *is* the case in constructions like he_i *is* [PRO_i *to come*] and he_i *is* [PRO_i *to be blamed*] but not in *he is to blame*. Consequently, type 3, which is reinforced by the existence of type 2, now personal, becomes the acceptable construction in Middle English, while type 4 slowly disappears.

There is one clear exception concerning the disappearance of type 4 and that is its survival in so-called Tough-movement constructions of the type 'He is easy to please'. It should be noted, however, that even here the passive infinitive began to occur in Middle English and has remained in use in certain cases until the present day (see Visser 1963–73: §§940, 1388). The reason why the passive infinitive did not become established in these cases is because of the structurally ambiguous use of the adjectives ('hard', 'easy', 'difficult', etc.) in the constructions concerned. They function as adjectival phrases to the subject as well as adverbial phrases to the infinitive. While turning the active infinitive into a passive one does justice to the adverbial reading ('He is easi(ly) to be pleased', i.e. 'one can easily please him'), it is decidedly strange in the adjectival reading because the adjective requires a structural subject and not a derived subject, as the subject of a passive infinitive inevitably is (i.e. it is thematically an object). In other words, the use of the passive infinitive emphasises the adverbial reading of the adjective, while the adjective itself remains morphologically an adjective. After the fifteenth century one occasionally comes across a true adverbial form, in which case the infinitive is always passive. An example given by Visser (1963–73: §1389) is:

(358) The olde Ewes... be easi/yer to be entreated

> (1586, B. Googe, in Heresbach's Husbandry III, 139)

The use of these passive infinitives in the late middle/early modern period was also affected by the peculiar characteristic of a number of adjectives borrowed from French/Latin to convey both an active and a passive reading. Thus, *profitable* could mean 'useful' (passive reading) as well as 'able, competent' (active). Sometimes this distinction was adopted for native adjectives as well:

(359)a. ... but certes what ende that shal therof bifalle, it is nat *light* to knowe.

> (*CT* VII.1040 [10: 1040])

'... it is not *easy* to know.' [passive]

b. And of the galle the goddesse,/ For sche was full of hastifesse/ Of wraththe and *liht* to grieve also,...

> (*CA* (Frf) v, 1481–3)

'... she was full of rashness, of wrath and *prone* to do harm' [active]

When these adjectives were employed in Tough-movement constructions, the presence of the passive infinitive could help to indicate that the reading was passive, not active:

(360) [thou] hast so woven me with thi resouns the hous of Didalus, so entrelaced that *it is unable to ben unlaced*,...

> (*Bo.* III, pr.12, 155–7)

(for more details, see Fischer 1991).

The meaning of construction type 3 is an amalgamation of the earlier meanings of types 2, 3 and 4. Most commonly, it expresses obligation or necessity, but other shades of meaning remain possible too. Type 1 remains and is not influenced by the other types since here the verb *to be* functions as a full verb, not an auxiliary; it has its own subject, i.e. there is no co-reference between the subject of *be* and the empty subject of the infinitive, which is an arbitrary PRO (PRO$_{arb}$ – see section 4.6.2.2).

4.6.2.10 The infinitive as direct object
Here only infinitival constructions occurring after full verbs will be discussed. For the infinitival complement after modal auxiliaries and the difference in usage between the bare and the *to*-infinitive, see section 4.6.2.3. There are two main types of object construction: (a) those that have an overt complementiser *for*:

(361) My Lord of G... desired for declaration of his worship to be yovyn to hym in writing

(Proc.Privy C 5.49)

but these are extremely rare in Middle English and do not really become current much before the nineteenth century (see Visser 1963–73: §2064); and (b) those without *for*, usually referred to as accusative and infinitive constructions, which can be divided into three subtypes:

(362)A God graunte thee thyn hoomly fo t'espye!

(CT IV.1792 [5: 548])

B & Godde we scullen bihaten, ure sunnen to beten.

(Brut (Clg) 9180)

'and we must promise God to atone for our sins'

C That he ne wol nat suffre it heled be,...

(CT VII.3055 [10: 3027])

On the surface all three subtypes look the same, they are all of the type $NP_1 \ V_{fin} \ NP_2 \ (for) \ (to) \ V$, but syntactically they differ in that the second NP can either be the subject argument of the infinitive as in (362 C), or the (in)direct object argument of the finite verb as in (362A) and (362B). In the latter case the infinitive has no overt subject, but empty PRO, which correlates either with the (in)direct object of the matrix verb, as in (A) or with the subject of the matrix verb, as in (B). All three constructions occurred in Old English (see vol. I, section 4.5.3.2), but since then there were a number of morphological and syntactic changes which affected the interpretation and currency of (A) and (C) in certain ways.

In Old English, types (A) and (C) were not only syntactically but also formally different in that in (A)-constructions NP_2 occurred normally in the dative, while in (C) NP_2 was accusative. Furthermore (A)-verbs are commonly followed by the *to*-infinitive, (C)-verbs by the bare infinitive. In Middle English, case syncretism completely wipes out the formal difference between dative and accusative, while the distinction in usage between *to*- and the bare infinitive also becomes less well-defined.

Another sign that the (A)- and (C)-constructions have become more closely related is that in Middle English many original (A)-verbs appeared with an inanimate NP_2, which in Old English was only possible with (C)-verbs. This means that in Middle English there are (A)-verbs that can appear in (A)- as well as (C)-constructions:

(363)A ... the kynge commaunded two knyghtes and two ladyes to take the child...

(Malory *Wks* (Add.59678) 11.10–11)

C And whan he had used hit he ded of hys crowne and commaunded the crowne to be sett on the awter.

(Malory *Wks* (Add.59678) 908.11–12)

Another example of such a verb is *require*:

(364)A ... he requeryd me to wryte on-to yow þat...

(Davis 1971–6: 409.48–9)

C Item, the seid John requerith an astate to be takyn in those londys lymyted to William the sone for deffaut of issu off Clement Paston...

(Davis 1971–6: 387.27–8)

Certain conditions which restricted the occurrence of (C)-constructions in Old English were lifted in the course of the Middle English period. These restrictions – associated with the use of only the bare infinitive in (C)-constructions in Old English – were: (a) the matrix verb and infinitive had to share the same tense domain; and (b) the action conveyed by the infinitive was concrete rather than abstract. Thus, Old English allowed *I saw him come* and *I found him lie along the road* but not *I saw him to have come* or *I found him to be a liar* because the last two examples violate conditions (a) and (b) respectively.[40] This means, in practice, that Old English only allowed the (C)-construction after physical perception verbs and causative verbs because only these verbs can obey the imposed conditions. In Middle English these conditions no longer hold, as can be seen from the fact that (C)-constructions occur after 'command'-type verbs whose infinitival complements – clearly for semantic reasons – always refer to some action in the future, and after verbs of mental perception, which naturally do not allow concrete or physical activities to appear in the infinitive:

(365) ... Which that he knew in heigh sentence habounde, ...

(*CT* VII.2748 [10: 2652])

Various explanations have been given for the developments described above. Borrowing from Latin and analogical extension (i.e. the (C)-

construction could spread to verbs of mental perception via verbs of physical perception) are the two factors that are most commonly offered to account for the spread of the (C)-construction. They undoubtedly played a role. However, they cannot form a complete explanation because in that case one would expect this development to have occurred already in the Old English period and in other Germanic languages such as German and Dutch, where (C) still occurs only after causatives and perception verbs.

A contributory factor was the loss of case inflections. The loss of verbal inflections, which in many dialects made the bare infinitive indistinguishable from certain indicative, subjunctive and imperative forms, may also have led to a confusion between infinitival and causal constructions (see Bock 1931; Fischer 1989), although in most cases context would have disambiguated the examples in question. Warner (1982: 134ff.) has shown that the (C)-construction after verbs of knowing spreads in certain unobtrusive ways in that it becomes available first in constructions which differ only minimally from existing ones, such as the extension of *I found him honest* to *I found him to be honest*, and also in constructions in which the new order does not occur on the surface, i.e. when NP-Preposing or wh-movement has taken place as in:

(366)   a perel in þe Chirche, þat Poul tauȝte for to come, is...

(Wycl.Sel.Wks I.303.23–4)

In Fischer (1989) I have noted that the spread of the (C)-construction coincides with a remarkable increase of the passive infinitive in that construction – cf. the (C) examples of (362)–(364). I believe this is related to the word-order change from Old English SOV to Middle English SVO. This made certain very frequent Old English (A)-type constructions containing an arbitrary PRO before the infinitive difficult to interpret in Middle English. Thus, in Old English grammar there is no problem with the analysis of

(367)   ...het   on his gesihðe þone diacon unscrydan
        ...commanded in his presence the   deacon undress

(ÆCHom. I, 29 424.11)

'...commanded the deacon to be undressed in his presence'

The NP *þone diacon* before the infinitive will be interpreted as object of the infinitive in a SOV language. In Middle English grammar, which has acquired SVO order, this NP will be interpreted as object of the preceding matrix verb (and consequently as subject of the infinitive). This would yield the wrong meaning: i.e. that the speaker commands the deacon to undress himself. It seems that in order to avoid possible misunderstanding it became more common to insert a passive infinitive in the place of the active one. This would make *diacon* subject and preserve the correct interpretation. One of the consequences of this replacement is that the relation between the matrix type (A)-verb and the following NP in Middle English was now very loose; the subject of the passive infinitive clearly is no longer a direct argument of the (A)-verb. It is not surprising that as soon as (A)-verbs start to appear in (C)-constructions (the essence of the (C)-construction was, as we have seen, that NP_2 is an argument of the infinitive, not of the matrix verb), whereby they destroy the conditions imposed earlier (in Old English) on the (C)-construction, other monotransitive verbs like *expect*, *know*, *desire*, etc. can begin to appear here as well. This is exactly what happens by the end of the Middle English period.

4.6.3 *Adverbial clauses*

4.6.3.1 Final and consecutive clauses

Final (or 'purpose') clauses and consecutive (or 'result') clauses are treated together because formal and semantic distinctions between them are slight. Generally, the purpose clause expresses a potential event, whereas the result clause expresses something factual. However, purpose comes close to result, since the outcome of purpose is a result; likewise a result may be hypothetical/non-factual, which brings it closer to purpose. Formally, the two are distinct in that the subjunctive mood is usual in purpose clauses, and the indicative in result clauses, but borderline cases show that the indicative and subjunctive may also occur in purpose and result clauses respectively. As in the complement clauses, what is expressed by the subjunctive mood may also be expressed by means of modal auxiliaries. The inflectional subjunctive, however, is still more common in Middle English, especially in the present tense. All through the period the auxiliary found most regularly in these clauses is *shal/sholde*, especially in the preterite. Next to *shal*, *may/mighte* is used, mainly in the present tense. *Mote* is also found, but is largely restricted to Early Middle English texts. *Wil/wolde* is occasionally found in Late Middle English.

The most common subordinators for both purpose and result clauses are *that* and *so(...)that*. Additionally, there are subordinators which formally distinguish purpose from result clauses. In final clauses we find a variety of conjunctive phrases (especially in prose) which strengthen the idea of purpose: *to that/the ende that*, *to that/the entente that*, *to theffect that*, etc.:

> (368) And whan ony man dyeth in the contree þei brennen his body in name of penance to þat entent þat he suffre no peyne in erthe to ben eten of wormes.
>
> > (*Mandev.* (Tit) 114.3–5)

We also find subordinators that indicate a mixture of purpose and cause: *for*, *for that*, *for as much as/that*, etc.:

> (369) And for his tale sholde seme the bettre,/ Accordant to his wordes was his cheere,...
>
> > (*CT* V.102–3 [4: 94–5])

Till that indicates a mixture of final (or consecutive) and temporal aspects:

> (370) And þanne þei schullen dyggen & mynen so strongly, till þat þei fynden the ȝates þat kyng Alisandre leet make...
>
> > (*Mandev.* (Tit) 178.19–21)

Similarly, (*so*) *that* or *so* by itself is occasionally used in clauses which are more temporal than final or consecutive:

> (371) And in sich wis weil long I can endwre,/ So me betid o wondir aventur.
>
> > (*Launc.* 79–80)

In negative purpose clauses *lest* (*that*) may be used:

> (372) 'Have do', quod she, 'com of, and speed the faste,/ Lest that oure neighebores thee espie.'
>
> > (*CT* I.3728–9 [1: 3721–2])

Lest expresses a purpose that is not desired, a fear that something might happen. For that reason it is also found in complement clauses after verbs expressing fear (see section 4.6.2.1). *That* + negative element (*ne* or *not*) is also used, but it simply denotes negative purpose.

The conjunction *that* can also be left out as long as a correlative element (*such*, *in such wise*, *thus*, etc.) is present in the main clause. This happens mainly in consecutive clauses and is on the whole more frequent in the more colloquial language of poetry than in Middle English formal prose (see Phillipps 1966a: 355):

> (373) Of clooth-makyng she hadde swich an haunt/ She passed hem of Ypres and of Gaunt.
>
> > (*CT* I.447–8 [1: 449–50])

Finally, there are instances of consecutive clauses which have often been interpreted as relative clauses with a resumptive pronoun[41] (see also section 4.6.1.1):

(374) þer passes non bi þat place so proude in his armes/ þat he ne
       dyngez hym to deþe with dynt of his honde...

(Gawain 2104–5)

Here the context makes clear that the reading is not 'there passes no one...whom he does not beat to death...' with hym as resumptive pronoun, but rather that it means 'no one of such pride in arms passes there that he does not beat him to death...', or in other words, 'no one passes there who is of such pride in arms that he does not get beaten to death...'. There is also a theoretical syntactic reason why this construction is more likely to be consecutive rather than relative: a resumptive pronoun in a relative clause is usual only when the relative pronoun has oblique case or when a clause intervenes between the relative pronoun and the rest of the clause (see section 4.6.1.1). The consecutive construction is formally distinct in that (a) both main and subclause are negative (explicit or implicit); (b) the predicate of the main clause is usually be or some existential verb; (c) the subject is often it or there or left out; and (d) the main clause usually contains a correlative element which links it strongly to the THAT-clause. Some typical examples:

(375)a. Was non of hem þat he ne gret...

(Havelok (Ld) 2160)

'there was not one of them [such] that he did not weep...'

b. Nas þar non so god wif... ʒif ʒeo were fair and fore/ þat he ne
    makede hire hore.

(Brut (Otho) 3502–3)

'there was never a good woman such...– if she was fair and flourishing[?] [forthcoming?] – that he did not make her a whore.'

c. ...went neuere wye in þis world þoruʒ þat wildernesse/ That he ne
    was robbed...

(PPl.B (Trin-C) xvii, 101–2)

'...never did a single man in this world go through that wilderness [in such a way] that he was not robbed (i.e. without being robbed)...'

4.6.3.2 Causal clauses
Causal clauses in Old English betrayed their paratactic origin, in that the causal marker for þæm (þe) still contained a deictic element (þæm) which

functioned as a kind of pragmatic connector between the two (independent) clauses (see vol. I, section 4.5.5). This made it possible for the causal marker to appear in various positions in both clauses. In Middle English this deictic element was lost, with the result that the causal marker became a conjunction with a fixed place, which in its turn influenced the relationship between the two clauses (for details see Wiegand 1982). With the exception of *for* and *forhwy*, all causal conjunctions are subordinating in Middle English. The co-ordinate causal clause has been discussed in section 4.6. The subordinate causal clauses are of two kinds: they either convey (a) new information or (b) given information (for an extensive discussion of this difference see vol. I, section 4.5.5).

1 The typical subordinator in Present-Day English is *because*. This came into use in the Late Middle English period and caught on very rapidly. At first it is found in conjunctive phrases of the type: *by (the) cause that*, *for the cause that*, etc., but already in Chaucer's time *by-cause (that)* was the more usual form:

> (376) And it is drye & no thing fructuous be cause þat it hath no moysture...
>
> *(Mandev. (Tit) 26.23–4)*

Earlier subordinators were *for (that)* (discussed in section 4.6) and the correlatives *for...for-thi/therfore*:

> (377) and for thow ne woost what is the eende of thynges, forthy demestow that...
>
> *(Bo.I, pr.6, 76–8).*

That is also very frequent in causal contexts. Although it is true that *that* may function in almost any kind of clause[42] – Jespersen called it 'the maid of all work' (for Middle English see Phillipps 1966a) – it is possible that causal *that* developed from OE *þæs (þe)*, which as a genitive indicated the source or cause, or functioned as a temporal conjunction (see vol. I, section 4.5.5):[43]

> (378) But *that* science is so fer us biforn,/ We mowen nat,.../ It overtake, it slit awey so faste.
>
> *(CT VIII.680–2)*

Notice that a prepositional source to indicate cause still occurs in Middle English:

> (379) And ek so glad *of that* she was escaped;
>
> *(LGW 815)*
>
> (other manuscripts have *that* or *that that*)

(380) Paraventure an heep of yow, ywis,/ Wol holden hym a lewed man
        in this/ *That* he wol putte his wyf in jupartie.

(CT V.1493–5)

That as a conjunction may also indicate given information. This may be
related to its possible source as a temporal conjunction (see below).

2 Two of the conjunctions in this category, *now* (*that*) and *siþ*/*sin* (*that*)
were originally temporal. This is not so surprising since these temporals
indicate that the activity expressed in the subclause is prior to that of the
main clause. Thus they could be used as causals to convey information
already known. *Now* (*that*) (< OE *nu*) was already usually causal in Old
English, but its temporal character remains prominent in its use in
Middle English (where it could also still be purely temporal, as is still
the case today):

(381) I am so sory, now that ye be lyght;

(Complaint to his Purse 3)

Sith or *sin* (< OE *siþþan*) was still exclusively a temporal conjunction in
Early Middle English. But the causal connotation spread very fast. In
Chaucer's works, for instance, *sin*/*sithen* is causal in about 75 per cent of
cases, *sith* in about 50 per cent (see Eitle 1914: 44). An example of
temporal *sin* is:

(382) For sikirly I saugh hym nat stirynge/ Aboute his dore, syn day
        bigan to sprynge.

(CT I.3673–74 [1: 3667–8])

Of causal *sin*:

(383) What sholde I tellen hem, syn they been tolde?

(CT III.56 [2: 56])

The indicative is the regular mood in causal clauses.

4.6.3.3 Conditional and concessive clauses

Conditional and concessive clauses are semantically very close in that in
both there exists a conditional relation between the main and the
subclause. In conditional clauses the effectuality of the circumstance(s)
described in the main clause depends on the condition expressed in the
subclause. In the concessive clause, the condition has, as it were, taken
effect already; the main clause, therefore, does not depend on it; rather,
it contrasts with it. Not surprisingly the conditional clause comes closest

to the concessive clause when there is a strong adversative relation between the main and subclause:

> (384) ... if it be a foul thyng a man to waste his catel on wommen, yet is it a fouler thyng whan that, ..., wommen dispenden upon men hir catel and substaunce.
>
> *(CT* X.849 [12. 849])

We also see that the subordinator used in the conditional clause often does service in the concessional clause and vice versa:

> (385) For though a man be falle in jalous rage,/ Lat maken with this water his potage,/ And nevere shal he moore his wyf mystriste, ...
>
> *(CT VI*.367–9 [9: 365–7])

For the close relation between these two types of clause, semantically and formally, and a historical overview of the similar ways of expressing conditionality and concessivity in English and related languages, see especially Harris (1989).

The most common subordinator in Middle English conditional clauses is (*ȝ*)*if* (*that*). (*ȝ*)*if* (*that*) can be accompanied by *ever* to indicate future:

> (386) And if that evere ye shul ben a wyf,/ Foryet nat Palamon, ...
>
> *(CT* I.2796–7 [1: 2792–3])

The (*ȝ*)*if* (*that*) clause is often accompanied by a correlative element in the main clause: *than(ne)*, *then(ne)* (cf. OE *þonne*), *tho*, *algates*, *certes*, etc. Later additions to the class of conditional subordinators are *and*,[44] *and if* (probably a development from the co-ordinator *and* – see Eitle 1914: 78) and conjunctive phrases such as *if so be/were that*, *be so* and (rare) *in cas that*:

> (387) For if so were I hadde swich myschaunce/ That I in hire ne koude han no plesaunce,/ Thanne sholde I lede my lyf in avoutrye ...
>
> *(CT* IV.1433–5 [5: 189–91])

To convey the sense of 'if only', 'provided that', Middle English uses *so* (*that*) (which shows the close connection between conditional and consecutive clauses) and *to that forward* (*that*).

> (388) So he may fynde Goddes foyson there,/ Of the remenant nedeth nat enquere.
>
> *(CT* I.3165–6 [1: 3159–60])

Instead of a positive main clause followed by *so* (*that*), we also find a negative main clause followed by *but if* 'unless', used with more or less the same meaning but with different emphasis:

(389) Bot I may not love þe so lyghtly,... bot if þi wil be conformed
       enterely to Goddes will.

(Allen 1931: 102.183–5)

That there is often little distance between conditional and temporal
clauses is shown by the following example, where two parallel clauses
show both *whan* and *if*:

(390) [he sins] eke *whan* he wol nat visite the sike and the prisoner, if he
       may; eke *if* he love wyf or child,... moore than resoun requireth;

(*CT* X.375 [12: 375])

Conditionality may also be expressed by other means, e.g. by inverted
word order (combined with the subjunctive, see below) as in (391);[45] an
imperative too may have conditional force (as in (392)):

(391) *Were þer* a belle on hire beiȝe [= collar].../ Men myȝte witen wher
       þei wente...

(*PPl.B* (Trin-C) Prol.165–6)

(392) *Swere* this, and heere I swere oure alliance.

(*CT* IV.357 [8: 357])

Likewise, clauses introduced by generalising or independent pronouns
often approximate to conditional clauses (note the use of *thanne* in the
main clause):

(393) For whoso wolde senge a cattes skyn,/ Thanne wolde the cat wel
       dwellen in his in;

(*CT* III.349–50 [2: 349–50])

(For more examples see Meier 1953: 202–9.) The fact that these three
alternative means of expressing conditionality are also used for
concessive clauses shows again how close the two types of clause are:

(394)a. Thurghout his armure it wole kerve and byte,/ Were it as thikke as
         is a branched ook;

(*CT* V.158–9 [4: 150–1])

  b. preise him, laste him, do him scheome, ...al him is iliche leof.

(*Ancr.* (Nero) 159: 12–13)

  'praise him, blame him, put shame on him, it is all the same to him.'

  c. That feele I wel, what so any man seith.

(*CT* VIII.711)

In contrast to Old English, where the indicative mood was usual
unless the main clause was non-indicative (see vol. I, section 4.5.6), in
Middle English conditional clauses are frequently found in the
subjunctive mood; in Late Middle English the subjunctive is almost the

rule, especially in the north. It is not quite clear what the basis was for subjunctive assignment in Middle English: different manuscripts often show different moods in the same text and sometimes indicative and subjunctive are found side by side within the same sentence:

(395) eke if he *apparailleth* (ind.) his mete moore deliciously than nede is, or *ete* (subj.) it to hastily by likerousnesse;

(*CT* X.376 [12: 376])

The subjunctive is the rule when conditionality is expressed by inverted word order. In other cases it seems to be more frequent when the condition is entirely 'open' i.e. when potentiality is stressed. Compare (396) to (397):

(396) But & sche *haue* (subj.) children with him þei leten hire lyue with hem to brynge hem vp…

(*Mandev.* (Tit) 114.8–9)

(397) If that a prynce *useth* (ind.) hasardrye,/… He is, as by commune opinioun,/ Yholde the lasse in reputacioun.

(*CT* X.599–602 [12: 599–602])

In (396) the subject may either have children or not and this is important for the effectiveness of the action expressed in the main clause. In (397) the speaker is not interested in whether a prince uses 'hasardrye' or not, but rather he wishes to state that every prince who *is* a 'hasardour' loses his reputation as a result of it. In the latter case the *if*-clause is almost equivalent to a temporal clause.

The past subjunctive is the rule in both main and subclause when the activity expressed is unreal or purely hypothetical. The subjunctive of the main clause is usually replaced by a modal auxiliary:

(398) …and I *were* a pope,/ Nat oonly thou, but every myghty man,/ …*Sholde have* a wyf;

(*CT* VII.1950–3 [10: 1950–3])

The typical conjunction in concessive clauses is *though* (< ON *þoh) or *theigh* (< OE *þeah*), the latter occurring mainly in early and southern texts. It may be accompanied by adversative particles in the main clause such as *yet, certes, nathelees,* etc. In the fourteenth century we also find *although* and longer phrases such as *though so be that, al be it (so) that. Although* is the result of the frequent co-occurrence of *though* and *al* in concessive clauses. Already in Old English *eall* was used as an emphatic adverbial in these clauses, especially when concession was expressed by inverted word order (for the use of *al* in concessive clauses in related languages, see Harris 1989). In Early Middle English *al* by itself became a conjunction, but it was still followed by inverted word order. The earliest example of this use of *al* given in the *Middle English Dictionary* (*MED*; Kurath, Kuhn & Lewis 1954–) is 1225, but *al* only becomes really frequent in the Late Middle English period:

(399)   ... That of hem alle was ther noon yslayn,/ Al were they soore yhurt, ...

(CT I.2708–9 [2708–9])

We have already seen that there were other means of expressing concessiveness: inverted word order (see (394a)), regularly accompanied by the intensifying phrase *never so*:

(400)   His manere was an hevene for to see/ Til any womman, were she never so wys, ...

(CT V.558–9 [4: 550–1])

the use of the imperative (see (394b)) and generalising clauses (see (394c)). The alternative or disjunctive concessive clause is also quite common, usually introduced by *whether* (*so*) ... *or*, but *though* ... *or* and *al* ... *or* are also found:

(401)   For whethir it be wel or be amys,/ Say on, lat me nat in this feere dwelle.

(Troilus II.313–14)

However, since concessive clauses are often used with a purely intensifying function, it is not surprising that there is a constant need of new ways of expressing it just as intensifying adverbs such as *terribly*, *awfully*, etc. are subject to constant change. Thus, concession can also be expressed through temporal, relative, comparative, co-ordinate and, as we have seen above, conditional clauses. Some examples:

(402)   For, God it woot, he sat ful ofte and song,/ *Whan that* his shoo ful bitterly hym wrong.

(CT III.491–2 [2: 491–2])

(403)   and thou, Virgine wemmelees,/ Baar of thy body – *and* dweltest mayden pure –/ The Creatour of every creature.

(CT VIII.47–9 [7: 47–9])

In Old English the subjunctive was the regular mood in concessive clauses even when the clause expressed something factual (see vol. I, section 4.5.6). In Middle English the use of the subjunctive continues but begins to be replaced later on in the period by the indicative when the subclause is factual, especially in the preterite. The increasing use of the indicative in concessive clauses is understandable since, even if the concessive clause is not necessarily a fact, it will be taken as such for the statement in the main clause to have effect. Below follow two examples showing the different moods in use:

(404)   And thogh youre grene youthe floure (subj.) as yit,/ In crepeth age alwey, as stille as stoon, ...

(CT IV.120–1 [8: 120–1])

(405)   And though that Salomon seith (indic.) that he ne foond nevere womman good, it folweth nat therfore that ...

(CT VII.1075 [10: 1075])

A reason why the preterite subjunctive is replaced more frequently by the indicative than the present (apart from the simple fact that the subjunctive and indicative forms were even less distinct in the past than the present – see chapter 2, section 2.9.2.4), is presumably that the preterite subjunctive came to be used more and more to express hypothetical/non-factual situations (see above); its use in a factual concessive clause became therefore counterintuitive.

4.6.3.4   Temporal clauses

The most common conjunction to indicate narrative sequence in Old English was *þa* 'when', which appeared usually in the combination *þa ...þa* 'then ... when/when ... then'. Another regular conjunction was *þonne*. Both these conjunctions disappear in the Middle English period. They still occur with some regularity in the early period:

(406)   Þeos Hule, þo heo þis iherde,/ 'Hauestu', heo seide ...

(Owl&N (Clg) 1667–8)

'This Owl, when she heard this, said 'Have you ...'

(407)   þo þat hit was a-yen þan euen ... þo seyde he to hem ...

(Ken.Serm. (Ld) 33.23–5)

'when [that] it was again evening ... then said he to them ...'

(408)   Þanne he komen þere þanne was Grim ded ...

(Havelok (Ld) 1204)

'when he came there, then Grim was dead'

but they are already being replaced by *whan(ne)*, *when* (*that*) (< OE interrogative pronoun *hwænne/hwanne*) in these same early texts:

(409)   Wan þe godemen þat sawe/ ... he stirten up sone onon, ...

(Havelok (Ld) 1963–5)

'When the worthy men saw that ... they leapt up all at once ...'

or *þo* is accompanied by *þat* to indicate its subordinate status, as can be seen from (407). In Chaucer, *þo* and *þonne* no longer occur as conjunctions. The only Late Middle English dialect that still makes regular use of these conjunctions is Kentish (*Ayenbite of Inwyt*), which is conservative in many respects. The disappearance of *þo* and *þonne* may be due to the fact that these forms served rather a lot of functions in Middle English;[46] and also because there was a tendency, as has been noted earlier, for correlative phrases to develop dissimilar forms for the adverb and conjunction.

Whan (*that*) may introduce a subclause that refers to a single occasion; sometimes *that* by itself is found:

(410) Þat Toilus [*sic*] ın þe toile þis torfer beheld,.../ He lyght doun full lyuely leuyt his horse,/ And dressit to Dyamede...

(*Destr.Troy* (Htrn) 7335–8)

'When Troilus saw this harm [afflicted] in the battle,... he alighted very quickly, left his horse and set upon Diomede...'

Whan (*that*) is also used to denote repeated action or a generalisation (cf. OE *þonne*):

(411) Ful many a deyntee hors hadde he in stable,/ And whan he rood, men myghte his brydel heere/ Gynglen...

(*CT* I.168–70 [1: 168–70])

Generalising *whan* is also encountered in the following forms: *whan that so ever*, *whan so that*, *ever whan that*, or it is preceded by *ay* or *alwey*:

(412) Yblessed be God that I have wedded fyve!/... Welcome the sixte, whan that evere he shal.

(*CT* III.44–5 [2:44–5])

Other conjunctions used in narrative sequence are *by that* (occurs from about 1300 but is fairly rare, more common is the phrase *by the time that*), and *as* (*that*). The latter is, however, more commonly used to express immediate sequence and also overlap in time (see below). *Now* (*that*) is hardly a pure temporal, it usually has causal overtones (see section 4.6.3.2).

The regular conjunction to express overlap in time is some form of (originally nominal) *while*: (*the*) *whyle*(*s*) (*that*), *therwhyle*, *whilst*. The article *the* represents the Old English feminine accusative demonstrative pronoun *þa*; *therwhyle*, which is rare, is a combination of the Old English temporal *þær* (see vol. I, section 4.5.7) and the noun *while*; the *-s* in *whyles* is an (adverbial) genitive ending (cf. *sithenes* below), while *whilst* is an elliptic form of *whiles that*. The latter only begins to occur at the end of our period:

(413)   ... þei holden hem self blessed & saf from all periles whil þat þei han hem [owl's feathers] vpon hem ...

(Mandev. (Tit) 149.5–6)

When the duration completely overlaps, we often find *whil* preceded by *ay*, and also the phrases *as long as, as longe time as*. The adversative meaning of *whil* is not attested in Old English and is extremely rare in Middle English. In Late Middle English it is found, but the temporal meaning is still clearly in the foreground:

(414)   ... I have thries in this shorte nyght/ Swyved the milleres doghter bolt upright,/ Whil thow hast, as a coward, been agast.

(CT I.4265–7 [1 : 4257–9])

Conjunctions indicating temporal sequence order events in two ways: (a) the event in the main clause follows the event in the subclause; (b) the event in the main clause precedes that of the subclause.

(a) can be further subdivided according to whether the conjunction (i) expresses simple sequence or (ii) limits the duration of the action of the main clause. In the first case the common conjunction is *after that*, in Late Middle English also *after* by itself. In Old English *siððan* could also be found in this sense, but in Middle English *siððan* > *sithen* develops primarily into a causal conjunction (see section 4.6.3.2). The following example shows the causal use of *sith(en)* where the original temporal meaning is still clearly present:

(415)   And now, sith I have declared yow what thyng is Penitence, now shul ye understonde that ...

(CT X.94 [12 : 94])

After that can also be used with comparative meaning 'in proportion to':

(416)   And we beleuen ... þat euery man schall haue his meryte after he hath disserued ...

(Mandev. (Tit) 87.12–13)

In the second case (ii), the regular conjunction is *sithen (that)* (other forms: *sith(e) (that), sin/sen (that), sithenes (that)*, etc.). The fact that *sithen*, as we have seen, also developed a causal sense, may account for the spread of the purely temporal conjunction *from that*, which first occurs in the *Peterborough Chronicle* (an. 1127). It is found all through the Middle

English period but it never becomes generally accepted. In Late Middle English *from* (*fra*) is also found by itself:

(417)   Bot fra þaa prude folk had hir sen,/ All spak of hir,

(Cursor (Vesp) 2415–16)

(Note the following forms in the other manuscripts: *quen* (Ffr), *Whenne that* (Trin) and *fra þat* (Gött).) Far more common is the phrase *from the/that time that*. The following mixed form is interesting:

(418)   O thow Fadir,...that comaundest the tymes to gon *from syn that* age
         hadde bygynnynge,...

(Bo. III, m.9, 1–5)

For the expression of immediate sequence, *as soon as* is used. Its negative counterpart in written Present-Day English, *no sooner ... than*, is not yet found in Middle English. Other expressions are used instead, such as *not so soone ... that/but*:

(419)   And nat so sone [he] departed nas/ Tho fro him, that he ne
         mette...

(HF 2068–70)

(b) When the event in the main clause precedes that of the subclause, we can again distinguish between simple sequence, in which case *er/or* (*that*) and *before* (*that*) are used, and cases in which the duration of the action in the main clause is limited by the conjunction, which in Middle English is *til* (*that*).

Er/or (*that*) is a development of OE *ær* (*þæm þe*) (with *or* going back to ON *ár*) with the by now familiar 'replacement' of *þe* by *that*. An earlier Middle English form is also *er than* (< *þæm*). *Before that* only occurs in Late Middle English; the earliest example of *before* by itself is found in *Pearl*, according to the *MED*:

(420)   ...On oure byfore þe sonne go doun...

(Pearl 530)

Once *before that* is introduced, *or* disappears fairly rapidly, presumably because it is easily confused with the co-ordinating conjunction. In *Mandeville's Travels*, for instance, *before that* is already the rule.

Til (*that*) occurs first in Late Old English prose and is common all through the period; *until* is not attested before 1600,

(421)   ...and wente so longe til þat he fond a chambre...

(Mandev. (Tit) 15.17)

Occasionally, the clause introduced by *til* (*that*) acquires consecutive meaning after a main clause containing *so*:

(422)   Ybeten hadde she hirself so pitously/ With bothe hir wynges til the rede blood/ Ran endelong the tree ther-as she stood.

(CT V.414–16 [4: 406–8])

The indicative is the rule in temporal clauses but the subjunctive can be used to indicate uncertainty, non-factuality or a prospective event. Not surprisingly, the subjunctive occurs most often after the conjunctions *till* (*that*) and *or/er/before* (*that*) because the action expressed in these clauses usually lies in the future if the clause is in the present tense. Thus, after *till* (*that*) etc. the indicative is the usual mood in the preterite, although the subjunctive occurs more often here than in Old English. In the present, the subjunctive is more frequent, especially in prose, and is more or less the rule when the *till*-clause depends on another subclause and when it occurs after an imperative or a volitional verb:

(423)   'Rys up', quod he, 'and faste hye,/ Til thou at my lady be;'

(HF 1592–3)

The indicative is found when the action is clearly factual:

(424)   Adoun by olde Januarie she lay,/ That sleep til that the coughe hath hym awaked.

(CT IV.1956–7 [5: 712–13])

After *or* etc. the subjunctive is the rule following negative main clauses to indicate the, as yet, non-factuality of the event (this in contrast to Old English – see vol. I, section 4.5.7):

(425)   He shal nat ryghtfully his yre wreke/ Or he have herd the tother partye speke.

*(LGW Prol.G.*324–5)

After positive main clauses the situation is rather similar to the use of mood after *till* (*that*), except that the use of the indicative does not always neatly correlate with factuality.

Modal auxiliaries replacing the subjunctive are found in temporal clauses (especially *shal*) but not very extensively.

4.6.3.5   Clauses of comparison

There are two main types of comparative clauses, those asserting equality and those asserting inequality. Unequal comparative clauses are always introduced by the conjunction *than/then* regularly followed by the general subordinator *that*:

(426) And yet he semed bisier than he was.

(CT I.322 [1: 324])

(427) Arveragus ... hadde levere dye in sorwe and in distresse/ Than that his wyf were of hir trouthe fals.

(CT V.1595–7 [6: 879–81])

In Old English these clauses had the subjunctive mood when they followed an affirmative main clause; otherwise they were indicative (see vol. I, section 4.5.8). In Early Middle English the indicative becomes the rule in the midlands but not in the south. Chaucer still prefers the subjunctive when the *than*-clause refers to a prospective event (428), and after phrases like *had lever*, which indicate uncertainty (see (427) and (429)). Instead of the subjunctive the auxiliary *should* is also found:

(428) It is ful lasse harm to lete hym pace,/ Than he *shende* alle the servantz in the place.

(CT I.4409–10 [1: 4401–2])

(429) For, by my trouthe, me were levere dye/ Than I yow *sholde* to hasardours allye.

(CT VI.615–16 [9: 613–14])

In Old English, clauses expressing comparison of equality were introduced by *swa* (*swa*) (...*swa*). In Late Old English *eall* could be added to strengthen the comparison. This gave a great variety of forms in Middle English: *alswa/alse/also/als/as/so* (main clause) ... *alswa/alse/ase/as* (subclause). *So* and *as* in turn could be strengthened by *right* in Late Middle English. *So* as part of the main clause could also be put at its end producing a new form *so as*. This in turn could develop the meaning 'in as far as',

(430) So as my troubled wit may hit atteyne,/ I wol reherse;

(Mars 161–2)

Of the rich abundance of forms quoted above, *as...as* is the most common pair. It is used when adjectives/adverbials (431) are compared. *As...so* is more usual when whole clauses are compared (432):

(431) ... Were it as thikke as is a branched ook;

(CT V.159 [4: 151])

(432) And right as the schipmen taken here avys here & gouerne hem be the lodesterre, right so don schipmen beȝonde þo parties be the sterre of the south,

(Mandev. (Tit) 119.27–9)

So can also be used before adjectives/adverbials. In that case it usually expresses degree (as in Present-Day English), but not necessarily, as (433) shows:

(433)   ..., for ye trespassen so ofte tyme as dooth the hound that
          retourneth to eten his spewyng.

(CT X.138 [12: 138])

When the verb in the two clauses is identical, it may either be repeated (see (431)) or replaced by *do* (see (432), (433)) or zero.

Example (432) shows that in Middle English main and subclause could be inverted. This emphatic form is found only from the fourteenth century onwards.

By the side of *as...as, swich/such...as* (< OE *swylc...swa*) was used where *such* functions as adjective to a following noun:

(434)   And such a smoke gan out wende/ Out of his foule trumpes
          ende, .../ As doth where that men melte led.

(HF 1645–8)

In these *such...as* constructions it often happened that *as* referred to the noun following *such* rather than to *such* itself. This turns the clause virtually into a relative clause:

(435)   Swich thyng as that I knowe, I wol declare.

(CT VIII.719)

The development is complete in clauses like

(436)   ...many of suche bestes þat I haue told before...

(Mandev. (Tit) 199.4)

where *as* has been replaced by *þat*. Examples with the relative pronoun *which* are also found.

Another type of comparative clause is the so-called conditional comparative clause (also often termed 'clause of rejected comparison'). It uses a hypothetical or counterfactual situation as a basis for comparison. The subclause is introduced by *as (that), as if, as though, lyk as*:

(437)   ...it is ȝit all broylly [= charred] as þough it were half brent,

(Mandev. (Tit) 72.3–4)

(438)   With lokkes crulle as they were leyd in presse.

(CT I.81 [1: 81])

A rather special case of comparative clause is the following,

(439)   As wisly Jupiter my soule save,/ As I shal in the stable slen thy
          knave, ...

(LGW 1806–7)

where the subclause expresses a certain truth (in the form of a wish that any man would want to see come true) which the speaker uses as a comparison in order to reach as high a degree of truth for the statement in the main clause. Very often this type of clause is used by itself as an asseverative phrase to give force to a promise or statement:

(440) Also moote I thee,/ Tomorwe wol I meete with thee,...

(*CT* VII.817–18 [10: 817–18])

The conjunction *as* could develop into a temporal subordinator when it was used to compare the duration of an activity in the main and subclause:

(441) Thus pleyneth John as he gooth by the way...

(*CT* I.4114 [1: 4106])

As does not yet have clear causal meaning in Middle English but many instances can be given where the beginnings of such a development are seen:

(442) help, god, in this nede!/ As thou art stere-man good/ and best, as I rede, Of all;/ Thou rewle vs in this rase [= rush],...

(*Towneley Pl.* (Hnt) 36.426–8)

In this example the phrase *As thou art stereman good* 'like the good helmsman you are' could also be interpreted as 'since you are a good helmsman'; both fit the context equally well.

As is used with consecutive force in example (443); next to *as...as*, *as...that* is also encountered:

(443) For me were levere thow and I and he/ Were hanged.../ As heigh as men myghte on us alle ysee!

(*Troilus* II.352–4)

In Old English *swa...swa* was used in so-called proportional comparatives:

(444) and swa he mare hæfð swa he grædigra bið
       and as he more has, so   he greedier is

(*ÆCHom.*II, 12.2 124.505)

'and the more he has the greedier he is'

In Present-Day English *the...the* is used. This instrumental *the* is also found in Old English (*þy/þon/þe*) but only absolutely, i.e. when the standard of comparison is not explicitly mentioned (see vol. I, section

4.5.8). In Early Middle English *swa ... swa* or forms developed from it may still be found:

(445) *Se* me deoppre wadeð i þe feondes leiuen, *se* me kimeð up leatere.

(Ancr. (Corp-C) 168.12–13)

'the deeper one wades into the fiend's swamp, the later one comes up'

The, however, replaces *swa* around the beginning of the fourteenth century, somewhat earlier in the south. The early examples are interesting in that they preserve the old word order of (444) and (445), i.e. the subject of the clause and not the comparative element follows *the* (*ðe*). Below follow an early and a late example:

(446) ðe he more is swaint   mid deules... ðe he strengere and betere is
the he more is troubled with devils... the he stronger and better is
on gode werkes.
in good works

(Vices&V(1) (Stw) 29.22–3)

'the more he is troubled with devils, the stronger and better he is in good works'

(447) The moore it brenneth, the moore it hath desir/ To consume every thyng...

(CT III.374–5 [2: 374–5])

(For more details and an explanation why *the* replaces *swa*, see Allen 1977: 277ff.)

The mood in clauses of comparison is as a rule the indicative unless non-factuality or potentiality is involved. Thus, we find the subjunctive in the following cases. (a) In *as if* clauses, the subjunctive indicates non-factuality. The tense is usually preterite even when the context is the present (tense shift, see section 4.3.2.2) – see (437). Instead of the subjunctive, the modal auxiliaries *sholde* and *wolde* are also used. (b) Subclauses as illustrated in (439) have a subjunctive because they express a wish. They are, as far as the subjunctive is concerned, very much like main clauses expressing a wish (see section 4.3.2.2). The auxiliary *mote* is a quite usual substitute for the subjunctive here – see (440). (c) When the comparative clause expresses the highest possible degree, a subjunctive is used in Early Middle English:

(448) Aþulf sede on hire ire/ So stille so hit were:

(Horn (Cmb) 309–10)

'Adolf said in her ear as quietly as possible'

In Late Middle English an auxiliary (*can*, *may* or *mighte*) is the rule; the conjunction itself is often accompanied by *ever*; *that* may also accompany *as* or be used instead of *as*:

(449)   And fleeth the citee faste as he may go.

(CT I.1469 [1: 1471])

(450)   And spedde hym fro the table that he myghte.

(CT II.1036 [3: 1036])

4.6.3.6   Non-finite adverbial clauses

In the previous sections we have seen that it is not always possible to separate the different types of adverbial clauses clearly. Although there are formal ways of distinguishing between them – mainly the form of the conjunction combined with the choice of mood – there are many cases where a clause could be both final and consecutive, causal and temporal, etc. In the literature it has been generally recognised that 'many of the categories traditionally used for the classification and characterisation of adverbial clauses are not discrete ones' (König, quoted in Harris 1989: 71). This is even more true if one attempts to classify non-finite clauses, which possess neither mood nor complementiser, to help make a decision. Thus, the function of a particular infinitive depends almost completely on the meaning of the noun, verb or adjective which governs it. Below follow some examples of infinitives depending on a noun, adjective and verb respectively:

(451)   ... þei fownden nothing to drynke.

(Mandev. (Tit) 37.18–19)

(452)   For þough þou se me hidouse & horrible to loken onne...

(Mandev. (Tit) 15.32–3)

(453)   ... he þat wil pupplische ony thing to make it openly knowen...

(Mandev. (Tit) 2.4–5)

It should be mentioned, however, that in quite a few cases it is not clear on which sentence element the infinitive depends. In the following instance, for example:

(454)   A Cook they hadde with hem for the nones/ To boille the chiknes
with the marybones, ...

(CT I.379–80 [1: 381–2])

the infinitive is classified by Quirk & Svartvik (1970: 397) as a noun modifier, but one could with equal justification say that it depends on the verb *hadde* (with its dependents) 'they had [acquired] him in order to cook...'. It is interesting to note that in the literature the infinitive is usually said to depend on the noun when the verb is semantically (almost) empty, i.e. with the verbs *be* and *have*, while it is said to depend on the verb if it is a full verb.

In Middle English, as now, the non-finite verb in these clauses can take three forms: infinitive, present and past participle. The infinitive typically expresses purpose, while the two participles usually denote the circumstances under which something takes/has taken place; this relates them most closely to a temporal clause or one of manner:

(455) Unto his chambres was he led anon/ *To take* his ese and *for to have* his reste,/ With al his folk, *to don* what so hem leste.

(LGW 1111–13)

(456) And after this, nat fullich al awhaped,/ Out of the temple al esilich he wente,/ *Repentynge* hym that he hadde evere ijaped/ Of Loves folk, ...

(Troilus I.316–19)

As was noted in section 4.6.2.3, the infinitive introduced by (*for*) *to* usually denotes a prospective event. This makes it understandable that purpose is the function associated with the *to*-infinitive. However, some infinitival purpose constructions are expressed by the bare infinitive in Middle English especially after the verbs *comen* and *gon* (cf. vol. I, section 4.5.3.2):

(457) Therfore I wol go slepe an houre or tweye, ...

(CT I.3685 [1: 3679])

(458) But certeynly she moste, by hire leve/ Come soupen in his hous with hym at eve.

(Troilus III.559–60)

Note, however, that in these examples the verbs *come* and *go* behave almost like auxiliaries, expressing some kind of aspect. In (457), for instance, *slepe* is not a separate action, and it therefore does not constitute a prospective event as *take* etc. does in (455). It is noteworthy, too, that these special *come/go* constructions usually depend on a modal auxiliary or a perception verb. When *come/go* is finite, a *to*-infinitive, which is always purposive, is the rule:

(459) For which I come to telle yow tydynges.

(Troilus II.1113)

When the notion of a prospective event is weakened, it is sometimes possible to ascribe a causal or concessive meaning to the infinitival construction; compare, for instance, (460) with (461):

(460) And they were glade for to fille his purs ...

(CT III.1348 [2: 1322])

(461)   And wondir glad was I to se/ That lusty place and that ryver.

(Rose 122–3)

The event of (461) is not situated in the future, so that a causal interpretation becomes possible. In the following example,

(462)   In al this world, to seken up and doun,/ There nys no man so wys that koude thenche/ So gay a popelote...

(CT I.3252–4 [1: 3246–8])

the infinitive literally refers to some possible future activity, but it is clearly used with modal colouring here, so that it can be interpreted as concessive or conditional.

When the activity expressed by the *to*-infinitive can be interpreted as taking place now as well as in the future, Present-Day English usually opts for a present participle or a gerund, while Middle English prefers an infinitive:

(463)   What joie hastow thyn owen folk to spille?

(Troilus V.588)

   'What joy do you find in destroying your own people?'

(464)   What sholde he studie and make hymselven wood,/ Upon a book in cloystre alwey to poure,...

(CT I.184–5 [1: 184–5])

   'Why should he study and make himself [go] mad by always poring over a book in the monastery...'

In a similar way, past or present participles denoting attendant circumstances can take on causal, final, concessive, etc. meaning:

(465)   But slep ne may ther in his herte synke,/ Thynkyng how she,.../ A thousand fold was worth more than he wende.

(Troilus III. 1538–40)

(466)   O bussh unbrent, brennynge in Moyses sighte,...

(CT VII.468 [10: 468])

Occasionally, a conjunction is used before the infinitive which indicates its function more clearly. Thus, *as* denotes cause in (467):

(467)   but he dede thanke þe Maistres... as for to have ʒove hym ʒifftes.

(Chambers & Daunt 1931: 182.1298–1301)

Usually the present and past participle constructions have reference to some element in the main clause – most often the subject or object (but see (465) for an example where it is related to the possessive pronoun in a prepositional phrase) – but in imitation of the so-called

Latin 'ablativus absolutus', the construction could also be used absolutely with a subject of its own. It occurs a few times in Old English but becomes more common towards the end of the Middle English period, partly also under the influence of French. In Early Middle English the subject is usually still found in the oblique case, on analogy with the Latin oblique form, but in Late Middle English the nominative begins to supplant it.

(468) Ful benyngly ... he suffred hir to sey hir entent & ʒaf a fayr answer, *hir supposyng* it xuld ben þe bettyr.

(MKempe A 37.11–12)

(469) What koude a sturdy housbonde moore devyse/ To preeve hir wyfhod and hir stedefastnesse,/ And *he continuynge* evere in sturdinesse?

(CT IV.698–700 [8: 698–700])

The infinitive is also used absolutely in a number of idiomatic expressions (especially with the verbs *witen*, *seyn* and *speken*) – see, for example, (462). For a discussion of the absolute infinitive containing a lexical subject see section 4.6.2.7.

4.7   Agreement

Concord or agreement is to some extent more loosely structured in Middle English than in Present-Day English: in Middle English both syntactic and semantic considerations play an important role, while in Present-Day English syntax alone determines most matters of agreement. This difference can be ascribed to the closer proximity that exists between the spoken and the written language in Middle English (see also section 4.6). A good deal of what are often seen as 'more logical' constructions in (especially written) Present-Day English found their origin in rules laid down by grammarians and schoolmasters in the Renaissance and after, who strove towards an English 'pure and undefiled', resembling Latin, which was considered to be perfect (see vol. III). Here follow some examples that illustrate the looseness even within one and the same sentence:

(470) This (sg.) glade folk (sg.) to dyner they (pl.) hem (pl.) sette;

(CT II.1118 [3: 1118])

(471) þanne the Mynstrall (sg.) begynnen (pl.) to don here (pl.) mynstralcye euerych (sg.) in hire (pl.) Instrumentes (pl.)...

(Mandev. (Tit) 155.16–17)

(472) In þat contre ... ben (pl.) gret plentee (sg.) of Cokodrilles (pl.), þat is (sg.) a maner of a long serpent...

(Mandev. (Tit) 192.16–18)

Concord or the lack of it seems to depend in general on the following three parameters in Middle English: (a) the nature of the NP triggering concord; (b) the relative positions of finite verb and subject NP; and (c) the presence/absence of generic context. In the discussion that follows the nature of these parameters and their interaction will be illustrated and explained.

4.7.1 Subject(–complement)–verb agreement

As in Present-Day English the subject normally agrees with the finite verb in number (in as far as number is still distinctive in Middle English—see ch. 2). Absence of concord is, however, quite frequent. Parameters (a) and (b) (see above) are at issue here.

(a) A distinction has to be made between simple and complex NPs. Simple NPs that represent collective nouns occur both with singular and plural verbal inflections. The tendency to treat these nouns as plural becomes stronger in Late Middle English but it also depends on the particular noun used. Thus, in Chaucer, *folk* tends to be treated as a plural noun while *people* is usually singular; cf. (470) and (473):

(473)a. I wolde that al this (sg.) peple were (subj.sg.; or pl.) ago.
(CT IV.1764 [5: 520])

    b. ...the peple that was (sg.) theere...
(CT VII.626 [10: 626])

Other frequent collective nouns are *host, countree, court, meynee,* etc. A rather special kind of collective noun is the group of nouns referring to animals. They are singular in form but clearly plural in meaning and usually take a plural verb:

(474) and þe fischer seide þat þey hadde i-solde þe fische (sg.) þat were (pl.) i-take...
(Trev.Higd. (StJ-C) vol. 3, 67.8–9)

It is possible that these nouns should be looked upon as unchanged plurals formed on analogy of original (Old English) plurals with zero inflection, such as *hors, swyn, sheep, deer.* On the other hand, these nouns may have acquired the character of collective nouns via their usage as material nouns. It is interesting to note in this respect that there are other material nouns in Middle English used as collectives: *board, rope, brick, candle,* etc. (see Mustanoja 1960: 60). Yet a third possibility is that these animal nouns developed a plural meaning because they were regularly used after numerals, with which a singular noun was fairly common (see also section 4.7.2).

The indefinite pronoun *man/men/me* can be followed by a singular as well as a plural verb. *Men/me* could be interpreted as a phonologically weak form of *man*, but also as a true plural (with *i*-umlaut). In Late Middle English the plural verb is far more frequent after *men* than in Early Middle English.

When the NP is complex, the inflection of the verb depends on whether the NP is seen as a unity or not (in the case of co-ordinate constructions (475)) or which part of the NP acts as the head: the grammatical subject or the 'logical' subject (in the case of subordinate constructions, i.e. *of*-adjuncts (476)):

(475)a.　...Wherof *supplant and tricherie/* Engendred is (sg.);

(CA (Frf) ii.2840–1)

    b.　so þat *rightwisness ne vengeance* han (pl.) nought to don amonges vs;

(Mandev. (Tit) 196, 4–5)

(476)a.　Þere ben (pl.) also in þat contree *a kynde of Snayles*...

(Mandev. (Tit) 128, 36)

    b.　Beȝonde þat yle is another yle where is (sg.) *gret multytude of folk*...

(Mandev. (Tit) 192, 1)

In both cases of complex nouns the plural inflection is more common.

(b) The position of the subject with respect to the predicate may also play a role in number agreement. Thus, lack of agreement occurs relatively more often when the subject follows the verb:

(477)　In that cytee was (sg.) the sittynges of the .xij. tribes of Israel...

(Mandev. (Tit) 71, 17–18)

(478)　And betwene the rede see & the see occyan toward the south is (sg.) the kyngdom of Ethiope & of libye the hyere,

(Mandev. (Tit) 95, 28–30)

In the following example the verb is plural because the part of the subject nearest the verb is plural:

(479)　And ȝif it so befalle þat the fader or moder or ony of here frendes ben (pl.) seke anon the sone goth to the prest...

(Mandev. (Tit) 132, 23–5)

This may also be the case in

(480)　...where the Arke of god with the relikes weren kept longe tyme...

(Mandev. (Tit) 70, 20–1)

In examples like (477) and (478) something else may be responsible for the use of the singular verb. Consider the following examples:

(481)   Hyllys, wodes and feldes wyde/ Was in that cuntre on euery syde.

(Guy(4) (Cmb) 6025–6)

(482)   And all aboute þer is ymade large nettes...

(Mandev. (Tit) 141, 26–7)

and many other instances with *þær/þer* and the verb *be* in Old English and Middle English (see Stoelke 1916). The verb *be* is used here to introduce the subject. It entails that the function of the plural NPs is more that of subject complement, the real subject is *ther*, which in Middle English could also be left out as is the case in (481). Breivik (1981) has called this the 'signal' function of *there*. (For similar examples with *it*, see section 4.7.3 and especially note 47.)

4.7.2   Agreement within the noun phrase

In Old English the attributive adjectives and pronouns agreed with the NP in number, case and gender. Due to the loss of inflections this type of agreement became largely irrelevant in the course of the Middle English period. (For this development and remnants of inflections see chapter 2 of this volume, sections 2.9.1.1 and 2.9.1.2.) Here we need only discuss the behaviour of collective nouns with attributive pronouns/articles and adjectives, and also the structure of NPs containing numerals or measurement nouns.

As we have seen in section 4.7.1, collective nouns behave syntactically like singular as well as plural nouns; consequently they collocate with singular as well as plural attributive words. Thus we find *this folk* – see (470) – as well as *þeise folk* (*Mandev.* (Tit) 80.35); *meche peple* beside *many dyuerse folk* (*Mandev.* (Tit) 83.3 and 104.15); *a fewe meynee* (*Mandev.* (Tit) 148.13), *a listes* (*CT* I.1713 [1: 1715]), etc.

After an expression of number or quantity a noun is often found in the singular rather than the plural, because number is in fact already expressed. Some of these nouns represent Old English unchanged plurals (*year*, *month*) or Old English genitive plurals which also became zero-inflected in Middle English (*mile*, *winter*), but the majority cannot be thus explained. Some examples are: *she was seven nyght old* (*CT* VII.2873 [10: 2845]), *an hundred punde* (*Owl&N* (Clg) 1101), etc.

4.7.3 Agreement between noun phrases

Appositional phrases in Old English normally agreed in case and number with the NP with which they were in apposition (see vol. I, section 4.2.2). In Middle English there is usually number concord, but, following the loss of case inflections, case concord disappeared except in the genitive, which could still be formally distinguished:

(483) Ælienor/ þe   wes Henries quene, þes heȝes kinges.
      Eleanor, who was Henry's queen, the high king's

                                                   (*Brut* (Clg) 22–3)

    'Eleanor, who was Henry the high king's queen.'

However, even here lack of concord soon became established. With quantifiers, number concord was not always necessary in Middle English as can be seen in

(484) My windowes were shette echon,

                                                   (*BD* 335)

where *echon* is singular and *windowes* plural. Number concord may also be absent with collective nouns (see parameter (a) p. 365).

Anaphoric pronouns (demonstrative, relative, personal, etc.) usually agree with their antecedent NP in number and natural gender in so far as these distinctions are made for each pronoun (for the loss of grammatical gender see ch. 2, section 2.9.1.1). The exceptions again are related to parameter (a) – cf. (470) and (485):

(485)a. the meynee (sg.) of the Soudan, … þei (pl.) ben aboute the souldan
         with swerdes drawen…

                                                   (*Mandev.* (Tit) 24.26–8)

    b. Vor harpe & pipe & fuȝeles song/ Mislikeþ ȝif hit (sg.) is to long.
                                                   (*Owl&N* (Clg) 343–4)

    c. Also y be-queythe to Robert … a reed bedde of worsteyd, with
        costers (pl.) [= side-hangings] þat langyth (sg.) þere-to, …
                                                   (*EEWills* an.1411, 19.1–2)

In the last example the singular nature of the relative pronoun (which itself has no number distinction) only becomes evident through the form of the verb *langyth* (other present plural forms in this will have the midland ending in -*n*). In the following instance,

(486) Prynt yow in [= express yourself in] sportys, whych best doth (sg.)
      yow plese…

                                                   (*Digby Pl.* 39.459)

it is not likely that *sportys* is treated like a collective noun; rather, it is part of an elliptical partitive construction, 'of the sports, the one that pleases you best'.

The following constructions may also belong here:

(487)   For hit ben eyres of heuene, alle þat ben ycrouned, ...

(PPl.C (Hnt 143) v, 59)

'For they are heirs of heaven, all who are tonsured'

(488)   And þere groweth a maner of fruyt as þough it weren Gowrdes,

(Mandev. (Tit) 175.25–6)

The examples show lack of agreement between subject and subject complement. Note, however, that (487) is an example of extraposition, i.e. empty *it* has taken the place of the original subject *alle þat ben crounede*. *It* has no argument status and therefore cannot enforce agreement on the verb. Example (488) looks rather similar to (481) and (482) except that here the verb is plural rather than singular.[47]

In generic contexts (parameter (c), p. 365), a singular (pro)noun is often referred to by a plural pronoun and the other way around:

(489)   ...that no man (sg.) sholde come to chese her (pl.) Mair but such as were (pl.) sompned, ...

(Chambers & Daunt 1931: 34.22–4)

(490)   Fele weren (pl.) on fote and fele (pl.) on hors,/ Wiþ meschief and kepten (pl.) his (sg.) corps...

(KAlex. (Ld) 3770–1)

In Middle English there is often lack of concord between NPs when used distributively, i.e. a singular rather than a plural noun is used with reference to another plural noun, when it concerns a thing or quality of which each individual person/item usually has only one. Many examples concern parts of the body (see also vol. I, section 4.2.3):

(491)a.   They ronne so hem thoughte hir herte (sg.) breeke. .

(CT VII.3388 [10: 3360])

'They ran so [fast] they thought their heart would break'

(cf. 'So priketh hem (pl.) nature in hir *corages* (pl.)'

(CT I.11 [1: 11]))

b.   And þei han allwey the throte (sg.) open,

(Mandev. (Tit) 193.18)

c.   ...as I haue herd hem seye in here confessioun (sg.)...

(Mandev. (Tit) 126.17–18)

Often we find plural and singular used side by side, especially in poetry to serve rhyme or metre:

(492)   Of latter date, of *wyves* hath he red/ That somme han slayn hir
        housbondes in hir *bed*,

(CT III.765–6 [2: 739–40])

The plural begins to gain ground in later Middle English.

4.7.4   Sequence of tenses

The use of the present tense in past-time context – the 'historical present' – has been discussed in section 4.3.2.1. In reported speech a present tense was normally reported by a preterite when the principal verb was in the preterite,

(493)   & the heremyte asked him what he was.

(Mandev. (Tit) 30.10)

However, if the statement in the subclause could be interpreted as generic, or referred to the future, the present tense is also found:

(494)   Somme seyde that oure hertes been moost esed/ Whan that we
        been yflatered and yplesed.

(CT III.929–30 [2: 903–4])

(495)   Men seyde eek that Arcite shal nat dye;

(CT I.2705 [1: 2705])

Sometimes we find a mixture of forms:

(496)   For I tolde hem þat in oure contree weren trees þat baren a fruyt
        þat becomen briddes fleeynge. And þo þat fellen in the water lyuen.
        And þei þat fallen on the erthe dyen anon; and þei ben right gode
        to mannes mete.

(Mandev. (Tit) 176.3–7)

4.8   Word order

This section will be concerned with the ordering of constituents within the clause, i.e. with the position(s) of nominal, verbal and adverbial phrases relative to one another. It will also deal with the position of a clause within the clause and refer to the internal structure of the verb phrase since both are relevant to the major divisions of the clause. The internal structure of the nominal phrase falls outside the scope of this section; a discussion of this is found in section 4.2.1.

The discussion will mainly centre on the changes that took place in the order of these clause elements between the Old and Middle English periods. I do not think it is too bold to state that we are dealing here with a major restructuring, one in which the language, which was largely verb final, changed into one that is clearly verb non-final. Linguists still argue on the point whether Old English was truly a SOV-type language that changed into a SVO language in the course of the Middle English period. The difficulty in deciding this matter lies in what kind of theoretical attitude the linguist wishes to adopt, i.e. to approach the question as a 'mentalist' or a 'behaviorist' (in the words of Chomsky). The former, the generative transformational linguist, will wish to look behind the surface word orders in order to find a basic or underlying word order that will explain the presence or absence of certain surface constructions in the language. The base order this linguist hypothesises need not necessarily be the most frequently attested surface order in a language. In most cases this type of linguist has come to the conclusion that Old English was verb final (see van Kemenade 1987: 14ff.; and cf. Denison 1986: 12) because this would explain among other things certain facts about the position of particles (Hiltunen 1983b; Koopman 1985), about verb clustering (van Kemenade 1985), about the rule of verb second (van Kemenade 1987), about extraposition (Stockwell 1977), etc. It would also correlate with the by now generally accepted theory that changes take place in root sentences before they percolate into subordinate clauses – see Bean (1983: 137), but see also Stockwell & Minkova (1991) (in Old English the non-final verb is predominant only in main clauses). The more taxonomically inclined linguist, however, who bases himself primarily on the percentages of SVO, SOV and other orders in both main and subclauses, would probably come to the conclusion that Old English cannot be said to represent any one *type* because of the amount of variation present. If pressed into a choice, he might well opt for SVO (see West 1973, who considers Old English SVO by about 900, and Denison 1986). The question as to whether Old English was SOV or SVO or some other type will remain open for quite a while yet – if it ever will be settled – but there is general agreement as to what type of language Middle English finally became, i.e. an almost pure SVO language. Thus, even if there is not a complete SOV > SVO change, there is certainly a strong tendency from verb final towards verb non-final in the course of the Middle English period, which coincides with the loss of the great variety of surface orders possible in Old English. In what follows we will look at some of these developments. It will not be possible to provide exact percentages and tables since the amount of research devoted to Middle English word order is still scanty and, more problematically, shows great methodological variation.[48]

4.8.1   Verb final vs verb non-final order and the position of the object

In Old English object pronouns tended to precede the verb in both main and subordinate clauses. Nominal objects, however, were as a rule postverbal in main clauses, while they could be both pre- and postverbal in subclauses and co-ordinate clauses. The position of the pronominal NP is usually explained by reference to its light weight in comparison to nominals. Van Kemenade (1987) gives substance to this suggestion by analysing the pronominals as a certain type of clitic; their clitic-like behaviour then provides an explanation for their distribution (see also below).[49] The changes taking place in the area of object placement are fairly rapid. Concerning the order in general in subclauses, Mitchell (1964) shows that in the two continuations of the *Peterborough Chronicle* (1122–54), the current Present-Day English word orders in subclauses (mainly SVO) rose to 72 and 88 per cent respectively compared to only 41 per cent in a sample of Late Old English prose. Palmatier's (1969: 51) figures in his study of the *Ormulum* do not distinguish between main and subclauses, but they show that the object precedes the verb in only 18 per cent of all cases when a noun, but still in 51 per cent of cases when a pronoun. For late east midland prose, MacLeish (1969: 15ff.) notes that in independent clauses SOV only occurs three times when the verb is simple; when it is complex it is quite usual for the object to precede the main verb, especially when the object is pronominal, but it normally follows the finite verb:

(497)   Thre of his olde foes han it espyed, ...

(CT VII.970 [10: 970])

His percentages are not very illuminating. They show that in independent clauses S(Aux)Vx order occurs in 71·8 per cent of all cases, compared to 84·4 per cent in dependent clauses, the opposite of what one would expect. This distortion is caused by the fact that he includes co-ordinate clauses under independent clauses, which ought to have been considered separately (see Mitchell 1964). Also his research is mainly aimed at distinguishing between SV and VS orders whatever other elements may intervene. Thus, the 28·2 and 15·6 per cent respectively of non-S(Aux)Vx orders includes inverted (VS) order, which naturally is far more frequent in main clauses. However, when one takes the above factors into consideration (and the exact figures given for each type of order in his conclusion (pp. 224ff.)) it is clear that SOV has become a fairly marginal type especially in main clauses. Verb-final patterns occur still far more often in late east midland poetry, according to MacLeish (1969) about five times as often in both main and subclauses. Many of these instances should be considered marked, however, i.e. used for stylistic or metrical effect, particularly when the object is nominal:

(498)   And Absolon his gyterne hath ytake;

(CT I.3353 [1: 3347])

This may also explain the much higher percentage of e.g. OVS patterns in poetry, about four times higher in poetry than in prose. Similarly, in a study of two versions of the *Morte Darthur*, i.e. those by Malory and Caxton (Šimko 1957), it is found that Malory's version has a much greater incidence of non-SVO orders than Caxton's. There is of course a small time difference here, but most of the archaic orders were probably put in for stylistic effect in Malory's prose. It can be shown in this case that Malory quite frequently changed SVO instances found in his source into word-order patterns such as were more unusual and therefore, presumably, more effective to his purpose.

From another study of fifteenth-century prose, Reszkiewicz's work on *The Book of Margery Kempe* (1962), it appears that SOV order has become the exclusive feature of pronominal objects or complements, and is very rare even there, both in main and in subclauses. SAuxOV order, on the other hand, occurs quite regularly also with nominals:

(499)   I may no rest haue a-mongys ȝow.

(MKempe A 122.19–20)

These facts reveal a clear tendency towards SVO in both main and subclauses. The vestiges of SOV order that remain give us some idea about the underlying causes for this development. The far greater frequency of preverbal pronominal objects was already apparent in Old English and has been connected with ordering principles related to weight (cliticisation) and theme–rheme structure, which are themselves presumably interrelated (see Denison 1986). Thus, NPs that are light (pronominals) and represent given information (pronominals are usually anaphoric) tend to occur early in the clause, whereas heavy NPs and NPs containing new information tend to occur late.[50] The question is why this multivariable but pragmatic Old English system (see vol. I, section 4.6) was slowly being replaced by an almost invariable one in the later periods. Many linguists have argued that this change is a result of the loss of inflections (e.g. Vennemann 1974; Weerman 1987; but see also Hock 1982 and Stockwell & Minkova 1991), which required other ways of indicating the function of sentence elements, such as (relatively) fixed word order and the use of prepositions. Developments in some of the Germanic languages seem to corroborate this. Gerritsen (1987: 62ff.) gives statistical evidence for Middle Dutch that there is a strong and significant interrelation between development from SOV to SVO and loss of inflections. With the loss of inflections, the greatest need was for subjects and objects to become distinguishable since both were normally represented by NPs. Because only pronominal subjects and objects could still be distinguished in case, SOV order first disappeared in the case of nominal NPs (for differences in the order of direct object and indirect object related to the use of nominal or pronominal NPs, see section 4.8.4). This, in a way, reinforced the Old English trends noted above, but, as it were, only by accident. It was suggested that the Old English organisation was based on principles of discourse structure, while the Middle English development is necessitated by syntactic factors. The fact that these two situations coincided may have speeded up the development. It is clear, however, that the syntactic needs finally overruled discourse strategies since even light elements moved eventually to (more) final positions.[51]

In this respect, it is interesting that Reszkiewicz (1962: 29) notes that wherever we have a sequence of two NPs, it is always the NP nearest (next) to the verb that is the subject. The reason for this must be again the loss of inflections, not just on the noun but also on the verb. It clearly shows the above-noted tendency to avoid SOV order, an order in which the subject is *not* placed next to the verb. We see a similar phenomenon in infinitival constructions. Already in the Early Middle English *Ormulum* (see Palmatier 1969: 96) an object of the infinitive normally follows it (in 84 per cent of cases), but preverbal placement is not at all infrequent (still 16 per cent). Interestingly enough, no distinction seems to exist here between nouns and pronouns – this is true also for Old English.[52] Proportionally as many nouns occur in preverbal position as pronouns. (This may well show the importance of theme–rheme ordering, i.e. the object of the infinitive would usually not constitute new information by itself and therefore was typically placed early (preverbally) in the phrase.) However, when the infinitival construction contained a subject as well as an object, the object directly precedes the infinitive in only 3·7 per cent of cases, and we find the subject always next to the infinitive.

Above, we described some functional reasons – related to morphological changes – why SVO may have become the regular order in Middle English. Stockwell (1977) approaches the change from a different direction. He starts from the notion that basic word order in Old English was SOV and that there operated a rule of verb second (V_2) in main clauses. Verb second is the name given to the phenomenon observed, e.g. in West Germanic languages, that in *main* clauses the verb is normally found in second position, i.e. immediately following the first constituent, which may be a subject or object NP, an adverbial phrase, etc. The application of this rule would result in a very high frequency of SVO order in main clauses (for the also regular XVS order, see section 4.8.2) when the verb was simple. When the verb was complex the regular order would be SvOV (where v expresses the finite verb, often an auxiliary). Stockwell then proceeds to show that this latter pattern is in fact not as frequent as one would expect, even in Old English, since it is often destroyed by a process which he terms 'exbraciation'. This is a process whereby the object is moved out to the right. As motivation for exbraciation he gives (a) the working of analogy (the overall greater frequency of SVO structures; according to Gerritsen (1984) this applies especially to English in contrast to, for example, German and Dutch); (b) the effect of a number of optional extraposition rules (which moved relative clauses, appositive phrases, etc. out to the right); (c) the position of NPs serving as afterthoughts. It should be noted that the so-called V_2 rule still operates in Middle English in that we find a large number of clauses showing SAuxOV (cf. SvOV above) and XVS orders. Van Kemenade (1987: 180ff.) shows how the V_2 rule became more and more limited in scope in the course of the Middle English period. By the fifteenth century it was mainly triggered when a wh-element or a negative element was the first constituent in the clause. In other words, what one sees happening is that a rule that once operated generally in main clauses as opposed to subclauses, whatever the nature of the first constituent, becomes restricted to only a selection of first constituents, where it then becomes grammaticalised (see also section 4.8.2).

4.8.2   *Inversion of subject and verb*

In Old English, as a rule, the subject and finite verb were inverted after pronominal temporal, locative and negative adverbs (see vol. I, section 4.6.1), especially after *þonne* and *þa*, although there is a tendency for a pronoun subject to retain a preverb position (see van Kemenade 1987 for an explanation of this distribution). Inversion is the traditional term; in the more recent (generative) literature, the phenomenon is subsumed under verb second. This does not change very much in Middle English. Mitchell (1964) notes even more occurrences of this in the continuations of the *Peterborough Chronicle* than in his Old English sample from Ælfric. In the *Ormulum* too, verb second is clearly the rule after the above-mentioned adverbs. For late east midland poetry and prose, MacLeish (1969: 224–5) shows that inversion is still the rule after adverbial elements (which in this study includes full adverbial phrases) in prose (in about 70 per cent of all cases), but that in poetry presence or absence of inversion is about equal. Inversion could well be a marked device in poetry, which also shows a much higher percentage of inversion after other than adverbial initial elements (e.g. after (in)direct objects, complements, etc.). In *The Book of Margery Kempe* too, inversion still seems to be the norm after adverbial phrases (Reszkiewicz 1962: ch. 2). According to Jacobsson (1951), a rapid decline occurs only after our period, with the sharpest drop taking place around 1600. One of the reasons why inverted patterns remained common so much longer than SOV patterns must be that the change in basic word order created no problems in syntactic analysis here, at least not as far as the most frequent type with initial adverb is concerned. In all cases the subject was still next to the verb. It was only when SV order became the standard in most clauses (to such an extent that subjectless clauses in the course of the Middle English period developed a dummy subject, *it/there*, to conform to the SV pattern – see Strang 1970: 211) that SV also became more and more the rule in adverb initiated clauses. For a more detailed discussion of what types of inverted patterns were retained, and what new patterns came into being, see Stockwell (1984), who also offers some tentative explanations. In general, inversion (or V_2) remained the rule after wh-elements and adverbial phrases in Middle English. In Old English inversion is also encountered after the negative element *ne*. *Ne* was always placed before the verb so, when initial, inversion of S and V would be as it were automatic. This situation changes in Middle English when *ne* begins to be lost (see section 4.5). The negative element that replaces it (or rather the element that is left, since *ne* was usually accompanied by another negative) normally followed the verb. This could have resulted in the disappearance of inversion in these negative clauses. However, the earlier system, and also the fact that many negatives, as adverbials, could be put in initial position, probably led to a renewed grammaticalisation of the inversion rule after negatives (see (500)) and implied negatives (see (501)).

(500)   ...and thus they lete hym lye;/ But *nevere gronte he* at no strook but oon, ...

(CT VII.2708–9 [10: 2612–13])

(501)   ...*scarsly shaltou* fynden any persone that may kepe conseil secrely.

(CT VII.1143 [10: 1143])

4.8.3   The position of the adverbial phrase

Not enough work has been done on the position of the adverbial phrase to advance more than general observations. Most of the investigations into Middle English word order concentrate on the main sentence elements i.e. S, V and O. Palmatier (1969) gives some information on adverb placement in his study of the *Ormulum*, and Reszkiewicz (1962) in his work on *The Book of Margery Kempe*. The only specialist studies are Borst (1910) on Chaucer's prose, and Jacobson (1981). The latter covers the Old English to the Modern English period but is only concerned with the placement of adverbs in relation to auxiliaries.

In principle, as in Old English, the adverbial phrase can be found in almost any position. However, the position is by no means free. There are clearly factors at work that influence the order, such as the type of clause the adverb(ial phrase) occurs in; the type of adverbial phrase (locative, temporal, etc.); the weight of the adverbial phrase; the weight of the object, if present. There are also diachronic and diatopic differences, not to mention stylistic differences (in most Middle English poetic texts the order is freer), but a lot more research is needed here to establish developments with more certainty. Palmatier (1969: 97) has found, for instance, that in the *Ormulum* adverbial modifiers to the infinitive tend to follow the infinitive (in 81 per cent of cases), whereas Borst's findings for Chaucer's prose show that with the infinitive preverbal position is preferred, although less so when the adverbial phrase is temporal or local in nature or when there is also an object. Borst, however, looks only at adverbs, while Palmatier includes all types of adverbial phrases.

In general, as is to be expected, the position of the adverbial phrase in Middle English is more varied than in Present-Day English (for the position of adverbials in Present-Day English see Greenbaum 1969, especially tables 6, 12, 13). In Middle English the adverbial phrase is frequently found between the finite verb and its object (see (502)) (an unusual position in Present-Day English unless the object is long or heavy), except when the object is pronominal. Another quite usual position is between the finite verb and the infinitive (503). In Chaucer's prose the following parameters seem to play a role in the position of the adverb.[53] Postverbal (especially postfinite) position is the norm (a) in main clauses (see (504)), (b) with manner and degree adverbs (see (505)).[54] Preverbal position is more regular in subclauses (ca 30 per cent is preverbal), especially in relative subclauses (50 per cent) (see (506)), and with temporal adverbs. In main clauses preverbal position is somewhat more common when there is also an object (14 per cent of cases). A note of caution is not amiss, however. These observations may well need to be corrected when more factors, such as the weight and length of nominal objects and of the adverbial phrases themselves, are taken into account.

(502)a. Lat us now considere whiche been they that ye holde *so greetly* youre freendes ...

(*CT* VII.1364 [10: 1364])

b. ... he scapyd of hard & left *per* hir scrippe [= bag].

(*MKempe A* 118.15)

(503) The fourthe signe is that he ne lette nat *for shame* to shewen his confessioun.

(*CT* X.995 [12: 995])

(504) he weneth *alwey* that he may do thyng that he may nat do.

(*CT* VII.1124 [10: 1124])

(505) but I wondre *gretly* how that thei may performe thynges ...

(*Bo.* I, pr.4, 188–90)

(506) he fareth lyk hym that handleth the scorpioun that styngeth and *sodeynly* sleeth thurgh his envenymynge;

(*CT* X.854 [12: 854])

For the position of the negative adverb, see section 4.5.

4.8.4   *The position of the indirect object*

Traditionally, the term 'indirect object' comprises what some grammarians have distinguished as the synthetic and the analytic indirect object, i.e. the oblique form (e.g. *him*, *her*, the common case of nouns) versus the prepositional phrase (introduced by *for* or *to*). Generative grammarians would distinguish between the two as follows: the synthetic indirect object is governed by the verb and distinct from the direct object in that it receives its case at deep-structure level, so-called inherent case (see Chomsky 1981), whereas the analytic indirect object receives its case from the preposition which governs it.

The position the indirect object can take in Present-Day English depends on, among other things, whether it is analytic or synthetic, which in its turn depends on other factors. This is not true for Middle English, although the later Present-Day English rules are already present as clear tendencies. The reason for this is that the analytic indirect object was a new development in Middle English. A new element normally does not emerge fully grammaticalised. It has to develop and spread first as an optional variant. For this reason it is necessary to have a look first at the emergence of the analytic indirect object before we can consider the position of both types of indirect object in Middle English.

4.8.4.1 The emergence of the analytic indirect object

In Old English the indirect object was expressed by the dative case. This was not the only function of this case. The dative was also employed in adverbial expressions, it could denote the role of experiencer or instrument, and it was inherent case with certain verbs, adjectives and nouns (e.g. *helpan* 'to help', *andswarian* 'to answer', *lað* 'disagreeable', *leof* 'dear') (for more uses of the dative consult Mustanoja 1960: 95ff.). With the loss of inflections in the Late Old English/Early Middle English period, the dative and accusative were no longer distinct, with the result that the dative lost most of its functions. In most cases the original dative was replaced by a prepositional phrase (i.e. after adjectives/nouns and when in instrumental or locative use), or it remained and changed syntactically into a direct object, as is the case after verbs like *helpan* (for the dative after impersonal verbs, see section 4.3.1.2). It was only in its role as indirect object that the dative could hold its place, albeit indistinguishable in *form* from the direct object. The reason why the original dative could be retained here is fairly clear. Since it always occurred together with the direct object, it could not be confused with it (only a handful of verbs govern(ed) two accusatives/direct objects). Secondly, the fact that this dative was practically always animate marked it off sufficiently from the direct object which was as a rule inanimate.

Nevertheless, the change-over to a prepositional phrase in other cases did not leave the indirect object undisturbed. In other words a variant, prepositional indirect object begins to develop by the side of the older synthetic one. At first only few instances are encountered. Nagel (1909) in his study of the dative in Early Middle English notes only four analytic indirect objects in the *Peterborough Chronicle*, while the inflectional dative has already almost disappeared there in its locative and instrumental functions. In later, thirteenth-century texts (*Vices and Virtues*, the *Katherine* group, *Ancren Riwle*), the number of analytic datives rises to about 10 per cent. Nagel also notes the lines of development of the analytic dative, which clearly show that its path is shaped by functional factors. Thus, the analytic dative is used more often when the object of the verb is animate rather than inanimate. It is more frequent when the indirect object is a noun rather than a pronoun (the noun, in contrast to the pronoun, early on lost all of its inflections, except for the genitive). It is especially common after *secgan* 'to say', presumably on analogy of *cweþan* 'to speak to', which was followed by *to* + NP in Old English. The analytic dative is also preferred when it is removed from its governor, the verb. Finally, it should be noted that the analytic construction is preferred after French (loan) verbs when they also govern a direct object. This seems to indicate that the inflectional dative was no longer part of a productive process. Later on, some French verbs do acquire synthetic indirect objects, presumably by the force of analogy, but the great majority of French (and Latin) verbs are still only found with the *to*-construction in Present-Day English. Mustanoja (1960: 110) refers to a possibly more direct influence of Old French here; he notes that prepositional phrases were used in Old French itself.

The development of datives after adjectives (and the same applies to nouns) is interesting too. In principle it should have been possible for a non-prepositional NP to be retained here. As long as the NP stood next to the adjective that governed it, confusion would not really arise (in contrast to locative and instrumental datives that had no outside governor). However, although these constructions were preserved in the Early Middle English period, the pull of the system must have become too strong. In Middle English it was the norm for oblique NPs to be governed by either verbs or prepositions. We see, therefore, that in most cases these adjectives early on in the period developed a preposition, e.g. *him lað* became *loath(some) to him*, *him nydbeðearf* became *necessary to/for him* etc.[55] In some cases the adjectives even turned into prepositions themselves: *near*, *like*, etc.:

(507)a. Þeos ne beoð nawt *ilihc* þe leane fuhel pellican,

$\qquad\qquad\qquad\qquad\qquad\qquad\qquad\qquad$ (*Ancr.* (Corp-C) 70.21–2)

$\qquad$ 'these are not similar to/like the lean bird [the] pelican'

b. ... & adrede/ Þat sum unhwate *neþ* [= neh] him beo,...

(Owl&N (Clg) 1266–7)

'...and fear that some misfortune may be close to/near him,...'

4.8.4.2 The positions of synthetic and analytic indirect objects

When the analytic or periphrastic dative first develops, almost all orders are still possible. Thus we come across examples such as the following, no longer usual in Present-Day English:

(508)a. Gif ic dale all ðat ic habbe *wrecche mannen*,...

(Vices&V(1) (Stw) 39.17)

'If I give all that I have [to] poor people'

b. ... þei xulde delyuyr *to hyr* þe keyyes.

(MKempe A 8.35)

c. & who so is absent... schal paie *to þe brotherede* [= brotherhood] a pound wex.

(Chambers & Daunt 1931: 42.21–2)

However, certain tendencies already present in the language, and functional needs discussed above, shaped the use of the analytic dative in the course of the Middle English period almost into its present-day form. Thus in Middle English, as in Old English, there was a preference for pronoun–noun order. Further, in Old English the indirect object tended to precede the direct object (see Fries 1940: 202; but see Mitchell 1985: §3940 and Koopman 1990a, 1990b: 133–223). Also, as we have seen, from the earliest times nouns rather than pronouns appeared in the analytic dative. These facts would strengthen a Middle English tendency, i.e. the use of the *to*-phrase rather than the inflectional dative whenever the dative was *not* next to the verb. These tendencies taken together would show the following picture for Middle English:

1   He gave him the book
2   He gave the book to him
3 (a) He gave Nero the book
   (b) He gave to Nero the book
4   He gave the book to Nero

These are possible and usual orders in Present-Day English with the exception of (3b), which is not an unusual construction in Middle English. Rantavaara (1962) shows that it is even more frequent than the construction without *to* at the end of our period. The reason why (3b) finally disappeared is not hard to find. The construction was not supported by a parallel pronominal construction. *He gave to him the book* is rare from the very beginning due to the tendencies noted above. Secondly, it clearly is the odd one out in the paradigm because normally the *to* NP occurs finally. In other words, systemic pressure leads naturally to the demise of this construction.

4.8.5 The position of the clause

All through the history of English there has been a tendency for the subclause to occur in final position. In Old English this is almost the rule. Even adverbial clauses tend to occur there with the exception of clauses of place, conditional and indefinite/generalising relative clauses. In most cases, the initial position of an adverbial clause is marked by the presence of a correlative phrase. In Middle English the initial position of adverbial clauses no longer has to be supported by correlation. Also a greater variety of adverbial clauses now occur initially (see e.g. section 4.6.3.5).

As we have seen in section 4.6.2.2, subject clauses do not occur in Old English, and are very rare in Middle English. Even in Present-Day English they tend to be avoided (cf. vol. I, section 4.6.3).

Relative clauses could immediately follow their head in Old English, but they had a tendency, too, to appear at the end of the clause (see vol. I, section 4.6.3; Stockwell 1977). With the word-order change to SVO, the object came to stand in final position so that its relative clause would now automatically occupy final position. Likewise, an indirect object followed by a relative clause would now normally follow the object, so that it was placed in final position together with its clause; a position that had become possible due to the introduction of the analytic indirect object (see section 4.8.4):

(509) that is to seyn, to yeven part to hem that han greet nede,

(CT VII.623 [10: 623])

When the antecedent of the relative clause was the subject, the clause would normally follow its antecedent immediately, although end position occurs too but not as frequently as in Old English.

In Old English there was a tendency for temporal and conditional clauses to occur before their complement (see vol. I, section 4.6.3) as in:

(510) ... þohte gif he hi   ealle ofsloge, þæt þæt an   ne ætburste
       thought if he them all   slew   that that one not would-escape
       þe   he sohte
       that he sought

(ÆCHom I 5 82.10)

'...thought that if he slew them all the one he sought would not escape'

This 'peculiar' order disappears in Middle English. Eitle (1914: 9) gives just one example, which he says goes back to Old English; but note the repetition here of the subordinator *that*:

(511) ...al be it so that whan he goth that it is necessarie that he goth.

(Bo. V, pr.6, 190)

4.9   Some grammatical processes

In this section two phenomena will be discussed which have attracted attention in the literature, both in the more theoretically inclined studies and in those which are more data-oriented. We refer here to the development of indirect object and prepositional passives, and to preposition-stranding constructions. From the point of view of the history of English, these constructions are interesting because in connection with them important changes occur between the Old and the Middle English periods. In the following sections, we will have a detailed look at the data, i.e. at the different surface structures that occur in the two periods. After that we will look at some of the explanations that have been given for these developments. I will suggest some interesting theoretical consequences, but a discussion of the more technical solutions that have been offered will be largely avoided (technical, in the sense that they are couched in formal rules, filters, principles, etc.) because this is not the place for a full discussion of the theoretical frameworks without which the full extent of the proposals cannot be properly understood (some of the more essential technical details are given in the further reading section at the end of the chapter).

4.9.1   *The passive in Old and Middle English*

The passive in Old English had a fairly narrow range in that only the direct object (expressed by the accusative case) could be passivised, i.e. become the subject (nominative) of a passive construction. In Present-Day English the subject of a passive construction can be related to (a) the direct object, (b) the indirect object, or (c) the prepositional object, in the corresponding active construction:

1   The book was selected by the committee
2   Nicaragua was given the opportunity to protest
3   His plans were laughed at
4   The library was set fire to by accident

There are two general paths along which one could look for an explanation of these developments. One can hypothesise that there was a change in the nature of the rule that generates passive constructions (see Lightfoot 1979, who posits a lexical rule for the derivation of Old and Middle English passives, and a structural rule for the later period). Another possibility is that there was a change in the application of the rule due to changes having taken place elsewhere in the system of the language (see Bennett 1980). The latter course seems to be the one now more generally followed. Additional factors that may have influenced the spread of passive constructions are the gradual loss of the Old English active construction with indefinite *man* (see section 4.2.3.1) (this construction could most easily be replaced by a passive) and the change in word order (see section 4.6.2.5).

For the indirect object and the prepositional object to become the subject of a passive construction, these two objects must have become syntactically similar to direct objects if we accept that the passive rule did not itself essentially change. This development is straightforward as far as the dative or indirect-object passive is concerned. Loss of inflections led to coalescence of dative and accusative in the pronominal system and to the coalescence of all cases (except the genitive) in the nominal system. Thus, verbs like *helpan* 'help', *andswarian* 'answer', which governed a dative in Old English, were no longer syntactically different from verbs like *ascian* 'ask', *seon* 'see', which governed an accusative. Van der Gaaf (1929) records unambiguous examples of nominative passive constructions with these verbs from about 1300 onwards (see also section 4.8.4.1).

More interesting from a syntactic point of view are the verbs that in Old English are construed with a dative and an accusative case (the so-called ditransitive verbs). Only the accusative case could become nominative in a passive construction in Old English, but it was possible for the dative to appear initially in topic position, as in:

(512) Þa   *him* wearð on slæpe swefen ætywed
      then himwas   in sleep dream shown

(*Dan.* 495)

'then he was shown a dream in his sleep'

These constructions remain frequent in Middle English up to the end of the period (see Visser 1963–73: §1966):

(513) ... Þat him was leued no catel.

(*Havelok* (Ld) 225)

'... so that "him" was left no goods.'

Given the ambiguous nature of these constructions in Middle English when the initial indirect object was a nominal phrase, a reanalysis from dative passive to nominative (subject) passive is no surprise. When one considers the increasing rigidification of SVO order, it is almost to be expected.

Thus, in the course of the Middle English period we see indirect-object passives appear, first, from about 1200, with (ambiguous) nominal indirect objects:

> (514) Nas neuere quene in þis lond ido so muche ssome...
>
> (Jacob&J (Bod) 229)
>
> 'never was a queen in this country done so much shame'

Later there appear also unambiguous examples with a pronoun as subject.[56]

> (515) And ther they were yolded all the hundret schyppys...
>
> (Gairdner 1910: I.68 p. 85)

Most of Visser's early examples (1963–73: § 1968) concern constructions in which a *that*-clause or infinitive takes the place of the direct object:

> (516) And afterward this knyght was bode appeere.
>
> (CT III.1030 [2: 1006])

It is interesting in this respect that in Modern Dutch, which does not allow an indirect-object passive, the following structure,

> (517) De mensen (pl.) worden (pl.) verzocht hun jassen hier te laten
>
> 'People are requested to leave their coats here'

in which the indirect object *mensen* has become subject, is now quite frequently heard beside the more 'correct' construction which has the verb in the singular. Note that here too we have an infinitival direct object. It appears, then, that an indirect-object passive is more likely to occur when the direct and indirect object are not both noun phrases.

Another factor that plays a role in the rise of the indirect-object passive (this is true also for the prepositional passive) is to what extent the indirect object functions in the role typical of a passive subject, i.e. as patient (see Denison 1985a: 194, and the literature quoted there). Most of Visser's infinitival and clausal instances (and see (514)) qualify highly in this respect.

Loss of case inflections, which plays such a large part in the development of the indirect-object passive, is often invoked as a cause in the rise of the prepositional passive (see van der Gaaf 1930; Lightfoot

1981a; van Kemenade 1987). Denison (1985a) convincingly shows, however, that in the latter case this is much less likely to be a factor because of the fact that the prepositional construction did not have a passive counterpart in Old English (i.e. *Her was talked to*), whereas the indirect-object passive did. Again, what is important to note here is in what ways the prepositional object began to look like a direct object.

The most notable new development in Middle English, involving prepositions, is the emergence of phrasal verbs like *to give up*, in which the particle may be a preposition or an adverb (see Strang 1970: 275–6). They almost completely replace the Old English prefixed verbs. Two types of Old English prefixed verbs are important here. First of all, (a), the type with an inseparable prefix (e.g. *besprecan* 'to speak about'). Since most Old English prefixes disappeared (cf. ch. 5, section 5.2.11), this type was presumably simply replaced by a new verb–particle combination. This new combination entered Middle English possibly by way of Old French and Old Norse models (see Mustanoja 1960: 362–3) but very likely also because of the developments described under (b), which follows. A second Old English type, (b), concerns verbs with a separable prefix. This particle could follow as well as precede the verb. It can be shown that the position of the particle depends heavily on whether the verb–particle combination occurs in a main or a subclause. As a rule, the particle precedes the verb in a subclause; in the main clause the particle follows the verb, or rather the verb has left it behind when it moved to second position in the clause (by the so-called verb-second rule, see also section 4.8.2). In other words, it is likely that in Old English the particle is base-generated before the verb and that other possible positions are derived. In the Middle English period, when the language became SVO, the particle acquired a new base position *after* the verb, i.e. the position it normally had in main (SVO) clauses in Old English (for this development see Hiltunen 1983a, b). Thus, in Middle English the position of the particle becomes fixed after the verb. This fixed position adjacent to the verb must have greatly favoured a reanalysis of V [P NP] to $V P$ [NP]. A reanalysis of this kind is assumed by most linguists and is considered to be necessary to explain the emergence of the prepositional passive.

Since many verbs included in the type described under (a) above were simply transitive verbs, it seems likely that these verbs remained semantically transitive even when they turned into verb–particle combinations. This also means that the semantic function of the new prepositional object equalled that of a direct object to a transitive verb so that it lent itself easily to passivisation. In this connection Strang (1970: 275) also notes that many of the verb–particle combinations already had a very specialised sense by the mid-twelfth century. In other words, these combinations were very soon lexicalised, i.e. they behaved like simple rather than prepositional verbs. Consequently, their prepositional objects came to be or could be interpreted as direct objects.

In the literature, additional factors are given that could have induced the new prepositional passive constructions. One of them is preposition stranding. Preposition stranding (discussed in the next section) became a more frequent phenomenon in Middle English. It could, therefore, have led to a closer association between the verb and its preposition, which now more often followed the verb rather than that it preceded its object. However, Denison (1985a : 197) notes that prepositional passives occur with the preposition *preceding* the verb. This seems to suggest that preposition stranding is no prerequisite for the development of the new passive. However, it seems entirely plausible that the reanalysis mentioned above furthered the development of the prepositional passive. For other possible factors involved in the development of the prepositional passive see Denison (1985a).

4.9.2 *Preposition stranding*

Preposition stranding is a phenomenon in which the preposition is left without its NP complement. It can be seen at work in such constructions as (a) *Who did you give it to*, which contrasts with (b) *To whom did you give it*, where the preposition occupies its normal place before the NP complement. The word 'stranded' has been chosen to convey the traditional notion in generative grammar that the NP complement (*who*) has been moved from its base-generated position to clause-initial position, whereby the preposition is left behind. This movement is necessary in the case of (a)–(b) because the basic structure has been questioned. Other cases of movement that can involve preposition stranding are passives (*He was laughed at*) and relative clauses (*This is the book I read about*), where again the NPs are moved to the head of the clause (by so-called NP-movement and wh-movement respectively). In the (b) example, the preposition is moved along with the NP complement. In generative literature this process is usually referred to as 'pied piping'.

In the Middle English period a number of changes occur concerning the possibilities of preposition stranding. Let us first consider the situation in Old English. Preposition stranding is obligatory in relative clauses initiated by *þe* and in non-introduced (or zero relative) clauses. It is also obligatory in infinitival relatives, which always have a zero relative; cf. the examples in (518):

(518)a. Seo gesyhð þe we god *myd* geseon scylon is angyt
         the sight   that we God with see   shall is understanding

                                                                     (*Solil.* 1 29.1)

      'The sight with which we shall see God is understanding'

    b. Ðonne is oþer stow elreordge men beoð *on*
        then   is other place barbarous men are   in

                                                                     (*Marv.* 18.1)

      'There is another place where barbarous people live'

    c. Eanflæd seo cwen ... bæd Osweo þone cyning ðæt he þær   forgefe
        Eanflæd the queen   bade Osweo the king   that he there gave
        stowe mynster *on* to timbrenne þæm foresprecenan   Godes
        place minster on to build   to the afore-mentioned God's
        þeowe Trumhere
        servant Trumhere

                                                                  (Bede 3 18.238.21)

      'Queen Eanflæd bade king Osweo to give the afore-mentioned Trumhere, God's servant, a place for building an abbey'

Pied piping is obligatory (i.e. preposition stranding does *not* occur) in relative clauses introduced by *se* or *se þe* etc. and in questions, both direct and indirect; cf. (519):

(519)a. ... þæt he us þingie wið ðone heofanlican cyning, *for þæs naman* he
        þrowode

                                                                 (*ÆCHom.* I 29 434.33)

      '... that he intercede for us with the heavenly king, for whose name he suffered'

    b. Ic nat   ful geare *ymb*   *hwæt* þu giet tweost
        I not-know full well   about what you still doubt

                                                                   (*Bo.* 5.12.26)

      'I do not quite understand what you are still doubtful about'

Finally, there are some constructions in which both preposition stranding and pied piping occur, but the occurrence of the former process is usually clearly defined. Thus, in topicalisation constructions preposition stranding is not found except when the topicalised NP is a personal or a locative (*þær*, *þyder*) pronoun,[57]

(520) & him þa siþþan se feondscipe wæs *betweonum* weaxende
and them then afterwards the enmity was between growing

(Or. 5.9.232.25)

'and then later between them the enmity grew'

In relative clauses introduced by a locative pronoun both constructions again are used, seemingly indiscriminately. However, the examples with pied piping given in Allen (1977: 100) – both of which show inversion of S and V, in contrast to the examples with preposition stranding – seem to suggest that these examples might be main clauses rather than subclauses.

In free relative clauses (i.e. clauses without a head) introduced by *se þe* and *swa hwa swa*, preposition stranding occurs, but only when *se* and *hwa* take their case from the function they have in the main clause. This is not surprising since this makes the construction very similar to a headed relative clause introduced by *þe* (n.b. *swa* is like *þe* in that it is indeclinable):

(521) & he tobrysð þone ðe he *onuppan* fylð
and it crushes that one that it upon falls

(Mt. (WSCp) 21.44)

'and it crushes whoever it falls upon'

Concerning the distribution of preposition stranding and pied piping in Old English, two general remarks can be made. First of all, preposition stranding is clearly more available in the case of personal and locative pronouns. This can be linked to the fact that there existed a looser connection between these pronouns and their prepositions than was the case in nominal prepositional phrases. Thus, in Old English, pronoun and preposition can be inverted (must be inverted in the case of locative pronouns), and the pronoun can easily be moved to another position in the clause away from the preposition (see van Kemenade 1987: ch 5, who also offers an explanation for this phenomenon). Secondly, preposition stranding is obligatory when the complementiser is zero or has no overt features (such as case, number, gender), i.e. when it takes the form of *þe* or *swa*.

In Middle English the possibilities for preposition stranding became greatly extended. In the thirteenth century we come across the first sporadic instances of preposition stranding in wh-relatives (522) and in questions (523), i.e. in cases where the complementiser does have overt features. It should be remarked, however, that the early examples in relative clauses mostly concern *which*, a pronoun that could hardly be said to show features like case, number and gender (cf. also the regular early use of preposition stranding in Middle English with relative indeclinable *þæt*, which replaced OE relative *þe* (see section 4.6.1.1)).

(522) And getenisse men ben in ebron,/ Quilc men mai get wundren *on*.

                                                 (*Gen.&Ex*.3715–16)

      'And giant men are in Hebron which one may still wonder at.'

(523) nuste nan kempe, whæm he sculde slæn *on*,

                                                 (*Brut* (Clg) 13718–19)

      'No soldier knew whom he should strike at'

The first instances of preposition stranding in passives (524) and topicalised constructions (525) are found at about the same time, but are also rare:

(524) þer wes sorhe te/ seon hire leoflich lich faren so reowliche *wið*.

                                      (*St.Juliana* (Roy) 22.195–6)[58]

      'it was painful to see her lovely body dealt so cruelly with.'

(525) ...ah þe gode ich ga aa   bisiliche *abuten*,...
       but the good I   go always busily   about

                                          (*St.Marg.(1)* (Bod) 30.35–6)

      'but the righteous ones I always war against constantly'

In all cases preposition stranding becomes only more common towards the end of the fourteenth century.

Examples like the following with a double preposition, which are quite frequent in Late Middle English,

(526) ...remembir *of* what kynne we be com *of*,...

                                   (Malory *Wks* (Add.59678) 408.23–4)

show the development of preposition stranding in wh-constructions. When in Late Middle English preposition stranding has become more common, it also spread to other constructions such as Tough-movement constructions (i.e. of the type *He is easy to please*), which allowed neither preposition stranding nor pied piping in Old English (see van der Wurff 1987: 4):

(527) ...the grete Roches, þat ben stronge and dangerouse to passe by.

                                        (*Mandev.* (Tit) 29.10–11)

Preposition-stranding constructions in which the preposition is not directly dominated by the verb phrase, as in PDE *What train did Shelagh arrive by?*, do not yet occur in Middle English.

What causes can be found for this extension of the process of preposition stranding? For the use of preposition stranding in relative wh-clauses we can distinguish three causes (for preposition stranding in the passive see section 4.9.1). First of all, it is possible that *which*-clauses (and later also *who*-clauses) acquired preposition stranding on the analogy of relative *that*-clauses (as noted above *which* was virtually indeclinable). Secondly, this process could have been further supported (or initiated) by the fact that the new wh-relatives developed from Old English free relatives. We have seen above that preposition stranding with free relatives was possible in Old English under certain conditions. Since wh-elements in (in)direct questions go back to the same source (see section 4.6.1.1), it is natural that preposition stranding became possible here too. Note in this light that the relative in (523) could still be interpreted as a free relative. Thirdly, the reanalysis of $V [P NP]$ to $V P [NP]$, discussed in section 4.9.1, which played an important role in the development of the prepositional passive, was of influence here too. It made it possible for the NP to be extracted out of the PP. This had not been possible in Old English, at least not for nominal NPs. Thus, preposition stranding was extended to topicalisation and Tough-movement constructions.

FURTHER READING

General

This chapter leans heavily, as the many references show, on Mustanoja's (1960) detailed work on Middle English syntax and on Visser's (1963–73) historical grammar. Their contributions frequently provided the basis or the starting-point for the discussion of a topic in this chapter, and any interested student would do well to get acquainted with these works. (Moessner's (1989) study on Early Middle English syntax was not yet available at the time this chapter was written. However, a cursory glance seems to indicate that this study will be of more use to a student of Axiomatic Functionalism than to someone who wishes to get access to the syntactic peculiarities of Early Middle English.) Other general studies on Middle English or, more widely, on historical English syntax which should be of help to the reader are Jespersen's monumental (historical) grammar (1909–49), Traugott (1972), Schibsbye (1974–7) and the short synopsis given in Mossé (1952). Of the general histories of the English language, Strang (1970) is the most useful and the most insightful as far as syntax is concerned. Older works on the history of English concentrate mainly on phonology and morphology, but syntactic information is found in Mätzner (1874), Einenkel (1887; 1916) and Brunner (1962). For more general information on the study and the theory of historical syntax and syntactic change I refer the reader to Rydén (1979) (a very accessible introduction to the topic), Lightfoot (1979), Romaine (1982), Warner (1982) and Hock (1986, ch. 13).

Although in the course of the chapter, and also in this section, a good number of references have been/will be discussed or touched upon, they represent no more than a small selection of the enormous amount of scholarship available on Middle English syntax. The reader interested in pursuing any given topic further should consult the bibliographical works provided by Fisiak (1987) and Tajima (1988), and the bibliographies given by Mustanoja throughout his work.

There is no separate section in this chapter on foreign influence on Middle English syntax but, where appropriate, reference has been made to it. For a general overview of Latin influence on English syntax see Sørensen (1957) and on European syntax in general, Blatt (1957). For foreign contacts that have been important for the development of Middle English syntax and for other external (social) factors, see Berndt (1965), Fisher (1977), Leith (1983), Hines (1984 and forthcoming) and Poussa (1982).

4.2 There are no general studies on word order in the noun phrase but some information may be gathered from syntactic studies based on individual authors such as van der Meer (1929) on *Mandeville's Travels* and Kerkhof (1982) on Chaucer. On the development, the use and the position of the indefinite article, consult Rissanen (1967). This work provides also the main source for the development of the propword *one*. More data on the use and the absence or presence of both the definite and the indefinite article will be found in Mustanoja (1960: 229–74). Information on the genitive is given in Mustanoja (1960, 70–93). More specialised studies concerning the emergence of new types of genitive are van der Gaaf (1927, 1932).

4.3.1.2 The impersonal construction has recently become a vigorously debated topic. A spate of studies have appeared of both a descriptive and a theoretical nature covering the Old as well as the Middle English period. For data on Old English consult Wahlén (1925), Elmer (1981), Ogura (1986) and Denison (1990a); for the Middle English and the transitional period, see van der Gaaf (1904) and Elmer (1981). Studies that address themselves primarily to an explanation of the developments and the use and meaning of impersonals are McCawley (1976), Fischer & van der Leek (1983, 1987), Lagerquist (1985), Allen (1986) and Anderson (1986).

4.3.2.1 and 4.3.3.2 Central works on tense for our period are Zimmermann (1968), Fridén (1948) and Bauer (1970). The first one covers the early period, the latter two the Late Middle English period and beyond. Fridén discusses in great detail the use of *have* and *be* as auxiliaries of the (plu)perfect (for this see also Fridén 1957 and Zimmermann 1973), and *shall* and *will* as auxiliaries of the future. A specialist study on the rivalry between *have* and *be* is Rydén & Brorström (1987). Their interest is mainly in the late modern period but they give a useful survey of earlier developments. The topic is also of synchronic interest because most of the modern Germanic languages have preserved the *have/be* variation. These synchronic data may in turn shed light on the historical situation in English. For references to studies on *have/be* usage in German and the Scandinavian languages, consult Rydén and Brorström (1987), for Dutch see de Rooy (1988). For the large number of specialised studies on the development of the future and the (plu)perfect consult the bibliography in Fridén (1948). For cross-linguistic similarities in the development of tense/aspect systems, which are also highly relevant to the developments of the perfect, progressive and future systems in English, see Bybee & Dahl (1989) and Bybee & Pagliuca (1987).

Beside these topics the most discussed subject is the use and the development of the historical present. All handbooks discuss this but no agreement has been reached so far. Of special interest is Steadman (1917). It is also possible that the historical present fulfils a discourse function in Middle English, as it does in Present-Day English (see Wolfson 1979). Brinton (1990: 44) suggests as much but does not go into any detail. A convenient overview of the uses of the present, past and (plu)perfect can be found in Visser (1963–73: §§ 710–811; 1898–1904; 2001–30), Mustanoja (1960: 479–509) and Schibsbye (1974–7, vol. II: 129–40).

4.3.2.3 More information on the replacement of the Old English instrumental/dative case by analytic agentive expressions can be found in Green (1914) and Knispel (1932).

4.3.3.1 A general history of the progressive in English is provided by Scheffer (1975). Mossé (1938) covers the Old and Middle English periods. Strang (1982) provides a good account of the later (i.e. in the modern period) grammaticalisation of the expanded form. An extensive discussion of the origin of the *-ing* form and the progressive is also given in Visser (1963–73: §§ 1001–38; 1800–89).

On the history of the gerund two studies have appeared recently: Tajima (1985) and Donner (1986). Tajima provides a large set of data covering the period from 1100 to 1500, enabling us to get a sense of the chronology of the syntactic changes taking place. Donner offers a statistical context for the occurrence of the gerund and comes to the conclusion that the quantitative validity of the evidence given for the gerund in Middle English is weak. The syntactic (rather than mere stylistic) use of the gerund only gets a real start in the late fifteenth/early sixteenth century. Mustanoja (1960: 566–81) offers a convenient overview and references of the earlier debate on the development of the gerund.

4.3.3.3 There is some controversy about the categorial status of the modals in the Old and Early Middle English periods. Lightfoot (1979) analyses them as full verbs. Warner (1990) shows how the modal verbs were already distinct from full verbs on a subcategory level in Old English and how they began to function as a full category by the Early Middle English period. Denison (1990b) grants the Old English modals the status of auxiliary verbs on the basis of syntactic and semantic evidence which he presents. Van Kemenade (1989) argues that the Old English modals could be both main verb and auxiliary, and that the former option disappears due to some internal changes later on in the grammar. This more distinct category status in turn led to greater opposition with full verbs. A central work on the development and the use of modal auxiliaries will be Warner (forthcoming). For a general overview see Visser (1963–73: §§1483–1710). Mustanoja (1960) has scattered information on the modals on pages 453–8; 489–96; 599–600. Traugott (1972: 198–9) provides a convenient chart setting out the functions of the modals between 800 and the present day.

4.3.3.4 A fair number of articles have been written on the development of aspect in English. References to the most relevant studies, especially on *gan*, have been given in the chapter itself. Brinton (1990) (which I saw too late to consider in the main body of the text) provides another interesting angle on the use of *gan* in Middle English narrative texts. She argues persuasively that *gan* developed from an aspectual marker into a discourse structure marker, following semantic and pragmatic principles of grammaticalisation also found elsewhere (see Traugott 1982, 1989). More general works on aspect for this period are Häusermann (1930) and Brinton (1981, 1988).

4.3.3.5 The essential reading on the emergence of periphrastic *do* is still Ellegård (1953), but the debate was not closed on the appearance of this book; see, for example, Visser (1963–73: §§1411–76), Traugott (1972) and Denison (1985b). Hausmann (1974) is a by now somewhat dated transformational generative attempt to explain the emergence of periphrastic *do* as a type of rule reordering. Stein (1990: ch. 2) reviews some of the post-Ellegård theories on the origin of periphrastic *do*. He himself suggests factors of a sociopragmatic nature, which may have influenced the development of non-causative periphrastic *do*. These factors may provide the bridge from perfectivity to the semantically meaningless periphrastic use of *do*, which was left open by Denison (1985b). The idea suggested by Traugott (1972: 139ff.) that periphrastic *do* may also have developed from what she has called 'affirming *do*' (due to the breakdown of the subjunctive system in Middle English *do* may have come to be used as a new marker of the opposition indicative/subjunctive, i.e. to assert the truth of a statement) is also incorporated in Stein's sociopragmatic explanation of the development. Kroch (1989) provides another perspective on the history of *do*. Using Ellegård's data-collection he observes the *processes* of change in the rise of periphrastic *do*. He notes that these can be better explained in psycholinguistic than in purely grammatical terms.

Studies not mentioned in the body of the chapter but which provide useful data on the actual uses of the auxiliary *do* in Late Middle English are Royster (1915), who discusses a number of authors, especially Lydgate; Moore (1918) on Robert Mannyng and Davis (1972) on Margaret Paston.

4.5 Mustanoja (1960: 339–41) deals only briefly with negation. More extensive data are given in Jack (1978a, c) on Early Middle English, and Jack (1978b) and Baghdikian (1979) on Late Middle English. These accounts do not attempt to give an explanation for the changes taking place in this period; this is done by Joly (1982), but in a highly idiosyncratic and not in every respect illuminating way. More insight into the English system of negation (and therefore also in its diachronic developments) is gained from reading Klima (1964). For a discussion of the use of unsupported *ne*, see also Warner (1982: 198–225).

4.6, 4.6.1 and 4.6.3 There is a clear paucity of material on the structure and behaviour of composite sentences in Middle English. The only general data study is by Eitle (1914) on sub- and co-ordinate clause structures in Chaucer. Negative co-ordination is treated in Jack (1978c). There are a few articles on adverbial clauses: a general study by Phillipps (1966a); König (1985a, b) and Harris (1989) deal with concessives; Wiegand (1982) with causal clauses. An interesting study on the use of *þa* as a narrative (discourse) marker rather than a syntactic marker strictly indicating sub- or co-ordination is Foster (1975). Stockwell & Minkova (1991) give a list of devices that helped to disambiguate between main and subclauses in Old English and they also discuss the various stages through which subordination passed from parataxis to hypotaxis in the course of the Old and Middle English period.

Information on relative clauses is the only kind that is not scanty. Not surprisingly, perhaps, since here the changes have been most obvious. For a convenient review of the developments taking place in this area, see Romaine (1982: 59ff.). The most relevant studies are discussed or referred to in the section concerned (4.6.1). On resumptive pronouns in relatives and other clauses, see also Mustanoja (1985). A detailed study of non-finite relative clauses and the changes they underwent between Old and Middle English is Allen (1977). Further discussion of zero relative clauses (also called contact clauses) can be found in van der Auwera (1984) and Moessner (1984: 68ff.). Moessner also offers a more general discussion of relatives and of relative clauses of the type '*Who* do you think *that* will come?' with a double complementiser, which were acceptable in Middle English but no longer are in Present-Day English.

Information on the type of mood used in subordinate clauses can be found most conveniently in Mustanoja (1960: 454–73) and in authors' studies such as van der Meer (1929) and Kerkhof (1982).

4.6.2.1 and 4.6.2.2 More studies have appeared on non-finite than on finite complements, the reason being that the important and most easily noticeable changes took place in the former, which extended themselves at the cost of the latter. The most detailed work on finite complements is Warner (1982). Lassaut & Dekeyser (1977) provide a general, theoretically oriented study on the changes that take place in subject and object clause embedding between 900 and the present day. Manabe (1989) studies the widening use in Middle English of infinitives as compared with finite clauses.

4.6.2.3 In the area of non-finite complements, the rise or expansion of the *to*-infinitive is of interest, explained lucidly and in great detail by Bock (1931). Following up this rise we see quite a few studies which attempt to clarify the difference in usage between the bare and the *to*-infinitive, such as Ohlander (1941), Kaartinen & Mustanoja (1958), Quirk & Svartvik (1970), Fischer (forthcoming b) and more general studies, i.e. Kenyon (1909), Sanders (1915) and Warner (1982: 115–33).

4.6.2.4 A Japanese study on the development of the perfect infinitive which I have not been able to consult is Miyabe (1954). This is complemented by Miyabe (1956).

4.6.2.5 The most convenient study dealing with all the positions in which the passive infinitive can occur in Modern English and the changes taking place there between the Old and the Middle English periods is Fischer (1991).

4.6.2.6 Data on the split infinitive can be found in van der Gaaf (1933), Mustanoja (1960: 515–16) and Visser (1963–73: §§977–82).

4.6.2.10 There are quite a few general studies on the use of the accusative and infinitive construction in English, such as Krickau (1877) and Zeitlin (1908). For Old English, Callaway (1913) is relevant. A more recent study on Late Middle English usage is Warner (1982). A more data-oriented account than is provided in Fischer (1989) of the relation between the rise of the accusative and infinitive and the role played in this by the passive infinitive will be found in Fischer (forthcoming a). It is shown there that the *passive* accusative and infinitive construction increases first after causative verbs (*let, do, make*) from where it spreads via 'persuade'-type verbs to genuine aci verbs (the so-called *verba sentiendi et declarandi*) because of causative connotations present in these verbs. This prepares the way for the more learned, Latin influenced accusative and infinitive constructions in English.

4.7 Some general information on agreement can be found under the headings concord or number in Mustanoja (1960: 55–66; 219–22), Mossé (1952: 110–11) and Traugott (1972: 133–4). Van der Meer (1929: 148ff.) and Kerkhof (1982: 198ff.) deal with agreement features in *Mandeville's Travels* and Chaucer. Stoelke (1916) is a monograph on subject–verb (dis)agreement, but he deals only with cases where the subject is singular and the predicate plural.

4.8 There is a vast amount of literature on word-order typology and word-order change, especially the change from OV to VO relevant here. For a general picture see Vennemann (1974, 1984), Hock (1982, 1986) and the literature quoted there. Gerritsen (1984) deals with word-order developments in Germanic languages. Narrowing the subject down to the history of English, Stockwell (1977, 1984) and van Kemenade (1987) provide a good starting-point for the deep-structure approach to word order, illustrating the changes taking place between the Old and the Middle English periods. Studies of word order combining both the deep- and surface-structure approaches are Bean (1983) for Old English and Kohonen (1978) for the transitional period (1000–1200). A critical review of Bean can be found in Denison (1986). Further word-order studies of specific Middle English texts, usually of a surface-structure approach, are mentioned in the section itself.

In the deep-structure-oriented literature on word order there is one exception to the generally accepted theory that changes take place in root sentences before they percolate down into subordinate clauses, and that is the study by Stockwell & Minkova (1991). This study, in fact, represents almost a reversal of Stockwell (1977). Whereas it was argued in 1977 that SVO order in main clauses in Late Old English was frequent, more frequent than the SvOV order which one would expect on the basis of the verb-second (V_2) rule, and that this SVO order served as a catalyst for the development of SVO in subordinate clauses, the new argument is that this SVO in main clauses does *not* represent subject–verb order but verb-second order; that in fact the two are quite distinct. If the word order in main clauses is analysed as verb second rather than subject–verb and if we accept that the V_2 rule remains active right till the end of the Middle English period (as Stockwell & Minkova assume with van Kemenade 1987), then indeed it can be said that subject–verb order occurred earlier in subclauses, where V_2 did not operate. The crucial question then becomes: could the language-acquiring child still deduce the V_2 rule in Middle English? In other words, how strong is the evidence for V_2?

Van Kemenade (1987) has investigated this, but her evidence is limited to only a few texts. More research is clearly needed to establish the case. The whole situation is aggravated by the fact that the V_2 rule is gradually taken over by the inversion rule (for the difference between the two, see Stockwell 1984). The new inversion rule takes care of the left-overs of the V_2 rule, i.e. of the orders that do not concur with the new subject–verb order, such as the verb–subject order after adverbials. At the same time the new rule represents a more limited domain in that the verb–subject order becomes restricted to (certain kinds of) adverbials (e.g. the Old English pronominal object–V–S order and the V–S order after locative and temporal adverbs disappears). Stockwell (1984) shows also that later on the new inversion rule widens its domain again; for instance, it becomes applicable after constituents that are of 'a predicative content' (p. 579) such as participles, adjective phrases, etc.

4.9.1 Further studies on the emergence of the new passive constructions not mentioned in the text are van der Gaaf (1929) and (1930) and Lieber (1979). (Since Lieber accepts the data from Visser, her account has to be read with caution; see note 55.) Mustanoja (1960) writes on the new passives on pp.

440–1; Visser (1963–73) discusses the prepositional passive in §§ 1947–57 and the indirect object passive in sections 1959, 1963–85.

One of the standard works on the emergence of phrasal verbs is Kennedy (1920). He is, however, more interested in the Modern English situation than in historical developments. His historical survey (pp. 11–18) shows that the new idiom only establishes itself slowly; that it occurs from the first in southern as well as northern dialects (which seems to argue for a native development, possibly reinforced by foreign patterns, rather than 'pure' foreign influence) and that it appears to be a feature more of colloquial than formal English. The latter would explain the fact noted by Strang (1970: 275) that, in spite of its infrequent occurrence, we find verb–particle combinations already by the mid-twelfth century that 'have so specialised a lexical sense ... that we must suppose the type to have become deeply entrenched even before period IV [i.e. the period between 1170 and 1370].' Kennedy also suggests that it is possible that the influx of Romance compound verbs stopped the development of new verb–particle combinations for a while, because they only begin to show real strength in the fifteenth century.

4.9.2 Allen (1977) explains the separate domains of pied piping and preposition stranding (P-stranding) with reference to the presence or absence respectively of a movement rule. Old English grammar had a prohibition against movement out of a prepositional phrase in the case of personal and locative pronouns. In Middle English this prohibition was lost. Van Kemenade (1987) believes that movement takes place in both cases but that P-stranding can only occur with movement of a clitic element to a non-argument position (for the latter see Chomsky 1981: 47). She shows that personal and locative pronouns, because of their different behaviour in comparison to nouns, are best interpreted as syntactic clitics. In relative *þe* clauses, she presupposes an empty clitic that is moved out of the prepositional phrase in order to explain the obligatory P-stranding in these clauses. The extension of P-stranding in Middle English is related mainly to two new developments: (a) the fact that in Middle English the preposition no longer assigns oblique case and can become a proper governor (in the sense of Kayne 1981); and (b) the reanalysis of the preposition into a particle of the verb, which becomes possible only in Middle English.

For the appearance of P-stranding in Tough-movement constructions, see van der Wurff (1987, 1990a).

TEXTUAL SOURCES

The illustrations in this chapter have been drawn from a large number of Middle English texts, early as well as late, representing a variety of dialects, although there is a clear bias towards the south east midlands, the dialect that provides us with the later standard. Apart from major authors like Chaucer I have used the references in the *MED*, part 1, Plan and Bibliography (1954) and in Supplement 1 (1984). Below, I provide an alphabetical list of the Middle English texts used, accompanied by the name of the editor(s), an indication of the date of the manuscript(s) used (and if possible the date of the original composition (in parentheses)) and an indication of the dialect in which the manuscript(s) was (were) written. This information has likewise been taken from the *MED* and from later studies or editions where appropriate. Whenever I have deviated from the edition referred to in the title abbreviations of the *MED* (indicated by '*'), a full reference will be provided. Texts marked with a dagger (†) occur widely in this volume and are referred to in this chapter either by a general abbreviation (see pp. xviii–xxi) or by editor and publication date. The references to Old English texts are the standard ones as given in Healey & Venezky (1980). The Old English sources are listed after the Middle English sources below.

Abbreviations

EML	East Midlands
Kt.	Kentish
Lnd.	London
ML	Midlands
NEML	Northeast Midlands
NML	North Midlands
No.	Northern
NWML	Northwest Midlands
Oxf.	Oxfordshire
S	Southern
Sc.	Scottish
SEML	Southeast Midlands
SW	Southwestern
SWML	Southwest Midlands
WML	West Midlands
WNorf.	West Norfolk

Sources of Middle English texts

Title abbreviation	Editor(s)	Date	Dialect
Ancr. (Corp-C)	J. R. R. Tolkien	ca 1230 (?a 1200)	SWML
Ancr. (Nero)	F. M. Mack	ca 1250 (a 1225)	SW/SWML
Ancr. (Tit)	M. Day	a 1250	SWML/NEML
Ayenb.	R. Morris & P. Gradon*	1340	Kt.
Barbour *Bruce*	W. W. Skeat*	1487 (1375)	Sc.
Bevis (Auch)	E. Kölbing	ca 1330 (?ca 1300)	SEML
†*Bk of Ldn Engl.*	R. W. Chambers & M. Daunt*	1384–1425	SEML

399

Title abbreviation	Editor(s)	Date	Dialect
Brut (Clg)	G. L. Brook & R. F.	ca 1275 (ca 1200)	SWML
Brut (Otho)	Lesley*	ca 1275 (ca 1200)	SWML
Brut-1333 (RwlB.171)	F. W. D. Brie	ca 1400	SEML
Brut-1419 (CmbKk)	F. W. D. Brie	ca 1450 (ca 1425)	SEML
Capgr.Chron. (Cmb)	P. J. Lucas*	a 1464	WNorf.
Caxton Eneydos	W. T. Culley & F. J. Furnivall*	1490	SEML
†Chaucer	L. D. Benson*	(1370–1400)	SEML
Cleanness	J. J. Anderson*	ca 1400 (?ca 1380)	NWML
Cloud (Hrl 674)	P. Hodgson	a 1425 (?a 1400)	North of central EML
Cursor (Vsp) and (Göt)	R. Morris	a 1400 (a 1325)	No
Cursor (Frf) and (Trin)	R. Morris	a 1400 (a 1325)	
Destr.Troy (Htrn)	D. Donaldson & G. A. Panton	ca 1450 (?a 1400)	WML
Digby Pl.	D. C. Baker, J. L. Murphy & L. B. Hall		
EEWills	F. J. Furnivall	1387–1439	Lnd, mixed
Emare	A. B. Gough*	a 1500 (ca 1400)	EML ·
Gawain	J. R. R. Tolkien & E. V. Gordon*	ca 1400 (?ca 1390)	NWML
Gen.&Ex.	R. Morris	a 1325 (ca 1250)	SEML
Glo.Chron.A (Clg)	W. A. Wright	ca 1325 (ca 1300)	SW
†Gower CA (Frf)	G. C. Macaulay	(a 1393)	SEML
Greg.Leg. (Vern)	C. Keller*	ca 1375 (ca 1300)	NEML
Guy(4) (Cmb)	J. Zupitza	15th cent. (?ca 1300)	SEML
Havelok (Ld)	G. V. Smithers*	ca 1300	Norfolk
Horn (Cmb)	J. Hall	ca 1260 (?ca 1240)	SW-SWML
Horn (Hrl)	J. Hall	ca 1325 (?ca 1240)	East of middle south
HMaid. (Bod)	B. Millett*	ca 1225 (?ca 1210)	SWML
Jacob&J (Bod)	A. S. Napier	?a 1300	SW
KAlex. (Ld)	G. V. Smithers	ca 1400 (?a 1300)	SEML
Ken.Serm. (Ld)	R. Morris	ca 1275	Kt.
Launc.	W. W. Skeat	(ca 1490)	Sc. + mixture of S and ML
Malory Wks (Add.59678) (formerly Win-College)	E. Vinaver (2nd edn)	ca 1485 (a 1470)	standard with No. + NML features

Title abbreviation	Editor(s)	Date	Dialect
Mandev. (Tit)	P. Hamelius	a 1425 (ca 1400)	SEML
Mannyng *Chron.Pt.2* (Petyt)	T. Hearne	ca 1375	
Mannying *HS* (Hrl)	F. J. Furnivall	a 1400 (ca 1303)	NEML
ME Sermons	W. O. Ross*	ca 1450 (1378–1417)	SWML
MKempe A	S. B. Meech & H. E. Allen	(a 1438)	SEML
Orfeo (Auch)	A. J. Bliss	ca 1330	SEML
Orm.	R. M. White & R. Holt	?ca 1200 (?a 1200)	NEML, Stamford
Owl&N (Clg)	E. G. Stanley*	ca 1275 (ca 1200)	SW (-SWML)
Palladius (Tit)	B. Lodge & S. J. H. Herrtage	a 1250 (?ca 1200)	SWML
†*Paston*	N. Davis	1422–1509	SEML
PC (Ld)	C. Clark*	a 1121–60	SEML
Pearl	E. V. Gordon	ca 1400 (?1380)	NWML
Pecock *Rule*	W. C. Greet	ca 1450	SEML
Perceval (Thrn)	W. H. French & C. B. Hale	ca 1440 (?a 1400)	No.
PPl.A[1] (Trin-C)	G. Kane	ca 1400 (a 1376)	WML
PPl.B (Trin-C)	G. Kane & E. T. Donaldson*	ca 1400 (ca 1378)	WML
PPl.C (Hnt 143)	D. Pearsall*	ca 1400 (?a 1387)	WML
Proc.Privy C	H. Nicolas		
Prov.Alf. (Trin)	O. S. A. Arngart*	ca 1250 (ca 1150)	S and ML
†Rolle *Engl.Wks*	H. E. Allen	ca 1440 (a 1349)	No.
†*Rose*	L. D. Benson*	(a 1380)	SEML (mixed)
7 Sages (1)	K. Brunner	ca 1520 (ca 1300)	SEML
Siege Troy(1)	M. E. Barnicle	ca 1400 (?a 1350)	SEML + WML
SLeg. (Ld)	C. Horstmann	ca 1300	SW
SLeg.Fran.(2)	C. Horstmann	a 1450	SW
St.Juliana (Bod) + (Roy)	S. R. T. O. d'Ardenne*	ca 1220 (?ca 1200)	SWML
St.Kath. (Bod)	S. R. T. O. d'Ardenne & E. J. Dobson	ca 1220 (?ca 1200)	SWML
St.Kath. (Tit)		a 1250 (?ca 1200)	SWML (mixed)
St.Marg. (Bod)	F. M. Mack	ca 1220 (?1200)	SWML
Stonor	C. L. Kingsford	1290–1483	Oxf.
Towneley Pl. (Hnt)	G. England & A. W. Pollard	a 1500 (a 1460)	NEML
Trev.Higd. (StJ-C)	C. Babington & J. R. Lumby	ca 1400	SW
Trin.Hom.	R. Morris	a 1225 (?a 1200)	SEML
Vices&V(1) (Stw)	F. Holthausen	a 1225 (ca 1200)	SEML

Wooing Lord (Tit)	W. M. Thompson*	a 1250 (?ca 1200)	NEML + AB language
Wycl..*Sel.Wks* (I)	T. Arnold	ca 1400	SML
Yonge S.Secr.	R. Steele & T. Henderson	a 1500 (1422)	

Sources of Old English texts (see Healey & Venezky 1980)

Reference	Description	Editor
ÆAdmon.1	*Admonitio ad filium spiritualem*	H. W. Norman (1848: 32–56)
ÆCHom.I	Ælfric's *Catholic Homilies* I	P. A. M. Clemoes (1955–6)
ÆCHom.II	Ælfric's *Catholic Homilies* II	M. Godden (1970, 1979)
ÆLS(Lucy)	Ælfric's *Lives of Saints*	W. W. Skeat (1881–1990: I, 210–18)
ÆLS(Oswald)	Ælfric's *Lives of Saints*	W. W. Skeat (1881–1900: II, 124–43)
And.	*Andreas*	G. P. Krapp (1932: 3–51)
Ap.T	*Apollonius of Tyre*	P. Goolden (1958)
Bede	Bede's *History*	T. Miller (1890–8)
Bo.	Alfred's *Boethius*	W. J. Sedgefield (1899)
*Chron.*A(Plummer)	*AS Chronicle*, Parker Chr.	C. Plummer (1892–9)
*Chron.*E(Plummer)	*AS Chronicle*: Ms Laud	C. Plummer (1892–9)
Dan.	*Daniel*	G. P. Krapp (1931: 11–32)
El.	*Elene*	G. P. Krapp (1932: 66–102)
Gen.	*Genesis*	S. J. Crawford (1922: 81–211)
HomU 34 (Nap 42)	*De temporibus Anticristi*	A. S. Napier (1883: 191–205)
Judg.	*Judges*	S. J. Crawford (1922: 401–14)
Lk.(WSCp)	The Gospel according to Luke	W. W. Skeat (1871–87)
LS 32 (Peter & Paul)	*The Blickling Homilies*	R. Morris (1874–80: 171–93)
Mald.	*The Battle of Maldon*	E. V. K. Dobbie (1942: 7–16)
Marv.	*The Marvels of the East*	S. Rypins (1924: 51–67)
Mk.(WSCp)	The Gospel according to Mark	W. W. Skeat (1871–87)
Mt.(WSCp)	The Gospel according to Matthew	W. W. Skeat (1871–87)
Or.	King Alfred's *Orosius*	H. Sweet (1883)
*Sol.*I	*Solomon and Saturn* (I)	J. M. Kemble (1848)
Solil.	St Augustine's *Soliloquies*	W. Endter (1922)
WCan.1.1.1(Fowler)	*Wulfstan's Canons of Edgar*	R. Fowler (1972: 2–18)
WHom.	*The Homilies of Wulfstan*	D. Bethurum (1957)

NOTES

1 For the knotty question 'When did Middle English begin?', consult chapter 2, section 2.1.2. This survey, too, will take 1066 as a symbolical starting point to be used with tact.

2 The only historical atlas that besides phonological and morphological data contains some maps on syntactic phenomena is that by Dees (1980) on Old French. Maps 269–81 provide information on subject–verb inversion, the omission of the subject, and the relation between the use of pronomina and changes in word order.

3 Sørensen (1957: 148) suggests that in certain biblical phrases, like 'God Almighty', Latin influence may have played a role as well.

4 According to Sørensen (1957: 147), Medieval Latin, where the title was always placed before the proper name, may have been of influence here too.

5 Object in (a) future, (b) modal or (c) negative scope means that the direct object is part of a clause that is (a) future in reference, (b) contains an element of modality, or (c) is negated.

6 It is interesting to note, however, in this connection that certain seventeenth-century grammarians, e.g. Wallis (1653), report that some people believe that *'s* stood for *his*. Wallis does not agree with this, but in spite of that he describes *'s* as a possessive adjective (see Kemp 1972: 305–11).

7 The expression can still be used in Present-Day English when it is immediately followed by a restrictive relative clause as in *The car of yours that I mentioned just now*. Here it is virtually equivalent to *That car of yours*.

8 The forms *dryveth* and *bryngeth* are two-syllabic in all other cases (fifteen) in which they are used in Chaucer with only two exceptions.

9 Sørensen (1957: 142–3) notes that Latin, 'with its rigorous sequence of tenses', may have influenced the use of the pluperfect in these cases.

10 Quite a few of the non-finite forms, especially the participials, have not been attested in Old English; they first appear in Late Middle English texts. See Campbell (1959) and the *MED* for more details on Old and Middle English respectively.

11 This remark constitutes no more than a mere suggestion because it would be impossible to prove that anything like what is described below actually happened in Middle English. By their very nature, structures like (156) would not have been recorded in older written texts. Another, but different, account that searches for the origin of periphrastic *do* in the use of a 'bleached' form of factitive *do* is that presented in Tieken-Boon van Ostade (1989).

12 Although examples in Visser (1963–73) show that other causative verbs do indeed appear in Middle English with infinitival constructions of the *do x* type (so without an infinitival subject NP), Ellegård emphasises that these constructions are, as in the case of *do*, not all that frequent (1953: 106–8).

13 At this stage it is not really correct to speak of progressive *be*. Not until the modern period does *be + V-ing* exist as a *grammatical* category expressing durative aspect. However, the use of *be +* present participle was one of the ways in which the *function* of duration could be expressed.

14 Lightfoot (1979: 28ff.) for that reason believes that this is an 'accidental gap' and that in fact modal and perfect *have* must have occurred together already in Old English. He argues likewise for the possibility of the combination passive and progressive *be*, which likewise has not been attested in Old English. Although one cannot disprove Lightfoot, I doubt whether this latter statement is correct. He does not take the fact into account that the perfect, passive and progressive forms were recent developments in Old English, which clearly had not become (fully) grammaticalised yet. Combinations of these forms within the VP are therefore not yet to be expected at this stage. Concerning the combination of modal and perfect *have*, he may be correct, but it is noteworthy that infinitival perfectives are also rare, if not non-existent, in Old English.

15 Cliticisation of *ne* is in Middle English a mainly southern feature.

16 This use of *ne* is very similar to the Middle Dutch use of the negative *en* (see van der Horst 1981: 49–51).

17 Matti Rissanen very kindly pointed out to me that there are a few examples of *not + any* in the Helsinki Corpus. They all seem to be late. An instance is:

> & ȝit was þat siȝt only by þe schewyng of oure Lorde whan hym likid to schewe it, & *not* for *any* deseert of his trauayle.
>
> *(Cloud* (Hrl 674) 128, 15–17)

18 This is the language used in the manuscript of the *Ancrene Wisse* (Corpus Christi College Cambridge 402) and in the Katherine Group (MS Bodley 34). Both manuscripts are written in the same west midland dialect. For a description see Tolkien (1929), but see also Hulbert (1946), Benskin & Laing (1981: 91ff.).

19 Klima (1964: 314) refers to the implicit negatives illustrated here as *adversative*. Notice that Present-Day English would use *any* in such constructions.

20 This is the reading given to it by Eitle (1914). For a different interpretation see Robinson (1957: 765).

21 Mitchell (1984) takes up a middle position. He believes that *þe* was originally a subordinating particle and that its use as a relative pronoun is 'probably a special adaptation' (p. 281). But he does not reject the possibility that it may have been originally of 'relatival nature' and that its presence in phrases like *þeah þe* etc. was due to analogical use (p. 282). He cannot agree with Geoghegan (1975: 43) that '*þe* can in no way be considered a pronoun' (p. 295, note 9).

22 The *OED* gives as the earliest occurrence *ȝiff þatt* from the *Ormulum*. Mitchell (1984: 273) has attested an earlier instance in Late Old English.

23 McIntosh (1948) stresses that this *þe* goes back to earlier Old English *þe*. It seems to me that the employment of *se*, *seo* with masculine and feminine nouns must also have influenced this use of *þe* since the *s-* in these forms was soon levelled out in favour of *þ-* (see also Kivimaa 1966: 135).

24 *Whose* is a special case since it comes to be used more and more with inanimate antecedents, presumably to avoid the clumsiness of *of which*.

25 I leave the use of the so-called zero relative out of account here.

26 Mustanoja (1960: 200) writes that *whose* does not occur with inanimate objects before the latter half of the fourteenth century. Instances given in Kivimaa (1966: 85, 90) from Early Middle English texts, however, show that this statement is not correct.

27 For the close proximity of possessive *have* and existential *be*, see Allan (1971).

28 This was first formulated by Emonds (1976), who showed that transformations should be structure preserving.

29 This is also true in Modern English varieties that have resumptive pronouns (e.g. Scots). These varieties generally have no relative pronouns proper (wh-forms) but only indeclinable *that*. I would like to thank Roger Lass for providing me with these observations.

30 In the case of *which* this is only true in so far as it allows a preposition in front of it (taking the place of the case form), something *þe* and *þat* do not allow.

31 Warner (1982: 65, 108) gives some Late Middle English examples from Chaucer's *Boece* and the Wycliffite sermons, which show finite and non-finite subject clauses in initial position.

32 See Warner (1982: 116ff.), who likewise argues for a structurally rather than a lexically conditioned selection between zero and (*for*) *to* in the case of the modals on the basis of their largely auxiliary status in the Late Middle English period.

33 The Old English verb *agan* 'to possess' developed into a modal verb in Middle English: *ought*. Since in the original construction *ought* was followed by an object noun and an infinitive 'to have/possess a thing to do' (see Kenyon 1909: 98), it normally took a *to*-infinitive. In later Middle English one also quite often finds a bare infinitive (especially in poetry); this could be an analogy of other modal verbs, or because *ought* also came to be used as an impersonal verb in Middle English, which verbs regularly took the bare infinitive (see below).

   Need was in Middle English still an impersonal verb and consequently appeared with the plain as well as the *to*-infinitive, although the latter is more frequent (see Visser 1963–73: §1345). The first instances of 'personal' *need* with infinitive date from the last quarter of the fourteenth century (Visser 1963–73: §1346).

   Dare is always followed by a plain infinitive in Middle English. Instances with *to* (not until the seventeenth century – see Visser 1963–73: §1385) only occur when *dare* develops full-verb next to its auxiliary status.

34 The same is true for the verbs *go* and *come*, which appear often with a bare infinitive when used 'aspectually':

> Therfore I wol *go slepe* an houre or tweye,...
>
> (CT I.3685 [1 : 3697])
>
> But certeinly she moste by hir leve,/ *Come soupen* in his hous with hym at eve.
>
> (Troilus III.559–60)

35 Two manuscripts have *to*, two have *ne* instead of *to*, and one has the bare infinitive.

36 Interesting in this connection is the use of *to* + -*yng* rather than just -*yng* to translate the Latin *future* participle in some Late Middle English texts (see Mustanoja 1960: 513, 516). Thus, *he was dying* becomes *he was to dying*.

37 In Fischer (1989, 1990) I also discuss reasons why a change from 'ordered the city to destroy' to 'ordered to destroy the city', which would also have solved the problem, was in most cases not the preferable option.

38 Mitchell (1985: §3782ff.) believes that there existed a so-called dative and infinitive construction (analogous to the accusative and infinitive construction) in Old English, in which the dative functions as subject of the infinitive. However, he gives no evidence of the kind presented here which shows convincingly that reanalysis *has* taken place. In all his examples the dative noun phrase can still be interpreted as governed by the matrix verb.

39 It is interesting to observe in connection with this that in the Late Middle English prose corpus analysed by Kaartinen & Mustanoja (1958) not a single bare infinitive is encountered, not even with impersonal verbs.

40 These kinds of examples do occur in texts based on Latin originals. However, since they do not occur outside these texts and since they are all word-for-word translations of Latin accusative and infinitives, these instances should not be considered as having been generated by the grammar of Old English (see Fischer 1989).

41 For the relative-clause interpretation see e.g. Mustanoja (1960: 202ff.); Visser (1963–73: §§75, 606); Kerkhof (1982: §541). For the opposite view see Kivimaa (1966: 41ff.) and references given there, and Diekstra (1984).

42 For instance, example (410) gives an instance of *that* used in a temporal clause. *That* is also regularly employed to continue the co-ordinate part of a subclause which itself was introduced by a more specific conjunction, as in:

> Men sholde hym brennen in a fyr so reed/ *If* he were founde, or *that* men myghte hym spye,...
>
> (CT VIII.313–14 [7: 313–14])
>
> Yit make hyt sumwhat agreable,/ *Though* som vers fayle in sillable;/ And *that* I do no diligence/ To shewe craft, but o [= only] sentence.
>
> (HF 1097–1100)

43 Dubislav (1916: 284) suggested that causal *that* developed from OE *for þæm*

þe. This seems unlikely, since in all other cases of conjunctive phrases, it was the preposition that survived (whether or not followed by *that*), not *that*.

44 For a discussion of the possible use of *and* as a conditional subordinator in Old English, see Mitchell (1985: §§3668–70).

45 This seems a new development in Middle English as far as concessive clauses are concerned; see below, example (394b); cf. Mitchell (1985: §§3440–1). The situation concerning the use of inverted word order in conditional clauses in Old English is somewhat unclear – see Mitchell (1985: §§3678–83).

46 *Þo* is also used as a demonstrative and relative pronoun, as an adverb and as a shortened form of *þoh* 'though'. *Þonne/þenne* functions as a temporal and locative adverb meaning 'then' and 'thence' and as the conjunction 'than'.

47 The reason why the verb is plural rather than singular, or, in other words, agrees with the subject-complement rather than with the subject is probably because in (488) after *it*, the verb *be* identifies *Gowrdes*. The emphasis is on *Gowrdes*, not on *it*. In (481) and (482) the verb *be* introduces what is in the subject-complement. Here the emphasis is on *be* (or *there*, if present) and not on the subject-complement.

48 Stockwell & Minkova (1991: note 14) show by means of some examples how notoriously difficult it is to compare word-order counts because of the different traditions in which, and the different assumptions with which, linguists work.

49 For some problems in relation to van Kemenade's theory that all Old English pronominals are clitics, see Koopman (forthcoming).

50 Van Kemenade (1987) relates the clitic behaviour of the pronominals to the inflectional morphology which is still a characteristic of Old English. She calls the Old English clitics syntactic clitics because they are distinguished by *position* but they behave like case affixes. Consequently, they are lost (i.e. the special position of the pronominals changes) when the case system disintegrates in the course of the Middle English period.

51 Swieczkowski (1962) has looked at the influence of what he calls 'semantic load' on word-order patterning in Late Middle English poetry and prose (i.e. the distribution of heavy (full nouns, verbs, etc.) and light (pronominals, prepositions, etc.) elements) (see also Reszkiewicz 1966 for Late Old English prose). Although he has found that weight is of influence (still) in Middle English, his evidence clearly shows that, especially in prose, rhythmical patterns are overruled by the syntactic need of having sentences conform as much as possible to the SVO pattern.

52 Mustanoja's (1985) study of a large body of Middle English texts confirms this. Of the objects preceding the infinitive, half were found to be nouns, half pronouns. Of the objects following, the majority were nouns.

53 These observations are mainly based on Borst (1910). It is difficult to

compare Borst's findings with those of Jacobson (1981) since the former only considers simple verb phrases but differentiates between main and subclauses with or without object. Jacobson looks at simple as well as complex verb phrases but makes no further distinctions.

54 Adverbs expressing negative degree occupy this position as long as *ne* precedes the finite verb. They become pre-finite when *ne* disappears.

55 Also, at the same time, the language was developing towards SVO order in which governors normally assign case to the right, or in other words, the NP dependent on the governing category (the adjective in this case) must be positioned to the right of it. This accounts for the differences in word order in the examples.

56 Contrary to what is stated in Visser (1963–73: §§ 1959ff.) and Lieber (1979), unambiguous indirect passives do not appear before 1500. This is shown conclusively by Mitchell (1979) and Russom (1982). See also Denison (1985a: 192, 196).

57 Preposition stranding with nominal NPs is extremely rare. For a discussion see Allen (1977: 72, note 4).

58 For a possible different interpretation of this example, see Denison (1985a: 191 n. 5).

5 LEXIS AND SEMANTICS

David Burnley

Lexis

Of all linguistic concepts, that of 'word' is the most fundamental, possessing a quality of homely familiarity which is lacking in more technical terms like 'phoneme', 'morpheme' or even 'syntax'. Words seem to have a reality either as pronunciations or as written characters, they have grammatical rules for combination, and they have meanings: and for everyday purposes we require little more than this in order to discuss them adequately. Yet, as soon as words become the object of serious study requiring more precise definition, it is apparent that our complacency is ill-founded. Difficulties are encountered in describing with precision what constitutes that composite of form and meaning we call a word. Our ready acceptance that words can be misspelt, mispronounced or inappropriately combined confirms that their use is governed by linguistic rules, but we assume too easily that such rules are founded on an ability to recognise words as the fundamental unit of analysis. In any period this is a troublesome business, but especially so in Middle English.

That written Middle English presents a problem in the definition of any individual word by its orthographic form is a fact vividly apparent to anyone who has ever used a computer to search a text. The machine's capacity to recognise forms is relatively inflexible, but inflexibility is not characteristic of scribal spelling. The scribe who, in the late fourteenth century, wrote MS Cotton Nero A.x, Art. 3, refers within a few lines of each other to *þyn aunt* and *þy naunt*, reflecting an uncertainty about word boundaries which is sometimes exploited in the patterns of alliterative verse: 'And *n*orisch him as *n*amely as he my*n*e awyn warre' (*Wars of Alexander* 582). The scribe of the Hengwrt manuscript of Chaucer's

Canterbury Tales writes both *at the* and *atte* as alternatives, and *the other* alongside *tother*. Such variation in the form of words is not normally found in printed Modern English, but before we scorn it as merely a medieval solecism, it is as well to recall that contractions like *tother* and assimilations like *atte* are quite common in modern *spoken* language and, moreover, that our modern words *apron, adder* and *another*, as well as the personal pronoun *my/mine* and the indefinite article *a/an*, are the standardised survivors of variation comparable with that recorded in *þyn aunt* and *þy naunt*. Medieval writing practice preserves for us variations of a sort common in the spoken language, which the standardised spelling of twentieth-century English will hide from scholars of the future. Variety in the forms of a word arose in Middle English in part from a more direct phono–graphic correspondence between spoken and written language than exists today. But this is by no means the only cause of such variation. For example, in the 1137 annal of the *Peterborough Chronicle* the scribe wrote five different forms of the word 'made' in a single short passage: *maket, maked, makede, macod, maced* (past participle). It is quite possible, of course, for an individual's spoken language to contain more than one pronunciation of a word, and because of the close correspondence between spoken and written modes this variation may be reflected in the written language; indeed *maket* faithfully records an assimilation in speech to the following fricative of *þurh*. But the remaining variation arises not from pronunciation but from the writer's inconsistency in rendering in writing the sounds of his speech: the same word, pronounced in the same way, has been given several different spellings. Such inconsistency reflects circumstances in which no national standard spellings of words existed, and in which a scribe could either choose between a regional spelling or an archaic standard spelling inherited from West Saxon, from some blend between them, or seek to reproduce his own pronunciation as best he could, employing his training in French or Latin orthography. That scribes rendered the phonetic details of their own dialectal pronunciations and exploited a variety of spelling systems to do so meant that at the orthographic level the identity of a word may become quite uncertain, and the bond between form and meaning which constitutes a word may become dissolved, so that even contemporary scribes might mistake the words they were copying (Matheson 1978). The *Middle English Dictionary* quotes under *forger*, 'a smith' an example from the fifteenth-century *Vegetius* spelt *forgeoure*, in which the context reveals that a scribe has confused the word with *fore-goer* 'one who goes ahead, a scout'. Other entries from different texts reveal confusions with *forager*. In extreme cases, the fact that a scribe might find nothing strange in his unfamiliarity with the word forms he was copying, could mean that he copied forms erroneously, creating new word forms which lacked any meaning: words which later scholars identify as 'ghost words'.

In addition to the variation of form arising from direct reproduction of the spoken language and from competing spelling practices, uncertainty as to the meaning of words might arise from the fact that Middle English is a conglomeration of separately developed dialects. English speakers of the time were well aware of the problems this raised. Referring to irregularities in the pronunciation of Yorkshire Middle English, Trevisa complained in 1387 that 'we Souþeron men may þat longage unneþe [hardly] vndurstonde' (Sisam 1955: 50). His view is endorsed nearly sixty years later by Osbern Bokenham, who goes on to identify as Scots the 'strange men and aliens' (Horstmann 1887: 31) whose language has so contaminated northern English. Although this failure of north–south communication may have been primarily a problem of pronunciation differences, there is ample evidence that northern Middle English possessed a vocabulary some-what distinct from that of the south (see 5.3.13). More dangerously, easily recognisable forms, familiar in both areas, may possess different senses in different parts of the country. Both Chaucer and Gower find it necessary to add some gloss to the context whenever they use the word *clippen*, which is a Scandinavian-derived word relatively recently introduced into their London language from the east midlands but which is identical in form to an Old English word meaning 'to embrace' (Burnley 1983: 148). The sense 'gear, accoutrements' of the word *fare* seems to have been exclusively a northern one (McIntosh 1973), although the form is common enough with other meanings elsewhere in the country. In the north the verb *dwellen* had the sense 'wait, stay', but in the south retained its older sense, 'live'. Chaucer, indeed, seems to make comic play of the discrepancy between the northern sense of the verb *hope* 'believe, think' and its southern one, 'hope', when John, his caricature of a northern student, declares 'Oure maunciple, I hope he wol be deed.' What is merely a prediction to a northern audience becomes an unholy desire to a southern one.

But we should not be too ready to accept that the meanings and forms of words were not known outside their home ground, and that communication was impossible when word forms differed. There is evidence in the deliberate translation of manuscripts from one dialect to another that, even when the sense might be guessed, grammatical forms and spellings which were unfamiliar could incur disapproval (Duncan 1981). Alleged failure to understand may be the expression of such disapproval in disguise. 'What', demands Caxton in his introduction to *Eneydos*, 'sholde a man in thyse dayes now wryte, "egges" or "eyren"', and he cites the example of a failure of communication between a southern countrywoman and a northern merchant. The context, however, is one of stylistic choice, and his allegations of unintelligibility are weakened by the fact that contemporary recipes contain both forms side by side. For practical communication, Middle English speakers tolerated considerable variation in the forms of a word, but like everyone else, they had their stylistic prejudices.

From the perspective which considers Middle English as a cultural whole, the concept of 'word' is much less clear-cut than we are accustomed to assume. The theoretical problems that this raises need not detain us at present (see 5.4.3), except that in the absence of a clear and unambiguous relationship between signifier and signified, between the form of a word and its meaning, a third category assumes great importance: that of context of occurrence. This category, upon which meaning depends to a great extent, is complex and can be subdivided in various ways. It is sufficient at present to distinguish the verbal context of discourse, or co-text, the context of the situation in which the word is used, and the much vaguer and more general context which the word inhabits in the associations familiar to competent and habitual users of the language. This complex of contexts serves to specify the probable sense of the word at each particular occurrence in Modern English too, but it would have been more important in Middle English in that the forms of words were more variable, and the meanings of even recognisable forms less predictable.

Although bilingual word lists and dictionaries were produced from the mid-thirteenth century onwards (Rothwell 1968; 1975-6), readers of Middle English manuscripts must normally have attributed meaning to unfamiliar written forms by a process of contextual glossing. This is the process commended to the translator by the author of the Prologue to the later translation of the Wycliffite Bible. Some Latin words subsume 'manie significacions under oon lettre'. The translator must establish the contextual sense of the original by considering its verbal context and choose his English rendering accordingly: 'a translatour hath greet nede to studie well the sentence both bifore and aftir, and loke well that such equivok wordis accorde with the sentence' (Forshall & Madden

1850: 59). Authors may contribute to this decoding process by co-ordinating difficult words in mutually defining pairs (*wene or suppose, for routhe and for pitee* Chaucer), and indeed it is possible that literary taste tolerated a degree of formulaic expression, a lack of originality in the choice and juxtaposition of words, precisely to facilitate communication. Contemporary commentators theorising on the choice of words in literary style are also apt to comment on the need for simplicity and clarity. Writing about 1387, Thomas Usk, perhaps echoing teaching on this matter to be found in Latin rhetorical theory, favours the avoidance of figurative terms and colours, recommending the use of chalk and charcoal in literary depiction. Simple and familiar words, he says, should be chosen, for 'rude wordes and boystous [plain] percen the herte of the herer to the innerest point, and planten there the sentence of thinges' (*Testament of Love*, in Skeat 1879: 7–8). It is a view echoed by Wyclif in his advice to preachers (Hargreaves 1966). Usk uses it to justify his choice of English rather than French as the medium for his work, but he does this by the rather surprising claim that there are many English words which he cannot understand: 'many termes there ben in English, of which unneth we Englishmen connen declare the knowleginge' (Skeat 1897: 2). That being so, how much less, then, can we understand the 'privy termes' of French?

These *termes*, to which both Chaucer and Usk refer, are a feature of Middle English vocabulary which seemed important to its original users and which also corresponds broadly to one of the modern categories of lexical analysis, that of register. *Termes* are lexical items recognised as being in some way restricted in their occurrence. This restriction may be a tendency for the lexical items to occur commonly in certain types of discourse: perhaps works on natural science or on alchemy; or they may be obviously of foreign origin and set aside from the common core of the vocabulary by this fact. For those familiar with technical discourse, the exploitation of such 'foreign' terms may be a conscious stylistic manoeuvre. Richard Rolle, in commencing his translation of the Psalter, shrinks from unusual English words, expecting adherence to the Latin to lend clarity:

> In þis werk I seke no strange Inglis, bot lightest and comunest and swilke þat es mast like vnto þe Latyn.
>
> (Allen 1931: 7)

It may seem strange that Latin should be viewed in this way, but consider too the remarks of Osbern Bokenham, who feels it necessary that men governed by the law should understand its terms: 'yn þe seyde lawis been mony termys vsid straunge to vndurstonde, þer-fore I wille rehersyne hem here withe here exposicyons' (*Mappula Angliae*). It is significant that the explanations he offers of difficult English words are sometimes in French: thus '*Mundebryche*: that is to sey on frensshe "blesmure de honneire," on Englyche "hurte of worschepe"' (Horstmann 1887: 21). The archaic English legal vocabulary was evidently less familiar than legal French, and the contemporary English translation of both is by a phrase patently modelled on French syntax, and using a French loan word.

That Latin and French should in this way be considered to lend clarity to English is not only the product of the circumstances of written English discussed in this introduction, but also the result of the familiar availability of these languages to readers in England. In the fourteenth and fifteenth centuries English was progressively reasserting itself in fields of discourse which for centuries had been dominated by Latin and French, so that Bokenham's words may be viewed as a microcosm of English lexical history in the medieval period. The Germanic compound *mundebryche*, which had come to seem so strange, represents the pre-Conquest period when Old English co-existed with the language of Scandinavian settlers; the legal French of *blesmure de honneire* represents a period extending until the first decades of the fifteenth century, when French existed alongside English as an official written language; and Bokenham's explanatory English rendering of it represents that anglicisation of official language which was in progress at the moment when he wrote. This co-existence of English first with the Germanic languages of Scandinavian settlers, and subsequently with French, with Latin as an ever-present background, has largely formed the English lexis which survives to this day.

5.1   Foreign influences

5.1.1   Scandinavian influence

5.1.1.1   The inhabitants of Britain since Gerald of Wales (*Description of Wales* 231) in the twelfth century have been content with the paradoxical view that, although they speak a language which matches in its diversity the various origins of the people, fresh influence from outside is to be regarded as a form of corruption. In the Renaissance period opposition by the proponents of pure English to that which they saw as foreign defilement was to become a serious intellectual debate, but in the Middle English period, when importations from French and Latin were generally regarded as a means of lending eloquence to style, the reproval of linguistic corruption was left to the protests of one or two individual voices. John of Trevisa, commenting in 1387 on the corruption of the mother tongue, asserts that it arose from the 'commyxstion and mellyng, first wiþ Danes and afterward wiþ Normans' and was promoted by the subsequent rise of French both for the purposes of instruction and as a mark of class distinction. As far as it goes, this account is not seriously at odds with the facts, but it is inadequate in several ways: notably that it neither credits the language of Scandinavian settlers with an important enough role, nor even mentions the effects of Latin influence. Modern etymology estimates that over 45 per cent of commoner words (25 per cent of the general lexis) in Present-Day English are of Germanic origin, nearly half of which are from sources other than Old English. Latin and French each account for a little more than 28 per cent of the lexis recorded in the *Shorter Oxford English Dictionary* (Finkenstaedt & Wolff 1973). Trevisa's failure to discuss Latin is explicable because it is the *spoken* languages of England which are under discussion and Latin influence was largely through the written language. Vagueness about the Scandinavian contribution is understandable too since, in marked contrast to French, its direct influence had been exclusively through spoken language many generations in the past, and by the fourteenth century its legacy was interpreted simply in terms of regional dialect features.

5.1.1.2 Cultural connections between England and Scandinavia are attested as early as the seventh century in the Swedish jewellery and arms among the grave goods at Sutton Hoo, but much of the Scandinavian influence on English lexis derives from contacts of a kind very different from these ancient aristocratic connections. In 787 three vessels were involved in a confused incident at Portland, in which the representative of the West Saxon king was murdered. According to the *Anglo-Saxon Chronicle*, these were the first ships of the Danes to visit England. Six years later Danish raiders sacked the monastery on Lindisfarne, and thus began a series of assaults on easy targets along the east coast which culminated in the major invasion led by Ivar the Boneless and Halfdan in 866. After a decade of plunder, the invaders began to settle in eastern England. The Danish presence was formally recognised in 886 when King Alfred of Wessex handed over to the

Danes control of all the land north of the Thames and to the east of Watling Street, the old Roman road running from London to Chester. North of the Tees, the Anglian kingdom of Northumbria maintained a precarious independence.

5.1.1.3   Although in terms of chronology, the events summarised here properly belong to volume I, the circumstances of settlement in the Danelaw are crucial to the understanding of lexical borrowing which became apparent only in the Middle English period. The Scandinavian newcomers were pagan and illiterate on arrival, leaving no contemporary account of their incursions, so that historical records of their settlement originate from outside their ranks and are partial, biased and scanty. The most reliable guide to the pattern of settlement may therefore be in place-name evidence, which is more fully treated in volume I. Within the Scandinavian-controlled region, settlement was somewhat uneven, but seems to have been heaviest in Lincolnshire, Nottinghamshire, Leicester and north and eastern Yorkshire (Fellows-Jensen 1975b). This is partly corroborated by dialectal evidence (Kolb 1965; Samuels 1985) which suggests that settlement was heaviest in a belt bounded to the north by a line running from the Solway to Teesmouth and to the south by a line running east from the mouth of the Ribble, and turning southward at the Humber to include Lindsey in north Lincolnshire. Place-name evidence (Fellows-Jensen 1972, 1978; Cameron 1975) also offers further insights of linguistic importance: firstly that the settlement concerned not only the aristocratic owners of large estates, but also the humbler occupants of the smaller thorps; and, secondly, that settlement seems to have been progressive. This corresponds to the suggestion that both place names and other Scandinavian loans preserve various sound changes characteristic of later periods than the original settlement. The change from /hj/ to /ç/, which takes place in the belt of heavy Scandinavian linguistic influence mentioned above, and is also exemplified in the name *Shetland* and probably the pronoun *she* (see chapter 7), seems to preserve the effects of a twelfth-century Scandinavian sound change (Dieth 1955). Place names with the contracted forms -*kill* and -*kell* of the personal-name element -*ketill* belong to a later period than that of the initial settlement, and may indeed date from renewed settlement after the accession to the throne of England of the Danish king, Knut (1017–35) (Fellows-Jensen 1978). Thus, although the English repossession of the northern Danelaw which followed the death of Eric Bloodaxe on Stainmor in 954 may have checked Scandinavian immigration, it did not finally halt it, and it is probable that it continued in some form until the Norman Conquest. The contact of Danish and English, then, was not simply a matter of a once for all conquest, but a process of infiltration lasting for two centuries. In this period the constitution of the population in the Danelaw must have become infinitely complex, and the relationship between the settled and the newcomers very various according to whether lands had been unceremoniously seized by force or purchased, perhaps with the proceeds of plunder gained elsewhere (Sawyer 1971: 100). The new settlers might be lords by conquest or neighbours by purchase; in the latter case, at least, racial origins would quickly have become confused. Generalisation about the Scandinavian settlement is therefore a peculiarly risky business.

5.1.1.4   Even the origins of the Scandinavian settlers are not a simple matter. The place name *Normanton* seems to be of a type given by neighbouring English to settlement by Norwegians rather than by Danes. The occurrence of this name alongside hybrids of the *Grimston* type (see chapter 7) in Leicestershire and Nottinghamshire suggests that groups of Norwegians were among the first settlers in these areas. The major areas of Norwegian settlement, however, which are indicated by place names with the modern elements *-scale*, *-gill*, *-fell*, *-slack* and *-thwaite*, were to the west of the Pennines in Cumbria, Lancashire, parts of Cheshire and the northwestern corner of Yorkshire. The last of these has been associated with a Cumbric substratum in the population (Hamp 1982). Celtic influence is evident also in the tenth-century stone cross at Gosforth (Cumbria), which depicts scenes from Scandinavian mythology as well as Christian ones, but in common with other monuments from this area has decorative motifs associated with Ireland and the Isle of Man (Wilson 1976). This is paralleled by a Celtic element evident in Cumbrian names, suggesting that Norwegian settlements took place from Ireland in the early tenth century after the Irish conquest of the Norse kingdom of Dublin in 903. In addition, Norse immigration took place by way of the Isle of Man, and in eastern England a similar Hiberno-Norse influence is found in place names to the east of York, reflecting perhaps their domination of York from 918 until 954.

5.1.1.5   To what extent did Scandinavian populations maintain their cultural and linguistic identity in England? Settlement names like *Irton* and *Irby* suggest that the English and anglicised Danes viewed Norse settlers as much as Irishmen as Scandinavians: any notion of a sentimental Scandinavian cultural unity is unlikely to be correct, although there is some evidence of the continuity of Scandinavian traditions of naming even in the southern Danelaw (Clark 1983a). As for language, the later *Gunnlaugssaga* (ca 1180) claims that in the reign of Ethelred II (978–1016) the same language was spoken in England as in Norway and Denmark, but the nicety of the author's linguistic judgement is not beyond question, and he may merely be making the point that a Germanic language has been replaced among the aristocracy by a Romance one after the Norman Conquest. Yet, in the Isle of Man, Scandinavian was spoken in the twelfth century, and even later in the Hebrides and the Shetlands. Direct evidence about the language of the Danelaw is hard to come by, but a few runic inscriptions from the early twelfth century show language mixtures (Ekwall 1930; Page 1971). That on the church at Aldborough (Yorks) has a Scandinavian personal name and third-person pronoun in an Anglo-Saxon sentence: 'Ulf het aræran cyrice for hanum and Gunware saule.' Lacking adequate written records, all that can safely be stated is that, although reinforcements of Scandinavian settlers must have done much to keep the understanding of the language alive *locally*, and local survival may have furnished the points of origin for some more widely disseminated sound changes, yet, in the absence of a written form or any standardising influence, Danish was in a very vulnerable position by comparison with English. Where the two languages were in close contact, something akin to pidginisation may have taken place quite quickly (Poussa 1982; Görlach 1986). The sociolinguistic situation is exceedingly complex, but over a longer period both this transient pidgin and the Scandinavian language itself died out (Hansen 1984), giving way to English, and bequeathing to it a rich legacy of lexical loans as it did so.

5.1.1.6 Perhaps the most striking feature of the lexical legacy of Scandinavian is the extent to which its emergence into written English is delayed. The major period of population mixing is over before the Middle English period begins, yet although the evidence of close contact is apparent quite early in Middle English from influence on word formation, function words and syntax, relatively few Scandinavian lexical loans (perhaps 150; see volume I, ch. 8) appear in Old English texts; indeed surprisingly few make their appearance until at least a century and a half after the Norman Conquest. This effect is due in part to the paucity of early written sources, but even works from areas of heavy Scandinavian settlement, such as the *Ormulum*, may contain no more than a 120 loans in 20,000 lines of text. Outside areas of heavy settlement, loans may be fewer. The southeast midland *Vices and Virtues* has only six; the southwest midland *Ancrene Riwle* seventy-three (Zettersten 1965), many of which seem to have been early borrowings (Caluwé Dor 1979); and the southwest midland text, Laʒamon's *Brut* 'less than forty' (Serjeantson 1935). By contrast, the nineteenth-century *English Dialect Dictionary* contains over 1,150 words beginning with /sk/, more than half of which are of Scandinavian origin. The explanation of this may be that throughout the period during which English and Scandinavian were in contact, the latter was never a literary language. Contact between the two languages took place in the spoken mode, and largely with reference to questions of immediate interest only to the local community. Most Scandinavian terms were adopted into English at the level of everyday communication and were barred from written expression both by the existence of a standardised form of written English, the West Saxon *Schriftsprache*, which was the official administrative language of the Anglo-Saxon state, and by the perception of Scandinavian-derived forms as belonging to comparatively non-literary registers. Scandinavian words filtered slowly into the written language only after the Conquest, when training in the West Saxon standard was terminated and scribes began once more to write on a broader range of topics in the forms of their own local dialects. The only serious exception to this state of affairs is in the case of certain formulaic phrases which may seem to belong to non-colloquial strata. In legal language, the early existence of Scandinavian-derived phrases such as *friþþ and griþþ*, 'peace and protection', *þwert nai* 'strongly deny' and *niþing* 'outlaw' testify to the prestige and independence of the Danes in legal matters (Olszewska 1935). In fourteenth-century alliterative poetry, formulaic phrases from outside the legal sphere are encountered: *glaum and gle* 'merriment and revelry', *more and mynne* 'greater and lesser'. These can be paralleled in Scandinavian literary sources, and may seem to suggest a Scandinavian literary culture in England, but it has been argued that, like the legal phrases, they had become established in the colloquial language (Turville-Petre 1977: 87).

5.1.1.7   In view of the historical circumstances, it is impossible to describe precisely the sociolinguistic situation, or rather situations, existing in the Danelaw. Linguistic developments continued over some hundreds of years amongst a population of various origins, changing constitution and shifting relationships, whose linguistic habits lack a written record for nearly three hundred years. One or two general statements only are possible. In areas of heavy Scandinavian settlement experience of both English and Norse would have been common enough, but extensive bilingual competence was probably much rarer, because in a simple agrarian economy, for practical everyday communication, there was neither the need nor the opportunity for either side to master the full resources of the other's language. In a complex literate society, literacy brings with it a degree of normalisation and conceptions of correctness in language use, which in turn become associated with social prestige. In conditions where simple communication is the sole aim, there is no such compulsion to learn a second language 'properly', and no stigma is felt in using syntactical structures from one language and word forms from another. A continuous interchange of linguistic forms took place in which the conception of the mere adoption of single word-forms would be an oversimplified account of the processes involved. When words are adopted by one language from another, depending on the competence of the language user, there takes place a certain degree of substitution of the forms of the borrower's language into the patterns adopted. According to the extent of the patterns taken over, substitution may be merely phonetic adaptation, substitution of phonemes or of morphs (Haugen 1950). No doubt both populations noticed that their languages possessed many forms in common which were differentiated by regular phonological contrasts: thus ON /sk/ often corresponds to a form with /ʃ/ in Old English, and ON /-g/ corresponds to either OE /-dʒ/ with a geminate consonant or /-j/, and initial ON /g-/ to /j-/. Once such correspondences were noted, it was a simple matter to make conscious modifications to aid comprehension. Such a process may explain the pronunciation of the modern verb *scatter*, first recorded in the *Peterborough Chronicle* (1154), where, in the absence of any Old Norse cognate, it is conjectured to derive from an unrecorded OE **sceatterian* – which would also account for modern *shatter* – with the substitution of Scandinavian pronunciation in the initial consonant cluster. For examples of similar processes in place-name formation, see chapter 7.

5.1.1.8   Especially in the dialects of the north, but also in the standard language, English was the lexical beneficiary of its historical contact with Scandinavian. The modern northern dialect words *laik* 'to play' (Yorks, Cumbria, Durham), *gowk* 'fool' (northern Northumbria and southern Scotland), *lug* 'ear' (north of a line from Cheshire to Suffolk), *lop* 'flea' (Durham, Yorks and northern Lincs), *brig* 'bridge' (north of a line from Morecambe Bay to the Wash) and *whin* 'gorse' (north of a line from Morecambe Bay to the Humber, also northern Norfolk) can be traced to this origin (Upton, Sanderson & Widdowson 1987); and the Middle English period saw the adoption of scores of words which today form familiar items of the common core of English lexis: *anger*, *bug*, *cake*, *dirt*, *flat*, *fog*, *happy*, *husband*, *ill*, *knife*, *law*, *leg*, *low*, *neck*, *odd*, *raise*, *scant*, *seem*, *silver*, *skin*, *sky*, *smile*, *take*, *Thursday*, *want* and *window*. Such borrowings illustrate the familiar and everyday contact between English and Scandinavian, and the adoption of function words into English alongside lexical words is confirmation that the major sociolinguistic process involved was not simply the rather distant cultural influence of an elite group, but a much more intimate cultural and linguistic mixing. Some of this 'grammatical' borrowing has also survived into modern English: *til* (as a conjunction), *though*, *they*, *their*, *them*, *both*, *same*, *against*. Other examples were lost during the Middle English period: *oc* 'but, and', *heþen* 'hence', *þeþen* 'thence', *fra* 'from', *summ* 'as', *wheþen* 'whence', *umb-* 'about'. In some cases the adoption of Scandinavian word forms resulted in doublets, some of which have survived, usually with differentiated meanings (in each of the following pairs the Scandinavian form precedes the English): *give/yive*, *gate/yate*, *skirt/shirt*, *dike/ditch*, *scrub/shrub*; and many which did not survive the Middle English period: *egg/ey*, *carl/churl*, *ere/are*, *loan/lene*, *worre/werre*, *silver/selver*, *sister/soster* (Rynell 1948). Dialect usage would, of course, add to those doublets to be found in Modern English: *laup/leap*, *garth/yard*, *kirk/church*, *trigg/true*, *nay/no*. Very often, however, Scandinavian words either replace or restrict the senses of their Old English equivalents: thus the modern word *anger*, from Scandinavian *angr*, steadily replaced OE *torn* and *grama* (this latter not until the end of the Middle English period). Scandinavian-derived *die* was in competition with *sweltan* and *steorfan*, *sky* with *wolcen* and *heofon*, *bark* with *rind*, *wing* with *feþer*, and *blom* with *blostma*.

5.1.1.9 In the Middle English period, as in modern dialects, the intensity of the influence of Norse on the vocabulary is more marked in the areas of heaviest settlement. Northern texts generally have more borrowings than those of southern or western origin, but the number of borrowings is in fact less telling than their quality, for southern texts tend to contain a selection of words which are of very general distribution, for example: *ay, calle, carpe, cast, felawe, griþ, give, hap, ille, knif*. Texts originating in local communities of strong Scandinavian influence, as we may presume the *Ormulum* to have done, may contain words which are rarely or never preserved elsewhere in writing (Ross 1970): *ammbohht* 'maidservant' (OE *ambiht* and ON *ambótt*, from a Celtic original), *naþe* 'grace' (ON *náþ*), *úsell* 'wretched' (ON *úsæll*). One of these, *benkedd* 'provided with benches', seems to be cognate with OSw. *bænker*, and together with *mensk* and *byrþ* may be traces of a minority Swedish element among the immigrants. It is rarely easy to distinguish the origins of Scandinavian borrowings since literary sources greatly postdate the most active periods of Scandinavian influence on English (Hoad 1984). Nevertheless, Strang cites the following as forms of distinctly Norwegian provenance: *bole* 'bull', *bon* 'boon', *bu* 'stock of cattle', *bu* 'inhabitant', *bun* 'bound for', *busken* 'to prepare', *lire* 'face', *weng* 'wing', *þreue* 'bundle'; and Danish derived forms are: *boþe, bulle* 'bull' and *wing* (Strang 1970). The Danish forms are generally those widespread in the dialect of the east midlands from which standard English derives, and so are more immediately recognisable as the modern forms. Norwegian forms are more common in the dialects of the north and west.

5.1.1.10 In conditions of oral contact between the two languages, English ignorance of the grammar of Scandinavian inflections led to the adoption of some words in which inflectional endings were mistaken for part of the stem. ME *busken* 'to prepare' and the surviving English *bask* both include the Scandinavian reflexive suffix *-sk*. The infinitive marker *at* has been incorporated into *ado* (from *atdo*). The genitive *-ar* is preserved in Chaucer's *nightertale* 'at night time' (modelled on ON *náttar þeli*) and the adjectival neuter inflection *-t* is found in *scant, want* and *athwart*. The word *hagherlych* 'skilfully', found in the northwest midlands poem *Cleanness* as well as the *Ormulum*, preserves the *-r* inflection of the Norse masculine noun.

5.1.1.11 Further effects of incomplete bilingualism were felt in terms of semantic shift and in word formation, and will be discussed below; and it is probably to the influence of Scandinavian that we owe two important characteristics of Modern English phrase structure: the common recourse to particled verbs (Denison 1985c), and the extensive use of the verbal operator *get*. The earliest record of the extensive use of verb + preposition/adverb colligations as phrasal verbs on the model of

Old Norse is in the *Peterborough Chronicle*: *gyfen up* (probably with Scandinavian initial /g/), *faren mid*, *leten up* and *tacen to*. The *Ormulum* contains numerous examples: *farenn forþ*, *commonn upp till*, *commenn off*, *kiddenn forþ* and *ȝedenn forþ*. The verb *get* (ON *geta*), whose Old English cognate *-gietan* occurs only in compounds, is most frequent, in a wide range of senses, in northern texts. It often occurs as a particled verb, and indeed the earliest occurrences of the common modern phrasal verbs *get up*, *get away*, *get out* are in the northern *Cursor Mundi* (ca 1300). (See further sections 5.2.9; 5.2.18.)

5.1.2 The influence of French

5.1.2.1 French influence upon the grammar and phonology of English was of relatively little importance, but the impact of that language upon the lexis was prolonged, varied and ultimately enormous. It commenced before the Conquest as the result of the political and religious contacts between Anglo-Saxon rulers and Normandy, where Ethelred II was forced to take refuge from the Danes, and it continued in one form or another, Norman, central French or Picard, throughout the medieval period. It was both that source of foreign influence of which people were most acutely conscious and, in quantitative terms, the most substantial source of new words in written Middle English. If we reflect that the army with which William of Normandy vanquished the Anglo-Saxons probably numbered no more than 7,000 men, and that estimates of the total French-born population of England vary between 2 and 10 per cent (Berndt 1965), it is immediately apparent that the process by which English underwent such immense influence from French cannot have been comparable with that which led to the majority of Scandinavian additions to the vocabulary. Clearly the influx of such a small proportion of French speakers, unevenly distributed around the country, cannot have had the effect it did simply by what Trevisa calls the 'commyxstion and mellyng' of the populations at large. In this connection it is worth quoting at length a less familiar translation of part of Ranulph Higden's *Polychronicon* on a supposed decree of William the Conqueror banning the use of English. It is that by Osbern Bokenham in his *Mappula Angliae*:

> children in gramer-scolis ageyns the consuetude and þe custom of alle
> oþer nacyons, here owne modre-tonge lafte and forsakyne, [lernyd
> here Donet on frenssh] and to construyn yn ffrenssh [and to maken

here latyns on þe same wyse]. The secounde cause was þat by þe same
decre lordis sonys and alle nobylle and worthy mennys children were
fyrste set to lyrnyn and speken ffrenssh, [or þan þey cowde spekyne
ynglyssh, and þat alle wrytyngis and endentyngis and alle-maner plees
and contrauercyes in courtis of the lawe, and alle-maner Reknyngis
and countis yn hows-oolde schulle be doon yn the same]. And þis
seeynge, þe rurales, þat þey myghte semyn þe more worschipfulle and
honorable and þe redyliere comyn to þe famyliarite of þe worthy and
þe grete, leftyn hure modre-tounge and labouryd to kunne spekyne
ffrensshe; [and thus by processe of tyme barbariȝid thei in bothyn and
spokyne neythyr good ffrenssh nor good Englyssh].

(Horstmann 1887: 30)

In this passage Higden, with supplements in brackets by Bokenham,
proposes in addition to the inscrutable results of a general mixing of
population, a much more precise explanation dependent upon social
prestige. The French language occupies a position of social esteem and
holds the key to advancement: it is therefore consciously and
deliberately learned by those who wish to rise in the world. Although
his reference to a decree of William I suppressing English as an official
language is based upon a fourteenth-century forgery (Woodbine 1943;
Richter 1979: 36–8), much of what Bokenham asserts in the passage
quoted is verifiable. It is worth examining each of his claims in detail:
that is, the general mixing of populations at the everyday level originally
advanced as a cause, the use of French as a learned language in law,
education and administration, and as a class dialect by the aristocracy,
and, finally, the resulting perception of it as the language of privilege.

5.1.2.2 Although following the Conquest, some speakers possessed
skills in French and Latin as well as English, our knowledge of the
linguistic situation in England for the first two generations after the
Conquest is by necessity fragmentary and anecdotal. Sources are few
and far between. It is likely that in mercantile centres and in the 'new
towns' established by the conquerors, such as those at Rhuddlan,
Hereford and Newark, some degree of functional French–English
bilingualism existed at an everyday level. French-derived nicknames are
found qualifying insular personal names in early twelfth-century Battle
(Beresford 1967; Clark 1980a). Nevertheless, the more general social
structure of the Norman settlement meant that equal competence in
both languages was rare, and even functional bilingualism was required
only at points of contact between the ruling elite and the population in

general, and it need not therefore have been very widespread. One such point of contact must have been that between the owners of land and the labourers who worked it. In twelfth-century Anglo-Norman romances a relatively familiar figure is the *latimier* or interpreter, whose title gives us the common English surname Latimer. Such a figure would be familiar on any Norman-held estate. Some must have been of Norman birth, for there is ample evidence that Normans made early attempts to learn English. According to Ordericus Vitalis, even William himself had tried but failed. But, as the century progressed English rapidly became the first language of many Anglo-Norman families, as an anecdote about Heloise de Moreville demonstrates. Her amorous advances had been rejected by a page, Lithulf, so that she sought vengeance by taking advantage of an entertainment in which Lithulf was to appear in the castle hall before her husband with sword drawn. At the crucial moment she turned the game to earnest by calling a warning: 'Huge de Moreville, ware, ware, ware, Lithulf heth his swerd adrage!' ('Hugh of Moreville, look out, look out, Lithulf has drawn his sword'). The unfortunate youth was quickly seized and put to death. The conventional nature of this story, with its parallels in romance, relieves us of the need to feel pity, indeed we may even doubt its truth. Its significance is in the fact that it did not seem incredible to a clerk writing about 1175 that, thirty years before, a dire warning might be shouted in English in a baronial household. A similar lesson is to be learned from the report of a spirit called Malekin haunting the house of Osbern de Bradewelle during the reign of Richard I and addressing the household in the Suffolk dialect, but using Latin to the chaplain (Richter 1979: 76). Baronial circles used English for domestic purposes in the twelfth century, but serious conversation with a clerk required Latin. However, it is significant that in the more elevated company of the royal court, which was more insulated from everyday contact with English, sudden anger could still be expressed by an exclamation in French as late as 1295 (Legge 1980).

5.1.2.3 A second major point of everyday contact between the rulers and the ruled was through the ministry of the Church, where, although both Latin and French were used among themselves, it was the duty of francophone clergy to preach comprehensibly to an English-speaking congregation. There are records of efforts made by senior clergy to reach their audience by preaching in English. Samson, abbot of Bury St Edmunds (1182–1211), and Odo, abbot of Battle (1175–1200), preached in English and so, probably, did Ranulf Flambard, bishop of Durham (1099–1101) (Wilson 1943). As for native-born Englishmen, their grasp of French often appears to reflect their position, education or aspirations in the world. A recluse like St Godric of Finchale, near Durham, expected Norman visitors to his cell to bring an interpreter; although his biographer, who himself possessed skills in Latin and French as well as his native English, tells how the uneducated Godric could understand conversations in these languages through divine intervention (Richter 1979: 82–7). The monk Ordericus Vitalis, whose father was a Norman and whose mother was English, learned French only after his arrival in Normandy at the monastery of St Évroult. On the other hand, for those who wished to pursue a career in ecclesiastical government French and Latin were essential. The *Life of St Wulfric* (1180–6) reports an incident in Somerset some fifty years before in which a dumb man miraculously gained the ability to speak both French and English: one of a number of similar miracles in contemporary texts (Richter 1979: 69–70). An attendant priest resents this miracle, complaining to Wulfric that he has been overlooked, for 'when I come before the bishop and archdeacon I am compelled to be silent like a dumb man: you have not given me the use of French'. This complaint of a man who feels himself disadvantaged by his lack of French would, in one sphere or another, have been equally as appropriate for the next three centuries. In brief, to the extent that it was necessary to communicate with the vast majority of the English people, French speakers must learn to speak English at an early stage or employ an interpreter; but to gain entry into that world of affairs controlled by the ruling elite, Englishmen must learn to speak, and even more emphatically, to read and write French, since this was to become the language of all official business.

5.1.2.4   The influence of French upon English is more complex than that of the Scandinavian languages, since in addition to the early oral contact between the two languages, there is a prolonged history in which French influenced English as a technical written language. Moreover, French influence came from two separate dialects of French: firstly from Norman, both as spoken and written language, and later, as an artificially acquired literary language, from the French of the Ile de France. At this later stage, there developed a distinction in prestige between the contemporary Anglo-French of England and the French of the Continent. Central French superseded both English and Anglo-French as the language of social prestige. The major watershed in this development of French in England, from a mother tongue to a social accomplishment, is that date at which the majority of the sons and daughters of the gentry could no longer expect to acquire French either in their parents' household or in those households where they were sent as children to learn *curteisie*; in other words, the point at which French ceased to be a language acquired in conversation with those around them and must be painstakingly learned with the help of books and tutors. It is impossible to give a precise date for this change, since it varied according to the social circles involved, and perhaps also geographically. Consequently, it has been the subject of some controversy. Taking the extreme limits, awareness of possible deviance from the language of Normandy is expressed by the Nun of Barking as early as 1160, and becomes widespread in the last quarter of the twelfth century; but such divergence does not necessarily imply a dead language. Indeed, it has been argued in contrast that French remained an independent vernacular in England until as late as the first third of the fourteenth century (Legge 1980; Rothwell 1985). All that can be stated with certainty is that the decline of French as a vernacular was a gradual process, commencing in some quarters within two or three generations of the Conquest, being hastened by the loss of Normandy in 1204, and its progress being marked by the appearance of grammar books and word lists, as well as by the hiring of French tutors by gentlemen in the mid-thirteenth century. By the end of that century very few families remained who could claim to have maintained their tradition of French speaking from earliest days, and indeed during the latter half of the thirteenth century, the domination of the French of Paris over all other regional forms of French established a newly prestigious variety which had to be consciously learned by any born outside the *francien* area. This co-existed with that Anglo-French which had developed as a technical language in administrative and legal circles. Thus, from a written language corresponding to a substantial spoken base, Anglo-Norman had become an accomplishment based upon a written language, preserving a pronunciation which, conditioned by contact with English (Pope 1952: 431), and contrasted with the newly prestigious French of Paris, was, in the next century, to become the butt of jokes about the French of Stratford atte Bowe.

5.1.2.5 The use of French as a technical language greatly outlived its use in the conversation of gentlemen. In education, although it appears that it had not been used as the language of instruction immediately after the Conquest, French was used throughout the thirteenth century. Indeed, when English was first restored as a language for the schools by the grammar teacher John of Cornwall in 1349, there are signs that it gained ground against considerable opposition. As late as 1380 the University of Oxford advised such grammar masters to construe Latin words in French as well as in English 'lest the French language be altogether lost', and in 1347 the Countess of Pembroke, as though to fend off such deterioration, had founded a college in Cambridge at which preference was to be given to teachers born in France (Tout 1922: 122).

5.1.2.6 In the administrative sphere, French had been used as an alternative to Latin since the early thirteenth century. The choice between the two languages seems to have depended upon the gravity of the occasion and upon the secular or ecclesiastical nature of the context. The Church preferred Latin for any formal contact or discussion. In the secular sphere too, although some writs continued to be written in English, royal letters are predominantly in Latin from the time of the Conquest; but from 1258, although letters on foreign diplomatic business, and those to important prelates continued to be written in Latin, French began to replace Latin as the language of royal letters patent (Suggett 1945). In the law courts, it was not until 1362 that Parliament formally acknowledged the right of English in place of Latin or French, and, although Parliament was opened in English as a nationalistic gesture at intervals throughout the fourteenth century, records of parliamentary debates were not written in English until 1386. Approximate parity between the numbers of French and English entries is not reached until 1430. As Bokenham noted, household accounts and inventories continued to be written in French well into the fifteenth century, and scribes destined for the commercial world had to be taught in the course of their training to 'escrire, enditer, acompter et fraunceys parler' (Berndt 1972). Handbooks for the Oxford schools concerned with commercial training continued to be produced in French until the middle of the fifteenth century (Richardson 1942). Thus, although French exerted a powerful influence on English life and cultural institutions for many generations, the fact that it had become a language to be learned whereas, from the later thirteenth century onwards, the English language had been associated with English nationhood, guaranteed the eventual triumph of the latter. This was not before English had been, as Bokenham puts it, *barbarizid* by French. By this he means nothing other than that English had adopted large numbers of French words.

5.1.2.7 The very earliest loan words from French appear in pre-Conquest documents, and reflect aristocratic values and tastes. Among them are *prūd* 'valiant'; *castel* 'castle' (see below, 5.5.4); *gingifer* 'ginger'; *capun* 'capon'. The word *tumbere* 'acrobat' is formed on a French stem *tumb-er* 'to fall', and *prȳd* 'pride' is probably derived from *prūd* by a derivational process modelled on that which produced the pair *foul* and *filth* from a native root, *fūl*. The earliest borrowing from the language of the conquerors, representing a period before French had become established as a culturally dominant written language, may be studied in the continuations of the *Peterborough Chronicle*, which were written irregularly between 1121 and 1154. French influence is not particularly heavy here, and in some cases it is possible that words borrowed from Latin were rendered with the spelling conventions proper to French. Such are: *natiuite, canceler* 'chancellor', *concilie* 'council', *carited* 'charity', *priuilegies, processiun* (alongside Latin *processionem*), *prior* (Clark 1952–3). A few are words of unique reference, such as the names of individuals (*Henri*) or of countries (*Normandie, France*), the battle of the *Standard*, or the *tur* of London; or of a technical nature, such as the term *tenserie*, which demands explanation in context as a toll exacted for military protection. A few, like *werre* 'war', *pais* 'peace', *iustise* 'justice', *acorden* 'come to agreement', are of a secular and political nature, and *castel* refers now to the new military fortifications rather than the villages which were its reference in Old English. The word *sotscipe* 'foolishness' is formed on the Old English borrowing *sot*. Another group clusters around ecclesiastical matters: *pasches* 'Easter', *miracle, canonie* 'canon', *messe* 'mass' (OE *mæsse* gives the form *masse*), *capitele* 'chapter', *clerc* 'scholar'. A final grouping is around the titles and concerns of the feudal aristocracy: *duc, cuntesse, emperice, rente* 'income', *curt* 'court', *tresor, prisun* 'arrest'.

5.1.2.8 Some of this rather limited list of words is clearly the result of cultural borrowing, in that the words refer to ideas or institutions not present or not viewed in that particular light in Old English: *tenserie* and *castel* are good examples. Yet most of these words were borrowed not to fill gaps in the structure of the English lexis, but because they seemed appropriate to the discourse. The technical term *dubbade* is adopted into English within a phrase into which English elements have been substituted: *dubbade to ridere* 'dubbed a knight' (AN *aduber a chevalier*). The phrase as a whole imitates the pattern of the French, but the fact that French forms are not taken over completely indicates not that there is a lexical gap in this area, but a deliberate stylistic choice. There is indeed ample evidence that Romance borrowing is by no means always motivated by lexical gaps revealed by cultural innovations (Gay 1899; Fischer 1979). Very many French words were adopted as part of phrases appropriate to the subject matter, into which native forms were substituted, leaving one or more French words untranslated either as a communicative convenience or a stylistic grace (Prins 1952). Such patterns are especially obvious in titles like the 1129 annal's use of the phrases *se duc of Sicilie* and *se kyng of France*. In both cases the word order represents French phrases into which English morphs have been substituted. Alongside the French type *þe king Stephne*, the native type *Henri king* occurs in the annal for 1137. In this annal, too, occur other phrases probably modelled on French, with partial (*iustise ne dide*; *makede pais*) or complete substitution (*manred makede* from French *faire hommage*). The discussion of examples in which English words are understood with French sense is deferred until section 5.5.6.

5.1.2.9   The earliest borrowing, which was from Norman, is dialectally distinct from later borrowing from central French, and the distinction is sometimes recognisable from spelling. The dialect of Normandy preserved – in some words until the twentieth century (von Wartburg 1969: 21) – the pronunciation /k/ initially before /a/, where central French had /tʃ/. Thus the Norman form of the verb *cachier* contrasted with the CF *chacer*. Similar doublets arise from other phonological alternations. In the following examples the first recorded occurrences (Mackenzie 1939) in English are given in parentheses:

Norman and Anglo-Norman	Central French
c	*ch*
canchelers (1066)	*chanceleres* (1300)
calange (1225)	*challenge* (1300)
w	*g/gu*
wile (1154)	*guile* (1225)
warrant (1225)	*guarantee* (1624)
warden (1225)	*guardian* (1466)
reward (1315)	*regard* (1430)
e/ei	*oi*
conveie (1375)	*convoye* (1425)

Norman and Anglo-Norman	Central French
lealte (1300)	*loialte* (1400)
-u-	*-o-*
prisun (1121)	*prison* (1225)
dulur (1300)	*dolour* (1330)
j [dʒ]	[ʒ]
gaol (1163)	*jail* (1209)
-issh	*-iss*
finisshed (1375)	*finissed* (1421)
-ti/ci- [ʃ]	*-ti/ci-* [s]
chi- [tʃ]	*ch-* [ʃ]

Norman spellings with *u + consonant* tend to be superseded after the mid-thirteenth century by Anglo-Norman spellings with *ou + consonant*. Although the situation is confused by the use of traditional spellings, the influence of translation, and the vagaries of survival, it is apparent from the material above that the emergence of central French spellings in general postdates the earlier Norman borrowings.

5.1.2.10 Although there are considerable problems of finding satisfactory comparisons among texts of like with like, it is apparent that the density of French loans increases with the passage of time, the rate of new adoptions into English reaching a peak in the second half of the fourteenth century as the uses of French were eroded by English (Jespersen 1962; Finkenstaedt, Leisi & Wolff 1970). But density of French loans in a text is also connected with the subject matter of the work – courtly literature tends to contain a higher incidence than popular poetry – and, at least in earlier texts, those from the southern counties may contain more French loans than texts from further north. Also, whether the text is an original work or a translation will affect the concentration of loan words throughout the period. The thirteenth-century Kentish sermons in MS Laud Misc. 471 (Bennett & Smithers 1966) are translated from French originals, and contain a far higher proportion of loan words than the original prose of the *Peterborough Chronicle* annals. More than 70 per cent of Romance borrowing into English is of nouns (Dekeyser 1986). Many of them are from the common core of French vocabulary: *age, bunte, nature, trauail, peril, auenture, custome, sergant, commencement*; others are associated with religious instruction: *religiun, prechur, deciples, miracle*; or the language of learning: *signefiaunce, contrarie*. A well-defined group are the names of vices and virtues, part of the pastoral language of the Church: *merci, anvie, lecherie, roberie, folie, large, umble, uertu.* Although these homilies cannot be dated with great precision, it is apparent that much of the borrowing which they contain is of a literary and abstract kind, carried over from their French source. In the fourteenth and fifteenth centuries still more borrowings were made through literary channels, and it is from this period that numerous abstract terms are borrowed with suffixes in *-ance, -ence, -ant, -ent, -tion, -ity, -ment*, and prefixes in *con-, de-, dis-, en-, ex-, pre-, pro-* and *trans-*.

5.1.2.11 It is worth noting that despite the great numbers of lexical items borrowed from French, the most frequently used words continued to be those of English and sometimes Scandinavian origin. In Early Middle English the lexicon still consisted of 91·5 per cent words of English origin; in later Middle English this figure had fallen to 78·8 per cent. But counted in terms of the number of occurrences of English-derived words in continuous text, the figures are 94·4 per cent for the earlier period, and falls only to 87·5 per cent for the later (Dekeyser 1986), reflecting both the more exotic nature of French borrowings, and the fact that the function words of the language remain English.

5.1.3 Latin and other foreign influences

5.1.3.1 The third major foreign influence upon English lexis throughout its history is Latin. As the language not only of the internal organisation and liturgy of the medieval Church, but also of scholarship until modern times, it has been continuous in its effect, although fluctuating in its intensity. Unlike either Scandinavian or Norman French, influence through contact between the spoken languages has been minimal. Since competence in Latin has always been the property of a literate minority, major contact between Latin and English was always in the learned sphere and mostly through the written language. There are, however, a few Early Middle English borrowings, such as *benedicitee, collatio, pater noster* and *dirige*, which may have been made from spoken language. Chaucer's use of *quoniam* 'female genitals' perhaps represents clerkish slang, and the earliest trace of the word *tup* 'ram', although probably of Scandinavian origin, is to be found in a Latin text as *tuppis* (Rothwell 1980–1).

5.1.3.2 The study and practice of the law and of administration, where the use of Latin alternated with French, have bequeathed many Latin words to Middle English which survive in modern use: *client* (1320), *arbitrator* (1424), *conviction* (1437), *executor* (1290), *executrix* (1395), *gratis* (1440), *implement* (1445), *legitimate* (1464), *memorandum* (1435), *proviso* (1434), *alias* (1465), *prima facie* (1500). Education and learning contributed many more: *abacus* (1387) and *allegory* (1384; both ultimately from Greek), *et cetera* (1150), *cause* (1225), *contradiction* (1382), *desk* (1363), *explicit* (1325), *formal* (1393), *incipit* (1400), *index* ('forefinger', 1398), *item* (1398), *major* (1390), *minor* (1410), *neuter* (1398), *scribe* (1200), *simile* (1400). Religion was a third major source of adoptions from Latin: *memento* (1400), *requiem* (1389), *limbo* (1400), *magnificat* (1225), *lector* (1387), *collect* (1225), *diocese* (1387), *mediator* (1384), *redemptor* (1438), *psalm* (1200; a learned form, restoring the Greek spelling lost in Old English). Many more entered the language from every sphere of medieval learning, from medicine, astronomy, alchemy, botany, zoology and from lapidaries.

5.1.3.3   Among the examples cited above, spellings show that many are adoptions direct from Latin: *memorandum*, *et cetera*, *index*. In others, however, this is less clear since spellings have been altered on reception into English: *allegory* (ME *allegorie*, Lat. *allegoria*), *desk* (ME *deske*, Med. Lat. *desca*). These alterations are the minor substitutions which are made at the level of pronunciation and orthography in order to make the borrowed items conform to the systems of the recipient language and are indications that an adopted word has been formally assimilated. But here a further difficulty arises, since the modifications made may conform to those necessary had the recipient language been not English but French. This circumstance is not especially surprising when for generations Latin had been taught in England through the medium of French. When the derivational affix is of a French type, it poses a particularly tricky problem for lexicographers, who may be uncertain whether a Latinate word was borrowed from French or whether its form represents the adoption into English of a Latin word using the French-based derivational processes which operated in England in literate circles. Indeed, it has been persuasively argued that many of the more abstract literary borrowings found in the fourteenth and fifteenth centuries, and conventionally ascribed to adoption from French sources, are in reality products of this latter type of word formation (Ellenberger 1974).

5.1.3.4   A clear distinction between these two sources may, however, be possible when dealing with the base morpheme (see 5.2.1) in those cases where it has undergone phonological change in French which would differentiate it from its Latin form. In each of the following pairs, the Latin derived form given first is clearly distinct from the phonologically altered French derived form which follows: *adulterie ~ avowtrie*, *Aprill ~ Avrill*, *perfect ~ parfit*, *providence ~ purveiaunce*, *debt ~ dette*, *confirmen ~ confermen*, *equal ~ egal*, *adventure ~ aventure*, *adorne ~ aorne*. Of these Latin forms, *providence* (1382), *debt* (1415, where the variation is found only in spelling and not in pronunciation) and *equal* (ca 1400) are first found in technical contexts and may represent independent adoptions from Latin. *Adventure* and *adorne*, which are first recorded in general contexts in Malory (1470), and Chaucer and Lydgate (ca 1400) respectively, represent a different process. They are not fresh adoptions from Latin, but the re-Latinisation of familiar French-derived English words. In the case of *adventure* the word is erroneously modelled on an imagined, but actually non-existent Latin original. *Perfect* is a sixteenth-century re-Latinisation of its Middle English doublet. Although *confirme* is recorded once in this Latin form in the thirteenth century, further examples of the Latin spelling are very rare until the last quarter of the fifteenth century, and the Latinisation of French derived *ferme* to *fyrme* does not occur according to the record of the *OED* until 1538. The Latinisation of pre-existing words, increased borrowing from Latin as French borrowing began to decline after 1375 (Dekeyser 1986), and the use afresh of less familiar Latin words mark a significant development in the influence of Latin upon literary composition. This increase in the Latinate lexical content of literary composition is first detectable in the works of Chaucer, Gower and Usk, but rapidly gains ground in the fifteenth century. Lydgate (ca 1370–1450) seems to have coined the word 'aureate' to describe his ideal of a diction which repudiated everyday language in favour of words which were unfamiliar and elevated in their associations, euphonious and often, but not necessarily, multisyllabic, and for these reasons usually of Romance, or more specifically, Latin origin. This conception of elevated diction was based upon the teaching of Latin rhetorics, and could appeal to an audience created both by the proliferation of grammar schools in the later fifteenth century, and by the tendency of young men intent upon secular careers to attend the universities of Oxford, Cambridge, St Andrews or Glasgow. Indeed, it has been remarked that as a percentage of the total population, the proportion of young men attending university in the

later fifteenth century was greater than that in Britain today. The esteem
accorded to Latinate diction resulted in works such as this stanza by
Lydgate from his *Commendation of Our Lady*:

> Of alle Cristen protectrix and tutele,
> Retour of exilid, put in proscrypcyoun,
> To hem þat erryn, þe path of her sequele,
> To wery wandrid, the tente, pavilioun,
> The feynte to fresshe, and pawsacioun,
> Vnto deiecte rest and remedye,
> Feyþlıfull unto all þat in þe affye.
>
> (Norton-Smith 1966: 26)

Diction such as this represents a literary taste which in the next
century was to lead to further Latin borrowing with the conscious
intent of 'improving' the expressivity of the language, and to the
'inkhorn controversy'.

5.1.3.5   The effects of the major sources of foreign borrowing upon the
language of the later Middle English period may be judged from a
comparison of three passages containing similar subject matter. Passage
(a), from *Pearl*, was written in the late fourteenth century in the
northwest midlands somewhere close to the junction of southeast
Lancashire, northeast Cheshire and northwest Staffordshire. Passage
(b), from Chaucer's *Prioress's Tale*, was written in London. Passage (c)
is the work of William Dunbar, who took his master's degree at the
University of St Andrews in 1479. Foreign borrowings are italicised in
all three passages.

(a)   '*Cortayse* Quen', þenne sayde þat *gaye*,
>   Knel*ande* to grounde, folde vp hyr *face*,
>   'Makeleʒ Moder and myryest *May*,
>   Blessed bygynner of vch a *grace*!'
>   Þenne ros ho vp and con *restay*,
>   And speke me towarde in þat *space*:
>   'Sir, fele here *porchaseʒ* and fongeʒ *pray*,
>   Bot *supplantoreʒ* none wythinne þys *place*.
>   Þat *emperise* al heuenʒ hatʒ,
>   And vrþe and helle, in her *bayly*;
>   Of *erytage* ʒet non wyl ho *chace*,
>   For ho is Quen of *cortaysye*.

'The *court* of þe kyndom of God alyue
Hatȝ a *property* in hytself beyng:
Alle þat may þerinne *aryue*
Of alle þe *reme* is quen oþer kyng,
And neuer oþer ȝet schal *depryue*,
Bot vchon fayn of oþereȝ hafyng,
And wolde her *corouneȝ* wern worþe þo fyue,
If *possyble* were her *mendyng*.
Bot my Lady of quom Jesu con spryng,
Ho haldeȝ þe *empyre* ouer vus ful hyȝe;
And þat *dyspleseȝ* non of oure *gyng*,
For ho is Quene of *cortaysye*.

(Gordon 1953: 16–17)

(b) 'O moder-mayde, o mayde-moder free,
O bussh vn*brent brennyng* in Moyses sighte,
That *rauysedest* doun *fro* the *deitee*
Thurgh thyn *humblesse* the goost that in th'alighte,
Of whos *vertu* whan he thyn herte lighte
Conceyued was the fadres *sapience*,
Help me to telle it in thy *reuerence*.
'Lady, thy *bountee*, thy *magnificence*,
Thy *vertu*, and thy grete *humylitee*,
Ther may no tonge *expresse* in no *science*.
For somtyme, lady, er men *praye* to thee
Thow goost biforn of thy *benygnytee*
And *get*est vs the lyght of thy *prayere*
To *gyden* vs vnto thy sone so deere.

'My konnyng is so *wayk*, o blisful queene,
For to *declare* thy grete worthynesse
That I ne may the weighte nat *sustene*,
But as a child of twelue-month old or lesse
That kan vnnethe any word *expresse*
Right so fare I. And therfore I yow *preye*
Gideth my song that I shal of yow seye.'

(*CT* II.1657–77 [10: 467–87])

(c) *Empryce* of *prys*, *imperatrice*,
Bricht *polist precious* stane;
Victrice of *vyce*, hie *genitrice*
Of Jhesu lord *soverayne*;
Our wys *pavys fro enemys*
Agane the Feyndis *trayne*;

Oratrice, mediatrice, salvatrice,
To God gret *suffragane*;
Ave Maria, gracia plena:
Haile, sterne, meridiane;
Spyce, flour delice of *paradys*
That baire the *gloryus grayne*.

Imperiall wall, *place palestrall*
Of *peirles pulcritud*;
Tryumphale hall, hie *trone regall*
Of Godis *celsitud*;
Hospitall riall, the lord of all
Thy *closet* did *include*;
Bricht *ball cristall, ros virginall*
Fulfillit of *angell* fude.
Ave Maria, gracia plena:
Thy *birth* has with his blude
Fra fall *mortall originall*
Us *raunsound* on the rude.

(Kinsley 1979: 6–7)

All three passages exhibit Scandinavian borrowings of a widely used kind: in passage (a) there are the words *may* 'maiden' and perhaps *gyng* 'company'; in passage (b) *get* and *wayk* 'weak' (from ON *veikr* rather than OE *wac*) and perhaps also the verb *brennen* 'burn'. Passage (c) has *haile*, *sterne* (the OE-derived form is *sterre*), *ball* and *birth*. Passages (b) and (c) both exhibit the Scandinavian-derived *fra/fro* rather than OE *from*. Passage (a) also includes some Norse influence of a more dialectally restricted sort, in the form of the northerly inflectional morph *-ande* in *knelande*. All the passages, despite the disparity between their dialectal origins, are full of words which have been transmitted through French from Latin: *sapience, reverence, magnificience, science, deitee, benyngnytee, humylitee, suffragane, possyble, victrice*; or which originated in French, but are associated with technical and elevated diction suitable for poetry in praise of the Virgin: *empryce, riall, spyce, cristall, prys, property, erytage, grace, rauysen, soverayne, flour delice*. The final passage has a highly wrought aureate diction, employing words which are conspicuously of Latin origin: *imperatrice, oratrice, mediatrice, salvatrice, regall, virginall, mortall, originall, pulcritud, celsitud*. The word *palestrall* may not be derived from Latin, but is probably a consciously elevated piece of poetic diction borrowed, but misunderstood, from the works of Lydgate or Chaucer, who are almost its only users in Middle English.

437

The latter seems to have adopted it from the Italian of Boccaccio. From these texts, it is clear that, in the late fourteenth century, there is no dialectal distinction in the incidence of French loan words. Although Romance loans were more scanty in the north and east during earlier Middle English, the relevant distinction now is in their stylistic quality: between the learned, overtly literary and perhaps recently coined, on the one hand, and the ordinary, familiar and long used, on the other.

5.1.3.6 Apart from Scandinavian, French and Latin, the only other source of substantial foreign influence directly upon Middle English lexis was that from the Low Countries. Borrowings from Dutch and Flemish, partly through commercial and military contacts, partly by the settlement of Flemish weavers and farmers in England and west Wales, began quite early. Thirteenth-century loans include *poll* 'head' (MDu. *polle*), *drivel* 'servant' (MDu. *drevel*), *doten* 'to be foolish, to rave' (MLG *doten*, from which *dotard* is derived by the use of a French derivational suffix), *luff* (MDu. *loefen*), *snecchen* (MDu. *snacken*, influenced by ME *lacchen* and AN *cacchen*). To the fourteenth century belong *ling* 'fish' (MDu. *lenge*) and three words connected with drinking: *bouse* 'to drink deeply', *gyle* 'a batch of ale brewed at one time' and *kilderkin* 'a cask'. *Waynscot*, originally a kind of fine oak imported from Holland and used for panelling is first recorded in 1352. The word *kit* (MDu. *kitte*) occurs in the sense of 'a tub'. *Skipper* 'master of a ship' is recorded from 1390 and *lollard* (MDu. *lollaerd*) was first applied to members of a fraternity guild caring for the sick and arranging funerals for the poor about 1300. A cynical association with sanctimonious piety may have led to the sense development which attached the word to the idealistic followers of Wyclif. Fifteenth-century loans are overwhelmingly of a maritime and commercial nature (Serjeantson 1935; Blake 1969c).

5.1.3.7 A small number of words from a surprisingly large number of other languages were transmitted into Middle English mostly by way of Latin and French, and act as testimony to the extensive cultural and trade contacts of the medieval world. More directly, Welsh contributed *cader* 'cradle' and the suffix in *baban* 'child' (Zettersten 1965). *Gannok* 'fortress' may be the corruption of the Welsh place name *Degannwy* (McIntosh 1940). The word *ambages* 'deceptive speeches', first recorded in *Troilus and Criseyde*, was taken directly from Italian by Chaucer, but words such as *ducat* and *Lombard* seem to have entered the language through French. Spanish loans in Middle English are limited to *cork* and *cordewan* 'Cordovan leather', and Portuguese to *marmalade* 'quince jam' (1480), but both seem to have entered the language by way of French. The Slavonic languages contributed *sable* (1225, from Russian *sobol* by way of Medieval Latin and French) and Irish the fifteenth-century loans *kern* and *lough*. The more extended trade routes to the east made some contribution also: the word *cendal* (1225) 'silken or linen cloth' is said to derive ultimately from Sanskrit (Serjeantson 1935), *elephant* (1330) and *ebony* (1398) may be of Semitic origin, *Caan, Khan* (1400) from Turkish. The words *paradise* (1200), *azure* (1325), *scarlet* (1185), *chesse* (1312), *rook* (1330), *check* (1330), *mate* (1225), *taffeta* (1373) and *orange* (1296) may be traced back to Persian sources, although Arabic, Latin, Italian and French intervene. Arabic itself contributed a substantial number of words in the fourteenth century, largely through French: *saffron* (1225), *admiral* (1225), *barbican* (1300) and *mattress* (1300, through Italian and French). A significant proportion are to do with mathematics, medicine, chemistry and astronomy, at which Arabic scholars excelled: *algorisme* 'Arabic numerals' (ca 1225); *algebra* (ca 1300), originally referring to the art of setting fractures; *alkarad* 'ankle bone' (ca 1400); *alkali* (1330); *zenith, nadir, azymuth* (ca 1400). Most exotic of all, the name of the spice *galingale* is claimed to have been transmitted by way of Persian, Arabic and French from Chinese.

5.2 Word formation

5.2.1   Additions to the lexis of Middle English took place not simply by the adoption of words from foreign sources outside the language system, but also by formation of new words from resources already existing within the system. The two methods of word formation which are of greatest importance in Middle English are *compounding* and *derivation*. In order to explain these processes, a preliminary note on word structure is necessary. The Modern English noun *unbelievers* is made up of individually recognisable parts: *un + believ + er + s*. Each is reusable in the formation of other words (e.g. *unseen, believable, loser, dogs*), and the *s* is the marker of plurality. These separate parts are known as morphemes. In terms of their combinatory properties, morphemes are of two kinds: free or bound. Bound morphemes are those which may occur only in combination with some other form, like *un-, -er* and *-s* above. These bound morphemes can be further divided into affixes and inflections. The bound morpheme *-s* is an inflection, and belongs to the very limited two-term system of number in English nouns, where the morpheme of plurality, *s*, contrasts with an uninflected form in the singular. Inflections, then, are bound morphemes which realise very restricted grammatical systems and which occur in very specific syntactic environments; for example, when bound to a preceding noun. The form, or string of forms, to which the inflection is attached – *unbeliever* – is known as the *stem*, so that the word *stem* contrasts with the word *inflection*. The second kind of bound morpheme, affixes, which are represented in *unbelievers* by *un-* and *-er*, are distinguished as *prefixes* when they occur before the base morpheme, and as *suffixes* when they are attached after it. Affixes may be distinguished from inflections by the fact that a change of inflection merely results in a new form of the same word (lexeme), but derivation by affixes creates a different word (lexeme). In addition, affixes are members of large, open classes rather than of limited contrastive systems. For example, the addition of a third term to the number system of English nouns ($-s \sim -\theta$) would radically alter the nature of the contrast, perhaps restoring dual number to the surviving singular and plural, but the adoption of a new method of deriving adjectives from nouns would not upset a much less highly structured process. Moreover, the occurrence of inflections may be specified by the syntactical rules of concord in a way which does not apply to affixes. Finally, when making a distinction between an affix and the form with which it is combined, we speak of the distinction between affix and *base*. Thus, *un-* is a prefix, *-er* a suffix and *believ* the base morpheme. Word formation by the combination of free morphemes is known as *compounding*; that by the addition of affixes to a base is called *derivation*. It is worth noting that in English both bases and affixes may form sequences: the word *antidisestablishmentarianism* can boast two prefixes and three suffixes. Even in Modern English the definition of compounds may not be easy, and in earlier stages of the language, with restricted access to language use, it can be considerably more difficult. Spelling is a poor guide to the distinction between compounds and syntactical groups in Middle English, and stress patterns can only be inferred uncertainly from verse. The best guide, therefore, is the semantic change which often accompanies compounding, and the conformity of the supposed compound to the morphological patterns of existing types of compound. Many compounds are formed from pre-existing syntactical groups, and so it may be expected that at a certain point in their development fluctuation will occur between their interpretation as compounds or syntactical groups: the Modern English word/group *headmaster* is a contemporary example. The boundary between compounds and derivations may also be obscured: the suffix -*ly* is related to the Old English noun *lic*, meaning 'form, shape, body'. In earlier Germanic this had been a free morpheme frequently used to create noun compounds. Thus, even in Old English, passages may be found in which the status of -*lic* as derivational affix or compound element may be in doubt. In the discussion which follows compounds and derivations which survive into the modern period are quoted in modern spelling.

5.2.2   In the Old English period compounding was an important means of addition to the lexis, particularly in the diction of poetry. The Norman Conquest, however, transformed poetic production rapidly. Even in that poetry which is closest to the Old English tradition, the fertility of invention of compounds declines markedly. In pre-Conquest poetry the rate at which compounds occur varies from two in just over eleven lines to two in just over three lines. The productivity of such poetic compounding is indicated by the fact that in *Beowulf* only about 22 per cent of its 1,069 compounds are repeated within the poem. By comparison Laȝamon's *Brut*, an alliterative work of about the year 1200, ten times as long as *Beowulf*, uses hardly over 800 compounds (Carr 1939). Yet Laȝamon is outstanding among Middle English poets for his use of compounding. Compounding had declined from a mainstay of poetic diction to an occasional device of poetic ornament.

5.2.3   In prose too, Old English had used both compounding and derivation freely. In particular, they are used under the pressure of foreign influences, when it is necessary to reproduce the significance of cultural borrowings: *tungol-cræft* for 'astronomy', for example, and *þrynes* for 'trinity'. In Middle English recourse to native resources of word formation for such purposes declined, and foreign word-forms were more freely adopted. Nevertheless, despite the fact that compounding was less fertile than in the Old English period, many of the Old English types of compounding continued to be productive, and some new types arose. Noun compounds were numerically the commonest in Old English and many types of these remained productive. Those of *Noun + Noun* structure were especially common: 268 have been counted in Laȝamon's *Brut*, of which 138 were new formations in Middle English (Sauer 1985). Examples from elsewhere which survive into Modern English include *bagpipe*, *bedchamber*, *birthday*, *bloodhound*, *schoolmaster* and *swordfish*. Those consisting originally of a noun in the genitive as modifier of a nominal head recruited to their ranks *doomsman*, *kinswoman* and *craftsman*. *Kinsman* occurs already in Old English as *cynnes man*, but it is uncertain whether the syntactical group was regularly considered a compound before the Middle English period (see vol. I, section 5.4.2.2.3). Nouns compounded from an *Adjective + Noun* within the Middle English period are: *blackberry*, *blackboard*, *grandfather*, *highroad*, *highway* and *shortbread* (Marchand 1969: 60–5). They represent the second most common type in Laʒamon with 18 new formations in a total of 37.

ˉ.2.4   A number of fresh types of compound noun emerged during the Middle English period. Especially worthy of note are those in which a verbal stem is completed by a nominal which in the underlying sentence would have acted as the subject of the verb: thus, *leap-year* (as far as any fixed festival is concerned, the year 'leaps' a day, so that the festival falls on the next weekday but one to that on which it fell in the previous year), *goggle-eye*, *bere-man* 'porter' (1226) and *plei-fere* 'play-fellow' (1225). Although compounds in which the second element was an agent noun with the first element the object of the underlying verb existed in Old English, none of them survived in Middle English records, so the revival of the type in the thirteenth century may be a fresh beginning, yet preserves an archaic syntactic pattern: *wæi-witere* 'guide' (1225), *wire-drawer* (1265 as an occupation by-name). The type became very productive in the fourteenth century: *moneymaker* (1297), *man-slayer* (1300), *lace-maker* (as a surname, 1305), *good-doer* (1340; *do-gooder* is not recorded until 1927), *house-breaker* (1340), *soothsayer* (1340), *law-maker* (1380), *householder* (1395), *peacemaker* (1436), *housekeeper* (1440) and *bricklayer* (1485). The use of personal names in the formation of noun compounds also belongs to the fourteenth century, at least in the case of *Tom* and *Jack* – *Tom-fool* dates from 1356 – but the use of other names belongs to the Renaissance period. Sex-determining compounds using personal pronouns are first recorded about 1300: *he-lamb*, *she-ape* (ca 1400), *she-ass* (1382) (Marchand 1969: 75–9).

5.2.5   All the noun compounds exemplified above are of a type known as *endocentric* compounds, which is to say that they have a modifier + head structure, and that the denotation of the compound word is included within the range of reference of the head word: a *man-slayer* is a kind of slayer; a *Tom-fool* a kind of fool. A second type of noun compound, which developed considerably in Middle English, is the *exocentric* compound, in which the denotation of the compound noun is not a subset of either the determiner or the head taken individually, but is rather included within the range of reference of some more general conception implied but unexpressed. Thus, the fifteenth-century poetic compound *burnwater* has the sense 'smith'. Similar personal substantives, often with pejorative associations, date from the early fourteenth century: *trailbastoun* (1305), *spurnwater* (1347), *spilltime* (1362), *cutpurse* (1350), Chaucer's *combreworld*, *pinchpenny* (1412), *wantwit* (1448) and *scattergood* (as a name 1226). This pattern, which became very productive in later English, is claimed to have been based ultimately upon French imperative phrases, since in French the name *coupe-bourse* 'cutpurse' is recorded from the twelfth century (Marchand 1969: 380–2). However, such formations contain no sense of an imperative, and very early Middle English examples used as nicknames suggest that they may equally well derive from English transitive clauses. The compounding of names alluding to some distinguishing feature of their referent is a second source of exocentric compound nouns. Thus Edward I received the nickname *Curtmantel* (1367). Other examples are: *whitethorn* (1265), *redbreast* (1401) and *Hotspur* (1460).

5.2.6   Copulative compounds, in which it is not clear which element is the grammatical head, both elements equally referring to the referent, had become unproductive in Old English, but are again represented in Middle English by a few thirteenth-century noun formations – *kayserr-kinng* (*Ormulum*) and *stane-roche* (*Vices and Virtues*) *leod-folk*, *gleo-drem*, *driht-folk* (Laȝamon) – whose tautology may have an interpretative function. The contrastive adjectival *bitter-sweet*, recorded in 1386, is not found again until the sixteenth century.

5.2.7   Compound adjectives include a type in which the first of two adjectival elements modifies a second, making fine distinctions in sense impressions: *icy-cold*, *red-hot* (1375), *lukewarm* (1398), *light-green* (1420), *brown-blue* (1450). The significance of this last is 'dark blue'. This type of compound is thinly represented in Old English, becoming much more productive in the late fourteenth century. The word *deorcegræg* 'dark grey' does, however, occur in Old English, but seems to have disappeared before the Middle English period; indeed, the word *dark* is not recorded in a compound in this way until the eighteenth century. Combinations of a noun and a past participle, which existed in Old English verse in examples like *goldhroden* 'adorned with gold', did not

443

survive into Middle English, but the type became productive once more in the fourteenth century: *moss-grown* (1300), *woe-begone* (1470), *moth-eaten* (1377), *book-learned* (1420), *wind-driven* (1387). Adjectival compounds formed with the past participle as head also include a type in which the determiner is an adjective or an adverb. Most extant examples date from the fourteenth century, but the major productivity of this pattern belongs to the later sixteenth century: *new-born* (1300), *high-born* (1300), *free-born* (1340), *new-sown* (1375), *hard-set* (1387) *free-hearted* (1415) (Marchand 1969: 92–5).

5.2.8   Although throughout its history English has readily formed verbs from compound nouns, the direct formation of verbal compounds is rare. But, like other Germanic languages, Old English possessed separable compounds, a type in which a verbal base was, in certain syntactical environments, combined with a particle (a locative adverb or a preposition), which in other syntactic environments could occur separated from this base. Thus, in Modern German the verb 'to come back' is *zurückkommen*. In some syntactical frames, the elements of the compound must be separated: *Kommen Sie zurück* 'Come back!' Old English possessed similar separable compounds, although the rules for their use were not so rigidly observed, and, as in Modern German, verbal compounds like *understandan* occurred in which the elements were no longer separable without a drastic change in sense. Compound nouns of similar structure were derived from both separable and inseparable verbal compounds, but were never separable themselves.

5.2.9   In Middle English all these types continued, but they began to be redistributed into: (a) inseparable particle + verb compounds (*understand, overtake*); (b) phrasal verbs consisting of verbal base + particle (*take up, write up*); and (c) derived nominal compounds of the two types (*outcry, write-off*). The stage at which particled verb was frequently matched by nominal compound was reached early in Old Norse (Bennett & Smithers 1966: xxxii–xxxiv), and it is probable that Scandinavian influence contributed to the development of particled verbs in Middle English (5.1.1.11). Moreover, Scandinavian particled verbs may sometimes have given rise to new pairs which resemble separable compounds: the verb *uthede* 'call out (a militia)' in *Havelok* seems to be derived from *bjóða út*. It is one of about a dozen such 'separable compounds' in the poem which are not paralleled in Old English (Smithers 1987: lxxxx). Among many examples of co-existing compound and particled verbs, may be quoted: *fall by* (1325) and *bifallen* (OE) 'happen, befall'; *fare out* (1393) and *outfare* (1150); *flee out* (1300) and *outflee* (1325) 'expel, banish'; *go out* (1325) and *outgo* (OE); *hente out* (ca 1400) and *outhente* (1450) 'grasp, seize'; *leap out* (1398) and *outleap* (1375) 'spring out'; *look over* (ca 1400) and *overlook* (ca 1400) 'survey from on high'; *pass over* (ca 1300) and *overpass* (1325) 'go over'. The compound *forþferan*, which was an Old English euphemism for 'to die' continues with this sense until the end of the fourteenth century, but then develops the new sense 'to set out', presumably re-adopting what was its original sense from the particled verb *fare forth*, recorded from 1225 onwards. This emphasis upon the particled verb as the focus of derivation is symptomatic of the change which took place during the fifteenth century by which the formation of verbs became concentrated on the production of particled verbs, and compound verbs ceased to be productive as a type of word formation. The derivation of agentive nouns from particled verbs, such as Chaucer's reference to Troilus as '*holder up* of Troye' or Lydgate's to Nimrod as '*fynder up* of false religions' also belongs to the turn of the fourteenth and fifteenth centuries.

5.2.10   The adoption of word forms by one language from another is often accompanied by a process of analysis which identifies the word structure of the adoption, usually retaining the stem and attaching to it the inflectional morphemes of the recipient language. Errors in analysis may result in the incorporation of inflectional morphemes of the original language into the stem of the adopted word, as with *scant* and *bask* (5.1.1.10), or perhaps in the omission of part of the stem which is wrongly thought to be an inflection, as, perhaps, in the word *hail* from ON *heilsa*. The adopted word form may also be analysed into base and affixal morphemes, so in the *Ancrene Wisse* (1225), the forms *i* + *weorr* + *et* and *bi* + *turn* + *ed* each exhibit a pattern in which both native inflectional ending and prefix have been attached to an Anglo-Norman verbal base. Such words are fully assimilated into both the derivational and grammatical systems of English.

5.2.11   Foreign words may be adopted with affixes as part of their structure, and these affixes may become productive in English. Here it is necessary to distinguish three successive stages. Firstly, the word containing affixes is adopted into English and assimilated into the grammatical systems of the language. Secondly, after analysis of the word structure, there follows a period during which the word is stylistically differentiated from the rest of the lexis. It is synchronically recognisable by speakers of the language as foreign, and its affixes may be used to produce new formations with a restricted set of bases also perceived to be foreign. Such affixes are productive only within a subset of the lexis. Finally, as coinages become more numerous, the affix ceases to be considered exotic, and is used to coin words on bases of any origin. At this point the affix has become part of the general derivational system of the language.

5.2.12   In the Middle English period, prefixation as a means of word formation was in retreat. Many of the Old English prefixes had become unproductive or disappeared altogether, and many new adoptions from French and Latin had not proceeded beyond the second stage mentioned above. One familiar Old English grammar (Quirk & Wrenn 1957: 109–14) lists thirty-four formally distinct prefixes in Old English, only a small proportion of which continued in use beyond the first half of the thirteenth century. Some, such as *a-*, *be-*, *for-*, *to-*, *ge-* and *ymb-*, were widely used in words inherited from Old English in the Early Middle English period, but the patterns declined in productivity. *Ge-* (spelt *i-*/*y-*) persists throughout the period in the south to mark the past participle of verbs, but although it survives into the fourteenth century in the south-east as a prefix with verbs, nouns and adjectives, and even longer in the adverb *iwis* 'certainly', it had not been productive in these positions for many centuries. OE *ymb-* is preserved in the thirteenth century through substitution by its Scandinavian cognate *umbe-* (*umbistode* 'stood around' (*Havelok*)). Many Old English prefixes, *ond-*, *æ-*, *æf-*, *ed-*, *el-*, *o-*, *sam-*, *sin-* and *wiþer-*, were no longer productive and rapidly disappeared altogether, sometimes by confusion with other prefixes of similar form, and sometimes by the loss of the words which contained them. Old English prefixes which remained productive sometimes changed their significance and the rules for their combination. Thus *un-*, which in Old English expressed the antithesis of the base morph with nouns and adjectives – *unlytel* 'notably large' – or gave it pejorative associations – *uncræft* 'malpractice' – or simply added intensity – *unfohrt* 'very afraid' – now lost the latter two functions. Many of the Old English combinations with this prefix disappeared altogether, but the combination with verbal bases became more common, and the reversative sense of the prefix, which had been connected with both *ond-* and *on-* in Old English, was developed: *unclose* 'to open' (Chaucer). From the fourteenth century, and probably by confusion with French and Latin *in-*, this prefix becomes especially common with the French suffix *-able*, and a large number of words of the type *unknowable* (1374) were formed (Marchand 1969: 230). Similarly, the Old English prefix *mis-* was greatly strengthened by the French *mes-*, with which it fell together, so that Middle English has many verbs and deverbal nouns formed with *mis-*: *misseyen* 'insult' (1225), *misgylt* 'misbehaviour' (thirteenth century).

5.2.13 In those cases where borrowed French or Latin prefixes were not paired with a pre-existing native one, many remained at the second stage until the end of the Middle English period. The prefix *de-/des-*, although available in borrowings from the late thirteenth century, is not combined with a native base until Lydgate's use of the Latin form *distrust* (1430). *Re-*, *sub-*, *super-* and *mal-* became available in the late fourteenth or early fifteenth century, but although a few coinages are recorded with Romance base morphs, these prefixes do not become fully productive until the Renaissance period. Similarly, *non-* is fairly widely used in Latinate law terminology from the mid-fourteenth century, but does not emerge from this restricted language until the seventeenth century, becoming most productive in modern times. The prefix *en-/em-*, which appears first with verbs in the writings of Wyclif, only begins to be used with native bases with the fifteenth-century search for elevated diction: *enthrallen* (1447).

5.2.14 If Middle English until the fifteenth century was somewhat depleted in its range of productive prefixes, it was better supplied with derivational suffixes. Of the forty or so which existed in Old English, about three-quarters persisted into Middle English, where they were joined by numerous additions from foreign sources. Of those native suffixes which survived, many underwent some modification in their function or senses. The suffix *-ful*, originally used to form adjectives from abstract nouns, now also formed adjectives from verbal bases: *forgetful* (1382), *weariful* (1454). The suffix *-ish*, which in Old English had been primarily a formative of the names of peoples and had been extended to refer to types of people (*ceorlisc*, *mennisc*), continued to be employed in this way – *elvisshe*, *wommanisshe* (Chaucer) – but in the late fourteenth century, as determinative colour compounds become more common, it is also extended to colour adjectives: *yellowish* (1379), *greenish* (1384), *reddish* (1398), *darkish* (1398), *bluish* (1400). The suffix *-ed* continued to form adjectives with the sense 'provided with' from nouns, but it was in Middle English that the very productive type with the prefix *well-* made its appearance: *well-weaponed* (1250), *well-boned* (1297), *well-lettered* (1303). It is matched by the appearance of similar compounds employing the Scandinavian borrowing *ill-*: *ill-tongued* (1400). The major productivity of this, as with other Scandinavian-derived prefixes (*bull-*, *flat-*, *low-*) belongs to a later period (Finkenstaedt & Wolff 1973: 135). The form *ill-* illustrates strikingly the process of transition from free morpheme and, therefore element of a compound, to bound morpheme, and therefore prefix, in Modern English. The development of exocentric compounds of the type mentioned above (5.2.5) led to combinations of the following kind: *heavy-handed*, *heavy-hearted*, *hard-hearted* (1225), *ill-tongued*, *long-lived*, mostly in the fourteenth and fifteenth centuries (Marchand 1969: 265–6). This type effectively replaced the exocentric adjectival (bahuvrihi) compounds of Old English, such as *heardheort*, *mildheort* and *bærfot*, which were now no longer productive.

5.2.15   A suffix of probable native origin which is of special interest for its associative force is *-ling*. It was derived by the metanalysis of the diminutive *-ing* (also productive in Middle English: *lording*, *sweeting*) when used with a base terminating in /l/, e.g. *ætheling*. The form *darling* in fact originated in Old English, but was followed in Middle English by a series of extensions to the significance of the suffix. Application was extended from humans to animals by 1220, when *youngling* with the sense 'young animal' is recorded. There followed *nestling* (1399) and *grayling* (1450), and coinages with a verbal base such as *suckling* (1440). An association with youth, perhaps arising from the form *youngling*, but perhaps inherent in the original meaning of *-ing*, gave rise to coinages with the meaning 'young' from the beginning of the fourteenth century: *wolfling*, *codling* (1314), *duckling* (1440), *gosling* (fifteenth century) and *sapling* (1415). Further associations of the diminutive, both favourable and contemptuous, are developed in the sixteenth century.

5.2.16   Suffixes from all the major sources of foreign influence achieved a limited productivity in Middle English. Under the influence of Flemish settlers, the diminutive suffix *-(i)kin* (MDu. *-kin*) is recorded in pet names from the thirteenth century – *Willekin*, *Malekin*, *Jankin*. Although common in the fourteenth century, they declined during the fifteenth, surviving only in common English surnames. The suffix was extended to common-noun bases in the fourteenth and fifteenth centuries: *baudekin* 'precious silk', *fauntekin* 'child' (both Langland), *napkin* (1420). The Scandinavian-derived suffix *-leik* found considerable currency as an alternative to *-ness* in the thirteenth century, and indeed Orm, when correcting his manuscript, substituted this for the native suffix, but it is also found far from the Danelaw in the *Ancrene Wisse*: *godlec* 'goodness, kindness'.

5.2.17　French and Franco-Latin are, however, by far the most prolific sources of foreign derivational suffixes. Many of the suffixes available, such as *-trix*, *-trice* or Latin *-ive* (with the exception of *talkative* (1420)) are not productive, remaining simply elements of borrowed word forms throughout the period. A second large group are productive only with a Romance base: *-able*, *-ate*, *-ee*, *-erie*, *-ment*, *-ous*, *-ic(al)*. But a substantial number are fully assimilated in Middle English: *-age*: *barnage* 'infancy' (from OE *bearn* 'child'; 1325); *-ard* entered the language by way of loans like *buzzard* and *bastard* and became productive as a pejorative suffix with English bases by the thirteenth century: *shreward* (1297), *dotard* (1386), *wizard* (1440). The diminutive *-erel* had become fully naturalised by the time *pickerel* 'young pike' was recorded in 1338, and this was followed in 1440 by *cockerel* and *mongrel* (1486). Finally, the suffix *-esse* is used to form the feminine equivalents of nouns with masculine reference from the fourteenth century: *hirdess* 'shepherdess' (Chaucer), *authoress*, *neighbouress*. *Hunteress* (1386) exhibits both the agentive *-ere* suffix and the feminine one. It should be noted that many of the French derivational suffixes which were adopted into English initially as word borrowings during the Middle English period were to have an importance not simply as isolated items. Many indeed formed derivational patterns which were to suggest even greater sources of lexical richness at a later period. Thus *-ate* (adj.) is paired with *-acy* (abstr. n.): *delicate*, *delicacy*; *-ate* (vb) with *-ation* (abstr. n.): *consecrate*, *consecration*; *-ent*, *-ency*: *innocent*, *innocency*; *-fy*, *-fication*: *justify*, *justification*. All these pairs existed in the fourteenth century, but others were added in the fifteenth: *-ize*, *-ization*: *solemnize*, *solemnization*; *-ic*, *-ician*: *arithmetic*, *arithmetician*.

5.2.18　Foreign sources which were of great importance to word formation in Middle English played equally as important a role in phrase creation. French in particular contributed a large number of phrasal idioms (Prins 1952), of which verbal phrases especially have proved productive. The structure of such phrases usually consisted of a verbal operator followed by an abstract noun or adverbial phrase; thus: *do homage, do mischief, do justice, make complaint, make moan, have compassion on, have mercy on, take pity on, take keep, hold dear, hold in despite*. Because some phrases can be paralleled in Old English, it is not always certain that they are formations on French phrases with *faire, avoir, prendre* and *tenir*. Nevertheless, because the pattern of the phrases corresponds so closely to the French, and many are apparently adoptions with partial substitution of native morphs, it is safe to assume that French influence played a major role in this important addition to English modes of expression. Prins, in his study of such phrases (1952), lists within Middle English more than fifty formations which have equivalents in, and are likely to be modelled on, French phrases with *faire*, fifteen with *avoir*, twenty-nine with *prendre* and eight with *tenir*. They are especially common from the second half of the fourteenth century. A parallel tendency exists in verbal phrases based upon the Scandinavian-derived verbal operator *get*, for phrases such as *get grace, get mercy* and *get leave* are recorded from 1300 onwards. The major contribution of this verb is, however, in a series of expressions with locatives: a dozen of the type *get away from, get up* and *get out* occur in the Middle English period.

5.3   The structure of the lexicon

5.3.1   It should not be assumed that the systems of word formation are the only systems operative within the lexis of English. Indeed, lexis, although not highly structured like grammar and phonology, is not merely an unordered list of items accumulated from the processes of word formation and foreign borrowing. Rather, it is structured and subclassifiable according to various criteria. Those structures which result from treating the lexical item as a form—meaning composite are dealt with in the discussion of semantics, but the vocabulary exhibits patterning at the purely formal level also. This formal patterning is of two kinds: that evident in the syntagmatic axis, that is the tendency of co-occurrence or combination within the string of words produced in connected discourse; and that dependent on a paradigmatic distinction between words in which choice is made according to the conditions of their use. In this latter case, words are differentiated from one another not by their meanings but by distinguishing features of the contexts in which they are likely to occur. Thus the words *pal* and *comrade*, which share much of their sense, are in sharp contrast in the conditions of their occurrence. In this conception of ordering, words are classed together according to the context of their occurrence. Judgement of likeness or unlikeness in context of occurrence is rarely a clear-cut decision, so that this kind of lexical patterning, which is dependent upon the 'architecture' of style, is a matter of open and intersecting classes, probabilities rather than mutually exclusive choices, and lacks the contrasts and oppositions of the more highly structured levels of analysis. Ultimately, such patterning depends on the conception of the world held by users of the language.

5.3.2 Patterning on the syntagmatic axis is usually discussed in terms of *collocability*, the potential for co-occurrence of word forms in the string of discourse. *Collocation* is thus a more inclusive category than *colligation*, which refers to the juxtaposition of lexical items within definable syntactic structures. The latter, however, is often treated under the heading *collocation*, and is so in this discussion (Firth 1957, 1968). In principle, the collocational patterning discernible in a corpus is derived from the probability of the co-occurrence of any two word forms, and this may be expressed statistically. Lexical sets may be established of items showing a high probability of collocation with any particular word chosen for investigation. Although a considerable amount of research has been devoted to this topic, the relationship of such lexical sets to the cognitive meaning of lexical items remains enigmatic (Jones & Sinclair 1974). Collocation, too, often reflects not contiguity of meaning, but reference to features of frequent situations of use or aspects of the user's world picture.

5.3.3 Among collocations of highest probability come those hardly variable idioms found in most languages, and the fixed formulas of literary composition common in Middle English. *To lien bolt upright*, the exclamation *a twenty devil way*, *ded as dorenail* or the archaic *eþer unker* in *Havelok* are probably idioms of speech; the formulas of verse are legion: *stille as stone*, *stif in stour*, *war and wis*, *joye and blisse*. Both speech idioms and verse formulas are often alliterative, or else co-ordinate pairs of semantically related words. Indeed alliteration may be the explanation of the fact that in Chaucer's poetry the phrase *hard herte* outnumbers *cruel herte* by a factor of about two to one. *Cruel corage* is found, but not *hard corage*. Not all such formulas are poetic. Some have their origins in religious or legal language. *Friþþ and griþþ* in the *Ormulum*, which pairs words of different linguistic origins (as many such pairs do), has a legal background, as does *heigh and lough* in Chaucer. The special stylistic status of this latter is emphasised by the fact that the scribe of the Hengwrt manuscript deviates from his usual spelling *lowe* in this phrase alone. The triplet *maiden, wife, widow*, which is a frequent collocation in the works of Chaucer and Gower, became a collocational set from frequent repetition in discourse reflecting contemporary Christian perceptions of the role of women. Collocational tendencies may not be so clearly marked as this. The application of adjectives sometimes shows a tendency to restriction which is easily overlooked. In the works of Chaucer, and indeed more widely in fourteenth-century literature, the word *buxom* 'submissive, obedient' is frequently applied to women, collocating especially with the word *wife*. The reason for this lies in the contemporary conception of the wife's role, to which she made assent in the marriage service using this very word. Other peculiarities of adjective + head colligation may be less easy to explain. Chaucer's use of the word *wood* 'furious, mad', for example, is commonly used to describe a lion, whereas his choice of epithet for a tiger is more likely to be *cruel*. When *grace* or *favour* is the object of the verb *send*, in Chaucer's works the subject is invariably *God*. Such partially ordered phrasings, as distinct from the alliterative formulas of poetry or the repetitive word pairs of fifteenth-century prose, have not been the subject of study in Middle English, but their existence serves to emphasise the fact that much of the language in use constitutes what has been characterised as 'repeated discourse' (Coseriu 1967). Phrases or schemata (Lyons 1968: 177–8) in use vary in the language from period to period, preserving in their formal structure archaic features of grammar and patterns of collocation which reflect traditional conceptions of the ordering of the world.

5.3.4　　Stylistic choice in lexis, arising from the uses to which language is put within a speech community, is an aspect of stylistics whose existence has been recognised for centuries. Full competence in the use of Latin demanded an awareness of the associations of its words – archaic, provincial, neologism or low-life – which was advocated by Quintilian and the Late Latin rhetorician Chirius Fortunatianus. This heritage, transmitted by lexicographical tradition, distantly underlies the division of vocabulary made by the editors of the *OED* where, in their General Explanation, they distinguish a common core of lexis from which they differentiate technical and dialectal words; a literary level, from which are distinguished scientific and foreign words; and a colloquial level, of which slang is a subcategory. To take one of these classes, it is apparent that the foreign element in the lexis is not adequately accounted for simply by listing individual word forms of foreign origin; even within the lexis, foreign influence will create patterning effects on both the syntagmatic and paradigmatic axes. Moreover, a style which is felt by the speakers of a language to exhibit foreign influence often does so at more than one level of analysis: syntactically or phonologically as well as lexically. It should be recognised, therefore, that the classification of lexis according to the styles in which lexical items are likely to be used is a lexicographer's abstraction, since the styles concerned are realised, if only intermittently, by marked items at all levels of analysis.

5.3.5   Style in the broader sense depends on use, and the concept of use can profitably be divided into two: the use to which language is being put, on the one hand, and the nature of the users of it, on the other (Halliday, McIntosh & Strevens 1964). Under the former it is possible to distinguish the *mode* of the language, written or spoken; the *field of discourse*, that is the general subject area to which the discourse belongs; the degree of *formality* of the utterance, which may vary from the informality of slang at one extreme to the rigid formality of technical written language at the other (Crystal & Davy 1969). Classification by user may be according to the *social status* of the user, which may be reflected in linguistic choice; or the geographical origins of the user, reflected in *dialect* usage or in foreign influence apparent in speech. These divisions are neither exhaustive nor mutually exclusive. They represent conceptual distinctions important to the speech community and reflected in the way it uses language. It would be possible, for example, to imagine – as actually happened in Thai – a society which made an important distinction between the language of royalty and commoners, or – as happens in Japanese and some Amerindian languages (Trudgill 1974b: 84–101; Hudson 1980: 120–2; Philips, Steele & Tanz 1987) – between that of men and that of women. The classifications are not mutually exclusive in the sense that a word may be marked not only by the fact of its dialectal use, but also by its social significance, or by its dual association with written mode and technical field of discourse. Just as much as by their participation in a common phonological or grammatical system, speech communities could in principle be defined by sharing a common understanding of the configuration of the associations of these styles and the lexical items habitually used in them. This is a rather different matter from the mere fact of having access to the same inventory of word forms, and indeed speech communities defined by a common appreciation of stylistic values are potentially very small groups of individuals. What is true in terms of stylistic values for one small group may be quite inapplicable to the linguistic usage of the other; for example, both Chaucer and Gower appear to avoid the serious, non-ironic use of certain common words – *lemman* 'lover', *oore* 'grace, mercy', *derelynge*, *hende* 'refined, gracious' – some of which are perfectly acceptable to their contemporary, the *Gawain*-poet. That he does not belong to the same stylistic community as Chaucer and Gower may be explicable on regional grounds, but that the poem *The Tournament of Tottenham* similarly deviates from Chaucer's usage is more probably explicable by divisions on the social scale.

5.3.6   Because the analysis of the stylistic associations of words in an early literary language is a delicate business, and because the classification of the lexis is essentially the work of contemporary users of a language, it is reassuring to find contemporary voices to confirm our analyses. Bokenham's identification of the terms of law (see p. 414), Usk's reference to recondite and technical terminology (see p. 413) and Chaucer's distinction of the terms of law (*CT* 3: 1189 [II.1189]), philosophy (*HF* 857), astrology (*CT* 6: 558 [V.1266]), physics (*Troilus* II.1038), alchemy (*CT* VIII.752), the schools (*CT* 6: 853 [IV.1569]), and love (*Troilus* II.1039) are particularly welcome in defining fields of discourse recognised by fourteenth and early fifteenth-century writers. The terms of alchemy occupy long passages of the *Canon's Yeoman's Tale*, where over fifty technical terms are used for the equipment, processes and materials of the science. Some of these are repeated by Gower and in the *Secretum secretorum*.

5.3.7   The Canon's Yeoman's alchemical list raises a problem about the classification of lexical items by fields of discourse. Many of the words which are clearly considered technical in context are so considered because of the particular sense they have, or collocations in which they occur in context. Nor is use in any one particular field of discourse a bar to similar technical use in a different field. Thus, many of the words for the materials of alchemy do not belong exclusively to this field of discourse: *lunarie* 'moon-wort' and *valerian* belong as much to herbals, *asshes* to the common core of the vocabulary. The words *matere* and *water* are clearly part of general vocabulary except when collocated respectively with *encorporyng* 'forming an amalgam' and *corosif* 'acidic'. In fact relatively few word forms or phrases are restricted to this context: *watres rubifying* 'liquids which cause reddening', *watres albificacioun* 'whitening by liquids (?)', *citrinacioun* 'turning to a lemon-yellow colour'. This potentiality for technical use in one particular field of discourse, yet also of possible broader use, is true of very many words in Chaucer's lexis. Many of the terms of law he uses have developed much wider privileges of occurrence through creative extensions of their use in literary texts. Phrases such as *under coverture* (used in *Kyng Alisaunder* of lovers), *by ... imaginacioun forncast* (used by Chaucer of a fox planning the downfall of a cock), *perpetuel prisoun* (used by Langland of Hell), *strong prisoun* and even *in newe cas lieth new avys* or *quit claim* all have legal associations, but are shifted in Middle English to use in other situations. The same is true of *adversarie*, *chalenge* 'claim' and *seize*, but *amercement* 'fine' remained a technical term. Terms of astrology include *ascensioun* (also found with a different sense in alchemical contexts), *aspect*, *elevacioun*, *equinoxial*, *elongacioun* and *perpendicular*. Some of these also form part of the technical vocabulary of geometry, which itself contributed *cercle*, *ligne*, *centre*, *equation*, *distaunce* and *equal*. In Chaucer's usage, the Latin-derived spelling distinguishes *equal* as the technical term from the French form *egal*, which is in more general use.

5.3.8   Particular occupations or definable areas of cultural interest contribute more or less restricted and technical vocabularies to Middle English, reflecting the diversity of its culture. Studies have been made recently of the terms of sheep farming in Norfolk (Davis 1969), grocers in London (Ross 1947–8, 1963, 1974), sailing and ships (Sandahl 1951–82), music (Carter 1961), cookery (Serjeantson 1938), horology (Rigg 1983), medicine (Wallner 1969), the English of merchants (Eberle 1983) and administrative English (Fisher, Richardson & Fisher 1984). The works of Chaucer, Gower and the *Gawain*-poet, taken together, contain about 140 words with references to the genres, effects, processes and authors of literature. This literary vocabulary, like every other technical vocabulary, contains very many words of much wider range of use, for example *entent*, *matere*, *forme* and *poynte*, but also a few words, especially those to do with genres, which are restricted to literary discussion: *balade*, *virelai* and *roundel* occur as a collocational set of recognisably French origin.

5.3.9　　Middle English has a number of lexical items which are restricted to particular fields of discourse and are technical terms in the narrowest sense, but it also possesses large numbers of terms which occur in more than one technical field, and even some which have an air of technicality but which are difficult to assign to any particular field of discourse at all: *assente, creature, dissolve, fixe, futur, permutacioun, notable, cavillacioun*. It is perhaps these which Chaucer calls *termes of philosophye* or *scole termes*; that is, a general category of technical terminology set apart from the common core of the lexis by belonging to the written mode, and obviously derived from Latin or French sources. Moreover, such words often exhibit characteristic derivational morphemes, such as *-acioun*, and are polysyllabic or of opaque morphemic structure, such as the Arabic-derived *alembik* and *alkali*. Two further important points may be noted about such words: firstly that as a superstrate upon the dialectally fragmented lexis of Middle English, they were not so subject to the variation in pronunciation or association which afflicted native words; secondly, since technical vocabulary is so rarely restricted for long to technical use, and since these words are almost all cultural borrowings from outside the language system, they act as an instructive demonstration of the channels by which foreign borrowings so frequently make their way into that language system. Much adoption of foreign words in the later Middle English period took place in technical written contexts from which they were then generalised.

5.3.10　　In medieval England social status expressed through language use could be simply summed up in the words of the author of *Arthur and Merlin*: 'Freynsche vse þis gentil man' ('Gentlemen use French'). As the fourteenth century wore on, this assertion was increasingly subject to qualification as competence in French declined, so that social discrimination tended to be made within the use of the English language alone. It is unlikely that Bokenham presented his explanation of the archaic terms of English law in the *Mappula Angliae* for the edification of any but gentlemen, although he purports to write it for the instruction of all those subject to the law. The compiler of a fifteenth-century list of the technical terms of hunting in MS Egerton 1995 makes no bones about stating that his work is intended to instruct young gentlemen in the 'propyr termys that longythe vnto hym'. These, according to Malory, are the technical language of the gentleman's recreation, hunting: 'the goodly tearmys that jantylman have and use and shall do unto the Day of Dome, that thereby in a maner all men of worshyp may discever a jantylman frome a yoman and a yoman frome a vylane' (I.375). By the close of the fifteenth century, it is claimed that discrimination of social class could be made in English by knowledge of the terms of particular fields of discourse considered appropriate to a gentleman, but, although Londoners may scorn provincialism (Blake 1976), dialect and accent were still irrelevant to the judgement of a claim to gentility.

5.3.11   French expressions, of course, did not lose their prestige even when used in an English co-text, and words of recognisably French provenance were common from the late thirteenth century in the language of those who wished to appear socially sophisticated. *Ma foy, maugree, madame, pardee, par compaignie, grant mercy, sanz* and *par chance* are all commonly found in fourteenth-century manuscripts. Social prestige, interpreted as worldly wisdom, adhered not only to such French phrases but also to that large technical vocabulary which betrayed by its form its Romance origins. A knowledge of the vocabulary of a particular skill was as likely to impress as traces of familiarity with French. Urbanity in speech, then, tended in the fourteenth and fifteenth centuries to presuppose a formality in lexis based upon knowledge of some part of that general technical vocabulary, a consequent Romance colouring to diction and elegant and appropriate phrasing. Although it might be suggested that there existed a courtly vocabulary – and certain words do designate concepts in courtly theory, for example *grace, curteisie, debonairetee, mercy, vylanye, conveyen, congeyen, avauntour, daunger, hende, pitee* and *servise* – it is impossible to find contemporary justification for the existence of *curtesie* as a field of discourse with its own distinctive terminology in the manner that such terminology is recognised in the spheres of alchemy or the law. *Faire speche* and speaking *curteisly* imply more in fourteenth-century texts than mere verbal choice or even any linguistically definable style. By contrast, however, words to be stigmatised are relatively clearly identifiable. Chaucer refers to *cherles termes* and the translation of the *Roman de la Rose* gives us some indication of their nature, condemning *foule wordes* and *wordes of ribaudye*. Although it is not easy to distinguish disapproval of the act of referring from stigmatisation of the lexeme itself, it seems probable that a fairly large number of words occurring in the works of Chaucer might have transgressed these strictures in the *Roman* against vulgar speech (Elliott 1974; Muscatine 1981; Ross & Brookes 1984). Regrettably, secure evidence of the status of many words is lacking, so that only a brief account can be given. On the evidence of the French text of the *Rose*, one stigmatised set of words seems to consist of those associated with sexual or excretory funtions: *coillons*, *toute*, *tayl*, *queynte*, *pisse*, *arse* and *swyve*. In the case of this last some fairly direct evidence to complement Chaucer's elaborate evasion of its use (*CT* 5: 1118 [IV.2362]) is the fact that the scribe of the Hengwrt and Ellesmere manuscripts, although writing it out in full within the line, preferred to complete the rhyme by writing down the first few letters of the word, ending with *etcetera* (*CT* 11: 256 [IX.256]).

5.3.12   A second and larger group of stigmatised lexis is that consisting of derogatory descriptive terms for people. Chaucer's *knarre* and *gnof* sound like pejorative terms, but proof is impossible. The words *boy* and *gadelyng*, however, were widely used to refer to servants, became associated with rogues and developed into insulting forms of description and address. The word *harlot*, also used frequently as an insulting form of address, had originally meant a rogue of either sex, a person of low social status and loose morals. The word *carl*, originally the Scandinavian equivalent of the English *cherle*, denoting the lowest class of freeman, likewise became an insult during the fourteenth century, and the use of both together cost fifteenth-century members of the Mercers' Company several pounds in fines. Other guild records and court rolls recording the consequences of slanderous abuse list among the most grievous examples of abuse: *fals man*, *ribaude*, *theefe*, *knave*, *traytour*, *swyn* and *Scot* (Thrupp 1949; Lindahl 1987). As a word descriptive of a young girl, *wenche* was quite acceptable in some circles in the fourteenth century, for John of Trevisa uses it without comment as a gloss for Latin *puella*, as does one of the translators of the later version of the Wycliffite Bible (Forshall & Madden 1850); but to Chaucer, and perhaps to a second anonymous translator of the Bible, it was socially marked and morally deprecatory, implying firstly a servant girl and, secondly, one who could be assumed to be immoral. *Lemman*, which means 'lover' and may refer to either sex, seems to be used by neither Chaucer nor Gower as an approved form of address. Indeed Chaucer employs the negative associations of *lemman* by comparison with the more acceptable *lady* to make a moral point in the *Manciple's Tale*. In this tale he collocates *lemman* and *wenche*, and the socially and morally derogatory associations of the latter word are confirmed by the contrast made between *wenche* and *gentil* in the *Merchant's Tale*: 'I am a gentil womman and no wenche' (*CT* 5: 958 [IV.2202]). Yet, although

Chaucer, Gower and Langland regarded *wenche* and *lemman* as forms of address to a woman to be avoided in polite discourse, neither word is at all objectionable to the translator of *William of Palerne*, who was doing his work expressly at the request of a member of the aristocracy. In this poem, the hero's betrothed is called his *worthi wenche* and his *lemman*. No pejorative implications are possible. There could scarcely be a clearer example of the distinct stylistic values attached to the same words by distinct speech communities. Such disjunction of the stylistic values attributed to words is undoubtedly the product of a society more fragmented and isolated than that of modern times.

5.3.13   Just as words may have distinct associations and therefore function in distinct stylistic roles in different social groupings, so, too, both different significances and different word forms may be found in geographically distinct communities: the dialect areas of Middle English have, to a certain extent, distinct lexical inventories (Kaiser 1937). The author of the mid fifteenth-century *Myroure of Oure Ladye* comments that 'oure language is also so dyuerse in yt selfe, that the commen maner of spekyng in Englysshe of some contre can skante be vnderstonded in some other contre of the same londe' (Blunt 1873: 7–8). He goes on to illustrate the geographical variation which may be found even within a restricted register:

> Ye shall vnderstonde that there ys a place in the bottome of a shyppe wherein ys gatheryd all the fylthe that cometh in to the shyppe...that place stynketh ryghte fowle, and yt ys called in some contre of thys londe, a thorrocke. Other calle yt an hamron, and some calle yt the bulcke of the shyppe.
>
> (Blunt 1873: 109)

This division is especially deep between north and south, where the divergence is largely due to the distinct foreign influences on Middle English (Kaiser 1937). In the north and north midlands, the Scandinavian settlements left their mark firmly impressed on the lexis of local dialect. Thus, as dialect speakers come into contact, variation occurs between the northern, often Scandinavian-derived, forms and those from Old English found in the south: *taken* ~ *nimen*, *ik* ~ *ich*, *though* ~ *theigh*, *carl* ~ *cherle*, *egg* ~ *ey*, *sterne* ~ *sterre*, *hundreth* ~ *hundred*. In some cases the northern and southern forms are geographically separated by an intermediary form, thus: *eight/d* occurs north of a line from Cumbria to the Wash, *eigth/þ*, south of a line from north

Shropshire to north Norfolk. The intervening belt is occupied by the intermediary form *eight* (McIntosh 1973).

5.3.14   The precise definition of a dialect form in Middle English may be somewhat difficult. To assign a term to a particular dialect, it should be recorded predominantly in Middle English texts from that dialect area, and if this distribution is supported by modern dialect distribution, so much the better. As far as northern dialect is concerned, derivation from Scandinavian sources would be corroboratory evidence. Thus word forms derived from Norse, such as *carl*, *ik* or *kirke*, may reasonably be considered northern dialect words. Common English words in northern dialectal spellings or with the morphemes of northern dialect grammar, such as *hame* for *home* or *gas* for *goth* 'goes', are better not regarded as northern for the purposes of lexical analysis. Northern meanings extended to common forms, such as *hope* with the sense 'suppose' rather than 'desire', *dwell* with the sense 'live' rather than 'stay' or *gate* (note the Scandinavian phonemic substitution) with the sense 'street, way', are a guarantee of the northern origin of the forms. Yet, whatever the dialectal origins of particular lexical items, their occurrence in a text is no warranty for the origins of the text. Quite apart from the dialectally mixed texts which arise through ordinary scribal copying, immigration into large centres can mean that geographical features are displaced. Gower preserves in his language features of East Anglian dialect learned during his years in Suffolk (Samuels & Smith 1981) and the clerk of the Tower of London ward in 1422 wrote among other northernisms the Scandinavian-derived form *gaytt* 'goat' (Chambers & Daunt 1931: 129).

5.3.15   In poetic texts this situation is further complicated by the fact that certain words achieved poetic status and were imitated outside their historically proper areas. The phonologically western form *bonkes* is used even in the eastern part of the country (Kaiser 1937), and certain northern texts, for example the *Kingis Quair*, the *Quare of Ielusy* and the *Scottish Troy Book*, consciously adopt diction of a Chaucerian or Lydgatian kind (McIntosh 1979). Statements about the dialect origins of Middle English lexis are therefore conditioned by the considerations discussed above, and further by the incomplete nature of the corpus upon which it is based. McIntosh (1973) states that at least 1,500 words in Middle English may be identified as having a northern dialectal provenance. Some of these – *barne* 'child', *unfrely* 'ugly', *greten* 'to weep', *ʒone* 'that' (demonstr.), *ner-honde* 'close by', *syte* 'grief', *belle* 'cauldron', *blishen* 'to look' – may be derived from Anglian forms. Others are of Scandinavian origin: *lende* 'to remain', *gar/geren* (causative), *till* and *intill*. Certain words seem to have withdrawn from southern usage during the Middle English period, becoming northern words by later Middle English: *belden* 'encourage', *ferly* 'marvel', *fliting* 'contention', *selkuth, inwith* (Heltveit 1964; McIntosh 1972, 1978).

Semantics

5.4   Meaning, use and structure

5.4.1   In its broader sense, the term 'semantics' presupposes a discussion not only of the meaning of words but also of sentences, including perhaps an account of such categories as negation, modals and even aspect. However, since this chapter is concerned primarily with lexis, for reasons of coherence as well as of space, such matter is not discussed, and the focus is upon lexical semantics, the meanings of words. Moreover, this treatment seeks to discuss the subject empirically and descriptively avoiding, as far as possible, unnecessary theoretical questions and hypothetical reconstructions. For the latter reason, nothing is said about the componential or distinctive-feature analysis of Middle English lexis.

5.4.2   The study of words in Middle English must have commenced when the language was still being spoken. But it began as the accidental effect of other more practical aims. It manifests itself first in the glossing of texts written in Latin or in Old English in the Worcester area in the early thirteenth century, but these are contemporary with the earliest bilingual word lists, the precursors of later dictionaries. In the mid-thirteenth century, instructional works on the French language, such as Walter of Bibbesworth's *Treatise*, contain parallel phrases in which English glosses French, thus: *un beu chivaler rous* 'a reed knyt'; *un destrer soor* 'a reed stede'; *l'eskou de gules* 'a reed cheeld'; *une lance rouge* 'a reed spere'; *vyn vermayl* 'reed wyn'. A fifteenth-century Anglo-Latin vocabulary has the following entries:

Hic gener	A sone-in-law
Hec amita	*soror patris*
Hec matertera	*soror matris*
Hic avus	A eld-fader
Hec avia	A eld-moder

(Wright 1857: 205)

Compiling entries such as these requires a degree of analysis of the system of the languages concerned so as to find forms of corresponding value in the two systems. In the above examples, where English uses a single colour adjective in various applications which provoke different adjectives in French, or in the English failure to make the Latin distinction between paternal and maternal aunt, discrepancies between the lexical structures of languages must have made themselves apparent, but this did not at first lead to study of the semantics of English for its own sake. For centuries translators had repeated the opinion of St Jerome that words in one language would not correspond exactly with the lexical inventory of another, and that therefore it may be necessary to paraphrase, but not until the later fourteenth century, and the translation of the Bible into English, did matters go beyond this. The author of the Prologue to the Later Version of the Wycliffite Bible warns of the dangers of translating words which may have more than one significance:

> But in translating of wordis equiuok, that is, that hath manie significaciouns vndur oo lettre, mai liȝtli be pereil... Ther-fore a translatour hath greet nede to studie wel the sentence, both bifore and aftir, and loke that suche equiuok wordis acorde with the sentence... this word *ex* signifieth sumtyme *of*, and sumtyme it signifieth *bi*... Manie such aduerbis, coniunccions, and preposiciouns ben set ofte oon for another, and at fre chois of autouris sumtyme; and now tho shulen be taken as it acordith best to the sentence.
>
> (Forshall & Madden 1850: I, 59)

About 1415, a Lollard author, producing a concordance to this very translation of the Bible with the purpose of aiding preachers in pursuit of suitable texts for sermons, found his task impeded by lexical variation and the orthographical instability characteristic of Middle English:

> In Englisch as in Latyn, ben wordis synonemus, þat is to seie, manie wordis betokenynge oo þing, as *kirke* & *churche*, *accesse* & *nyȝcomynge*, *clepe* & *calle*, *ȝyue* & *gyue*, *ȝift* & *gift*, *bigyle* & *disceyue* & *defraude*. And sumtyme suche wordis varyen or diuersen al oonly in oo lettre, as *flax* & *flex*, *invie* and *envie*, *lomb* & *lamb*. And oþirwhile haþ þat oon a lettre more þan þat oþir, as *epistle* & *pistle*.
>
> (Kuhn 1968: 271)

Any future user of this concordance is asked, if a word seems to have been omitted, to search for it under its synonyms, since the Bible text is acknowledged to vary from scribal copy to copy. Later the compiler turns his attention to:

wordis equiuouse, þat is, whanne oon word haþ manye significaciouns or bitokenyngis. As, þis word *kynde* bitokeneþ *nature*, and also such a man clepen we *kynde* which is a free-hertid man & þat gladly wole rewarde what þat men don for hym. An instrument wherwiþ we hewen, clepen we an *axe*, & I *axe* God mercy of synnes þat I haue don. Such wordis in þis concordaunce ben maad knowen bi sum word addid to hem, wherby it may be wist whanne þei ben taken in oon significacioun & whanne in a-noþir.

(Kuhn 1968: 272)

The essential linguistic insights implicit in these passages are three: firstly, that words are a composite of form and meaning; secondly, that the relation within this composite is an unstable one; and, thirdly, that context and colligations may be used to determine sense in any particular occurrence of a word. Yet, from the point of view of Modern English, some of the classifications used seem strange. The term 'synonymy' is used of pairs of words whose relationship with one another is quite disparate. *Accesse* and *nyʒcomynge*, for example, are quite distinct words, whereas *lamb* and *lomb* are mere dialectal variants, and *pistle* is simply an aphetic form of *epistle*.

The medieval commentator worked quite unanalytically, concentrating simply on the substance of his word forms and classing together any two diverse forms which possess similar senses as synonyms. Most modern readers of Middle English are likely to have a more sophisticated theoretical outlook, even if they are not aware of it, making certain abstractions from the individual occurrences of forms, classifying them into canonical forms with their variants and only then making any decision on synonymy. Similarly, in the case of *equiuok wordis*, the modern reader would seek to make a distinction between the case of *ex*, with its different senses, and the distinct meanings of *axe*. In the first, and in similar, cases we may feel that the two locative senses are more closely related to one another than the two separate 'words' spelt *axe*. This discrepancy between medieval observation and modern interpretation emphasises that, however unaware of it we may be, we bring our own interpretative hypotheses, based on our understanding of the structure of language, to the reading of Middle English. It is important to discuss some of these linguistic presuppositions before we continue.

5.4.3   Middle English exists as forms written or printed on the page. These 'word forms' are subject to variation, for example: *invie* or *envie*, *ȝift* or *gyft*. We class word forms together as representatives of a single word, but in this process we regard some kinds of formal variation as important, other kinds as irrelevant. Thus that variation which is predictable from a knowledge of the inflectional morphology of the language is ignored, so that *sing*, *sings* and *sang*, although quite different in form and substance, are classed together as representatives of the same word, whereas derivational variants like *body* and *embody* or *loose* and *unloose* would be considered different words. In the case of the former group, beneath the variation in word forms, we recognise an abstract lexical form, which could be represented as **sing**. This lexical form **sing** is realised in various contexts by the various word forms we have noted, and it occurs repeatedly with a single significance. The contextual significance of the lexical form, we shall call its 'sense'. The composite of lexical form and sense may be called a 'lexical unit' (Cruse 1986). The lexical unit will occur on many different occasions with the same sense, but some lexical forms, occurring in a large number of contexts, may vary in sense from context to context. If there seems to be a continuity in the sense range associated with a particular lexical form, it may be justifiable to posit a lexical item of a higher order, the lexeme. Thus the different senses of tree implicit in references to 'a rose tree', 'a palm tree', 'a family tree' and 'a tree diagram' may all be considered as representing distinct lexical units belonging to the same lexeme, TREE. In terms of traditional semantic analyses, different senses subsumed under a single lexeme were referred to as constituting a case of polysemy. When two word forms are identical, but they belong to different lexemes, the word homonymy would be used. Thus, in these terms, although *ex* may be classed as an example of polysemy, *axe*, with its two quite distinct significances, would be regarded as an example of homonymy. As we shall see, this distinction is less essential to synchronic linguistic processes than it is to etymology. Indeed, perhaps the compiler of our medieval concordance had a firmer grasp of semantic reality than our own inherited linguistic prejudices allow him.

5.4.4   Sense is to a considerable extent a *product* of context, as was clearly apparent to the Lollard writers quoted above. Outside verbal contexts, however, the meaning of a lexeme may be much less specific, consisting rather of a potential for occurrence which becomes realised only by use in context. This potential meaning attaching to lexemes out of context may be called 'denotation'. Considered from the point of view of the analysis of senses in context it might be assumed that the meaning of a lexeme is the range of senses which correspond to the inventory of lexical units from which it is composed. But this view would be too simply arithmetical. The denotational meaning is not simply an aggregate of the senses of a lexeme. When judged against the range of senses, the denotational meaning of a lexeme is vague, but seems to be adumbrated by certain meaning criteria (Waldron 1967). Such meaning criteria include those which are felt to be essential and others which are peripheral, or at least not activated until the required context, verbal or non-verbal, evokes them.

5.4.5   Lexicographical research in Middle English, lacking the information about the denotational meaning, use and associations of a lexeme which can be contributed by a native speaker, must work from the level of the particular, that is from the occurrence of word forms in texts, classing these together into lexical units and only then proceeding to identify lexemes and state their characteristic denotations. The final part of this process is fraught with practical difficulties, so that the majority of the discussion in this chapter will be concerned with the study of senses and their relationships.

5.4.6   Before going on to discuss the senses of Middle English words, however, it is necessary to make reference to a common distinction made between cognitive or propositional meaning, on the one hand, and expressive, connotative or associational meaning, on the other. Depending upon exactly which terms are used to frame this dichotomy, it asserts that lexemes possess two distinct kinds of meaning, one of which is central and primary, shared and therefore communicative, and the other, which is in some respects secondary, peripheral or individual, a less than certain inference from an encounter with the word form. The central meaning is cognitive, whereas the secondary meaning is emotive or expressive. Thus, the word form *cold* in Middle English cognitively means 'lacking heat', but may also have the expressive meanings 'fatal', 'dread' or 'threatening' (Salmon 1959). Similarly, the word *grene* has the simple colour significance, but may also carry powerful associations of youth and the concomitants of youth in medieval moral mythology, lust, vigour and folly. It is, however, unnecessary to regard the two kinds of meaning attributed to a lexeme as qualitatively different if we consider that the denotation of a lexeme is conditioned by its relationship to the senses-in-context of its constituent lexical units, and vice versa. So-called connotative meaning may exist as an association of a lexeme because it has been encountered, realised as a sense, in certain contexts: thus Chaucer's is the first recorded use of the lexical unit *grenehede* with the sense 'youthful folly', in effect lexicalising a 'connotative' meaning which is also a contextual sense of *grene*. The related connotation 'fresh vigour of plants' is similarly lexicalised about 1340 in the *Ayenbite of Inwit*. There is, therefore, a continuity between cognitive and associational meaning, the true difference between them being that which is currently regarded as criterial and that which is peripheral in the denotation of the lexeme. Indeed, studies of semantic change have shown how peripheral significances may be created by context, both verbal and situational, and progress to become central to the meaning of lexemes. The history of the senses of the words *bead* and *money* are good examples (Stern 1931; Ullmann 1967). This continuity between the periphery and the centre of denotational meaning raises a question concerning proper limits of the study of semantics, and this too deserves some initial discussion.

5.4.7 When discussing the problem of whether it is possible to distinguish a vocabulary characteristic of the Lollards, Anne Hudson (1981) identifies certain phrases commonly but not exclusively used in Lollard texts. In some cases neither the lexical forms themselves nor even their contextual senses can be identified with any confidence as deviating from any norm of Middle English usage. Yet in the case of the use of the phrase *poor prest* and that of the phrase *bishops and prelatis*, Hudson feels that there is some special significance. This is dependent upon both the frequency of the use of these phrases and the awareness of an approving or a derogatory attitude implicit in the co-text. Thus, whereas *poor prest* and *bishops* attract approval, the word *prelatis* seems to imply the author's distaste. Is this distaste part of the meaning of *prelatis*? If so, is it general in Middle English or restricted to Lollard authors? Clearly, if the lexeme does in fact carry such associations, they are never realised as a sense of the word in the way that *grenehede* came to mean 'folly'. Rather a derogatory association is part of the use of the word by people of a certain outlook. Is that association, therefore, to be regarded as part of the semantics of *prelatis*? Consider a second example: commonly in Middle English texts, from at least as early as the early thirteenth-century *Vices and Virtues* until the fifteenth-century Rolls of Parliament, the plural demonstrative, *these*, is used exophorically to refer to groups of people or things which are assumed to be familiar, but which have not previously been mentioned in the discourse: *as thise clerkes seyen, as don these louyeres alle, these Merchantys Ytaliens*. In many contexts the implied familiarity seems also to imply contempt; yet in others this is not so. It may be argued therefore that the semantics of *these* in Middle English – and probably in Modern English too – includes a contemptuous sense, as has been argued for Jacobean *your* (Wales 1985).

5.4.8　　An alternative to locating such meaning in the semantics of a word is to introduce a distinct level of meaning into the analysis, that of pragmatics, to deal with such particularities of the use of lexical units. Once again, however, it is important not to insist on an impenetrable barrier between that meaning which belongs to semantics and that which is proper to pragmatics. The use of language items in context (which is the concern of pragmatics) feeds associations with certain characteristic contexts back into the denotational meaning of the lexeme. Thus, in actuality, we may assume a cline from the individual association, through the institutionalised and widely recognised association, to the cognitive meaning, and also from the pragmatic rule to the widely accepted denotation.

For convenience in analysis and discussion, however, it is useful to make a distinction by which the senses of lexical units may be considered to constitute the study of semantics. Information about the associations of words which are not themselves individually realised as contextual senses, together with a great deal of encyclopedic knowledge, and that awareness of the appropriate circumstances of use which constitutes the stylistic skill of a competent language user, may best be considered to fall within the domain of pragmatics (Bloomfield 1933: 141). Pragmatics is crucial to the study of literary language, historical stylistics and the sensitive reading of literature. It is also important to the dynamism of language; thus pragmatic concerns will arise repeatedly in this chapter, but, because the identification of pragmatics as a distinct field of study in Middle English has scarcely begun (Schroeder 1983; Sell 1985a, 1985b), there is no extended discussion of this topic as a subject in its own right.

5.4.9　　Some discussion of the borderline between semantic and pragmatic meaning is, however, justified. This may be approached initially through the example of the lexeme GUERDOUN in the works of

Chaucer. *MED* gives two senses: (a) reward, recompense, remuneration; (b) punishment, retribution, retaliation. These may be exemplified by the following quotations:

(1) At after-soper fille they in tretee
What somme sholde this maistres gerdoun be
To remoeuen alle the rokkes of Britayne.

(*CT* 6: 511–13 [V.1219–21])

(2) This is the mede of lovynge and guerdoun
That Medea receyved of Jasoun
Ryght for hire trouthe and for hire kyndenesse.

(*LGW* 1662–4)

Despite the fact that *mede* is co-ordinate with *guerdoun* in quotation 2, neither *MED* nor *OED* lists sense (b) as one of the senses of MEDE. It is clear that senses (a) and (b) are closely related in the criterion of repayment, but they are directly opposed in respect of the desirability of the kind of repayment referred to: in extract 1 a handsome reward is contemplated; in 2 desertion is the recompense for constancy. This opposition is explicitly stated in other Chaucerian contexts:

(3) good and yvel, and peyne and medes, ben contrarie

(*Bo.* IV, p. 3, 60)

(4) that is to seyn that shrewes ben punysschid or elles that good folk ben igerdoned.

(*Bo.* V, p. 3, 166)

Is it justifiable for *MED* to list sense (b) as a sense of the lexeme GUERDOUN, or for that matter for *OED* to list 'recompense or retribution for evil-doing; requital, punishment' as a sense of REWARD? Both groups of lexicographers are citing interpretations of occurrences of the words in context, but since both omit a similar interpretation for MEDE, they have at least proceeded inconsistently. It may indeed be better to dispense with this supposed opposition within the denotational meaning of the lexemes GUERDOUN, MEDE and REWARD, and instead consider sense (b) to be an example of pragmatic meaning. These words are frequently used by Middle English authors in a way in which their context gives them an interpretation diametrically opposed to their usual sense – in short, they are often used ironically.

5.4.10 The tendency to use words with strong evaluative associations to imply meanings somehow in conflict with their ordinary sense is a common characteristic of linguistic behaviour, and was as familiar a feature in Middle English as it is today. Perception of such usage in Early Middle English texts is less easy than in the time of Chaucer. However, Chaucer's language furnishes a wealth of lexical units used deviantly and ironically. Describing the Summoner, he says:

> He was a gentil harlot and a kynde,
> A bettre felawe sholde men noght fynde.
> He wolde suffre for a quart of wyn
> A good felawe to haue his concubyn
> A twelf monthe and excusen hym at the fulle.

> (*CT* 1: 649–53 [I.647–51])

The usual senses of *gentil* and *kynde* are here compromised by application to *harlot*, a word which more than once in the fifteenth century provoked a fine for insulting language in polite company (see 5.3.12). *Kynde*, we are told by the compiler of the Lollard concordance, is the adjective we should apply to 'a man...which is a free-hertid man & þat gladly wole rewarde what þat men don for hym' (see 5.4.2). If this is really the sense of *kynde*, is it misused of the Summoner? He certainly rewards the gift of a couple of pints most generously. The adjective *gentil*, when applied to persons, ordinarily means 'noble' or 'exhibiting the characteristics proper to nobility'. But it is also frequently used simply as an approbatory epithet. This approbatory use is presumably what we find here. Thus, in terms of the definable senses of the lexemes, neither *kynde* nor *gentil* is here used deviantly. What is strange about their occurrence is that the approbatory use of *gentil* is bestowed upon a scoundrel, and the affability indicated by *kynde* is associated with corruption. Irony arises here from awareness of behavioural values which would not condone the Summoner's conduct. It is not a part of the semantics of the words, but arises from recognition of their inappropriateness to such a context.

5.4.11   The use of words in inappropriate contexts is a fertile source of verbal irony in the *Canterbury Tales*. At the beginning of the Shipman's fabliau tale, a monk, 'a fair man and a boold', about thirty years old, is introduced in the company of a merchant's errant wife. The narrative recommences with the words 'This yonge monk...' (*CT* 10: 28 [VII.28]). Yet, in medieval England, thirty would have been considered the age of full maturity. Thus, because there is a discrepancy between linguistic usage and presupposition, the reader is forced to seek a resolution through the associations of vigour and lust which attach to the word YONG in Middle English usage.

The word *pitously* in Chaucer's usage means (a) 'with pity; compassionately; mercifully'; (b) 'in a manner arousing or deserving of pity, pitiably'; (c) 'devoutly, reverently, righteously'. Sense (c) is evidently distinct from senses (a) and (b), which, indeed, are simply a subjective and objective application of the same sense: that is, an individual feels pity on the one hand, or an external object is such as to arouse pity on the other – pitying or pitiable. In the Wife of Bath's Prologue we encounter the following account of her dealings with her old husbands:

> As help me god I laughe whan I thynke
> How pitously a nyght I made hem swynke,
> And by my fey I tolde of it no stoor.

(*CT* 2: 201–3 [III.201–3])

Clearly the sense here must be the objective one, sense (b). The sentence is perfectly well formed, yet the context makes the use of *pitously* inappropriate, for the objective sense (b) should surely be reciprocally related to the subjective sense (a). However, the agent causing the pitiable condition is represented as laughing, and she 'tolde of it no stoor'. The context once again contradicts the implications of the sense relations, so that we are forced to seek into our knowledge of human behaviour beyond the bounds of semantics for an explanation of the situation described, which is explicable in terms of unusual lack of sympathy.

Alongside this scene, we may set another marital reminiscence of the Wife:

> I wol perseuere, I nam nat precius:
> In wifhode wol I vse myn instrument
> As frely as my makere hath it sent.
> If I be daungerous, god yeue me sorwe.
> Myn housbonde shal it han bothe eue and morwe.

(*CT* 2: 148–52 [III.148–52])

In this passage, the word at issue is *daungerous*. The three senses found in Chaucer's writings according to *MED* are (1) 'domineering, overbearing'; (2a) 'unapproachable, aloof, haughty, reserved'; (2b) 'hard to please, fastidious'; (3) 'niggardly'. The sense in the above passage must be either (2a) or (3), and the implied opposition with *frely* suggests the latter. The lexeme DAUNGER is, however, frequently used in contexts of courtly love (Barron 1965), where sense (2a) is the one required, and this is indeed hypostatised as the personification Daunger in the courtly love theory of the *Romaunt of the Rose*. This powerful association of DAUNGER with the decorum of courtly love therefore evokes sense (2a) despite the necessary contextual reading in terms of sense (3). Semantic analysis is once more complicated by pragmatic knowledge, and we are forced to conclude that either Chaucer has here made an incompetent choice of lexical unit or, alternatively and more persuasively, that his choice was deliberate and added to the ironic complexity of his statement by exploiting the discrepancy between pragmatic and semantic aspects of meaning.

There is space only for one further illustration of the literary exploitation of the discrepancies between semantic and pragmatic meaning. In Chaucer's Reeve's Tale occur the words:

> ... this millere stal bothe mele and corn
> An hondred tyme moore than biforn,
> For therbiforn he stal but curteisly,
> But now he was a theef outrageously.

(CT 1: 3987–90 [I.3995–8])

The senses of *curteisly* listed in *MED* are (a) 'in a courtly manner; courteously, politely'; (b) 'kindly, graciously; benevolently, mercifully; generously'; (c) 'respectfully, deferentially, meekly'; (d) 'decently [used ironically]'. The last of these, sense (d), is exemplified only by the above passage; evidently the lexicographers felt it necessary to add a new sense to the spectrum to account for this one occurrence, although they specify it as an ironic use. The gloss 'decently' adequately captures the contextual meaning, but would be more precise if the implied opposition with the sense of *outrageously* could have been given more prominence. If *curteisly* means 'decently', then the outrage in *outrageously* is one of excess, for this is the commonest meaning of that word. Consequently, the opposition with *curteisly* implies that the earlier decency was manifested in moderation, so that *curteisly* should probably be understood in the more specific contextual sense of 'moderately'. A word with precisely this sense, *mesurably*, existed and was indeed associated with the ideals of courtly behaviour, but Chaucer preferred the word *curteisly*, used in an uncharacteristic sense, and probably in an unparalleled colligation, no doubt for the comic appropriateness which those familiar with the characteristic *use* as well as the senses of the words involved would at once recognise. The word *curteisly* as well as the sense 'moderately', suggested by opposition with 'excessively', had the advantage of association with a whole panoply of ideals of social behaviour, of decorum, propriety, decency – ideals which, elsewhere, Chaucer shows to be the aspirations of the miller and his wife. Once more, knowledge of the uses of words, of their consequent associations, contributes complex meaning beyond that apparent from the immediate sense of the lexical units involved.

This discussion illustrates a number of important points for lexical meaning in Middle English. Firstly, it is possible, and indeed desirable for the purposes of clear illustration, to draw a distinction between semantic and pragmatic meaning. Secondly, and equally importantly, simultaneous awareness of both kinds of meaning is necessary for the competent interpretation of medieval discourse; indeed, although the distinction is a descriptive convenience, in the absence of guidance from native speakers, there is no natural or certain boundary between the two kinds of meaning in the everyday use of language. Associational meanings may be present alongside a particular contextual sense at any occurrence of a lexical unit, and may arise from awareness of the frequent situational conditions of use of a lexical unit or from consciousness of secondary senses within the sense spectrum of the lexeme to which the lexical unit belongs. Such factors must have been as important to the daily communication of medieval Englishmen as they are in their more urbane literature. Moreover, as we shall see, the interpenetration of pragmatic meaning in the form of knowledge of situations of use, and the sense spectra of lexemes, may be a crucial prerequisite of semantic change.

5.4.12   In the preceding discussion of the borderline between pragmatic and semantic aspects of meaning, the point has implicitly been made that lexical units do not exist in splendid isolation from one another. Just as words may be categorised by details of their use and grouped by style and register, so also, within the more narrowly limited sphere of semantics which we have adopted for this discussion, categories and relationships exist. The simplest and most familiar sense relationship, already mentioned by the compiler of the Lollard concordance, is that of sameness of meaning, synonymy. Although synonymy is the most familiar of the relations existing between the meanings of words, it must be recognised that it is, to be more precise, a relationship of sense; complete denotational sameness is rare, and rarer still is equivalence in terms of both semantic and pragmatic meaning.

5.4.13   A rough test for synonymy when dealing with the language of
earlier texts is occurrence in identical contexts. It is not always easy to
find occurrences of two words in identical contexts in Middle English,
but there are numerous examples where contexts are very similar, for
example:

(5)   Leon rorynge and bere hongry been like to the crueel lordshipes in
      withholdynge or abreggynge of the shepe or the hyre or the wages
      of seruauntz.

$\hfill$ (*CT* 12: 568 [X.568])

(6)   Of coucitise comen thise harde lordshipes thurgh whiche men been
      distreyned by taylages, custumes and cariages moore than hir
      duetee or resoun is.

$\hfill$ (*CT* 12: 752 [X.752])

(7)   'Certes,' quod dame Prudence, 'this were a cruel sentence and
      muchel ageyn reson.

$\hfill$ (*CT* 10: 1836 [VII.1836])

(8)   'Youre prynces erren as youre nobleye dooth,'
      Quod tho Cecile, 'and with a wood sentence
      Ye make vs gilty, and it is nat sooth.

$\hfill$ (*CT* 7: 449–51 [VIII.449–51])

In passages (5) and (6) it is apparent that the lexical units *cruel* and *hard*
have a very similar sense; in (7) and (8) *cruel* seems to have the same
sense as *wood*. Can we go further and say that the senses in (5)–(8) are the
same, so that *cruel*, *hard* and *wood* are synonymous? What then of *shepe*,
hyre and *wages* in passage (5)? It would be possible to make short lists of
lexemes which in Middle English share much of their sense spectra:

stibourn	hyre	hals	maistresse	sweven	pley
sturdy	shepe	swire	lemman	dreme	game
stout	guerdoun	necke	lotebie	mettynge	disport
strong	mede	throte	lady	avisioun	laik
stif	wages		wenche		
stern					
stoor					

The group beginning with *stibourn* is interesting as an apparently
phonaesthetic grouping, where the initial /st/ seems to be associated
with an attitude of hostility and intractability. Yet, although the words
in each column have very similar senses, readers familiar with Middle
English texts will be reluctant to allow that they are all synonyms. They
may differ according to social status (*hyre* and *guerdoun*), geographical

distribution (*hals* and *swire*), derogatory or approbatory associations (*lemman* and *lady*) or technical as opposed to general use (*avisioun* and *sweven*). Indeed, the tendency for synonyms to become differentiated has repeatedly been the subject of comment by semanticists (Bréal 1964; Ullmann 1967; Palmer 1981).

Thus, although *cruel, hard* and *wood* may appear synonymous because all refer to the oppressive behaviour of a tyrannous lord, they are not pragmatically equivalent. It has been shown that in translated works *wood* frequently renders Latin *saevus* whereas *cruel* corresponds to *crudelis*. In Latin technical writings, *saevitia* is associated with tyrannical madness, whereas *crudelitas* may indicate strict justice. Something of this distinction seems to have been transferred into Chaucer's English (Burnley 1979). But is this merely a matter of the kind of encyclopedic knowledge which should be excluded from the proper field of semantics? The question cannot be answered with certainty, but it may be significant that in passage (7) the qualifier *muchel ageyn reson* is added to *cruel*. The word *wood* does not receive such qualification, perhaps because irrationality is felt to be an important criterion in the meaning of the lexeme.

Let us consider two further examples of contextual synonymy:

(9) ... thow shalt come into a certeyn place,
     There as thow mayst thiself hire preye of grace.

(Troilus II.1364–5)

(10) This Diomede al fresshly newe ayeyn
      Gan pressen on, and faste hire mercy preye.

(Troilus V.1010–11)

(11) And hym of lordshipe and of mercy preyde.
      And he hem graunteth grace.

(CT 1: 1829–30 [I.1827–8])

It is clear that in passages (9) and (10) *grace* and *mercy* are synonymous; this is confirmed in a different situation in passage (11). In other contexts, of course, the lexeme GRACE may be synonymous with *destine*, and the lexeme MERCY with *pitee*. Moreover PITEE and MERCY may, like WOOD and CRUEL, be separable according to the criteria of, respectively, irrational and rational impulses. These lexemes may be synonymous at the level of individual senses, although their denotational meanings are not identical. But compare MERCY and GRACE in their shared sense of the 'erotic favour of a lady' with a third such term:

(12) Lemman, thy grace, and, swete bryd, thyn oore.

(CT 1: 3718 [I.3726])

Although the sense of the word *oore* is here cognitively equivalent to that just discussed, this word's meaning would have felt quite different to a Chaucerian audience, for it has been shown how this is the unique use in Chaucer of a word from an unaccustomedly popular stylistic register, exploited by Chaucer for satirical effect (Donaldson 1951). Semantically equivalent to MERCY and GRACE it may be, but it is pragmatically quite distinct.

Concentrating upon the lexeme CURTEISIE in Chaucer's language, we may examine this matter of sense relations further. Within the specific situational context of the judgement of wrongdoers, CURTEISIE is used to imply sympathetic and merciful sentences:

(13) yow moste deme moore curteisly; this is to seyn, ye moste yeue moore esy sentences and iugementz.

(CT 10: 1855–6 [VII.1855–6])

This sense we shall call 'merciful'. Chaucer's works reveal other examples of this sense, but realised by other lexical units, thus:

(14) oure swete lord Iesu Crist hath sparid vs so *debonairly* in oure folies that if he ne hadde pitee of mannes soule a sory song we myghten alle synge.

(CT 12: 315 [X.315])

(15) For, syth no cause of deth lyeth in this caas,
Yow oghte to ben the lyghter *merciable*.

(LGW F 409–10)

Thus we have evidence that with regard to the sense 'merciful', *curteisie* is synonymous with DEBONAIR and MERCY. This synonymy does not, of course, extend to other senses which may be realised by the lexical form *curteis*; we have seen, for example, that the latter, when realised as an adverb, can have the sense 'moderately'. CURTEISIE is, however, realised in a context which demonstrates a third sense, that of 'kindliness', and here it becomes synonymous with the lexical unit *kyndenesse*:

(16) But nathelees I wol of hym assaye
At certeyn dayes yeer by yeer to paye,
And thonke hym of his grete curteisye.

(CT 6: 851–3 [V.1567–9])

(17) Seend me namoore vnto noon hethenesse,
But thonke my lord heere of his kyndenesse.

(CT 3: 1112–13 [II.1112–13])

Thus we have two distinct senses of CURTEISIE, and the strong suggestion of a third. The situation may be represented diagrammatically as follows:

		CURTEISIE	
senses	'merciful'	'moderate(ly)'	'kind'
lexical units	*curteis*	*curteisly*	*curteisie*
	merciable	*mesurably*	*kyndenesse*
	debonair		

The senses 'merciful' and 'kind' are realised respectively by the forms *curteis*, *merciable* and *debonair*, on the one hand, and by *curteis* and *kyndenesse*, on the other. The lexical forms *curteisly* and *mesurably* with the sense 'moderate(ly)' are deduced from Chaucer's usage and that of wider Middle English sources.

5.4.14   A structure such as that above, in which one lexical unit is placed superordinate to others which are, among themselves, incompatible in sense, is termed a hyponymic structure. CURTEISIE is the superordinate term and the other lexical units are co-hyponyms. It is important, however, to realise that hyponymy is a sense structure operating between lexical units, with their distinct senses, rather than between lexemes, which may have multiple significance, and cannot therefore be subsumed under a single superordinate.

Turning now to sense opposition, we shall find that in the situation of judgement a clear opposition to the sense 'merciful' is demonstrated in scenes where a judge exacts unsympathetic and harsh penalties. This sense, we shall call 'merciless':

(18)   I resceyve peyne of fals felonye for guerdoun of verrai vertue. And what opene confessioun of felonye hadde evere juges so accordaunt in cruelte...that either errour of mannys wit, or elles condicion of fortune...ne enclynede some juge to have pite or compassioun?

(*Bo.* I p. 4 226–34)

(19)   Ther shal the stierne and wrothe iuge sitte aboue, and vnder hym the horrible pit of helle open to destroye hym that moot biknowen hise synnes.

(*CT* 12: 170 [X.170])

(20)   'Youre prynces erren as youre nobleye dooth,'
Quod tho Cecile, 'and with a wood sentence
Ye make vs gilty, and it is nat sooth.

(*CT* 7: 449–51 [VIII.449–51])

The lexical units *stern*, *cruel* and *wood* are used in contexts which strongly suggest a sense opposition to those lexical units which realise the sense 'merciful'. Taking CRUEL as the lexeme for further investigation, we again discover a hyponymic structure, this time of more extended hierarchical form:

	CRUEL			
	CRUEL 1		CRUEL 2	
sense	'merciless' (just)	'merciless' (unjust)	'oppressive tyranny'	'repressive tyranny'
lexical forms	cruel stern	cruel wood irous tiraunt	cruel wood irous felonous	cruel hard dangerous

Here it is possible to make a distinction between mercilessness justified by the crime of the prisoner, and mercilessness without justification, motivated by tyranny. Such tyranny is represented by senses outside the judicial situation: 'oppressive tyranny' covers various acts of cruelty and injustice on the part of a feudal lord; 'repressive tyranny' means his withholding of various rights. The lexeme CRUEL is used to realise all four senses, but each one is realised also by the lexical forms listed beneath each sense. It is apparent that CRUEL will be opposed in sense to CURTEISIE within the particular situation of judgement, and that as a consequence the hyponyms *merciable* and *debonair*, on the one hand, and *stern, wood, irous* and *tiraunt*, on the other, enter this opposition.

The manner in which hyponymy is represented in the diagrams illustrates a further important feature about this structure. This is that it may be used to represent not only the relations of different lexical forms to one another, but also that of related lexical units belonging to the same lexeme. Since hyponymy is a sense relationship, the lexical units *cruel*, with their distinct senses, are just as much co-hyponyms of the lexeme CRUEL as the lexical units *wood* or *hard*. Hyponymy thus presents a model of the relationship of individual senses to the denotational meaning of the lexeme. As mentioned above (5.4.4), it is certainly misleading to think of this more generalised level of meaning as consisting of an inventory of discrete senses, and it would be better to regard it rather as a meaning potential which both makes available and places restrictions on the senses which can be realised in context. The denotation of a lexeme, therefore, is not a precisely definable concept; nevertheless, even out of context, certain criteria of meaning are likely to be more prominent than others. These may be so either from the frequency of occurrence of particular senses, or from some other cause of psychological salience. Indeed, the details of the relation between mental actuality and the senses of lexical units are beyond the scope of this discussion, but the matter is worthy of some discussion, since it may help to explain a peculiarity of the data examined above.

This data, constructed from a limited number of occurrences of lexical units, has illustrated hyponymic sense structures whose members seem to be semantically opposed. To those familiar with Middle English literature, the opposition may have seemed strange. Asked for an antonym of *cruel*, most such readers would no doubt suggest *pitous* rather than *curteis*. Similarly, they would be likely to suggest *vylayn* as the antonym of *curteis*. A search of contexts to validate these latter oppositions would not be in vain, although, as it happens, Chaucer's language is not sufficiently rich in parallel contextual frames to illustrate these oppositions fully. Nevertheless, it is true that the hyponymic sense structures just demonstrated probably do not represent the habitual associative structure of the lexemes concerned in Middle English. Other senses were more salient and ensured a different associative structure: PITEE: CRUELTE and CURTEISIE: VYLAYNYE. To reconstruct this, we should have needed to possess a perspective over the occurrences and senses of many more lexemes. This would then have demonstrated to us that the particular structure represented by the CURTEISIE hyponymy arises as the artefact of our decision to choose that particular lexeme as the starting point of our investigation.

5.4.15   The general direction of the discussion of the semantic structure of Chaucer's Middle English has been from the simple concept of synonymy between two lexical units towards greater complexity in sense relations. At the close of the last paragraph it was stated that the analysis of sense relations requires to be verified by the examination of many contextual occurrences and by comparison between more than two lexemes at a time. Implicit in this is the assumption that semantic structure extends beyond the small systems examined so far, so that whole groups of lexemes may turn out to be semantically related.

This claim, that the items which make up the lexis of a language are related on a larger scale, has been repeatedly made, but most influentially by Jost Trier, who also initiated the application of this hypothesis to the study of medieval languages by his account of intellectual terminology in Old High German (Trier 1931). Trier's contention was that the entire lexis of a language consisted of lexemes whose denotations were inter-related in such a way that the extent of one was defined and delimited by the extent of those adjacent to it in the structure. Trier's use of the descriptive imagery of the 'field' and the 'mosaic' to explain his conception has led to much valid criticism of it. The picture of a mosaic, with its individual and distinct *tesserae* cemented side by side, is a particularly unfortunate one to represent the complexity, the vagueness and the dynamism of the lexicon. Denotational meanings, unlike pieces of tile, are often not easily distinguishable from one another: they are vague; they may seem to overlap or to leave gaps. Moreover the two-dimensionality of a mosaic is especially unsuited to represent the multiplicity of axes of meaning in the lexis. More recent writers on semantic-field theory have, however, answered many of these ob-jections, modifying their conceptions so that current semantic-field theory differs considerably from that of earlier versions, reflecting better the findings of empirical research (Weisgerber 1953; Ducháček 1960; Geckeler 1971).

Field research into Middle English commenced with a study of morally evaluative terminology in the vocabulary of Chaucer (Hér-aucourt 1939) and has more recently developed into studies based closely upon analysis of the senses of words in context, usually within precisely defined areas, which acknowledge the importance of structural relations within their chosen areas, but owe no special homage to the simplistic assumptions of the earlier Trier theory. A study of the lexical field of *boy/girl – servant – child* finds that the forms *boy* and *servant* (borrowed from French) and *girl* (raised from lower-class usage) were connected with alterations in sense, or the complete loss of *knight, knape, knave* and *wenche* during the course of the Middle English period (Diensberg 1985). The word *boy* entered the language meaning 'servant'. A feminine equivalent, *boiesse* briefly existed but was discouraged by the existence of *maiden, wenche* and *girl*, used to mean 'female servant'. *Boy*, however, was more readily adopted, first of all probably in lower-class usage, where it contrasted with upper-class *page, garsoun* and *bacheler*. The word *knight*, which earlier had meant 'boy, servant, retainer', developed military significance early, and the polysemy of *knave*, 'male child', 'servant' or 'common peasant' encouraged its replacement in the first two senses by *boy*. The forms *lad* and *lass* were restricted to northern Middle English. *Maiden* split into *maid* and *maiden*, and the senses were distributed between the two forms, 'servant girl' and 'unmarried girl' respectively.

A study of the words for 'play' in Middle English is openly critical of Trier's early conception of the semantic field, finding in its two-dimensionality sufficient cause for its rejection (Aertsen 1987). Once again, in this study, the Saussurean unities of time and place are rejected in favour of an approach which incorporates dialectal and stylistic variation and their role in sense development. A detailed analysis of the senses of the words *game*, *pley*, *leik* and *disport* reveals extensive synonymy but differentiation by pragmatic restrictions. Thus the loanwords *leik* and *disport* are differentiated by dialectal and sociolectal appropriateness: the former is a northern dialect word, the latter a word of upper-class speech.

The necessity of multidimensionality in modelling lexical meanings is clearly evident in studies which transgress the limits of synchrony and which incorporate words from different linguistic systems; but it may also be necessary even when dealing with much more narrowly restricted semantic data. Consider, for example, the field of colour terms in Middle English. For this purpose, in order to eliminate as far as possible variation according to chronological development, class and dialect, we may concentrate on the works of a single author.

5.4.16   In Chaucer's writings there are at least thirty-three lexemes which have colour denotation. Many occur in both substantival and adjectival use, and this presents an immediate problem in interpreting contexts like 'Hir hosen weeren of fyn scarlet reed' (*CT* 1: 458 [I.456]) or 'A long surcote of pers vpon he haade' (*CT* 1: 619 [I.617]). The problem arises from the fact that both *scarlet* and *pers*, and indeed many other terms with colour denotation, have etymological origins as designations of materials of a characteristic colour. It may not therefore be obvious whether reference is being made to colour or material. When Chaucer refers to the complexion of Sir Thopas with the words 'His rode is lyk scarlet in grayn' (*CT* 10: 727 [VII.1917]) the words *in grayn* betray the fact that he is referring to the fast-died red cloth from which the name of the colour adjective is derived. The decision on which word forms are truly colour words is not obvious. If we include all words occurring in such expressions as *hewed lyk* N or *of coloure of* N, the range of colour terms would be greatly increased; however, if we exclude all terms in Chaucer's work with a material denotation alongside a colour one, the number of colour terms would be reduced by about half. Substantival occurrence is no guide to the distinction between colour and material denotation, as examples like *a cote of grene of cloth of Gaunt* (*Rose* 573–4) illustrate.

Colour adjectives are often applied conventionally to objects which would not represent their normal denotation. This is as apparent in medieval English as in modern, and leads to oppositions between colour adjectives which are quite at odds with the assumption that colour denotation is simply a graduated spectrum. We have encountered this peculiarity of the restricted application of colour adjectives in Walter of Bibbesworth's presentation of French equivalents of red (5.4.2), and in Chaucer too there are conventional applications: thus *red* is contrasted with *whit* as descriptions of wine. This is a familiar contrast today, but the opposition between *blak* and *whit* explained as brown bread and milk (*Hir bord was serued moost with whit and blak,/ Milk and broun breed*) in the Nun's Priest's Tale (10: 2815–16 [VII.4033–4]) needs further interpretation. Here, in fact, we are probably dealing with a conscious metonymy by which the frugal diet of the old widow in whose farmyard the action of the tale takes place, is emphasised by the use of two words within the field of colour terms, whose collocation seems already to have implied a certain simplicity or severity when placed in implicit contrast to more gaudy hues. Indeed, this opposition is explicit in Usk's *Testament of Love*, where he contrasts the telling of a tale in a simple style – like drawing in chalk and charcoal – with the use of rhetorical skills called 'colours'. Clearly a complex opposition of this kind does not derive from the relation between the potential sense range of the lexemes involved and a single verbal context. It belongs to that large body of pragmatic meaning attached to many lexemes in Middle just as in Modern English.

Encyclopedic and cultural information is required to explain the evaluative opposition between *gold* and *blak*, in particular in reference to the letter forms in books, or the opposition between *whit* and *broun* when representing respectively the beauty or ugliness of complexion. The associations of the word GRENE with youth, vigour, springtime and folly are to some extent opposed by the associations of the word HOOR. In Old English the latter had been applicable to a wide range of grey or whitish objects from rocks to wolves, as well as to the hair of old men. In Middle English, however, it became almost restricted to this last, occurring commonly elsewhere only in fixed phrases such as *hoor-frost* and the poetic *holtes hor*. The association of the word with age became so strong that in some contexts it may be best interpreted as having the sense 'aged'. Thus a sense opposition emerges between GRENE and HOOR modelled upon that between youth and lustiness and age and gravity. Compare the following:

(21) I wol with lusty herte fressh and grene
    Seye yow a song to glade yow I wene.

(CT 8: 1173–4 [IV.1173–4])

(22) But she was neither yong ne hoor,
    Ne high ne lowe, ne fat ne lene,
    But best as it were in a mene.

(Rose 3196–8)

The sense of *grene* in (21) is not easy to define precisely, but 'youthful' with its appropriate associations seems a reasonable interpretation. In passage (22) the sense of *hoor* is undeniably 'old'. Chaucer was alive to this implicit opposition and exploits it by word play with the colour and age senses of these lexemes:

(23) I feele me nowher hoor but on myn heed.
    Myn herte and alle my lymes been as grene
    As laurer thurgh the yeer is for to sene.

(CT 5: 220–2 [IV.1464–6])

This passage is nonsense unless the words in question are given the two senses which we have seen lie within their sense range. There could scarcely be a clearer example than this of the way in which pragmatic meaning contributes to new senses and sense relations.

More extensive, even if less well delineated, oppositions are associated with colour changes in the face to accompany states of health or emotional changes. The lexemes RED, RODY and SANGWYN are associated with good health and vigour; WAN, PALE, and GRENE are associated with the opposite. Shifts of colour from an unspecified norm, caused by shame or embarrassment, are to *red* and *rosy*. Fear, sorrow and anger cause one to turn *pale* or *grene*.

Something of the symbolism of colours has already been mentioned in relation to the significance of GRENE, but it may be added that, as the symbol of inconstancy, GRENE is opposed to BLEW, the symbol of fidelity. Similarly, RED, which may symbolise both military force and harsh justice, is opposed to WHIT, the colour of mercy and peace. Thus, the colour lexicon of Chaucer's English is very much more complex than assumptions of simple colour denotation would lead us to believe. Plainly, the two-dimensional mosaic is hopelessly inadequate as an image if we wish to incorporate pragmatic meaning into our account of semantic structure. It may be objected, however, despite the contrary examples of *grene* and *hoor*, that colour denotation is a distinct category from this encyclopedic and pragmatic meaning, and that the semantic field exists within colour denotation alone. We may investigate this objection.

5.4.17 The lexemes used for colour denotation by Chaucer are the following; they may be divided into basic colour terms (in small capitals) and their hyponyms (in parentheses): BLAK, RED (rosen, rosy, rody, sangwyn, scarlet, purpre), GRENE, WHIT (snowisshe), YELOW (citryn, saffroun), BLEW (asure, inde, pers, waget), GRAY (grys, hoor), BROUN. A number of other colour words are difficult to locate within this structure: *gold, gilte, sonnysshe, silver, pale, asshen, wan, bloo, dun, falwe*.

With a few exceptions, the denotation of basic colour terms seems to be comparable to that of the Modern English counterparts. RED, which is used of coral, rubies and blood, is also used of beard, hair, the sun and roses as in Modern English, but it is applied too to gold, where it alternates with YELLOW perhaps originally to distinguish alloys but too freely to normally imply such technical usage. Elsewhere in Middle English, RED is applied to ripe oranges, pomegranates and wheat. It may be, therefore, that the lexeme had a somewhat broader range of application than currently. BLAK is used of coal, pitch and a raven's feather, just as it might be today, but also refers to the colour of sunburnt skin, and even the face flushed with blood. BROUN, too, has the former application, but more surprisingly, like BLAK, can be applied to mourning clothes. There is some degree of synonymy between BLAK and BROUN which is uncharacteristic of Modern English.

The probable explanation of this synonymy lies in the fact that colour denotations may not be simple concepts. Indeed, sporadic distinctions are made between the categories of hue, saturation and luminosity in describing colour sensations. The adjective *deep* is applied to colour words to indicate full saturation. *Pale* suggests desaturation, but can also be used to refer to levels of ambient light, or more commonly to light radiated from some source (e.g. *pale moon*). In such uses it is opposed to *bright* and synonymous with *dim*. Modern English *black* is used both of lack of hue, and also of low lighting levels, and *dark* is used for this latter sense, but also to qualify hues, indicating lack of luminosity. Thus, the Modern English system may represent conceptual distinctions such as hue, desaturation of hue and brightness of light. Of the words used for such purposes, only *black* would normally be considered a colour term. In Middle English, however, the lexical representation of these distinctions also existed but was rather differently distributed.

BLAK and BROUN exhibit some degree of synonymy in Chaucer's English since both have senses expressing low degrees of luminosity. These senses are, however, less well exemplified in Chaucer than elsewhere in Middle English. In works from the north and west, *broun* may express lack of brightness ('briȝtter oþer broun, beter oþer worse' *William of Palerne*, in Bunt 1985: 470) and the darkness of night ('Sone þe worlde bycom wel broun; þe sunne watȝ doun and hit wex late' *Pearl* 537–8). *Broun* is also found more widely as a premodifier of colour adjectives like modern *dark*: Mandeville tells of diamonds called *violastres* 'for here colour is liche vyolet, or more browne þan the violettes' (Hamelius 1919–23). Juliana of Norwich describes the livid appearance of the dying Christ as turning 'in to blew, and after in browne blew, as the flessch turned more depe dede' (Colledge & Walsh 1978). The denotation of *blew* has here been influenced by association with the sense 'livid' of the Scandinavian borrowing *blo*.

Many Middle English lexemes seem to have had luminosity senses or associations: BROUN, BLAK, DUN, WHIT, SILVER, GOLD, SONNYSSHE, YELOW, CITRYN and PALE. *Whit* translates Latin *candidus*, and may be used of glittering precious stones that 'schynes so schyr' (*Cleanness*, in Anderson 1977: 1121). In Chaucer's translation of the *Roman de la Rose* the French adjective *blonde* is rendered variously as *yelow* and *hewed bright*. The adjective is also used to describe the sun. GRAY, when applied to the eyes, renders French *vairs*, and may imply brightness, as it does when applied to weapons. Paradoxically, in view of its darkness senses, BROUN can signify brightness when applied to weapons, as it had done in Old English (Barley 1974). This sense is commonest in, although not confined to, the verse of the alliterative tradition, where the sense is indeed extended to applications to objects other than weapons: 'glemande glas burnist broun' (*Pearl* 990).

We may conclude that the case of BROUN alone demonstrates the fallacy of regarding even the simplest of colour denotations as structured after the pattern of a mosaic. Indeed, the semantic space of colour vocabulary in Middle English cannot be plotted in two dimensions, even when the variables of place and time are unified and various aspects of pragmatic meaning are excluded. Not only do we have to make provision for sense relations upon the scale of hue, but we must also take into account luminosity values, and we must be prepared to account for special restricted subsystems of denotation, as when *gray* and *broun* are used to indicate the brightness of weapons. Even an idealised representation of colour denotation turns out on close inspection to be complex. Moreover, a full understanding of this area of the lexis must recognise that such idealised representations do not adequately represent medieval usage. In the end, if we are to view language as a functional system of communication in all its complexity, semantic and pragmatic meaning cannot be separated.

5.5 Semantic change

5.5.1   Ye knowe ek that in forme of speche is chaunge
Withinne a thousand yeer, and wordes tho
That hadden pris, now wonder nyce and straunge
Us thinketh hem.

(Troilus II.22–5)

That words change their meaning in the course of time is a truism which has been assumed without comment in earlier discussion. Precisely what is meant by change in meaning has not been questioned. Chaucer's words are often quoted to illustrate his awareness of semantic change, but this does not seem to be exactly what he is talking about. In more extended context, it is apparent that he is referring to formulations of speech used in social situations to bring about a particular effect: that is, to persuade a lady of a young man's love. He goes on to say not that we cannot understand the phrasing of the past, but that we find it ridiculous and inappropriate. The matter is not therefore one of cognitive meaning but of competence in usage; not semantics but pragmatics. The word *hlæfdige*, which in Old English had been in common use as a title, is in Middle English extended to use as a form of address. As such, from the fourteenth century it becomes correlated with the use to a single addressee of the plural form of the second person pronoun, *ye*. Together they represent part of a system of polite address inspired by French usage (Finkenstaedt 1963; Shimonomoto 1986); but there has been no change in the meaning of these words, the change is rather in the conditions of their occurrence. This development is quite different from that of the adjective *gesælig*, which in Old English had meant 'happy, blessed', but which by the end of the Middle English period had developed a whole range of new senses – 'pious', 'innocent', 'harmless', 'helpless', 'deserving of pity', 'weak' – and had lost its Old

English ones (Samuels 1972: 66–7). The changes to *hlæfdige* and *ye* are changes in the pragmatics of the words; those to *gesælig* are changes to its sense. It is these semantic changes which form the subject of this section.

5.5.2   We cannot proceed to discuss semantic change exclusively in terms of sense history, since this begs a further question about what can in fact be considered semantic change. Has the lexeme FIRE undergone semantic change between Old English and the present day because it can now be used to refer to radiant heaters fuelled by gas or electricity? If we were to define semantic change as an alteration of the relationship between a word form and a material object, an alteration in its extension (Lyons 1977: 158; Hurford & Heasley 1983: 76–88), this would be the case. It has indeed been claimed that the lexeme SHIP has changed its meaning because of technological developments (Stern 1931). This may be true, but it is not simply the result of a relationship between the material object and the lexical form. Indeed, such a definition would presume a relationship which probably does not exist, for it disregards the fact that a wide variety of distinct objects may equally well be synchronically designated by a single lexical form. Indeed, their variety may be as great as the disparateness between chronologically remote objects which is offered as an example of change. The discussion of semantic change, therefore, needs a more complex model of the relationship of language to the world, and the best-known attempt to provide one is that of the semiotic triangle (Ogden & Richards 1949: 11), of which the diagram below is an adaptation.

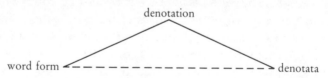

This triangle represents a mentalistic explanation of meaning relations in which the word form, *fire* or *ship*, is related to a meaning (denotation), which itself is related to the objects (denotata). The denotation is conditioned by its relation to denotata, but, except in the case of sound symbolism, there is no direct relationship between word form and denotata. As we have seen above, the denotation may also be related to senses and be conditioned by them, as well as providing a potential for the realisation of senses in context. Semantic change, then, is not an alteration in the relationship between word form and denotata, but a change in the relationship between word form and denotation, observable by changes to the senses realised with a particular word form in context. In the case of the lexeme FIRE, the denotata have been increased in range, that is, the extension of the term is broader, but it is less clear that the essential criteria of meaning which make up its denotation have changed very greatly. A prototypical fire in Modern English is close to what it was in Middle English: a bonfire is still more typical of what is understood by this word than a gasfire. Changes may have been made to what some linguists call the intension or stereotype (Lyons 1977: 159; Hurford & Heasley 1983: 89–100). It is possible that light and heat have become more salient than smoke and flame among the defining characteristics of fire, but in the absence of detailed analysis certainty is impossible. It does seem certain, however, that in the sphere of colour terminology discussed above, the criterion of luminosity has become generally less important among colour words than the differentiation of hue.

Attempts to categorise semantic change into types may be divided into two major kinds: those which simply observe the most salient meaning of a lexeme at chronologically distant periods and by a comparison of the two states make a declaration about the results of processes which remain uninvestigated; and those which endeavour to trace the processes of change diachronically. The two types are not always easy to distinguish, however, because observed effects are often spoken of as though a process were being described. Thus in Old English *deor* meant all kinds of wild creatures, but by the mid-fourteenth century *deor* was rarely used of wild animals in general and had become restricted to the modern sense 'deer'. This semantic development is described as 'narrowing' or 'specialisation'. The word *barn*, which allegedly had meant a building for storing barley, would be considered to have broadened in meaning. Other types, such as ameliorative and pejorative developments, or transitions from abstract to concrete and the reverse, or the change of verbs from intransitive to transitive, and vice versa, are similar kinds of classification. Such classifications may give a spurious sense of order in handling meaning change, but, operating as they do with selective and abstracted data, and disregarding the mechanisms of change, they cannot claim a place in a history of the language.

5.5.3   Serious attempts to explain the mechanisms of change by exploiting analysis of senses often tend, through the very bulk of data required, to become atomistic, dealing with one or two words at a time. Nevertheless, interesting generalisations about the processes of change have been made by a number of scholars (Stern 1931; Ullman 1967; Waldron 1967). Among them, certain voices, especially among Romance lexicographers, have called for a structural approach to semantic change, uniting the diachronic and synchronic axes of Saussure into a 'panchronic' perspective (Ullmann 1957; von Wartburg 1969). From such a 'panchronic' perspective, which is fostered also by recent work on style and sociolinguistics, descriptive variation and stylistically differentiated variables may be seen as the symptoms of change which becomes apparent in a subsequent synchronic state.

5.5.4   The motivation for this variation may originate extra-linguistically, as for example when a change in denotata leads on to a modification of the denotation of a lexeme. A familiar example of such extralinguistic motivation is the proliferation of senses of the word *horn*, where the denotation has been affected by the development of the electric automobile horn. Semantic change as the result of extralinguistic developments is rarer in Middle English, but it might be argued that the development of the sense 'sensibility' for the lexeme CONSCIENCE, first recorded in Chaucer, was brought about by the extralinguistic values of courtliness. It is less easy to find examples among words with material denotata. The word *castel* had in Old English meant a 'fortified village' but came by the twelfth century to mean a 'stone-built fortress'. The earlier sense co-existed in restricted contexts throughout the Middle English period with this newer one, but became increasingly rare. However, alongside the technological advance, which may have brought about this change, social developments also played a part. The role in the development of the new sense of Norman French cultural influence and renewed linguistic borrowing cannot be separated from the extension of the native term.

The *Peterborough Chronicle* records in the annal for 1085 that King Henry's son was *dubbade to ridere* at Westminster. This phrase gives the native agentive noun *ridere* an entirely new significance, for it is an expression based upon a French phrase which has undergone partial substitution by the English form for the French *chivaler*. Laȝamon's *Brut* also uses this native form instead of the French, but couples it with the more familiar term *cniht*: 'Iulius hæfde to iueren þritti hundred riderne, cnihtes i-corene' (4297–8). The Norman Conquest introduced into England the institution of the armed, mounted retainer, and in the spirit of Old English practice, an attempt was made to meet the lexical need by the use of native resources. *Ridere* – perhaps an etymological translation of French *chivaler*, perhaps simply descriptive – emphasises his role as a horseman. *Cniht*, which in Old English had meant 'boy, servant, retainer', focuses upon his relationship to his lord. The words emphasised different criteria of the role of the knight, but both continued in use throughout the Middle English period. As Diensberg has suggested, the further borrowings *boy* and *servant* made available words to duplicate the function of *cniht* in denoting 'servant', and so it lost this sense. Furthermore, as chivalric theory developed, the clearly agentive formation of *ridere* must have made its associations more and more inappropriate, and the relative opacity of the form *cniht* made it more adaptable to semantic changes arising from the growing complexity of the institution. Thus, before 1300, it was already possible to write a line like the following, quoted from *King Horn*, in which the contrast between the estates of thrall and knight is the whole point of the utterance: 'Þanne is mi þralhod/ Iwent in to kniȝthod' (Allen 1984: 445–6).

5.5.5 Generally speaking, it may be assumed that the lexical resources of a language are sufficient to fulfil the communicative needs of the society in which it is used. Radical alterations to that society and to its communicative needs, such as those which followed the Norman Conquest, may leave a language lacking words for the new circumstances. The same situation may, however, arise more slowly as the product of cultural evolution, and in either case, if the deficit occurs in some highly structured area of the lexis, it is often referred to as a 'lexical gap'. In discussing Middle English colour vocabulary, it was noted that the denotational area of RED seemed to be somewhat broader than is the case today. Ripe oranges, wheat and pomegranates were called *red*. Gold is variously called *red* and *yelow* partly, although probably not exclusively, as the result of a real metallurgical difference. These peculiarities of usage correspond with the fact that the word *orange* is not recorded as a colour adjective before the sixteenth century. Since *orange* is one of the eleven basic colour *foci* considered to be universal in human language (Berlin & Kay 1969: 2), it is reasonable to enquire whether Middle English may not have had a lexical gap at this point.

Since the notion of the lexical gap depends on the perception of a requirement for a word which does not currently exist, such a gap can not be seen as the motivation of change unless the existence of communicative need can be shown. It is as pointless to compare the Middle English situation with universals erected by comparative studies as it would be to argue a lexical gap in Present-Day English on the grounds that we do not possess an equivalent of the French verb *foudroyer* 'to strike with a thunderbolt' or distinct words for mother's brother and father's brother, like those found in Latin. No need is felt for any of these. There is, however, evidence in Chaucer's usage to imply a need for greater lexical representation in the red–yellow area of the spectrum. This is indicated by the means taken to remedy the lack. Chaucer exploits the derivational rules of his language to create the word *sonnyssh* to describe the colour and brightness of Criseyde's hair, probably as an effective alternative to *golden*, but more persuasively he repeatedly resorts to paraphrase to capture this colour, as for example in his description of Lycurge with the orange pupils of a bird of prey:

> The cercles of his eyen in his heed
> They gloweden bitwixen yelow and reed.
> And lyk a griffon loked he aboute.

> (CT 1: 2133–5 [I.2131–3])

The conditions may therefore seem to exist which in the sixteenth century suggested a third remedy, the shift of *orange* from a count noun to a colour adjective.

5.5.6   When *orange* was adapted to its new purpose, it had long been an English word; but some changes of meaning are more directly motivated by influences from outside the language system concerned. In some cases this takes the form of a kind of semantic merger effected between native lexical units and those imported, such as that already noted in the case of *castel*. Thus, in Old English, *blæw* had meant 'hue', 'blue' and, perhaps under the influence of Scandinavian *blá*, an indistinct 'dark colour'. The importation of *bleu* from French, followed by its formal assimilation to ME *blew*, contributed to the greater salience of the sense 'blue', whilst the other senses declined. A very similar process took place in the case of OE *rice* 'powerful', which is used in the 1137 annal of the *Peterborough Chronicle* in a context which demonstrates that it has already begun to assimilate the sense of the French *riche* 'wealthy': 'sume ieden on ælmes þe waren sum wile rice men'. The sense 'powerful', however, continued to occur alongside the French sense until well into the sixteenth century.

Contact with Scandinavian languages causes similar effects upon the senses of English words. OE *drēam* 'mirth, joy' was affected by contact with ON *draumr* 'dream', and the new sense is first attested in English in the east midlands, an area of heavy Scandinavian influence. The Old English sense survived into the thirteenth century, and the related sense 'musical entertainment' into the fifteenth. OE *brēad* was a relatively rare word, with the sense 'morsel, mouthful', and the sense 'bread' belonged to the lexical unit *hlāf*. However, the modern sense of *brēad* first makes its appearance in Northumbrian Old English, and by 1200 it had replaced *hlāf* in this mass noun sense, and the latter had become a count noun. Contact with Scandinavian *brauð* seems to have facilitated this development. The addition of the sense 'live in' to OE *dwellan* 'delay, linger', which is recorded from the first quarter of the fourteenth century, takes place under the influence of Scandinavian *dvelja*. In this case, however, both senses survive side by side until the present day, although the Scandinavian one may now be felt to be rather formal or legal, as in the compound *dwelling-house*.

5.5.7   The economy of language as a system of communication is illustrated by the fact that it contains very few total and complete synonyms. That is to say that, although many lexemes share senses, few are capable of precisely the same range of occurrence: they are differentiated either by some discrepancies in sense or by pragmatic meaning. There is, it is reasonable to assume, a general tendency towards the differentiation of lexemes in any particular language system, so that synonyms which arise for whatever reason usually undergo a process of differentiation. Thus, after the borrowing of Scandinavian *wing*, the Old English synonym *feþer* became restricted in its sense, referring now only to an individual feather. Similarly, the word *rind*, when referring to the 'skin' of a tree, began during the fourteenth century to be replaced from the north by the Scandinavian *börkr* 'bark', and the Old English words *wolcen* 'cloud, sky' and *heofon* were affected by the importation of Scandinavian *sky*. *Heofon* gradually became restricted to religious contexts and those derivative from them, and, except for some survival in poetic contexts, *wolcen* with the sense 'sky' entirely disappeared by the end of the Middle English period. The word *sky* itself was challenged in the south by the separate sense development of OE *clūd* 'rock, hill', which had developed the modern sense 'cloud' by about 1300. Thus although *sky* could still mean 'cloud' in the works of Chaucer, it lost this sense by the mid-sixteenth century. The importation of the Scandinavian word *deyja* 'to die' may have reinforced an unrecorded Old English form, and the word is first attested in 1175, when it emerged in competition with the Old English derived words *swelten* and *sterven*, which at this time meant no more than 'to die'. Throughout the Middle English period it gained ground against both these words, so that the former became rare after the mid-sixteenth century, and from this same period the latter was restricted to death from hunger, also developing a causative sense 'to kill by starvation'. Already in Chaucer's time, *swelten* appeared in contexts where it had the sense 'to be overcome by heat' and these became common in the sixteenth century, giving the modern verb *swelter*.

The Old English word for 'flower' was *blostm*, so that when King Alfred collected a bouquet of the flowers of the thoughts of St Augustine, he entitled it *Blostman*. Today the word *blossom* is normally used of the massed flowers of trees or productive crops, and this restriction has come about as the result of the borrowing of the words 'bloom' and 'flower', respectively from Scandinavian and French. *Blom*, which first occurs at the close of the twelfth century, has both mass- and count-noun senses, but remained rare outside the north and north midlands until the end of the fourteenth century. The French-derived *flour* probably therefore played a more important role in restricting the sense of *blosm*. *Flour* is first recorded in English about 1225 in *Ancrene Wisse*, and it rapidly became the most common of the three words, usually as a count noun, so that a useful distinction began to emerge between this word and the native *blosm*.

The importation into English of the French word *fleur*, although later developments created a useful distinction between it and its synonyms, cannot have been motivated by communicative need, that is, by any lexical gap. Indeed, the redistribution of senses in the semantic field, which was a consequence of its adoption, might be viewed as a disruption which had little to offer the users of the language. The precise reason for the adoption of *fleur* cannot be given, but it is quite possible that the motivation was extralinguistic and connected with social prestige, that the word became familiar from French cultural values represented by poetry extolling the delights of the spring season, its birdsong and flowers. The lesson which may be learned from this is that, as part of a communicative system, the lexis of the language does not operate with an unerring sense of purpose and an unfailing accomplishment in its execution. It is not a well-designed machine working infallibly towards maximum economy and precision. Innovation may indeed be disruptive to the system, and be imposed upon it by external factors. Economy then enters the picture more readily in terms of the restoration of regularity and differentiation following such a disruption.

5.5.8   We have discussed above how formally similar lexemes entering the language system from external sources lead by a kind of merger to the broadening of sense ranges and, as earlier senses are lost, to semantic change. We have also considered the case where formally distinct lexemes with similar senses lead to a redistribution of the senses of existing lexemes as the availability of near-synonyms facilitates subtler distinctions in reference, fulfilling newly felt communicative needs. We may now discuss in some detail a mechanism by which, having established broader sense ranges for formal items by processes like the first, certain senses are made obsolete. If these are the earlier ones, we then have a case of semantic change; if they are the newly imported ones, the importation of the new item may be judged to have failed.

Homonymic conflict is a concept which is associated with the lexical studies connected with the French dialect atlas compiled by Gilliéron (von Wartburg 1969: 138–41), and which has been persuasively applied to Middle English examples in a variety of special studies (Menner 1936; Williams 1944). Although the objects of such study have usually been homophones, there is no difference in the principle involved between these and studies of polysemous lexemes (Menner 1945; Rudskoger 1952). In both cases a single word form has a range of senses associated with it among which two or more are capable of confusion with one another so as to hinder effective communication. They are then said to be in conflict. The result of this conflict may then be the avoidance of the word in contexts where such confusion may arise, and the consequent loss of one or more senses, or even of the word form itself. Thus the fact that in most Middle English dialects the Old English word *breād* 'morsel' (and later under the influence of Scand. *brauð*, 'bread'), came to be pronounced identically to the form *brǣde* 'roast meat' meant that an annoying potential for misunderstanding arose. Remedial action could be taken by using instead of the ambiguous form *brede* the French loan word *rost*, which from the early fourteenth century rapidly replaced *brede*. *OED* records the last occurrence of the sense 'roast meat' for *brede* in 1535.

Precisely what factors are necessary for conflicts of this sort to arise is not exactly predictable, and any attempt to explain the process purely in terms of propositional meaning and the analytic patterns of structural linguistics may not be entirely satisfactory. Indeed, some scholars have contested the functionalist assumptions of homonymic conflict *in toto* (Lass 1980). Linguistic logic would predict that sense conflict should occur only if the words involved are of the same grammatical class, phonologically identical, semantically related and used in the same sphere of the discourse, so that cognitive ambiguity may result. In fact, it has been demonstrated by the development of the third-person pronouns, and the clash in southern Middle English of *þei* 'though' and *þei* 'they' that identicality of word class is not a necessary condition (Samuels 1963). It may be assumed that none of the above conditions is absolute. Moreover, in speech, because of performance and situational features, it is unlikely that the confusion created by conflict ever extends to a complete breakdown of communication. Rather, it is probable that homophones bring to a spoken exchange inappropriate and distracting associations, creating, as it were, 'noise' in the channel of communication. In the written language, which offers less opportunity to rectify the communicative ambiguity, homographs may be genuinely confusing, so that writing systems have often attempted to differentiate homophones by spelling. This may well account for the rather sudden adoption in London English in the fourteenth century of the form *though* in preference to *þei* – spelling practice leading linguistic change – and it has been suggested as the explanation of Orm's use of accents to distinguish homographs in the late twelfth century (Bennett & Smithers 1966).

A final, more extended, example will illustrate the functioning of homonymic conflict. The Old English word *draca* was an early borrowing from Latin which, about the year 1000, had the following senses:

1(a) 'a dragon'
1(b) 'a battle standard (with the image of a dragon)'
2 'a serpent'
3 'a water monster'
4 'Satan'

Senses 1(a), 1(b) and 4 persisted into Middle English. In the early thirteenth century, however, the word *dragon* (originally formed on the Latin accusative *draconem*) was imported into English from French. It was used with the following senses from the dates marked:

1(a)   'a dragon' (1225)
1(b)   'a battle standard etc' (1297)
2   'a serpent' (1220)
3   'a water monster' (1350)
4   'Satan' (1340)
5   'Death' (1500)

Clearly, ME *drake* and *dragon* were substantially synonymous, so that the opportunity existed for some differentiation of the senses. In the latter half of the thirteenth century, a third word joined this group with the emergence from an obscure origin of the word *drake* 'male duck'. Now, if *drake* 'dragon' had been made vulnerable to change by the adoption of the French *dragon*, the conflict with *drake* 'male duck' very greatly increased its peril. Yet the process was a slow one. Senses 2 and 3 persisted to the close of the fifteenth century, and rather later in antiquarian literary use, and sense 4 until the end of the fourteenth century. New senses parasitic upon the attributes of dragons as airborne fire-breathers emerged, so that *drake* was applied to shooting stars and comets, and in the post-medieval period to a variety of cannon, but alongside these developments the frequency of use with the former primary sense of 'dragon' steadily declined.

Why is it that the sense changes of *drake* follow the pattern recorded? Clearly, there is no real difficulty in distinguishing from context whether your interlocutor is discussing a duck or a dragon. But this is probably a pseudo-problem. Indeed, it is probable that *drake* 'male duck' had been current in English long before it was recorded in the thirteenth century, but such creatures, unlike dragons, do not figure prominently in literary sources. The homophones were therefore stylistically and situationally separated: ducks belonged to everyday conversation; dragons to literary narrative. However, when reference to both becomes more common in literary texts, the homographs are in much greater danger of confusion. They are pronounced and spelt in the same way, belong to the same word class and are semantically related as hyponyms of the same superordinate term, *beast*. Even so, it is unlikely that conflict occurred at the level of contextual sense; much more likely that the identical word form created a danger of the awareness of inappropriate associations: the conflict occurs in pragmatic rather than semantic terms. This, of course, would be disastrous to a story of suspense in which a knight-errant faces a *drake*. Collocation with the form *fire*, of course, tended to head off such inappropriate associations, so that the compound *fire-drake* (OE *fyr-draca*) survives much later than the simplex, indeed is still listed by contemporary popular dictionaries. Senses concerned with astronomical reference, which are also developed by *fire-drake*, survive because they are both semantically and contextually distant from the senses in conflict. But the developments cannot be explained purely in terms of structural factors. The disappearance of senses 4 and 5 are presumably not caused by the danger of ambiguity with the 'monster' senses, but rather by changes in theological concepts.

This extended example involves the effect upon the lexis of importation from foreign sources, and illustrates well the role played by different registers, as well as the effects of word formation, upon sense history. It illustrates, too, how disruption of the system can occur, but how the system proves self-regulating. The concept of a system is that of an abstraction, but the process of regulation is not itself idealised or abstract. It lies in the use of the language by those who wish to communicate with one another. For the results of homonymic conflict to come about, language users have to be inconvenienced by the existing state of affairs: structural disfunction provides only the occasion for change; pragmatic factors implement it when speakers or writers take steps to ensure that their language is fit for its major purpose of communication. This example, then, provides a fitting end to a chapter on lexis and semantics which has throughout sought to present lexis as structured, but above all as subject to the processes imposed upon it by its users in the act of using it.

FURTHER READING

The primary resource for work on the lexicography and semantics of Middle English texts is the *Middle English Dictionary* (*MED*), which has fuller coverage than the *Oxford English Dictionary* (*OED*), but which is appearing in fascicles and is not yet complete. The etymologies offered by the Oxford dictionary have not been superseded, but dates given for the first recorded occurrence of many words differ between the two works not only because of the inclusion of new source material, but more significantly as the result of the decision to cite the dates of manuscript sources by the later dictionary in preference to dates of original composition. Consequently the dates cited in *MED* frequently postdate those of *OED* by many years. A useful bird's-eye view of additions to the English lexicon is available in Finkenstaedt, Leisi & Wolff (1970), which is based upon the *Shorter Oxford English Dictionary*. It may be expected that the publication of the materials gathered at the University of Glasgow for a Historical Thesaurus will contribute substantially to the resources available for the study of Middle English lexis. Discussion of the nature of the word as a linguistic unit is perennial, and may be found in Lyons (1968), Matthews (1974) and Cruse (1986). A useful account of Middle English spelling practice is that by Scragg (1974), although its handling of the structural aspects is a little confusing. Stimulating remarks on the variety of English, its co-existence with other languages and the effects upon literary composition and everyday life can be found in Chaytor (1945), Blake (1977) and Clanchy (1979). Burnley (1977, 1984) discusses the special category of marked *termes*. Two recent bibliographies (Fisiak 1987) and (Tajima 1988) are valuable guides to secondary sources, and may be supplemented by the annual reports in *Annual Bibliography of English Language and Literature*, *Year's Work in English Studies* and the reports of research in *Neuphilologische Mitteilungen*.

5.1 Two major studies of the expansion of English vocabulary from foreign sources in general are those by Serjeantson (1935) and Sheard (1954). The former is a useful compendium, but is theoretically unsophisticated and dated in outlook. More detailed and often more reliable work is available with more specialised focus. For Scandinavian influence, the standard work has for long been Björkmann (1900–2), who is perhaps too ready to claim Scandinavian influence in doubtful cases. Some of the uncertainties are the subject of an article by Hoad (1984). A detailed study illustrating the competition between native and Scandinavian synonyms is offered by Rynell (1948) and a fuller but more popular account in Geipel (1971). Hansen (1984) gives a resumé of recent scholarship on the settlement and sociolinguistic situation in relation to their linguistic effects. The role of place-name research is particularly important here too (Fellows-Jensen 1975b).

The circumstances of French influence upon the lexicon have been charted most fully by Berndt (1965, 1972, 1976) and Richter (1979), and in more detail in a series of articles on the role of Anglo-Norman contributed by W. Rothwell (1968, 1975–6, 1985). That foreign influence upon the lexicon is not restricted to the adoption of individual words is well demonstrated by Prins (1952, 1959, 1960), although some of the constructions he cites with *taken* could as well derive from Old English constructions with *nimen* as French ones with *prendre*. Estimates of the rate of adoption of French borrowings first offered by Jespersen (1909–49) and Baugh (1935) are updated by Caluwé Dor (1983) and Dekeyser (1986).

The major study of aureate diction has long been Mendenhall's (1919). More recently, the influence of Latin upon Middle English and Scots has been studied by Ellenberger (1974, 1977), who believes that many apparently French borrowings may in fact be derived directly from Latin. Contributions dealing with a few words in the works of various authors, largely from a literary viewpoint, are fairly frequent; e.g. (Ebin 1977). The only other source of borrowing which has been the subject of extended study is Dutch (Bense 1926–39). The work of Mersand (1937) and Kaplan (1932) on Romance loan words in Chaucer and Gower respectively remains interesting, but has been justifiably criticised on methodological grounds. Käsmann (1961) is a more subtle study of Romance influence in the restricted domain of ecclesiastical terminology. Much sociolinguistic work on language contact, creolistics and the mechanisms of linguistic interference is potentially relevant to the Middle English linguistic situation (Haugen 1950; Weinreich 1953; Ferguson 1959; Gumperz 1964, 1969; Todd 1974; Görlach 1986). Weinreich, Labov & Herzog (1968) make a strong case for the importance of prestige as a motivating factor in linguistic development.

5.2 Expansion of the lexicon by word formation is less studied than by borrowing, and the major resource here is Marchand (1969). More general treatments of English word formation are by Adams (1973) and Bauer (1983). Although concerned with the earlier period, Carr (1939) complements the work of Oakden (1935) on nominal compounds. Sauer (1985) is a more recent and a thorough study of similar material. Frankis (1983) deals with some formations by blending to be found in alliterative verse.

5.3 The importance of collocability as an analytic tool, by which lexical sets are compiled from commonly collocated items belongs to the London School associated with J. R. Firth and is described in his writings and those of his followers (Firth 1957, 1968; McIntosh & Halliday 1966; Jones & Sinclair 1974). The conception of stylistic register derives largely from the same source (Halliday, McIntosh & Strevens 1964; Crystal & Davy 1969). The study of lexical variety in Middle English is extensively recorded by Tajima (1988), and there are many studies of the words of certain specialised domains (Sandahl 1951–82; Carter 1961; Burnley 1979; Lohmander 1981). Less fully represented is dialect geography. Here the standard work is that of Kaiser (1937) which supplements Jordan (1906). More detailed studies, especially on northern texts, have emerged from the Edinburgh project on Middle English dialects (McIntosh 1973, 1978). See also Hudson (1983). Later dialectal resources may also be relevant to the study of dialectal lexis in Middle English: for example, the *English Dialect Dictionary* and publications arising from the Survey of English Dialects (Orton & Wright 1974; Upton, Sanderson & Widdowson 1987).

5.4 Introductions to synchronic semantics may be either general and exhaustive (Lyons 1977), or more selective and accessible (Palmer 1981; Hurford & Heasley 1983). They may be directed towards the lexicon (Cruse 1986), towards sentences (Kempson 1977) or towards pragmatics (Levinson 1983). None is specifically concerned with Middle English. The synchronic approach to the semantics of Middle English may be informal and restricted to studies of individual words (Barron 1965) or structural and directed towards groups of words (Diensberg 1985); such groups are sometimes explicitly (Héraucourt 1939; Aertsen 1987) investigated in relation to semantic-field theory (Trier 1931; von Wartburg 1969). Although pragmatic meaning is frequently accidentally incorporated into Middle English word studies, it has rarely been the subject of deliberate and separate investigation. In those examples which exist (Schroeder 1983; Sell 1985a, 1985b), the author's purpose is essentially literary critical.

5.5 The diachronic study of Middle English semantics is frequently embedded in more general accounts of semantic change (Stern 1931; Ullmann 1967; Waldron 1967), although detailed studies of some words exist which include some account of development within the Middle English period (Rudskoger 1970). The role of form and function in semantic change is illustrated by the claims made for homonymic conflict (Menner 1936, 1945; Williams 1944). More recently, examples of homonymic conflict breaching the expectation of identicality of word class between the forms concerned have emerged from the study of Middle English dialects (Samuels 1963, 1972). These claims have, however, been contested (Lass 1980), and subsequently defended (Samuels 1987).

6   THE LITERARY LANGUAGE

Norman Blake

6.1   Introduction

6.1.1   The title of this chapter, 'The literary language', suggests that there is a clear division between literary and non-literary languages in the Middle English period. As is true of any period in English, there exists a highly literary style at one end of the spectrum and an equally clear non-literary style at the other end, but in between there are so many gradations that it is difficult to draw a precise boundary between them. One can, however, say that if one were to attempt to draw such a boundary, it would for the Middle English period be drawn in a rather different place from the one which we would recognise as appropriate for the modern situation. Today *literature* is traditionally regarded as both an exclusive and an evaluative term; works which lack an aesthetic structure or an emotional appeal are readily dismissed as being not literature. The growth of a book-buying market has led to literature being advertised and sold as something quite separate from other printed material. The word *literature* comes ultimately from Latin *littera*, 'that which is written', and this definition reflects Middle English attitudes to literature more adequately than contemporary ones do, though the beginnings of a modern attitude can be traced at the end of the medieval period. It is in the fifteenth century that literary texts like the *Canterbury Tales* begin to be produced by themselves in de luxe manuscripts as though they were special texts which needed a specialised form of reading. Until that time, and in most cases long afterwards as well, literary texts appeared with other written material in compendia of one type or another. What we would now classify as literary texts do not have a different status in presentation or format.

6.1.2   This situation makes the concept of literary English difficult to apply to the written material in Middle English, because whatever survives is usually thought of as literary and it cannot be judged against non-literary English, which to all intents and purposes has not survived. If rhetoric, for example, was taught, it would not be assumed that its teaching had relevance only to a special form of written output; it was more generally available. Rhetorical conventions may be found as much in a letter as in a romance. Furthermore, the period was witness to considerable upheavals in the use of English and to variation in its written forms. The effect of the Norman Conquest was to promote the use of French in England, so that there appears to be a gap between those early texts whose English suggests a close link with Old English literary expression and the texts written after the re-emergence of English for literary use in the fourteenth century. In both the earlier and the later periods not only do texts from many different parts of the country survive but they are also written in the prevailing regional forms. Towards the end of the Middle English period London emerges as the most important centre for the production of literary works, but even then it is by no means the only one. The question naturally arises as to whether separate areas have different literary languages; a question which has been raised particularly in relation to the variation between alliterative and non-alliterative styles. Because of these conditions it is much more difficult to focus on Middle English literary language than on that from the preceding or following period. In the Old English period there is far less material available, and for various historical reasons most of what survives is extant in a relatively homogeneous linguistic form. Most Old English poetry was written in what some have called a 'poetic koiné' and was relatively uniform in its metre and approach to lexical embellishment. The bulk, but by no means all, of Old English prose was written in Late West Saxon and was dominated by two writers, Ælfric and Wulfstan. In the Early Modern English period the introduction of printing, the dissolution of the monasteries and the dominance of London led to the centralising of literary output in and around London so that writers more readily responded to the same stylistic pressures and their books are printed in an increasingly standardised language. The Middle English period was far more diffuse in its output and hence it is more difficult to chart the development of its literary language.

6.1.3   The Middle English period also differs from the Early Modern English period in that it contained almost no discussion in English about the type of language and style which might be appropriate for writings in English; what little there was came right at the end of the period. Consequently, there is no foundation upon which one might build a theoretical approach to the literary language of the time. It is true that in England as in the rest of Europe works about literature and its language were written in Latin about Latin, and it is not unreasonable to suppose that writers in English were aware of some of these discussions and proposals and may have been influenced by them when they wrote. For example, Chaucer in his Nun's Priest's Tale refers to 'O Gaufred, deere maister souerayn' (*CT* 10: 3319 [VII.3347]), by whom he means Geoffrey of Vinsauf, a medieval rhetorician who included instructions on how to write a poem in his *Poetria nova*. Such references do not in themselves prove that English writers were influenced in their choice of words and styles by what was written in Latin rhetorical handbooks, if only because the information such handbooks contained may not have been readily adaptable to an English situation. Nevertheless, two modern scholars have studied the Latin background with a view to its influence on vernacular writing, Ernst Curtius and Alastair Minnis, and it may be worthwhile to consider what they have concluded.

Curtius explored the writings of the Latin Middle Ages in so far as they responded to the teachings of the rhetoricians, particularly in the organisation and presentation of material. The choice of particular styles is not a matter which bulks large in his book (Curtius 1953). Yet the encouragement such handbooks gave to writers to present their material within certain themes such as the brevity formula or the ideal landscape may have led English writers to copy the words as well as the topoi of their Latin counterparts, though the differing structures of each language would provide a limit to the extent of this similarity. Nevertheless, the Latin models might have encouraged the adoption of a foreign-based vocabulary and such stylistic features as parallelism, though if they did they would only have been reinforcing a tendency which can be traced elsewhere. Minnis' book (Minnis 1984) is concerned with the historical development of the theory of authorship in schools of philosophy and theology. This development takes place in Latin about Latin writings and is channelled into two major types of academic prologue. It is suggested that the theoretical position and approach which lie behind these prologues were known to later Middle English writers such as Gower and Chaucer. Because of the differences between

Latin and English vocabulary, this influence can usually be traced only at a general level which is reflected in some of the themes presented by English authors. It may also be traced in some of the Latin commentaries which occasionally accompany English works, as is true of Gower's *Confessio amantis*. However, these commentaries represent a high level of learning and would not be familiar in a detailed way to the average English writer. It is improbable that they influenced many English writers in their choice of vocabulary and style, though they may have had some impact on the general presentation of material. Furthermore, their influence is not likely to have been felt before the fourteenth century in English works, and so the implications of the development of the academic prologue are restricted in their applicability to the whole of the Middle English period. It does not seem as though either of these books provides a way in to the study of the literary language.

The Latin background has been exploited differently by such scholars as Atkins, who concentrated on the development of rhetorical techniques in Latin handbooks and the influence these exerted on English writers (Atkins 1943). The general influence of these rhetoricians was partly to encourage a distinction between different styles and the appropriateness of certain styles for particular types of writing, and partly to encourage the elaboration of English writing through the use of tropes, figures and an ornamental vocabulary. The disposition of the words in a sentence and the choice of individual words may have been dictated by the wish to use rhetorical figures or to present a florid style. These features are more characteristic of the later Middle English period, though they may be found to some degree throughout the period. For example, when Richard Rolle writes 'Þi lovely face so wan and so bolnyd with bofetynge and with betynge, with spyttynge, with spowtynge' (Allen 1931: 21), we assume that he was influenced by rhetorical practice to arrange the adjectives and nouns in pairs, and to link the last two pairs partly through alliteration and partly through *similiter cadens*. These features in turn dictate the vocabulary which is employed, since the words which alliterate together and the words which cover a similar lexical field are restricted. That restriction could operate on the vocabulary by keeping alive words which might otherwise fall out of use entirely or by introducing new, particularly foreign, words.

6.1.4   Although this influence is clear, it remains rather too wide to use as a marker of literary language, because the conventions of the rhetoricians could be employed by any writer. More recently, attempts to chart the influence of Latin or French have concentrated on particular styles or genres. Richardson (1984) has suggested that the medieval *ars dictaminis* or art of letter writing had a profound effect upon the style not only of letters but also of other prose in the fifteenth century. The *dictamen* influenced in particular the material issued by the Chancery, and as that was extensive the language and style promoted through it must have become very familiar. At first the letters and documents were in Latin, but from about 1420 they tended increasingly to be in English. Hence the knowledge of the formulas advocated by the *dictamen* and the elegance of style which was encouraged spread first to English letter writers and then more generally to literature. Many of the scribes employed in government offices also undertook copying on a commercial basis and even, as in Hoccleve's case, indulged in poetic composition. As a scribe turned from official correspondence to literary composition it is natural to assume that he would take over to the latter many of the stylistic attitudes which he had acquired in copying the former.

This style with its Latinate constructions, clausal qualifiers and innumerable doublets is associated with Caxton and it has been suggested that he acquired it from French courtly models, in particular those linked with the duchy of Burgundy (see Blake 1968). Bornstein (1978) showed that this style was found much earlier, for examples of it can be found in Chaucer's Tale of Melibee, a translation of the French *Livre de Mellibee et de Prudence*. Even earlier, Workman (1940) had showed how important translation was as an influence on English prose. More recently, David Burnley (1986) has called this style 'curial style', which he suggests is a more accurate title than the 'clergial style' proposed by Bornstein. Burnley makes the same observation as Richardson, namely that this style was developed in literary works through the scribes' familiarity with the administrative style which had been developed in such centres as the Chancery. This style, which we shall return to later, is simply one of those current in the later Middle English period. Its importance is that it offers one way of looking at the material being produced then. It may well be that this style was favoured by many, but it was certainly not the only one available. We must also recognise that styles are not so distinct in this period to allow us easily to attribute a text to one style or the other.

6.1.5 Increasing attention is now being given to scribes and their handling of texts since their reactions to the material they copy should give some indication of their stylistic prejudices. It has for long been known that scribes altered the language of the texts they copied. Reasons for doing so can include the obsolescence of the vocabulary or the unfashionable nature of the style. Sometimes the changes may be arbitrary and unplanned, as seems to be the case when a scribe copied the same passage twice and one copy differs in many linguistic matters from the other (see Brook 1972). Unfortunately, it cannot always be determined which manuscript represents the original text best, and so it may be difficult to decide in what direction the changes were being made. For example, it was customary to think that the Ellesmere manuscript of the *Canterbury Tales* reflected Chaucer's language well, and most modern editions of the poem use that manuscript as their base text. However, it has become accepted more recently that the Hengwrt manuscript is older and represents Chaucer's intentions more faithfully. If that is the case, then the changes which are made in the text of Ellesmere probably represent scribal interference. Certain features of Ellesmere have been highlighted in this connection. Ellesmere is more likely to have parallelism of linguistic structure than Hengwrt (see Pearsall 1985). This can be illustrated by the following pairs of examples:

1   *Hengwrt*   As wel in cristendom as hethenesse (1: 49 [I.49])
     Ellesmere   As wel in cristendom as in hethenesse
2   *Hengwrt*   As wel of ioye as tribulaciouns (10: 2952 [VII.2980])
     Ellesmere   As wel of joye as of tribulaciouns.

It appears as though the Ellesmere scribe insisted on a pedantic level of syntactic regularity, and this may reflect certain stylistic prejudices which were becoming widespread in the fifteenth century, and may well have been influential earlier. Scribes altered the lexis of their texts as much as the syntax as an examination of the *apparatus criticus* of any modern edition reveals, but the matter has not been studied in any regular way as yet to provide guidelines as to what stylistic attitudes were operative at any one time.

6.1.6 A slightly different approach has been suggested for those texts which have glosses attached to them (Blake 1988). Why are glosses included and what effect are they intended to have on the reader? Glosses consist of three types: single words which do little more than provide a Latin or French translation of a word in the text; short explanations of something that is in the text, such as identifying an individual referred to there; and longer glosses which provide some intellectual background for an understanding of the passage as a whole and which may have been taken from a Latin text which deals with the matters raised in the text. From a stylistic point of view it is the first type of gloss which is significant. For example, in the Knight's Tale where the text reads:

> Nat oonly lyk the loueris maladye
> Of Hereos, but rather lyk manye
>
> (1: 1375–6 [I.1373–4]),

the Hengwrt manuscript, together with some later ones, has a marginal gloss *mania*. This provides the Latin form of the word *manye* which occurs in the text. It can hardly have been introduced to inform readers of the word's meaning. It is a word of Latin origin in English and only educated readers are likely to have been familiar with the word. The gloss would emphasise the learned origin of the word and perhaps suggest to readers that there were connotations to this word in Latin which they should bear in mind for its English equivalent. More importantly it would highlight this word in the text and show that the poem was one in which words of Latin origin were used. It would concentrate attention on the lexis of the text and encourage the reader to think that the learned associations of words were significant. Once again one has to accept that insufficient work has been done in this area to know how common such glosses are and whether they can all be interpreted in a similar way.

6.1.7   Many of the points raised so far can be brought together under the general concept of the influence of translation on English literary language. Throughout the Middle English period the bulk of literary output was modelled, directly or indirectly, on foreign originals. The closer the English works kept to those foreign originals the more their vocabulary and syntax were influenced by the other language. To some extent, therefore, the history of Middle English literary language may be said to embody the accommodation between native traditions and foreign influences. This can be most clearly seen in the relationship between alliterative and courtly styles. The influence of translation meant that there was in the period no sense of tradition as we understand it today. English texts did not exist in a stable form because scribes could change the wording and content; many English texts were localised in their distribution; and most had no system of referring to passages or lines within them. Hence it was not possible to refer from one text to another, except perhaps in a very general way. Latin texts had authors who were known, were copied carefully to preserve what had been written by the author because the words were authoritative and were studied and repeated endlessly. Hence Latin words may well carry far more connotation than English words, which were not associated with particular contexts or themes. This makes English texts very different from Latin ones, and in particular the language found in Middle English works did not carry the same associations as those found in Latin or in Modern English. It has been suggested that the use of one word rather than another was not significant provided both came from the same register (Blake 1977). If a word was likely to be replaced by a scribe as soon as the text was copied, it might be difficult for an author to put too much meaning into his choice of single words. It would be safer to concentrate on developing themes on a stylistic level which would be recognised. Similarly, the absence of a standardised written language made certain types of syntactic dislocation impossible at the time. Today, when certain grammatical expectations are inculcated into educated people, deviations from those expectations are regarded as deviations from the norm which help to foreground the style. It is difficult, if not impossible, to introduce such deviations into Middle English literary language except at a very general level.

6.1.8   As such an approach seems somewhat negative, other scholars have tried to devise different approaches to the study of medieval literary language. Burnley (1979) has suggested that scholars should pay attention to the 'language architecture' of a literary work. A study of Middle English literary texts would thus imply an understanding of the historical language architecture of the period. The language architecture of a period is related to the complexity of the culture which produced it, and since the intellectual and cultural milieu of the fourteenth century, for example, was complex, it is not possible to accept the views of those who see Middle English language as simple. In his book Burnley traces some of the themes which were used by Chaucer in order to show the complexity of the language architecture found in them. However, the themes he considers are all of foreign origin and consequently many of the overtones which he detects in their English usage are attributable to the antiquity of the theme and to its recorded history. This approach, while very fruitful, is somewhat limited in that it is more difficult to trace the language architecture of those concepts which do not have this background. His book is a useful corrective against the assumption that the literary language in the Middle English period was relatively unsophisticated and that its vocabulary had few connotations. While this is true, our ability to trace those connotations depends on factors which are varied and difficult to interpret.

To close this introductory section it should be stated that so far there has been little application of modern linguistic techniques to the study of Middle English literary language. Some scholars have begun to apply the principles of pragmatics and discourse analysis to some major works, such as the *Canterbury Tales* (see Sell 1985b), but so far the studies have been more in the nature of outlining how such investigations should be conducted and what results they might obtain. Few concrete results have emerged, and those which have deal with issues like themes and discourse rather than specifically with the nature of the literary language.

6.2 Early Middle English literature

6.2.1 At the end of the Old English period there was a well-developed prose tradition associated with Winchester and centres dependent upon it. This type of prose followed the stylistic model of Ælfric's writings, which were noted for their alliterative organisation and syntactic clarity. The influence of his work in the Middle English period may be recognised because it was copied frequently, particularly in monastic centres in the west of the country. Knowledge of Ælfric's prose style, which has so many points of contact with Old English poetry, was extensive in that part of the country. For its part Old English poetry is largely extant in manuscripts which were copied about 1000, and there is no evidence that poetry composed before the Conquest was preserved in post-Conquest manuscripts or even known about at that time. This situation presents the problem of what knowledge of the alliterative style which we associated with Old English poetry and of the language associated with it existed in the Middle English period.

6.2.2 A problem in tracing the development of literary style in this period is that there is very little poetry which survives from the period immediately after the Conquest, and it is not easy to decide whether what does survive is poetry or prose. The so-called *Worcester Fragments* are a case in point. A manuscript, now at Worcester, contains some leaves with fragments of an address of the soul to the body. Significantly, this same manuscript also contains a copy of Ælfric's *Grammar* and *Glossary*. The address of the soul to the body is usually printed as poetry in modern editions, though it may in fact be prose (see Johansen-Aase 1984). Whichever it may be, what is noticeable about the vocabulary is that the compounds which were such a familiar feature of Old English poetry have largely disappeared. Among those which survive are *lorþein* 'scholar', *lifdawes* 'life', *burtid* 'nativity', *feorþsiþ* 'death' and *goldfæt* 'treasure box'. Equally, kennings, which we regard as so typical of Old English poetry, are rarely encountered. Although alliteration is common, it is by no means the only means of linking phrasal units together, for rhyme is found in such examples as *þeo moder greoneþ and þet bearn woaneþ* 'The mother wails and the child cries.' However, the alliteration is sufficiently strong to preserve many words of Old English origin, such as *isceaften* 'creatures' and *balewen* 'griefs', which were shortly to be replaced by French words. Indeed, it is striking that French appears to have made little inroad into the vocabulary of this text, which is usually dated to the end of the twelfth century. This didactic text is still part of an English tradition, and has not been unduly influenced by Latin or French models.

6.2.3   The most important alliterative poem in the Early Middle English period is Laȝamon's *Brut*. This survives in two manuscripts and was written at the beginning of the thirteenth century. Of the two manuscripts Cotton Caligula A.ix preserves a more archaic language and style than Cotton Otho C.xiii, which has eliminated a great deal of the elaboration found in the other manuscript. Otho has modernised the poem, even though the two manuscripts seem not to be far apart in date. Laȝamon used as his main source a French chronicle by Wace, the *Roman de Brut*, which is in its turn an adaptation of Geoffrey of Monmouth's *Historia regum Britanniae*. Laȝamon's poem is written in an alliterative long line which falls into two half-line groups. Each half-line normally consists of from six to nine syllables, at least two of which are stressed. The two half-lines are linked by alliteration or by rhyme or assonance. Sometimes alliteration is used together with rhyme or assonance; and sometimes the two half-lines may be linked through similar syntactic patterns in the language rather than through alliteration.

There are certain important differences between the *Brut* and Old English poetry. In the *Brut* major syntactic units terminate at the end of each line rather than at the caesura as is characteristic of Old English poetry. Litotes, such a prominent feature of Old English, is missing in Laʒamon, as is the kenning. The few examples which remain have none of the evocative power of Old English. Hence the Old English poetic variation of language and development of stylistic ornamentation are largely lacking in the *Brut*. However, the *Brut* does contain a large number of what have been termed 'epic formulas'. The use of these formulas has been adduced as one reason why the *Brut* is almost twice as long as its French source. These formulas usually occupy a whole half-line, and occur particularly frequently in the second half-line where they seem to be little more than tags. As sentences usually start at the beginning of the line, the formulas at the end of the lines provide a means of finishing the sentence without adding extra information. Some of these formulas represent phrases that had been found in Old English poetry, but many of them are new. Often they consist of two words belonging to the same word class which are linked together by *and* as well as by alliteration: *mid sæhte and mid sibbe* 'in friendship and peace', *þan strongen and þan richen* 'the powerful and noble' and *lude and stille* 'loudly and quietly'. Some consist of a noun group such as *aðelest kingen* 'noble kings', a group which may be varied with different nouns like *cnihten*, *folken* or *mannen*, and *aðelest alre kinge* 'noblest of all kings'. Others may be either full clauses such as *balu þer wes riue* 'there was great misfortune' and *he lette blawen beomen* 'the trumpets resounded' or non-finite clauses such as *ærhðen bidæled* 'deprived of possessions', a phrase which has many antecedents in Old English poetry. It would appear as though these formulas are not borrowed from Wace, though similar ones occur in French *chansons de geste* which may have provided the model.

Although the *Brut* is based on a French source, another characteristic feature of its language is that it contains very few French loan words. In view of the fact that it was written about 150 years after the Norman Conquest, this is surprising. It has been estimated that not more than a hundred French loan words occur in both manuscripts. But the Otho text has perhaps as many as 160 additional loans which are not found in the Caligula manuscript. These changes presumably reflect that scribe's intention to modernise the language of the text, which meant recourse to many new words borrowed from French. The French words found in the *Brut* are those which became part of the ordinary language such as *abbey*, *admirail* and *appostolic*. The absence of significant numbers of French words in this poem has been explained on the grounds that, because it deals with epic warfare, which had been the subject of Old English poetry, the author was fond of using archaic vocabulary characteristic of that earlier poetry. Many words which are common in Old English are still used in the *Brut*, though they were not to be found in Middle English literature after his time very frequently, if at all. These include *drihten* 'God', *eitlond* 'small island', *fæie* 'doomed', *gume* 'man, hero', *ofslean* 'kill', *underfon* 'receive' and *uppen* 'up, upon'. Even within the poem words like this do not occur regularly throughout, for they seem to be found in groups (Iwasaki 1986b). Elsewhere in Caligula, and more widely in Otho, they may be replaced, so that, for example, *drihten* frequently gives way to *god*, and *fæie* to *deʒe* or *dead*.

As an example of the language and its features which have already been commented on, let us consider the following passage quoted from both manuscripts:

Caligula
Nu haueð Vortigernes cun   Aurilien aquald.
nu þu ært al ane   of aðele þine cunne.
Ah ne hope þu to ræde   of heom þat liggeð dede.
ah þenc of þe seoluen   seolðen þe beoð ʒiueþe.
for selde he aswint   þe to him-seolue þencheð.
þv scalt wurðen god king   & gumenene lauerd.
& þu to þere mid-nihte   wepne þine cnihtes.
þat we i þan morʒen-liht   mæʒen come forð-riht.

Otho
Nou haueþ Vortigerne his cun   Aurelie acwelled.
nou hart þou al one   of alle þine kunne.
Ac ne hope þou to reade   of hamþat liggeþ deade.
ac þench ou þou miht þi-seolf   þine kinedom werie.
for sealde he aswint   þat to him-seolue tresteþ.
þou salt worþe god king   and steorne þorh alle þing.
And þou at þare midniht   wepne þine cnihtes.
þat þou at þan moreliht   maʒe be a-redi to þe fiht.

           (Brook & Leslie 1978: 8948–55, with caesura marks replaced by gaps)

('Now that Vortigern's family has killed Aurilie, you are the sole survivor of your family. But do not expect any support from him who lies dead. Put your trust in yourself that help is granted you, for seldom is he disappointed who puts his trust in himself. You will become a worthy king and ruler of people. And arm your followers at midnight so that we may advance in the morning.')

Each line constitutes a sense unit. The two half lines are usually linked by alliteration, but rhyme is found in *nihte*:*cnihtes* and *liht*:*riht*, and perhaps also in *ræde*:*dede* (which Otho represents as *reade*:*deade*). An epic formula is seen in *of aðele þine cunne*, the last word of which repeats the *cun* of *Vortigernes cun*. There are no elaborate kennings or elaborate noun groups which we may regard as characteristic of Old English poetry, though *gumenene lauerd* is reminiscent of Old English poetry. Some of the vocabulary is becoming distinctly archaic such as *aquald*, *aðele*, *ræde*, *gumenene* and *morʒen-liht*. The last of these is the only compound word which echoes the compounding so common in Old English. Repetition of single words and epic formulas have replaced elaborate kennings and heavy noun groups. The alliteration is also different in that it need not fall upon the main lexical words such as nouns and adjectives. Verbs, adverbs and pronouns are more likely to have the alliteration even where nouns and adjectives are present in the half line. This makes the poetry seem less compressed than its Old English counterpart. The developments within the language have accentuated that process. The loss of inflections led to the use of more determiners and prepositions so that the number of grammatical words increased within a sentence. This made the language of poetry seem more diffuse and may have undermined the dominant position of noun groups in the literary language. The effect is to make the literary language of this period rather more dynamic and less static than that of the earlier period.

6.2.4   The *Brut* and other poems in the Early Middle English period have points of contact with Old English poetry, but by no means work on the same structural principles. They have, on the other hand, textual links with French models, but they do not seem to have been influenced by these models to any great extent in their vocabulary. Two explanations have been offered for this state of affairs. The first is that there was a popular poetry which either existed alongside the more courtly Old English poetry or superseded it (Tatlock 1923). It was from this popular poetry that literary Middle English poetry derives, and this origin is offered to explain the differences between Old and Middle English alliterative styles. Because there is no evidence that such a popular poetry ever existed, an alternative theory has proposed that Late Old English prose style borrowed many of the techniques of Old English poetry (Blake 1969b). This prose style survived into the Middle English period, as we have already seen, in that works by such writers as Ælfric were copied particularly in the west up till the thirteenth century. Ælfric's writings are highly alliterative and they are sometimes printed as verse by modern editors. They also exhibit other rhetorical features such as rhyme and parallelism which are found in Early Middle English alliterative poetry. In this hypothesis it is suggested that alliterative prose and poetry are not far apart; they differ in their rhythmical assumptions rather than in kind. Classical Old English poetry may have generated Ælfrician prose, and its Middle English successor may in its turn have generated the re-creation of alliterative poetry. At first this poetry was of the type found in the *Brut*, but later in the Middle English period it developed towards more regular alliteration.

6.2.5   In view of this possible development it is time to consider the prose of the Early Middle English period. In addition to the copies made of Old English works, many new texts were produced during the twelfth and early thirteenth centuries. The most important include the so-called *Wooing* group (that is, texts associated with the lyrical prose treatise *The Wooing of Our Lord*), the *St Katharine* group (mainly lives of saints and didactic texts) and the *Ancrene Wisse*. Some of the characteristics of this prose style may be seen in a passage from *Ancrene Wisse*:

> Ich halsi ow, he seið, as elþeodie & pilegrimes, þet ȝe wiðhalden ow from fleschliche lustes þe weorrið aȝein þe sawle. Þe gode pilegrim halt eauer his rihte wei forðward. Þah he seo oðer here idele gomenes & wundres bi þe weie, he ne edstont nawt, as foles doð, ah halt forð his rute & hiheð toward his giste. He ne bereð na gersum bute his speonse gnedeliche, ne claðes bute ane þeo þet him to neodeð. Þis beoð hali men þe, þah ha beon i þe world, ha beoð þrin as pilegrimes, & gað wið god liflade toward te riche of heouene.

> (Shepherd 1959: 3–4)

('I implore you, he says, as strangers and pilgrims to avoid the sins of the flesh which fight against the soul. The good pilgrim keeps always to the straight road. Although in his journey he sees or hears vain games and amusements, he does not linger on the way as fools do, but he keeps to his path and hastens towards his lodging. He takes with him no treasure except the expenses necessary for his journey, and he takes only those clothes which are required. By this we understand those holy men who, although they live in this world, they are there like pilgrims who proceed with righteous lives towards the kingdom of heaven.')

In this passage we may see that the typical vocabulary of Old English poetry is not present. There are no compounds, and the vocabulary associated with heroic poetry is also missing. The archaic words found in Laȝamon's *Brut* are not found here. There is no attempt to seek out exotic words, though some words may well be unfamiliar to us as they have since dropped out of the language. A word that was to disappear very soon in Middle English is *elþeodie* whose original meaning was 'stranger' but which is here joined in a doublet to the French *pilgrim*, for pilgrims who visited foreign lands were strangers there. It is the latter word which occurs most often in this text, and *elþeodie* may have been introduced simply to create the doublet, for it is typical of this style as it is of the *Brut* to have phrasal units consisting of two words linked by *and*. Another example in this passage is *gomenes & wundres*. Equally characteristic of this passage is the repetition of words, for the variety which was so characteristic of Old English is no longer found. Words like *god, pilegrim, wei* and *halt* are repeated and this repetition forms one of the cohesive devices of the text. It is not only words which are linked together by *and*. Phrases and clauses operate in much the same way, as for example *halt forð his rute & hiheð toward his giste*, where the alliteration on *h* helps to point the similarity of structure between each clause.

Because the nouns themselves are often lighter than in Old English, there being few compounds, this is compensated for by the use of doublets or of adjectives so that an adjective and noun often come to be linked together as a collocational set. In this passage *fleschliche lustes* and *rihte wei* could be said to fall into this category. Indeed, such pairs of words often stand in contrast to one another so that in the opening lines *fleschliche lustes* and *idele gomenes* are parallel to each other and stand in opposition to *gode pilegrim* and *rihte wei*. The style of the passage is one which is constructed in brief phrases, usually held together paratactically rather than hypotactically, and this structure accentuates the use of parallelism and contrast. The words and sentence patterns are employed for the overall effect of hammering home the contrast between the good pilgrim who keeps his eyes firmly fixed on the goal of heaven and the others who get sidetracked by the temptations of this world, a contrast which is emphasised by the specific pairing of *þe world* and *te riche of heouene* at the end of the passage.

In essence, texts like this rely rather more on rhetorical conventions than was characteristic of Old English poetry. In this feature Middle English prose texts make use of the rhetorical teaching of the twelfth century associated with the *artes prædicandi*, for sermons in Latin were becoming far more rhetorical and contrived in this period. Even the new approaches to dialectic may have influenced the way in which man considered the world and hence how authors wrote about it. A view of a structured universe divided into contraries lies behind the style of texts like *Ancrene Wisse*. Figures of sound are used to buttress this world picture, particularly those which involve repetition. Hence repetition of successive words at the beginning of clauses, at the end of clauses or within a phrase occurs frequently. Alliteration is a feature which may provide the linking device between or within clauses, although it tends to occur only in patches. It is found particularly in passages of great emotional intensity, in which the rhythm becomes more insistent and the phrasal structure more uniform. Several examples are listed in Shepherd (1959: lxviii).

6.2.6   In the meantime secular tastes were catered for by the development of the secular lyric and the rise of romance. The latter is either modelled on or translated from Anglo-Norman or French versions, as is true of *King Horn* and probably of *Sir Orfeo*. Despite their French background texts like this have a relatively simple style which does not show a heavy preponderance of French words or phrases. The simple vocabulary and style are new features in English, but the absence of many French loan words is characteristic of much of the literature of the time. Some links with the earlier English literary tradition is possible in that certain stock phrases and an occasional use of alliteration occur. Consider a brief passage from *Sir Orfeo*, which survives in one form in the famous Auchinleck manuscript from ca 1330 but which may have been written in the latter half of the thirteenth century. It may be an adaptation of an Anglo-Norman version which no longer survives.

> In Breteyne þis layes were wrouȝt
> First y-founde & forþ y-brouȝt,
> Of auentours þat fel bi dayes,
> Wher-of Bretouns maked her layes.
> When kinges miȝt our y-here
> Of ani meruailes þat þer were,
> Þai token an harp in gle & game
> & maked a lay & ȝaf it name.
> Now, of þis auentours þat weren y-falle
> Y can tel sum, ac nouȝt alle:
> Ac herkneþ, lordinges þat beþ trewe,
> Ichil ȝou telle Sir Orfewe.

(Bliss 1966: 13–24)

('These lays were composed, first uttered and issued in Brittany; they deal with adventures which happened in days gone by and out of these the Bretons made their lays. When kings heard of any remarkable events which had taken place, they took a harp in joy and merriment and composed a lay to which they gave a name. Now I can relate some, but not all, of those adventures which took place; but faithful lords pay attention because I will recite to you the lay of Sir Orfeo.')

The octosyllabic lines arranged in couplets do not encourage the use of a vocabulary with compound words. There are a number of words of French origin such as *layes*, *auentours*, *meruailes* and *Sir*. Most of these are common words; there is no suggestion that the poet looked for any unusual French words. Many words are of Old English origin and most of these are monosyllabic. Alliteration is found in lines like *First y-founde & forþ y-brouȝt*, a line which also exhibits parallelism in its phrasal structure, and in phrases like *in gle & game*. This particular phrase occurs frequently in a variety of different texts in the second half of the Middle English period, particularly alliterative ones. It is possible that a phrase like *bi dayes* is a reflex, however weak, of the Old English expression *in ȝeardagum* which is found in *Beowulf* and subsequently in *Havelok the Dane*.

6.2.7   Although only a few passages have been looked at in detail, a general assessment of the Early Middle English period, till approximately the beginning of the fourteenth century, is now desirable. The Norman Conquest interrupted the production of poetry in English, though there is evidence to suggest that Old English poetry was already by the eleventh century in something of a decline. There is a recognisable continuity only in prose writing from the Old to the Middle English period. English itself was undergoing changes which accelerated its movement from a synthetic to an analytic language. In addition, the availability of three languages in the country, with English being the least elevated, may have inhibited the enlargement of the literary potential of English. It is characteristic of the literary language in the Early Middle English period that it shows few signs of a deliberate policy of upgrading by borrowing foreign words, by introducing new compounds or by adapting unusual syntactic patterns. Some element of archaic vocabulary is certainly present, though it becomes less noticeable as the period progresses. Old English compounds and variation are replaced by a heavier reliance on modification and on the grouping of words into parallel units such as doublets. A certain amount of influence from rhetorical practice is detectable in the more sophisticated prose writings, though that influence should not be pressed too far. The picture is very much one in which authors accept the language as it is and make use of it as best they can. Conscious attempts to manipulate it or to enrich it for specific purposes are few.

6.3   Later Middle English literature

6.3.1   This situation changed quite dramatically in the fourteenth and fifteenth centuries, which in contrast to the earlier period were far more conscious of stylistic considerations and mannered in their use of language. Although comments about literary language remain relatively uncommon, they do start to appear. Even more importantly, writers show an awareness of an English literary tradition and are prepared to write about it. Chaucer, Gower and Lydgate became established as the great literary triumvirate. Several reasons are responsible for this change in attitude. The most important is undoubtedly the changing status of the English language itself. During the course of the fourteenth century English won acceptance as the main spoken language and gradually extended its primacy into the written variety as well. As it grew in stature so people became concerned about its expressiveness and took steps to improve it. At the same time the amount of written English increased dramatically both through new writing and through translation. Translation in its turn encouraged writers to think about the respective merits of each language, and faults which were detected in English had remedies applied which were taken from other languages, particularly Latin and French. At the same time developments in educational ideas and in writing techniques affected all languages. Even though the primary target for improvement in expressiveness was writing in Latin, it was inevitable that there was some spill-over into English. In particular, new codifications of rhetorical practice in reference to different genres of writing and new approaches to grammatical investigation increased a general awareness of the importance of language and the presentation of information in the most effective way. After the upheavals of the Norman Conquest and the transition to a synthetic language, the fourteenth and fifteenth centuries witnessed growing stability in the language and an increasing tendency towards standardisation. Schools of literature sprang up in various parts of the country so that a sense of continuity became more marked. Later writers extended the practices of earlier ones in their own area or school.

It seems likely also that the audience for works in English became more sophisticated as the use of French diminished among the upper classes, and this exerted greater pressure on authors to increase the sophistication of their language.

6.3.2   Some of this attitude can be seen in the works of Richard Rolle. As he was born about 1300, his birth marks a convenient division between the earlier and later periods. He attended Oxford through the patronage of the archdeacon of Durham, but left before he could take a degree. Nevertheless, he had more formal education than had been common hitherto in writers of English literature and he went on to write many works in Latin as well as in English. His Latin works are elaborate and mannered in style, for they show considerable influence of rhetorical teaching as found in the handbooks of the time. His English writings show many points of contact with the earlier religious writing as represented by the *Wooing* and *St Katharine* groups. Some of the themes and subject matter of Rolle's writing may be seen in this extract from his first *Meditation on the Passion*:

> I aske not, dere Lady, kastelys, ne towrys, ne oþer worldys wele, þe sonne, nor þe mone, ne þe bryȝt sterrys; but woundys of reuthe is al my desyr, peyne and compassyoun of my Lord Jhesu Cryst. Werste and unworthyest of alle mennys haldyng, I have appetyte to peyne, to beseke my Lorde a drope of hys reed blod to make blody my soule, a drope of þat watur to waschyn it with. A, Lady, for þat mercy, þat modur art of mercy, socoure of al sorewe, and bote of alle bale, modur mad of wrecchys and of wooful, herken to þis wrecche, and vysyt thy chyld. Soue in myn herte, þat is hard os ston, a sparcle of compassyoun of þat dere passyoun, a wounde of þat reuthe to souple it with.
>
> (Allen 1931: 23–4)

('I do not ask, dear lady, for castles, towers or other worldly goods, or for the sun, the moon or the bright stars. The wounds of pity are all I require, the pain and compassion of my lord Jesus Christ. I, who am the worst and most unworthy of all mankind, seek suffering and I beg my lord for a drop of his red blood to make my own soul bloody and for some of that water to wash it in. Madam, on account of your mercy, because you are the mother of mercy, the balm of all sorrow, the soother of all pain, the mother of all those who are wretched and in sorrow, listen to this wretch and comfort this child. Kindle in my heart, which is as hard as stone, a spark of that suffering Our Lord endured at his passion and implant a wound of that pity to make my heart more pliable.')

This passage shows links between both Latin and English writings. The series of phrases which are applied to the Virgin Mary, 'modur of mercy', 'socoure of al sorewe' and 'bote of alle bale', echo similar phrases found in Latin texts such as hymns which will be found in later English writings by authors such as Lydgate. Often in Latin they are rather more elaborate and ornate. Here each phrase is bound internally by alliteration, and although alliteration is a feature of some Latin writing, its presence in this passage is attributable to the English prose tradition going back to Old English. In addition certain words are repeated, often in parallel phrases: 'a drope of hys reed blod...a drope of þat watur'. Other words may be repeated in a slightly different form, as in 'blod to make blody; of wrecchys... þis wrecche'; and 'compassyoun of þat dere passyoun'. Other words are arranged in a type of catalogue, as is true of the first clause in the passage, and there is imagery of a traditional nature, such as the heart as stone being cultivated to make it supple. It is difficult with many of these features to be certain whether they come from a Latin tradition or from the survival of an English rhetorical prose style. No doubt both contributed to some extent, and it may not matter too much if we cannot attribute exact proportions to one or the other. What is important is that a more ornate style is used by an author who was himself to become very popular in the fourteenth and fifteenth centuries. Many works were to be attributed to his pen, and the style he stood for exerted considerable influence.

What is noteworthy is that in some of his works his writing reached an intensity of emotion so that the rhetorical features in it were sufficiently frequent to make modern editors assume that the prose had slipped into alliterative poetry (Allen 1931: 64). This happens in *Ego dormio*, in which Hope Emily Allen prints lines 104–13 as poetry. This may well be correct, for elsewhere in that prose text Rolle included pieces of rhyming poetry. The occurrence of this poetry may indicate that Rolle was familiar with the traditional style of alliterative poetry. Inevitably, both the prose and the poetry rely on a larger vocabulary with many borrowings from French and Latin in order to accommodate the more elaborate rhetorical presentation of the material. The vocabulary and syntax of works like *Ego dormio* are more wide-ranging than those found in earlier works like *Sir Orfeo*. However, there are indications that poetry continued in some forms at least to remain rather less elaborate in its language and style than prose. Rolle's *The Form of Living* is a prose work which was adapted as a poem, probably during the fourteenth century. Whereas the prose form is a somewhat specialised text of a mystical nature, for it was written for a woman recluse to guide her in her spiritual devotions, the poetic version is intended for a wider audience; hence much of the prose is omitted in the poetic version. The poem is in couplets and this metre has caused some simplification of the syntax and vocabulary of the original, for each couplet tends to be no more than a simple declarative statement. As far as vocabulary is concerned both prose text and poem contain many polysyllabic words, usually of Latin origin, such as *abstinens*, *discrecioune*, *transfigures* and *turmentand*. But where in the prose these had often occurred in doublets, in the poem the doublets are simplified to a single word. Those doublets which remain are those which are very traditional or alliterative. It is a notable feature of the poetic version that it increases the amount of alliteration found in the prose original. As compared with poetic texts of the thirteenth century, this poem also shows an increase in the amount both of polysyllabic vocabulary and of alliteration. Syntactically, it remains relatively straightforward, for each couplet generally equates with a complete sentence; it is only in catalogues and suchlike features that a sentence may run on for a number of lines (see Blake 1974).

6.3.3   This close relationship between poetry and prose, particularly of an alliterative kind, is one which continues throughout the fourteenth century. A volume of sermons, British Library MS Additional 41321, dated to about 1380, contains many passages which fall easily into alliterative lines of poetry. Significantly on folio 72v of this manuscript a marginal entry in a contemporary hand notes 'ista prosa est edita instar cadencie'. The punctuation of the manuscript helps to make clear the alliterative composition of the text, which is arranged in phrasal units linked through alliteration. Some of the sermons in this manuscript contain echoes of *Piers Plowman* and of other poems, though it is not certain that these represent direct borrowings in either direction. The poets may have found much of their material and inspiration in prose texts, and it may have been through the tightening up of the prosaic cadences that they were able to create poetry in the alliterative long line (see Salter 1978: 34).

6.3.4   The first datable poem of the so-called Alliterative Revival, which saw the re-emergence of alliterative poems in English, is *Winner and Waster*, which is dated in the period 1352–3. However, the confidence with which the poet handles the metre and style indicates that he was not the first alliterative poet of the Revival. What is characteristic of the Revival is the common assumption about vocabulary and content which lies behind all the poems. These poets use a distinctive vocabulary which is rarely found elsewhere in Middle English. How strict the metre of Middle English alliterative poetry was in comparison to classical Old English remains disputed, but recent scholars have suggested that the metre was much stricter than was previously imagined (see Duggan 1986). This matter of metre has an important bearing on the diction because the standard alliterative line contains at least three alliterating words. This demand put a heavy strain upon the resources of the vocabulary, for it meant that many words were needed to express the same idea so that the alliteration in any line could be completed. In Old English this demand had been met partly through the use of a large poetic vocabulary and partly through the development of kennings and formulas. It is worth considering the development of these features by looking in detail at two passages from alliterative poems of the Middle English period.

6.3.5   The first is from *The Parlement of the Thre Ages*, a poem often thought to have close links with *Winner and Waster*. It is from the opening May setting, a common theme in all poems of this period.

> The cukkowe, the cowschote, kene were þay bothen,
> And the throstills full throly threpen in the bankes,
> And ich foule in that frythe faynere þan oþer
> That the derke was done & the daye lightenede.
> Hertys and hyndes one hillys þay gouen,
> The foxe and the filmarte þay flede to þe erthe;
> The hare hurkles by hawes & harde thedir dryves,
> And ferkes faste to hir fourme & fatills hir to sitt.
>
> (Offord 1959: 13–20)

('The cuckoo and the wood-pigeon were both active, and the thrushes contend vigorously with one another on the hedgerows; and every bird in the meadow was happier than the next one that the darkness was past and the day had broken. The harts and hinds betook themselves to the hills, the fox and the pole-cat took to their burrows. The hare crouches by the hedgerows and runs vigorously here and there, and it goes quickly to its nest and gets ready to lie low in its lair.')

An interesting feature of this passage is that it falls into the typical pattern of the opening of love and dream poems in Middle English.

Many of the ideas and expressions in it are those which could readily be found in poems of other metrical bases. The names of the animals and birds are in no way unusual. There are no compound words as there had been in Old English, and there are equally no kennings. There are many formulas of a type which are common in Middle English though of a different structure from Old English. In Middle English they consisted of two or more words which collocated together. In this passage expressions like 'throstills...threpen', 'foule in that frythe' and 'hertys and hyndes' are ones which occur in non-alliterative poems, particularly lyrics. They indicate a stock of formulas, often alliterative, which were available to a wide range of poets. There are, however, two words which are somewhat rare in Middle English and are almost certainly restricted to an area that might be described as 'northern' at that time. They are *hurkles*, for which no Old English equivalent exists, and *fatills*, which may be related to Old English *fetel* 'a belt'. It is not surprising that both words refer to the activities of the animals, since many verbs to express such activity were needed. The word *cowschote* may have been principally dialectal by this time, as is its modern equivalent *cushat*.

One could have chosen a passage with a higher proportion of words of restricted currency. Alliterative poetry had a specialised vocabulary in some areas. It had a large number of synonyms for 'man', many of which came from Old English and did not survive in other contexts. They include words like *beryn, douth, freke, gome, hathelle, lede, segge* and *wy*. There are also words which were by then archaic like *axles* 'shoulders', *brande* 'sword', *bowes* 'goes' and *dreped* 'slew', to name only a few. Some words are restricted to the north, and this applies especially to those of Scandinavian origin, among which may be included *grathely* 'promptly', *irkede* 'grew tired' and *layke* 'to play'. The vocabulary of Middle English had been subject to considerable French influence. Although it is probably true that alliterative poems contain fewer French words than poems written in or around London, they could not escape the penetration of French into the language. Certain themes show a high proportion of French words, such as the description of Youth's attire and the account of hawking. The descriptions of the accomplishments and pursuits of a gentleman would have been impossible without recourse to the more fashionable language of French. Alliterative poems are as courtly and chivalric as non-alliterative ones, and hence they must employ the vocabulary which is part and parcel of the more sophisticated life-styles and attitudes.

6.3.6   Some of these features may be seen in *Sir Gawain and the Green Knight*, as can be seen in this passage from the fourth fitt:

> 'Now iwysse,' quoþ Wowayn, 'wysty is here;
> Þis oritore is vgly, with erbez ouergrowen;
> Wel bisemez þe wyȝe wruxled in grene
> Dele here his deuocioun on þe deuelez wyse.
> Now I fele hit is þe fende, in my fyue wyttez,
> Þat hatz stoken me þis steuen to strye me here.
> Þis is a chapel of meschaunce, þat chekke hit bytyde!
> Hit is þe corsedest kyrk þat euer I com inne!'

(Tolkien & Gordon 1967: 2189–96)

('Gawain said: "This is indeed a desolate spot. The chapel, which is overgrown with weeds, is oppressive. It is very appropriate that the knight clad in green should say his devotions here following the devil's use. In each of my five wits I feel that it is the devil who has made this appointment with me in order to destroy me. This is a chapel of evil – may ill-luck befall it. This is the most evil church I have ever entered."')

In this passage there are many words of French extraction: *oritore*, *erbez*, *deuocioun*, *chapel* and *meschaunce*. There is one of the poetic words for 'man', namely *wyȝe*, though words of this type tend to occur when they are required by the alliterative metre. There are several traditional phrases and collocations, such as 'on þe deuelez wyse', 'fyue wyttez' and 'stoken me þis steuen'. There are no words which are specifically northern in this passage, though the poem does contain some, such as *brent* 'steep', *farand* 'splendid', *ron* 'bush', *snayp* 'to nip', *snart* 'to snick' and *stange* 'pole'. The poem contains words of both French and Scandinavian origin, as is true of almost any poem written in the fourteenth century. Some of the Scandinavian words are restricted to northern situations. Some which are common enough today had not by the fourteenth century become adopted nationally. A word like *ille* is restricted to the north in the fourteenth century; it is significant that it is used by Chaucer only in the northern speech of the undergraduates in the Reeve's Tale. Some Scandinavian words echo the Norse literary tradition; *mynne* in the phrase *more and mynne* 'the greater and the smaller, i.e. everybody' is an Anglicised version of *meiri ok minni*, found frequently in Old Norse alliterative poetry. However, such words in *Sir Gawain* are less common than in some other northern poems. The poem has many words for 'man' which are reminiscent of the Old English poetic tradition, and it also employs a number of verbs in alliterative positions to express the sense of going. In this latter aspect the poem differs from Old English, which has fewer verbs in alliterative positions and does not show the same variety in vocabulary. In *Sir Gawain* these words include *cach* 'catch', *chose* 'choose', *driue* 'drive', *found* 'hasten', *glyde* 'hasten' and *hale* 'draw' among many others. The French words found in the poem may be divided into two main types: one which represents the common stock of borrowing from French and could be found in almost any text, and the other words of a technical nature which are used because of some of the specialised descriptions. This latter group includes words referring to armour, etiquette and hunting, though it may also be said to incorporate more abstract words referring to morals and religious practices. For the most part there appears to be no attempt by the poet to look out for new and unusual words, though his chosen metre and his subject matter have led him to use words less familiar to us because they are archaic or technical.

6.3.7   Because of the greater use of French lexis and because many of the alliterative words and compounds had fallen out of use, it could be said that the difference between alliterative and non-alliterative poetry at the end of the fourteenth century was much less than it had been in the Early Middle English period. Not only our own perception today but also the attitude of people in the fourteenth and fifteenth centuries acknowledged a great gulf between the alliterative and non-alliterative writings in this period. In part this is because as people became more stylistically conscious they attempted to emphasise the differences which separated these two styles. Chaucer himself in the prologue to the Parson's Tale has the Parson say:

> But trusteth wel I am a Southren man,
> I kan nat geste rom ram ruf by lettre

> (*CT* 12: 42–3 [X.42–3])

('You must realise that, as I am a southerner, I cannot tell tales in the 'rom, ram, ruf' alliterative style.')

Although the Parson seems to attack all kinds of poetic embellishment, he identifies alliterative style as non-southern. A much fuller view of these differences can be found in the prologues and epilogues of William Caxton, who, as the first English publisher, had to promote the stylistic virtues of the texts he had printed and wanted to sell. He does not refer to alliterative style as such, but he divides his audience into what may be termed courtly and non-courtly groups. The alliterative style was non-courtly in so far as it represented the old-fashioned style which had been characteristic of the whole country at one time. It was Chaucer who provided England with a new style which had completely revivified the literary scene and it is this style which Caxton recommended to his readers. It is worth looking at what he has to say in greater detail.

When he published Chaucer's translation of Boethius' *De consolatione philosophiae* Caxton said of Chaucer that he was the 'first translatour of this sayd boke into Englissh and enbelissher in making the sayd langage ornate and fayr' (Blake 1973: 59). Elsewhere he praised Chaucer for his 'crafty and sugred eloquence' which had transformed the rude English of earlier days into the courtly elegance of his own time. Caxton does not specify precisely what it was that Chaucer had done to the literary language, but it is clear that two features of style which he approved of were the use of many words of French or Latin origin and the employment of rhetorical figures. In many of his own translations Caxton emphasised how closely he has kept to his original and he apologised for not using more rhetorical figures. In his praise of Chaucer he followed Lydgate, and it has been suggested that he saw Chaucer through Lydgate's eyes. A tradition grew up in the fifteenth century which accepted that a new start in English literary style had been made by Chaucer and confirmed by Gower and Lydgate. These three poets were recognised as the main luminaries of this development, and they appeared frequently in this capacity in writings of the fifteenth and early sixteenth centuries.

This tradition is one which is thought of by its promoters as a poetic one and it represents the first time that the language of individual English authors was remembered and repeated. Up till this time it was difficult to guarantee that the words of any writer would be preserved without substantial scribal alteration and indeed much of what had been written was not attributed to a named author, as still remained true of the alliterative poems. A fifteenth-century writer could imitate a Chaucerian poem as the author of *The Boke of Cupide* (perhaps Sir John Clanvowe) did and expect his readers to pick up the allusion. This poem opens:

> The god of love, a! benedicite,
> How myghty and how grete a lord is he!
>
> (Scattergood 1975: 35)

and this opening reflects almost exactly two lines in the Knight's Tale (1: 1787–8 [I.1785–6]). One might not have expected lines in the middle of a Chaucerian tale to be so familiar, and yet presumably readers would be able to recognise the allusion if they thought of this poem attributed to Clanvowe as 'Chaucerian'. There is nothing in the style of the lines which is very different from those in other works which were written either before or at the same time as Chaucer's poem. They stand out because they apostrophise the God of Love, a Chaucerian theme, they come at the beginning of the poem, and they occur in a poem with other Chaucerian allusions.

6.3.8   If one analyses a passage from the *Canterbury Tales* the major impression one gets is how ordinary the vocabulary appears. Take, for example, the opening of the description of the prioress in the General Prologue:

> There was also a nonne, a prioresse,
> That of hir smylyng was ful symple and coy;
> Hir gretteste ooth was but by seint Loy.
> And she was clepyd madame Eglentyne.
> Ful wel she soong the seruyce dyuyne
> Entuned in hir nose ful semely.
> And Frenssh she spak ful faire and fetisly
> After the scole of Stratford-at-the-Bowe
> For Frenssh of Parys was to hire vnknowe.
>
> (*CT* 1: 118–26 [I.118–24])

('In addition there was a nun, who was a prioress, whose smiling was unaffected and modest. The most violent oath she swore was 'By Saint Eligius'; and her name was Madame Eglantine. She chanted the divine service with propriety through her nasal passages. And she spoke French elegantly and properly after the manner of Stratford-at-Bow, because she was ignorant of the French of the manner of Paris.')

There is in this passage no seeking after unusual French or polysyllabic words; there are no compound words; there are no unusual constructions, for most sentences are simple declaratives which extend to two or at most three lines; and the personal names do not seem out of place, for they could hardly be thought of as exotic. The group 'symple and coy' is a traditional expression found in many French poems. There are in the description as a whole a number of adjuncts which are repeated like *ful*, and there are many phrases with an alliterative linkage like 'faire and fetisly'. In various analyses of Chaucer's style which have been made, it is not so much the choice of individual words which has attracted attention as the variety of styles and the exploitation of words in a context in which they are not normally found. The *Canterbury Tales* itself is a collection of stories written in different metres, on different subjects and in different styles. It tended to break down the more traditional approach to style, which saw a particular style as suitable for a certain poem. It made readers aware of the possibilities of stylistic mixing and encouraged them to look beyond the traditional use of vocabulary. A typical way in which a word may be highlighted is Chaucer's use of *hende* in the Miller's Tale. This word is a conventional epithet of praise which is frequent in Middle English poetry. It appears from the rest of the poem that Chaucer felt the word had become somewhat tarnished, for he used it only in what might be called non-courtly situations; for example, the Wife of Bath used it to describe her fifth husband, Jankin. It is used almost as a defining feature of Nicholas in the Miller's Tale, who is regularly *hende Nicholas* (1: 3193 [I.3199]). The word which seems unexceptional in the rest of Middle English poetry is made to have significant overtones in Chaucer (see Donaldson 1970: 13–29), though how far his contemporaries recognised this linguistic feature is not certain. They did not imitate it. They saw in Chaucer a man who used rhetoric and called attention to his rhetorical masters by referring to rhetoricians. The scribes responded to this use of rhetoric by marking purple passages in the tales with a *Nota* or an *Auctor* in the margin. They admired Chaucer as a man who exploited French styles and motifs. They recognised that he admitted many serious references into his work, because he produced such things as catalogues of famous ladies or of trees. His exploitation of these lists could involve more exotic vocabulary, but more often they relied upon less common personal names. These lists also make clear the varieties of style used by Chaucer, for a tale may suddenly change from narration to a highly rhetorical list in which the author produced some generalised comment on the action. His use of classical authorities in these passages can only have increased his readers' admiration of his literary skill.

6.3.9 Chaucer's successors, particularly Lydgate, developed this new style in a more pedestrian way, and they produced that style which we now label 'aureate'. This style concentrated specifically on vocabulary and in Lydgate's case it implied the use of a vocabulary formed from liturgical or classical Latin in secular as well as in religious poems. This vocabulary is clustered thickly around certain stock themes and images so that, particularly in religious verse, it produced a richly celebratory style (see Norton-Smith 1966: 192–5). A good example of the style is found in a stanza from *A Balade in Commendation of Our Lady*:

> O souerraynest, sowht out of Syon,
> O punycall pome agens all pestilence,
> And auryat vrne, in whom was book and boun
> The agnelet that fought for oure offence
> Aȝens the serpent with high defence
> That like a lyoun in victory he was founde
> To Him commende vs, of mercy moost habounde.
>
> (Norton-Smith 1966: 28)

('O most royal one who came from Sion, O pomegranate who are proof against all disease, and O golden urn in whom was prepared and made ready the little lamb who with mighty power redeemed our sin against the serpent so that He was shown to be a lion in victory, commend us to Him, who is most rich in mercy.')

Here the first six lines consist of a long noun group referring to the Virgin, and the elaboration of noun groups is a feature of this style, which makes it seem rather like a bejewelled shrine. The vocabulary is Latinate: 'punycall pome' is a 'pomegranate' and 'agnelet' appears to be a Lydgate coinage based on the Latin *agniculus* applied to Christ. The word *auryat* is based on Latin and was introduced into English by Lydgate. The syntax has many echoes of Latin, particularly in the order of the last line with the indirect object before the verb and the post modifier 'of mercy moost habounde' separated from its head. This style made a greater impact and was easier to imitate than Chaucer's, which was much more sophisticated, and so it is not surprising that Lydgate's reputation was high in the fifteenth century. The concentration on vocabulary and the construction of elaborate noun groups remained the dominant stylistic technique in poetry until Skelton introduced a wider variety of style at the end of the fifteenth century.

6.3.10   Translation from Latin or French had remained a regular feature of English prose in the Middle English period. Usually this translation stayed fairly close to its originals, perhaps for no better reason than that it is the technique which makes least demand on the translator. To that extent it seems to have been a relatively unself-conscious approach at least until the middle of the fourteenth century and probably later. The focus on poetic style which was generated by the emphasis on Chaucer, Gower and Lydgate as the creators of a new courtly style was bound to make people more conscious of prose style as well. After all, it was just as possible to write alliterative prose as alliterative verse; and we have seen that writers like Richard Rolle exploited the potentialities of alliteration in their prose. If it was fashionable to write poetry in the Chaucerian or Lydgatian manner, it would be equally so to extend that example to prose. This would mean replacing the vocabulary which was traditional and linked to alliteration by a courtly vocabulary which was made up of words of Latin or French origin. In addition, the syntax could be much more complicated as parataxis gave way to hypotaxis with many of the grammatical and other words associated with it. No doubt the influence of Latin and French would have been felt even without this poetic 'revolution' in style, but it probably expedited and reinforced tendencies already felt in the language. As far as prose is concerned the influence of the forms used in the royal administration by such people as the Chancery scribes may have been as important as the influence of the poetic style.

As an example of the prose that could be produced at the beginning of the fifteenth century let us consider a letter from the Mayor and Aldermen of London to Henry V which is dated 6 September 1419:

> Our most dred and most souueraign ertly ['earthly'] lord, we recomande vs ['commend ourselves'] vnto þe souueraign excellence of your kyngly mageste in þe most humble and lowely wyse þat any pouere ['poor'] or simple lieges can best imagine or deuise, lowely thankyng your souueraign excellence and noble grace of þe right gracious and right confortable lettres, which ye liked late to sende vs fro your town of Maunt, be Johan Palyng. The which lettres, with al maner of honour and lowely reuerence, we haue mekly ['humbly'] resceyued and vnderstonde. And trewely, most dred and souueraign lord, gladder ne moor confortable tithinges might neuer haue come, nor in better tyme, for to satisfie and refresshe þe feruent desir of your poure lieges, þat haue loong thrusted ['thirsted'] aftur knowlech of your prosperite, than were your sayd gracious lettres, the which amongs al oþer special graces most Principalich for our hertly confort conteyned þe souueraign helþ and parfit prosperite of your most souueraign and gracious persone.
>
> (Chambers & Daunt 1931. 79)

The style is pompous and wooden, as perhaps befits a letter to a king. Most nouns have an accompanying adjective, and many of these groups are coupled with another adjective or noun as a doublet. A phrase like 'souueraign excellence and noble grace of þe right gracious and right confortable lettres' is typical. There is no attempt to find particularly exotic words, though many of the words which occur are of French or Latin origin, presumably because they carry more weight than Old English words. Many words like *souueraign*, *right* and *gracious* are repeated throughout the letter, for the aim is dignity of tone rather than variety of style. Although the sentences can be long, the basic syntactic pattern is often simple, for the elaboration is provided by lexical embellishment through the abundance of adjectives and doublets. The result comes close to pure verbiage which expresses little thought.

This prose style has been called 'curial' or 'clergial' style by modern scholars, and it has been assumed that it was characteristic of the fifteenth century and popularised by William Caxton. It was previously accepted that Caxton learned this style through his translation of French works associated with the court of the Dukes of Burgundy; but Bornstein showed that this style was found in England as early as Chaucer's translation of the *Livre de Mellibee et de Prudence* (Bornstein 1978). Burnley has subsequently shown that many of the features of this style – Latinate constructions, extensive clausal qualifiers, doublets and anaphoric cohesive devices – can be found in the documentary practice of the English royal administration (Burnley 1986). At first this documentary style was written in French, but gradually it was transformed into English. Much of this style was in its turn generated by the various dictaminal arts which flourished in the Middle Ages. Many of the letters and documents, as Burnley shows, combined congratulatory ceremoniousness with continuous clarity, but during the fifteenth century the tendency was for the former to encroach on the latter. This is precisely what we have seen in the letter quoted in the previous paragraph. To some extent, therefore, the ground for this courtly style in prose was already well prepared. Documentary practice in England, and French and stylistic prejudices combined to reinforce in prose the type of style which was commonly ascribed as a new invention to Chaucer, Gower and Lydgate. Certainly, one can accept that their example made people more conscious of style; and as they became more aware of it they would naturally try to drive the style further along the road of ornamentation and elaboration in order to make it seem different from other styles.

6.3.11   One effect was to change people's attitude towards lexis. The vocabulary which was old-fashioned and which could be linked with alliteration gave way to French words. This process was already in train in the fourteenth century, but it received new impetus from this new attitude to style. This can be seen in the way Caxton treated some older authors when he reprinted their works. Prose works by Chaucer were reprinted without change. But Malory, who had written his *Le Morte Darthur* only a few years before Caxton printed it, was revised by Caxton particularly in those passages which were based on the alliterative poem *Morte Darthure*. What in Malory appeared as

> Than the kynge yode ['went'] up to the creste of the cragge, ['the summit of the rock'] and than he comforted hymself with the colde wynde; and than he yode forth by ['passed'] two welle-stremys, and there he fyndys two fyres flamand full hyghe ['burning brightly']. And at that one fyre he founde a carefull wydow wryngande hir handys, syttande on a grave that was new marked ['a sorrowful widow wringing her hands and sitting by a newly made grave'].

became in Caxton

> And soo he ascended vp in to that hylle tyl he came to a grete fyre and there he fonde a careful wydowe wryngynge her handes and makynge grete sorowe syttynge by a graue newe made.
>
> (Vinaver 1967: 200)

Caxton avoided the alliteration of the original like 'creste of the cragge' and 'fyre flamand full hyghe', often through simple omission. He replaced Malory's vocabulary with words which are usually of French origin and which tended to be general rather than specific; *grete* is a good example which occurs twice in the Caxton version. The one addition in his version, which is otherwise shorter than the original, acts almost as a doublet to a noun group, because to *wryngynge her handes* he adds what is little more than a variant, *makynge grete sorowe*. The result is a book which in style is no different from the many romances being issued at the time, for all specific and particular vocabulary was replaced by generalised vocabulary of French origin. In his translations from French Caxton also increased the number of words of French origin by adding doublets to the words in the original. For the most part his interest in language was limited to vocabulary. He seems not to have paid much attention to syntax, though as he translated his French sources fairly literally he often produced sentences with more subordination than was otherwise normal in English. The desire to produce a literary language which was different from the less sophisticated alliterative style, as southerners thought, led to a concentration on ornamentation and elaboration through the choice of vocabulary supplemented to some extent by various rhetorical and syntactic features.

6.4   Special features of the literary language

In this final section of this chapter I would like to consider some particular linguistic features which have figured in discussions of the literature of the period. These are firstly colloquial style and its relation to oral, popular and formulaic types of composition and secondly the variation in use between the second singular and second plural personal pronouns. I do not imply that these are the only features which have been the subject of discussion; they must stand as examples of the others which are not treated here.

6.4.1   'Colloquial' is an adjective which is frequently employed in discussions of Middle English literature, and when it occurs it is used more often than not in an approving way. The reason for this is no doubt that a colloquial style is valued in Modern English, and we tend to carry that attitude back to earlier periods. By the same token, the elaborations of the aureate style are not often regarded highly today because our taste has turned away from the exploitation of polysyllabic vocabulary towards syntactic ambiguity or a more straightforward style. As Rygiel (1981) has shown, the term 'colloquial' can be used in an almost unthinking way and it is characteristic of those who use the term that they rarely analyse the features which are supposed to be colloquial. If a passage is not stylistically elaborate and if its content is homely or low-class, this is often sufficient to make a modern critic think that its style is colloquial.

Before the invention of the gramophone or tape-recorder it was impossible to record the spoken language with any accuracy. It is true that transcripts of trials purport to contain a verbatim account of what was spoken. Not only is the language of such trials rather formal, but also no transcripts in English survive from the Middle English period. Consequently, there is no way to find out what colloquial language was like in our period. Not unnaturally some types of literature have encouraged the view that its authors were trying to create a colloquial language. Generally, poetry has been regarded as rather literary and hence even its fictional dialogue is thought to be idealised. Only Chaucer has attracted attention as a poet who may have introduced colloquial features into his language (Schlauch 1952). Letters and diaries are not satisfactory repositories of colloquial language, for the former are literary and conventional in their language and the latter do not exist. But one source which it has been suggested may contain colloquialisms is the sermon, because it often contains *exempla* drawn from everyday life couched in a language which has a simplicity, if not a colloquialism, which makes it suitable for a non-literary audience. In fact, what is noticeable is that passages of discourse in such sermons tend to be in a different style from those of ordinary narration. Clark has shown how in the dialogue of sermons 'qualifying elements are both rarer and less elaborate, attributive adjectives being more sparsely used and adverbial phrases, so common elsewhere, largely eschewed in favour of plain adverbs' (Clark 1978c: 346). The sentences in the dialogues are shorter and have less subordination, and they often exhibit ellipsis. Such passages also contain many exclamations, contain fewer poetic or archaic words and generally avoid learned French loans. But all this exhibits is that the author of a text like *Ancrene Wisse* can write in two different styles; it does not show that one of those styles is colloquial.

6.4.2   The same may be said to apply to the style which has been labelled as colloquial in Chaucer's works. As Schlauch has stated, his 'more colloquial passages show characteristics of informal English which are recognizable as deviations from the contrasting formal usages of both Chaucer's age and ours' (Schlauch 1952: 1104). These characteristics include the following features. Large or small units may be repeated. In

> Thow seydest eek that ther ben thynges three
> The whiche thynges troublen al this erthe
>
> > (*CT* 2: 362–3 [III.362–3])

('Also you said that there are three things, and these things afflict the whole world.')

thynges is repeated. A special case of repetition is the use of a dummy pronominal subject so that the real subject can be delayed or in some cases introduced earlier. Ellipsis is found frequently in this style. In the following lines the Wife of Bath omits any antecedent for *it*, which is understood from the context:

> And walke I wolde as I hadde doon biforn
> From hous to hous, althogh he hadde it sworn.
>
> > (*CT* 2: 617–18 [III.639–40])

('And I intended to go from house to house as I had done previously, although he had sworn to prevent it.')

A rather different kind of ellipsis is the abandonment of a sentence because the speaker cannot carry through with his train of thought. In this type of style parataxis is found more frequently than hypotaxis, and it might be said that the sentence structure is in general much looser so that it is sometimes difficult to produce a coherent analysis of its make-up. In

> I seigh today a corps born to chirche
> That now a Monday last I seigh hym wirche
>
> <div align="right">(<i>CT</i> 1: 3423–4 [I.3429–30])</div>
>
> ('Today I saw a corpse carried to church of a man that I saw at work last Monday.')

it is difficult to fit the relative pronoun *that* within a normal analytical framework which corresponds with what might be considered standard usage.

6.4.3　Both in the prose and in the Chaucerian examples what has been called 'colloquial' are various features which are more characteristic of a certain style or register. They are not found so frequently in more formal styles, though this in no way indicates that they are indeed colloquial. For it needs to be emphasised that these features do occur in more formal styles and this is hardly surprising. The looseness of structure tends to occur in many varieties of Middle English writing, if only because the period antedates the involvement of the grammarians in the regulation of English style. The recommendations of the rhetoricians did not encompass the niceties of grammar. Inevitably, the features which have been categorised as colloquial are somewhat literary because they occur in literary texts. As long as we accept that colloquial in Middle English literature means no more than a level of style, it may do no harm; but it is probably more sensible to think of this style as informal rather than as colloquial.

6.4.4　What has been thought of as colloquial style is often linked with popular and oral literature. As we saw in an earlier section, it has been suggested that the alliterative poetry of Late Middle English was linked with classical Old English poetry through a popular poetry which flourished in the transition period, but of which no trace has survived. In addition, it has been suggested that many of the Middle English romances were composed for oral delivery because the stereotyped diction which is common to them indicates such a delivery (see Crosby

1936; Baugh 1959). A characteristic feature of this diction is the use of tags and formulas, and they in turn produce a high level of stylistic redundancy. Although repeated phrases and stock vocabulary are typical of the romances, they are found in all types of Middle English literature. Often within the romances these stock phrases resemble formulas which are used to develop stock themes (Wittig 1978). Hence the introduction of a romance will be developed through the use of stock motifs expressed in formulas. This was appreciated by Chaucer who was able to exploit this usage in his Tale of Sir Thopas. That begins

> Listeth, lordes, in good entent
> And I wil telle verrayment
>   Of myrthe and of solas,
> Al of a knyght was fair and gent
> In bataille and in tornament.
>   His name was sir Thopas.
>
> (*CT* 10: 712–17 [IX.712–17])

('Lords, listen attentively and I will truly tell a story of entertainment and joy about a knight who was neat and handsome and his deeds in battle and tournament; his name was Sir Thopas.')

The junction of *list* with *lord* or *lording* occurs in over thirty Middle English poems, and Chaucer himself repeated it later in the Tale of Sir Thopas (see Burrow 1984: 66). Chaucer did not use this formula elsewhere in his work, and perhaps he felt it had become too debased through overuse. In this opening stanza the groups 'of myrthe and of solas', and 'fair and gent' have the nature of formulas, for they occur many times elsewhere.

The end of the tale is broken off by the Host's interruption. But even there one can detect formulas. The incomplete last stanza runs:

> Hymself drank water of the well
> As dide the knyght, sir Percyuell,
>   So worly vnder wede,
> Til on a day...
>
> (*CT* 10: 915–18 [IX.912–18])

('He himself so valiant in his armour drank water from the well, as the knight, Sir Percival, had done, until on a day...')

The unfinished line must be based on the common formula 'It befell one day', and from this fact and from the rhyme one can deduce that line would have been 'Til on a day it so bifel' (Burrow 1984: 74). The previous line also represents a type of alliterative formula which was extremely common in romances. The pattern was *x under y*, where *x* represents an adjective or adverb of commendation and *y* an item of clothing or material from which clothing is made. Although such collocations are extremely frequent, Chaucer does not use them elsewhere. This is not to say that Chaucer does not use other formulas and tags in his writings such as *for the nones* and *shortly for to seye*. Although the romances contain the highest proportion of formulas and tags, they are found throughout Middle English poetry for they were a useful tool to fill up a line and to provide a rhyming or alliterative word. The problem that such expressions pose is whether they are evidence of a popular or oral poetic culture. They are certainly not examples of a colloquial level of language, for they occur commonly enough in very literary works and in translations. At best they might be thought of as some form of literary colloquialism, by which I would understand linguistic features included in a literary text to suggest to the reader an informal style, though even this is doubtful. Although it may be true that oral poetry is often formulaic, it is not true that formulaic poetry is oral. There is evidence to suggest that most Middle English poetry, including the romances, was written by sophisticated and literary people who exploited the conventions available to them. Even if some of those conventions originated through oral composition or oral delivery it is not likely that they reflect such a position in Middle English.

6.4.5   The other feature of Middle English I shall comment on is the variation in use between *you* and *thou*. Originally in Old English *thou* and its associated forms *thy* and *thine* were used of the second-person singular, and *ye*, *you* and the associated forms *your* and *yours* of the second-person plural. The distinction between *thou* and *you* was one of number. Gradually the plural forms like *ye* and *you* were extended to singular use, while still remaining the plural forms. It is not certain when this began, but examples are found from the latter half of the thirteenth century, probably under the influence of French (Mustanoja 1960: 126). Although Mustanoja thinks that the use of plural for singular was developed from the plural of majesty, this is far from proved. In Old French the use of the singular and plural forms was not consistent. In any event the use of the plural for the singular meant that the difference between the two forms was no longer one simply of number. The tendency was to use *thou* forms as marked forms indicating either intimacy or contempt, whereas *you* forms were neutral and polite. As far as Middle English is concerned, Skeat has expressed what is perhaps the prevailing view: '*thou* is the language of a lord to a servant, of an equal to an equal, and expresses also companionship, love, permission, defiance, scorn, threatening; whilst *ye* is the language of a servant to a lord, and of compliment, and further expresses honour, submission, entreaty' (Skeat 1867: xlii). However, it must be remembered that this view expressed by Skeat represents an ideal and that the reality was often far different. It might not be unfair to say that the system opened up the possibility of nice discriminations in language use to literary authors, but that not all authors took advantage of it. The problem is to know whether a particular author does use these forms in a meaningful way, and if so whether he does so consistently.

If a text is long enough one may often detect a careful use of these forms from a detailed examination of all occurrences, but even here it need not follow that care in one part of the text is matched by equal care in another. Otherwise one needs to take other linguistic features into account, such as forms of address, since these may provide a helpful guide to the tone of the dialogue, though one can never be certain that any given example does match the rest of the usage in the text. Some of these points may be considered in reference to *Sir Gawain and the Green Knight*. In the opening fitt there is a distinction between the attitude of Gawain and of the Green Knight towards King Arthur. Gawain consistently uses ʒe, which is the regular subject form in this poem, but the Green Knight uses þou. Even though Arthur is a king and technically superior to the Green Knight, the latter uses þou forms to indicate his contempt for the Arthurian knights, who he refers to in an uncomplimentary way as 'berdlez chylder' (280). To children this þou form may well seem not inappropriate. Gawain, as the pattern of courtesy, naturally uses the polite form to his king and his superior. The king refers to both Gawain and the Green Knight by þou forms, presumably to the former through intimacy and to the latter as a mark of scorn. At the end of the poem Gawain addresses the Green Knight with þou forms, though when the knight is transformed into Sir Bercilak he turns to the ʒe forms. The Green Knight/Sir Bercilak uses the þe forms to Gawain, though he does occasionally relapse into *yow* forms, as when he says:

> 'With my wyf, I wene,
> We schal yow wel acorde
> Þat watz your enmy kene,'
>
> (Tolkien & Gordon 1967: 2404–6)

('I anticipate that we will reconcile you to my wife who was your mortal enemy.')

It would be dangerous to look for any significance in this switching. The same applies to Gawain at the castle of Hautdesert. Generally, he addresses his host with ȝe forms, though occasionally he relapses into a þou form. Although in the temptation scenes the lady uses þou forms to Gawain, he uses ȝe forms to her except for an occasional lapse. Shortly before she offers Gawain a ring in the third temptation scene, he relapses into using one þy:

> 'Now iwysse,' quoþ þat wyȝe, 'I wolde I had here
> Þe leuest þing for þy luf þat I in londe welde.'
>
> (Tolkien & Gordon 1967: 1801–2)

("'Now truly", said that knight, "I wish that for your sake I had the most valuable thing on earth that I own here".'.)

It has been suggested that his lapse 'makes the mental turbulence dramatic – is a concrete indication of how far the lady has driven him' (Evans 1967: 42), though this is perhaps to read too much into a single example which may have arisen for a variety of reasons including scribal corruption.

6.4.6 Other fourteenth- and fifteenth-century authors, such as Chaucer and Malory, are able to exploit this difference between the two forms. By Malory's time it may well be that the *thou* of intimacy was becoming less common, for it has been largely abandoned by the Pastons in their correspondence, and this has left it as a mark of contempt or as a social marker. Field has pointed out a notable use of *thou* forms in *Le Morte Darthur* (Field 1971: 101). When Gareth first appears in Arthur's court the king is sufficiently impressed by the young man to use *ye* forms, which would be the polite form of address in any case. When Gareth asks for food and drink for a year, the king switches to *thou* forms, for the request seems to suggest someone of a low social rank who has come to beg. Later, when it is revealed that Gareth is his nephew the king reverts to *ye* forms. This switching of forms indicates that Malory was aware of the potential for social and other implications of the *thou* and *you* forms and was prepared to exploit them.

As for the *Canterbury Tales* Keiko Shimonomoto has examined the relationship of *you* and *thou* forms with both forms of address and forms of the imperative (Shimonomoto 1986). The use of the polite *you* forms appears to be a characteristic of genre in so far as they occur regularly in courtly romances. In the Franklin's Tale *you* forms are used by all the characters among themselves, though they use *thou* forms to gods and goddesses and the clerk uses them in his final speech to Aurelius (*CT* 6: 897–902 [V.1613–18]). Since the clerk is not an aristocratic character, his use of *thou* forms may indicate his status. He may behave magnanimously by waiving his fee, but his language reveals him to be of a different class. Terms of address also have a significance in indicating the genre of the tale. Ladies in courtly romance can expect to be called *madame*, whereas those in other tales are apt to be addressed as *dame*. The latter is not used in tales like the Knight's Tale, but it is found in the Reeve's Tale, where it is said of the miller's wife 'Ther dorste no wight clepen hire but dame' (*CT* 1: 3948 [I.3956]). The forms of the imperative, whether they have the base form or the ending -*eth*, seem to be interchangeable in Chaucer. What is more significant in requests is the overall syntax rather than the form in which the verb itself appears. In more courtly language commands become concealed as gentle requests or wishes, as is found in the Host's request to the Prioress to tell a tale (*CT* 10: 447–51 [VII.447–51]). Inevitably there is switching between *you* and *thou* forms, and in most cases it can be attributed to the author attempting to manipulate an effective response on the part of the reader. Because courtly romances use the *you* forms as a marker of genre, there are not many examples where a courtly speaker switches to *thou* forms. When this happens, it may be interpreted usually as a sign of high emotional tension. Arveragus switches briefly to *thou* forms in the Franklin's Tale when he forbids Dorigen to reveal to anyone that he has instructed her to keep her word to Aurelius (*CT* 6: 771–6 [V.1481–6]). The switching is probably more characteristic of other tales such as the Nun's Tale in which Cecilia at first addresses the judge Almachius with *you* forms, but then switches to *thou* forms as her contempt for him grows. Such large shifts in attitude are not characteristic of courtly romances and hence shifting is less likely to be found there. Once again one cannot be certain that all these switches are significant, and the forms are liable to corruption in scribal transmission, but one can often provide some check on the reasons for the change by considering forms of address and the syntax of commands.

Both these examples indicate that writers were becoming more sophisticated in their exploitation of linguistic features at the end of the Middle English period. To some extent this was because linguistic conditions were becoming more stable and also because increasing attention was being paid to English style, which it was increasingly felt needed to be elevated to make it a suitable vehicle for literary expression. The Middle English period represents a series of adjustments to changes taking place in the language and society generally. It is hardly surprising that the literary language should appear to be somewhat fragmented and that stability and cohesiveness should appear only towards the end of the period.

FURTHER READING

Useful background studies may be found in Curtius 1953, Minnis 1984 and Eric Auerbach, *Literary Language and its Public in Late Latin Antiquity and in the Middle Ages* (London: Routledge and Kegan Paul, 1965) who explain some of the features of literary language and the reception of literature from a European standpoint, dealing particularly with the Latin background. H. J. Chaytor, *From Script to Print* (1945), tackles vernacular, particularly French, literature, and Atkins (1943) and Pamela Gradon, *Form and Style in Early English Literature* (London: Methuen, 1971) deal more specifically with the English background. A work dealing only with the end of our period is A. J. Gilbert, *Literary Language from Chaucer to Johnson* (London and Basingstoke: Macmillan, 1979).

The continuity of prose style was first proposed by R. W. Chambers, *On the Continuity of English Prose from Alfred to More and his School* (London: Oxford University Press, 1932), but this approach was questioned by N. Davis, 'Styles in English prose of the late Middle and early Modern period', *Langue et littérature* (1961: 165–84) and by R. M. Wilson 'On the continuity of English prose', *Mélanges de linguistique et de Philologie* (1959: 486–94). More recent work on Middle English religious prose includes Riehle (1981) and Elizabeth Salter, *Nicholas Love's 'Myrrour of the Blessed Lyf of Jesu Christ'* (Salzburg: Institut für englische Sprache und Literatur, 1974). A more general book on prose style is Robert K. Stone, *Middle English Prose Style* (The Hague and Paris: Mouton, 1970). On Malory there are good books in M. Lambert, *Style and Vision in Le Morte Darthur* (New Haven, CT: Yale University Press, 1975), P. J. C. Field, *Romance and Chronicle* (1971), and Larry D. Benson, *Malory's Morte Darthur* (Cambridge, MA, and London: Harvard University Press, 1976). On the Lollards and the Wycliffite translation of the Bible one may consult Anne Hudson, *Lollards and their Books* (1985) and C. C. Butterworth, *The Literary Lineage of the King James Bible 1340–1611* (Philadelphia: University of Pennsylvania Press, 1941). On Caxton see Blake (1968).

On the continuity of the Old English style through to Middle English see Tatlock (1923) and Blake (1969b). For the language of Laȝamon the more recent study of Iwasaki (1986b) supplements earlier studies such as Tatlock (1923), H. C. Wyld, 'Studies in the diction of Layamon's *Brut*', *Language* 9 (1933): 47–71, 171–91 and 10 (1934): 149–201, and D. Everett, *Essays on Middle English Literature* (Oxford: Clarendon, 1955, 28–45). A major study of Laȝamon's language and style remains an important desideratum. Several essays in David

A. Lawton (ed.), *Middle English Alliterative Poetry and its Literary Background* (Cambridge: Brewer, 1982), deal with style, as does T. Turville-Petre, *The Alliterative Revival* (1977). The style of *Sir Gawain and the Green Knight* is dealt with in Marie Boroff, *Sir Gawain and the Green Knight: a Stylistic and Metrical Study* (New Haven, CT: Yale University Press, 1962). Also important is R. A. Waldron, 'Oral formulaic technique and Middle English alliterative poetry', *Speculum* 32 (1957): 792–804, and Crosby (1936). The formulas used in alliterative poetry are collected in J. P. Oakden, *Alliterative Poetry in Middle English* (1930–5).

For the influence of translation the standard work is still Workman (1940), though it now needs updating. Work on the influence of features of Latin and French style may be found in Richardson (1984), Bornstein (1978) and Burnley (1986). The use of glosses to help appreciate the register of words is dealt with in Blake (1988). Works which try to focus on the colloquial elements of style are Schlauch (1952) and Clark (1978c). Many of these matters are treated also in N. F. Blake, *The English Language in Medieval Literature* (1977). The question of applying some modern linguistic advances, such as politeness theory, to medieval texts is looked at in Sell (1985a and b).

The language and style of Chaucer is examined in Burnley (1979), J. D. Burnley, *A Guide to Chaucer's Language* (1983) and R. W. V. Elliott, *Chaucer's Language* (1974). Gregory Roscow, *Syntax and Style in Chaucer's Poetry* (Cambridge: Brewer, 1981) is largely concerned with syntactic features; for vocabulary see J. Mersand, *Chaucer's Romance Vocabulary* (1937). Two books by Michio Masui can also be consulted with profit: one a collection of essays, *Studies in Chaucer's Language of Feeling* (Tokyo: Kinseido, 1988), which deal with various aspects of Chaucer's style; and the other his *The Structure of Chaucer's Rime Words: an Exploration into the Poetic Language of Chaucer* (Tokyo: Kenkyusha, 1964, but frequently reprinted) remains valuable for showing how Chaucer exploited rhyme. For Chaucer's followers one may consult Norton-Smith (1966) for Lydgate and J. C. Mendenhall, *Aureate Terms: a Study in the Literary Diction of the Fifteenth Century* (1919) for Chaucer's influence on the fifteenth century.

Features of romance style including traditional formulas and expressions are treated in Wittig (1978) and Baugh (1959). For particular studies, that by Burrow (1984) shows how Chaucer exploited the romance style in Sir Thopas.

For a study of the language of the Middle English lyric the two fullest studies are still D. Gray, *Themes and Images in the Medieval English Religious Lyric* (London: Routledge and Kegan Paul, 1972) and Rosemary Woolf, *English Religious Lyric in the Middle Ages* (Oxford: Clarendon, 1968). For the relation of alliteration to the lyric see M. Fifield, '13th century lyrics and the alliterative tradition', *JEGP* 62 (1963): 111–18.

7 ONOMASTICS

Cecily Clark

7.1 Sources and methodology

7.1.1 General principles

Names, whether of places or of people, have by definition a distinctive standing *vis-à-vis* the language at large. Although ultimately derived from elements of common vocabulary (not necessarily that of the language they currently grace), they have become emptied of their original etymological denotation; and this is true even for those whose form still coincides with that of the related lexical items: no-one expects to find cattle wading across the river at Oxford and, should a Mr Butcher actually be in the meat trade, the coincidence almost excites mirth.

On the one hand, this semantic detachment promotes cross-cultural survival: some Present-Day 'English' place names are traceable to Celtic forms at least two millennia old, a few even suspected of going back to pre-Celtic times; some 'English' baptismal names have Hebrew origins. On the other, it lays names open to phonological attrition, for no more of any form need survive than is required for acting, in context, as an unambiguous signal or pointer. Name compounds are thus subject to early obscuration, to having their unstressed syllables reduced more drastically than similar ones of analogous 'meaningful' forms, and to being 'folk-etymologised' (Lass 1973; Coates 1987; Colman 1989a and b; Clark 1991). As well as complicating the etymologising process, this makes name material an unreliable guide to the incidence and the chronology (though not the nature) of general sound changes; it raises, indeed, a possibility of there having been specifically onomastic changes, related to the general ones but carrying them further (see further below, pp. 593–4).

Name studies are also distinctive in that they stand upon what is – in conventional terms – the boundary between 'linguistics' and 'history'. Onomastic source-materials are mainly ones otherwise associated with socio-economic and administrative history. Likewise, the aims and the findings of onomastics bear at least as closely upon cultural, social and economic circumstances, often, indeed, on settlement history, as upon linguistic developments: a reminder of how artificial the conventional compartmentalisation of disciplines is (see further Clark 1990).

7.1.2 Source materials

For onomastics, and especially for anthroponymy, placing the notional break between 'Old' and 'Middle' English at 1066 corresponds with a certain reality. What it means for the specific sorts of name will be considered under the relevant heads. Contrasts bearing upon general methodology involve the range as well as the volume of source material available. Whereas study of Old English naming, personal naming in particular, is hamstrung by dearth of material, for the Middle English period there is so much documentation extant – much of it as yet neither published nor onomastically searched – that work can proceed only selectively, and therefore provisionally. As always, each type of source, and often each individual document, requires separate assessment.

The sources for name study of all kinds normally consist of administrative records; and for the Middle English period this means that most name forms found are at least perfunctorily Latinised (for some problems of interpretation that this raises, see below, pp. 548–9). The vast bulk of records surviving from this period is in itself of moment, for it reflects a growth of bureaucracy at all levels from central government to manor court (for the period before 1300, an excellent general introduction is given by Clanchy 1979; detailed references will be given under the separate heads).

For the opening of this new period, the chief group of sources is the same as for the close of the Old English one: Domesday Book (DB) and its 'satellites', the fruits of the great inquest initiated by the Conqueror in 1086 (vol. I, pp. 453–4; for recent scholarship see Sawyer 1985 and Holt 1987, and for further reading Bates 1986). The focus of study has, however, shifted. The fact that DB offers the earliest extant record of many place names ceases to be central, in so far as most 'major' English place names had long since become fixed (see below, pp. 588–91). Personal naming was, by contrast, at this very time beginning to undergo its most far-reaching changes, those that were to result in the present-day system. In this context, the evidential value of DB is enhanced by its consisting of two strata: one representing 1086 and the other *tempus regis Edwardi*, that is, 1066 or shortly before. For each date the principal landholders, under-tenants as well as tenants-in-chief, are specified; and DB thus provides, for the socio-economic classes in question, two contrasting yet comparable name corpora. Despite the scope thus offered, only the earlier corpus has so far enjoyed intensive analysis (Feilitzen 1937; cf. Dodgson 1985a; for the 1086 stratum Hofmann 1934 is interesting as a pioneer effort but its premises, and in consequence its conclusions, are now outdated).

Interpreting DB material is never easy. The two main volumes – known as 'Great' and 'Little' DB – represent, in varying degrees, recastings of the preliminary returns made by the several panels of circuit commissioners. Recasting meant risk of scribal error, and some forms are now explicable (if at all) only by comparison between the main texts and corresponding passages in the various 'satellites', such as *Liber Exoniensis, Inquisitio Comitatis Cantabrigiensis, Inquisitio Eliensis*, the *Domesday Monachorum* of Christ Church, Canterbury, and others (see, e.g. H. B. Clarke's paper in Sawyer 1985). Errors apart, orthography is a problem here. Old English spelling traditions, although to be maintained in some quarters for a further thirty-five years or more, were largely disregarded by the DB scribes, who, engaged as they were in compiling a Latin record, usually adopted Latin conventions ill-suited to the English sound system (see, e.g., Clark 1984a: 100–3). That the difficulties are best regarded as orthographic must be emphasised: approaching DB name forms, or those of any other post-Conquest records, through speculation as to 'Anglo-Norman sound-substitution' imports a needless additional level of uncertainty (see below, pp. 548–9, and 592–4; also Clark 1991).

DB represents only the first fruits of the new bureaucracy. Many series of governmental records followed, including numerous quasi-national ones, such as the Hundred Rolls of 1279 (see Cam 1930 and Kosminsky 1956: 7–46), the many sets of Lay Subsidy Rolls and especially those running from 1290 to 1332 (see Beresford 1963: 1–7; also Willard 1934) and the Poll Tax Rolls of 1377, 1379 and 1381 (Beresford 1963: 19–29). In principle, such records not only covered the whole country in uniform style but did so with a socio-economic scope far exceeding that of any pre-Conquest ones. No series, however, survives in its entirety. All are, besides, circumscribed by their compilers' aims, listing only individuals liable to tax and mainly therefore heads (90 per cent of them male) of prosperous households (see, e.g., Ekwall 1951 : *passim*); even the Poll Tax Rolls, which do often name servants and other subsidiary adult members of households, omit not only children under fourteen, beggars and successful tax evaders but also wives (see, Owen 1984: 221–34). Consequently, no tax-roll furnishes a fair sample of women's names, and few embrace the least prosperous members of society. Explicit genealogical information is sparse. What such records do offer are localisations – to a village or, in large towns, to a particular ward (they therefore give forms of all relevant place names) – and, except with the flat-rate Poll Taxes, fiscal assessments based on relative degrees of prosperity, together with occasional indications of trades practised. Within its limitations, each roll, or local section of a roll, provides a cross-section of personal-name patterns, analysable in geographical and/or socio-economic terms (the latter dimension thus far largely ignored by modern scholars); when, as with the Lay Subsidy Rolls, there survives a chronological run of similar lists for the same localities, the cross-sections can be built up into diachronic patterns. In this chapter, two Lay Subsidy Rolls for London that are fortunately available in an excellent edition (Ekwall 1951) will be used to illustrate the name fashions current among well-to-do burgesses of ca 1292 and ca 1319.

The Middle English period is thus the earliest for which documentation is ample enough to permit of viewing personal naming in a socially stratified geographical and chronological framework: a possibility that gives anthroponymics primacy among sociolinguistic studies. For, alongside the governmental records, there also survive others which, less systematic though they are in coverage, put flesh on the statistics, sometimes indeed allowing identification of particular taxpayers and the compilation of thumbnail biographies for them (see the notes to Ekwall 1951: *passim*).

Thus, there survive from ca 1200 onwards voluminous records – each sort again in its own way selective – from the various types of lawcourt: the King's Bench, the county assizes and the periodical eyres dealing with the graver crimes, the coroners' courts, the manorial courts and also the church courts responsible for matrimonial causes and some other kinds of case (editions of some of the earliest of these records have appeared among the publications of the Selden Society and in some of the county record series). The collections of *miracula* appended to saints' *Vitae* also in a sense belong under this head, in so far as constituting evidence for the canonisation process. The onomastic information afforded by judicial records is, in comparison with that from tax-rolls, sparse as well as random; but it is better backed by evidence of familial links and social standing.

Most valuable of all are the many local archives, civic and manorial as well as monastic, that survive, some going back to ca 1100 or even earlier (for early borough records, see G. H. Martin 1960–4 and 1963; and for examples, see, e.g., Bateson 1899 and Owen 1984; for the sorts of material to be expected from a religious house, see, e.g., Owen 1976; J. Martin 1978; Thomson 1980). For the twelfth century, there survive schedules of peasants dwelling on the estates of abbeys such as Bury St Edmunds (Douglas 1932: 25–44; Davis 1954; cf. Clark 1987a), Burton (Bridgeman 1916), Glastonbury (Jackson 1882) and Ramsey (Hart & Lyons 1884–93: III, 218–315) and others listing the urban tenants of houses like Battle (Searle 1980: 52–9; cf. Clark 1980a) and Christ Church, Canterbury (Urry 1967: 221–382; cf. Clark 1976a). After ca 1200 borough records grow to rival the monastic ones: there are, for instance, extensive gild-rolls surviving, together with supporting information, from towns like Leicester (Bateson 1899: 12–35) and King's Lynn (Owen 1984: 295–313; cf. Clark 1982a and 1983a). Also in the thirteenth century there begin many series of manor-court rolls detailing routine village business (Harvey 1984, and for examples, see, e.g. Holt 1964 and Harvey 1974; DeWindt & DeWindt 1981 and Raftis 1982, although not themselves onomastic studies, make clear the anthroponymical potential of the types of document used). Substantially antedating as many of them do the main series of tax-rolls, these local records afford the earliest extensive evidence extant for non-aristocratic English personal naming (Clark 1987a; cf. vol. I, pp. 461–2); and at the same time they offer authentic forms of place names, especially those of the 'minor' kinds (see below, pp. 595–604). Again coverage is selective, being centred on individuals (under 10 per cent of whom were, on average, women) responsible for property and the obligations stemming therefrom. At their fullest, on the other hand, these local materials allow of studying names in the context of neighbourly and familial relationships. Among sources of this kind often to be cited here are the earlier of the two Bury St Edmunds estate surveys already mentioned (Clark 1987a) and also the late-thirteenth-century *Carte Nativorum* or 'peasants' charters' from Peterborough Abbey (Brooke & Postan 1960; cf. King 1973: 99–125 and Clanchy 1979: 34–5).

Choosing, from among this *embarras de richesses*, which type of source to investigate depends upon the questions to be asked; for each has shortcomings as well as strengths. Thus, the Lay Subsidy Rolls cover large parts of the country systematically and at precisely datable intervals but, indications of relative prosperity apart, give little background information. Their textual reliability is, besides, like that of all the other sorts of record that survive mainly in copies at several removes from the original, sometimes suspect (McClure 1973; Rumble 1980: xiv–xvi, xxv, and 1984: 42–4; cf. McKinley 1988: 22; Hunnisett 1971 on the similar unreliability of coroners' rolls). The London Lay Subsidy Rolls have none the less been chosen as illustrative material to be cited here, mainly because of their availability in an edition whose rich annotation compensates for the documents' own bareness. In general, the records likely to be soundest as well as most forthcoming on matters of detail will be either originals, *viz*. rough rather than fair copies, or at least copies made by scribes familiar with the localities concerned rather than by ones serving a remote bureaucracy. Such local records, on the other hand, lend themselves less well than do the more stereotyped materials, such as tax-rolls, to comparison with ones from other localities or even from the same locality but of different date.

7.1.3   Statistics

The variability as well as the bulk of medieval onomastic source material has long made the applicability to it of statistical analysis a vexed question, and the increasing use of computers now makes it a pressing one. Some scholars have doubted, mainly on the grounds that no two samples are truly comparable, whether any such analysis of medieval personal-name material can ever be valid (e.g. Michaëlsson 1947 and 1954). Records do, however, as indicated, fall into groups based upon similar types of selectivity, listing gildsmen, or prosperous burgesses, or customary tenants, or people allegedly involved in crime, and so on; and this seems to authorise either some cautious comparison of like with like for different areas or different dates or, alternatively, for a single place and date, a no less cautious contrasting of different socio-economic groups (see Clark 1990: 62–4).

   That said, all personal-name records – modern censuses not excluded – carry an irreducible randomness due to the perpetual fluctuations of population, and therefore of name patterns, caused by deaths and births. To calculate percentages, as is sometimes done, to several decimal places therefore gives only a spurious exactitude. Indeed, although a wisely chosen sample ought to be broadly representative of usages at the place and time in question and among the social class concerned, to stand upon small differences in name ratios must always be risky.

Name statistics can, besides, be based in at least two different ways: either upon the number of individuals named or else upon the stock of forms represented; and each mode has its own appropriateness. Reckoning by individual name bearers can show, for instance, how eagerly a new fashion is being taken up; but it does require accurate distinction among those individuals and that, as long as by-name usage remains thin or capricious, poses problems. Analysing the name stock is simpler, but represents the swings of fashion less well; where this is valuable is for revealing, say, the long-term contribution made by a spent cultural influence to local cultural patterns.

The imbalance between the names of the sexes already noted as characterising most types of medieval record means, furthermore, that all name patterns may initially be best assessed in terms of men's names alone (see below, pp. 583–7).

7.1.4   Languages of record

For this period even more than for the Old English one, name studies depend mainly upon Latinised materials. From Domesday Book onwards, some administrative currency also of (Anglo-)French may at times need to be taken into account; but it must be borne in mind that – except in the generations immediately following the Norman settlement, and even then only among a small group of families, mostly aristocratic ones, of immigrant stock – French was no less than Latin a language deliberately learnt, not a cradle-tongue (Shelly 1921; Woodbine 1943; Rothwell 1968, 1975–6, 1978 and 1983; Richter 1979 and 1985; cf. Clark 1991). To speak, therefore, as some do, of 'Anglo-Norman scribes ignorant of English' is likely to be untrue, except when some specific document of early post-Conquest date is involved (see Clark 1987c). What constantly complicates modes of interpretation are scribal intentions of writing in languages other than English.

Orthography is, as always in historical linguistics, a basic problem, and one that must be faced not only squarely but in terms of the particular type of document concerned and its likely sociocultural background. Thus, to claim, in the context of fourteenth-century tax-rolls, that 'OE þ, ð are sometimes written t, d owing to the inability of the French scribes to pronounce these sounds' (Hjertstedt 1987: 45) involves at least two unproven assumptions: (a) that throughout the Middle English period scriptoria were staffed chiefly by non-native speakers; and (b) that the substitutions which such non-native speakers were likely to make for awkward English sounds can confidently be reconstructed (present-day substitutes for /θ/ and /ð/, for what they are worth, vary partly according to the speakers' backgrounds, often involving, not /t/ and /d/, but other sorts of spirant, e.g., /s/ and /z/, or /f/ and /v/) Of course, if – as all the evidence suggests – (a) can confidently be dismissed, then (b) becomes irrelevant. The orthographical question that nevertheless remains is best approached in documentary terms; and almost all medieval administrative documents, tax-rolls included, were, in intention, Latin documents (see Ekwall 1951: 25–6, 29–31). A Latin-based orthography did not provide for distinction between /θ/ and /t/ or between /ð/ and /d/, and so spellings of the sorts mentioned may reasonably be taken as being, like the associated use of Latin inflections, matters of graphic decorum rather than in any sense connected with pronunciation.

Indeed, Latinate graphic decorum masks vernacular usages in many ways. Baptismal names, as well as being equipped with Latin inflections, were sometimes represented by conventional archaisms, such as *Radulfus/Radulphus*, abbreviated as *Rad'*, for the name spelt in the vernacular first as *Raulf*, later as *Raul* or *Rafe* (cf. PDE *Ralph*, traditionally [reif]). The descriptive phrases constituting early forms of personal by-names and of 'minor' place names (*viz.* field names and street names) were likewise commonly Latinised. In so far as it underlines the artificiality of the record and also the pre-onomastic status of the forms concerned, such translation can be salutary; but it does create uncertainty. The naming of a man, as say, *Robertus tincter* conceals not only the colloquial form of the baptismal name but also whether the local term for 'dyer' was ME *deier*, *dextere* or *litestere* (Fransson 1935: 104–6; cf. OE *dēagian* 'to dye' and ME *liten* < Scand. *lita* 'to dye'). It further leaves it unclear whether the phrase means 'Robert, who works as a dyer' or 'Robert Dyer/Dexter/Lister': a point crucial to the history of family naming. Similarly, the Latinising of an early street name as *vicus tinctorum* conceals the local term for 'street' as well as that for 'dyer'. Because modern translators and indexers often decide quite arbitrarily how to render such forms, onomastic work must always be based on the original texts themselves. Even a printed edition of the Latin text may prove a trap, if by arbitrary capitalisation it implies onomastic status for phrases not yet possessing it (for further comments on some dangers of relying on printed sources, see Löfvenberg 1942: xxv).

With Anglo-French materials, problems can be more subtle. From about the mid-thirteenth century onwards, French (by then current in England almost wholly as a second language) functioned as a secondary language of record, sometimes interchanging with Latin within one and the same document (Ekwall 1951: 26–8, 31–3). It was also the source of many loan words widely current in Middle English. Judging the status of French forms figuring in documents is thus a delicate business. Some Gallicisation is patently superficial, as when a vernacular personal by-name *atte grene* 'dwelling beside the village green' is rendered as *de la grene* (Löfvenberg 1942: 82–3); even the more consistent *de la verte place* betrays its own artificiality. With French terms that had provided loan words into Middle English, uncertainties grow: for instance, current Middle English terms for 'blacksmith' included not only the native *smith* but also the more specialised *ferrour* < OF *ferreour* and *marshal* < OF *mareschal*, both meaning 'farrier' (see Fransson 1935: 142–5); and, in so far as Present-Day English family names perpetuate Middle English personal by-names (see below, pp. 577–83), the existence of *Farrer* and *Marshall* alongside *Smith* implies that both loan words did figure as vernacular by-names. So, forms such as *le ferrour* and *le mareschal* found in English medieval records might either have been reflecting colloquial usage or else have represented scribal rendering of 'the (shoe)smith'. On the other hand, some Present-Day English family names certainly represent Old French terms that were apparently unknown, or at most very rare, in the Middle English current vocabulary: e.g. *Rous(e)* < ME *(le) Rus* (Mod.F *Leroux*), the Middle English lexical equivalent of which was rare indeed; and this suggests some specifically onomastic transmission of French by-names (see Clark 1985). Interpretation of French items figuring in the records thus involves judging between multiple possibilities, with certainty seldom attainable unless the records themselves happen to reveal relationships between bearers of variant forms.

7.1.5   Caveat

The accounts to be given here of Middle English onomastic history will represent only overcompressed summaries of what is accepted in the early 1990s. Vast masses of records remain unanalysed, and findings therefore remain provisional. This is one of the fundamental differences between the Old English situation and the Middle English one: although analysis of the extant materials is not yet complete for the Old English period either, those materials are so limited as, on the one hand, to allow of one day being fully exploited yet, on the other, to put a complete survey for ever out of reach; but for the Middle English period documents are so plentiful that – except perhaps for the personal names of the very poorest people, who escaped record unless accused of crime – a truly comprehensive survey might well be possible, but only in the very long run indeed. Development of family naming could, for instance, be clarified by establishing tens of thousands of late-medieval and early-modern genealogies. Early forms of field names and street names could be collected and collated to form the basis of a systematic history, interlinked with that of rural and urban developments in the wider sense. No findings described here are to be taken as definitive. A vast uncultivated tract of name material still lies available for the breaking in.

7.2   Anthroponymy

7.2.1   A change of system

Neither the structure nor the content of the Present-Day English personal-name system owes much to pre-Conquest styles. The typical Old English personal designation consisted of a single distinctive name (or 'idionym'), such as *Dudda*, *Godgifu* or *Wulfstan*; and only occasionally was this supplemented by a qualifying by-name (usually postposed), such as *sēo dæge* 'the dairymaid' or *sē hwīta* 'the white(-haired man)' (see vol. I, pp. 469–70). A Present-Day English 'full name', on the other hand, necessarily involves two components: the second denoting a patrilinear family group and the first (which may consist of one unit or of several), an individual within that group. In Present-Day English usage, moreover, the familial, hereditary component is the crucial one for close identification, whereas in Old English usage, as in early Germanic ones generally, the idionym was central, any addition being optional. Beside this total change of structure, it is trivial that, out of the hundreds of Old English idionyms, only a handful, and those mainly ones which, like *Edith*, *Edmund* and *Edward*, were associated with widely venerated saints, are today represented among Present-Day English first-names.

The change of system demands a change of terminology. The special term 'idionym', no longer appropriate, will be replaced by 'baptismal name' ('Christian name' is needed for a more specific sense, neither 'forename' nor 'first name' is appropriate until family naming is well established, and 'font name' is unidiomatic). For an optional identifying component, the term 'by-name' will be retained. Only when continuity between generations is demonstrable will the term 'family name' be used ('surname' is rejected as insufficiently precise).

This twofold shift in English personal naming was a specifically Middle English process. Among the mass of the population, the name system of ca 1100 was still virtually the classic Late Old English one, modified only by somewhat freer use of *ad hoc* by-names (Clark 1987a); but by ca 1450 a structure prefiguring the present-day one had been established, with hereditary family names in widespread use, though not yet universally adopted. As for the ousting of pre-Conquest baptismal names by what were virtually the present-day ones, that had been accomplished by ca 1250. This series of changes involved several convergent processes.

The shift away from single idionyms to combinations of family name with baptismal name affected most of western Europe. One cause of it may have been the general decline, in some areas manifest well before 1000, in the old Germanic custom of permutating the conventional name elements (or 'themes': see below, p. 554) in such ways as continually to create fresh idionyms. What was crucial, however, was the subsequent reliance not merely on a finite stock of set forms but largely on a very few disproportionately favoured ones. This latter practice seems to have arisen spontaneously in many areas, for it shows itself in the native name patterns of late-eleventh-century England as well as, for instance, in those of pre-Conquest Normandy (Clark 1987a; Fauroux 1961: index). A corollary of this was that, from the early eleventh century onwards, by-names came everywhere to be more and more needed for distinguishing between individuals of like idionym (see, e.g., Aebischer 1924: 120–41; Beech 1974: 85–7; Clark 1987a). Then practical convenience, essential to the growing bureaucracy and sometimes abetted by family pride, soon led to passing of the distinctive by-names from generation to generation, albeit at first mainly from father to heir.

In England, the Norman Conquest complicated these processes. Within a few years of it all but a few of the pre-Conquest landholders had, as Domesday Book shows, been replaced by foreigners, partly but by no means exclusively 'Normans'. New appointments of bishops and abbots likewise brought foreigners into positions of prestige. Some English towns experienced influxes of merchants from Normandy, France and Flanders (it was from such stock that St Thomas Becket sprang). All these immigrants brought with them name fashions current in their homelands; and these fashions so swiftly captivated the native English that within hardly more than a generation baptismal names characteristic of the settlers were beginning to appear among towns-people and peasantry alike (Ekwall 1947; Clark 1987a). By ca 1250 these borrowed names had ousted virtually all the pre-Conquest ones; and thenceforth the typically 'English' baptismal names were reflexes, not of Old English ones like *Ælfgifu*, *Gōdwine*, *Lēofþryð*, *Wulfstān* and so on, but of typically 'continental' ones like (to give them in their PDE forms) *Alan*, *Alice*, *Christine*, *Geoffrey*, *John*, *Maud*, *Robert*, *Stephen*, *Susan*, *Walter* and *William* (for a classification of the sorts of name involved, see below, pp. 556–8). Adoption of so many fresh forms brought, however, no increase in variety. Already existing tendencies towards disproportionate reliance on a very few of the many names available were indeed reinforced, with the result that, for instance, the London sections of the Lay Subsidy Roll for 1292 show *John* as accounting for over a sixth of the men's names recorded and *William* for over a seventh, the two together thus making up almost a third of the total (Ekwall 1951: 35).

Patently, such baptismal-name patterns were scarcely adequate for social identification, far less for administrative and legal purposes. By-naming – that is, supplementation of baptismal names by phrases specifying their bearers in genealogical, residential, occupational or characteristic terms – became, in England as elsewhere, a general necessity. Such specifying phrases had been in occasional use among English people since well before the Conquest (see vol. I, pp. 469–70), and all signs are that shrinkage of the name-stock would in any case have soon compelled their general adoption. The Norman Conquest may well, however, have acted as a catalyst to the process, in so far as it brought in a new aristocracy among whom, as is clear not only from Domesday Book but also from the early records surviving from the settlers' homelands in Normandy, France and Flanders, use of by-names, and of territorial ones especially, was already widespread, with even some tentative movements towards family naming (see further below, pp. 580–1). The prestige thus accruing to use of a by-name would hardly have hindered wider adoption of them among the general native population. Exactly how colloquial usages may have developed in this respect we cannot know. In the sorts of record that constitute our main source material, use of an unqualified baptismal name had at all events become by the early thirteenth century rare even in reference to the peasantry. Nor is this development hard to understand: where rents, taxes and duties were concerned it was in the lord's interest to ensure that the individuals concerned were specified precisely; and, where holdings, rights and inheritances were concerned, it was greatly in each individual's own interest to be so specified. The processes of change then spiralled: just as disproportionate favouring of a certain few baptismal names had evoked recourse to by-naming, so in its turn the universalisation of by-naming reduced checks upon the disproportionate favouring of just a few baptismal names.

7.2.2   Insular name styles and their post-Conquest survival

The pre-Conquest English personal-name stock (to which the term 'insular' will be applied) had incorporated various strains reflecting aspects of the country's social and political history (see vol. I, pp. 456–68; also Clark 1987a, 1987b: 33–40, and Feilitzen 1937). The fifth-century West Germanic settlers had brought with them a stock that consisted, not of set names, but of name elements or 'themes', mostly carrying heroic meanings, the permutation of which could produce both simplex ('monothematic') and compound ('dithematic') idionyms in endless variety. The Vikings who from the late ninth century on settled north and east of Watling Street, in what became known as the Danelaw, observed analogous yet distinctive North Germanic naming customs, soon widely adopted in the districts where they settled. The whole pre-Conquest period also saw continual, though light, influence from continental West Germanic styles, which were introduced by visiting clergy, by merchants and, during the Confessor's reign, also by immigrant nobility. Along the borderlands, in Cornwall, in the Welsh Marches and in Cumbria, Celtic styles partly survived. The basic geographical patterns are clear, even though much remains to be discovered about the distributions of particular items. Much less clear is what forms, if any, social stratification of personal naming might have taken (see vol. I, pp. 461–2).

Even apart from the outside influences just mentioned, pre-Conquest usages had never been uniform or static. Sometimes it is asserted that, except among the peasantry, simplex names and 'short-forms' of dithematic ones lost favour after ca 900 (see vol. I, pp. 461–2); but such a generalisation now seems too sweeping. As already pointed out, the crucial development, in England no less than on the Continent – and in all areas partly, no doubt, as a consequence of familial theme permutation – was that there grew up during the eleventh century a grossly disproportionate favouring of just a few out of the many name forms current. Thus, English personal naming had on the eve of the Conquest been variegated, long since receptive of outside influences and approaching a crisis of its own.

The post-Conquest swamping of native styles by foreign ones, although virtually complete in under two centuries, was far from being catastrophically sudden. Indeed, some of our knowledge of pre-Conquest uses comes by extrapolation from post-Conquest materials, these being geographically more representative as well as more plentiful and socially more comprehensive than most earlier ones. Twelfth-century records offer many previously unrecorded forms, feminines especially, of authentic Old English kinds (Reaney 1953). How far any of these late-recorded forms represented fresh creations can hardly be determined; but certainly twelfth-century familial name patterns show theme permutation as still practised to a limited extent. Moreover, the new wealth of local records gives retrospective insight into localised fashions, such as the currency at Canterbury of *Ælfhēah* and *Dunstān* (Urry 1967: 459, 457) and the favouring in Cumbria of names associated with the former earls (Insley 1982). For Anglo-Scandinavian styles in particular, the dearth of pre-Conquest records from the Danelaw means that most relevant ones date from the twelfth century. Here, even more than with the native Old English tradition, the most enlightening studies are proving to be localised ones (e.g. Fellows-Jensen 1968; Insley 1979, 1982, 1985a and b, 1987; cf. Clark 1982a: 52–5). These show that average levels of Scandinavian influence varied from district to district, being graded from 15–20 per cent in Bedfordshire and in Suffolk, through 35–40 per cent in the east midlands and in Norfolk, to 60 per cent and more in Yorkshire and in north Lincolnshire: figures which roughly correlate with the durations of Scandinavian lordship over the districts concerned and also with the general levels there of Scandinavian linguistic and cultural influence (how far they might correlate with densities of settlement is a question that here is best left unbroached).

Medieval baptismal-name usages and distributions can be further investigated through those of patronymic by-names (see below, pp. 568–9), with the advantage of then being able to exploit the plentiful documentation surviving from the later thirteenth century. With caution, modern family names, many of which retain to this day geographically circumscribed distributions, may also be pressed into service; doing so does, of course, entail assuming in advance of the discussion below (pp. 568–9) that family names of apparently patronymic form adequately reflect early medieval styles of baptismal naming. If that be granted, then fair survival of native Old English names into at least the early thirteenth century, the date when fixing of family names seems likely to have begun, seems implied by modern surnames like *Aylmer* (< OE *Æðelmǣr*), *Edrich* (*Ēadrīc*), *Goodwin* (*Gōdwine*), *Wooldridge* (*Wulfrīc*) and so on. Similar survival of Anglo-Scandinavian ones is implied by *Arkell* (< Scand. *Arnke*[*ti*]*ll*), *Brand* (*Brandr*), *Gamble* (*Gamall*), *Grimes* (*Grímr*), *Thorburn* (*Þorbjǫrn*) and so on. Admittedly, the distributions of the Present-Day English names give only the roughest indications of what the medieval patterns might have been, and serious study must therefore aim at working back – perhaps by genealogical methods – to groups of clearly localised medieval materials. Of these, an excellent example is given by the late-thirteenth-century Peterborough *Carte Nativorum*, which show that on the abbey's estates, for which the tenth-century list of *festermenn* offered a name stock comprising over 40 per cent of Scandinavian-derived items, the patronymics of medieval peasants also included numerous Anglo-Scandinavian forms such as *Arketyl*, *Brand*, *Gamel*, *Gubbe* (< Scand. *Gubbi*), *Harold* (*Haraldr*), *Teyt* (*Teitr*) and so on (Brooke & Postan 1960: *passim*; cf. vol. I, pp. 465–8).

7.2.3 The new baptismal-name stock

The name styles favoured by the Norman duke's followers are recorded not only in the 1086 stratum of Domesday Book and in post-Conquest English charters and chronicles but also in records concerning Normandy itself and the other regions, including Brittany, Picardy and Flanders, from which settlers were drawn (this wide background makes the widespread use of 'Norman' as a code term for such names misleading).

Throughout those regions, the dominant eleventh-century styles were of West Frankish origins. Structurally, the names concerned partly resembled the native Old English ones, in so far as likewise created from a battery of 'themes' that had at one time been fairly freely permuted. Although not all themes were common to all the Germanic onomastic dialects, some were widely enough current to make a good few names ambivalent, at least in their documentary forms: e.g. *Wimund*, formally attributable equally to OE *Wīgmund*, Scand. *Vígmundr* or CWGmc *Wigmund*. Moreover, CWGmc names like *Wilhelm* possessed a general familiarity of structure that perhaps eased their adoption by English-speakers. In the main, however, CWGmc names were distinctive. Partly this was because certain of them were based on themes, such as *Grim-/-grim* and *Rod-* < Common Gmc *Hrōð-*, absent from the original Old English system, although sometimes known through the Scand. as well as the CWGmc forms borrowed from the late ninth century on. It was due also to differentiation through the normal phonological processes of those themes that were held in common, so that CWGmc *Ans-* corresponded to OE *Ōs-* (Scand. *Ás-*), CWGmc *Aud-* > *Od-/Ot-* to OE *Ēad-* (Scand. *Auð-*) and so on. Distinctiveness was also due to the Continental West Germanic favouring of a wide range of hypocoristic suffixes, some of which were foreign to native Old English usages (see especially Marynissen 1986). With the disuse of theme permutation, the set names thenceforth current evolved, no matter what their original structure, as single units, subject to the various local sound laws.

There were, in addition, certain specifically 'Norman' types of name, chiefly the Scandinavian ones handed down by the early-tenth-century Viking colonists (see Adigard 1954). Some of these are – at all events, in their conventional documentary forms – not easy to tell from the corresponding West Frankish ones; and, in England, some are hard to tell from their Anglo-Scandinavian equivalents. Although there are philological rules to go by – such as that *Ansketil*, with *Ans-* by analogy with the Frankish reflex of the theme, is Norman, whereas *Osketel/-cytel* is Anglo-Scandinavian – allowance has to be made, when dealing with medieval English materials, for scribal (or even colloquial) substitution of the more prestigious Norman variant. (In the early post-Conquest period, on the other hand, substitution sometimes went the other way, so that, for instance, the name of the Norman Turstein, archbishop of York 1119–40, often appears under the Anglo-Scandinavian spelling *Þurstan*.) A minor, and historically related, group of 'Norman' names consisted of Irish forms brought by Vikings who had reached Normandy via Dublin: e.g., *Brian, Murdac, Muriel* and *Neil* – the latter Latinised as *Nigellus*, which formally was a diminutive of Latin *niger* (Musset 1975: 48). Then, too, Normandy, like many parts of western France as well, saw some currency of names, such as *Alan*, that had been borrowed from the neighbouring Bretons.

Throughout medieval western Europe, the main competition to Continental West Germanic name styles came not from such minor and local influences, but from the specifically Christian tradition of taking names from the Old and New Testaments and from saints and Fathers of the Church. Disparate as were the ultimate origins of these names, often involving Greek or Hebrew, in western Christendom all had been transmitted through the Latin traditions of the Church, their current forms being necessarily modified by local speech habits. Because such 'Christian' names, although not unknown in pre-Conquest England, had been little favoured there, their great post-Conquest popularity may fairly be ascribed to the reinforced continental influences. Certainly, such names as *John*, *Peter*, *Simon*, *Stephen* and *Thomas* had in the pre-Conquest period been more popular in Normandy than in England (see index to Fauroux 1961), although even in Normandy characteristic, it would seem, of the clergy rather than of the nobility.

7.2.4 *Baptismal naming: rates and processes of change*

The great quantities of post-Conquest records extant might seem to facilitate a detailed charting of this major change that came over English baptismal naming between the late eleventh century and the mid-thirteenth; but, even apart from the difficulties of searching and controlling so vast a mass of material, there are obstacles. Close dating is hardly obtainable; for, because few records mention any name bearer's age (beyond a general implication of adulthood), any name corpus is likely to mingle inextricably fashions characteristic of at least two, sometimes three generations. And, with a matter so intertwined with social stratification, the uncertain comparability of the different types of record becomes especially frustrating.

The new styles (to which the term 'continental' will be applied) might at first sight seem to have caught on earliest in towns. In the tiny new town of Battle, for instance, over 40 per cent of the men listed ca 1110 bore names of continental sorts, and for the Winchester of the same date the figure is over 70 per cent (Clark 1978a: 245, and 1980a; the figures given by Feilitzen 1976: 185 make no distinction between the sexes). In London, although the extant materials of this period hardly lend themselves to statistical treatment, a shift towards continental styles can be observed from ca 1080 onwards and was by ca 1100 well advanced (Ekwall 1947: 87, 91–6). Among the peasantry, by contrast, the Bury St Edmunds survey of perhaps ca 1100 or somewhat later shows under 5 per cent of men bearing continental names, and the Burton Abbey ones datable to 1115 and 1126 show respectively 18 and 24 per cent (Clark 1987a; Bridgeman 1916: 212–47; cf. Clark 1978a: 238). These comparisons are not, however, of like with like; for, whereas peasants may be assumed generally to be all of native stock, Battle was expressly described as peopled partly from overseas, and at Winchester many Anglo-Norman magnates figured among the propertyholders. That fashion as well as immigration was at work in both towns is, on the other hand, clear from conjunctions of continental baptismal name with insular patronymic or metronymic, as in Winchester's *Herbertus filius Edwini* (CWGmc *Her(e)bert*; OE *Ēadwine*) and Battle's *Robertus f. Siflet* (CWGmc/OF *Ro(d)bert*; OE *Sigeflǣd* fem.); and similar combinations appear for London residents. The balance between the two processes remains, however, unquantifiable.

At all events, the later twelfth century seems to have seen some levelling-out between urban and rural fashions. A partial survey of Canterbury in the 1160s shows 75 per cent of men as bearing continental names, and a Newark tax-list of the 1170s, some 80 per cent; and for the peasantry of this period figures of 70–75 per cent emerge from the surveys already mentioned of those attached to the estates of Glastonbury, Ramsey and Bury St Edmunds (Urry 1967: 221–43; Cameron, Barley & Stevenson 1956: 1–4; cf. Clark 1976: 238–9). By the mid-thirteenth century insular names had virtually died out even among the peasants, being borne by only some 6 per cent of those listed for the Lincolnshire estates of the bishopric of Lincoln and by some 2–8 per cent of those listed for its east and central midland ones (Fellows-Jensen 1973: 87; 1975a: 41). Similar findings have emerged from studies of other areas, such as East Anglia (Seltén 1972: 38–43; also Insley 1985a: 74–7). Among burgesses, the shift of fashion seems, on the evidence of records such as a Canterbury rent-roll of ca 1200 and gild-rolls from Leicester (admissions dating from 1196 on) and from King's Lynn (a bede-roll or necrology, running probably from ca 1220 to post-1300), to have reached a comparable stage perhaps half a century sooner (Urry 1967: 249–83; Bateson 1899: 12–23; Owen 1984: 295–313; cf. Clark 1982a: 55–6). All attempts at dating are, as must never be forgotten, bedevilled by the uncertain age-ranges of the lists; for, in general, records represent baptisms of at least fifteen years previously and possibly as much as seventy or more previously (see Clark 1987a: 24, n. 29), with scant means of discriminating between the generations; a necrology might, of course, be surmised to represent name patterns more old-fashioned than an admissions list or even a rent-roll of similar date.

Statistics offer a skeleton history; anecdotal evidence fleshes this out, revealing possible motivations as well as contexts for the choices observed. What implications an insular name might carry in post-Conquest court circles is plain from a mocking reference to Henry I and his quarter-English queen Edith-Matilda as *Godric* and *Godgifu* (Stubbs 1887–9: II, 471). The chronicler concerned, William of Malmesbury, himself of mixed blood and probably well-born, elsewhere refrained from citing the names of several pre-Conquest saints on the grounds of their 'grating somewhat barbarously' on the ear ('quia barbarum quiddam stridunt': Hamilton 1870: 237–8). By about the 1120s similar prejudice had taken a strong enough hold among non-aristocratic children in Northumbria for a lad baptised by the Anglo-Scandinavian name of *Tósti* (short for *Þórsteinn*) to have been mocked into changing it for the more up-to-date *William* (Arnold 1882–5: I, 296). Even in the 1080s parents of as humble condition as those of the future St Godric might sometimes choose to call a son *William* rather than by any traditional insular name, a tendency that explains, for instance, the sprinkling of continental name forms among those of the Bury peasants listed perhaps ca 1100 or soon after (Stevenson 1845: 23; cf. Clark 1987a: 14–17).

So early and so marked a favouring of the name *William*, as evidenced not only in anecdote but by statistical evidence (e.g. Feilitzen 1976: 177, 187; also Fellows-Jensen 1973: 87; Insley 1985a: 75–6) might at first sight suggest royalty as a chief name model; but that supposition hardly bears scrutiny. In general, neither the names of pre-Conquest kings (e.g. *Alfred, Edgar, Edward, Harold*) nor those of other post-Conquest ones (e.g. *Henry*) enjoyed any similarly overwhelming favour; the immense popularity that *John* did enjoy began well before 1199 (see below, pp. 561–2). Perhaps people mostly found their name models nearer to hand: among the Bury peasants of perhaps ca 1100, for instance, the few continental names by then adopted show fascinating, albeit inconclusive, resemblances with those of local immigrant gentry (Clark 1987a).

Although the new post-Conquest styles of baptismal naming have *grosso modo* been retained to the present day, the shift of fashion must not be envisaged as any once-for-all adoption of a set and finite name stock. Whether in England, in France, in Flanders or elsewhere, medieval name fashions were constantly evolving, one widespread tendency being for the rarer Continental West Germanic forms to be discarded and, most importantly, for the specifically 'Christian' ones to become ever more popular (for various continental developments, see, e.g. Aebischer 1924: 112–20; Le Pesant 1956: 48–51; Leys 1958; Gysseling 1966: 9–11; Morlet 1967: 23–4; Beech 1974: 87–95).

For England too, a rising popularity of 'Christian' forms is clear. Thus, the successive Winchester surveys, datable from ca 1110 to 1207, show Continental West Germanic names, as a category, keeping fairly stable at between 50 and 60 per cent of total name occurrences but 'Christian' ones rising over the century from 4 per cent to more than 30 per cent (Feilitzen 1976: 185–6). As for particular names of the latter type: *John* accounted for little more than 1 per cent of occurrences in ca 1100 and again in 1148 but for 5 per cent in 1207; *Peter* (*Piers*), absent in ca 1100, accounted for 1 per cent in 1148 and nearly 4 per cent in 1207; *Adam*, barely represented at all until 1207, then accounted for over 3 per cent of occurrences; and the less dominant names show corresponding rises in frequency (Feilitzen 1976: 187, 191). So, too, at Canterbury ca 1200 'Christian' forms had come to account for roughly a third both of the masculine name stock and of name occurrences, whereas in the mid-1160s, although already constituting a third of the continental stock current, they accounted for no more than a quarter of occurrences; *John*, rising from just over 5 per cent of occurrences to 8 per cent, had overtaken all Continental West Germanic names other than *William* (14 per cent) and *Robert* (9 per cent), with *Simon* also rising from 2 to 6 per cent. Although percentages as well as details of name choice vary somewhat from place to place, the underlying trend is constant: thus, the Leicester gild admissions of ca 1200 show 'Christian' names as running at just under 25 per cent, whereas the patronyms of some of those enrolled (forming, it is true, a smaller and perhaps less representative corpus) suggest only 18 per cent for the preceding generation (Bateson 1899: 12–17). Similar developments appeared among the peasantry, so that among, for instance, the tenants listed ca 1190 for the Bury estates the frequencies of *Adam* and of *John* (both absent from the lists of perhaps ca 1100), although not yet equalling those of *William* and of *Robert*, had come to rival those of the CWGmc *Gilbert, Henry, Ralph, Roger* and *Walter*, with *Jordan, Martin, Peter, Salomon* and *Stephen* all now favoured here (Davis 1954, the section analysed being 6–23). The trend continued to such effect that by the 1290s *John* had become far and away the most frequent name among London taxpayers, followed by *William*, *Robert*, *Richard*, and *Thomas*, in that order, and its dominance became even more marked by 1319 (Ekwall 1951: 35, 36; for analogous trends on the Continent, see, e.g., Le Pesant 1956: 52, 55–7).

To suppose any simple opposition between these two broad categories would, however, be false; for, within each, the popularities of individual items waxed and waned from generation to generation. Among prosperous Londoners, for instance, *Adam*, *Matthew* and *Stephen* lost favour between 1292 and 1319, while *Nicholas* and *Simon* gained it. There were also local variations, with *Salomon*, for instance, favoured at Canterbury ca 1200 but not at Leicester. The rare names might well make a more rewarding study than the overwhelmingly popular ones. A minor category of great interest consists of names with literary or learned associations (e.g. Rumble 1985: 1405–6), although evidence for these is often too sparse to lend itself to statistical analysis. In the twelfth century there may have been a special fondness for such names among clerical families: a canon of St Paul's by the name of *Quintilian* called his son, also to be a canon, *Cyprian*; the chronicler–archdeacon Henry of Huntingdon had a grandson called *Aristotle* (Clay 1961). Those particular choices seem not to have caught on; but others did, most notably *Alexander* (in its colloquial form, with elision of the initial syllables unstressed in French, to be the source of the Present-Day English family-name *Sa(u)nders*), which in the London of 1292 and 1319 enjoyed a popularity comparable to those of *Nicholas* and *Philip* and much greater than those of, for instance, *Andrew*, *David*, *James* and *Michael*. Motivations behind the adoption of particular names are seldom plain: thus, the limited yet persistent currency of *Oliver* might have been attributed to the *Chanson de Roland*, were it not for the scarcity of the name *Roland* itself. How far close study of particular names and of their known individual bearers might throw light upon patterns of transmission and imitation remains to be determined (for a tentative beginning in that line, see Clark 1987a).

A vast amount of work does indeed remain to be done on the chronological, regional and social variations in the popularity of individual name forms as well as of the categories into which they fall (for the roles of godparents, see, e.g., Niles 1982 and Haas 1989). In every study, as much account as evidence allows should be taken of all potential influences, such as, for instance, the possible role of the Becket cult in encouraging the thirteenth-century rise in the frequency of the name *Thomas*. Of all the types of variation, the socio-economic one is that least explored, an omission that cries out to be remedied.

7.2.5   Current Middle English forms of baptismal names

Thus far, names have been cited in normalised forms usually based upon their Present-Day English equivalents. What the current Middle English ones were is often unclear. Attention has already been directed to the Latinate artificiality of almost all the source materials available; normally, the forms under which baptismal names, and especially those from the continental stock, were actually current were hidden under the Latinisation and abbreviation that filled the records with forms, such as *Pet(rus)* and *Rad(ulphus)*, that had deliberately been distanced from everyday usages. Modern translators and commentators, whose interests usually lie with the content of such records rather than with their language, generally render such forms straightforwardly as 'Peter' or 'Ralph'; but, from a linguist's point of view, to take it thus for granted that the colloquial Middle English forms coincided (give or take the standard early modern sound changes) with their apparent Present-Day English counterparts would be indefensible.

For the most part, names were necessarily transmitted through the spoken languages. The vernaculars through which continental forms became known in England were mainly, though not exclusively, Romance ones in which names of all types had undergone, in the measure appropriate to the dialect concerned, such typically French sound changes as effacement of medial and final dentals, vocalisation of preconsonantal [ł], loss of final palato-velars, and so on (see, e.g., Pope 1952). Thus, CWGmc *Adalheidis* is represented by *Aðeliz* (cf. the Middle English 'phonetic' spelling *Æðelic* found in several independent early-twelfth-century records) > *Aeliz* > *Alis*, CWGmc *Alberic* (equivalent to OE *Ælfrīc*) by *Aubri*, and the Latin acc. *Petrum* gives *Peðre* (another Early Middle English 'phonetic' spelling) > *P(i)erre* beside *P(i)ers* < nom. *Petrus*. Some Middle English forms show specifically northeast French (Picard) features: e.g. *Walter* and *William*, with initial [w] retained, in contrast with its shift > [gw] > [g] in CF (Francien) *Guillaume* and *Gautier*. The varied origins of the post-Conquest settlers meant that with some names Middle English usages reflected French dialectal variations: e.g. EME *Rikard* with Picard [k] retained before /a/, a pronunciation preserved in the Present-Day English family name

Rickard(s), beside later *Richard* with Francien assibilation of [k] to [ʧ] (>
Mod.F [ʃ]); likewise *Guy* from the Francien reflex of CWGmc *Wido*
beside the Picard form of the hypocoristic *Wiot*, as preserved in the
Present-Day English family names *Guy/Guise* and *Wyatt* respectively.
Post-Conquest linguistic and cultural influences were never exclusively
'Norman', for which reason one must deplore the frequent use of that
term by some modern commentators as shorthand for 'of post-Conquest
introduction'. Nor indeed were all such influences 'French' in even the
broadest sense: in the east-coast ports especially, trading contacts with
Low German speakers – Flemings, Frisians, Saxons, people from the
Hanseatic ports – led to adoption of name forms like *Hildebrand* (Clark
1982a: 56–8; 1983a: 77).

Investigation of colloquial name usages in medieval England is, as
already said, hampered by the pervasive Latinisation of formal records,
coupled with a dearth of naturalistic vernacular ones (such informal
papers as are extant – notably the letters of the Cely, Paston and Stonor
families – are for this purpose inconveniently late). Not all official
usages were, however, perfectly self-consistent: thus, in the London
Lay Subsidy Rolls of 1292 and of 1319 there appear – alongside the
conventional and usually abbreviated Latinisations – forms such as
Benoit, Denys, Maheu and *Matheu, Peres*, and so on. These, rather than
solving the original puzzle, in the event raise a fresh one; for in
documents of this date spellings so emphatically French, far from
suggesting a lapse into colloquialism, raise a possibility of documentary
Gallicisation as alternative to Latinisation (Ekwall 1951: 5, 26–8, 31–3,
cf. 29). If, as a control, we again examine the relevant Present-Day
English family names, we find *Bennett, Dennis/Dennison, Mayhew/
Matthew(s), Pearce/Pears/Pierce/Pearson/Peters*: a complex pattern
which, while not excluding some deliberate Frenchification (e.g. *Benoit*
for *Benet* < older F *Beneit*), seems in general to confirm that the current
Middle English forms of 'Christian' names, no less than those of
Continental West Germanic ones, had mainly been adopted through a
Romance vernacular, rather than directly from Latin.

Foreign influences can be traced in finer detail. As noted in passing,
medieval French and Flemish personal naming had been characterised
by lavish use of hypocoristic suffixes of many kinds, including *-el,
-echon/-esson, -et/-ot, -in, -elin* (see e.g. Le Pesant 1956: 58–60; Morlet
1967: 24–31; Marynissen 1986: *passim*). Unlatinised baptismal names
in the London Lay Subsidy Rolls include forms like *Baudechon* (representing *Baudouin*), *Gosselin* (various names based on CWGmc

Gaut- > *Goz-*), *Houchun* (*Hugues*), *Jacolin* (*Jacques*) and so on, together with asyndetic patronyms like *Eliot* (*Elias, Elie*), *Lambin* (*Lambert* < *Landberht*) and *Thomasyn* (*Thomas*). Nor was adoption of such forms limited to the bourgeoisie: *Goscelin* and *Houchun*, together with *Lancelyn* (Continental West Germanic names in *Land-*) and *Raulyn* (*Raoul* < *Radulf*), figure among the patronyms of late-thirteenth-century east midland peasants (Brooke & Postan 1960: *passim*). Fair Middle English currency of such forms seems confirmed by Present-Day English family-names like *Bodichon, Elliott, Goslin* (and probably some instances of *Gosling*), *Hutchins/Hutchinson, Rawlins/Rawlinson*; likewise with, for instance, PDE *Bartlett* (< OF *Berthelet/Berthelot* for *Barthélemy*), *Collins/Collinson* (OF *Colin* for *Nicolas*), *Perrin(s)* and *Parrott/Perrott* (OF *P(i)errin, P(i)errot* for *Pierre*), *Philbin/Philpin* and *Philpott(s)* (OF *Phillipin, Phillipot* for *Phillippe*), *Robin/Robbins/Robinson* (OF *Robin* for *Robert*), fifteenth-century *Simnel* and PDE *Simnett* (OF *Simonel, Simonnet* for *Simon*), *Wilmot* (Old North F *Willemot*, cf. PDE *guillemot* < Francien *Guillemot* for *Guillaume*) and so on. Family-name etymologies like these, even though seldom as yet genealogically proven (Reaney 1976 does not pretend to offer more than possible pointers towards etymologies, see further below, p. 579), seem acceptable as confirmatory evidence for the Middle English vernacular currency of the diminutives recorded in the source materials (the PDE /-t/ shown by several names the Mod.F equivalents of which have /θ/ reflects the partial OF maintenance of such a /-t/, especially *in pausa* and therefore in citation forms, into the sixteenth century and even beyond; see Pope 1952: 220–4).

Is Middle English baptismal naming therefore to be envisaged as predominantly Gallic in style? The dearth of naturalistic Middle English writing remains a hindrance here; but perhaps fantasy may be allowed to have sometimes been spiced with realism. Thus, amid all the allegorical naming in *Piers Plowman*, some of the low-life scenes offer a few apparently realistic forms, of two main types: (a) short, virtually monosyllabic ones like *Gibbe, Hikke, Phippe, Symme, Thomme, Watte*; and (b) ones showing the borrowed Flemish suffix *-kin* added either to one of these clipped forms or else to an original monosyllable, e.g. *Haukyn* (difficult to etymologise), *Perkin* from *P(i)ers* and *Watkyn*. Clipped forms seem to have been authentic colloquialisms, characteristic of the peasantry and of the humbler sorts of townsman, the *locus classicus* for this link being the often-quoted passage in Gower's *Vox clamantis* (Macaulay 1902; I, 783–92) that, as it were 'generically', names rebellious peasants in this style. The morphological tradition has been seen as stretching from the Old English, and indeed the Common Germanic, use of short forms of 'full' names through to Present Day English demotic ones like *Dave* and *Pete* (cf. vol. I, pp. 459–60; and Sundén 1904); certainly, the consonantal simplifications and geminations seen in Middle English short forms like *Gibbe* for *Gi(l)b(ert)*, *Phippe* for *Philip*, *Watte* for *Walter* and so on look closely akin to those found in Old English, Scandinavian and Continental West Germanic ones. Several of the most frequent clipped forms spawned rhyming variants: Old North F *Rik(ard)* gave *Dick* and *Hick* (as above) and Francien *Rich(ard)* gave *Hitch*, *Rob(ert)* gave *Dobb* and *Hobb*, *Rog(er)* gave *Dodge* and *Hodge*, *Will(iam)* gave *Bill* and so on. Then, as already noted, a clipped form could be re-extended by use of a diminutive suffix, not only the borrowed Flemish *-kin* but also the apparently native *-cock*: thus, *Ad(am)cock* and *Adkin* > *Atkin* by assimilation, *Hickock* and *Hitchcock*, *Hobkin > *Hopkin*, *Hodgkin*, *La(u)r(ence)kin*, *Sim(on)cock* and *Simkin*, *Thomkin*, *Wilcock* and *Wilkin* and so on. Although direct investigation of such colloquialisms is again partly hampered by the documentary conventions, their widespread currency is, also again, confirmed by the frequency of such originally patronymic Present-Day English family names as *Gibb/Gibbs/Gibson*, *Perkin/Parkin/Perkins/Parkinson*, *Phipps*, *Rix/Dick/Dix/Dixon/Hicks/Hickson/Hickock/Hitchcock*, *Robb/Robson/Dobbs/Dobson/Hobbs/Hobson/Hopkins/Hopkinson*, *Syme/Simms/Simpson/Simcock/Simcocks/Simpkins/Sinkinson*, *Thom/Thomson/Thom(p)kins/Thomkinson*, *Watt/Watts/Watson/Watkins/Watkinson*, *Wills/Wilson/Wilcox/Wilcockson/Wilkins/Wilkinson/Bill/Bilson*. Reshortening of suffixed *Perkin* and *Wilkin* is implied by family names like *Perks* and *Wilks*; *Wilke* is indeed well evidenced in Leicester records of ca 1200. These multiple variants being formed upon mainly continental name forms imply a vigorous vernacular tradition that was firmly and ungenteelly making the imported name stock its own.

7.2.6   Middle English by-names and their categorisation

The most salient contrast between the English personal-name patterns of ca 1100 and those of ca 1300 involves the universalisation of by-naming; for, whereas in tenth- and eleventh-century records by-names scarcely appeared except when needed for distinguishing between individuals of like idionym, late-thirteenth-century documentary practices seldom allowed any baptismal name to stand unqualified.

As observed, several convergent causes were at work here: need to compensate for over-reliance on just a few of the baptismal names available, and that at a time when communities were expanding; growth of bureaucracy, and a consequent drive towards onomastic precision; and imitation of the new aristocracy's customs. The precise aetiology of the process is probably undiscoverable, in so far as virtually the only twelfth- and thirteenth-century usages accessible are administrative ones, from which the underlying colloquial ones have to be inferred (see further pp. 568–77 below).

Although this generalised by-naming was what underlay the development of family naming, the two types of system must not be confused; for a by-name works differently from a family name. A by-name is literally descriptive (and therefore often translatable) and, in actual usage, applies only to one specific individual (to say which is not in the least, however, to deny the existence of conventional stocks of such descriptive phrases). It is, therefore, unstable and thus interchangeable with other formulations, as context or even whim might dictate, so that one and the same man might be specified in documents either as 'John son of William' or as 'John the tanner', probably according to whether his inheritance or his trade was in question, and might also perhaps have been known among his cronies as 'John with the beard' (cf. Ekwall 1944–5a; also Harvey 1965: 126–8). Such literal and shifting descriptions were no more than embryonically onomastic; and some of the more elaborate thirteenth-century formulas, such as *Robertus filius Simonis ad crucem de Wytherington*, were hardly even that. Yet, by showing how identity was being defined, even these artificial formulas contribute to onomastic history; and they may be supposed to have reflected, albeit distantly, everyday naming practices.

As examples have implied, by-names fall into several semantic categories (universal ones, as it happens): (a) familial ones, *viz.* those defining an individual by parentage, marriage or other tie of kinship; (b) honorific and occupational ones (categories that in practice overlap); (c) locative ones, *viz.* those referring to present or former domicile; and (d) characteristic ones, often called 'nicknames' (see vol. I, pp. 469–71).

7.2.6.1 The type of by-name most widely applicable is the familial one: not everyone possesses a distinctive rank or trade, a fixed domicile or memorable bodily or moral characteristics, but few lack known kin. Thus, the Bury St Edmunds survey of perhaps ca 1100 gives roughly half the individuals listed (mainly ones whose baptismal names are duplicated within the same vill) what may, in the widest acceptance of the term, be called 'by-names'; and, of these by-names, roughly half specify family relationships (Clark 1987a: 10–12). This usage was not untypical. In early records, any sort of relationship might be invoked: daughter/son, wife/widow, brother/sister, father/mother, *nepos* 'nephew; grandson', *cognatus* 'kinsman', also *socius* 'business partner' or *serviens* 'employee, apprentice'. In time, filiation and, for women, marriage came to constitute the standard forms of reference, partly at least because, in the usual context of landholders' rights and obligations, these relationships were relevant as well as obvious.

The better-drawn a document, the more thoroughly every element that could be Latinised was Latinised. This applied especially to expressions of kinship, and so now hinders attempts to analyse their history. The ubiquitous *filius* formula, as in *Johannes filius Willelmi*, might either have translated a colloquial name phrase or else have been a scribal addition made in response to administrative requirements; either way, it now gives all too little clue as to the details of vernacular usage (the discussion in Seltén 1972: 46–50 is far from adequate; cf. Sørensen 1983). Such few forms as did slip through unlatinised show usages as variable, even within a single document: thus, the Bury survey of perhaps ca 1100 employs, alongside its prevailing *filius* formulas, three vernacular styles of patronym: to wit, asyndetic ones, simple genitives and genitive phrases involving *dohtor/sunu* (for the corresponding Old English usages see vol. I, p. 469). All three survive in Present-Day English family names: thus, *Rickard*, *Richards*, *Richardson* (see above, pp. 563–4). No full survey of their distributions in the extant medieval English records has yet been attempted and restricted space allows here no more than scanty sampling. Broadly speaking, the asyndetic style prevailed up to ca 1300: the late-thirteenth-century *Carte Nativorum*, for instance, shows regular interchangeability between *filius* formulas like *Robertus fillius Brand* and the asyndetic *Robertus Brand*, together with numerous unchecked asyndetic patronyms and metronyms of all etymological types, but only a handful of vernacular phrasal forms like *Cecilesone*, *Collesone*, *Sandersone*, and fewer still bare genitives, as in *Johannes Jonis*; the London Subsidy Rolls of 1292 and 1319, representing a different documentary tradition as well as a different milieu, regularly show asyndetic forms, hardly varied either by *filius* formulas or by vernacular genitival formulations. From ca 1300, however, the suffixal forms in -*s* and in -*sone* became ever more frequent; and that they were by then the only ones still productive is implied by the fact that, whereas Present-Day English family names representing asyndetic patronyms and metronyms involve baptismal names current in the twelfth and thirteenth centuries (including some that had survived from pre-Conquest times, such as *Æðelmǣr* > *Aylmer* and *Wulfrīc* > *Wooldridge*), forms in -*s* and in -*son* seem limited to ones current from the fourteenth century onwards (in the sample series quoted earlier, the asyndetic *Rickard* involves the Picard form introduced soon after the Conquest, whereas the suffixal *Richards* and *Richardson* are based on the Francien doublet that superseded it). In addition, the suffixal styles show a general geographical differentiation, bare genitives being characteristic of southern England and forms in -*son* of the north, with a wide band of overlap running across the midlands (for the West Riding of Yorkshire, see Redmonds 1973: 23–6, 29–37; for East Anglia, McKinley 175: 127–38; for Oxfordshire, McKinley 1977: 211–35, noting the southwest midland currency of an -*en* suffix also; for Lancashire, McKinley 1981: 313–34; for Sussex, McKinley 1988: 305–23, 325–35; for a recent discussion of possible Scandinavian influence, see Sørensen 1983).

There is also a socio-onomastic element in the distribution of familial by-names; for their universal applicability made them especially frequent among peasants, although by no means peculiar to them (McKinley 1977: 199–200). Frequently humble associations are reflected, as already illustrated, in the not-uncommon forming of Present-Day English family names in -*s* and in -*son* upon clipped and otherwise colloquial name forms. Among the prosperous Londoners of ca 1300, on the other hand, patronymic forms accounted for no more than 8 per cent of all by-name occurrences and those that did occur seldom involved the more demotic name styles.

7.2.6.2   In contrast with the universally applicable by-names of family relationship, occupational forms were characteristic of towns, the *raison d'être* of which was trade. It is, however, a matter of proportion, not absolute distinction. The Bury survey of perhaps ca 1100 identifies by trade or office under 10 per cent of the 600 or so individuals, peasants mostly, that it lists (figures cannot be exact, because some terms may be locative rather than occupational, see below, p. 575), specifying some twenty-five or so occupations – bakers, horsemen, millers, priests, reeves, smiths, also two merchants, two skinners and two goldsmiths; fourteen terms are Latinised, some ten are English, none clearly French. The contemporaneous rental from Battle, with only a sixth the number

of entries, identifies by trade some 30 per cent of the householders it
lists, again specifying about twenty-five occupations; twenty-one terms
are Latinised (two being difficult to interpret and one a periphrasis), one
is English, two are French and one ambivalent. The also contemporaneous survey from Winchester likewise has twenty-three Latin
terms and two French ones; but that of 1148 offers seventy-seven Latin
terms, twelve English ones and eight French, many being applied to
several individuals. Both the London Lay Subsidy Rolls identify by such
means about a quarter of those listed (some instances being by then,
however, familial rather than literal in implication); within the Latin
frameworks, terms in all three languages appear, with French dominant
in 1292 but by 1319 giving ground to English (tellingly, the incidence
of the three languages varies from ward to ward).

This sampling (random in so far as choice of texts has turned on
availability rather than content) shows early by-name records as fairly
reticent about vernacular occupational terms (what they provide in
plenty is evidence for the economic basis and daily activities of the
community concerned). When French forms appear, it is seldom clear
whether they represent borrowing into Middle English or mere use of
French as a secondary language of record (see Ekwall 1951: 29; and cf.
above, p. 550): a matter which, upon scrutiny, reveals a further
dimension. In exploring this, the evidence of Present-Day English
family names will again be invoked, along with that of Middle and
Present-Day English common vocabulary. Thus, the name *Frobisher*,
the verb *to furbish* (first recorded 1398) and the agent-noun *furbisher*
(1400; beside the more frequent *furbur* from 1260 on) combine to
suggest that documentary *le fourbisseur* represents not so much
Gallicisation as formalised spelling of a term current both in colloquial
vocabulary and as a personal by-name. By contrast, the frequent
documentary *le pestour* 'baker' corresponds neither to any present-day
family name nor (*pace* the *MED*, s.v *pastere*) to any current Middle
English agent-noun, and so must be taken as simply a documentary
alternative to Lat. *pistor*. Each item thus demands separate assessment.
Many originally French terms – such as *barber*, *butcher*, *carpenter*,
cordwainer/cordiner, *draper*, *farrier*, *mason*, *mercer*, *tailor* – had early been
adopted into Middle English usage (the near coincidence of OF -*eor* <
Lat. -*ātor* with OE/ME -*er(e)* might have eased some adoptions) and
likewise came in time to figure as Present-Day English family names.
Others seem limited to documentary use; but if a French by-name form
that lacks an equivalent among Middle English common nouns proves

to have parallels among medieval French by-names and also among Present-Day English as well as Modern French family names, then it may be guessed to have come in on the back of an immigrant merchant (see Clark 1985).

Native Middle English terms fall, structurally speaking, into several categories. A small but basic group comprises simplex forms inherited from Old English: e.g. *cok* 'cook', *herde* 'herdsman', *smith*, *webbe* < OE *webba* 'weaver', *wrighte* < OE *wyrhta* 'craftsman'. Most were, however, derivatives or compounds. The agent-suffix *-er(e)*/fem.*-estre*, which in Middle English gradually seems to have superseded the obsolete *-a* > *-e* (so that, for instance, *webbe* slowly yields place to *webbere*/*webster* and the later-formed *weaver*), could be affixed to either (a) verbal bases or (b) substantive ones: (a) *bruere*/*breuster* < OE *brēowan* 'to brew', *heuere* < OE *hēawan* 'to hew', *hoppere*/*hoppestre* < OE *hoppian* 'to dance', and so on; (b) *bureller* < ME *burel* 'coarse cloth', *glovere* < OE *glōf* 'glove', *glasier* < OE *glæs* 'glass', *madrer* < OE *mædere* 'dyestuff', *nailere* < OE *nægl* 'nail', *ropere* < OE *rāp* 'rope', *skinnere* < Scand. *skinn* 'pelt' and so on. Some original feminines, e.g. ME *baxter* < OE *bæcestre* 'baker' and ME *breuster* especially, came – mainly in the old 'Anglian' areas – to be applied indifferently to both sexes (Fransson 1935: 41–5; in brewing at least, women were dominant enough for some relevant borough ordinances to be drafted in the feminine). Terms of type (a), *-makere* in particular, could be focused by prefixing of the verb's object: *bokebynder*, *bowestrengere*, *cappmaker*, *lanternemaker*, *lymbrenner*, *medmowere*, *rentgaderer*, *sylkthrowster*, *waterladestre* (for further exemplification, see Fransson 1935: 209–10; Thuresson 1950: 276–8). Compounds roughly equivalent to *-er(e)* forms of type (b) could be formed with *-knave*, *-grom* or *-man* and with *-wif* or *-wymman*, thus *burelman*, *candelwif*, *horseknave*, *maderman*, *plougrom*, *sylkewymman*; and also with the more specific *-herde*, *-monger* < OE *mangere* 'dealer', *-reve* 'overseer', *-ward* 'keeper' and *-wrighte* 'maker', thus, *couherde*, *swynherde*, *madermongere*, *stocfisshmongere*, *ripreve* 'harvest overseer', *bulleward*, *wodeward*, *wheelewrighte*. With the genitive of a personal name or by-name prefixed, *-man* meant 'servant' in general.

The full range of Middle English occupational terms may well not yet be known: over 250 unknown to *OED* were listed by Thuresson in 1950, and others have since been noted casually (e.g. Sundby 1952; Mills 1968; Clark 1976b). Nor are dates and distributions as fully analysed as they might be. For instance, the Bury survey of perhaps ca 1100 – in print by 1932 and excerpted in Tengvik 1938 but since then disregarded

– offers not only the otherwise, it seems, unrecorded OE *inn-gerēfa ?'overseer of lodgings' (see Feilitzen 1939: 130) but also antedatings of blodletere (MED 1221), cropper(e) 'tree-pruner' (1221), demere 'arbitrator' (1225), hayward (1165) and wheelwright (1274; Fransson 1935), as well as of the ambivalent chircheman (1229) and halleman (1297). Little has been done towards mapping the various sets of synonyms such as fullere, tuckere and walker, deiere, dexter and litestere, madrer, maderman and madermongere and so on (see the brief notes by Thuresson 1950: 273–5; these are not the sorts of term studied in McIntosh et al. 1986); what is clear is that there is more to this than just the effects of Scandinavian influence upon usages in the old Danelaw.

7.2.6.3 Middle English locative by-names – viz. ones referring to their bearers' present or former homes – fall into two linguistic categories: (a) toponymical, that is, involving proper place names; and (b) topographical, that is, specifying some feature of the bearer's homestead. Because these partly differ in their social implications, some scholars prefer to regard them as distinct. Semantically, however, they overlap; for, although toponymical forms, unlike topographical ones, mainly marked people who had left the places named, there was no hard-and-fast distinction, in so far as great landholders took such names from their chief residences, just as peasants took topographical ones from the sites of their cottages.

Toponymical by-names were among the earliest recorded. In England, ad hoc resort to them appeared already in tenth-century records (cf. vol. I, pp. 470–1). In Normandy, and also in other parts of the Continent, some nobles were taking names from their principal estates well before 1066 (e.g. Aebischer 1924: 142–51; Loyd 1951; Musset 1976: 94–5; Bates 1982: 99–121, esp. 113–14; Holt 1982: 11–16); and in England, as Domesday Book makes clear, many immigrants retained these designations. Other settlers, lesser gentry in the main, soon took similar names from their new English holdings: a custom that perhaps gave toponymical by-names, in England previously mere descriptions, some social cachet. Subsequently, such forms became characteristic of well-to-do and rising townspeople. The Winchester survey of ca 1110 offers about thirty different toponymical by-names, two-thirds of which refer to places in France; but in that of 1148 (containing over three times as many entries) more than half the eighty-three such names used refer to English places – a sign, perhaps, of new coinage in progress. True, Winchester, where many messuages were held by Anglo-Norman magnates, was not typical of English towns; but such fashions were not long in appearing elsewhere, with names usually taken not from landed property but from the village that an upwardly mobile migrant had left. Thus, early entries in the King's Lynn necrology, begun perhaps ca 1220, show toponymical forms running at 30–5 per cent of by-name occurrences, and by ca 1300 gild admissions there and at Norwich show them at 50 per cent or more (Owen 1984: 295–302; McKinley 1975: 82–4; cf. for medieval Oxford, McKinley 1977: 88–106). In the London of ca 1300 40–5 per cent of citizens comfortably off enough to be taxable bore such names. Not unexpectedly, there are unevennesses in the pattern: thus, in the Leicester admissions rolls of 1196–1214 (Bateson 1899: 12–23) toponymical forms account for only 18 per cent of by-name occurrences; this low ratio, complemented as it was by a high one for patronyms, might perhaps have been partly due to an *ad hoc* emphasis on the filial relationships often underlying such admissions. Among villeins, whose physical as well as social mobility was restricted, use of such by-names was correspondingly slight (e.g. McKinley 1977: 199, also 203–4).

Linguistically, the main interest of toponymical by-names might lie in their potential as evidence for the uninhibited development of the place names in question (see below, pp. 592–4); but, at any level beyond the impressionistic, such study demands firm genealogical linkage between each family name and the locality whose name it represents. Because so much personal-name investigation has been, and is, focused upon the history of population movements, that has in the event been the aspect of toponymical by-naming which has thus far received most attention, being, for instance, a main theme of the English Surnames Series. A notable contribution was Ekwall's 1956 monograph on London, aimed at elucidating the regional background to London English and so, ultimately, to the standard language. Such investigations are, it must be stressed, less simple than some amateurs suppose, partly because of the multiple reference of many place-name forms (see McClure 1979).

By contrast with toponymical by-names and their frequent assertion of mobility, topographical ones imply their bearers to have been, at the time of coinage, living or working at the place described ('at the cross', 'at the green', 'under the wood', 'at the kitchen' and so on), further implying that to be the most distinctive thing about him or her. Typical of the settled peasantry, such as those figuring in the late-thirteenth-century *Carte Nativorum* (cf. also Harvey 1965: 126), and seen also among modest townsfolk, such names hardly appear among the early-to mid-twelfth-century propertyholders of Winchester, the early-thirteenth-century gildsmen of King's Lynn and Leicester, or the London taxpayers of ca 1300: their distributions are thus, as noted above, in part complementary to those of toponymical ones (see McKinley 1977: 41–5, 199–200, 203–4; 1988: 11–14, 105–7).

A topographical by-name consists of an adverbial phrase, *viz.* a preposition (most often *at*, sometimes *above*, *by*, *in*, *of*, *on*, *over*, *under* or *up*) plus a form of the definite article (proof that the term following was, at time of coinage, a common noun, not a 'name') plus a term indicating a landmark or, sometimes, a place of employment. That such formulas were until well into the fourteenth century still perceived as descriptive is shown by their general translatability: *atte grene*, for instance, might be rendered as *ad placeam* or *de placea*, as *de la* (*verte*) *place* or, perfunctorily, as *de la* (more rarely, *del*) *grene*. Rather as with occupational terms, the standing of French forms may be uncertain; and each case must again be assessed according to whether it possesses a counterpart either in current Middle English vocabulary or among present-day family names. 'French' terms early adopted into Middle English (e.g., *abbey*, *castle*, *forest* and so on) count as naturalised. Ones coinciding with Old French place names, major or minor (e.g. *del pre*), might be chance results of scribal translation or might, alternatively, represent genuine Old French names belonging to immigrants, and only investigation of the family concerned, a precaution sometimes neglected, will resolve the ambiguity. Terms authenticated as current, whether native or naturalised, constitute our main evidence for Middle English topographical vocabulary, which, being poorly evidenced in the extant literary materials, is therefore under-represented in the general dictionaries. Such terms may be simplex, as illustrated, or compound like (*atte*) *tounesende*, Latinised as (*ad*) *caput villa*; their full range may not yet be fully established. Sometimes they offer embryonic forms of 'minor' place names (e.g. Rumble 1985: 1408–9; cf. below, pp. 595–9). The standard monographs are, as it happens, orientated towards lexical and etymological concerns rather than onomastic ones *stricto sensu* (Löfvenberg 1942; Kristensson 1970; cf. Mawer 1930).

The phrasal structure of these by-names throws incidental light on Middle English forms of the definite article. The most frequent is an indeclinable *þe*, often assimilated and merged with a preceding *at* (*at þe* > *atte*). Some postprepositional inflections do, however, occur, usually as *atten* < OE masc./neut. *æt þǣm/þām* or *atter* < OE fem. *æt þǣre*. Except before terms beginning with a vowel or /h-/, *atten* is rare but, in some areas at least, *atter* appears also before consonants. By this time choice between *atten* and *atter* was only partly governed by Old English genders: *atten* can appear with Old English feminines like *āc* > ME *ok(e)* and *burg*/dat. *byrig* (cf. PDE *Attenborough*) and, proportionately more often, *atter* is extended to Old English masculine and neuter nouns (Löfvenberg 1942: xxx–xxxiii). A comprehensive survey, such as has not yet been undertaken, might perhaps reveal some regional patterns in usage. Once such forms had become fixed (a matter not easy to date) and denotation had faded, false divisions might occur, as with dative-based place names (see vol. I, pp. 476–7) and occasionally with common vocabulary, so that ME *atten ashe* > PDE Nash and OE **æt þǣre ēa* 'beside the stream' > ME *atter ee* > PDE *Ree, Ray* or *Rea*.

Semantically, this latter category is far from clearly demarcated. A phrase referring to a probable workplace, such as bakehouse, cellar, kitchen, malthouse, mill, pound, and so on, might be tantamount to an occupational term, e.g. baker, cellarer, cook, maltster, miller, pinder, and so on. Conversely, some by-names apparently formed like occupational terms, *viz.* with *-er* or with *-man*, either, as with, for instance, *Hiller* and *Hillman*, resist occupational interpretation, or else prove to vary, for the same individuals or families, with phrases in *at*, as with *Waterer/atte water* (Fransson 1935: 192–202; McClure 1982; McKinley 1988: 141, 145–7, 152–61, 173–7, 179–80). This topographical application of the suffix *-er(e)* seems restricted to southern England and, in those areas where it does occur, forms are often, as just observed, ambivalent (see Thuresson 1950: 27–8). Further synonymous sets of Present-Day English family names therefore include groups like *Ashe, Asher, Ashman, Nash*.

7.2.6.4 Linguistically, the most fascinating, because far and away the most perplexing, category of by-name consists of 'nicknames': that is, expressions which in some way – physically or morally, literally or ironically – characterise their bearers. The idiomatic, sometimes even cryptic, nature of such forms to some extent discouraged their scribal translation: thus, the Bury survey of perhaps ca 1100 offers several vernacular phrase names – among them *Brenebrec*, which (*pace* Tengvik 1938: 385; Reaney 1967: 280) surely means 'burn clearing' rather than 'burn breeches', and *Crep under hwitel* 'crawl under blanket' – unlikely to have been scribal inventions (see vol. I, p. 470). In form, nicknames range from phrases like these to simple and freely translatable epithets such as 'the red-haired' (*the Rede, le Rus, Rufus*). Semantically, many of the latter have widespread counterparts: e.g. *White*, *de Wit*, *Weiss*, *Leblanc*, *Blanco*, *Bianchi* and so on.

One frequent device in medieval usage involves an asyndetically postposed substantive referring variously to a feature or a limb, a garment, tools of trade or wares, or to a metaphorical animal: the London Lay Subsidy Roll of 1292 offers, for instance, *Jeffrey Fot* 'foot', *Ric. Heued* 'head', *Rob. Hod* 'hood', *Rob. Oingnon* 'onion', *Laur. Bulloc* 'bullock', *John. Heyrun* 'heron', *Adam Hering* 'herring' and *Th. Pecoc* 'peacock', all of which find counterparts among present-day family names. Import is often uncertain. A garment name like *Hod* might denote either characteristic attire or stock-in-trade (here the bearer seems identifiable as a corn merchant); this particular one might, alternatively, involve a literary allusion. Animal nicknames sometimes involve a further level of ambiguity; for, because by-names like *Bucca* 'he-goat' and *Crāwa*/fem. *Crāwe* 'crow' seem already in Old English times to have come to figure simply as idionyms, the corresponding Middle English by-names might have been asyndetic patronyms rather than current nicknames. That apart, uncertainties as to occupational or personal reference are rife: 'heron' and 'peacock' must be presumed to have normally been (at least in genesis) characterisations, the quoted instance of 'herring' applies to a fishmonger, and 'bullock', the quoted instance of which seems not to apply to a butcher, might have been either physically descriptive or else inherited from a forebear who had been a butcher or a stockman. Onomastic interpretations must never, therefore, be based upon etymology alone but always upon as full study as records allow of the individual name bearers and their families: a procedure splendidly exemplified in Ekwall's edition of the two London Lay Subsidy Rolls but all too seldom followed in more recent work on nicknames (see McClure 1981: 101–3).

Prefixing an adjective to such a substantive produced a so-called 'bahuvrihi' form, such as *Gretheved* '(with the) big head' or *Grenehod* '(with the) green hood': a type of formation frequent also in early Scandinavian and Old French styles of by-naming (Seltén 1975). Although descriptive intent may seem more obvious here, implications are again often obscure; for, behind seemingly commendatory expressions such as *Clenehond* '(with the) clean hand', *Freburs* '(with the) open purse' and *Swetmouth* '(with the) dainty mouth', irony may be suspected but hardly now proved. Formally similar but semantically distinct are the names apparently based on characteristic sayings, like

Godchep '(I offer a) good bargain' – also perhaps given an ironical ring by customers or rival traders.

The so-called 'Shakespeare' or 'pickpocket' names are formed – like the poet's and like the *Brenebrec* (whatever its exact meaning) quoted above – from transitive verb plus object. The aetiology of this pattern is obscure. Currency of analogous forms in Old French (e.g. *Gâteblé*) has led their appearance in England to be ascribed – on the *post hoc*:*propter hoc* principle all too often applied to post-Conquest phenomena – to imitation of French fashions (e.g. Tengvik 1938: 383–4; Seltén 1969: 119–20 (sees both sides); Hjertstedt 1987: 23). Sociolinguistically, however, this is hard to square with the evidence: the Bury survey of perhaps ca 1100 or shortly after, from which *Brenebrec* has already been cited, contains a fair number of such forms, mostly involving native terminology, and it is hard to suppose several groups of Suffolk peasants, among whom continental idionyms had barely begun to be adopted, as having by that date so thoroughly assimilated French nickname syntax as to be freely inventing for one another native forms based on its patterns; indeed, a form *Wulfwine spillecorne* 'ruin-grain' was apparently given to a peasant of *ante* 1066 (Stubbs 1887–9: 273–4; cf. Reaney 1967: 269–80). The type is, besides, widespread in medieval German dialects as well as in the Romance languages (Schützeichel 1983). Structure too has been disputed: sometimes these forms have been called 'imperative names', as though *spillecorne* meant 'Go on – spoil the grain!', but the verbal component may more acceptably be taken as a stem form (Reaney 1967: 279; Sauer 1988: 200).

Authentic nicknames constitute virtually our only direct link with colloquial Middle English, offering many antedatings of words and of idioms, slang ones especially (e.g. Tengvik 1938: 23–7; Feilitzen 1976: 229) If rightly interpreted, they might also illuminate social attitudes: for instance, the frequent reference to purses – deep, open and locked – suggests censure of stinginess. It would not be an easy enterprise; but as yet little has even been attempted on these lines.

7.2.7 The spread of by-naming and the rise of family naming

Virtually universalised by-naming makes name styles of ca 1300 look almost modern; misleadingly so, for a by-name, as observed above (p. 567), works differently from a family name. Evolution from the one to the other was by no means inevitable; for, as the Present-Day

Icelandic system of true patronyms demonstrates, identification through individual by-name can without inconvenience be prolonged indefinitely. The previous exposition has nevertheless, perhaps rashly, taken it for granted that Present-Day English family-names are reflexes of Middle English by-names. How, when and – if possible – why English usage underwent this shift of system remains to be shown.

The spread of by-naming is less amenable than baptismal-name fashion to statistical analysis, owing to the even less certain correlation between colloquial styles and incidences and documentary ones, a correlation that may, moreover, vary, even synchronically, from document to document. There is, besides, a problem of definition: a genealogical formula like the late-thirteenth-century *Willelmus filius Symonis filii Walteri de Undele* (Brooke & Postan 1960: 144), clearly though it testifies to a need to specify individuals and to choice of ancestry and abode as means of so doing, is not in itself a 'name' in the full sense. Between Common Germanic usages and Present-Day English ones, some five stages of development might be postulated: (a) use of bare idionyms; (b) frequent addition of *ad hoc* descriptions; (c) use of set by-names for many individuals; (d) sporadic passing of such by-names from parent to child; (e) universal family naming. The difficulty is not only to distinguish in documentary records between stages (c) to (e) but, even more, to determine the underlying colloquial usages.

Twelfth- and thirteenth-century usages hardly lend themselves to systematisation. The marked over-reliance on just a few of the many baptismal names available required recourse to means of distinguishing between the numerous individuals of like idionym – to by-names, in short; that this was so in everyday life as well as in the drafting of administrative documents is confirmed by the currency of untranslatable nicknames, but colloquial usages are not otherwise accessible. Social class was a variable, and an influence: from 1066 on, members of the immigrant nobility and gentry regularly sported distinctive by-names, often territorial ones but sometimes nicknames, whereas for the peasantry even documentary usage could admit bare idionyms well into the thirteenth century (e.g. Fellows-Jensen 1975a: 41–2); and so snobbery, a motive likewise not easily accessible to modern scholarship, may have encouraged social, as well as documentary, adoption of by-naming and ultimately also of family naming.

Getting behind the documentary styles to the colloquial ones is not impossible. As previously remarked, even for early-twelfth-century peasants the by-names recorded include some, not only nicknames but also asyndetic patronyms, that must have been carried over from everyday usage; but at that stage the colloquial incidence of such forms remains unquantifiable. By the 1290s and among prosperous burgesses the lightly Latinised/Gallicised styles of the London Lay Subsidy Roll involve asyndetic patronyms and other by-names of seemingly colloquial form so often as to allow of assuming that, among people such as those listed, everyday by-naming had by then become widespread, if not universal; and it was against the background of such an assumption that Ekwall, exceptionally well-versed as he was in the personal naming of medieval London, carried out his studies into by-name variation (1944–5a). On the other hand, the Poll Tax returns of ca 1380 sometimes, though not invariably, show household servants entered by baptismal name alone (e.g. Owen 1984: 221–34); whether or not colloquial usages accorded by-names to such individuals, administratively the context (equivalent to a form in -*man* preceded by the genitive of the master's name) apparently obviated any need for such addition. Universalisation of non-hereditary by-naming, let alone therefore of family naming, was of very slow growth.

Ideally, the rise of family naming would be studied by establishing, for the period 1100–1500, tens of thousands of annotated genealogies representing all social classes and all areas of the country: an undertaking scarcely practicable even if scholars were more numerous than they are and records less discontinuous. As it is, except for the nobility and gentry and for a few groups of urban patricians, even such genealogical work as the documentation permits has so far hardly been attempted. Few family names therefore possess other than provisional etymologies. The existing so-called *Dictionary of British Surnames* (Reaney 1976), remarkable though it is as a repertory of Middle English personal-name forms, makes no pretence at genealogical verification of etymologies but simply collocates Present-Day English family names with some likely Middle English antecedents; lacking though it is in authority, as a starting-point for investigations it is invaluable.

Before any Middle English by-name can be claimed as a 'true family name' (and it is a matter always of individual cases, not of general development), certain criteria must be fulfilled. It is not enough for the same form to reappear in successive generations, because occupation, abode or physical characteristics can all be transmitted from father to son in such ways as to maintain the literal applicability of a by-name. To be onomastically hereditary, a name must be retained and transmitted after ceasing to be literally true. To be a family name, it needs to be passed not only from parent to heir(ess) but to all the children of a family and then (given that the underlying social system was a patriarchal one) on to all those of each son, indefinitely. Because this transmission goes in parallel with loss of denotation, family naming thus further exemplifies how naming comes to crystallise out of literal description (see vol. I, pp. 452–3).

The rise of family naming can thus be studied only through documents giving adequate background information (on their own, Lay Subsidy Rolls are virtually useless here). With a toponymical by-name, the bearer must represent the second generation at least after migration from the place concerned; with an originally patronymic or metronymic one, he or she must be the grandchild at least of the person named; and with an occupational one, he or she must not be practising the trade in question; preferably, he or she should not be the heir to any family property. Documents must be studied only in reliable editions (to say, only in manuscript, would be a counsel of perfection), never in translation or from calendars and indexes, in which convenience of reference sometimes seduces historians and archivists into unwarrantedly extending a by-name from one member of a family to the rest. Modern historical custom must never be accepted uncritically: there seems, for instance, no contemporary authority for the conventional reference to Thomas son of Gilbert Beket, afterwards St Thomas of Canterbury, as 'Thomas Becket' (Barlow 1986: 12; see also Rigg 1987).

The earliest instances on English soil of apparently hereditary by-naming involve Norman immigrants. Well before 1066, as observed, some Norman nobles had begun passing by-names from parent to heir; and settlers in England continued this custom, sometimes with pre-Conquest continental by-names, sometimes with new ones derived from English estates. In assessing the import of this custom, caution is indicated. No territorial by-name can be deemed truly hereditary as long as its successive bearers hold the lands in question. Similarly, a descriptive by-name – such as *Crispin*, taken by the family itself to refer to their curly hair (Robinson 1911: 13–18) – becomes hereditary only when applied, for us unverifiably, to family members lacking the characteristic in question. Nor must early continuities of name be overstressed: the expression 'from parent to heir' was just now used advisedly, because eleventh- and twelfth-century Normandy and England abound in cases of brothers taking distinct by-names, often (but not necessarily) alluding to the estates each held, one well-known instance involving Hugh of Montgomery (whose father had named his

Welsh castle after his Norman one, *dép*. Calvados) and Robert of Bellême (who took his mother's estates).

From the mid-twelfth century on, continuities of name spread gradually (McKinley 1988: 29–67) and irregularly through most ranks of English society, encouraged not only by continuities of trade, residence and physical feature but also by the value of a firm familial identity to anyone having even a modest inheritance to claim. The keyword is 'gradually'. In mid- to late-twelfth-century Canterbury, for instance, some citizens were passing non-descriptive by-names from father to heir (e.g. *Hamo Coppe filius Henrici Coppe*, ca 1200, where the by-name probably derives from a patronymic use of OE *Coppa*), others figured under two or more interchangeable designations each, and yet others were specified only by lengthy periphrases (Clark 1976a: 14). Analogous situations obtained in other towns, including, for instance, King's Lynn, Winchester and Oxford; in the last-named, family naming appeared among the patricians up to two centuries earlier than among the humbler citizens (Clark 1983a: 66–9; Rumble 1985; McKinley 1977: 25–30). London is the town thus far most intensively studied: that denotation was by ca 1290 receding even from occupational by-names is clear from Lay Subsidy Roll entries such as *Joh*. *le Clerc pestur*, *Rob*. *le Mareschal surgien* and *Will*. *le Taverner chaucer* (in quoting, capitalisation has been normalised); but by-naming nevertheless retained a fair degree of flexibility at least up to the middle of the fourteenth century and perhaps beyond (Ekwall 1944–5a, 1951). Among rural populations, transmission of names from generation to generation soon began, but apparently more gradually than among burgesses (e.g. McKinley 1977: 22–5). The mid- to late-thirteenth-century Peterborough *Carte Nativorum*, for instance, show clear examples of continuity alongside equally clear ones of discontinuity: thus, *Galfrido* (dat.) *Prodom filio Roberti Prodhom de Empingham* (1225), *Thome* (gen.) *Palmer de Castre* beside *Thomas filius Willelmi Palmer de Castre* (ca 1300), but also *Warinus de Glinton filius Ascelini Hereward* beside *Warinus filius Ascelini Hereword* (a 1290), and the prize specimen *Johannes de Bardeneye manens in Lee filius Leticie Raynberd de Haytheby* (1333). The degree of variation still possible well into the fourteenth century can be illustrated from the titles and colophons relating to the works of a well-known writer: *Richard Rolle heremyt of hampolle*, *Richard Rolle hermyte*, *holi richard þe hermit of hampulle*, *Richard hermite of hampole*, *Richard the Ermyte*, *Richard hermyte*, *seynt rycharde of hampole*, *Richarde of hampole*, *Richard hampole*, *Richard hampole heremyte*, with a similar range of variation in the

Latinised versions (Ogilvie-Thomson 1988). Even by the mid-fifteenth century fixed by-names were by no means universal: witness some alternative styles given in the Paston correspondence, such as 'Pyrs Waryn, otherwyse callyd Pyrs at Sloth ["beside the marsh"]' or 'John Botillere, oþerwyse callid John Palmere' (Davis 1971–6: 295, 323). For parts of the north, parish registers (first instituted in 1539) show some of the humbler families as even in the seventeenth century still relying on true patronyms in -*daughter*/-*son* (McKinley 1981: 46, 355–8). The conventional definition of the so-called 'surname-creating period' as running from ca 1100 to ca 1400 is thus unduly circumscribed.

Nevertheless, the decisive innovation in name custom seems to have been virtually accomplished by the mid-fifteenth century, with the shift of primacy from baptismal name (or 'idionym') to family name. This is revealed by growing tendencies to use the latter, with or without handle, as a regular mode of public reference: a style found, for instance, in the correspondence of the Pastons and of the Celys (e.g. Davis 1976: 224; Hanham 1975: 191–2) and a century later fully established, as shown by the names of Shakespeare's *Master* and *Mistress Ford, Mistress Quickly* and other realistic characters. For all the slowness of its evolution, this shift from a name system based on a multitude of idionyms optionally supplemented by by-names to one based on a huge range of family names supplemented by a limited one of baptismal names was drastic. Common to most of western Europe, it presumably reflected a general shift in concepts of social structure.

The loss of denotation resulting from the transmutation of descriptive by-names into fixed family names had much the same phonological consequences as the analogous semantic emptying of place names. Both types of name were for centuries transmitted chiefly by word of mouth rather than in writing, and both were therefore subject to unrestrained phonetic attrition (Reaney 1967: ch. 1; cf. below, pp. 593–4). This process is clearest with the prepositional phrase names, whose evolution partly parallels that of some place names (see vol. I, pp. 476–7). Mostly the phrase was clipped down to the bare substantive, so that ME *atte grene* > PDE *Green, atte stighele* > *Stiles* (with -*s* added by analogy with patronymic pairs like *Gibb*/*Gibbs*). Alternatively, the preposition might be procliticised: ME *atte rigge* > PDE *Attridge, bi the watere* > *Bywater(s), aboue the toune* > *Bufton, under the hille* > *Undrill*, and so on. Occasionally, procliticisation is limited (as also with place names) to the final consonant of an inflected demonstrative: ME *atten ashe* > *Nash*,

(OE *æt þǣre ēa >) ME *atter ee* 'beside the stream' > *Rea/Ree/Ray* (see above, p. 575).

Again as with place names, topographical family names must never be approached primarily through Present-Day English forms, many of which are ambiguous: thus, PDE /rei/ (howsoever spelt) may represent not only a reflex of ME *atter ee* (as above) but equally a northern, and especially a Scottish, one of OE *rā* 'roe-deer' (> southern *Roe*). As already noted, toponymic family names may show phonological developments freer than those underlying the present-day forms of the place names themselves; but investigating these would demand much expert and painstaking genealogical spadework. That is true of family-name etymology in general: without a firm genealogical connection between the Present-Day English form and an explicit Middle English one, nothing definitive can be said.

7.2.8   Women's names

For many reasons, women's names demand partly separate treatment. In medieval English records they are less adequately represented than men's: in estate surveys they seldom amount to even a tenth of the total and in tax-rolls ratios may be lower still, e.g. a twentieth in the 1319 Lay Subsidy Roll for London and a thirtieth in that of 1292. Such gross imbalance makes statistical comparison problematic. There are, besides, indications that in Middle English times – by contrast with what is known of Old English as well as of Common Germanic usages (see vol. I, pp. 458–9) – the principles governing the naming of the two sexes may partly have differed; and this makes the paucity of evidence all the more frustrating.

Thus, although baptismal names for women necessarily fall into the same general categories as those for men, patterns of choice among those categories often seem to differ.

For what the patchy and scanty evidence is worth, there seems, for instance, to be a lower ratio of Scandinavianised forms among women's names. Unfortunately, the problems inherent in under-recording are exacerbated by some modes of analysis. For instance, out of more than 750 Anglo-Scandinavian name forms collected from records concerning Yorkshire and Lincolnshire, feminines number only fifty-three, some 7 per cent; but, because the plan of collection excluded the complementary Old English name stock, the import of the discrepancy cannot be determined (Fellows-Jensen 1968). In fact, when insular name stocks from Danelaw records are analysed as wholes, then differences appear not just in totals of name forms (influenced by the grossly differing sample sizes) but also in the ratios of Anglo-Scandinavian forms to Old English ones: a Bury survey of ca 1190 shows Scandinavian forms as constituting under 20 per cent of the stock of women's names as against over 30 per cent for men's, some Norfolk records show 10–20 per cent as against 40–5 per cent, and some Lincolnshire ones, 40 per cent as against over 60 per cent (Clark 1979: 17–18; 1982: 59–60). Despite the inadequacy of each feminine sample, a pattern so recurrent looks significant, and all the more so because of the similar but greater discrepancy seen in Norman styles (Adigard 1954: 251–3). The seeming paucity of Anglo-Scandinavian names for women might be ascribed to fashion, especially as the English records mostly date from two to three centuries after the Viking settlements assumed to have brought such names in. On the other hand, an imbalance in name styles might have reflected one in the original cultural impact, *viz*. a low proportion of women among the settlers, perhaps combined with a tendency for culturally mixed couples to name daughters, rather than sons, according to maternal traditions. The question remains unresolved.

Somewhat better documented is a post-Conquest divergence and its demographic background. Almost consistently, women's names appear as slower than those of the corresponding men in reflecting continental influences, discrepancies often looking too great to be explicable by a likelihood that women figuring in records might, being mostly widows, have had a higher average age than the men listed alongside them. Clear, although patchy, evidence for post-Conquest marriages between men of continental origin and Englishwomen (sometimes heiresses) but seldom for the converse suggests a settlement pattern by which men, especially perhaps those who were to constitute the lesser gentry (the knightly class), arrived single and married as a means of improving their title to lands. If this were so, then the consequent paucity, during the first generation or so after the Conquest, of models for feminine continental name fashions might have affected current styles in much the way observed (Clark 1978a).

As noted above (pp. 560–3), neither in their homelands nor when adopted in England were 'continental' name fashions static, one widespread trend involving a rising popularity of 'Christian' forms. About women's names, two related generalisations are often made: (a) that they tended to be less stereotyped, even more fanciful, than men's (see Rumble 1985: 1406–7); and (b) that they reflect the 'Christian' fashion both earlier and more extensively. *A priori*, there is nothing unlikely about either proposition (see the observations made about Present-Day English fashions in Lassiter 1983: 23–6); but the imbalance in recording hinders verification. Thus, the 1292 Lay Subsidy Roll for London shows twenty-seven women sharing seventeen names, but 787 men sharing seventy-four; the 1319 one shows ninety-five women sharing thirty-two names but 1,757 men sharing seventy-five. If, however, 100 men are taken consecutively and at random from each list, they prove to share thirty and twenty-seven names respectively; and this suggests that the complete figures illustrate the law of diminishing returns, and not necessarily a differential variability in the naming of the sexes. Certainly, uneven frequency patterns affected both sexes: in 1292 *John* was borne by 143 men out of 787 and by 431 out of 1,757 in 1319; *Alice* was borne by four women out of twenty-seven and fourteen out of ninety-five respectively. In 1292 the leading seventeen names for men, accounting for 653 occurrences, included only six 'Christian' or 'literary' items, against eleven so classifiable for women; and in 1319, the leading thirty-two names for men, accounting for 1,672 occurrences, included nineteen such forms, many admittedly in the lower-frequency bands, against seventeen amongst women's. How far comparison between samples so different in size can be valid is a question for statisticians (preferably ones versed also in record studies and in historical anthroponymics). If parents did indeed favour fanciful names or overtly religious forms when naming daughters, this might be taken as reflecting particular views of the social and moral role of women.

Certainly, such views seem to have influenced development of family naming. In its Present-Day English form, conventional family naming involves two independent customs: (a) the transmission of a (usually paternal) surname from generation to generation; and (b) extension to a married woman of her husband's family name. In so far as (a) by no means entails (b), it cannot be assumed *a priori* that the two conventions developed *pari passu*. Among the post-Conquest nobility, with their pride in descent and possessions, a woman might in the twelfth century retain her own familial by-name after marriage and, if she were an heiress, pass it to whichever of her sons received the relevant lands. Such customs seem partly to have continued during the thirteenth century, but after ca 1300 it became conventional for a husband's family name, especially (although not solely) when derived from his principal estate, to be extended also to his wife (McKinley 1977: 181–6; and 1988:

66–7). Among humbler people, usage was – just as with men's by-names – even slower to settle. Thirteenth-century materials often specify women just as they do men, but perhaps proportionately more frequently, by complex periphrases detailing family relationships: e.g. *Agnes filia Ade filii Willelmi de Thorp*, *Matilda condam uxor Thome de Bernak de Burgo*, *Margareta filia Radulphi quondam uxor Willelmi de Elmede* (Brooke & Postan 1960: 6, 35, 102) – phrases that give little clue as to colloquial usage. Partly at least because the usual context is property transmission, a married woman or a widow is, as the examples have just illustrated, often identified – as a man scarcely ever is – by reference to her (deceased) spouse. That it was a matter of context is emphasised by the few exceptions, such as a grant by which *Alicia filia Gilberti bercarii de Irtlingburg'* passed on to her daughter lands that had come down from her own family, for here the husband and father figures merely as 'Henry' (Brooke & Postan 1960: 123, cf. 125). The governing of name custom by property rights is further illustrated by the practice in at least one Oxfordshire village by which a second husband taking over the first one's tenement took also his by-name (Harvey 1965: 127–8; McKinley 1977: 190). The thirteenth century thus saw some independent by-naming of man and wife among peasants much as among the gentry (McKinley 1977: 187–9). Fluidity of usage for both sexes does, however, make judging from isolated references risky: thus, *Willelmus de Arderne et Agnes de Bradecroft uxor sua* might be taken to show independent naming, were it not for a previous mention, in connection with the same property, of a *Willelmus de Bradecroft* with a wife Agnes (ca 1300; Brooke & Postan 1960: 135). Unambiguous cases nevertheless occur: e.g. *Roberto* (dat.) *Pacy et Emme* (dat.) *Godzer uxori sue*, with a parallel reference to *Emme* (dat.) *filie Walteri Godzer* (ca 1290; Brooke & Postan 1960: 139–40). Some women had at this time, besides, personal seals showing names distinct from those of their husbands (McKinley 1977: 188, 195 n. 76). The need for parallel and supplementary records again limits the value of the Lay Subsidy Rolls. An entry such as that in the 1292 Roll for London of *Roys le Clerk* reveals only that her by-name was derivative, not whether it had been originally her father's or her husband's; so likewise with all isolated instances of women bearing by-names which, like *Cartere* or *Pyteman*, are masculine in denotation and/or in form. Nor need a specifically feminine form indicate more than scribal punctilio: that *Leticia la Aylere*'s by-name was (a) transferred from her husband, (b) already in his case hereditary and (c) scribally Gallicised and feminised is revealed by other, more discursive documents recording a Luke *le Garlecmonger* (*ob. a* 1292) as trading in stockfish and leaving his wife Lettice properties in the relevant ward (Ekwall 1951: 146). From this and other instances it appears that well before 1300 the merchant class had at least sporadically come to adopt matrimonial by-naming of women.

In so far as they are known, women's independent styles of by-naming – ones, that is, derived neither from father nor from husband – followed slightly different patterns from men's. Except in the north, patronyms in *-dohter* (as distinct from descriptive phrases using *filia*) are rare, perhaps because in the pre-1300 period when independent by-names are mostly recorded it was the asyndetic style that prevailed. Although true occupational by-names do occur, as, for instance, *Juliana Selkwomman, Margeria le Goldescherster* (Ekwall 1951: 259, 319), these too are rare, probably because few women were publicly defined by occupations of their own. As for descriptive or humorous nicknames, these hardly appear (see Jönsjö 1979: 44; Hjertstedt 1987: 47), perhaps because they were eschewed by or unknown to officials, perhaps – although this cannot be verified – because they were uncommon in colloquial usage as well: the *Carte Nativorum* do offer a *Mabillie* (dat.) *Brounlady*, apparently sister of a *Radulphus Motyn*, and it may not be irrelevant that she had a daughter but no husband worth mentioning (Brooke & Postan 1960: 119–20; cf. McClure 1981: 98).

Exactly when matrimonial by-naming of women became the rule seems not to have yet been fully investigated. The partial surveys so far made suggest that, whereas in much of the country this apparently happened in the course of the fourteenth century, in the north, where hereditary naming was also slow to become established, the independent naming of married women partly continued into the sixteenth (McKinley 1977: 188–91; 1981: 53–4; 1988: 66–7).

7.3   Toponymy

For semantic rather than lexical or morphological reasons, place names are conventionally classified into 'major', *viz.* names of regions and of mountains and rivers as well as those of settlements, and 'minor' (or 'microtoponyms'), *viz.* those of subsidiary or small-scale features of the rural or urban scene, such as fields, farms, manor-houses, bridges, brooks, landmarks, tracks, streets and city-gates (see Mawer 1933; Cameron 1988: 194–211, 240). Some linguistic distinction also obtains, in so far as the ranges of generic partly differ: but this is far from absolute, for often a sizeable settlement has arisen at a spot bearing a landmark name, e.g. *Dunstable* < ME *Dunestaple*, probably < OE *(*æt*) *Dunnan stapole* '(at) Dunna's boundary-pillar' and *Oswestry* < ME *Osewaldestre* < OE *Ōswaldes trēo 'Oswald's tree (or, cross)' (*PN Beds. & Hunts.*: 120; Gelling, Nicolaisen & Richards 1970: 140–1; Gelling 1989: 188–9). What dictate separate consideration of the two categories are general contrasts of context and especially of chronology.

Study of the various kinds of 'minor' place name is indeed scarcely feasible until the Middle English period, partly because that is the earliest for which relevant documentation is adequate, more essentially because only then did socio-economic organisation become complex enough to require widespread systematisation of such kinds of name. For other reasons too, it would be unwise to attempt retrospective extrapolation from the Middle English evidence. Minor names are of their nature less stable than major ones, not simply because subject to the whims of farmers (and, nowadays, of town councils) but even more because the very entities they denote are subject to obliteration. Current names for fields and for streets are therefore far younger than those of most settlements and of the main landscape features; and a similar discrepancy may well have characterised twelfth-century name patterns. Certainly, the creation of minor names extends far beyond the *terminus ad quem* of the present volume, continuing actively into the present and on into the foreseeable future.

Middle English toponymical studies thus fall into two barely connected parts: that of the relatively stable major names; and that of the minor ones whose development is just beginning. The latter, from their earliest extant records on, fall into two further subcategories: (a) field names; and (b) street names – categories that correspond to the two main theatres of socio-economic life: the land and its cultivation; towns and their trade.

7.3.1 *Major place names: Middle English coinages and innovations*

Present-Day English has lost virtually all power of creating fresh names for centres or regions of settlement – witness the naming by transference of the unhistorical 'counties' instituted in 1974: e.g. *Avon* from the river, *Cleveland* from the hill range, *Cumbria* and *West Mercia* from the Anglo-Saxon past. Recent coinages thus mostly ring false, like *Bournville* with its un-English generic and *Peacehaven* with its rare one and its probably unique specific (see Smith 1956, which admits neither *peace* nor *ville*). A comparatively felicitous invention was that of *Camberley* for the military town founded near Aldershot in 1862, originally called *Cambridge Town* in honour of its ducal founder but soon renamed 'for postal convenience' (*PN Surrey*: 127).

Most English settlement names had become established and fixed well before the Conquest: hence the Domesday Book forms available for so many of them. By 1086 some compounds were already well on the way to becoming obscured: hence the frequent difficulty of interpreting those Domesday Book forms. Name material, semantically divorced as it has become from common vocabulary, lies especially open not only to phonological change of all kinds – vowel shortening in polysyllables, consonant assimilations, dissimilations and elisions, syncope and so on – but also to analogical reformation, of which 'folk etymology' is the type best known (see, for instance, Lass 1973; Coates 1987; Clark 1991). As a basis for etymology, no Present-Day English form has therefore any standing; many now give wholly false impressions of the name's original structure (for some confusions of generic see vol. I, pp. 486–7). Nor can name forms of any date be taken as a sure guide to general phonological developments, and especially not to their chronology. Allowance should perhaps, as will later be urged in more detail, be made for some occurrence of specifically onomastic sound changes, the results of giving free rein to tendencies elsewhere curbed by need to maintain formal links between related items of vocabulary.

Some limited toponymical creativity did survive into the Middle English period. Well into the twelfth century a transparently possessory place-name form, *viz.* one consisting of OE *-tūn* or AScand. *-by* preceded by the genitive of a personal name, might be modified in line with a change of lordship (Lund 1975; Fellows-Jensen 1984; Insley 1986; cf. Ekwall 1962 and 1964; and Clark 1983–4). Likewise, an occasional fresh name of such type might be created, such as *Royston*, first recorded in 1286, for the twelfth-century town grown up *apud crucem Roesie* 'beside Rohais's cross' (*PN Herts.*: 161–2). The names of the 140-odd post-Conquest 'planted' towns are much to the point (Beresford 1967: 386–99, 414–526, the Cornish instances being omitted for linguistic reasons). Almost half bear names of traditional, sometimes even archaic, Old English types, including four with *-ing(-)* and six in *-hām* (for the Old English place-name elements and their chronology see vol. I, pp. 477–9); a good many others have topographical generics, with *-bridge* found four times, *-mouth* six times and *-ford* eighteen times, reflecting the sorts of site favoured for plantation. Sixteen further names show the specific *New-*, thus *Newborough, Newcastle* (with a very early Old French loan word as generic), *Newport, Newto(w)n* and so on. Nine new towns received purely French names: *Battle* (for the abbey, *monasterium de Bello*, founded on the site of the Norman victory – *æt þære bataille*, as the annal for 1094 puts it – and also for the associated town), *Beaulieu, Belvoir, Devizes, Egremont, Mountsorrel, Pleshey* (cf. OF *plessis* 'enclosure'), *Pontefract* (*olim* ['pɑmfrɪt] < OF *pont freit* 'broken bridge') and *Richmond* (Yorks., see further, p. 591). Two bore names transferred from foreign localities: *Caus*, Salop, this being commonly supposed to have been taken from the Pays de Caux, and *Baldock*, for a town founded by the Templars, after Baghdad.

As that list suggests, the lexical impact of the Norman Conquest upon English toponymy was slight; and the contrast this makes with the profound as well as widespread effects of the ninth-century Scandinavian colonisation of the Danelaw (see vol. I, pp. 482–5) suggests, as has been remarked by others, a corresponding contrast in modes, and perhaps also densities, of settlement. Not only were pre-Conquest place names almost always retained but, more often than not, a new settlement was given a commonplace native name, either a fresh coinage or a form transferred from an Old English landmark name. Now and then, however, a village adopted as military strongpoint or manorial seat was renamed by its new overlords in their own language: thus, a place by the Old English name of *Depenbech* < *(*æt þǣm*) *dēopan bece* '(in the) deep valley by the stream' had by ca 1121 received the almost synonymous alternative one of *Malpas* 'difficult crossing'; this, derived from a current Old French common noun that provided a good few continental microtoponyms, was still transparent, as is confirmed by the joke that Gerald of Wales retailed in his *Itinerarium Kambriae*, II, 13 (Dimock 1868: 146). The English form remained current, however, until the fifteenth century at least (*PN Cheshire*, part 4: 38–40). Some nobles named their English, or Welsh, seats after their Norman ones, from which they had sometimes already taken territorial by-names (see above, p. 572): thus, Roger of Montgomery had by 1086 given his Welsh castle the name of his seat in Calvados. Others gave their castles or manor-houses simple complimentary names, several of which have already been cited: e.g. *Belvoir* 'beautiful view' > PDE ['biːvə] *Belvoir* (cf. the frequent F *Beauvoir*), for a Derbyshire castle set on a scenic as well as strategic vantage point and *Belrepaire* 'fine dwelling place' > PDE ['belpə] *Belper* – as has been commented elsewhere, the parallels with modern house naming are irresistible. For forms as commonplace as these only scrutiny of the particular landholder's background will reveal whether allusion is likely to have been intended to any specific French place. The name *Richmond* 'splendid hill' given (in replacement, it seems, of an older *Hindrelac*) to the castle that Count Alan the Red built upon a cliff above the Swale later furnished the title for an earldom and, as such, was transferred by Henry VIII to his rebuilt palace at Sheen (< OE *scīene* 'beautiful'; see *PN Surrey*: 65–6, cf. *PN NYorks.*: 287 and Watts 1981–2). Some post-Conquest religious foundations likewise received French names, such as *Dieulacres* (= (*que*) *Dieu l'accroisse!*; alternatively, *Dieulencres*) and *Haltemprice* 'noble undertaking' (Greenslade 1970: 230; *PN EYorks.*: 208).

Despite the paucity of new coinages and the banality of the few recorded, the Middle English period did see one toponymic innovation: the adoption of so-called 'affixes' (a specialised sense of the term to be sharply distinguished from the regular morphological one) for distinguishing between places which, whether because of subdivision or of simple commonplaceness of name, would otherwise have been inadequately specified (the treatment in Tait 1924 is confused; see Cameron 1988: 100–9). Thus, the Essex names *Helion('s) Bumpstead* and *Steeple Bumpstead* distinguish the two parishes (adjacent, although assigned to different hundreds) by means of reference, respectively, to an early Breton overlord's territorial by-name (from Helléan in Morbihan) and to a visual feature (indicated in early records by *ad turrim, a la tour* or *atte tour*) (*PN Essex*: 419, 508–9). Such 'affixes' are, because sometimes derived from 'Norman' familial by-names, often classed among effects of 'Anglo-Norman influence'; but that is, at best, a partial truth. Affixation of this sort, far from being a phenomenon of the early post-Conquest period, developed from perhaps the mid-thirteenth century onwards, and was probably – rather like personal by-naming (see above, pp. 566–7) but perhaps to a greater extent – promoted by the administrative exigencies of that period. Apart from tenurial specifiers (*viz.* family names and terms such as *Abbot's, Bishop's, King's*), 'affixes' may define a place by its relative size (*Great* or *Much* contrasted with *Little*, usually paired; official Present-Day English forms sometimes show revival of documentary Latin *Magna, Parva*), by its relative situation (*North, South, East* or *West*, again usually in a set; *Nether* or *Lower* contrasted with *Over, Upper* or *High*, sometimes with *Middle* as well), by its soil quality (*Dry, Fen(ny), Stone(e)y*), by a characteristic crop (*Cherry, Saffron*), by its proximity to a river or to a better-known settlement (*Walton-on-Thames*, Stoke-*by*-*Clare*), or by any other distinctive feature (*Castle*; *Chipping* or *Market*; *Church*, or the specific dedication). Tenurial 'affixes' are mostly, despite the above-cited *Helion Bumpstead*, postposed, as in *Swaffham Bulbeck* (involving the territorial by-name *Bolebec* derived from the Norman *Balbec*) in contrast with neighbouring *Swaffham Prior*, likewise *Easton Maudit* (from the Old French sobriquet *Mauduit*, Latinised as *Maleductus* 'ill-behaved'), *Hemingford Grey* (earlier *Turbervill*) in contrast with *Hemingford Abbots* and so on. So, too, are church dedications, as in *Deeping St James* contrasted with *Deeping St Nicholas*; and also, necessarily, prepositional phrases. Otherwise, most types of 'affix' are, as is usual with English specifiers, prefixed to the main name: e.g. *Castle Rising*, *Chipping Camden*, *Market Rasen*, *Dry Drayton*, *Stony Stratford*, *Much Hadham*, *Saffron Walden*, *Cherry Burton*. With the most commonplace and frequent name forms, such as *Barton*, *Kingston*, *Newton*, *Stanton*, *Stoke* and so on, 'affixation' of one kind or another has become almost *de rigueur* (see *Dictionary of English Place-Names* (*DEPN*), Ekwall 1960, under names quoted).

7.3.2 Major place names: pronunciation

The paucity of French lexical influence on Middle English place naming bears upon that aspect of it often supposed to have been widely subject to 'Anglo-Norman influence': its pronunciation. Ever since the publication in 1909 of Zachrisson's monograph on this topic (handily summarised in Zachrisson 1924), many English toponymists have accepted its claims that any apparent deviation from the supposed native phonological norms can safely be ascribed to 'French' influence.

More than mere passage of time now dictates reassessment of that thesis. To begin with, its sociolinguistic premise no longer commands universal assent. Zachrisson postulated a continuing and widespread presence in England, until the late thirteenth century at least, of native speakers of French, not only nobles and prelates but also schoolmasters, scribes and artisans. Recent studies, however, suggest that by shortly after ca 1200, if not indeed before, French had even among the gentry become an acquired accomplishment rather than a cradle-tongue shaping the basis of articulation (Shelly 1921; Woodbine 1943; Rothwell 1968, 1975–6, 1978 and 1983; Richter 1979 and 1985; Short 1979–80). Some Anglo-Normanists have indeed seen Middle English as exercising phonological and structural influences on Anglo-French (Pope 1952: 432–50; Rothwell 1983: 268–9). Zachrisson's analyses made, besides, little distinction between medieval documentary spellings, regular or occasional, and long-term phonological developments. As earlier emphasised (pp. 548–50), spellings must always be interpreted in terms of the conventions governing the documents where they occur; and for Middle English place-name forms those conventions were normally Latin ones. In any event, scribal practices are in the long term neither here nor there; the crucial question is how to explain the evolution of Present-Day English forms from their postulated etyma.

The slightness of Old French lexical influences on English toponymy has already been taken as pointing to less than overwhelming Gallicisation of post-Conquest England. And, not only were French-based coinages few but such as did appear were speedily adapted to English speech habits, with stress shifted to the initial syllable and frequent reformation by analogy with native structures: thus, the Worcestershire *Beaulieu* (originally identical with the Hampshire one now ['bju:li]), now *Bewdley*, was already by ca 1350 being spelt with -*ley*, as if derived from OE -*lēah*, and the Bedfordshire one, now *Beadlow*, was by the sixteenth century showing -*low* spellings, as if derived from OE -*hlāw*; similarly at Oxford the Anglo-Norman *Real Liu* (*Regalis Locus*), the name of an abbey dedicated in 1281, was less than a decade later spelt *Rewley* (*PN Worcs.*: 40–1; *PN Beds. & Hunts.*: 147; *PN Oxon.*: 22–3). Such observations might seem to justify a methodological principle the converse of Zachrisson's: to wit, assuming that any phonological development shown by an English place name ought – unless there be incontrovertible evidence to the contrary – to be ascribed to native processes. Zachrisson himself remarked on the difficulty of deciding between effects of 'Anglo-Norman influence' and those of 'non-standard' native tendencies. An alternative strategy might, as already suggested, be to postulate a non-standard, indeed specifically onomastic, branch of English phonology, compatible rather than identical with the general one and owing its more far-reaching operation to the special semantic status of names.

If that be granted, then some apparently difficult forms become explicable in terms of unfettered operation of native assimilatory and reductive processes, often finding parallels in Present-Day English casual or vulgar speech (see Brown 1977; Lass 1987: 118–21). One frequent process involves, for instance, syncope of a medial syllable of three, a toponymical instance of this being PDE ['lemstə] < OE *Lēōmynster* and one involving common vocabulary, PDE ['strɔ:bri] *strawberry*. The operation of that on, e.g., OE *Exanceaster* would produce ['ekstʃstə], the six successive palatal, alveolar and dental consonants of which would in rapid speech inevitably be assimilated and simplified. Acceptance of such probabilities may be thought to remove need to invoke foreign influences as explanation for the frequent though sporadic reductions of weak-stressed OE *-ceaster* > PDE [-stə]. Likewise, a dissimilatory lightening of consonant groups such as is daily heard in the casual PDE pronunciations ['febjuri] *February*, ['sekɪtri] *secretary* and ['vetɪnri] *veterinary* might be thought partly to explain the development of PDE *Cambridge* < OE *Grantanbrycg*. As for the unvoiced initial consonant of *Cambridge*, name material is especially subject to false divisions of the spoken chain, as shown by the sporadic procliticisations of articles and prepositions or of reduced forms thereof (see vol. I, pp. 476–7), and this might account for some apparently aberrant initial consonant developments. Initial [g] might have been unvoiced by contact with the [t] of preceding *at*; and, similarly, occasional replacement of initial [j] by [dʒ], as in *Jarrow* < OE *Gyrwe*, might have been due to assibilation produced by such a [t]. As yet, this alternative approach to the phonology of English place names remains tentative, so that whether or not it will in time prove acceptable is uncertain (see further Clark 1991). No claim to definitiveness is made for any of the explanations just proposed. What is urged is that in no case of supposedly aberrant development ought recourse to be had to invoking outside influences until all possibilities of explanation in native terms have been ruled out.

On the other hand, recent times have witnessed occasional seeming reversals of the sort of free phonological development just postulated as characteristic of name material. Place names are especially subject to 'spelling-pronunciation', that is, rejection of an historically developed form in favour of one based upon the official spelling, howsoever derived (see Gelling 1978: 26–9). This too is, in all likelihood, a further effect of semantic divorce from the rest of the language. Its immediate causes are sociolinguistic, including not only the increased personal mobility and the wider dissemination of news that combine to bring places and their names to the notice of people unfamiliar with the local speech (a case in point being the embarrassment aroused at the time of the Prince of Wales's wedding by the Northamptonshire village name ['ɔːltrʌp] *Althorp*) but also a self-conscious semi-literacy that can lead even local people to reject as slipshod and shameful the historically developed form of their town's or village's name (a case in point here being the local ['saʊθ,wel] reported for the Nottinghamshire ['sʌðl] *Southwell*). Many cases of spelling-pronunciation involve the initial <h-> of several Old English place-name generics. Medially and in weak stress this would regularly be lost; but in official spelling it has often been restored, only to fall foul of semi-literate prejudice. Thus, the Suffolk ['heivrıl] *Haverhill* is often heard as ['heivə‚hıl], probably because of the social stigma attached to '*h*-dropping'. Should a specific end, as often when representing the genitive of a personal name, in < -s >, the resultant < s-h > may be read as < sh > for [ʃ]; and similarly with a specific in < -t >, < t-h > may be read as < th > for [θ]. So, although ['bɒzm̩] *Bosham* retains its historical pronunciation, many other names of comparable form, such as *Amersham*, *Evesham* and so on, are by now irrecoverably distorted. This can be so even for names of smallish places seldom much mentioned outside their own districts, such as the Essex *Coggeshall* < OE *(*æt*) *Cocces h(e)ale* '(at) Cocc's nook of land'; this, although already by the mid-twelfth century spelt *Cogsale*, is nowadays usually called ['kɒgi‚ʃɔːl] (*PN Essex*: 265–6). Further instances include *Grantham* < OE *Grantan hām* probably 'Granta's estate', now commonly called ['grænθm̩], *Waltham* < OE *w(e)ald hām* 'forest estate', for which historical ['wɔːltm̩] now varies with the artificial ['wɔːlθm̩]. Attributing such pronunciations to 'semi-literacy' is, of course, an oversimplification; for even English people otherwise well educated seldom have the least notion of the history of their own language, let alone of the structure of their native place names. If the point has been somewhat forcefully put, this is because a prerequisite of historical study is an intelligent appreciation of what the present has inherited from the past.

7.3.3   *Minor names*

7.3.3.1   Field names form the largest and best-known category of rural microtoponym. Present-Day English forms necessarily apply to current agricultural arrangements, sometimes embodying allusions datable to the nineteenth century and after; but it by no means follows that all those now in use are of recent coinage. Tracing the history of field names involves not only seeking, as always, the earliest documentation available but also taking account of changing agrarian practices.

Throughout most of England, and in the Midlands especially, medieval agriculture was based upon division of a village's arable land into (notionally, not always literally) three 'great' or 'open' fields, each several hundreds of acres in extent, that were cultivated and fallowed according to a three-year cycle: a system that has, exceptionally, survived at Laxton in Nottinghamshire (for the variety and complexity of English field systems, see Baker & Butlin 1973; for the three-field system in particular, see further Orwin & Orwin 1967; also Chambers 1964). Each field (in Latin, *campus*) was divided, according to the lie of the land, into 'furlongs' (*culturae*); this Middle English term, < OE *furh* 'furrow' + *lang* 'long', denoted primarily the distance, varying with soil quality, that an ox-team could plough before needing to rest and, by extension, a piece of ground of which that was the operative dimension. Across each end of the furlong ran a 'headland' (*forera*), on which the team turned. Each furlong was subdivided into 'strips' (*seliones*), each notionally representing a single day's stint of ploughing; and these strips were shared out, as equitably as might be, among the villagers (the beautiful Laxton map of 1635, reproduced in Orwin & Orwin 1967, shows such a layout in detail). Each village also possessed hay-meadow (*pratum*), likewise shared out in sections for mowing, together with common pasture and woodland, and often some supplementary lands, or 'assarts', brought under cultivation through recent clearance of woodland or drainage of fens. There would also have been enclosures of various kinds, such as garden-plots, orchards and paddocks. For administrative purposes all these elements needed to be specified precisely, and many of them were in fact named.

The main sources for medieval field names are estate surveys (like the Cambridge one edited in Hall & Ravensdale 1976), variously called 'extents' and 'terriers', and also small-scale land-conveyances like those constituting the *Carte Nativorum* (Brooke & Postan 1960). The general term for 'great field' was ME *feld* < OE *feld* 'open plain' (see Gelling 1984: 235–7); and particular ones mostly figure under straightforward designations – such as, in modern spelling, *Church Field*, *Mill Field*, *West Field* and so on – that specify them in terms of compass-point or nearby landmark (see, e.g., Lobel 1969–75: Cambridge, map 3). The incorporation of such vernacular phrases into mid-thirteenth-century Latin documents implies them to have already by that time been perceived as 'names' rather than as translatable descriptions. Their scheme of reference is none the less compatible with the standard documentary mode of specifying in terms of relative position any piece of ground concerned in a survey or a conveyance. (Nowadays, the names of former great fields and of their furlongs sometimes serve as those of suburban housing estates.) Apart from *furlong* itself, regular Middle English terms for sections of field included *flat* (cf. ON *flatr* adj. 'level'), *schot* (of complex origin, and usually referred to a stress-shifted development from OE *scēat*, meanings of which included 'piece of ground' as well as 'surface'), and *wang/wong* (< ON *vangr* 'field'). Modes of specification vary more than for great fields: although often based upon shape or upon relative position, they also include occasional transferences of the name of an access road (a crucial point of organisation when standing crops are concerned) or of some minor landmark: thus, *Hiderfurlong, Middelfurlong* or *Middelwong, Brocfurlong*, the pejorative *Brembilfurlong, Rygweye* (alternatively and more explicitly, *cultura que uocatur* Ryggeweye), *Appeltre* (or, *cultura que uocatur Appeltre*) and so on (Brooke & Postan 1960: 6, 8, 9, 15, 16, 27, 31, 47, 54; Hall 1976–7). Where the lie of the land produced not a neat 'furlong' but an irregularly shaped parcel of strips, especially one at a junction between furlongs, then a group of short ones might be called *The Buttes* (perhaps < OE **butt* 'stump' rather than OF *bout*) and a triangular group, a *gore* (< OE *gāra* 'point'). Terms for 'strip' included ME *aker* (< OE *æcer*/ON *akr* 'plot of arable land'), again not to be confused with the Present-Day English unit of measurement, with which the average area of a 'strip' only occasionally coincided, and also sometimes *land*. Usually, a strip was specified only in terms of the ownership of the contiguous ones but, exceptionally, one might be named, as with the *Lampe Aker* at Cambridge (and also elsewhere), the revenue from which went to providing a lamp for the hospital (Hall 1976–7: 15; cf. Mawer 1933: 196). Terms for 'meadow' included *eng/ing* (< ON *eng* 'pasture'), as well as the two pairs of doublets, *lese/leswe* (< OE *lǣs*, obl. *lǣswe*) and *mede/medwe* (< OE *mǣd*, obl. *mǣdwe*; cognate with *māwan* 'to mow'). Meadows were specified in terms similar to those applied to great fields, thus, *Suthmede, Westeng* and so on. A share of meadow was often called a *dole* (< OE *(ge)dāl* 'portion'), so that a modern field name such as *The Doles* usually indicates former common meadow (but cf. Hall & Ravensdale 1976: 19). For forest 'assarts', there were many Middle English terms current, including *breche* (< OE *brǣc* 'breach in the woodland cover'), *ridding* (< OE *hryding* 'clearing'), *stocking* and the doublets *stibbing/stubbing* (all three meaning 'place of tree-stumps'), and *thweit* (< ON *þveit* 'clearing'); such land seems often to have been named from an individual, presumably the one chiefly responsible for the breaking-in, thus, *Berengeres Stibbyng*, associated with the named man's descendants (Brooke & Postan 1960: 36, cf. 7, 37). For fenland reclamations, one frequent term was *neuland*, a rarer one *inlik* (this latter neither in *MED* nor in Smith 1956; Hallam 1965 gives a good idea of the medieval terminology in context). For enclosures, terms current included ME *clos* (< OF *clos* < Lat. *clausum*: one of the few Middle

English agrarian terms seemingly not of pre-Conquest origin), *croft* (<
OE *croft* 'small field'; also sometimes applied to a section of open field),
garth (< ON *garðr*, cognate with OE *geard* > PDE *yard*), *pichtel* (of
vexed etymology: that suggested in *MED* fails to explain the /ç/, and
a more acceptable one is from *piȝt*, a form of the past participle of *picchen*
'to mark out with stakes', see *PN Cheshire*, 5, section 1, 2: 304, 305) and
its supposed variants *pingel*, *pingott* and *pringel*.

A general summary like this cannot but oversimplify matters, and to
that extent misrepresent them; but as yet there is, unfortunately, no
synthesis of Middle English field naming to which to refer. The English
Place-Name Survey has always in principle embraced field naming,
which from the early 1950s on has been comprehensively treated under
each parish (see also the separate monographs Keene 1976 and Standing
1984); but, even so, pressure of space sometimes means that names are
given out of context and without definition of the sort of entity
designated. Study is certainly best pursued village by village, and in the
light of local topography, with the aim of bringing out the principles of
specification and determining what balance was kept between continuity
and innovation. For minor names are, as previously remarked,
observably less stable than major ones. In particular, name transfers
seem to have been not uncommon: not only might a furlong be known,
as instanced above, by the name of a road or a landmark but occasionally
a field name might be transferred to a landscape feature, as happened at
Cambridge when the phrase *binne brok* 'on this side of the stream', at
first denoting land to the south of a rivulet, came later, after the land in
question had been subsumed into the great Carme Field (named from a
house of Carmelites), to denote the stream itself (*PN Cambs.*: 1–2, 44;
Hall 1976–7: 17–18; Hall & Ravensdale 1976: 45–6).

In the wider linguistic context, Middle English field names afford
evidence for otherwise little-known dialect vocabulary, supplementing
the thin 'literary' record of agricultural terminology and allowing
isoglosses to be more precisely drawn. With linguistic datings,
admittedly, they offer little help, in so far as the earliest extant record of
a name may substantially postdate its coinage. Where minor place
names, more numerous as well as less fixed than major ones, have time
and again proved to have the edge is as indicators of cultural influences.
Along the Welsh Marches, for instance, field names show where Welsh
linguistic influences have been strong (Foxall 1980: 68–71; Dodgson
1985b). It is, however, with regard to degrees of Scandinavianisation
that such names have been most intensively, and most rewardingly,

studied. Time and again, they have revealed strong Scandinavian lexical influences in districts, ones in the east midlands and East Anglia in particular, where the major names look purely English (Mawer 1932; Fellows-Jensen 1974; Cameron 1975, also 1978; Sandred 1979 and 1982; Insley 1985c; also Wainwright 1945 and 1962: 86–8). Relevant Anglo-Scandinavian terms already cited include *eng* 'meadow', *garth* 'enclosure', *thweit* 'clearing' and *wong* 'field, esp. furlong'; others are *beck* 'stream' (cognate with OE *bæce*/*bece*, for which see Gelling 1984: 12–13), *brigg* 'bridge' (cognate with OE *brycg*), *deil* 'share' (cognate with OE *(ge)dāl*), *dike* 'boundary ditch or mound' (cognate with OE *dīc*), *gate* 'track' (cognate with OE *gān* 'to go'), *holm* 'water-meadow', *ker* 'marshy scrubland', *lund* 'grove' (when weak-stressed, sometimes subsequently replaced by *-land*), *mire* 'swampy ground', *rigg* 'ridge' (cognate with OE *hrycg*), *sike* 'ditch' and, by transference, 'water-meadow' (cognate with OE *sīc*), *toft* 'house-plot' (< ON *topt*), and *wro* 'nook' (< ON *vrá*). In culturally ambivalent areas, such as Northamptonshire, native and Anglo-Scandinavian synonyms – e.g. *weye* and *gate*, *stibbing* and *thweit* – were sometimes used interchangeably. As yet, no comprehensive mapping of the distributions of Middle English field-name elements has been attempted; if accomplished, such a survey would throw great light on linguistic and cultural patterns. In addition to their lexical value, field names also form a supplementary, though not easily datable, source for personal names current among local groups of early medieval peasantry: in this context, their special value lies in showing such names in colloquial rather than documentary form (see Insley 1979).

Between the medieval and the modern periods, field naming shows only a limited continuity, having been reshaped by the processes of 'enclosure' – *viz.* consolidation of individual holdings of 'strips' into compact blocks and the consequent establishment of separate farms – that began piecemeal during the late fourteenth century and were from the mid-eighteenth onwards extended and systematised by private Acts of Parliament (the paperwork for which, when it survives, constitutes valuable evidence for the former layouts and name patterns). In place of the 'great' fields, each covering several hundreds of acres, there appeared around each village a patchwork of fenced or hedged 'closes' ranging in size from, say, 5 to 50 acres; concomitantly, the more substantial farmers (sometimes called 'yeomen') left the village nucleus for new houses amid their own allotments of land. The new closes and the new farmhouses all needed naming. Often the farms were named from the families concerned or from landmarks, sometimes from places in the news at the time, as with *Quebec Farm* (1760) in Sileby, Leicestershire (Hoskins 1955: 157). For the new small fields, fresh names were usually created, some of which, such as *Gas Close* (situated beside the gas-works), *Waterloo Close* and *Pylons*, proclaim their modernity (for a general account, see Field 1972, from which the forms cited are taken; for a regional one, see Foxall 1980). Recent formation is shown also by the tendency for generic and specific to remain separate words, each with its own accentual pattern, instead of being reduced to elements of a single-stressed compound. Between medieval and modern modes of naming there are also apparent semantic differences; for postmedieval field names are one of the few sorts of toponym in which personality, sometimes even playfulness, is given any rein. Biblical allusions appear, as with *Babylon* at Ely and elsewhere (land beyond the river, perhaps with humorously pejorative intent). Distant plots are named from countries on the other side of the globe, such as *Australia* and *California*. And for describing soil quality various picturesque phrases have been coined (for complimentary ones, see Field 1986, and for derogatory ones, Field 1976–7; one striking case of the latter, *cat's brain*, goes back, however, at least to the fourteenth century). The general capacity of name material to survive loss of lexical sense means that not all the medieval forms have, however, been wholly lost, although some have been transmogrified. Thus, ME *Austemor/Oustmor* 'eastern wasteland' (with ON *austr*) is now represented by *Horsemoor*, no doubt because the land served as rough pasture and so */'ɔːs.mɔː/ came to be understood in that sense (*PN Northants.*: 281; Insley 1985c: 122). The analogous *Austreng* 'eastern meadow' has, on the other hand, been replaced – with a coincidental etymological appropriateness – by *Austrian Meadow*, which shows a modern fancifulness in its way of dealing with the obsolete and obscured generic that has been supplemented by a current synonym.

Present-day usages are themselves, of course, far from stable. Postwar reversal of the trend towards enclosure has meant loss, through obliteration of the individual plots they designated, of many eighteenth- and nineteenth-century names; for such lost forms, the Tithe Awards compiled from ca 1836 onwards are a vital source. At the same time, the new layouts are calling forth a new nomenclature: thus, a Leicestershire prairie formed by the amalgamation of fourteen former closes has been called *Bulldozer* (personal communication from Mr J. Field).

7.3.3.2　Street naming, required only in settlements of some size, first appeared in England, as also in most continental countries, mainly as a concomitant to the urban expansion taking place from ca 1100 onwards (see Platt 1976; also Beresford 1967; cf. Langenfelt 1954). Pre-Conquest instances are rare; but the many urban rentals and surveys available for the period beginning in the mid-twelfth century regularly provide (albeit often in Latinised form) names not only for streets but also for other urban features such as bridges, churches, crosses, fortifications, guildhalls, markets, wells, wharves and occasionally individual houses, often in contexts permitting establishment of town plans (see Lobel 1969–75).

Like most other sorts of early toponym, a medieval street name usually began as a straightforward description; naming in compliment to, say, politicians, local or international, is a recent mode (in what follows, forms from London are taken from Ekwall 1954; those from Winchester from Biddle & Keene 1976: 231–9; those from Canterbury from Urry 1967 and Clark 1976a: 22–3; those from York from Palliser 1978; and those from other towns, when not otherwise indicated, from the relevant volume of the English Place-Name Survey). Thus, the few names preserved from tenth-century Winchester refer to trades and their practitioners: *cēap strǣt* 'the market street', *flǣscmangera strǣt* 'the butchers' street', *scyldwyrhtena strǣt* 'the shieldwrights' street', *tænnera strǣt* 'the tanners' street' (spellings, as often, normalised). The extant pre-Conquest records for London are – despite their mentions of churches, city-gates and even some individual properties, such as *Cēolmundinghaga* 'Ceolmund's messuage' – virtually silent as to streets; but some forms whose first record now survives only in twelfth-century materials did apparently date back far earlier, as with OE **candelwyrhtena strǣt* 'the chandlers' street' > ME *Candelwrichstrete* and variants > PDE *Cannon Street* and OE **beardceorfera lanu* 'the barbers' alley' > ME *Bercheruere(s)lane* > PDE *Birchin Lane* (Ekwall 1944–5b: 32–4; 1954, see under names quoted). Late-twelfth-century Canterbury similarly had its *Croccereslane* 'the potters' alley', *Sporiereslane* 'the spurriers' alley' and *Webbenelane* 'the weavers' alley' (the first two translations assume genitive plural forms with analogical *-s*); and so likewise had other towns whose early medieval records survive. Alternatively, a trade might be invoked in terms of product or wares, as with London's *Bread Street* < ME *Bredstret* (a 1170) and its EME (only perfunctorily Latinised) *Cornhilla* < OE *corn* 'grain' + *hyll* 'slope'. A procedure too frequent to need exemplification is naming from a landlord or leading resident. Another regular mode of specification invoked, as with fields, the points of the compass, witness London's *Eastcheap* 'the eastern market (by contrast with *Cheap* or *Westcheap*, later *Cheapside*)' (ca 1100), York's *North Street* (a 1180), and countless other such. Other names referred to destination, as with Chester's *Northgate Street* (= *vicus a porta de North usque ad ecclesiam*), York's *Fossgate* 'street leading to/from the river Foss', Nottingham's *Derbigate*, and various ubiquitous forms like *Bridge Street* (or *Briggate*), *Church Street* (or *Kirkgate*) and so on. Many were simple descriptions, like London's *Broad Street* < ME *Bradestrete* 'the wide street' (a 1200), Canterbury's *Niewestrete* (a 1200), and York's *Micklegate* 'the big, main street' (a 1185) and so on. Other forms reappearing in town after town include, in particular, *King Street*, seemingly the equivalent of *via regia* 'public highway (conforming to legal requirements)'. Paradoxically, some of the most widespread forms, like *Pepper Street* (see Dodgson 1968: 45–6; the equivalent is widespread also in the Low Countries) and *Silver Street*, are among those whose precise implications are often questioned; an especially controversial one is the Danelaw *Finkle Street*, found in Hull, Norwich, Nottingham, York and several other towns, and variously taken to involve ME *fenkel* 'fennel' or else an homonymous term for 'sharp bend' (see, for instance, Ekwall 1954: 76–7; Smith 1956: I, 169; Palliser 1978: 9, 15, and *PN Cheshire*, 5, I, 1: 17–18; *PN Lincs*, I, 65–6, and *PN Norfolk* I, 104–5).

As already tacitly illustrated, medieval street names mostly followed the standard English toponymic pattern of generic modified by preposed specific, the range of generics being narrowly circumscribed. Apart from OE *strāt* 'metalled road' (< Lat. *(via) strata*) > ME *strete* 'urban thoroughfare lined with buildings' (rendered in Latin by *via* or *vicus*) > PDE *street* (cf. Du. *straat*, G. *Strasse*) and OE *lanu* > ME/PDE *lane* 'alleyway' (rendered as *venella*; for distinction between the two Middle English terms, see Dodgson 1968: 46–8), there were also their Anglo-Scandinavian equivalents: to wit, respectively, ME *gate* < Scand. *gata* 'track' (cognate with OE *gān* 'to go'; cf. G. *Gasse*), as already instanced, and ME *gayl/gil* < Scand. *geil* 'ravine; narrow alleyway', as in York's *Nowtgail* (ca 1400), where the specific is Scand. *naut* 'cattle' (cognate with OE *nēat*). Subsidiary generics included Late ME *aleye* < OF *alée* 'path, passage (often semi-private)', ME *bicht* < OE *byht* 'corner, bend', ME *hell/hill/hull* < OE *hyll* 'slope', ME *rowe* < OE *rāw* 'alignment (of houses or shops)', and ME *twitchel/twitchen* 'narrow path' (cf. OE *twycen* 'forked path'). Partly because their generics have over the centuries remained so few and so transparent, street names mostly – like field names of recent coinage – retain a composite structure, with each element keeping its separate identity and stress pattern. Such obscuration as has occurred has usually been limited to the specific, as in London's already-cited *Birchin Lane* and *Cannon Street* and also in York's *Blossom Street* and Ripon's *Blossomgate*, each representing an original ME *plouswayngate* 'ploughman-street'. Even when unobscured, a specific may have become so fully onomasticised as to constitute only an otherwise 'meaningless' label.

As with the other categories of name, the distributions of the various elements cast light on Middle English dialectal and cultural patterns. French loan words are only a little less uncommon in urban than in rural 'minor' naming (on this and its implications, see especially Ekwall 1954: 19–23; also Clark 1976a: 22–3). Thus, apart from the Late ME *aleye* already cited, we scarcely find more than the occasional commonplace commercial loan word, such as *Drapery*, *Poultry*, *Vintry*, and occupational terms like *butcher* and *mercer*. By contrast, the Anglo-Scandinavian elements again prove of particular interest. AS *gate* 'road, street' (to be firmly differentiated from general ME *gate* 'barrier' < OE pl. *gatu/gata/gatum*, varying with *yat/yett* < sg. *geat* etc.) was the regular term in, for instance, York, Lincoln, Nottingham and Peterborough, whereas in towns south and west of Watling Street, including Chester, it was absent, with native *street* holding sway (see Dodgson 1968: 52–3); in those on the borders of the old northern Danelaw, like Derby and King's Lynn, both terms were current. AS *gayl(e)* 'alleyway' had a more restricted currency, appearing only in the most heavily Scandinavianised towns like York. With some pairs of cognates, like *bridge/brigg* and the reflexes of OE *stæð*/ON *stǫð*, the ambiguities of medieval spelling partly obscure the distributions; to say which is not by any means to deny that a painstaking investigation might prove worthwhile. As noted above, certain occupational terms occur in seemingly synonymous sets with complementary distributions (e.g. *barker/tanner*, *deiere/dexter/litster*, *fuller/tucker/walker* and others); and here too it might be profitable to map the occurrences of the various terms in street names as well as in personal by-names.

Occasionally, a street name of unusual form turns out to have been transferred from some other sort of local feature. This is, in particular, the explanation for the street names in *-gate* found in southern towns like London and Colchester; for these represent transfers of forms originally applying to the nearby city gates. So, too, names appertaining to other features of a town's defences were not uncommonly transferred to neighbouring streets, as with York's *Aldwark* < ME *Aldewerke* 'the old fortifications' (a 1190), and with London's (*Old*) *Bailey* (a 1290) and *Barbican* (late fourteenth century). Still in London, miscellaneous instances include *Houndsditch* (as a street name, sixteenth century) from a section of the ditch running along the outside of the city wall, (*Old*) *Change* (ca 1300) from the royal mint, *Minories* (sixteenth century) from a house of Minoresses and *Old Jewry* from the former Jewish quarter. York's *Bootham* is also an original district name, < ME *Bouthum* < ON dat. pl. *búðum* '(at) the place where the booths are'.

For street names even more than for field names, no account breaking off in the early modern period tells more than a fraction of the story. All that it can hope to do is indicate some traditional principles of formation and at the same time emphasise the antiquity and the historical bearings of many seemingly unremarkable Present-Day English forms. Study of early street naming can thus be seen as a branch of urban archaeology.

FURTHER READING

Most of the bibliographical and periodical references listed in the corresponding section of volume I remain valid for the Middle English period, and also indeed for all later ones. The best guide to current work again consists of the annual bibliographies published in *Nomina*, occasionally supplemented by the sections on onomastics included in the *Annual Bibliography of English Language and Literature* and in *Year's Work in English Studies*; for international perspectives, the relevant portions of the worldwide listings in *Onoma* are indispensable. Apart from *Nomina*, the only other English onomastic periodical is the more specialised *Journal of the English Place-Name Society*, which also publishes bibliographies, and regularly includes in its purview studies of field names as well as of major names. Related work also appears from time to time in journals such as *Economic History Review*, *Genealogists' Magazine*, *Local Historian*, *Medieval Prosopography* and so on, and especially in those of the numerous local-history societies. Materials essential for background and for comparison are regularly presented in *Beiträge zur Namenforschung*, *Naamkunde*, *Namn och Bygd*, *Nouvelle Revue d'Onomastique*, *Studia Anthroponymica Scandinavica* and elsewhere.

For this period, the locating, identifying and evaluating of potential source material is a more complex, and therefore more crucial, matter than it was for the Old English one. Many texts of cartularies, surveys, court records and tax-lists have been published by the various record societies, local as well as national; but anyone wishing to use such printed texts as a basis for onomastic research must heed the warnings given above against miscopyings and misinterpretations and, above all, against the expedient but sometimes false normalisation of names practised by many compilers of calendars and indexes (translations and modernised texts are, and this cannot be too often emphasised, useless for onomastic purposes). Much material nevertheless remains only in manuscript, and anyone wishing to explore this must first seek training in archive studies and in palaeography (for a summary guide to such sorts of material, see Rumble 1973–4, and for a specimen guide to a county record office, Emmison 1969).

For every branch of English name study, a good grounding in the social and economic history of the relevant period as well as in English philology is essential. So, too, as has just been implied, are the abilities to use dog-Latin source material and to identify influences on English usage from other medieval languages. Personal-name study, in particular, regularly involves comparison with materials collected in Dutch, French, German and Scandinavian reference works (see further below).

For work on specifically Middle English developments in place naming, the county surveys being published by the English Place-Name Society remain the prime basis; especially so the more recent volumes, with their systematic collections of field names, street names and other 'minor' forms (in compensation for their shortcomings on this score, the surveys published in the Society's pioneering days offer great scope for supplementary research). Collections of minor names, as well as the editions of potential source materials already mentioned, also appear from time to time in the publications of local-history societies. In this chapter English Place Name Society volumes are cited by the abbreviation *PN* followed by the name of the county or counties concerned.

For Middle English personal naming, there are as yet no authoritative works of general reference; in an onomastic context, the term 'dictionary' is, in any case, even less than usual to be taken as implying definitive authority. Withycombe 1977 is unreliable; and, although Reaney 1967 and 1976 offer many starting-points for investigation, neither has ever been claimed to be either comprehensive or definitive (see Clark 1980b). The sound and scholarly county surveys being produced in the English Surnames Series (in progress since the mid-1970s) represent historical rather than linguistic points of view. Thus, the main works of reference available consist at the moment of specialised monographs: in particular, the classic studies by Olof von Feilitzen (1937 – now a little dated – and 1976; also 1939, 1945, 1963, 1964, 1968), the remarkable series of publications on medieval London by Eilert Ekwall (1944–5a, 1947, 1951, 1956, 1965), and the more limited one on East Anglia by Bo Seltén (1965, 1969, 1972, 1975, 1979). Taking study of baptismal names further therefore requires co-ordinating the various sets of findings and extending them both by analysis of fresh source materials and by comparison with findings from that of continental records (e.g. Lind 1905–15, 1931 and 1920–1; Knudsen *et al.* 1936–48, 1949–64; Adigard 1954; Schlaug 1955; Morlet 1967 and 1968–72; Tavernier-Vereecken 1968; Marynissen 1986, amongst others). For by-names, the range of categories renders matters more complex still. Tengvik (1938), never a safe guide (see Feilitzen 1939), is now outdated. Occupational terms have been collected by Fransson (1935), Otto (1938) and Thuresson (1950), with occasional supplementation by others; topographical ones, mainly by Löfvenberg (1942) and Kristensson (1970). When aiming to elucidate toponymical forms, it is essential to consult not only compendia of place names (e.g. *DEPN* plus the relevant English Place-Name Society surveys; Dauzat and Rostaing (1963) plus the relevant *Dictionnaires topographiques*) but also such primary and secondary sources of prosopographical and tenurial information as may lead to closer identification of the individual or family concerned. As for 'nickname' forms, selections are given in Seltén (1965, 1969 and 1975), Jönsjö (1979) and Hjertstedt (1987); but for some caveats as to the latter two works, see Clark (1982b), Fellows-Jensen (1980), Mills (1988) and especially McClure (1981), the best introduction to this topic yet written. With certain of these monographs, emphasis on etymology and/or dialectology to the exclusion of social and prosopographical considerations undermines their value as contributions to the history of personal naming as such; with Erlebach (1979), shortcomings are compounded by failure to consult any primary sources whatsoever.

Immense scope thus exists for further research into all aspects of English naming from the Conquest to the Renaissance, and indeed up to the present day. Any topic that involves place naming may best be approached under the auspices of the English Place-Name Society, which brings together all scholars in this field and also maintains a specialised library (at present housed at Nottingham University) as well as research collections. For personal naming, no corresponding organisation at present exists, and ways forward have therefore to be found through individual initiatives: the most fruitful approaches are likely to be ones not only based on analyses of clearly dated and localised source materials studied from authentic texts but also backed by firm grasp of the socio-economic, genealogical and prosopographical structures of the communities concerned.

GLOSSARY OF LINGUISTIC TERMS

This glossary aims only to give brief working definitions of the more important or difficult linguistic terms used in this work, omitting such terms as phonetic classifications, for which the reader in difficulty should consult a relevant textbook. It is not a comprehensive dictionary of linguistic terms, and the explanations offered are intended only to be sufficient to allow the reader who is unacquainted with such terminology to gain a more complete understanding of this volume's contents. Readers requiring a more comprehensive dictionary should consult Crystal (1985).

abduction　See **metanalysis.**

ablaut　Variation in the root vowel as in PDE *sing, sang, sung.* See **gradation.**

accidence　The morphological means of signalling grammatical categories; inflectional **morphology.**

accountability (to the data)　A term in dialectology indicating that all data should be accounted for so that inconvenient data should not be quietly ignored because it does not fit into a preferred pattern.

active　A construction typically involving the subject as actor; in **passive** the subject is not actor.

adversative co-ordination　The linking of two co-ordinate clauses by means of contrastive conjunctions (typically *but*).

affix　A type of **morpheme** consisting of derivational and inflectional affixes. Affixes may be prefixes attached to the beginning of words, e.g. *un-like*, suffixes attached to the end of words, e.g. *like-ly*, or infixes embedded within a word, though this type is rare in English. Derivational affixes are found in the formation of new words; inflectional affixes mark grammatical relations.

agent　The semantic role of a noun phrase as doer of an action, e.g. *Jane came home.*

agglutinative Of a language or form that strings out grammatical morphs in sequence with only one category represented on each, e.g. *cat-s* 'cat + plural'.

agreement See **concord**.

allograph See **grapheme**.

allomorph Different realisations of the same **morpheme**, e.g. /z/ in *dogs* and /s/ in *cats* are different allomorphs of the PDE plural morpheme.

allophone The particular individual sounds or phones which are all members of the same **phoneme**. In PDE [p] and [pʰ] are allophones of the phoneme /p/.

ambisyllabic A phonological term referring to a sound which belongs to both of two abutting **syllables**, like the medial /t/ in *sitting*.

analogy A term referring to the historical process whereby irregular forms are replaced by regular ones. In morphophonology the process usually involves either the extension of a change, which permits it to occur where it should not phonologically speaking, or the levelling of a change so that it does not occur where it might have been expected. A typical analogical form is PDE *roofs* with final /fs/ alongside *rooves* with final /vs/ showing allomorphic variation of the **root**.

analytic A term referring to language or even grammatical categories to indicate an organisation through separate words in a particular order rather than one through affixes in words, which is referred to as **synthetic**. Grammatically, *more lovely* is analytic as compared with *loveli-er*, which is synthetic.

anaphoric A term used of linguistic elements, such as pronouns, which have no referential meaning of their own, that refer back to another constituent within the clause or discourse. (**Cataphoric** elements are those which refer forwards.) In *I saw John and then he left*, the *he* is an anaphoric pronoun referring back to *John*.

anchor (text) A term in historical dialectology referring to those historical texts whose provenance can be plotted on non-linguistic evidence and can therefore be considered secure.

antepenult A term referring to the third last **syllable** in a word.

anthroponym The name of a person; hence *anthroponymy* is the study of such names.

aorist One of the past-tense forms of the Greek verbs not marked for **aspect**, and usually represented in English by the simple past, e.g. *walked, ran*. In linguistic discussions the issue is most often the phonological shape rather than the semantic nature of the aorist.

aphetic The loss of a short unaccented vowel at the beginning of a word, e.g. *esquire/squire*.

apocope Deletion of word-final vowel(s).

apposition A syntactic construction in which there is a sequence of two constituents with the same grammatical role and semantic reference, as in *I, Henry Smith, declare...*, in which *Henry Smith* is in apposition to *I*.

argument A term used of a noun phrase which is a member of the predicate.

argument structure A term used of the configuration in which a predicate may occur, i.e. it consists of a verb and its dependants.

artes praedicandi Rhetorical manuals for writing sermons.

aspect A category indicating the manner by which the grammar of a language refers to the duration or type of temporal activity of a verb. In English the clearest aspectual contrast is between perfective and imperfective (as in *I have read the book* compared with *I read the book*).

assimilation A phonological process by which two sounds become closer in pronunciation.

asyndetic Formed by apposition only, without preposition, inflection or other linking device. See also **parataxis**.

athematic See **theme**.

auxiliary verb A 'helping' verb such as PDE *may, can, have, be, do*. It typically carries information about **tense, aspect** or **modality.**

back-derivation The morphological process by which a shorter word is formed by the deletion of a morpheme interpreted as an **affix**, e.g. *peddle* < *pedlar*.

bahuvrihi A compound in which the semantic reference of the compound is to an entity to which neither of its elements refers. Structurally bahuvrihi compounds are **exocentric**.

baptismal name An onomastic term referring in ME to the primary component in a personal-name phrase, since any **by-name** was at this time a secondary, and optional, addition.

base See **root**.

bilingual The property of being proficient in two languages; contrast **diglossia**.

bimoric See **mora**.

by-name An onomastic term used of any qualifying phrase apposed (usually postposed) to an **idionym** or a **baptismal name** to prevent misunderstanding of which person is referred to. In *Richard the Redeless*, the phrase *the Redeless* is the by-name which specifies which *Richard* is intended.

cataphoric See **anaphoric**.

causative A verb expressing as part of its meaning the sense 'cause to' e.g. *set* 'cause to sit'.

chain shift A sequence of changes in which one change is claimed to depend on another or others. The most notable example is the Great Vowel Shift.

Christian name A baptismal name taken from the name of a biblical character or saint.

cleft construction A construction in which a clause is divided into two parts, each with its own verb, e.g. *It's John who left* compared with *John left*.

clitic A form which in general depends upon the existence of a neighbouring lexical item. In phonology and morphophonology a clitic is always attached to another unit. If attached at the front it is a proclitic, e.g. *ne is* > *nis*; and if attached at the end it is an enclitic, e.g. PDE *is not* > *isn't*. Syntactically, *the* is a clitic because it demands the existence of a noun. But a syntactic clitic can also be an unstressed element like a pronoun whose behaviour differs from full nouns in that it can take up an exceptional position in the clause.

coda That portion of **rhyme** of a syllable following the peak or **nucleus** as the /t/ in *cat* /kæt/ (simple) or the /mpst/ in *glimpsed* /glɪmpst/ (complex). See further chapter 2, section 2.5.1.

cognate A language or form which has the same source as another language or form, e.g. English and German are cognate languages as both have the same source, namely Germanic.

colligation The relationship between linguistic items at both lexical and syntactic levels, as in *dark night* or *blue sky*. The term is frequently confused with **collocation**.

collocation The habitual co-occurrence of lexical items in the speech chain irrespective of whether they are syntactically related. Collocates constitute a lexical set of words which frequently co-occur.

compensatory lengthening The phonological process by which one phonetic segment (usually a vowel) is lengthened to compensate for the loss of a following segment in the same syllable.

complement A clause functioning as a noun phrase dependent on a transitive verb, e.g. *I believe that you are right*.

complementiser Grammatical markers that occur in initial position to introduce a **complement** or an infinitive. In *I believe that you are right* the complementiser is *that* which introduces the complement *(that) you are right*.

composite (text) A text which contains the linguistic forms of two or more scribes who have written different parts of it.

concord The formal relationship between one or more units whereby the form of one word dictates a corresponding form or grammatical category in another word. In PDE the verb is marked for number in the third person to correspond to the number of the subject, e.g. *he walk-s*, but *they walk*.

concrete case A form that marks a semantically definable case function such as location (ablative or dative), direction (accusative) or source (genitive).

conjugation The set of inflectional forms or **paradigm** of a verb; a class of verbs whose forms are generally the same in some major respect, e.g. the weak conjugation.

connotation A term used to mean the peripheral significances of a lexical item such as affective or emotional associations.

conspiracy A set of rules or changes that are formally unrelated but appear to 'act in concert' or 'serve a single goal', e.g. lengthenings or shortenings whose effect is to favour certain syllable types to the exclusion of others.

constraint(s) The arbitrary and usually subconscious limits to the amount of variation tolerated in individual forms or structures within a particular dialect or speech community at a spoken or written level.

context A term broadly understood to include all the circumstances relevant to any particular occurrence of a linguistic item, whether verbal, situational, social or psychological.

continental A term used in onomastics as a portmanteau description (in contradistinction to **insular**) of the types of **baptismal name** favoured by post-Conquest immigrants, mainly ones of Continental Germanic and of **Christian** types but also including some Breton and Normano-Scandinavian forms.

contracted verbs A set of verbs in which the **stem** and inflection have become fused as a result of the loss of a stem-final consonant.

copula A linking verb, typically a verb of being, e.g. *This is a glossary*.

copulative co-ordination The linking of two co-ordinate clauses by means of a semantically neutral conjunction (typically *and*).

correlative A construction in which the relationship between two or more units is marked on each unit, e.g. *either...or*.

co-text A term which contrasts with **context** by referring only to the verbal context accompanying the occurrence of a linguistic item.

creole A **pidgin** language which is the mother-tongue of a group of speakers.

de-adjectival Formed from adjectives by morphophonemic processes.

declension See **paradigm**.

degemination The phonological process whereby a double consonant is reduced to a single one.

deictic Of an item reflecting the orientation of discourse participants in time and space, normally with reference to the speaker, along a **proximal** (toward-speaker) versus **distal** (away-from-speaker) axis, e.g. *I*:*you*; *this*: *that*; present:past.

demonstrative A **deictic** pronoun or adjective like *this* or *that*.

denotation The meaning of a lexical item free of **co-text**, which, though imprecise, is partially determined by cultural norms. Although usually contrasted with **connotation**, in chapter 5 it is also contrasted with **sense**.

derivation See **morpheme**.

determiner The term covering articles, **demonstratives** and **quantifiers**.

diachronic A term used to refer to linguistic differences through time.

diacritic A term used of a mark or letter which has no phonetic value in itself, but which modifies the phonetic realisation of a graph.

diatopic A term which contrasts with **diachronic** and refers to linguistic differences existing at a particular point in time.

dictamen A rhetorical manual advocating formulas and styles for particular genres.

diglossia The state where two radically different varieties of a language co-exist in a single speech community. In German-speaking Switzerland both High German and Swiss German exist; and in Britain a diglossic situation exists in some parts of Scotland where both Scots and Scottish English are used.

digraph A combination of two graphs (as a **trigraph** is of three graphs) to represent a single graphic unit, as PDE < th > in *the* as compared with the sequence of these two graphs separately in *hotheaded*.

diphthong A vowel in which there is a noticeable change in quality during the duration of its articulation in any syllable. The diphthong is usually transcribed by means of the starting- and finishing-points of articulation. It may have prominence on the first (*falling diphthong*) or the second (*rising diphthong*) element, though the former is more common in all periods of English. The term diphthongisation refers to the process by which a **monophthong** becomes a diphthong.

direct argument   See **structural case**.

dissimilation   A phonological process by which two (nearly)adjacent and similar or identical sounds are made less similar; cf. Lat. *peregrinus* and PDE *pilgrim* where the first /r/ is dissimilated to /l/.

distal   See **deictic**.

distribution   There are two important types of distribution: (a) complementary distribution, where the environment in which the two elements may occur consists of two disjoint sets, each associated with only one element; and (b) contrastive distribution where the environment consists of two overlapping sets. In PDE /p/ and /b/ contrast, for they can occur in the same environment, while [l] and [ł] are in complementary distribution.

dithematic   An onomastic term used of a name formed from two Germanic name **themes**.

ditransitive   A term referring to verbs which can take two objects. These may be both direct objects (in OE two accusatives) or a direct and an indirect object (in OE an accusative and a dative). The term contrasts with **monotransitive** verbs, which can take only one object.

dual   A term used of number category indicating 'two and only two' as opposed to the terms *singular* and *plural*.

dummy   A term referring to a formal element which is semantically empty but required syntactically, e.g. the *do* in *Do you like coffee?*

dynamic   See **stative**.

enclitic   See **clitic**.

endocentric   A term used of a construction in which one of the elements is functionally equivalent to the construction as a whole, i.e. acts as **head**. In a noun group such as *the tall man* the head is *man* and could stand for the whole group.

epenthesis   A phonological process by which a segment is inserted between two other segments. PDE *empty* contains an epenthetic /p/, cf. OE *æmtig*.

epistemic   A term referring to the semantics of probability, possibility and belief. The sentence *They must be married* implies the sense (*From what is known to me*) *I conclude that they are married*.

existential A **copula** construction which refers to being in existence (e.g. *There is a plant on my windowsill*) rather than to definition (e.g. *The plant is drooping*).

exocentric A type of construction in which none of the elements is functionally equivalent to the group as a whole. Basic sentences are typically exocentric, for in *The man fell* neither *the man* nor *fell* can act as a sentence itself. Cf. **endocentric**.

exophoric reference In discourse, reference may be **anaphoric, cataphoric** or exophoric, which refers to the world outside the linguistic discourse itself.

experiencer The semantic role of the noun group referring to an entity or person affected by the activity or state of the verb, e.g. *Jane* in *Jane knew the answer* or *Jane heard the music*.

extraposition The process of moving a clause from its normal position to one near the end or beginning of another clause. Compare *It was obvious that she had taken the book* with *That she had taken the book was obvious*.

factitive Of a verb indicating the 'bringing-into-existence' of a state, such as *strengthen*.

finite A term used to describe a verb marked for **tense** and person/number. A finite clause contains a subject and a finite verb.

fit In dialectology a term used of the technique for plotting dialect forms on a map to enable other texts to be fitted into an appropriate point on the map.

foot A rhythmic unit of a stressed syllable and any other syllables to its right before the next stress; see chapter 2, section 2.5.1.

foregrounding A term used in discourse analysis to refer to the relative prominence of an item, most often a clause. In the sentence *While Donna played the piano John sang* the first clause is the background and the second is foregrounded.

gap A term used in syntax to refer to the absence of a unit in the clause where one might have been expected; thus *the man* is not repeated in *That is the man they arrested____yesterday*.

geminate A term used in phonology to describe a sequence of two identical segments which are each short but which together are interpreted as one long segment. It thus refers to a cluster of two identical vowels or consonants.

gender There are two types of gender; (a) natural gender refers to the sex of the item; and (b) grammatical gender refers to the inflectional endings of items, particularly nouns, which are arbitrarily classified as masculine, feminine and neuter and which have no reference to natural gender.

generic A term used to describe an expression where the whole class of referents is referred to, e.g. *Cats are mammals, a cat is a mammal.*

glide A vocalic sound which occurs as the result of transition between one articulation and the next, as in the /ə/ in PDE /bɪərɪ/ *beery.*

government A term referring to the government of the case forms of nouns or pronouns by verbs or prepositions.

gradation The modification of a vowel in **ablaut**; and *grade* refers to the particular ablaut form of a vowel associated with a particular tense or tense/number form.

grammaticalisation The process whereby a device developed for stylistic or topicalisation purposes or an element of full referential meaning comes to be employed as the regular grammatical exponent of a particular category. In English the change in use of the progressive form of verbs from a stylistic device to an expression of duration is an example of grammaticalisation.

grapheme The minimal contrastive unit in the writing system of a language. Thus the grapheme <a> contrasts with the grapheme <b>, but each grapheme may take a variety of forms or allographs so that <a> may appear as <A, a, *a*, ɑ>.

hapax legomenon A word which occurs only once in the relevant corpus.

harmony A term used in phonology to indicate the process by which one segment in a string of segments is influenced by another segment in the same string so that some degree of **assimilation** takes place between the two.

head The central or essential element in a larger unit, e.g. *man* in *the large man.*

heavy syllable One whose **rhyme** consists of a short vowel plus two or more consonants or of a long vowel or diphthong (with or without following consonants), e.g. *asp, eye.*

hiatus The abutting of two vowels belonging to adjacent syllables with no intervening consonant: (a) internally in a word as in *royal, neon*; and (b) between words as in *the only, China is.*

homonymy A term describing the situation in which two distinct significances are represented by the same word form, either (a) phonologically as in *mail/male* (*homophones*), or (b) graphemically as in *wind* as verb and noun (*homographs*).

homophone   See **homonymy**.

homorganic   A term describing adjacent phonological segments which have the same place of articulation, as in PDE *impossible*. Its opposite is *heterorganic*, as in OE *cniht*.

hortative   A term referring to expressions of exhortation and advice, e.g. *Let's go*.

hypercorrection   The term used to refer to the production of anomalous forms through the faulty imitation of prestige norms and their extension to inappropriate environments. For example, the dropping of initial /h/ in many dialects leads some speakers to add it to words which do not have it etymologically as in *hable* 'able' *Hamsterdam* 'Amsterdam'.

hypermetric   A term used in poetry to indicate that a line contains one or more stresses than the norm.

hypocoristic   A pet name, e.g. PDE *Lizzie*.

hyponymy   A semantic term referring to the hierarchical structure of meaning whereby the significance of several items is contained within that of a superordinate word. The significance of *deer*, *rabbit*, *cat* and *dog* may be said to be contained within the superordinate word *animal*.

hypotaxis   A term in syntax referring to the sequencing of constituents by means of subordinating conjunctions in contrast to **parataxis**. In the sentence *He went to the cinema after he bought a newspaper*, the two clauses are linked by the subordinating conjunction *after*.

idionym   A quasi-unique personal name, usually of Germanic origin, adequate for identification without recourse to by-naming, e.g. *Æthelweard*; by extension, sometimes used as equivalent to **baptismal name**. Cf. **anthroponym**.

impersonal   A construction lacking a subject, such as the archaic *Methinks*.

indicator   A term in dialectology used to refer to those features of a dialect or dialects which best signal differences between one dialect and others.

inflectional   Pertaining to the marking of grammatical categories like case, number, tense, etc. on linguistic grounds.

inherent case   A case assigned at deep-structure level which is lexically determined. Its opposite is **structural case**.

insular   A term used in onomastics as a portmanteau description (in contrast to **continental**) of the types of **baptismal name** or **idionym** current in pre-Conquest England which are mainly of Old English, Anglo-Scandinavian, Welsh or Cornish origin.

intensifier A word (usually an adverb) which has a heightening or lowering effect on the meaning of another element, e.g. PDE *very*.

interlanguage A simplified or otherwise special variety of a language used between a fluent and less-fluent speaker of that language.

interlinear gloss The translation of a text written usually on a word-for-word basis between the lines of the original with the glosses of each word appearing immediately above the corresponding words in the text.

inverse spelling The term used of a graph whose phonetic value has changed over time which is then inserted into an environment where it is representationally 'correct', but historically not justified. When <gh> ceased to represent /x/, it was inserted into forms with no etymological /x/ such as *delight* < F *deliter*.

isogloss A line on a dialect map separating a regionally distinct feature; a dialect boundary is made up of a bundle of isoglosses.

kenning A type of compressed metaphor frequent in OE poetry, e.g. *swanrad* 'swan road' for the sea.

laryngeal In phonetics this refers to a sound whose place of articulation is in the larynx. In Indo-European studies the term refers to a set of sounds which have been hypothesised for Proto-Indo-European.

lengthening The phonological process by which a short vowel is converted into a long one.

lexeme The minimal distinctive unit in the lexical system and the abstract unit underlying a set of grammatical variants; hence close to popular notions of a word. The forms *sing*, *sings*, *sang* and *singing* all belong to the lexeme *sing*; and the forms *rose tree*, *beech tree*, *tree diagram* are **lexical units** which are related through the lexeme *tree*. The head words in a dictionary are usually lexemes.

lexical form The abstract lexical item underlying various word forms which differ only in inflections.

lexical rule This refers to a local rule which identifies the idiosyncratic properties (morphological, syntactic, semantic) of a particular lexical item and the relationships between lexical items. A syntatic or **structural rule** is a general rule which applies to (a configuration of) syntactic categories irrespective of their (idiosyncratic) properties. See Wasow (1977).

lexical unit **colligations** which share the same **lexeme**.

lexicalisation A process whereby an element or construction acquires lexemic status of its own. In derivational morphology it refers to the process by which a derived **lexeme** comes to be viewed as underived.

lexicon The inventory of **lexemes** in any given language, its vocabulary. The term *lexis* is sometimes used as an equivalent, but more usually to contrast with *grammar* at the level of analysis.

light syllable A syllable whose **rhyme** contains a short vowel and either zero or one consonant, e.g. *at*, unstressed *a*. See chapter 2 section 2.5.1.

liquid A traditional term for *r* sounds and laterals; some writers use it for all non-nasal sonorant consonants, i.e. /r l j w/.

loan (word) A word used in a language other than the one in which it originated. In English *biscuit* is a loan from French.

marked The terms *marked* and **unmarked** form a contrastive pair, in which the unmarked element or rule has a greater distribution and is semantically more neutral. In the opposition *deep*:*shallow*, the unmarked form is *deep* since we ask the question *How deep is the water?* rather than *How shallow is the water?* since the former implies nothing about depth.

merger The falling together of two or more originally distinct categories; e.g. OE /a/ (*catt*) and /æ/ (*rætt*) merge into ME /a/ (*cat, rat*). See also **syncretism**.

metanalysis The reanalysis of constituent structure. In morphology it involves the faulty signalling of a boundary resulting in the formation of a new lexical item, e.g. *a nadder* > *an adder*. In syntax the term **abduction** is more usual; it involves the assignment of a new structural analysis to an existing string, e.g. *It is bad for you* [*to smoke*] > *It is bad* [*for you to smoke*].

metathesis A phonological process in which the order of two adjacent or nearly-adjacent segments is reversed, e.g. PDE *wasp* and *wopse*.

minimal pair A pair of words which are differentiated only by one sound, e.g. PDE *bat* and *pat*.

Mischsprachen A term used in dialect study to indicate where a text in one dialect is incompletely copied into another dialect so that the copy contains forms from both dialect areas.

modal verbs A closed set of verbs which have a common primary meaning of the expression of **modality**, e.g. PDE *shall, may*.

modality A term referring to attitudes to obligation, necessity, truth and belief which in PDE are usually restricted to **auxiliary verbs** such as *can* and *may* and to sentence adverbs such as *apparently*. See **epistemic** and contrast **mood**.

modifier   In a noun phrase an element which adds meaning to the **head**.

monomoric   See **mora**.

monophthong   A vowel in which there is no distinctive change in quality for the duration of its articulation in any given **syllable**. The term contrasts with **diphthong**. The term *monophthongisation* refers to the process by which a diphthong becomes a monophthong.

monothematic   An onomastic term referring to a name formed from a single Germanic name **theme** with or without the addition of a diminutive or other suffix.

monotransitive   See **ditransitive**.

mood   The cover term for indicative, subjunctive and imperative. The choice may be controlled by specific constructions or by the semantic function of expressing doubt, hypothesis or unreality.

mora (pl. *morae*)   A phonological unit of length by which the **weight** of a syllable is measured. Short vowels and consonants contain a single *mora* (and are **monomoric**), whereas long vowels, long consonants and (usually) diphthongs contain two *morae* (and are **bimoric**).

morpheme   The minimal distinctive unit in grammar (as opposed to phonology). Morphemes may be either lexical or syntactic, as in the two morphemes of PDE *boy + s*. Words of only one morpheme are said to be *monomorphemic*. Free morphemes can stand alone as words, e.g. *boy*, whereas bound morphemes must be attached to another morpheme whether they are used in inflection, e.g. plural *-s*, or in derivation, e.g. the prefix *un-*.

morphology   The structure and form of words, either in terms of inflections (*inflectional morphology*) or word formation (*derivational morphology*).

morphophonemics   The study of the phonological factors which affect the form of morphemes, as in PDE *cats* with plural /s/ compared with *dogs* with plural /z/. This distribution is known as *morphophonemic alternation*.

morphosyntactic   A term referring to a grammatical category or property which is defined by both morphological and syntactic criteria, e.g. number, which affects both syntax (as in subject–verb **agreement**) and morphology (as in the plural inflection).

negative-raising   A transformation which optionally moves the negative element out of an embedded clause to the immediately higher clause.

Negative-raising is only possible with certain verbs, such as those expressing belief or expectation (*think, hope*, etc.), e.g. *I think he is not coming > I don't think he is coming*.

Neogrammarian   A group of German linguists who rose to prominence in the 1870s and are best known for their slogan that sound laws admit no exceptions, though this characterisation is a gross simplification of their views.

neutralisation   A term used in phonology to describe a situation where a contrast between two **phonemes** is lost in certain environments. Thus in LOE the unstressed vowels /e, a, o/ are neutralised as /ə/.

nickname   Any descriptive personal-name form, whether functioning as **idionym** or as **by-name**.

non-rhotic   A term in phonology referrring to dialects in English which permit /r/ to occur only before vowels. Such a dialect would have no preconsonantal /r/ and none finally unless the next word begins with a vowel. So /kaːt/ *cart*, /faː/ *far*, but /faːr awei/ *far away*.

NP-Preposing   Also known as *NP-Movement*. A transformation whereby a noun phrase is fronted from a postverbal position.

NP-role   The semantic function of a noun-phrase, such as **agent, experiencer**.

nucleus   The constituent of a **rhyme** of a **syllable** containing the syllabic element (normally a vowel), e.g. /æ./ in *cat* /kæt/. Otherwise used more generally for all vocalic elements in a language, short, long or diphthongal.

object-control   See **subject-control**.

oblique   A term referring to all the case forms of a word other than that of the unmarked case, which in OE and EME is the nominative.

obstruent   A stop (fricative or affricate) as opposed to a sonorant (nasal or liquid).

onomastic   A term indicating the study of names.

onset   The constituent of a syllable preceding the **rhyme**, e.g. /k/ in *cat* /kæt/, zero in *at* /æt/. Also used of the first element of a diphthong. See chapter 2, section 2.5.1.

orthography   A term used of the way in which words are conventionally spelled and of the nature and value of letters.

paradigm The set of forms belonging to a single word or grammatical category. *Conjugation* refers to the paradigm of a verb; *declension* refers to the paradigm of a noun, adjective or pronoun.

paradigmatic See **syntagmatic**.

parataxis A syntactic construction in which clauses or phrases are linked without any overt connecting device such as subordinating conjunctions. If co-ordinating conjunctions are used, it is referred to as *syndetic parataxis* (e.g. *He went out and bought a paper and went to the library*), but linkage without a conjunction is referred to as *asyndetic parataxis* (e.g. *He went out, bought a paper, went to the library*). The opposite of parataxis is **hypotaxis**.

particle An invariable item with grammatical function which usually cannot be easily classified within the traditional parts of speech. A frequent particle in OE and EME is *þe*, often used in the introduction of subordinate clauses. Particles typically are constrained in position, function and meaning.

passive See **active**.

patronym A formulaic term which indicates that a **by-name** refers to actual parentage.

penult The next-to-last syllable of a word.

performative utterance/verb A performative utterance is a type of sentence where an action is 'performed' by virtue of the sentence being uttered (e.g. *I promise...*). Verbs used in such utterances are called performative verbs.

periphrasis Phrasal as opposed to inflectional expression of case, mood or temporal relations. Thus *of the man* is the periphrastic counterpart of *man's*. The term is used more loosely to refer to any structure where several words are found where one would suffice.

phonaestheme A **phoneme** or sequence of phonemes which has the property of sound symbolism. In PDE *sl-* appears to carry connotations of 'furtive movement', e.g. *slink*.

phoneme The minimal unit in the sound system of a language. The simplest test for a phoneme is substitution, i.e. if one sound, e.g. /p/, can be substituted by another, e.g. /b/, with a resulting contrast in meaning as *big*:*pig*, then the two sounds are each realisations of different phonemes. If a sound is substituted for a similar sound, e.g. [pʰ] for [p], with no consequent difference in meaning, the two sounds are **allophones** of a single phoneme. Technically, different phonemes are in contrastive **distribution,** i.e. can appear in the same environment, whereas allophones of a single phoneme are in complementary distribution, i.e. cannot appear in the same environment.

In transcription phonemes are indicated by slant brackets, e.g. /p/, as compared with the square brackets, e.g. [p], of phonetic transcription.

phonographic   Referring to the writing systems which reflect the sound system of a language. Hence *phonographic correspondence* is the relation between the sounds of a language and the spelling system used to express them.

phonology   The study of the sound systems of languages.

phonotactic   A term in phonology referring to the constraints on the occurrence or sequence of phonemes in a language.

phrasal verb   A verb + particle combination which acts syntactically and semantically as a single unit, e.g. PDE *dig in* 'to construct a fortified trench or dug-out' as compared with the verb + preposition of *dig in* as 'to dig (e.g. in the garden)'.

pidgin   A language which results from the mixture of two or more distinct languages as a result of attempts to communicate between two separate speech communities. The pidgin language has a much reduced linguistic structure and is not the mother-tongue of any speaker. Cf. **creole**. Hence pidginisation is a process involving the reanalysis by adult speakers with one linguistic background of the grammatical structures of a different ('target') language. The result is usually simplification in grammatical complexity of the target language, especially in the area of inflectional morphology.

pied piping   See **preposition-stranding**.

polysemy   The term used when a single word-form has more than one significance. In polysemy new senses have arisen for a single root, whereas in *homonymy* the divergence of meaning in the single word-form is caused by the historical convergence in the form of two originally distinct roots.

postdeterminer   An element following **determiner** and preceding **modifier** (if any) in a noun phrase, usually indicating quantity.

predeterminer   An element preceding **determiner** in a noun phrase, usually indicating quantity, e.g. *half the cake*.

predicate   A term in syntax referring to all the obligatory elements in a sentence apart from the subject, e.g. the bracketed constituents in *John [gave Mary a kiss] last week*.

prefix   See **affix**.

premodal   A verb cognate to one of the PDE **modals**, with many of the semantic but not the syntactic properties of the PDE forms.

premodifier   In syntax an element which precedes the **head** and modifies its meaning; an element which follows the **head** is a *postmodifier*.

preposition-stranding   A process in which a preposition and its complement do not form one constituent but are separated, whereby the preposition is left in its original position and its complement has been moved. The opposite of this is **pied piping**, whereby the preposition and its complement remain together. Compare *The boy he gave the book to* with *He gave the book to the boy*.

preterite   Past **tense**; the term is often specifically used in morphology to refer to the past-tense forms of verbs.

preterite-presents   A class of verbs in which the original preterite comes to acquire present-tense meanings and where subsequently a new **preterite** is formed. Thus OE *witan* 'know' and Lat. *novi* 'I know' (not etymologically related) are both preterite in form but present in meaning.

PRO   An empty, abstract pronominal noun phrase which may function as the underlying subject of a subjectless infinitival clause. Its reference is determined by an antecedent with which it is co-referential/co-indexed. The antecedent may be situated in the same clause, e.g. *John$_i$ [PRO$_i$ to be successful]*, or it may be situated outside the clause in which case PRO is arbitrary in reference, e.g. *It is unclear [what PRO$_{arb}$ to do]*.

proclitic   See **clitic**.

proto-   A prefix to indicate a theoretical ancestor of a given language, e.g. Proto-Old English refers to the reconstructed ancestor of OE for which there is no direct evidence. See also **theme,** sense 2.

proximal   See **deictic**.

punctual   A term used of verbs expressing a complete and precise activity of short duration.

quantifier   A word which expresses general quantity (amount or number) and not specific quantity, e.g. *some, every, many*.

raising   A term used in certain linguistic analyses to refer to the phenomenon whereby a constitutent of a subordinate clause becomes part of the superordinate clause.

Received Pronunciation   The regionally neutral accent of British (especially English) English, usually considered to be a mark of education and social position.

reduplication   A morphological process by which certain features of the **root** are used in the formation of a **prefix** or **suffix**. Thus Gothic *slepan* 'sleep' has the past-tense form *saislep*, where the initial consonant is repeated in the prefix attached to the unchanged root *slep-*.

register   A variety of language which is defined according to the social situation in which it is employed, e.g. formal vs informal.

relativiser   A grammatical marker introducing a relative clause, e.g. PDE *that, who, which*.

resumptive pronouns   Pronouns which fill the gap left by a moved noun phrase. These do not occur in standard PDE, but are found in OE and ME. A marginal modern example is *the man who, I don't believe the claim that anyone saw him*. The position occupied by the relative pronoun *who* (the object of *saw* in deep structure) has been taken up by a pronoun that is co-referential with the relative after the relative itself has been moved (by wh-movement).

rheme   See **theme**.

rhotic   A term in phonology referring to dialects which allow /r/ both before consonants and finally (as well as before vowels as in **non-rhotic** dialects).

rhyme   The syllable containing the **nucleus** plus any following material, e.g. /æt/ in *cat*, /iː/ in *see*. See chapter 2, section 2.5.1.

root   The single **morpheme** within a complex form which carries the primary lexical meaning of a word; i.e. that part of a word which remains when affixes and inflections are deleted. In historical linguistics the term is often used to denote the original morpheme from which a word is etymologically derived, e.g. *see* in *unseeing*. An equivalent term is *base*.

rounding   A phonological term indicating a change in quality of a vowel through rounding of the lips in its pronunciation.

sandhi   A term indicating the processes which occur at the margins of words or morphemes when they are found in sequence, e.g. the dropping of /r/ before a word beginning with a consonant in **non-rhotic** dialects, as in /fɔː/ *for me* vs /fɔːr ʌs/ *for us*.

schemata   Lexico-grammatical formulas in which a single element can be varied, e.g. *Go home … *or *It is my pleasure (and privilege) to welcome …*

Schriftsprache   See **standard**.

schwa   The name of the central vowel [ə], often found in unstressed syllables in English as in *another* /ənʌðə/.

sense   The meaning attached to a lexical form in context; also its meaning in contrast with those of other lexical forms. The kind of meaning involved in sense relations such as synonymy and hyponymy.

short form   An onomastic term referring to an abbreviated form of a **baptismal name** or **idionym**, often, but not necessarily, a colloquialism.

similiter cadens   A rhetorical device by which words are linked through a similar final morpheme.

simplex   Used to describe a word containing only the **root** morpheme.

sonorant   See **obstruent**.

split   A term in phonology referring to the process whereby a single linguistic category divides into two or more, e.g. ME /u/ (*put*, *cut*) splits into PDE /ʊ/ (*put*) and /ʌ/ (*cut*).

standard (dialect, language)   The prestigious variety of a particular language, often an institutionalised norm, which cuts across regional differences. In ME written forms of a given dialect which is spelled consistently and which has spread over a geographical area greater than that in which the original dialect was spoken often fulfil the function of a standard and may be referred to as **schriftsprache**.

stative   A term referring to the **aspect** category of verbs. Semantically, stative verbs refer to states rather than actions, e.g. *I know* vs *I walk*. There may be syntactic restrictions on stative verbs. In PDE, for example, the stative verb *know* is not used in **Know!* or **He is knowing the answer*. *Stative* stands in contrast to **dynamic**.

stem   That part of a word to which inflections are attached, e.g. PDE *boy-s*. Only in a **simplex** is the stem equivalent to the **root**, for a stem may consist of more than one **morpheme**, e.g. PDE *overthrow-s*.

stimulus/source   The semantic role of the noun phrase referring to the place, perception or idea *from* or *out* of which something comes.

stop   See **obstruent**.

stranding   The phenomenon whereby an element can be left unattached after the rest of its constituent has been moved. In PDE *Where do you come from?* the preposition *from* has been stranded, because *where* has been moved to the front of the clause.

stress   A complex of phonetic features which refers to the degree of force used in producing a **syllable.** In PDE *about*, the first syllable is unstressed and the second is stressed. Stressed syllables may carry the main stress in a word, in which case they are primary-stressed, or not, in which case they are secondary-stressed. In PDE *rhododendron* the third syllable is primary-stressed, the first is secondary-stressed and the remainder are unstressed.

strong adjective A Germanic adjective declension with relatively rich marking for gender, number and case, as compared with the more poorly marked weak adjective. See chapter 2, section 2.9.1.2.

strong syllable A stressed syllable; cf. **stress**.

strong verb A verb which forms its **preterite** by internal vowel change rather than through affixation, *drive*:*drove*, *bite*:*bit* vs weak verbs like *walk*:*walked*, *keep*:*kept* that form their preterites with a dental suffix (even if there is also some vowel alteration). See chapter 2, sections 2.9.2.2–3

structural case A case that serves to mark a grammatical relation, e.g. subject, direct object. In generative grammar it is a case assigned at surface level.

structural rule See **lexical rule**.

subject-control Control is the relation that exists between PRO and its antecedent. When the antecedent is the subject of the matrix verb, we speak of subject-control e.g. *John$_i$ tries* [PRO$_i$ *to do his best*]. When the antecedent is the (indirect) object of the matrix verb, we speak of object-control, e.g. *John asks Mary$_i$* [PRO$_i$ *to do her best*].

suffix See **affix**.

superheavy syllable One whose **rhyme** consists of a long vowel or diphthong and at least two consonants, e.g. *east* /iːst/. See chapter 2, section 2.5.1.

suppletion A morphological process whereby different inflectional forms of an individual word are taken from different **roots** to produce irregular alternation within a paradigm. In PDE *go*, *went*, the latter derives from the **preterite** of a verb *wend*, which is now archaic.

suprasegmental A term in phonology used to describe phonetic features which have an effect over more than one segment. A suprasegmental feature characteristic of English (and other languages) is **stress**, which is a property of **syllables** rather than of individual segments.

syllable No phonetic definition for syllable has yet been found which is entirely satisfactory, though phonologically the syllable is a unit into which sequences of consonants and vowels are grouped with the requirement that no syllable may contain more than one vowel or diphthong.

synchronic A term referring to the state of a language or variety at a particular time without a historical dimension.

syncope   Deletion of vowel(s) within a word, as in OE *heafod* 'head' which has a genitive singular *heafdes*.

syncretism   The merger of two distinct inflectional forms into one such as is usually the case for the OE nominative and accusative plurals, which were formerly distinct and separate but had become identical in OE. See **merger**.

syntagmatic   A term referring to the co-occurrence or combination within the string of words of co-ordinated discourse. It contrasts with **paradigmatic**, which refers to the choice available to replace a single item in the discourse.

synthetic   See **analytic**.

telic   A term used of verbs denoting an activity which is purposive, directed towards a definite end.

tense   A morphological and semantic temporal category. Morphologically, PDE tense distinguishes past (*walked*) and non-past (*walks*). Semantically, it distinguishes past, present and future as well as past of past (pluperfect) and future of the past (by means of the *will have X-ed* construction).

thematic role   The semantic function that a subject or complement has in relation to its head, the verb, e.g. that of agent, recipient, goal, etc.

theme   A term used in a variety of different technical ways: (1) In morphology used to denote an element which, when added to the **root**, forms a **stem** to which inflections may be added. Thus Gmc **luf-oj-an* 'love' consists of root + theme (stem) + inflection. Forms in which an inflection is added directly to the root, as in Gmc **mann-iz*, OE *menn*, are said to be *athematic*. (2) In onomastics the term refers to the conventional elements, usually of 'heroic' meaning, from which traditional Germanic **idionyms** were formed. The name *Wulfstan* contains two themes: a prototheme (*wulf*) and a deuterotheme (*stan*). (3) In syntax the distinction between theme and rheme is similar to the topic–comment contrast. The theme constitutes that part of the sentence that presents given information and is the first major constituent of the clause. The **rheme** contains new information and follows the theme; it is communicatively likely to be the most important element.

topicalisation   The process by which particular attention is drawn to an element, generally a noun phrase. Usually the noun phrase is moved to an initial position so that it becomes the theme or topic of a clause. The process in PDE may involve contrast, as in *The wine he loved, the beer he hated*.

toponym   The name of a place; hence *toponymy* is the study of place names.

Tough movement   A transformation by which a structure like *This house is* *difficult to clean* is derived from *It is difficult to clean this house*. In other words, the surface-structure subject has been moved from the deep-structure infinitival object position.

trigraph   See **digraph**.

unmarked   See **marked**.

valency   A term referring to the relationship that exists between a verb and its dependents/complements (i.e. (in)direct objects, prepositional objects).

variable   In dialectology a linguistic feature, often a phoneme, which is realised by different forms in dialects throughout the country.

verb second   A term referring to the phenomenon found in certain languages in which the (finite) verb is usually found in second position in the main clause whatever the nature of the first constituent.

vocalisation   A phonological process by which an approximant (also called a semivowel) takes on the functions of a vowel, as in the shift from disyllabic OE /nerje/ (*nerie* 'I perform') to trisyllabic /nerie/.

weak adjective   See **strong adjective**.

weak syllable   One that is (relatively) non-prominent or unstressed.

weak verb   See **strong verb**.

weakening   A term in phonology referring to any change involving opening of articulation (stop > fricative, fricative > approximant), voicing or shift from oral to glottal articulation. The changes [t] > [θ], [t] > [d], [t] > [ʔ] are all examples of weakening.

weight   Also known as *quantity*. A structural property of syllables defined by the configuration of the **rhyme**. A **syllable** with either a complex **nucleus** or **coda** is heavy; and one with a simple nucleus or coda is light. See chapter 2, section 2.5.1.

wh-movement   A transformation whereby wh-elements (i.e. interrogative pronouns and adverbs and relative pronouns) are moved to the first position in the clause, as happens in relative clauses and questions; e.g. *Where is he going?*

word form   A term in semantics referring to the spoken or written representation of a **lexical form** as encountered in speech or writing.

zero derivative   A word derived from another word without the presence of an overt marker such as a suffix to indicate this difference in category, as in the PDE verb *mother* from the noun *mother*.

BIBLIOGRAPHY

Primary sources

Allen, H. E. (1931). *English Writings of Richard Rolle Hermit of Hampole*. Oxford: Clarendon.

Allen, R. (1984). *King Horn: an Edition Based on Cambridge University Library MS Gg.4.27(2)*. New York and London: Garland.

Anderson, J. J. (1977). *Cleanness*. Manchester: Manchester University Press.

Arngart, O. S. A. (1942). *The Proverbs of Alfred*. Lund: Gleerup.

Arnold, T. (1869–71). *Select English Works of John Wyclif*. 3 vols. Oxford: Clarendon.

(1882–5). *Symeonis Monachi Opera Omnia*. 2 vols. (Rolls Series.) London: Longman.

Babington, C. & J. R. Lumby (1865–8). *Polychronicon Ranulphi Higden Monachi Cestrensis*. 9 vols. (Rolls Series.) London: Longman.

Baker, D. C., J. L. Murphy & L. B. Hall Jr (1982). *The Late Medieval Religious Plays of Bodleian MSS Digby 133 and E Museo 160*. (EETS 283.) Oxford: Oxford University Press.

Barnicle, M. E. (1927). *The Seege or Batayle of Troye*. (EETS 172.) London: Oxford University Press.

Bateson, M. (1899). *Records of the Borough of Leicester 1103–1327*. London: Clay.

(1904). *Borough Customs I*. (Publications of the Selden Society 18.) London: Quaritch.

Bennett, J. A. W. & G. V. Smithers (1966). *Early Middle English Verse and Prose*. 2nd edn. Oxford: Clarendon.

Benson, L. D. (1987). *The Riverside Chaucer*. (Based on F. N. Robinson's *The Complete Works of Geoffrey Chaucer*.) 3rd edn. Boston, MA: Houghton Mifflin.

Blake, N. F. (1973). *Caxton's Own Prose*. London: Deutsch.

(1980). *The Canterbury Tales by Geoffrey Chaucer*. London: Arnold.

Bliss, A. J. (1966). *Sir Orfeo*. 2nd edn. Oxford: Clarendon.

Blunt, J. H. (1873). *The Myrroure of Oure Ladye*. (EETS e.s. 19.) London: Trübner.

Bridgeman, C. G. O. (1916). The Burton Abbey twelfth-century surveys. *Collections for a History of Staffordshire edited by the William Salt Archæological Society*, 209–310.

Brie, F. W. D. (1906–8). *The Brut or The Chronicles of England*. 2 vols. (EETS 131, 136.) London: Oxford University Press.

Brook, G. L. & R. F. Leslie (1963–78). *Laȝamon: Brut*. 2 vols. (EETS 250, 277.) London: Oxford University Press.

Brooke, C. N. L. & M. M. Postan (1960). *Carte Nativorum*. (Publications of the Northamptonshire Record Society 20.) Oxford: Oxford University Press.

Brown, C. (1932). *English Lyrics of the XIIIth Century*. Oxford: Clarendon.

Brunner, K. (1933). *The Seven Sages of Rome (Southern Version)*. (EETS 191.) London: Oxford University Press.

Bunt, G. H. V. (1985). *William of Palerne: an Alliterative Romance*. Groningen: Bouma's Boekhuis.

Cameron, K., M. W. Barley & W. H. Stevenson (1956). *Documents relating to the Manor and Soke of Newark-on-Trent*. (Thornton Society Records Series 16.) Nottingham: Derry.

Chambers, R. W. & Marjorie Daunt (1931). *A Book of London English 1384–1425*. Oxford: Clarendon. (Rptd 1967.)

Clark, Cecily (1958/1970). *The Peterborough Chronicle 1070–1154*. 2nd edn., 1970. Oxford: Clarendon.

Cockayne, O. (1864–6). *Leechdoms, Wort-cunning, and Starcraft*. 3 vols. (Rolls Series.) London: Longman.

College, Edmund, O. S. P. & J. Walsh SJ (1978). *A Book of Showings to the Anchoress Julian of Norwich. Part I*. Toronto: Pontifical Institute.

Crotch, W. J. B. (1928). *The Prologues and Epilogues of William Caxton*. (EETS 176.) London: Oxford University Press.

Culley, M. T. & F. J. Furnivall (1890). *Caxton's Eneydos 1490* (EETS e.s. 57.) London: Oxford University Press.

d'Ardenne, S. R. T. O. (1936). *An Edition of Þe Liflade ant te Passiun of Seinte Iulienne*. (Bibliothèque de la Faculté de Philosophie et Lettres de l'Université de Liège LXIV.) Liège: Université de Liège; Paris: Droz.

d'Ardenne, S. R. T. O. & E. J. Dobson (1981). *Seinte Katerine*. (EETS s.s. 7.) London: Oxford University Press.

Davis, Norman (1971–6). *Paston Letters and Papers of the Fifteenth Century*. 2 parts. Oxford: Clarendon.

Davis, R. H. C. (1954). *The Kalendar of Abbot Samson of Bury St Edmunds and Related Documents*. (Camden 3rd Series 84.) London: Royal Historical Society.

Day, M. (1952). *The English Text of the Ancrene Riwle edited from Cotton Nero A. xiv*. (EETS 225.) London: Oxford University Press.

Dickens, B. & R. M. Wilson (1956). *Early Middle English Texts.* 3rd edn. London: Bowes & Bowes.

Dimock, J. F. (1868). *Giraldi Cambrensis Opera.* 6 vols. (Rolls Series.) London: Longman.

Dobson, E. J. (1972). *The English Text of the Ancrene Riwle edited from B. M. Cotton MS. Cleopatra C. vi.* (EETS 267.) London: Oxford University Press.

Donaldson, D. & G. A. Panton (1869–74). *The Gest Hystoriale of the Destruction of Troy: an Alliterative Romance.* 2 vols. (EETS 39, 56.) London: Trübner.

Douglas, D. C. (1932). *Feudal Documents from the Abbey of Bury St Edmunds.* London: Oxford University Press for the British Academy.

Ekwall, E. (1951). *Two Early London Subsidy Rolls.* (Acta Regiæ Societatis Humaniorum Litterarum Lundensis 48.) Lund: Gleerup.

England, G. & A. W. Pollard (1897). *The Towneley Plays.* (EETS e.s. 71.) London: Kegan Paul, Trench, Trübner.

Fauroux, M. (1961). *Recueil des actes des ducs de Normandie (911–1066).* (Mémoires de la Société des Antiquaires de Normandie 36.) Caen: Caron.

Fisher, John H., Malcolm Richardson & Jane L. Fisher (1984). *An Anthology of Chancery English.* Knoxville: University of Tennessee Press.

Forshall, J. & Sir F. Madden (1850). *The Holy Bible, made from the Latin Vulgate by John Wycliffe and his Followers.* 4 vols. Oxford: Clarendon.

French, W. H. & C. B. Hale (1964). *The Middle English Metrical Romances.* 2 vols. New York: Russell & Russell. (First published 1930.)

Furnivall, F. J. (1882). *The Fifty Earliest English Wills of the Court of Probate, London, A.D. 1387–1439.* (EETS 78.) London: Trübner.

(1901–3). *Robert of Brunne's Handlyng Synne.* 2 vols. (EETS 119, 123.) London: Kegan Paul, Trench, Trübner.

Gairdner, J. (1910). *The Paston Letters 1422–1509 AD.* 4 vols. Edinburgh: Grant.

Gerald of Wales (1978). *The Journey through Wales and the Description of Wales,* tr. Lewis Thorpe. Harmondsworth: Penguin.

Gordon, E. V. (1953). *Pearl.* Oxford: Clarendon.

Gough, A. B. (1901). *Emaré.* (Old and Middle English Texts 2.) London: Low Marston.

Greet, W. C. (1927). *The Reule of Crysten Religioun by Reginald Pecock D.D.* (EETS 171.) London: Oxford University Press.

Hall, C. P. & J. R. Ravensdale (1976). *The West Fields of Cambridge.* (Cambridge Antiquarian Society 3.) Cambridge: Cambridge Antiquarian Record Society.

Hall, J. (1920). *Selections from Early Middle English 1130–1250.* 2 vols. Oxford: Clarendon.

Hamelius, P. (1919–23). *Mandeville's Travels.* 2 vols. (EETS 153, 154.) London: Oxford University Press.

Hamilton, N. E. S. A. (1870). *Willelmi Malmesburiensis Monachi de Gestis Pontificum Anglorum Libri Quinque.* (Rolls Series.) London: Longman.

Hanham, A. (1975). *The Cely Letters 1472–1488.* (EETS 273.) London: Oxford University Press.

Hart, W. H. & P. A. Lyons (1884–93). *Cartularium Monasterii de Rameseia.* 3 vols. (Rolls Series.) London: Longman.

Harvey, P. D. A. (1974). *Manorial Records of Cuxham, Oxfordshire, c. 1200–1359.* (Oxfordshire Record Society 50.) Oxford: Oxfordshire Record Society.

Hodgson, P. (1982). *The Cloud of Unknowing and Other Treatises.* (Analecta Cartusiana 3.) Salzburg: Institut für Anglistik und Amerikanistik.

Holt, N. R. (1964). *The Pipe Roll of the Bishopric of Winchester 1210–1211.* Manchester: Manchester University Press.

Holthausen, F. (1888–1921). *Vices and Virtues.* 2 vols. (EETS 89, 159.) London: Oxford University Press.

Horstmann, C. (1878–81). *Sammlung altenglische Legenden.* 2 vols. Heilbronn: Henniger.

(1887). Osbern Bokenham: Mappula Angliae. *Englische Studien* 10: 1–34.

Jackson, J. E. (1882). *Liber Henrici de Soliaco Abbatis Glaston.* London: Roxburghe Club.

Johansen-Aase, J. G. (1984). 'The Worcester Fragments' (Worcester Cathedral MS F.174 ff. 63r–66v). Unpublished PhD thesis. Sheffield University.

Kane, G. (1960). *Piers Plowman: the A Version.* London: Athlone.

Kane, G. & E. Talbot Donaldson (1975). *Piers Plowman: the B Version.* London: Athlone.

Keller, C. (1914). *Die mittelenglische Gregoriuslegende.* Heidelberg: Winter.

Kingsford, C. L. (1919). *The Stonor Letters and Papers 1290–1483.* 2 vols. (Camden Society 3rd series 29–30.) London: Camden Society.

Kinsley, J. (1979). *The Poems of William Dunbar.* Oxford: Clarendon.

Kölbing, E. (1885–94). *The Romance of Sir Beues of Hamtoun.* 3 vols. (EETS e.s. 46, 48, 65.) London: Kegan Paul, Trench, Trübner.

Lester, G. (1988). *The Earliest English Translation of Vegetius' De Re Militari.* (Middle English Texts 21.) Heidelberg: Winter.

Lodge, B. & S. J. H. Herrtage (1873–9). *Palladius on Husbondrie.* 2 vols. (EETS 52, 72.) London: Trübner.

Lucas, P. J. (1983). *John Capgrave's Abbreuiacion of Chronicles.* (EETS 285.) London: Oxford University Press.

Macaulay, G. C. (1900). *The English Works of John Gower.* 2 vols. (EETS e.s. 81, 82.) London: Oxford University Press.

(1902). *John Gower: the Complete Works,* vol. IV: *Vox clamantis.* Oxford: Clarendon.

Mack, F. M. (1934). *Seinte Marherete þe Meiden ant Martyr.* (EETS 193.) London: Oxford University Press.

(1963). *The English Text of the Ancrene Riwle edited from Cotton Titus D. xviii.* (EETS 252.) London: Oxford University Press.

Macrae-Gibson, O. D. (1973–9). *Of Arthour and Merlin*. 2 vols. (EETS 268, 279.) London: Oxford University Press.

Madden, Sir F. (1847). *La3amon's Brut or Chronicle of Britain*. 3 vols. London: Society of Antiquaries.

Manzalaoui, M. A. (1977). *Secretum Secretorum*. (EETS 276.) London: Oxford University Press.

Meech, S. B. & H. E. Allen (1940). *The Book of Margery Kempe*. (EETS 212.) London: Oxford University Press.

Millett, B. (1982). *Hali Meiðhad*. (EETS 284.) London: Oxford University Press.

Mills, A. D. (1971). *The Dorset Lay Subsidy Roll of 1332*. (Dorset Record Society 4.) Dorchester: Dorset Record Society.

Morris, R. (1872). *An Old English Miscellany*. (EETS 49.) London: Trübner.

(1873a). *Genesis and Exodus*. (EETS 7.) London: Trübner.

(1873b.). *Old English Homilies of the Twelfth Century*. 2nd series. (EETS 53.) London: Trübner.

(1874–92). *Cursor Mundi (The Cursor o the World)*. 6 vols. (EETS 57, 59, 62, 66, 68, 99.) London: Kegan Paul, Trench, Trübner.

Morris, R. & P. Gradon (1965–79). *Dan Michel's Ayenbite of Inwyt*. 2 vols. (EETS 23 (reissue) and 278.) London: Oxford University Press.

Mossé, F. (1957). *A Handbook of Middle English*. Baltimore, MD: Johns Hopkins.

Napier, A. S. (1916). *Jacob and Josep: a Middle English Poem of the Thirteenth Century*. Oxford: Clarendon.

Nicolas, Sir H. (1837). *Proceedings and Ordinances of the Privy Council of England*. (Record Commission Publications 16.) London: Record Commission.

Norton-Smith, J. (1966). *John Lydgate: Poems*. Oxford: Clarendon.

Offord, M. Y. (1959). *The Parlement of the Thre Ages*. (EETS 246.) London: Oxford University Press.

Ogilvie-Thomson, S. J. (1988). *Richard Rolle: Prose and Verse*. (EETS 293.) Oxford: Oxford University Press.

Owen, D. M. (1984). *The Making of King's Lynn: a Documentary Survey*. (Records of Social and Economic History n.s. 9.) London: Oxford University Press for the British Academy.

Pearsall, D. A. (1978). *Piers Plowman by William Langland: an Edition of the C-Text*. London: Arnold.

Robinson, F. N. (1957). *The Works of Geoffrey Chaucer*. 2nd edn. Boston, MA: Houghton Mifflin.

Ross, W. O. (1940). *Middle English Sermons edited from British Museum MS. Royal 18 B. xxiii*. (EETS 209.) London: Oxford University Press.

Rumble, A. R. (1980). *The Dorset Lay Subsidy Roll of 1327*. (Dorset Record Society 6.) Dorchester: Dorset Record Society.

Scattergood, V. J. (1975). *The Works of Sir John Clanvowe*. Cambridge: Brewer.

Searle, E. (1980). *The Chronicle of Battle Abbey*. Oxford: Clarendon.

Shepherd, G. (1959). *Ancrene Wisse Parts Six and Seven*. London: Nelson.

Sisam, K. (1955). *Fourteenth Century Verse and Prose*. 3rd edn. Oxford: Clarendon.

Skeat, W. W. (1865). *Lancelot of the Laik*. (EETS 6.) London: Trübner.

(1867). *William of Palerne*. (EETS e.s. 1.) London: Trübner.

(1874–89). *The Bruce*. 2 vols. (EETS e.s. 11, 55.) London: Trübner.

(1886). *The Wars of Alexander*. (EETS e.s. 47.) London: Trübner.

(1897). *Thomas Usk: The Testament of Love*. In *Supplement to the Works of Geoffrey Chaucer*. London: Oxford University Press.

Smithers, G. V. (1952–7). *Kyng Alisaunder*. 2 vols. (EETS 227, 237.) London: Oxford University Press.

(1987). *Havelok*. Oxford: Clarendon.

Stanley, E. G. (1960). *The Owl and the Nightingale*. London: Nelson.

Steele, R. & T. Henderson (1898). *Three Prose Versions of the Secreta Secretorum*. (EETS e.s. 74.) London: Kegan Paul, Trench, Trübner.

Stevenson, J. (1845). . *Libellus de Vita et Miraculis S. Godrici*. (Surtees Society 20.) London: Nichols.

Stubbs, W. (1887–9). *Willelmi Malmesbiriensis Monachi de Gestis Regum Anglorum Libri Quinque*. 2 vols. (Rolls Series.) London: Longman.

Thompson, W. M. (1958). *Þe Wohunge of Ure Lauerd*. (EETS 241.) London: Oxford University Press.

Tolkien, J. R. R. (1962). *The Ancrene Wisse edited from MS. Corpus Christi College Cambridge 402*. (EETS 249.) London: Oxford University Press.

Tolkien, J. R. R. & E. V. Gordon (1967). *Sir Gawain and the Green Knight*, rev. by Norman Davis. 2nd edn. Oxford: Clarendon.

Urry, W. (1967). *Canterbury under the Angevin Kings*. London: Athlone.

Vinaver, E. (1967). *The Works of Sir Thomas Malory*. 2nd edn. London: Oxford University Press.

White, R. M. (1878). *The Ormulum*, rev. by R. Holt. 2 vols. Oxford: Oxford University Press.

Wright, T. (1857). *A Volume of Vocabularies*. London: privately printed by Mayer.

Wright, W. A. (1887). *The Metrical Chronicle of Robert of Gloucester*. 2 vols. (Rolls Series.) London: Longman.

Zupitza, J. (1875–91). *The Romance of Guy of Warwick*. 5 vols. (EETS e.s. 25, 26, 42, 49, 59.) London: Trübner.

Secondary sources

The following abbreviations of journal titles are used in this section.

Archiv	*Archiv für das Studium der neueren Sprachen und Literaturen*
ASE	*Anglo-Saxon England*
ChR	*The Chaucer Review*

E&S	Essays and Studies
ES	English Studies
FLH	Folia Linguistica Historica
JEGP	Journal of English and Germanic Philology
JEPNS	Journal of the English Place-Name Society
JL	Journal of Linguistics
MLN	Modern Language Notes
MLR	Modern Language Review
MP	Modern Philology
NB	Namn och Bygd
NM	Neuphilologische Mitteilungen
NOWELE	North-Western European Language Evolution
N&Q	Notes and Queries
PMLA	Publications of the Modern Language Association of America
RES	Review of English Studies
SAP	Studia Anglica Posnaniensia
SN	Studia Neophilologica
TPS	Transactions of the Philological Society
ZAA	Zeitschrift für Anglistik und Amerikanistik

Abercrombie, D. (1964). Syllable quantity and enclitics in English. In Abercrombie et al., 216–22.

Abercrombie, D., D. B. Fry, P. A. D. McCarthy, N. C. Scott & J. L. M. Trim (eds.) (1964). In Honour of Daniel Jones. Papers contributed on the Occasion of his Eightieth Birthday, 12 September 1961. London: Longman.

Adams, V. (1973). An Introduction to Modern English Word-formation. London: Longman.

Adamska-Sałaciak, A. (1984). Some notes on the origins of Middle English /a/. SAP 17: 51–62.

Adamson, S., V. Law, N. Vincent & S. Wright (eds.) (1990). Papers from the 5th International Conference on English Historical Linguistics. Amsterdam: Benjamins.

Adigard des Gautries, J. (1954). Les Noms de personne scandinaves en Normandie de 911 à 1066. (Nomina Germanica 11.) Lund: Blom.

Aebischer, P. (1924). L'Anthroponymie wallone d'après quelques anciens cartulaires. Bullétin du dictionnaire wallon 13: 73–168.

Aertsen, H. (1987). Play in Middle English: a Contribution to Word Field Theory. Amsterdam: Free University Press.

Ahlqvist, A. (ed.) (1982). Papers from the 5th International Conference on Historical Linguistics. Amsterdam: Benjamins.

Allan, K. (1971). The source of There in existential sentences. Foundations of Language 7: 1–18.

Allen, C. L. (1977). Topics in Diachronic Syntax. PhD thesis. Amherst, Mass.;

Ann Arbor, Mich.: University Microfilms. (Published by Garland, New York, 1980.)

(1986). Reconsidering the history of *like*. *JL* 22: 375–409.

Allen, W. S. (1965). *Vox Latina*. Cambridge: Cambridge University Press.

Anderson, H. (1973). Abductive and deductive change. *Language* 49: 765–93.

(1986). Center and periphery: adoption, diffusion and spread. Privately distributed in manuscript.

Anderson, J. M. (1986). A note on Old English impersonals. *JL* 22: 167–77.

Anderson, J. M. & C. J. Ewen (1987). *Principles of Dependency Phonology*. Cambridge: Cambridge University Press.

Anderson, J. M. & C. Jones (eds.) (1974). *Historical Linguistics. Proceedings of the First International Conference on Historical Linguistics, Edinburgh, 2–7 September 1973*. 2 vols. Amsterdam: North-Holland.

(1977). *Phonological Structure and the History of English*. Amsterdam: North-Holland.

Anttila, R. (1972). *An Introduction to Historical and Comparative Linguistics*. New York: Macmillan.

Árnason, K. (1980). *Quantity in Historical Phonology. Icelandic and Related Cases*. Cambridge: Cambridge University Press.

Arngart, O. (1978). Three English hundred-names. *NB* 66: 13–17.

Atkins, J. W. H. (1943). *English Literary Criticism: the Medieval Phase*. London: Methuen.

Auwera, J. van der (1984). More on the history of subject contact clauses in English. *FLH* 5:171–84.

Baghdikian, S. (1979). *Ne* in ME and EModE. *ES* 60: 673–9.

Bailey, C.-J. N. & K. Maroldt (1977). The French lineage of English. In Meisel, 21–53.

Baker, A. R. H. & R. A. Butlin (eds.) (1973). *Studies of Field-systems in the British Isles*. Cambridge: Cambridge University Press.

Bammesberger, A. (ed.) (1985). *Problems of Old English Lexicography. Studies in Memory of Angus Cameron*. Regensburg: Friedrich Pustet.

Barley, N. F. (1974). Old English colour classification: where do matters stand? *ASE* 3: 15–28.

Barlow, F. (1986). *Thomas Becket*. London: Weidenfeld & Nicolson.

Barron, W. R. J. (1965). Luf-daungere. In F. Whitehead, A. H. Diverres & F. E. Sutcliffe (eds.) *Medieval Miscellany Presented to Eugene Vinaver*. Manchester: Manchester University Press, 1–18.

Bates, D. (1982). *Normandy before 1066*. London: Longman.

(1986). *A Bibliography of Domesday Book*. Woodbridge: Boydell & Brewer.

Bauer, G. (1970). *Studien zum System und Gebrauch der 'Tempora' in der Sprache Chaucers und Gowers*. (Wiener Beiträge zur englischen Philologie 73.) Vienna: Braumüller.

Bauer, L. (1983). *English Word-formation*. Cambridge: Cambridge University Press.

Baugh, A. C. (1935). The chronology of French loan-words in English. *MLR* 50: 90–3.

(1959). Improvisation in the Middle English romance. *Proceedings of the American Philological Society* 103: 418–54.

Baugh, A. C. & T. Cable (1978). *A History of the English Language*. 3rd edn. London: Routledge & Kegan Paul.

Bean, M. C. (1983). *The Development of Word Order Patterns in Old English*. London: Croom Helm.

Beech, G. T. (1974). Les Noms de personne poitevins du IXe au XIIIe siècle. *Revue internationale d'onomastique* 26: 81–100.

Bennett, M. (1979). Spiritual kinship and the baptismal name in traditional European society. In L. O. Frappell (ed.) *Principalities, Power and Estates*. Adelaide: Adelaide University Union Press, 1–13.

Bennett, P. A. (1980). English passives: a study in syntactic change and relational grammar. *Lingua* 51: 101–14.

Bennett, W. H. (1955). The southern English development of Germanic initial *[f s þ]. *Language* 31: 367–71. (Rptd Lass 1969.)

Bense, J. F. (1926–39). *A Dictionary of the Low Dutch Element in the English Vocabulary*. London and The Hague: Nijhoff and Oxford University Press.

Benskin, M. & M. Laing (1981). Translations and *Mischsprachen* in Middle English manuscripts. In Benskin & Samuels, 55–106.

Benskin, M. & M. L. Samuels (1981). *So meny people, longages and tonges: Philological Essays in Scots and Medieval English Presented to Angus McIntosh*. Edinburgh: privately printed.

Benson, L. D. (1961). Chaucer's historical present, its meaning and use. *ES* 42: 65–77.

Beresford, M. W. (1963). *Lay Subsidies and Poll Taxes*. Canterbury: Phillimore.

(1967). *New Towns of the Middle Ages: Town Plantation in England, Wales and Gascony*. London: Lutterworth.

Berlin, B. & P. Kay (1969). *Basic Color Terms*. Berkeley and Los Angeles: California University Press.

Berndt, R. (1965). The linguistic situation in England from the Norman Conquest to the loss of Normandy. *Philologica Pragensia* 8: 145–63. (Rptd Lass 1969.)

(1972). The period of the final decline of French in medieval England (fourteenth and early fifteenth centuries). *ZAA* 20: 314–69.

(1976). French and English in thirteenth-century England: an investigation into the linguistic situation after the loss of the Duchy of Normandy and other continental dominions. In *Aspekte des anglistischen Forschungen in der DDR: Martin Lehnert zum 65. Geburtstag*. Berlin: Akademie-Verlag, 129–50.

Biddle, M. & D. J. Keene (1976). The early place-names of Winchester. In their *Winchester in the Early Middle Ages*. (Winchester Studies 1.) Oxford: Clarendon, 231–9.

Björkmann, E. (1900–2). *Scandinavian Loan-words in Middle English*. 2 vols. Halle: Karras.

(1910). *Nordische Personennamen in England*. (Studien zur englischen Philologie 37.) Halle: Niemeyer.

(1912). *Zur englischen Namenkunde*. (Studien zur englischen Philologie 47.) Halle: Niemeyer.

Blake, N. F. (1968). Caxton and courtly style. *E&S* n.s. 21: 29–45.

(1969a). *Caxton and his World*. London: Deutsch.

(1969b). Rhythmical alliteration. *MP* 67: 118–24.

(1969c). Some Low Dutch loan-words in fifteenth-century English. *N&Q* 16: 251–3.

(1974). *The Form of Living* in prose and poetry. *Archiv* 211: 300–8.

(1976). Born in Kent. *Lore and Language* 2, 5: 5–9.

(1977). *The English Language in Medieval Literature*. London: Dent. (Rptd London: Methuen, 1979.)

(1988). Literary and other languages in Middle English. In A. Torti & P. Boitani (eds.). *Themes and Images in Middle English Literature*. Cambridge: Brewer, 166–85.

Blake, N. F. & C. Jones (eds.) (1984). *English Historical Linguistics: Studies in Development*. Sheffield: Centre for English Cultural Tradition and Language (Sheffield University).

Blatt, F. (1957). Latin influence on European syntax. *Travaux du cercle linguistique de Copenhague* 11: 33–69.

Bloomfield, L. (1933). *Language*. New York: Holt. (Also London: Allen & Unwin, 1935.)

Bock, H. (1931). Studien zum präpositionalen Infinitiv und Akkusativ mit dem *TO*-Infinitiv. *Anglia* 55: 114–249.

Bødtker, A. T. (1908–10). *Critical Contributions to Early English Syntax*. 2 series. Christiania: Videnskabsselskabets Skrifter.

Bøgholm, N. (1944). *The Layamon Texts. A Linguistic Investigation*. (Travaux du cercle linguistique de Copenhague 3.) Copenhagen: Munksgaard.

Bornstein, D. (1978). Chaucer's *Tale of Melibee* as an example of 'style clergial'. *ChR* 12: 236–54.

Borst, E. (1910). Zur Stellung des Adverbs bei Chaucer. *Englische Studien* 42: 339–62.

Bourcier, G. (1981). *An Introduction to the History of the English Language*, tr. and arranged by C. Clark. Cheltenham: Thornes.

Bréal, M. (1964). *Semantics: Studies in the Science of Meaning*, tr. N. Cust. New York: Dover.

Breivik, L. E. (1981). On the interpretation of existential *there*. *Language* 57: 1–25.

Breivik, L. E., A. Hille & S. Johansson (eds.) (1989). *Essays on English Language in Honour of Bertil Sundby*. Oslo: Novus.

Brinton, L. J. (1981). The historical development of aspectual periphrasis in English. PhD Thesis. University of California. (Ann Arbor, MI: University Microfilms.)

(1983). Criteria for distinguishing the non-aspectual functions of ME *ginnen*. *General Linguistics* 23–4: 235–45.

(1988). *The Development of English Aspectual Systems: Aspectualizers and Post-verbal Particles*. Cambridge: Cambridge University Press.

(1990). The stylistic function of ME *gan* reconsidered. In Adamson *et al.*, 31–53.

Brook, G. L. (1972). A piece of evidence for the study of Middle English spelling. *NM* 73: 25–8.

Brown, G. (1977). *Listening to Spoken English*. London: Longman.

(1982). The spoken language. In R. Carter (ed.) *Linguistics and the Teacher*. London: Routledge and Kegan Paul, 75–87.

Brunner, K. (1962). *Die englische Sprache*. 2nd edn. Tübingen: Niemeyer.

(1963). *An Outline of Middle English Grammar*, tr. G. K. W. Johnston. Oxford: Blackwell.

Bryan, W. R. (1921). The Midland present plural indicative ending in *-en(n)*. *MP* 18: 457–73.

Burnley, J. D. (1977). Chaucer's *termes*. *Yearbook of English Studies* 7: 53–67.

(1979). *Chaucer's Language and the Philosophers' Tradition*. Cambridge: Brewer.

(1983). *A Guide to Chaucer's Language*. London and Norman, OK: Macmillan and Oklahoma University Press. (Reissued as *The Language of Chaucer* 1989.)

(1984). Picked terms. *ES* 65: 195–204.

(1986). Curial style. *Speculum* 61: 593–614.

Burrow, J. A. (1984). *Essays on Medieval Literature*. Oxford: Clarendon.

Bybee, J. L. & Ö. Dahl (1989). The creation of tense and aspect systems in the languages of the world. *Studies in Language* 13: 51–103.

Bybee, J. L. & W. Pagliuca (1987). The evolution of future meaning. In A. G. Ramat, O. Carruba & G. Bernini (eds.) *Papers from the VIIth International Congress on Historical Linguistics*. Amsterdam: John Benjamins, 109–22.

Bynon, T. (1977). *Historical Linguistics*. Cambridge: Cambridge University Press.

Callaway, M. (1913). *The Infinitive in Anglo-Saxon*. Washington: Carnegie Institution.

Caluwé Dor, J. (1979). The chronology of the Scandinavian loan-verbs in the *Katherine Group*. *ES* 60: 680–5.

(1983). Chaucer's contribution to the English vocabulary: a chronological survey of French loan-words. *NOWELE* 2: 73–91.

Cam, H. M. (1930). *The Hundred and the Hundred Rolls*. London: Merlin. (Rptd 1963.)

Cameron, K. (1973). Early field-names in an English-named Lincolnshire village. In Sandgren, 38–43.

(1975). Scandinavian settlement in the territory of the Five Boroughs. In K. Cameron (ed.) *Place-name Evidence for the Anglo-Saxon Invasion and Scandinavian Settlements: Eight Studies*. Nottingham: English Place-Name Society, 115–38.

(1978). The minor names and field-names of the Holland division of Lincolnshire. In T. Anderson & K. I. Sandred (eds.) *The Vikings*. Uppsala: Almqvist & Wiksell, 81–8.

(1988). *English Place-names*. 4th edn. London: Batsford.

Campbell, A. (1959). *Old English Grammar*. Oxford: Clarendon.

Carr, C. T. (1939). *Nominal Compounds in Germanic*. London: Oxford University Press.

Carter, H. H. (1961). *A Dictionary of Middle English Musical Terms*. Bloomington: Indiana University Press.

Chambers, J. D. (1964). *Laxton: the Last English Open-field Village*. London: HMSO.

Chaytor, H. J. (1945). *From Script to Print*. Cambridge: Heffer. (Rptd London: Sidgwick & Jackson, 1966.)

Chédeville, A. (1974). L'Immigration bretonne dans le royaume de France du XIe au début du XIVe siècle. *Annales de Bretagne* 81: 301–43.

Cheshire, J. (1982). *Variation in an English Dialect*. Cambridge: Cambridge University Press.

Chomsky, N. (1981). *Lectures on Government and Binding*. Dordrecht: Foris.

Chomsky, N. & M. Halle (1968). *The Sound Pattern of English*. New York: Harper.

Clanchy, M. T. (1979). *From Memory to Written Record: England 1066–1307*. London: Arnold.

(1983). *England and its Rulers 1066–1272: Foreign Lordship and National Identity*. London: Fontana.

Clark, C. (1952–3). Studies in the vocabulary of the 'Peterborough Chronicle', 1070–1154. *English and Germanic Studies* 5: 67–89.

(1957). Gender in the *Peterborough Chronicle*. *ES* 35: 109–15, 174.

(1976a). People and languages in post-Conquest Canterbury. *Journal of Medieval History* 2: 1–33.

(1976b). Some early Canterbury surnames. *ES* 57: 294–309.

(1977–8). Winchester in the early Middle Ages. *Archives* 13: 84–9. (Review article based on Biddle *et al.* 1976.)

(1978a). Women's names in post-Conquest England: observations and speculations. *Speculum* 53: 223–51.

(1978b). Thoughts on the French connections of Middle English nicknames. *Nomina* 2: 38–44.

(1978c). 'Wiþ scharpe sneateres': some aspects of colloquialism in *Ancrene Wisse*. *NM* 79: 341–53.

(1979). Clark's first three laws of applied anthroponymics. *Nomina* 3: 13–19.

(1980a). Battle *c*. 1110: an anthroponymist looks at an Anglo-Norman new town. In R. A. Brown. (ed.) *Proceedings of the Battle Conference on Anglo-Norman Studies 1979*. Woodbridge: Boydell & Brewer, 21–41 and 168–72.

(1980b). Review of Reaney 1967 (rptd 1980). *Nomina* 4: 88–90.

(1982a). The early personal names of King's Lynn: an essay in socio cultural history, Part I: baptismal names. *Nomina* 6: 51–71.

(1982b). Review of Jönsjö 1979. *ES* 63: 168–70.

(1983a). The early personal names of King's Lynn: an essay in sociocultural history, Part 2: by-names. *Nomina* 7: 65–89.

(1983b). On dating *The Battle of Maldon*: certain evidence reviewed. *Nottingham Medieval Studies* 27: 1–22.

(1983–4). Starting from Youlthorpe (East Riding of Yorkshire): an onomastic circular tour. *JEPNS* 16: 25–37.

(1984a). L'Angleterre anglo-normande et ses ambivalences socio-culturelles. In R. Foreville (ed.) *Les mutations socio-culturelles au tournant des XIe–XIIIe siècles*. (Spicilegium Beccense 2.) Paris: Centre National de la Recherche Scientifique, 99–110.

(1984b). L'Anthroponymie cantorbérienne du XIIe siècle: quelques exdamples de l'influence normanno-picarde. *Nouvelle revue d'onomastique* 3–4: 157–66.

(1985). Certains éléments français de l'anthroponymie anglaise du Moyen Age: essai méthodologique. In G. Taverdet (ed.) *L'Onomastique, témoin de l'activité humaine*. Fontaine les Dijons: Association Bourguignonne de Dialectologie et d'Onomastique, 259–67.

(1987a). Willelmus Rex? vel alius Willelmus? *Nomina* 11: 7–33.

(1987b). English personal names *ca*. 650–1300. *Medieval Prosopography* 8, 1: 31–60.

(1987c). Spelling and grammaticality in the Vespasian homilies: a re-assessment. *Manuscripta* 31, 1: 7–10.

(1990). Historical linguistics – linguistic archaeology. In S. Adamson, V. A. Law, N. Vincent & S. Wright (eds.) *Proceedings of the Fifth International Conference on English Historical Linguistics*. Amsterdam: Benjamins, 55–68.

(1991). Towards a reassessment of 'Anglo-Norman influence on English place-names'. In P. S. Ureland & G. Broderick (eds.) *Eighth International Symposium on Language Contact in Europe: Language Contact in the British Isles*. Tübingen: Niemeyer, 275–93.

Clark, C. & D. Owen (1978). Lexicographical notes from King's Lynn. *Norfolk Archaeology* 37: 56–69.

Clay, C. (1961). Master Aristotle. *English Historical Review* 76: 303–8.

Coates, R. (1987). Pragmatic sources of analogical formation. *JL* 23: 319–40.

Coghill, N. (1966). Chaucer's narrative art in *The Canterbury Tales*. In D. S. Brewer (ed.) *Chaucer and Chaucerians*. London: Nelson, 114–39.

Colman, F. (1981). The name-element *Æðel-* and related problems. *N&Q* 206: 195–201.

(1984). Anglo-Saxon pennies and Old English phonology. *FLH* 5: 91–143.

(1989a). Neutralisation: on characterizing distinctions between Old English proper names and common names. *Leeds Studies in English* n.s. 22: 249–70.

(1989b). The crunch is the key: on computer research on Old English personal names. In B. Odenstedt & G. Persson (eds.) *Instead of Flowers*. Umeå: Umeå University Press,

Comrie, B. (1981). *Language Universals and Linguistic Typology*. Oxford: Blackwell.

Cooper, C. (1687). *The English Teacher*, ed. B. Sundby, 1952. Lund: Gleerup.

Coseriu, E. (1967). Lexical structures and the teaching of vocabulary. In A. Haigh (ed.) *Linguistic Theories and their Application*. Strasburg and London: AIDELA and Harrap, 9–123.

Crosby, R. (1936). Oral delivery in the Middle Ages. *Speculum* 11: 88–110.

Cruse, D. A. (1986). *Lexical Semantics*. Cambridge: Cambridge University Press.

Crystal, D. (1985). *A Dictionary of Linguistics and Phonetics*. 2nd edn. Oxford: Blackwell.

Crystal, D. & D. Davy (1969). *Investigating English Style*. London: Longman.

Curme, G. O. (1912). A history of the English relative construction. *JEGP* 11: 10–29, 180–204, 355–80.

Curtius, E. R. (1953). *European Literature and the Latin Middle Ages*, tr. W. R. Trask. (Bollingen Series 36.) New York: Pantheon.

Dal, I. (1952). Zur Entstehung des englischen Participium Praesentis auf *-ing*. *Norsk Tidskrift for Sprogvidenskap* 16: 5–116.

Dauzat, A. & C. A. Rostaing (1963). *Dictionnaire étymologique des noms de lieux en France*. Paris: Larousse.

Davenport, M., E. Hansen & H.-F. Nielsen (eds.) (1983). *Current Topics in English Historical Linguistics*. Odense: Odense University Press.

Davis, G. R. C. (1958). *Medieval Cartularies of Great Britain: a Short Catalogue*. London: Longmans, Green.

Davis, N. (1969). Sheep-farming terms in medieval Norfolk. *N&Q* 214: 404–5.

(1972). Margaret Paston's uses of *do*. *NM* 73: 55–62.

Davis, N. & C. L. Wrenn (eds.) (1962). *English and Medieval Studies presented to J. R. R. Tolkien*. London: Oxford University Press.

Debrabandere, F. (1980). *Kortrikse Naamkunde 1200–1300*. (Anthroponymics 22.) Leuven: Instituut voor Naamkunde.

Dees, A. (1980). *Atlas des formes et des constructions des chartes françaises du 13e siècle*. (Beihefte zur Zeitschrift für romanische Philologie 178.) Tübingen: Niemeyer.

Dekeyser, X. (1986). Romance loans in Middle English: a reassessment. In Kastovsky & Szwedek, I, 253–65.

Denison, D. (1985a). Why Old English had no prepositional passive. *ES* 66: 189–204.

(1985b). The origins of periphrastic *do*: Ellegård and Visser reconsidered. In Eaton *et al.*, 45–60.

(1985c). The origins of the completive *up* in English. *NM* 86: 37–61.

(1986). On word order in Old English. *Dutch Quarterly Review* 16: 277–95.

(1990a). The Old English impersonal revived. In Adamson *et al.*, 111–40.

(1990b). Auxiliary + impersonal in Old English. *FLH* 9: 139–66.

DeWindt, A. R. & E. B. DeWindt (1981). *Royal Justice and the Medieval English Countryside*. (Studies and Texts 57.) Toronto: Pontifical Institute of Medieval Studies.

Dickens, B. (1941–2). The Names of Grim's children in the Havelok story. *SN* 14: 114.

Diekstra, F. N. M. (1984). Ambiguous THAT-clauses in Old and Middle English. *ES* 65: 97–110.

Diensberg, B. (1985). The lexical fields BOY/GIRL – SERVANT – CHILD in Middle English. *NM* 86: 328–36.

Dieth, E. (1955). Hips: a geographical contribution to the *she* puzzle. *ES* 36: 208–17.

Dobson, E. J. (1962). The affiliations of the manuscripts of *Ancrene Wisse*. In Davis & Wrenn, 128–63.

(1968). *English Pronunciation 1500–1700*. 2nd edn. 2 vols. Oxford: Clarendon.

(1976). *The Origins of Ancrene Wisse*. Oxford: Clarendon.

Dodgson, J. McN. (1968). Place-names and street-names at Chester. *Journal of the Chester Archaeological Society* 55: 29–61.

(1985a). Some Domesday personal-names, mainly post-Conquest. *Nomina* 9: 41–51.

(1985b). The Welsh element in the field-names of Cheshire. In Schützeichel, 154–64.

(1987). Domesday Book: place-names and personal names. In Holt, 121–35.

Donaldson, E. T. (1951). Idiom of popular poetry in the Miller's Tale. In A. S. Downer (ed.) *English Institute Essays 1950*. New York: Columbia University Press, 116–40. (Rptd Donaldson 1970, 13–29.)

(1970). *Speaking of Chaucer*. London: Athlone.

Donner, M. (1986). The gerund in Middle English. *ES* 67: 394–400.

Dubislav, G. (1916). Studien zur mittelenglischen Syntax I and II. *Anglia* 40: 263–96, 297–321.

Ducháček, O. (1960). *Le Champ conceptuel de la beauté en français moderne*. (Opera Universitatis Brunensis, Facultas Philosophica 71.) Prague: Státní Pedagogické Nakladatelství.

Duggan, H. N. (1986). Alliterative patterning as a basis for emendation in Middle English alliterative poetry. *Studies in the Age of Chaucer* 8: 73–105.

Duncan, P. (1972). Forms of the feminine pronoun in modern English dialects. In Wakelin, 182–200.

Duncan, T. G. (1981). A Middle English linguistic reviser. *NM* 82: 162–74.

Eaton, R., O. Fischer, W. Koopman & F. v. d. Leek (1985). *Papers from the 4th International Conference on English Historical Linguistics, 10–13 April 1985.* Amsterdam: Benjamins.

Eberle, P. J. (1983). Commercial language and the commercial outlook in the *General Prologue. ChR* 18: 161–74.

Ebin, L. (1977). Lydgate's views on poetry. *Annuale Medievale* 18: 76–105.

Einenkel, E. (1887). *Streifzüge durch die mittelenglische Syntax unter besonderer Berücksichtigung der Sprache Chaucer's.* Münster: Schöningh.

— (1914). Die Entwicklung des englischen Gerundiums. *Anglia* 38: 1–76.

— (1916). *Geschichte der englischen Sprache*, II: *Historische Syntax.* 3rd edn. Strasburg: Trübner.

Eitle, H. (1914). *Die Satzverknüpfung bei Chaucer.* (Anglistische Forschungen 44.) Heidelberg: Winter.

Ekwall, E. (1913). Die Ortnamensforschung ein Hilfsmittel für das Studium der englische Sprachgeschichte. *Germanisch-romanische Monats-schrift* 5: 592–608.

— (1917). *Contributions to the History of Old English Dialects.* Lund: Gleerup.

— (1930). How long did the Scandinavian language survive in England? In N. Bøgholm, A. Brusendorff & C. A. Bodelsen (eds.) *A Grammatical Miscellany offered to Otto Jespersen on his Seventieth Birthday.* Copenhagen: Levin and Munksgaard, 17–30. (Rptd in *Selected Papers*, 1963. Lund: Gleerup, 54–67.)

— (1933). Names of trades in English place-names. In J. G. Edwards, V. H. Galbraith & E. F. Jacob (eds.) *Historical Essays in Honour of James Tait.* Manchester: privately printed 79–89.

— (1944–5a). Variation in surnames in medieval London. *Kungl. Humanistiska Vetenskapssamfundet i Lund Årsberättelse 1944–1945.* Lund: Gleerup, 207–62.

— (1944–5b). Notes on some Middle English place-names. *SN* 17: 25–34.

— (1947). *Early London Personal Names.* (Acta Regiae Societatis Humaniora Litterarum Lundensis 43.) Lund: Gleerup.

— (1954). *Street-names of the City of London.* Oxford: Clarendon.

— (1956). *Studies on the Population of Medieval London.* (Kungliga Vitterhets Historie och Antikvitets Akademiens Handlingar, Filologisk-Filosofiska Serien 2.) Stockholm: Almqvist & Wiksell.

— (1960). *Concise Oxford Dictionary of English Place-names.* 4th edn. Oxford: Clarendon.

— (1962). Variation and change in English place-names. *Vetenskaps-Societetens i Lund Årsbok*, 3–49.

— (1964). Some cases of variation and change in English place-names. In

English Studies Presented to R. W. Zandvoort on the Occasion of his Seventieth Birthday. (Supplement to *ES* 45.) Amsterdam: Swets & Zeitlinger, 44–9.

(1965). Some early London by-names and surnames. *ES* 46: 113–18.

(1975). *A History of Modern English Sounds and Morphology*, tr. and ed. Alan Ward. Oxford: Blackwell.

Ellenberger, B. (1974). On Middle English *mots savants*. *SN* 46: 142–50.

(1977). *The Latin Element in the Vocabulary of the Earlier Makars Henryson and Dunbar.* Lund: Gleerup.

Ellegård, A. (1953). *The Auxiliary 'do': the Establishment and Regulation of its Use in English.* Stockholm: Almqvist & Wiksell.

Elliott, R. W. V. (1974). *Chaucer's English.* London: Deutsch.

Elmer, W. (1981). *Diachronic Grammar: the History of Old and Middle English Subjectless Constructions.* Tübingen: Niemeyer.

Emmison, F. G. (1969). *Guide to the Essex Record Office.* 2nd edn. (Essex Record Office Publications 51.) Chelmsford: Essex County Council.

Emonds, J. (1976). *A Transformational Approach to English Syntax: Root, Structure-preserving and Local Transformations.* New York: Academic Press.

Engblom, V. (1938). *On the Origin and Early Development of the Auxiliary 'Do'.* (Lund Studies in English 6.) Lund: Gleerup.

Erlebach, P. (1979). *Die zusammengesetzten englischen Zunamen französischer Herkunft.* (Anglistische Forschungen 137.) Heidelberg: Winter.

Erdmann, P. (1980). On the history of subject contact clauses in English. *FLH* 1: 139–70.

Evans, W. M. (1967). Dramatic use of the second-person singular pronoun in *Sir Gawain and the Green Knight. SN* 39: 38–45.

Feilitzen, O. Von (1937). *The Pre-Conquest Personal Names of Domesday Book.* (Nomina Germanica 3.) Uppsala: Almqvist & Wiksell.

(1939). Notes on Old English bynames. *NB* 27: 116–30. (Review article based on Tengvik 1938.)

(1945). Some unrecorded Old and Middle English personal names. *NB* 33: 69–98.

(1963). Some continental Germanic personal names in England. In A. Brown & P. Foote (eds.) *Early English and Norse Studies presented to Hugh Smith.* London: Methuen, 46–61.

(1964). Notes on some Scandinavian personal names in English twelfth-century records. In *Personnamnstudier 1964 tillägnade minnet av Ivar Modéer 1904–1960.* (Anthroponymica Suecana 6.) Stockholm: Almqvist & Wiksell, 52–68.

(1968). Some Old English uncompounded personal names and bynames. *SN* 40: 5–16.

(1976). The personal names of the Winton Domesday. In M. Biddle & D. J. Keene (eds.) *Winchester in the Early Middle Ages.* (Winchester Studies 1.) Oxford: Clarendon, 143–229.

Fellows-Jensen, G. (1968). *Scandinavian Personal Names in Lincolnshire and Yorkshire.* (Navnestudier udgivet af Institut for Navneforskning 7.) Copenhagen: Akademisk Forlag.

(1972). *Scandinavian Settlements in Yorkshire.* (Navnestudier 11.) Copenhagen: Akademisk Forlag.

(1973). The names of the Lincolnshire tenants of the Bishop of Lincoln *c.* 1225. In Sandgren, 86–95.

(1974). English field-names and the Danish settlement. In P. Andersen *et al.* (eds.) *Festskrift til Kristian Hald.* (Navnestudier udgivet af Institut for Navneforskning 13.) Copenhagen: Akademisk Forlag, 45–55.

(1975a). The surnames of the tenants of the Bishop of Lincoln in nine English counties *c.* 1225. In T. Andersson (ed.) *Binamn och Släktnamn Avgränsning och Ursprung: Handlingar från NORNA's tredje Symposium i Uppsala 27–28 April 1974.* (NORNA-Rapporter 8.) Uppsala: Almqvist & Wiksell, 39–65.

(1975b). The Vikings in England: a review. *ASE* 4: 181–206.

(1978). *Scandinavian Settlement Names in the East Midlands.* (Navnestudier 16.) Copenhagen: Akademisk Forlag.

(1979). *Hungate:* some observations on a common street-name. *Ortnamssällskapets i Uppsala Årsskrift:* 44–51.

(1980). On the study of Middle English by-names. *NB* 68: 102–15. (Review article of Jönsjö 1979.)

(1984). Place-names and settlements: some problems of dating as exemplified by place-names in *-by. Nomina* 8: 28–39.

(1988). Review of Hjerstedt 1987. *NB* 76: 220–3.

Ferguson, C. A. (1959). Diglossia. *Word* 15: 325–40.

Field, J. (1972). *English Field-names: a Dictionary.* Newton Abbot: David & Charles.

(1975). Size and shape in English field-nomenclature. *Names* 23: 6–25.

(1976–7). Derogatory field-names. *JEPNS* 9: 19–25.

(1986). *Compliment and Commemoration in English Field-names.* 2nd edn. Hemel Hempstead and Edinburgh: Dacorum College and Council for Name Studies in Great Britain and Ireland.

Field, P. J. C. (1971). *Romance and Chronicle: a Study of Malory's Prose Style.* London: Barrie & Jenkins.

Finkenstaedt, T. (1963). *'You' and 'Thou'. Studien zur Anrede im Englischen.* Berlin: de Gruyter.

Finkenstaedt, T. & D. Wolff (1973). *Ordered Profusion: Studies in Dictionaries and the English Lexicon.* Heidelberg: Winter.

Finkenstaedt, T., E. Leisi & D. Wolff (eds.) (1970). *A Chronological English Dictionary.* Heidelberg: Winter.

Firth, J. R. (1957). *Papers in Linguistics, 1934–51.* London: Oxford University Press.

(1968). *Selected Papers of J. R. Firth, 1952–59*, ed. F. R. Palmer. London: Longman.

Fischer, O. C. M. (1979). A comparative study of philosophical terms in the Alfredian and Chaucerian Boethius. *Neophilologus* 63: 622–39.

(1985). Gower's *Tale of Florent* and Chaucer's *Wife of Bath's Tale*: a stylistic comparison. *ES* 66: 205–25.

(1988). The rise of the *for NP to V* construction: an explanation. In G. Nixon & J. Honey (eds.) *An Historic Tongue: Studies in English Linguistics in Memory of Barbara Strang*. London: Routledge, 67–88.

(1989). The origin and spread of the accusative and infinitive construction in English. *FLH* 8: 143–217.

(1990). *Syntactic Change and Causation: Developments in Infinitival Constructions in English.* (Amsterdam Studies in Generative Grammar 2.) Amsterdam: Faculteit der Letteren.

(1991). The rise of the passive infinitive in English. In Kastovsky, 141–88 (prepublished in *Amsterdam Papers in English* 1, 2 (1988): 54–107).

(forthcoming a). Syntactic change and borrowing: the case of the accusative and infinitive construction in English.

(forthcoming b). Factors influencing the choice of infinitive marker in late Middle English.

Fischer, O. C. M. & F. C. van der Leek (1981). Optional vs radical re-analysis: mechanisms of syntactic change. *Lingua* 55: 301–50. (Review of Lightfoot 1979.)

(1983). The demise of the Old English impersonal construction. *JL* 19: 337–68.

(1987). A 'case' for the Old English impersonal. In W. Koopman, F. van der Leek, O. Fischer & R. Eaton (eds.) *Explanation and Linguistic Change*. Amsterdam: Benjamins, 79–120.

Fisher, J. H. (1977). Chancery and the emergence of standard written English in the fifteenth century. *Speculum* 52: 870–99.

Fisiak, J. (1965). *Morphemic Structure of Chaucer's English*. University: Alabama University Press.

(1968). *A Short Grammar of Middle English. Part One: Graphemics, Phonemics and Morphemics*. Warsaw: PWN.

(1977). Sociolinguistics and Middle English: some socially motivated changes in the history of English. *Kwartalnik Neofilolgiczny* 24: 247–59.

(ed.) (1978). *Recent Developments in Historical Phonology*. The Hague: Mouton.

(ed.) (1984a). *Historical Syntax*. Berlin: Mouton.

(1984b). The voicing of initial fricatives in Middle English. *SAP* 17: 3–16.

(1985). *Historical Semantics. Historical Word Formation*. Berlin: Mouton de Gruyter.

(1987). *A Bibliography of Writings for the History of the English Language*. Berlin: Mouton de Gruyter.

(ed.) (1988). *Historical Dialectology*. Berlin: Mouton de Gruyter.

Forssner, T. (1916). *Continental-Germanic Personal Names in England in Old and Middle English Times*. Uppsala: Appelberg.

Förster, M. (1925). Die Französierung des englischen Personennamenschatzes. In *Germania: Festschrift für Eduard Sievers*. Halle an der Saale: Niemeyer, 327–40.

Forström, G. (1948). *The Verb 'to be' in Middle English: a Survey of the Forms*. Lund: Gleerup.

Foster, R. (1975). The use of *þa* in Old English and Middle English narratives. *NM* 76: 404–14.

Foxall, H. D. G. (1980). *Shropshire Field-names*. Shrewsbury: Shropshire Archaeological Society.

Francis, W. N. (1962). Graphemic analysis of late Middle English manuscripts. *Speculum* 37: 32–47.

Frankis, J. (1983). Word-formation by blending in the vocabulary of Middle English alliterative verse. In E. G. Stanley & D. Gray (eds.) *Five Hundred Years of Words and Sounds: a Festschrift for E. J. Dobson*. Cambridge: Brewer, 29–38.

Franklin, P. (1986). Norman saints and politics: forename-choices among fourteenth-century Gloucestershire peasants. *Local Population Studies* 36: 19–26.

Fransson, G. (1935). *Middle English Surnames of Occupation, with an Excursus on Toponymical Surnames*. (Lund Studies in English 3.) Lund: Gleerup.

Fridén, G. (1948). *Studies on the Tenses of the English Verb from Chaucer to Shakespeare with Special Reference to the Late Sixteenth Century*. Uppsala: A.-B. Lundeqvistska Bokhandeln.

(1957). On the use of auxiliaries to form the perfect and the pluperfect in late Middle English and early Modern English. *Studia Linguistica* 11: 54–6.

Fried, V. (1969). The notion of diacritics in Modern English graphology. *Brno Studies in English* 8: 62–7.

Fries, C. C. (1940). On the development of the structural use of word-order in Modern English. *Language* 16: 199–208.

Funke, O. (1922). Die Fügung *ginnen* mit dem Infinitiv im Mittelenglischen. *Englische Studien* 56: 1–27.

Gaaf, W. van der (1904). *The Transition from the Impersonal to the Personal Construction in Middle English*. Heidelberg: Winter.

(1927). A friend of mine. *Neophilologus* 12: 18–31.

(1928a). The predicative passive infinitive. *ES* 10: 107–14.

(1928b). The post-adjectival passive infinitive. *ES* 10: 129–38.

(1929). The conversion of the indirect personal object into the subject of a passive construction. *ES* 11: 1–11, 58–67.

(1930). The passive of a verb accompanied by a preposition. *ES* 12: 1–24.

(1932). The absolute genitive. *ES* 14: 49–65.

(1933). The split infinitive in Middle English. *ES* 15: 15–20.

Gardiner, A. H. (1940). *The Theory of Proper Names: a Controversial Essay*. Oxford: Clarendon.

Gay, L. M. (1899). Anglo-French words in English. *MLN* 14: 40–3.

Geckeler, H. (1971). *Strukturelle Semantik und Wortfeldtheorie*. Munich: Fink.

Geipel, J. (1971). *The Viking Legacy: the Scandinavian Influence on the English and Gaelic Languages*. Newton Abbot: David & Charles.

Gelling, M. (1978). *Signposts to the Past: Place-names and the History of England*. London: Dent.

(1984). *Place-names in the Landscape*. London: Dent.

(1989). The early history of Western Mercia. In S. Bassett (ed.) *The Origins of the Anglo-Saxon Kingdoms*. Leicester: Leicester University Press, 184–201.

Gelling, M., W. S. H. Nicolaisen & M. Richards (1970). *The Names of Towns and Cities in Britain*. London: Batsford.

Geoghegan, S. G. (1975). Relative clauses in Old, Middle and New English. *Working Papers in Linguistics* (Dept. of Linguistics, University of Ohio) 18: 30–71.

Gerritsen, M. (1984). Divergent word order developments in Germanic languages: a description and a tentative explanation. In Fisiak, 107–35.

(1987). *Syntaktische Verandering in Kontrolezinnen, een Sociolinguistische Studie van het Brugs van de 13e tot de 17e Eeuw*. PhD Thesis. University of Leiden. Dordrecht: ICG Printing.

(1988). Naar een atlas van de Nederlandse dialektsyntaksis. Unpublished paper read at the Nineteenth Annual Meeting of the Dutch Linguistic Society at Leiden on 23 January 1988.

Giegerich, H. (1985). *Metrical Phonology and Phonological Structure: German and English*. Cambridge: Cambridge University Press.

Givón, T. (1981). On the development of the numeral 'one' as an indefinite marker. *FLH* 2: 35–53.

Gneuss, H. (1972). The origin of standard Old English and Æthelwold's school at Winchester. *ASE* 1: 63–83.

Goossens, L. (1984). The interplay of syntax and semantics in the development of the English modals. In Blake & Jones, 140–59.

Görlach, M. (1986). Middle English – a creole? In Kastovsky & Szwedek, I, 329–44.

Gougenheim, G. (1929). Étude sur les périphrases verbales de la langue française. Doctoral thesis. University of Paris.

Graves, E. B. (ed.) (1975). *A Bibliography of English History to 1485*. Oxford: Clarendon.

Green, A. (1914). The analytic agent in Germanic. *JEGP* 13: 514–52.

Greenbaum, S. (1969). *Studies in English Adverbial Usage*. London: Longman.

Greenberg, J. H. (1966). Some universals of grammar with particular reference to the order of meaningful elements. In J. H. Greenberg (ed.) *Universals of Language*. Cambridge, MA: MIT Press, 73–113.

Greenslade, M. W. (ed.) (1970). *A History of the County of Stafford.* Vol. III. (Victoria History of the Counties of England.) Oxford: Institute of Historical Research.

Guiraud, P. (1971). Modern linguistics looks at rhetoric: free indirect style. In J. P. Strelka (ed.) *Patterns of Literary Style.* (Yearbook of Comparative Criticism 3.) University Park: Pennsylvania State University Press, 77–89.

Gumperz, J. (1964). Linguistic and social interaction in two communities. *American Anthropology* 66, 2: 137–54.

　(1969). Communication in multilingual societies. In S. Tyler (ed.) *Cognitive Anthropology.* New York: Holt Rinehart, 435–49.

Guy, G. (1980). Variation in the group and the individual: the case of final stop deletion. In Labov, 1–36.

Gysseling, M. (1966). *Overzicht over de Noordnederlandse Persoonsnamen tot 1225.* (Anthroponymica 16.) Groningen: Wolters.

Haas, L. (1989). Social connections between parents and godparents in late medieval Yorkshire. *Medieval Prosopography* 10, 1: 1–21.

Haas, W. (1970). *Phono-graphic Translation.* Manchester: Manchester University Press.

Hall, C. P. (1976–7). Application of field-names in the Cambridge West Fields. *JEPNS* 9: 12–18.

Hallam, H. E. (1965). *Settlement and Society: a Study of the Early Agrarian History of South Lincolnshire.* Cambridge: Cambridge University Press.

Hallé, M. & S. J. Keyser (1971). *English Stress: its Form, its Growth, and its Role in Verse.* New York: Harper & Row.

Halliday, M. A. K., A. McIntosh & P. Strevens (eds.) (1964). *The Linguistic Sciences and Language Teaching.* London: Longman.

Hamp. E. (1982). Thwaite. In J. Anderson (ed.) *Language Form and Linguistic Variation: Papers Dedicated to Angus McIntosh.* Amsterdam: Benjamins, 161–7.

Hansen, B. H. (1984). The historical implications of the Scandinavian linguistic element in English: a theoretical evaluation. *NOWELE* 4: 53–95.

Hargreaves, H. (1966). Wyclif's prose. *E&S* 19: 1–17.

Harmer, F. E. (1950). *Chipping* and *market*: a lexicographical investigation. In C. Fox & B. Dickins (eds.) *The Early Cultures of North-west Europe.* Cambridge: Cambridge University Press, 335–60.

Harris, J. (1984). Syntactic variation and dialect divergence. *JL* 20: 303–27.

　(1985). *Phonological Variation and Change: Studies in Hiberno-English.* Cambridge: Cambridge University Press.

Harris, M. (1978). *The Evolution of French Syntax: a Comparative Approach.* London: Longman.

　(1989). Concessive clauses in English and Romance. In J. Haiman & S. A. Thompson (eds.) *Clause Combining in Grammar and Discourse.* (Typological Studies in Language 18.) Amsterdam: Benjamins, 71–99.

Harvey, P. D. A. (1965). *A Medieval Oxfordshire Village: Cuxham 1240–1400*. Oxford: Oxford University Press.

(1984). *Manorial Records*. (Archives and the User 5.) London: British Records Association.

Haugen, E. (1950). The analysis of linguistic borrowing. *Language* 20: 210–31. (Rptd in Lass 1969.)

Häusermann, H. W. (1930). *Studien zu den Aktionsarten in Frühmittelenglischen*. (Wiener Beiträge zur englischen Philologie 54.) Vienna: Braumüller.

Hausmann, R. B. (1974). The origin and development of Modern English periphrastic *do*. In Anderson & Jones, I, 159–89.

Healey, A. & R. L. Venezky (1980). *A Microfiche Concordance to Old English*. Toronto: Center for Medieval Studies, University of Toronto.

Heltveit, T. (1953). *Studies in English Demonstrative Pronouns: a Contribution to the History of English Morphology*. Oslo: Akademisk Forlag.

(1964). Dialect words in the *Seven Sages of Rome*. *ES* 45: 125–34.

Héraucourt, W. (1939). *Die Wertwelt Chaucers, die Wertwelt einer Zeitwende*. Heidelberg: Winter.

Hill, A. A. (1940). Early loss of [r] before dentals. *PMLA* 55: 308–21.

Hiltunen, R. A. (1983a). The Decline of the Prefixes and the Beginnings of the English Phrasal Verb: the Evidence from some Old and Early Middle English Texts. DPhil. thesis. University of Oxford.

(1983b). Syntactic variation in the early history of the English phrasal verb. In S. Jacobson (ed.) *Papers from the Second Scandinavian Symposium on Syntactic Variation*. Stockholm: Almqvist & Wiksell, 95–108.

Hines, J. (1984). *The Scandinavian Character of Anglian England in the Pre-Viking Period*. (BAR British Series.) Oxford: British Archaeological Records.

(forthcoming). Scandinavian English: a creole in context.

Hjertstedt, I. (1987). *Middle English Nicknames in the Lay Subsidy Rolls for Warwickshire*. (Acta Universitatis Upsaliensis: Studia Anglistica Upsaliensia 63.) Uppsala: Almqvist & Wiksell.

Hoad, T. F. (1984). English etymology: problematic areas in the vocabulary of the Middle English period. *TPS* 27–57.

Hock, H. H. (1982). Aux-cliticization as a motivation for word order change. *Studies in the Linguistic Sciences* 12: 91–101.

(1986). *Principles of Historical Linguistics*. Berlin: Mouton de Gruyter.

Hockett, C. F. (1958). *A Course in Modern Linguistics*. New York: Macmillan.

Hofmann, M. (1934). *Die Französierung des Personennamenschatzes im Domesday Book der Grafschaften Hampshire und Sussex*. Munich: Buchdrückerei Furst.

Hogg, R. M. & C. B. McCully (1987). *Metrical Phonology: a Coursebook*. Cambridge: Cambridge University Press.

Holdsworth, C. (ed.) (1986). *Domesday Essays*. Exeter: Exeter University.

Holt, J. C. (1982). *What's in a Name? Family Nomenclature and the Norman Conquest*. (Stenton Lecture, 1981.) Reading: University of Reading.

(ed.) (1987). *Domesday Studies*. Woodbridge: Boydell & Brewer.

Homann, E. R. (1954). Chaucer's use of 'gan'. *JEGP* 53: 389–98.

Horst, J. M. van der (1981). *Kleine Middelnederlandse Syntaxis*. Amsterdam: Huis aan de drie Grachten.

Hoskins, W. G. (1955). *The Making of the English Landscape*. London: Hodder & Stoughton.

Hudson, A. (1981). A Lollard sect vocabulary? In Benskin & Samuels, 15–30.

(1983). Observations on a northerner's vocabulary. In E. G. Stanley & D. Gray (eds.) *Five Hundred Years of Words and Sounds: a Festschrift for Eric Dobson*. Cambridge: Brewer, 74–83.

(1985). *Lollards and their Books*. London: Hambledon.

Hudson, R. A. (1980). *Sociolinguistics*. Cambridge: Cambridge University Press.

Hulbert, J. R. (1946). A thirteenth-century English literary standard. *JEGP* 45: 411–14.

Hunnisett, R. F. (1971). The reliability of inquisitions as historical evidence. In D. A. Bullough & R. L. Storey (eds.) *The Study of Medieval Records: Essays in Honour of Kathleen Major*. Oxford: Clarendon, 206–35.

Hurford, J. R. & B. Heasley (1983). *Semantics: a Coursebook*. Cambridge: Cambridge University Press.

Insley, J. (1977–8). Addenda to the survey of English place-names: personal names in field- and minor names. *JEPNS* 10: 41–72.

(1979). Regional variation in Scandinavian personal nomenclature in England. *Nomina* 3: 52–60.

(1981–2). Review of K. Forster's *Englische Familiennamen aus Ortsnamen*, Nuremberg, 1978. *JEPNS* 14: 37–44.

(1982). Some Scandinavian personal names from south-west England. *NB* 70: 77–93.

(1985a). The names of the tenants of the Bishop of Ely in 1251. *Ortnamnssällskapets i Uppsala Årsskrift* 58–78.

(1985b). Some Scandinavian personal names from south-west England from post-Conquest records. *Studia Anthroponymica Scandinavica* 3: 23–58.

(1985c). Field-names and the Scandinavian settlement of England: a comparative study of the evidence provided by the English Place-Name Society's survey of Northamptonshire. In Schützeichel, 113–28.

(1986). Ortsnamen und Besitzwechsel im Altenglischen und Mittelenglischen. In R. Schützeichel (ed.) *Ortsnamenwechsel*. (Beiträge zur Namenforschung, n.s. supplement 24.) Heidelberg: Winter, 83–95.

(1987). Some aspects of regional variation in early Middle English personal nomenclature. *Leeds Studies in English* n.s. 18: 183–99.

Iwasaki, H. (1986a). Case and rhyme in Laʒamon's *Brut*. In Kastovsky & Szwedek, 387–96.

(1986b). A few notes on the vocabulary of Laʒamon's *Brut*. *Poetica* (Tokyo) 24: 1–15.

Jack, G. B. (1975). Relative pronouns in language AB. *ES* 56: 100–7.

(1978a). Negation in later Middle English prose. *Archivum Linguisticum* n.s. 9: 58–72.

(1978b). Negative adverbs in early Middle English. *ES* 59: 295–309.

(1978c). Negative concord in early Middle English. *SN* 50: 29–39.

Jacobson, S. (1981). *Preverbal Adverbs and Auxiliaries: a Study of Word Order Change.* (Stockholm Studies in English 55.) Stockholm: Almqvist & Wiksell.

Jacobsson, B. (1951). *Inversion in English with Special Reference to the Early Modern English Period.* Uppsala: Almqvist & Wiksell.

Jacobsson, U. (1962). *Phonological Dialect Constituents in the Vocabulary of Standard English.* Lund: Gleerup.

Jakobson, R. (1929). *Remarques sur l'évolution phonologiques du Russe comparée à celle des autres langues slaves.* (Travaux du cercle linguistique de Prague 2.) Nendeln: Kraus. (Rptd 1968.)

Janda, R. D. (1980). On the decline of declensional systems: the overall loss of Old English nominal case inflections and the Middle English reanalysis of -ES as HIS. In E. C. Traugott, R. Labrum & S. Shepherd (eds.) *Papers from the 4th International Conference on Historical Linguistics.* Amsterdam: Benjamins, 243–52.

Jespersen, O. (1909–49). *A Modern English Grammar on Historical Principles.* 7 vols. Copenhagen: Munksgaard.

(1935). *The Philosophy of Grammar.* London: Allen & Unwin.

(1962). *The Growth and Structure of the English Language.* 9th edn. Oxford: Blackwell.

Joly, A. (1982). The system of negation in later ME prose. In Ahlqvist, 176–89.

Jones, C. (1967). The grammatical category of gender in early Middle English. *ES* 48: 289–305.

(1972). *An Introduction to Middle English.* New York: Holt, Rinehart & Winston.

(1988). *English Grammatical Gender 950–1200.* London: Croom Helm.

Jones, S. & J. McH. Sinclair (1974). English lexical collocations: a study in computational linguistics. *Cahiers de Lexicologie* 24: 15–61.

Jönsjö, J. (1979). *Studies on Middle English Nicknames,* I: *Compounds.* (Lund Studies in English 55.) Lund: Gleerup.

Jordan, R. (1906). *Eigentümlichkeiten des englischen Wortschatzes.* Heidelberg: Winter.

(1934). *Handbuch der mittelenglischen Grammatik,* I: *Lautlehre,* rev. edn by Charles Matthes, 1968. Heidelberg: Winter. (English tr. E. J. Cook, 1974, as *Handbook of Middle English Grammar.* The Hague: Mouton.)

Jud-Schmid, E. (1956). *Der indefinite Agens von Chaucer bis Shakespeare: die Wörter und Wendungen für 'Man'.* (Schweizer anglistische Arbeiten 39.) Bern: Francke.

Kaartinen, A. & T. F. Mustanoja (1958). The use of the infinitive in *A Book of London English 1384–1425. NM* 59: 179–92.

Kain, R. J. P. & H. C. Prince (1985). *The Tithe Surveys of England and Wales.* Cambridge: Cambridge University Press.

Kaiser, R. (1937). *Zur Geographie des mittelenglischen Wortschatzes.* Leipzig: Mayer & Müller.

Kaplan, T. J. (1932). Gower's vocabulary. *JEGP* 31: 395–402.

Karlberg, G. (1954). *The English Interrogative Pronouns: a Study of their Syntactic History.* (Gothenburg Studies in English 3.) Stockholm: Almqvist & Wiksell.

Käsmann, H. (1961). *Studien zum kirchlichen Wortschatz des Mittelenglischen 1100–1350.* Tübingen: Niemeyer.

Kastovsky, D. (ed.) (1991). *Papers from the Kellner Conference on English Historical Syntax.* Berlin: Mouton de Gruyter.

Kastovsky, D. & A. Szwedek (eds.) (1986). *Linguistics across Historical and Geographical Boundaries in Honour of Jacek Fisiak*, I: *Linguistic Theory and Historical Linguistics.* Berlin: de Gruyter.

Kayne, R. (1981). ECP extensions. *Linguistic Inquiry* 12: 93–135.

Keene, C. H. (1976). *Field-names of the London Borough of Ealing.* (English Field-name Studies 1.) Nottingham: English Place-name Society.

Kemenade, A. van (1985). Old English infinitival complements and West-Germanic V-raising. In Eaton *et al.*, 73–84.

(1987). *Syntactic Case and Morphological Case in the History of English.* PhD thesis. University of Utrecht. Dordrecht: ICG Publishing.

(1989). Syntactic change and the history of English modals. *Dutch Working Papers in English Language and Linguistics* 16: 1–27.

Kemp, J. A. (ed.) (1972). *John Wallis, Grammar of the English Language with an Introductory Grammatico-physical Treatise on Speech.* London: Longman.

Kempson, R. M. (1977). *Semantic Theory.* Cambridge: Cambridge University Press.

Kennedy, A. G. (1920). *The Modern English Verb–Adverb Combination.* (Stanford University Publications in Language and Literature 1.) Stanford: Stanford University Press.

Kenyon, J. S. (1909). *The Syntax of the Infinitive in Chaucer.* 2nd edn. Leiden: Brill and Leiden University Press.

Kerkhof, J. (1982). *Studies in the Language of Geoffrey Chaucer.* 2nd edn. Leiden: Brill.

Keyser, S. J. & W. O'Neil (1985). *Rule Generalization and Optimality in Language Change.* Dordrecht: Foris.

King, E. (1973). *Peterborough Abbey 1086–1310.* Cambridge: Cambridge University Press.

Kiparsky, P. (1988). Phonological change. In Newmeyer, I, 362–414.

Kirkman, K. (1983–4). Field-names at Woodhall, Pinner, Middlesex. *JEPNS* 16: 50–7.

Kivimaa, K. (1966). *Þe* and *þat* as clause connectives in early Middle English with special consideration of the emergence of the pleonastic *þat*. *Commentationes Humanarum Litterarum* 39, 1: 1–271.

(1967). The pleonastic *that* in relative and interrogative constructions in Chaucer's verse. *Commentationes Humanarum Litterarum* 39, 2: 1–37.

Klima, E. S. (1964). Negation in English. In J. A. Fodor & J. J. Katz (eds.) *The Structure of Language: Readings in the Philosophy of Language*. Engelwood Cliffs, NJ: Prentice Hall, 246–323.

Klöpzig, W. (1922). Der Ursprung der *to be to* Konstruktion. *Englische Studien* 56: 378–89.

Knispel, E. (1932). *Der altenglische Instrumental bei Verben und Adjektiven und sein Ersatz im Verlaufe der englischen Sprachgeschichte*. Breslau: Eschenhagen.

Knudsen, G. & M. Kristensen (1936–48). *Danmarks Gamle Personnavne*, I: *Fornavne*. Copenhagen: Gad.

Knudsen, G., M. Kristensen & R. Hornby (1949–64). *Danmarks Gamle Personnavne*, II: *Tilnavne*. Copenhagen: Gad.

Kökeritz, H. (1961). *A Guide to Chaucer's Pronunciation*. Stockholm: Almqvist & Wiksell.

König, E. (1985a). On the history of concessive connectives in English. Diachronic and synchronic evidence. *Lingua* 66: 1–19.

(1985b). Where do concessives come from? On the development of concessive connectives. In Fisiak, 263–82.

Kohonen, V. (1978). *On the Development of English Word Order in Religious Prose around 1000 to 1200 AD*. PhD thesis. University of Turku. (Publications of the Research Institute of the Åbo Akademi Foundation 38.) Åbo: Åbo Akademi.

Kolb, E. (1965). Skandinavisches in den nordenglischen Dialekten. *Anglia* 83: 127–53.

Koopman, W. F. (1985). The syntax of verb and particle combinations in Old English. In H. Bennis & F. Beukema (eds.) *Linguistics in the Netherlands, 1985*. Dordrecht: Foris, 91–100.

(1990a). The double object construction in Old English. In Adamson *et al.*, 225–43.

(1990b). *Word Order in Old English, with Special Reference to the Verb Phrase*. (Amsterdam Studies in Generative Grammar 1.) Amsterdam: Faculty of Arts.

(forthcoming). Old English clitic pronouns: some remarks. In F. Colman (ed.) *Edinburgh Studies in English* 2.

Koskenniemi, I. (1968). *Repetitive Word Pairs in Old and Early Middle English*. Turku: University of Turku.

Kosminsky, E. A. (1956). *Studies in the Agrarian History of England in the Thirteenth Century*. Oxford: Blackwell.

Krickau, C. (1877). Der Accusativ mit dem Infinitiv in der englischen Sprache, besonders im Zeitalter der Elisabeth. PhD thesis. University of Göttingen.

Kristensson, G. (1967). *A Survey of Middle English Dialects 1290–1350: the Six Northern Counties and Lincolnshire.* (Lund Studies in English 35.) Lund: Gleerup.

(1969). Studies on Middle English local surnames containing elements of French origin. *ES* 50: 1–22.

(1970). *Studies on Middle English Topographical Terms.* (Acta Universitatis Lundensis I, 13.) Lund: Gleerup.

(1976). Lay subsidy rolls and dialect geography. *ES* 57: 51–9.

(1979). A piece of Middle English word geography. *ES* 60: 254–60.

(1987). *A Survey of Middle English Dialects 1290–1350: the West Midland Counties.* (Publications of the New Society of Letters at Lund 78.) Lund: Lund University Press.

(1989). Place names and linguistic geography. In Breivik *et al.*, 55–64.

Kroch, A. S. (1989). Function and grammar in the history of English: periphrastic *do*. In R. W. Fasold & D. Schiffrin (eds.) *Language, Change and Variation.* Amsterdam: Benjamins, 133–72.

Kuhn, S. (1968). The preface to a fifteenth-century concordance. *Speculum* 43: 258–73.

Kurath, H. (1956). The loss of long consonants and the rise of voiced fricatives in Middle English. *Language* 32: 435–45.

Kurath, H., S. M. Kuhn & R. E. Lewis (eds.) (1954–). *Middle English Dictionary.* Ann Arbor: University of Michigan Press.

Labov, W. (1966). *The Social Stratification of English in New York City.* Washington DC: Center for Applied Linguistics.

(1972a). Contraction, deletion and inherent variability of the English copula. In his *Language in the Inner City*. Philadelphia: University of Pennsylvania Press, 65–129.

(1972b). *Sociolinguistic Patterns.* Philadelphia: University of Pennsylvania Press.

(ed.) (1980). *Locating Language in Time and Space.* New York: Academic Press.

(1981). Resolving the neo-grammarian controversy. *Language* 57: 267–308.

Lagerquist, L. M. (1985). The impersonal verb in context: Old English. In Eaton *et al.*, 123–36.

Laing, M. (1988). Dialectal analysis and linguistically composite texts in Middle English. *Speculum* 63: 83–100.

(ed.) (1989). *Middle English Dialectology. Essays on some Principles and Problems by Angus McIntosh, M. L. Samuels and Margaret Laing.* Aberdeen: Aberdeen University Press.

(1990). A linguistic atlas of early Middle English: the value of texts surviving in more than one copy. Paper delivered at the Sixth International Conference on English Historical Linguistics, May 1990, Helsinki.

Langenfelt, G. (1954). Street-names, old and new. In J. Sahlgren, B. Hasselrot & L. Hellborg (eds.) *Quatrième congrès international de sciences onomastiques.* Lund: Blom, 331–40.

Lass, R. (ed.) (1969). *Approaches to English Historical Linguistics*. New York: Holt, Rinehart & Winston.

  (1973). Review article of Reaney 1967. *Foundations of Language* 9: 392–402.

  (1974). Linguistic orthogenesis? Scots vowel quantity and the English length conspiracy. In Anderson & Jones, II, 311–52.

  (1976). *English Phonology and Phonological Theory: Synchronic and Diachronic Studies*. Cambridge: Cambridge University Press.

  (1977a). On the phonetic characterisation of Old English /r/. *SAP* 9: 3–16.

  (1977b). 'Centers of gravity' in language evolution. *Die Sprache* 23: 11–19.

  (1980). *On Explaining Language Change*. Cambridge: Cambridge University Press.

  (1981). John Hart *vindicatus*? A study in the interpretation of early phoneticians. *FLH* 1: 75–96.

  (1983). Velar /r/ and the history of English. In Davenport *et al.*, 67–94.

  (1984a). Quantity, resolution and syllable geometry. *FLH* 4: 151–80.

  (1984b). *Phonology: an Introduction to the Basic Concepts*. Cambridge: Cambridge University Press.

  (1985). Minkova *noch einmal*: MEOSL and the resolved foot. *FLH* 6: 245–6.

  (1986). On *schwa*. *Stellenbosch Papers in Linguistics* 15: 1–30.

  (1987). *The Shape of English: Structure and History*. London: Dent.

Lass, R. & J. M. Anderson (1975). *Old English Phonology*. Cambridge: Cambridge University Press.

Lass, R. & S. Wright (1986). Endogeny vs. contact: 'Afrikaans influence' on South African English. *English World-Wide* 7: 201–24.

Lassaut, J. & X. Dekeyser (1977). Aspects of sentence embedding in Old and Middle English. *Leuvense Bijdragen* 66: 327–44.

Lassiter, M. (1983). *Our Names, Our Selves: the Meaning of Names in Everyday Life*. London: Heinemann.

Leek, F. C. van der (1989). Casting a cold eye on generative practice. PhD thesis, University of Amsterdam.

Legge, M. D. (1941–2). Anglo-Norman and the historian. *History* n.s. 26: 163–75.

  (1980). Anglo-Norman as a spoken language. In R. Allen Brown (ed.) *Proceedings of the Battle Conference on Anglo-Norman Studies II, 1979*. Woodbridge: Boydell & Brewer, 108–17.

Lehmann, W. & Y. Malkiel (eds.) (1968). *Directions for Historical Linguistics*. Austin: University of Texas Press.

Leith, D. (1983). *A Social History of English*. London: Routledge & Kegan Paul.

Leonard, A. G. K. (1984). *Stories of Southampton Streets*. Southampton: Paul Cave.

Le Pesant, M. (1956). Les Noms de personne à Évreux du XIIe au XIVe siècle. *Annales de Normandie* 6: 47–74.

Levinson, S. C. (1983). *Pragmatics*. Cambridge: Cambridge University Press.

Leys, O. (1958). La Substitution de noms chrétiens aux noms préchrétiens en Flandre occidentale avant 1225. In L. Cortés *et al.* (eds.) *Actes et mémoires du Ve congrès international de toponymie et d'anthroponymie.* (Acta Salmanticensia, filosofia y letras 11.) Salamanca: University of Salamanca, I, 403–12.

Lieber, R. (1979). The English passive: an argument for historical rule stability. *Linguistic Inquiry* 10: 667–88.

Lightfoot, D. W. (1979). *Principles of Diachronic Syntax.* Cambridge: Cambridge University Press.

(1981a). The history of noun phrase movement. In C. L. Baker & J. McCarthey (eds.) *The Logical Problem of Language Acquisition.* Cambridge, MA: MIT Press, 86–119.

(1981b). A reply to some critics. *Lingua* 55: 351–68.

Lind, E. H. (1905–15; 1931). *Norsk-isländska Dopnamn ock fingerade Namn från Medeltiden; with Supplementband.* Uppsala: Lundequistska Bokhandeln.

(1920–1). *Norsk-isländska Personbinamn från Medeltiden.* Uppsala: Lundequistska Bokhandeln.

Lindahl, C. (1987). *Earnest Games: Folkloric Patterns in the Canterbury Tales.* Bloomington and Indianapolis: Indiana University Press.

Lobel, M. D. (ed.) (1969–75). *Historic Towns: Maps and Plans of Towns and Cities in the British Isles, with Historical Commentaries, from Earliest Times to 1800.* 2 vols. London: Lovell Johns & Cook, Hammond & Kell.

Löfvenberg, M. T. (1942). *Studies on Middle English Local Surnames.* (Lund Studies in English 11.) Lund: Gleerup.

Lohmander, I. (1981). *Old and Middle English Words for 'Disgrace' and 'Dishonour'.* (Gothenburg Studies in English 49). Gothenburg: Acta Universitatis Gothenburgensis.

Long, M. M. (1944). *The English Strong Verb from Chaucer to Caxton.* Menasha: Banta.

Longnon, A. (ed.) (1886–95). *Polyptyque de l'abbaye de Saint-Germain des Prés.* 2 vols. Paris: Champion.

Loyd, L. C. (1951). *The Origins of some Anglo-Norman Families.* (Publications of the Harleian Society 103.) Leeds: Harleian Society.

Luhmann, A. (1906). *Die Überlieferung von Laȝamons Brut nebst einer Darstellung der betonten Vokale und Diphthonge.* (Studien zur englischen Philologie 22.) Halle: Niemeyer.

Luick, K. (1914–40). *Historische Grammatik der englischen Sprache.* 2 vols. Stuttgart: Tauchnitz. (Rptd 1964: Oxford: Blackwell.)

Lund, N. (1975). Personal names and place-names: the persons and places. *Onoma* 19: 468–85.

Lyons, J. (1968). *Theoretical Linguistics.* Cambridge: Cambridge University Press.

(1977). *Semantics.* 2 vols. Cambridge: Cambridge University Press.

McCawley, N. (1976). From OE/ME 'impersonal' to 'personal' constructions:

what is a 'subjectless' S? In S. B. Steever, C. A. Walker & S. S. Mufwene (eds.) *Papers from the Parasession on Diachronic Syntax*. Chicago: Chicago Linguistic Society, 192–204.

McClure, P. (1973). Lay subsidy rolls and dialect phonology. In Sandgren, 188–94.

(1978). Surnames from English place-names as evidence for mobility in the Middle Ages. *Local Historian* 13: 80–6.

(1979). Patterns of migration in the late Middle Ages: the evidence of English place-name surnames. *Economic History Review* 32: 167–82.

(1981). The interpretation of Middle English nicknames. *Nomina* 5: 95–104. (Review article of Jönsjö 1979.)

(1982). The origin of the surname *Waterer*. *Nomina* 6: 92.

McIntosh, A. (1940). Middle English 'Gannockes' and some place name problems. *RES* 16: 54–61.

(1948). The relative pronouns þe and þat in early Middle English. *English and Germanic Studies* 1: 73–87.

(1956). The analysis of written Middle English. *TPS* 26–55. (Rptd Lass 1969 and Laing 1989.)

(1963). A new approach to Middle English dialectology. *ES* 44: 1–11. (Rptd Laing 1989.)

(1966). 'Graphology' and meaning. In McIntosh & Halliday, 98–110.

(1972). Some words in the Northern Homily Collection. *NM* 73: 196–208.

(1973). Word geography in the lexicography of medieval English. *Annals of the New York Academy of Sciences* 211: 55–66.

(1974). Towards an inventory of Middle English scribes. *NM* 75: 602–24. (Rptd Laing 1989.)

(1975). Scribal profiles from Middle English texts. *NM* 76: 218–35. (Rptd Laing 1989.)

(1976). The language of the extant versions of *Havelok the Dane*. *Medium Ævum* 45: 36–49. (Rptd Laing 1989.)

(1978). The Middle English poem *The Four Foes of Mankind*: some notes on the language and text. *NM* 79: 137–44.

(1979). Some notes on the language and textual transmission of the *Scottish Troy Book*. *Archivum Linguisticum* 10: 1–19. (Rptd Laing 1989.)

McIntosh, A. & M. A. K. Halliday (eds.) (1966). *Patterns and Ranges: Papers in General, Descriptive, and Applied Linguistics*. London: Longman.

McIntosh, A. & M. F. Wakelin (1982). John Mirk's *Festial* and Bodleian MS Hatton 96. *NM* 83: 443–50. (Rptd Laing 1989.)

McIntosh, A., M. L. Samuels, M. Benskin, with assistance of M. Laing and K. Williamson (1986). *A Linguistic Atlas of Late Mediaeval English*. 4 vols. Aberdeen: Aberdeen University Press.

Mackenzie, B. A. (1928). *The Early London Dialect*. Oxford: Clarendon.

Mackenzie, F. (1939). *Les Relations de l'Angleterre et de la France d'après le vocabulaire*. 2 vols. Paris: Droz.

McKinley, R. (1975). *Norfolk and Suffolk Surnames in the Middle Ages*. (English Surnames Series 2.) Chichester: Phillimore.

(1976). The study of English surnames. In Voitl, 119–25.

(1977). *The Surnames of Oxfordshire*. (English Surnames Series 3.) London: Leopard's Head Press.

(1981). *The Surnames of Lancashire*. (English Surnames Series 4.) London: Leopard's Head Press.

(1988). *The Surnames of Suffolk*. London: Leopard's Head Press.

(1989). *The Surnames of Sussex*. (English Surnames Series 5.) London: Leopard's Head Press.

McLaughlin, J. C. (1963). *A Graphemic–Phonemic Study of a Middle English Manuscript*. The Hague: Mouton.

MacLeish, A. (1969). *The Middle English Subject–Verb Cluster*. The Hague: Mouton.

Malone, K. (1930). When did Middle English begin? In J. T. Hatfield, W. Leopold & A. J. F. Zieglschmid (eds.) *Curme Volume of Linguistic Studies*. (Language Monographs 7.) Baltimore, MD: Waverley Press, 110–17.

Manabe, K. (1989). *The Syntactic and Stylistic Development of the Infinitive in Middle English*. Fukuoka: Kyushu University Press.

Marchand, H. (1939). Review of Engblom 1938. *ES* 21: 121–5.

(1969). *The Categories and Types of Present-day English Word-formation*. 2nd edn. Munich: Beck.

Martin, G. H. (1960–4). The origins of borough records. *Journal of the Society of Archivists* 2: 147–53.

(1963). The English borough in the thirteenth century. *Transactions of the Royal Historical Society* 5th ser. 13: 123–44.

Martin, J. D. (1978). *The Cartularies and Registers of Peterborough Abbey*. (Northamptonshire Record Society 28.) Peterborough: Northamptonshire Record Society.

Marynissen, C. (1986). *Hypekoristische Suffixen in Oudnederlandse Persoonsnamen, inz. de -ʒ- en -l- Suffixen*. Ghent: Secretariaat van den Koninklijke Academie voor Nederlandse Taal- en Letterkunde.

Matheson, L. (1978). An example of ambiguity and scribal confusion in 'Piers Plowman'. *English Language Notes* 15: 263–7.

Matthews, P. H. (1974). *Morphology: an Introduction to the Theory of Word Structure*. Cambridge: Cambridge University Press.

Mätzner, E. (1874). *An English Grammar: Methodological, Analytical, and Historical*, tr. C. J. Grece. 3 vols. London: Murray; Boston, MA: Roberts.

Mausch, H. (1986). A note on late Middle English gender. *SAP* 18: 89–100.

Mawer, A. (1930). Some unworked sources for English lexicography. In N. Bøgholm, A. Brusendorff & C. A. Bodelsen (eds.) *A Grammatical Miscellany Offered to Otto Jespersen on his Seventieth Birthday*. London: Allen & Unwin, 11–16.

(1932). The Scandinavian settlement of Northamptonshire. *NB* 20: 109–23.

(1933). The study of field-names in relation to place-names. In J. G. Edwards, V. H. Galbraith & E. F. Jacob (eds.) *Historical Essays in Honour of James Tait*. Manchester: privately printed, 189–200.

Meer, H. J. van der (1919). *Main Facts concerning the Syntax of Mandeville's Travels*. PhD thesis. University of Amsterdam. Utrecht: Kemink & Zoon. 1929. *Main Facts concerning the Syntax of Mandeville's Travels*. Utrecht: Kemink.

Meier, H. H. (1953). *Der indefinite Agens im Mittelenglischen 1050–1350: die Wörter und Wendungen für 'Man'*. (Schweizer anglistische Arbeiten 34.) Bern: Francke.

(1967) The lag of the relative 'who' in the nominative. *Neophilologus* 51: 277–88.

Meisel, J. M. (ed.) (1977). *Langues en contact: pidgins, créoles*. (TBL 75.) Tübingen: TBL-Verlag Narr.

Mendenhall, J. C. (1919). *Aureate Terms: a Study in the Literary Diction of the 15th Century*. Lancaster, PA: Wickersham Print.

Menner, R. (1936). The conflict of homonyms in English. *Language* 12: 229–44.

(1945). Multiple meaning and change of meaning in English. *Language* 21: 59–76.

Mersand, J. (1937). *Chaucer's Romance Vocabulary*. Brooklyn: Comet.

Mertens-Fonck, P. (1984). The place of the Vespasian Psalter in the history of English. *SAP* 17: 17–28.

Michaëlsson, K. (1947). Questions de méthode anthroponymique. *Onomastica* 1: 190–204.

(1954). L'Anthroponymie et la statistique. In J. Sahlgren, B. Hasselrot & L. Hellborg (eds.) *Quatrième congrès international de sciences onomastiques*. Lund: Blom, 308–94.

Mills, A. D. (1968). Notes on some Middle English occupational terms. *SN* 40: 35–48.

(1988). Review of Hjertstedt 1987. *Studia Anthroponymica Scandinavica* 6: 171–4.

Milroy, J. (1981). *Regional Accents of English: Belfast*. Belfast: Blackstaff Press.

(1983). On the sociolinguistic history of /h/- dropping in English. In Davenport *et al.*, 37–54.

(forthcoming). Social network and prestige arguments in sociolinguistics. In H. Kwok & K. Bolton (eds.) *Papers from the First Hong Kong Conference on Language in Society*. London: Routledge.

Milroy, J. & J. Harris (1980). When is a merger not a merger? The MEAT/MATE problem in a present-day English vernacular. *English World-Wide* 1: 199–210.

Milroy, J. & L. Milroy (1978). Belfast: change and variation in an urban vernacular. In Trudgill, 19–36.

(1985). Linguistic change, social network and speaker innovation. *JL* 21: 339–84.

Minkova, D. (1982). The environment for open syllable lengthening in Middle English. *FLH* 3: 29–58.

(1983). Middle English final *-e* from a phonemic point of view. In Davenport *et al.*, 191–210.

(1984). Early Middle English metric elision and schwa deletion. In Blake & Jones, 56–66.

(1991). *The History of Final Vowels in English: the Sound of Muting*. Berlin: Mouton de Gruyter.

Minnis, A. (1984). *Medieval Theory of Authorship: Scholastic Literary Attitudes in the Later Middle Ages*. London: Scolar.

Mitchell, B. (1964). Syntax and word-order in the Peterborough Chronicle 1122–1154. *NM* 65: 113–44.

(1979). F. Th. Visser, *An Historical Syntax of the English Language*: some caveats concerning Old English. *ES* 60: 537–42.

(1984). The origin of Old English conjunctions: some problems. In Fisiak, 271–99.

(1985). *Old English Syntax*. 2 vols. Oxford: Clarendon.

Miyabe, K. (1954). On the development of the perfect infinitive. *Studies in English Literature* 31, 1: 51–70.

(1956). Some notes on the perfect infinitive in early Middle English. *Anglica* 2: 13–19.

Moessner, L. (1984). Some English relative constructions. *La Linguistique* 20: 57–79.

(1989). *Early Middle English Syntax*. Tübingen: Niemeyer.

Moore, S. (1918). Robert Mannyng's use of *do* as auxiliary. *MLN* 33: 385–94.

(1921). Grammatical and natural gender in Middle English. *PMLA* 36: 79–109.

(1927). Loss of final *-n* in inflectional syllables of Middle English. *Language* 3: 232–59.

(1928). Earliest morphological changes in Middle English. *Language* 4: 238–66.

Moore, S. & A. H. Marckwardt (1964). *Historical Outlines of English Sounds and Inflections*. Ann Arbor, MI: Wahr.

Moore, S., S. B. Meech & H. Whitehall (1935). Middle English dialect characteristics and dialect boundaries. *Essays and Studies in English and Comparative Literature*. Ann Arbor: University of Michigan Press, 1–60.

Morlet, M.-T. (1967). *Étude d'anthroponymie picarde: les noms de personne en Haute Picardie aux XIIIe, XIVe, XVe siècles*. Amiens: Musée de Picardie.

(1968–72). *Les Noms de personne sur le territoire de l'ancienne Gaule*. 2 vols. Paris: Centre National de la Recherche Scientifique.

Mossé, F. (1938). *Histoire de la forme périphrastique 'être + participe présent' en germanique: I Partie*. Paris: Klincksieck.

(1945). *Manuel de l'anglais de moyen âge. I.1-2 Vieil Anglais*. Paris: Aubier.

(1952). *A Handbook of Middle English*, tr. J. A. Walker. Baltimore, MD: Johns Hopkins University Press.

(1957). Refléxions sur le genèse de la forme progressive. In S. Korninger (ed.) *Studies in English Language and Literature Presented to Professor Karl Brunner on the Occasion of his Seventieth Birthday*. (Wiener Beiträge 65). Vienna and Stuttgart: Braumüller, 155–74.

Mühlhäusler, P. (1986). *Pidgin and Creole Linguistics*. Oxford: Blackwell.

Mullins, E. L. C. (1958). *Texts and Calendars: an Analytical Guide to Serial Publications*. (Royal Historical Society Guides and Handbooks 7.) London: Royal Historical Society.

Muscatine, C. (1981). Courtly literature and vulgar language. In G. S. Burgess & A. D. Deyermond (eds.) *Court and Poet. Selected Papers of the Third Congress of the International Courtly Literature Society*. Liverpool: Francis Cairns.

Musset, L. (1975). Pour l'étude comparative de deux fondations politiques des vikings: le royaume d'York et le duché de Rouen. *Northern History* 10: 40–54.

(1976). L'Aristocratie normande au XIe siècle. In P. Contamine (ed.) *La Noblesse au Moyen Age, XIe–XVe siècles: essais à la mémoire de Robert Botruche*. Paris: Presses Universitaires de France, 71–96.

Mustanoja, T. F. (1958). *The English Syntactical Type 'One the Best Man' and its Occurrence in other Germanic Languages*. Helsinki: Société Néophilologique.

(1960). *A Middle English Syntax Part I*. (Mémoires de la Société Néophilologique de Helsinki 23.) Helsinki: Société Néophilologique.

(1983). Chaucer's use of *gan*: some recent studies. In D. Gray & E. G. Stanley (eds.) *Middle English Studies Presented to Norman Davis in Honour of his Seventieth Birthday*. Oxford: Clarendon, 59–64.

(1985). Some features of syntax in Middle English main clauses. In M.-J. Arn & H. Wirtjes (eds.) *Historical and Editorial Studies in Medieval and Early Modern English for Johan Gerritsen*. Groningen: Wolters-Noordhoff, 73–6.

Nagel, F. (1909). Der Dativ in der frühmittelenglischen Prosa mit besonderer Berücksichtigung von Synthese und Analyse. PhD thesis. University of Greifswald.

Nehls, D. (1974). *Synchron–diachrone Untersuchungen zur Expanded Form im Englischen*. Munich: Hueber.

Newmeyer, F. J. (ed.) (1988). *Linguistics: the Cambridge Survey*. 4 vols. Cambridge: Cambridge University Press.

Nickel, G. (1966). *Die Expanded Form im Altenglischen: Vorkommen, Funktion und Herkunft der Umschreibung 'beon/wesan' + Partizip Präsens*. Neumünster: Karl Wachholtz.

Niles, P. (1982). Baptism and naming of children in late medieval England. *Medieval Prosopography* 3: 95–107.

Norman, J. (1988). *Chinese*. (Cambridge Language Surveys.) Cambridge: Cambridge University Press.

Oakden, J. P. (1930). *Alliterative Poetry in Middle English: Dialectical and Metrical Survey*. Manchester: Manchester University Press.

(1935). *Alliterative Poetry in Middle English: a Survey of the Traditions*. Manchester: Manchester University Press.

Ochs, E. (1983). Planned and unplanned discourse. In E. Ochs & B. Schieffelin *Acquiring Conversational Competence*. London: Routledge, 129–57.

O'Donnell, W. R. & L. Todd (1980). *Variety in Contemporary English*. London: Allen & Unwin.

Ogden, C. K. & I. A. Richards (1949). *The Meaning of Meaning*. 10th edn. London: Routledge & Kegan Paul.

Ogura, M. (1986). *Old English 'Impersonal' Verbs and Expressions*. (Anglistica 24.) Copenhagen: Rosenkilde & Bagger.

(1989). *Verbs with the Reflexive Pronoun and Constructions with 'Self' in Old and Early Modern English*. Cambridge: Brewer.

Ohlander, U. (1941). A study on the use of the infinitive sign in Middle English. *SN* 14: 58–66.

(1981). Notes on the non-expression of the subject pronoun in Middle English. *SN* 53: 37–49.

Olszewska, E. S. (1935). Types of Norse borrowing in Middle English. *Saga-book of the Viking Society for Northern Research* 11: 153–60.

Orton, H. & N. Wright (1974). *A Word Geography of England*. London and New York: Seminar.

Orton, H., S. Sanderson & J. Widdowson (eds.) (1978). *A Linguistic Atlas of England*. London: Croom Helm.

Orton, H., W. J. Halliday, M. Barry, M. Wakelin & P. M. Tilling (eds.) (1962–71). *Survey of English Dialects*. 4 vols. Leeds: Arnold for University of Leeds.

Orwin, C. S. & C. S. Orwin (1967). *The Open Fields*. 3rd edn. Oxford: Clarendon. (1st edn 1938.)

Otto, G. (1938). *Die Handwerkernamen im Mittelenglischen*. PhD thesis. Friedrich-Wilhelms University, Berlin. Bottrop: Postberg.

Owen, D. (1976). The muniments of Ely cathedral priory. In C. N. L. Brooke, D. E. Luscombe, G. H. Martin & D. Owen (eds.) *Church and Government in the Middle Ages: Essays Presented to C. R. Cheney on his 70th Birthday*. Cambridge: Cambridge University Press.

Page, R. I. (1971). How long did the Scandinavian language survive in England? In P. Clemoes & K. Hughes (eds.) *England before the Conquest: Studies in Primary Sources Presented to Dorothy Whitelock*. Cambridge: Cambridge University Press, 165–81.

Palliser, D. M. (1978). The medieval street-names of York. *York Historian* 2: 2–16.

Palmatier, R. A. (1969). *A Descriptive Syntax of the Ormulum*. The Hague: Mouton.

Palmer, F. R. (1981). *Semantics: a New Outline*. 2nd edn. Cambridge: Cambridge University Press.

Pearsall, D. (1985). *The Canterbury Tales*. London: Allen & Unwin.

Perrott, A. M. J. (1980). The field-names of the parishes of Deepingate, Northborough and Maxey. *Northamptonshire Archaeology* 15: 133–7.

Philips, S. U., S. Steele & C. Tanz (eds.) (1987). *Language, Gender and Sex in Comparative Perspective*. Cambridge: Cambridge University Press.

Phillipps, K. C. (1965). Asyndetic relative clauses in late Middle English. *ES* 46: 323–9.

 (1966a). Adverb clauses in the fifteenth century. *ES* 47: 355–65.

 (1966b). Absolute construction in late Middle English. *NM* 67: 282–90.

Phillips, B. S. (1983). Middle English diphthongization, phonetic analogy and lexical diffusion. *Word* 34: 11–23.

Pilch, H. (1955). Der Untergang des Präverbs e- im Englischen. *Anglia* 73: 37–64.

Plank, F. (1983). Coming into being among the Anglo-Saxons. In Davenport *et al.*, 239–78.

 (1984). The modals story retold. *Studies in Language* 8: 305–64.

Platt, C. (1976). *The English Medieval Town*. London: Secker & Warburg.

Pope, M. K. (1952). *From Latin to Modern French, with Especial Consideration of Anglo-Norman*. 2nd edn. Manchester: Manchester University Press.

Poussa, P. (1982). The evolution of early standard English: the creolization hypothesis. *SAP* 14: 69–85.

 (1988). The relative WHAT: two kinds of evidence. In Fisiak, 443–74.

 (1990). A contact-universals origin for periphrastic *do*, with special consideration of OE–Celtic contact. In Adamson *et al.*, 407–34.

Poutsma, H. (1929). *A Grammar of Late Modern English*, Part I: *The Sentence*. 2nd edn. Groningen: Noordhoff.

Prins, A. A. (1952). *French Influence in English Phrasing*. Leiden: Universitaire Pers.

 (1959). French influence in English phrasing: a supplement. *ES* 40: 27–32.

 (1960). French influence in English phrasing (continued). *ES* 41: 1–17.

Prior, O. H. (ed.) (1924). *Cambridge Anglo-Norman Texts*. Cambridge: Cambridge University Press.

Quirk, R. (1957). Relative clauses in educated spoken English. *ES* 38: 97–109.

Quirk, R. & J. Svartvik (1970). Types and uses of non-finite clauses in Chaucer. *ES* 51: 393–411.

Quirk, R. & C. L. Wrenn (1957). *An Old English Grammar*. 2nd edn. London: Methuen.

Raftis, J. A. (1982). *A Small Town in Late Medieval England: Godmanchester 1278–1400*. (Pontifical Institute of Medieval Studies: Studies and Texts 52.) Toronto: Pontifical Institute of Medieval Studies.

Rantavaara, I. (1962). On the development of the periphrastic dative in late Middle English prose. *NM* 63: 175–203.

Reaney, P. H. (1952). Pedigrees of villeins and freemen. *N&Q* 197: 222–5.

(1953). Notes on the survival of Old English personal names in Middle English. *Studier i Modern Språkvetenskap* 18: 84–112.

(1967). *The Origins of English Surnames*. London: Routledge & Kegan Paul.

(1976). *A Dictionary of British Surnames*. 2nd edn, rev. R. M. Wilson. London: Routledge & Kegan Paul.

Redmonds, G. (1973). *Yorkshire: West Riding*. (English Surname Series 1.) Chichester: Phillimore.

(1976). English surnames research. In Voitl, 75–82.

Reed, D. W. (1950). The history of inflectional *n* in English verbs before 1500. *University of California Publications in English* 7, 4: 157–328.

Reszkiewicz, A. (1962). *Main Sentence Elements in the Book of Margery Kempe: a Study in Major Syntax*. Warsaw: Komitet Neofilologiczny Polskiej Akademii Nauk.

(1966). *Ordering of Elements in Late Old English Prose in Terms of their Size and Structural Complexity*. Wroclaw: Ossolineum.

(1971). The elimination of the front rounded and back unrounded vowel phonemes from medieval English: a reinterpretation. *Kwartalnik Neofiloligiczny* 18: 279–95.

Rettger, J. F. (1934). *The Development of Ablaut in the Strong Verbs of the East Midland Dialects of Middle English*. (Language Dissertations 18.) Philadelphia: Linguistic Society of America.

Reuter, O. (1937). Some notes on the origin of the relative combination 'the which'. *NM* 38: 146–88.

(1938). On continuative relative clauses in English. *Commentationes Humanarum Litterarum* 9, 3: 1–61.

Richardson, H. G. (1942). Letters of the Oxford *dictatores*. In H. E. Salter, W. A. Pantin & H. G. Richardson (eds.) *Formularies which Bear on the History of Oxford*. Oxford: Historical Society n.s. 5: 331–450.

Richardson, M. (1984). The *dictamen* and its influence on fifteenth-century English prose. *Rhetorica* 2: 207–26.

Richter, M. (1979). *Sprache und Gesellschaft im Mittelalter: Untersuchungen zur mündliches Kommunikation in England von der Mitte des elften bis zum Beginn des vierzehnten Jahrhunderts*. (Monographien zur Geschichte des Mittelalters 18.) Stuttgart: Hiersemann.

(1985). Towards a methodology of historical socio-linguistics. *FLH* 6: 41–61.

Riehle, W. (1981). *The Middle English Mystics*, tr. B. Standring. London: Routledge & Kegan Paul.

Rigg, A. G. (1983). Clocks, dials and other terms. In D. Gray & E. G. Stanley (eds.) *Middle English Studies Presented to Norman Davis*. Oxford: Clarendon, 255–74.

(1987). Nigel of Canterbury: what was his name? *Medium Ævum* 56: 304–7.

Rissanen, M. (1967). *The Uses of ONE in Old and Early Middle English*. Helsinki: Société Néophilologique.

Robinson, F. N. (1985). Metathesis in the dictionaries: a problem for lexicographers. In Bammesberger, 245–66.

Robinson, I. (1971). *Chaucer's Prosody: a Study of Middle English Verse Tradition*. Cambridge: Cambridge University Press.

Robinson, J. A. (1911). *Gilbert Crispin, Abbot of Westminster*. Cambridge: Cambridge University Press.

Romaine, S. (1982). *Socio-historical Linguistics, its Status and Methodology*. Cambridge: Cambridge University Press.

(1984). The socio-linguistic history of t/d deletion. *FLH* 5: 221–55.

Rooth, E. (1941–2). Zur Geschichte der englischen Partizip-Praesens-Form auf *-ing*. *SN* 14: 71–85.

Rooy, J. de (1988). *Van HEBBEN naar ZIJN*. Amsterdam: Publikaties van het P. J. Meertens Instituut.

Ross, A. S. C. (1947–8). The vocabulary of the records of the Grocers' Company. *English and Germanic Studies* 1: 91–100.

(1963). Three lexicographic notes. *English Philological Studies* 8: 30–5.

(1970). The rare words of the *Ormulum*. *English Philological Studies* 12: 42–7.

(1974). Dub. *N&Q* 219: 209–10.

Ross, T. W. (1972). *Chaucer's Bawdy*. New York: Dutton.

Ross, T. W. & E. Brooks Jr (1984). *English Glosses from BL Additional Manuscript 37075*. Norman, OK: Pilgrim.

Rothwell, W. (1966). A study of the prefix *de/des* in Anglo-Norman. *TPS* 24–41.

(1968). The teaching of French in medieval England. *MLR* 63: 37–46.

(1975–6). The role of French in thirteenth-century England. *Bulletin of the John Rylands Library* 58: 445–66.

(1978). A quelle époque a-t-on cessé de parler français en Angleterre? In *Mélanges de philologie romane offerts à Charles Camproux*. Montpellier: Université Paul-Valéry, 1075–89.

(1980–1). Lexical borrowing in a medieval context. *Bulletin of the John Rylands Library* 63: 118–43.

(1983). Language and government in medieval England. *Zeitschrift für französischen Sprache und Literatur* 93: 258–90.

(1985). Stratford atte Bowe and Paris. *MLR* 80: 39–54.

Royster, J. F. (1915). The *do* auxiliary 1400–1500. *MP* 12: 189–96, 449–56.

(1918). The causative use of *hatan*. *JEGP* 17: 82–93.

Rudskoger, A. (1952). '*Fair, Foul, Nice, Proper*': a Contribution to the Study of Polysemy. Stockholm: Almqvist & Wiksell.

(1970). *Plain: a Study in Co-text and Context*. (Stockholm Studies in English 22.) Stockholm: Almqvist & Wiksell.

Ruggiers, P. G. (ed.) (1984). *Chaucer: the Great Tradition*. Norman, OK: Pilgrim.

Rumble, A. R. (1973–4). Onomastic and topographical sources in English local record offices, September 1970: a summary guide. *JEPNS* 6: 7–43.

(1984). The status of written sources in English onomastics. *Nomina* 8: 41–56.

(1985). The personal-name material. In D. Keene & A. R. Rumble (eds.) *Survey of Medieval Winchester*. (Winchester Studies 2.) Oxford: Clarendon, 1405–11.

(1987). The Domesday manuscripts: scribes and scriptoria. In Holt, 79–99.

Russom, J. H. (1982). An examination of the evidence of OE indirect passives. *Linguistic Inquiry* 13: 677–80.

Rydén, M. (1979). *An Introduction to the Historical Study of English Syntax*. (Stockholm Studies in English 51.) Stockholm: Almqvist & Wiksell.

(1983). The emergence of *who* as a relativiser. *Studia Linguistica* 37: 126–34.

Rydén, M. & S. Brorström (1987). *The Be/Have Variation with Intransitives in English, with Special Reference to the Late Modern Period*. (Stockholm Studies in English 70.) Stockholm: Almqvist & Wiksell.

Rygiel, D. (1981). *Ancrene Wisse* and 'colloquial' style. *Neophilologus* 65: 137–43.

Rynell, A. (1948). *The Rivalry of Scandinavian and Native Synonyms in Middle English, especially TAKEN and NIMEN*. Lund: Gleerup.

Salmon, V. (1959). Some connotations of 'cold' in Old and Middle English. *MLN* 74: 314–22.

Salter, E. (1978). Alliterative modes and affiliations in the fourteenth century. *NM* 79: 25–35.

Samuels, M. L. (1949). The *ge-* prefix in the Old English gloss to the Lindisfarne Gospels. *TPS*, 62–116.

(1963). Some applications of Middle English dialectology. *ES* 44: 81–94. (Rptd Lass 1969 and Laing 1989.)

(1972). *Linguistic Evolution*. Cambridge: Cambridge University Press.

(1985). The great Scandinavian belt. In Eaton *et al.*, 269–81. (Rptd Laing 1989.)

(1987). The status of the functional approach. In W. Koopman, F. van der Leek, O. Fischer & R. Eaton (eds.) *Explanation and Linguistic Change*. (Current Issues in Linguistic Theory 45.) Amsterdam: Benjamins, 239–50.

Samuels, M. L. & J. J. Smith (1981). The language of Gower. *NM* 82: 295–304. (Rptd Smith 1989.)

Sandahl, B. (1951–82). *Middle English Sea Terms*. 3 vols. Stockholm: Almqvist & Wiksell.

Sanders, H. (1915). *Der syntaktische Gebrauch des Infinitivs im Frühmittelenglischen*. (Kieler Studien zur englischen Philologie 7.) Heidelberg: Winter.

Sandgren, F. (ed.) (1973). *Otium et Negotium: Studies in Onomatology and Library Science presented to Olof von Feilitzen*. (Acta Bibliothecae Regiae Stockholmiensis 16.) Stockholm: Norstedt.

Sandred, K. I. (1973). Anglo-Saxon heritage in East Anglia. *NB* 61: 83–92. (Review article based on Seltén 1972.)

(1979). Scandinavian place-names and appellatives in Norfolk: a study of the medieval field-names of Flitcham. *NB* 67: 98–122.

(1982). Scandinavian place-names and appellatives in Norfolk: a study of the microtopy of Flitcham. In K. Rymut (ed.) *Proceedings of the Thirteenth International Congress of Onomastic Sciences*. Cracow: Universitas Iagellonica, 357–63.

Sandved, A. O. (1985). *Introduction to Chaucerian English*. (Chaucer Studies 11.) Cambridge: Brewer.

Sankoff, D. (ed.) (1978). *Linguistic Variation: Models and Methods*. New York: Academic.

Sapir, E. (1921). *Language*. New York: Harcourt Brace.

Sauer, H. (1985). Laȝamon's compound nouns and their morphology. In Fisiak, 483–532.

(1988). Compounds and compounding in early Middle English: problems, patterns, productivity. In M. Markus (ed.) *Historical English*. Innsbruck: University of Innsbruck, 186–209.

Sawyer, P. H. (1971). *The Age of the Vikings*. 2nd edn. London: Arnold.

(ed.) (1985). *Domesday Book: a Reassessment*. London: Arnold.

Scheffer, J. (1975). *The Progressive in English*. Amsterdam: North Holland.

Scheler, M. (1961). Altenglische Lehnsyntax. PhD thesis. University of Berlin.

Schibsbye, K. (1974–7). *Origin and Development of the English Language*, II, III: *Morphology and Syntax*. Copenhagen: Nordisk Sprog- og Kulturforlag.

Schlauch, M. (1952). Chaucer's colloquial English: its structural traits. *PMLA* 67: 1103–16.

Schlaug, W. (1955). *Studien zu den altsächsischen Personennamen des 11. und 12 Jahrhunderts*. (Lunder Germanistische Forschungen 30.) Lund: Gleerup.

Schmittbetz, K. (1909). Das Adjektiv in 'Sir Gawayn and the Grene Knyȝt'. *Anglia* 32: 1–59, 163–89, 359–83.

Schroeder, P. R. (1983). Hidden depths: dialogue and characterization in Chaucer and Malory. *PMLA* 98: 374–87.

Schützeichel, R. (1983). Shakespeare und Verwandtes. In *Münsteraner Familiennamen-Kolloquium: Natur, Religion, Sprache*. (Schriftereihe der Westfälischen Wilhelms-Universität Münster 7.) Münster: Aschendorff, 103–26.

(ed.) (1985). *Giessener Flurnamen-Kolloquium*. (Beiträge zur Namenforschung n.s. Supplement 23.) Heidelberg: Winter.

Scragg, D. G. (1974). *A History of English Spelling*. (Mont Follick Series 3.) Manchester: Manchester University Press.

Seefranz-Montag, A. von (1983). *Syntaktische Funktionen und Wortstellungsveränderung: die Entwicklung 'subjektloser' Konstruktionen in einigen Sprache*. Munich: Fink.

Sell, R. (1985a). Tellability and politeness in 'The Miller's Tale': first steps in literary pragmatics. *ES* 66: 496–512.

(1985b). Politeness in Chaucer: suggestions towards a methodology for pragmatic stylistics. *SN* 57: 175–85.

Seltén, B. (1965). Some notes on Middle English by-names in independent use. *ES* 46: 165–81.

(1969). *Early East-Anglian Nicknames: 'Shakespeare' Names*. (Scripta Minora Regiae Societatis Humaniorum Litterarum Lundensis 1968–9: 3.) Lund: Gleerup.

(1972). *The Anglo-Saxon Heritage in Middle English Personal Names: East Anglia 1100–1399*. Vol. I. (Lund Studies in English 43.) Lund: Gleerup.

(1975). *Early East-Anglian Nicknames: Bahuvrihi Names*. (Scripta Minora Regiae Societatis Humaniorum Litterarum Lundensis 1974–5: 3.) Lund: Gleerup.

(1979). *The Anglo-Saxon Heritage in Middle English Personal Names: East Anglia 1100–1399*. Vol. II. (Acta Regiae Societatis Humaniorum Litterarum Lundensis 72.) Lund: Gleerup.

Serjeantson, M. S. (1927). The dialects of the West Midlands in Middle English. *RES* 3: 54–67, 186–203, 319–31.

(1935). *A History of Foreign Words in English*. London: Routledge & Kegan Paul. (Rptd 1961.)

(1938). The vocabulary of cookery in the fifteenth century. *E&S* 23: 25–37.

Sheard, J. A. (1954). *The Words We Use*. London: Deutsch.

Shelly, P. van D. (1921). *English and French in England 1066–1100*. Philadelphia: University of Pennsylvania.

Shields, K. (1980). Fast speech and the origin of the standard English verbal suffix -*s*. *Journal of English Linguistics* 14: 24–35.

Shimonomoto, K. (1986). The use of *ye* and *thou* in the *Canterbury Tales* and its correlation with terms of address and forms of the imperative. MA dissertation. Sheffield University.

Short, I. (1979–80). On bilingualism in Anglo-Norman England. *Romance Philology* 33: 467–79.

Simko, J. (1957). *Word Order in the Winchester Manuscript and in William Caxton's Edition of Thomas Malory's Morte Darthur: a Comparison*. Halle: Niemeyer.

Sisam, K. (1915). *Havelok the Dane*. 2nd edn. Oxford: Clarendon.

Skeat, W. W. (1897). The proverbs of Alfred. *TPS* 399–418.

Smith, A. H. (1928–36). Early northern nicknames and surnames. *Saga-book of the Viking Society for Northern Research* 11: 30–60.

(1956). *English Place-name Elements*. 2 vols. (English Place-name Society 25–6.) Cambridge: Cambridge University Press.

Smith, J. J. (1989). *The Language of Chaucer. Essays by Michael Samuels and J. J. Smith on the Language of Late Medieval Authors and Scribes*. Aberdeen: Aberdeen University Press.

(forthcoming). Tradition and innovation in South-West Midland English.

Smyser, H. M. (1967). Chaucer's use of *gin* and *do*. *Speculum* 42: 68–83.

Sørensen, J. K. (1983). *Patronymics in Denmark and England*. (Dorothea Coke Memorial Lecture in Northern Studies 1982.) London: University College.

Sørensen, K. (1957). Latin influence on English syntax. *Travaux du Cercle Linguistique du Copenhague* 11: 131–55.

Southworth, J. G. (1954). *Verses of Cadence*. Oxford: Blackwell.

Standing, R. W. (1984). *Field-names of Angmering, Ferring, Rustington, East Preston and Kingston (West Sussex)*. (English Field-name Studies 2.) Nottingham: English Place-Name Society.

Steadman, J. M. (1917). The origin of the historical present in English. *Studies in Philology* 14: 1–46.

Steel, D. J. (1968–78). *National Index of Parish Registers*. 12 vols. London: Society of Genealogists.

Stein, D. (1990). *The Semantics of Syntactic Change: Aspects of the Evolution of* do *in English*. Berlin: Mouton de Gruyter.

Stern, G. (1931). *Meaning and Change of Meaning, with Special Reference to the English Language*. Bloomington: Indiana University Press.

Stevick, R. D. (1964). The morphemic evolution of Middle English *she*. *English Studies* 45: 381–8.

Stockwell, R. P. (1961). The Middle English 'long close' and 'long open' mid vowels. *Texas Studies in Literature and Language* 2: 250–68. (Rptd Lass 1969.)

(1977). Motivations for exbraciation in Old English. In C. Li (ed.) *Mechanisms of Syntactic Change*. Austin: Texas University Press, 291–314.

(1978). Perseverance in the English vowel shift. In Fisiak, 337–48.

(1984). On the history of the verb-second rule in English. In Fisiak, 575–92.

(1985). Assessment of alternative explanations of the Middle English phenomenon of high vowel lowering when lengthened in the open syllable. In Eaton *et al.*, 303–18.

Stockwell, R. P. & D. Minkova (1991). Subordination and word order change in the history of English. In Kastovsky, pp. 367–408.

Stoelke, H. (1916). *Die Inkongruenz zwischen Subjekt und Prädikat im Englischen und in den verwandten Sprachen*. (Anglistische Forschungen 49.) Heidelberg: Winter.

Stoffel, C. (1894). *Studies in English Written and Spoken*. Zutphen: Thieme.

Strang, B. M. H. (1970). *A History of English*. London: Methuen.

(1982). Aspects of the history of *BE + ing* construction. In J. M. Anderson (ed.) *Language Form and Linguistic Variation. Papers Dedicated to Angus McIntosh*. Amsterdam: Benjamins, 427–74.

Suggett, H. (1945). The use of French in England in the later Middle Ages. *Transactions of the Royal Historical Society* 28: 61–83.

Sundby, B. (1952). Some Middle English occupational terms. *ES* 33: 18–20.

(1963). *Studies in the Middle English Dialect Material of the Worcestershire*

Records. (Norwegian Studies in English 10.) Bergen & Oslo: Norwegian Universities Press; New York: Humanities Press.

Sundén, K. (1904). *Contributions to the Study of Elliptical Words in Modern English*. Uppsala: Almqvist & Wiksell.

Swieczkowski W. (1962). *Word Order Patterning in Middle English*. The Hague: Mouton.

Tait, J. (1924). The feudal element. In A. Mawer & F. M. Stenton (eds.) *Introduction to the Survey of English Place-names*. (English Place-Name Society 1.1.) Cambridge: Cambridge University Press, 115–32.

Tajima, M. (1975). The Gawain-poet's use of CON as a periphrastic auxiliary. *NM* 76: 429–38.

(1985). *The Syntactic Development of the Gerund in Middle English*. Tokyo: Nan'un-do.

(1888). *Old and Middle English Language Studies: a Classified Bibliography 1923–1985*. Amsterdam: Benjamins.

Tatlock, J. S. (1923). Laȝamon's poetic style and its relations. In *The Manly Anniversary Studies in Language and Literature*. Chicago: Chicago University Press, 3–11.

Tavernier-Vereecken, C. (1968). *Gentse Naamkunde van ca. 1100 tot 1252*. Tongeren: Belgisch Interuniversitair Centrum voor Neerlandistiek.

Ten Brink, B. (1884). *Chaucer's Sprache und Verskunst*. Leipzig: Weigel. (English translation by M. Bentinck Smith. 1901. *The Language and Metre of Chaucer*. London: Macmillan.)

Tengvik, G. (1938). *Old English Bynames*. (Nomina Germanica 4.) Uppsala: Almqvist & Wiksell.

Terasawa, Y. (1974). Some notes on the Middle English 'gan' periphrasis. *Poetica* (Tokyo) 1: 89–105.

Thomas, H. M. (1987). A Yorkshire thegn and his descendants after the Conquest. *Medieval Prosopography* 8, 2: 1–22.

Thomson, R. M. (1980). *The Archives of the Abbey of Bury St Edmunds*. (Suffolk Record Society 21.) Woodbridge: Boydell & Brewer.

Thrupp, S. L. (1949). *The Merchant Class of Medieval London 1300–1500*. Chicago: Chicago University Press.

Thuresson, B. (1950). *Middle English Occupational Terms*. (Lund Studies in English 19.) Lund: Gleerup.

Tieken-Boon van Ostade, I. (1990). The origin and development of periphrastic auxiliary *do*: a case of destigmatisation. *NOWELE* 16: 3–52.

Todd, L. (1974). *Pidgins and Creoles*. London: Routledge & Kegan Paul.

Tolkein, J. R. R. (1929). *Ancrene Wisse* and *Hali Meiðhad*. *E&S* 14: 104–26.

Toon, T. (1978). Lexical diffusion in Old English. In D. Farkas, W. M. Jacobsen & K. W. Todrys (eds.) *Papers from the Parasession on the Lexicon*. Chicago: Chicago Linguistic Society, 357–64.

(1983). *The Politics of Early Old English Sound Change*. New York: Academic Press.

Tout, T. F. (1922). *France and England in the Middle Ages and Now*. Manchester: Manchester University Press.

Traugott, E. C. (1972). *A History of English Syntax: a Transformational Approach to the History of English Sentence Structure*. New York: Holt, Rinehart & Winston.

(1982). From propositional to textual and expressive meanings: some semantic–pragmatic aspects of grammaticalization. In U. P. Lehmann & Y. Malkiel (eds.) *Perspectives on Historical Linguistics*. Amsterdam: John Benjamins, 245–71.

(1989). On the rise of epistemic meanings in English: an example of subjectification in semantic change. *Language* 65: 31–55.

Trier, J. (1931). *Der deutsche Wortschatz im Sinnbezirk des Verstandes. Geschichte eines sprachlichen Felde*. Heidelberg: Winter.

Trnka, B. (1930). *On the Syntax of the English Verb from Caxton to Dryden*. (Travaux du Cercle Linguistique de Prague 3.) Prague: Cercle Linguistique de Prague.

Trudgill, P. (1974a). *The Social Differentiation of English in Norwich*. Cambridge: Cambridge University Press.

(1974b). *Sociolinguistics: an Introduction*. Harmondsworth: Penguin.

(ed.) (1978). *Sociolinguistic Patterns in British English*. London: Arnold.

(ed.) (1984). *Language in the British Isles*. Cambridge: Cambridge University Press.

(1986). *Dialects in Contact*. Oxford: Blackwell.

Turville-Petre, T. (1977). *The Alliterative Revival*. Cambridge: Brewer.

Tyrwhitt, T. (1798). Essay on the language and versification of Chaucer. *The Canterbury Tales*, I: *Preface*. London: Payne.

Ullmann, S. (1957). *The Principles of Semantics*, 2nd edn. Oxford: Blackwell.

(1967). *Semantics: an Introduction to the Science of Meaning*. Oxford: Blackwell.

Upton, C., S. Sanderson & J. D. A. Widdowson (1987). *Word Maps: a Dialect Atlas of England*. London: Croom Helm.

Vachek, J. (1945–9). Some remarks on writing and phonetic transcription. *Acta Linguistica* 5: 86–93.

van Draat, F. (1902–3). The loss of the prefix ʒe- in the Modern English verb and some of its consequences. *Englische Studien* 31: 353–84; 32: 371–8.

Vennemann, Th. (1974). Topics, subjects and word order: from SXV to SVX via TVX. In Anderson & Jones, I, 339–76.

(1984). Verb-second, verb late, and the brace construction: comments on some papers. In *Fisiak*, 627–36.

Visser, F. Th. (1963–73). *An Historical Syntax of the English Language*. 3 vols. Leiden: Brill.

Voitl, H., K. Forster & J. Insley (eds.) (1976). *The Study of the Personal Names of the British Isles*. Erlangen: Universität Erlangen-Nürnberg.

von Wartburg, W. (1969). *Problems and Methods in Linguistics*, rev. S. Ullmann, tr. J. M. H. Reid. Oxford: Blackwell.

Wahlén, N. (1925). The Old English Impersonalia. Part I. PhD thesis. University of Gothenberg.

Wainwright, F. T. (1945). Field-names of Amounderness hundred. *Transactions of the Historic Society of Lancashire and Cheshire* 97: 181–222.

(1962). *Archaeology and Place-names and History: an Essay on Problems of Co-ordination.* London: Routledge & Kegan Paul.

Wakelin, M. F. (1972a). *English Dialects: an Introduction.* London: Athlone.

(ed.) (1972b). *Patterns of Folk Speech in the British Isles.* London: Athlone.

(1984). Rural dialects in England. In Trudgill, 70–93.

Wakelin, M. F. & M. V. Barry (1968). The voicing of initial fricative consonants in present-day dialectal English. *Leeds Studies in English* n.s. 2: 47–64.

Waldron, R. A. (1967). *Sense and Sense Development.* London: Deutsch.

Wales, K. (1985). Generic 'your' and Jacobean drama: the rise and fall of a pronominal usage. *ES* 66: 7–24.

Wallner, B. (1969). A note on some Middle English medical terms. *ES* 50: 499–503.

Walters, K. (1988). Dialectology. In Newmeyer, IV, 119–49.

Wang, W. S.-Y. (1969). Competing changes as a cause of residue. *Language* 45: 9–25.

Warner, A. R. (1982). *Complementation in Middle English and the Methodology of Historical Linguistics.* London: Croom Helm.

(1990). Reworking the history of English auxiliaries. In Adamson *et al.*, 537–58.

(forthcoming). *English Auxiliaries: Structure and History.* Cambridge: Cambridge University Press.

Wasow, T. (1977). Transformations and the lexicons. In P. W. Culicover, T. Wasow & A. Akmajian (eds.) *Formal Syntax.* New York: Academic Press, 327–60.

Watts, V. E. (1981–2). The place-names of *Hindrelac. JEPNS* 15: 3–4.

Weerman, F. (1987). The change from OV to VO as a 'possible change'. In F. Beukema & P. Coopmans (eds.) *Linguistics in the Netherlands 1987.* Dordrecht: Foris, 223–32.

Weinreich, U. (1953). *Languages in Contact: Findings and Problems.* New York: Linguistic Circle of New York; The Hague: Mouton.

Weinreich, U., W. Labov & M. I. Herzog (1968). Empirical foundations for a theory of language change. In Lehmann & Malkiel, 95–188.

Weisgerber, L. (1953). *Von den Kräften der deutschen Sprache,* II: *Vom Weltbild der deutschen Sprache.* 2nd edn. Part I: *Die inhaltbezogene Grammatik.* Düsseldorf: Schwann.

Wells, J. C. (1982). *Accents of English.* 3 vols. Cambridge: Cambridge University Press.

(1984). English accents in England. In Trudgill, 55–69.

West, F. (1973). Some notes on word order in Old and Middle English. *MP* 71: 48–53.

Wiegand, N. (1982). From discourse to syntax: *for* in early English causal clauses. In Ahlqvist, 385–93.

Willard, J. F. (1934). *Parliamentary Taxes on Personal Property 1290–1334*. (Monographs of the Medieval Academy of America 19.) Cambridge, MA: Medieval Academy of America.

Williams, E. R. (1944). *The Conflict of Homonyms in English*. (Yale Studies in English 100.) New Haven, CT: Yale University Press.

Wilson, D. M. (1976). The Scandinavians in England. In D. M. Wilson (ed.) *The Archaeology of Anglo-Saxon England*. London: Methuen, 393–403.

Wilson, R. M. (1943). English and French in England 1100–1300. *History* 28: 37–60.

Withycombe, E. G. (1977). *Oxford Dictionary of English Christian Names*. 3rd edn. Oxford: Clarendon.

Wittig, S. (1978). *Stylistic and Narrative Structures in the Middle English Romances*. Austin: University of Texas Press.

Wolfson, N. (1979). The conversational historical present alternation. *Language* 55: 168–82.

Woodbine, G. E. (1943). The language of English law. *Speculum* 18: 395–436.

Workman, S. K. (1940). *Fifteenth Century Translation as an Influence on English Prose*. Princeton: Princeton University Press.

Wrenn, C. L. (1943). The value of spelling as evidence. *TPS* 14–39. (Rptd in *Word and Symbol: Studies in English Language*. London: Longman, 1967.)

Wright, J. (1905). *The English Dialect Grammar*. Oxford: Frowde.

Wright, J. & E. M. Wright (1928). *An Elementary Middle English Grammar*. 2nd edn. Oxford: Clarendon.

Wurff, W. van der (1987). Adjectives plus infinitive in Old English. In F. Beukema & P. Coopmans (eds.) *Linguistics in the Netherlands 1987*. Dordrecht: Foris, 233–42.

(1990a). The 'easy-to-please' construction in Old and Middle English. In Adamson *et al.* 519–36.

(1990b). *Diffusion and Reanalysis in Syntax*. PhD thesis. University of Amsterdam. Amsterdam: Faculteit der Letteren.

Wyld, H. C. (1913). The treatment of OE *y* in the dialects of the midland and south-eastern counties in ME. *Englische Studien* 47: 145–66.

(1927). *A Short History of English*. 3rd edn. London: Murray.

(1936). *A History of Modern Colloquial English*. 3rd edn. Oxford: Blackwell; New York: Smith.

Zachrisson, R. E. (1909). *A Contribution to the Study of Anglo-Norman Influence on English Place-names*. (Lunds Universitets Årsskrift n.s. 1.iv.3.) Lund: Gleerup.

(1924). The French Element. In A. Mawer & F. M. Stenton (eds.) *In-*

troduction to the Survey of English Place-names. (English Place-Name Society 1.1.) Cambridge: Cambridge University Press.

Zandvoort, R. W. (1949). A note on inorganic *for*. *ES* 30: 265–9.

Zeitlin, J. (1908). *The Accusative with Infinitive and some Kindred Constructions in English*. New York: Columbia University Press.

Zettersten, A. (1965). *Studies in the Dialect and Vocabulary of the Ancrene Riwle*. Lund: Gleerup.

Zimmermann, R. (1968). *Untersuchungen zum frühmittelenglischen Tempussystem*. PhD thesis. University of Kiel. Heidelberg: Groos.

(1973). Structural change in the English auxiliary system: on the replacement of BE by HAVE. *Folia Linguistica* 6: 107–17.

INDEX

THE CAMBRIDGE HISTORY
OF THE ENGLISH LANGUAGE

GENERAL EDITOR Richard M. Hogg

VOLUME III *1476–1776*

EDITED BY Roger Lass

VOLUME VI *English in North America*

EDITED BY John Algeo
(in alphabetical order by contributor)